PSYCHOLOGICAL TESTING

Principles, Applications, and Issues

FOURTH EDITION

ABOUT THE AUTHORS

Robert M. Kaplan is professor and chief of health care sciences in the Department of Family and Preventive Medicine at the University of California, San Diego. He has studied psychometrics and testing for over 25 years. Dr. Kaplan's research has been supported by a variety of agencies, including the National Institutes of Health, the National Science Foundation, NATO, the National Center for Health Services Research, the American Diabetes Association, and the Arthritis Foundation. He has served on many advisory committees to the United States Government and the governments of countries in Europe, Asia, and Australia. Having spent most of his career in San Diego, Dr. Kaplan has been active in the development of many new training programs there: He helped found a new graduate school of public health at San Diego State, and he was active in the development of a new Ph.D. program that combined the resources of an academic psychology department and a school of medicine. He is the former recipient of an NIH Research Career Development Award and the Award for Outstanding Scientific Contribution to Health Psychology from the American Psychological Association. He is currently an associate editor for *Annals of Behavioral Medicine,* and he serves on several other editorial boards. He has held elected offices in several organizations, including the Society of Behavioral Medicine, the American Association for the Advancement of Science, and the American Psychological Association. Dr. Kaplan is president of the Society of Behavioral Medicine and president of the International Society for Health-Related Quality of Life Research. He is past president of the Division of Health Psychology of the American Psychological Association and is also vice president of the International Association of Health Psychology, headquartered in Japan. Dr. Kaplan is the author or editor of 14 books and over 250 publications.

Dennis P. Saccuzzo is professor of psychology at San Diego State University and adjunct professor of psychiatry at the University of California, San Diego. He is a California licensed psychologist and Board Certified in forensic medicine and as a forensic examiner. He holds a Ph.D. in clinical psychology and is a Diplomate of the American Boards of Forensic Medicine, Forensic Examiners, and Assessment Psychology. He is a Fellow of the American Psychological Association, American Psychological Society, and Western Psychological Association for outstanding and unusual contributions to the field of psychology. Dr. Saccuzzo is the author of over 200 peer-reviewed papers and publications and four textbooks. He is the co-principal investigator on Project SERVE, a three-year grant from the U. S. Department of Education, and is presently pursuing a juris doctorate at California Western School of Law.

PSYCHOLOGICAL TESTING

Principles, Applications, and Issues

FOURTH EDITION

Robert M. Kaplan
University of California, San Diego

Dennis P. Saccuzzo
San Diego State University

BROOKS/COLE PUBLISHING COMPANY

I(T)P®   *An International Thomson Publishing Company*

Pacific Grove • Albany • Belmont • Bonn • Boston • Cincinnati • Detroit • Johannesburg • London
Madrid • Melbourne • Mexico City • New York • Paris • Singapore • Tokyo • Toronto • Washington

Sponsoring Editor: *Jim Brace-Thompson*
Marketing Team: *Gay Meixel and Romy Taormina*
Editorial Associate: *Terry Thomas*
Production Coordinator: *Fiorella Ljunggren*
Production: *Greg Hubit Bookworks*
Manuscript Editor: *Molly Roth*

Permissions: *Carline Haga*
Interior Design: *Christy Butterfield*
Cover Design and Illustration: *Cloyce Wall*
Interior Illustrations: *Lotus Art*
Typesetting: *Monotype Composition, Inc.*
Cover Printing: *Phoenix Color Corporation, Inc.*
Printing and Binding: *Quebecor Printing, Fairfield*

For more information, contact:

BROOKS/COLE PUBLISHING COMPANY
511 Forest Lodge Road
Pacific Grove, CA 93950
USA

International Thomson Editores
Seneca 53
Col. Polanco
11560 México D. F. México

International Thomson Publishing Europe
Berkshire House 168-173
High Holborn
London WC1V 7AA, England

International Thomson Publishing GmbH
Königswinterer Strasse 418
53227 Bonn
Germany

Thomas Nelson Australia
102 Dodds Street
South Melbourne, 3205
Victoria, Australia

International Thomson Publishing Asia
221 Henderson Road
#05-10 Henderson Building
Singapore 0315

Nelson Canada
1120 Birchmount Road
Scarborough, Ontario
Canada M1K 5G4

International Thomson Publishing Japan
Hirakawacho Kyowa Building, 3F
2-2-1 Hirakawacho
Chiyoda-ku, Tokyo 102, Japan

Library of Congress Cataloging-in-Publication Data
Kaplan, Robert M.
   Psychological testing : principles, applications, and issues /
   Robert M. Kaplan, Dennis P. Saccuzzo.
          p.   cm.
       Includes bibliographical references and indexes.
       ISBN 0-534-26364-X
       1. Psychological tests.   I. Saccuzzo, Dennis P., [date]–
   II. Title.
   BF 176.K36 1997
   150'.26'7—dc20
                                                    96-16325
                                                    CIP

To Cathie and Lorraine

Brief Contents

Contents

List of Sample Test Profiles

Preface

Psychology is a broad, exciting field. Psychologists today work in a variety of settings, including everything from schools and clinics to biochemical laboratories and industrial settings. Despite this diversity, all psychologists have at least two things in common: They all study behavior, and they all depend to some extent on its measurement. This book concerns a particular type of measurement, psychological tests, which measure characteristics pertaining to all aspects of behavior in human beings.

Psychological Testing is the result of a deep interest its authors share. As active participants in the development and use of psychological tests, we became disheartened because far too many undergraduate college students view psychological testing courses as boring and unrelated to their goals or career interests. In contrast, we view psychological testing as an exciting field. It has a solid place in the history of psychology, yet it is constantly in flux because of challenges, new developments, and controversies. A book on testing should encourage, not dampen, a student's interest. Thus, we provide an overview of the many facets of psychological tests and measurement principles in a style that will appeal to the contemporary college student.

To understand the applications and issues in psychological testing, the student must learn some basic principles, which requires some knowledge of introductory statistics. Therefore, some reviewing and a careful reading of Part I will pave the way for an understanding of the applications of tests discussed in Part II. Part III examines the issues now shaping the future of testing. Such issues include test anxiety, test bias, and the interface between testing and the law. The very future of applied psychology may depend on the ability of psychologists to face these challenging issues.

Throughout the book, we present a series of focused discussions and focused examples. These sections illustrate the material in the book through examples or provide a more detailed discussion of a particular issue. We also use technical boxes to demonstrate material such as statistical calculations.

Students today often favor informal discussions and personally relevant examples. Consequently, we decided to use models from various fields and to write in an informal style. However, because testing is a serious and complicated field in which major disagreements exist among scholars and experts, we have treated the controversial aspects of testing with more formal discussion and detailed referencing.

It has been fifteen years since the first edition of *Psychological Testing: Principles, Applications, and Issues* was published. On completion of the first edition, we believed that future revisions would be easy because psychological testing is a field that changes slowly. However, because there have been many major developments since 1982, we have attempted to reflect these developments in the second, third, and fourth editions.

Since the initial publication of *Psychological Testing,* many of the major tests—including the Stanford-Binet intelligence scales, the Wechsler Intelligence Scale for Children, and the Strong-Campbell Interest Inventory—have been revised. We have done our best to provide updates on all of them as well as descriptions of new psychological tests. Further, we have attempted to grow with the field. For example, fifteen years ago psychological testing was relatively rare in medical settings. Today, psychological testing in hospitals and clinical medical settings is common. To address these changes, we have added updated chapters on testing in health-care settings and have expanded our coverage of new developments, such as clinical neuropsychology. Also, many social and political developments have affected testing. For example, the changes in affirmative action policies that occurred in the mid-1990s may significantly impact how tests are developed and used for student selection. Changes in the practice of psychology under managed care have also greatly affected the development and application of psychological tests. We respond to all these developments in this fourth edition of the book.

Producing four editions of *Psychological Testing* over fifteen years has been challenging and rewarding. We are honored that hundreds of professors have adopted our text. However, some professors have suggested that we reorganize the book to facilitate their approach to the class. The challenge is that there are so many different ways to organize a course on psychological testing. In order to accommodate these different approaches, we have tried to keep the chapters independent enough for professors to teach them in whatever order they choose. For example, one approach to the course is to go through the book in the sequence that we present. Professors who wish to emphasize psychometric issues, however, might assign Chapters 1 through 8, followed by Chapters 20 and 21. Then, they might return to certain chapters from the Applications section. On campuses that require a strong statistics course as a prerequisite, Chapters 2 and 3 might be dropped. Professors emphasizing applications might assign Chapters 1 through 5 and then proceed directly to Part II, with some professors assigning only some of its chapters. Though Chapters 9 through 13 are the ones most likely to be used in a basic course, we have found sufficient interest in Chapters 14 through 19 to keep them. Chapters 17 through 19 represent newer areas into which psychological testing is expanding. Finally, Chapters 20 and 21 were written so that they could be assigned either at the end of the course or near the beginning. For example, some professors prefer to assign Chapters 20 and 21 after Chapter 5.

As with the previous editions, a student workbook is available. Further, professors have access to an instructor's manual and a bank of electronic test items.

Acknowledgments

We are highly indebted to the many reviewers and professors who offered feedback on this and the previous editions. Special thanks go to Jeff Bryson of San Diego State University, who neatly edited the second edition of the book. His contribution was invaluable. Raul Betterncourt of California State University, Fresno, and Mary Allen of California State University, Bakersfield, also provided many useful suggestions. We are also indebted to Darrell Anderson of the University of New Mexico; Robert Grissom of San Francisco State University; Leonard Jacobson of the University of Miami; Calvin Janssen of Tennessee Temple University; Frank Rosekrans of Eastern Washington University; James R. Barclay; Nancy S. Breland of Trenton State College; Richard D. Draper of Montclair State College; Lisa Friedenberg of the University of North Carolina at Asheville; Tim Hartshorne of Central Michigan University; Elaine M. Heiby of the University of Hawaii; Richard A. Hudiburg of the University of North Alabama; Ron Jewett of North Central Bible College; Terry Newell of California State University, Fresno; Allen L. Shoemaker of Calvin College; and Mark T. Smircina of Blackburn College for their thoughtful analyses.

The reviewers of the fourth edition were Israel Cuellar of the University of Texas-Pan American; Robert Grissom of San Francisco State University; Margaret A. Herrick of Kutztown University of Pennsylvania; Martin Johnson of Missouri Western State College; Vance Maloney of Taylor University; Faye Plascak-Craig of Marian College; Frank Rosekranz of Eastern Washington University; Eva D. Vaughan of the University of Pittsburgh; and Naomi Wagner of San Jose State University. We thank them all for their constructive criticisms and useful suggestions.

The four editions of this book have been developed under five different editors at Brooks/Cole. The earlier editions benefited from the patient and inspired supervision of Todd Lueders, C. Deborah Laughton, Phil Curson, and Marianne Taflinger. We are particularly indebted to Jim Brace-Thompson for his patience, wisdom, and support in the development of the current edition. Although we have had many editors, we have learned from each of them. We are most indebted to Greg Hubit for the high-quality production of the book, to Molly Roth for her excellent editing of the manuscript, and to Christy Butterfield for the elegant interior design. And we are also indebted to the expert production team at Brooks/Cole, especially Fiorella Ljunggren, who supervised the production process, and Roy Neuhaus and Cloyce Wall, who created the cover for the book.

We are very grateful to Nancy Johnson, who helped extensively with literature searches and the integration of new materials, and Liz Berkin, who did an exceptional job of collating references. Arlene Vine and Arlysse Kienle typed several portions of the manuscript and corrected several errors in early drafts. Finally, Beverly Jones coordinated several aspects of the fourth edition, including many of the interactions between the authors and the publisher.

Robert M. Kaplan
Dennis P. Saccuzzo

PSYCHOLOGICAL TESTING

Principles, Applications, and Issues

FOURTH EDITION

Principles

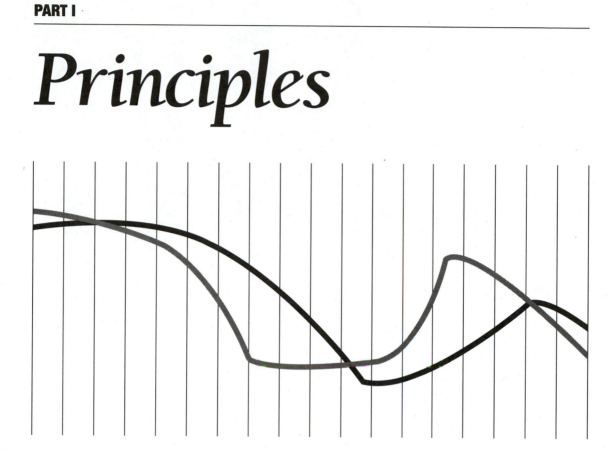

CHAPTER 1

Introduction

LEARNING OBJECTIVES

When you have completed this chapter, you should be able to:

- Define the basic terms pertaining to psychological and educational tests

- Distinguish between an individual test and a group test

- Define the terms *achievement, aptitude, and intelligence* and identify a concept that can encompass all these terms

- Distinguish between ability tests and personality tests

- Define the phrase *structured personality test*

- Explain how structured personality tests differ from projective personality tests

- Explain what a normative or standardization sample is and why such a sample is important

- Identify the major developments in the history of psychological testing

- Explain the relevance of psychological tests in contemporary society

Y ou are sitting at a table. You've just been fingerprinted and have shown a picture ID. You look around and see another 40 nervous or frightened-looking people. A stern-looking "test proctor" with a stopwatch in one hand and stack of booklets in the other passes out the booklets. You are warned not to open the booklet until told to do so, lest you face possible disciplinary action. This is not a nightmare or some futuristic fantasy—this is real.

Finally, after what seems like an eternity, you are told to open your booklet to page 3 and begin working. Your mouth is dry; your palms soaking wet. You open to page 3. You have 10 minutes to solve a five-part problem based on the following information.[1]

Eleven books are arranged from left to right on a shelf. Of the eleven, two are novels, two are art books, three are history books, and four are chemistry books. The two art books are next to each other. The two novels are not next to each other. The history books are next to each other. A novel is on one end of the row, and a history book is on the other.

A bit bewildered, you examine the first two questions.

Question 1. If the second book is a chemistry book, and the four chemistry books are next to each other, then which one of the following books must be an art book?
  A. The fifth
  B. The sixth
  C. The seventh
  D. The eighth
  E. The ninth

Not quite sure how to proceed, you look at the next question.

Question 2. If the second, third, fourth, and seventh books are chemistry books, which of the following must be true?
  I. The sixth book is an art book.
  II. The eighth book is a novel.
  III. Each novel is next to at least one chemistry book.

  A.   I only
  B.   II only
  C.   III only
  D.   I and II only
  E.   I, II, and III

Your heart beats a little faster and your mind starts to freeze up like an overloaded computer with too little working memory. You glance at your watch and notice that about two minutes have elapsed and you still don't have your bearings. The person sitting next to you looks a bit faint. Another three rows up someone storms up to the test proctor and complains frantically that

---

[1]From the Law Services Analytical Reasoning Workbook, a publication of Law School Admissions Council/Law School Admissions Services. (Note: answer to Question 1 is *C*; answer to Question 2 is *E*.)

he cannot do this type of problem. While the proctor struggles to calm this person down, another makes a mad dash for the restroom.

Welcome to the world of competitive standardized psychological tests. The questions you just faced were actual problems from a past version of the LSAT—the Law School Admissions Test. Whether or not a student is admitted into law school is almost entirely determined by that person's score on the LSAT and undergraduate grade point average. Thus, one's future can depend, to a tremendous extent, on a single score from a single test given in a tension-packed morning or afternoon. Similar problems appear on the GRE—the Graduate Record Exam, a test that plays a major role in determining who gets to study at the graduate level in psychology and other disciplines. (Later in this book we will discuss issues such as preparing for such tests and their significance, or predictive validity.)

Tests like the LSAT and GRE are among the most difficult of the modern psychological tests. The scenes we've described are real; careers do ride on a single test. Perhaps you've already taken the GRE or LSAT. Or perhaps you have not graduated yet, but are thinking about applying for an advanced degree or professional program and soon will be facing the GRE, LSAT, or MCAT (Medical College Admissions Test). Clearly, it is in your best interests to have some basic understanding of these and the multitude of psychological tests people are asked to take throughout their lives. In this book, we hope to teach you the fundamentals of testing. We believe that understanding these fundamentals is essential in negotiating the complexities of such personally relevant issues as entrance requirements for educational opportunities and job placement. Psychological tests may also have national or even international significance.

Thirteen-year-old children in 12 industrialized nations were given problems such as the following from the International Assessment of Education Progress (IAEP):

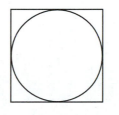

The length of a side of this square is 6. What is the radius of the circle?
A. 2   B. 3   C. 4   D. 6   E. 8   F. 9   G. Don't know

Only one of the 12 countries ranked below the United States in the percentage of 13-year-olds who had mastered such concepts (see Figure 1-1).

The results were similar for an IAEP science knowledge test (see Figure 1-2), which had questions such as the following:

Group A	Water vapor
	Oxygen
	Air
Group B	Ice
	Aluminum
	Iron
Group C	Alcohol
	Water
	Gasoline

The substances above, each at room temperature, have been classified into groups. On what property is the classification based?

A. Chemical composition

B. Specific heat

C. State of matter

D. Abundance within the earth's crust

How useful are tests such as these? Do they measure anything meaningful? How accurate are they? Such questions concern not only every American but also all members of the highly competitive international community. To answer them, you must understand the principles of psychological testing that you are about to learn.

Whether you like it or not, tests have a profound effect on you and your family, and they will continue to do so. Tests can play a decisive role in which college you attend, whether you get into an advanced degree program, and even whether you will be accepted for employment after graduation. They may even

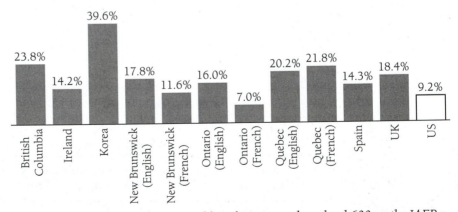

FIGURE 1-1 *Percentage of 13-year-old students at or above level 600 on the IAEP mathematics scale.*

(From "Performance at the Top: From Elementary Through Graduate School," p. 15. Copyright 1991 by Educational Testing Service. Reprinted by permission of Educational Testing Service, the copyright holder.)

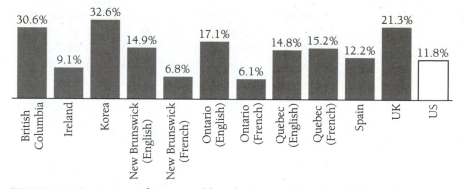

FIGURE 1-2   *Percentage of 13-year-old students at or above level 600 on the IAEP science scale.*

(From "Performance at the Top: From Elementary Through Graduate School," p. 15. Copyright 1991 by Educational Testing Service. Reprinted by permission of Educational Testing Service, the copyright holder.)

be used to determine whether you or someone in your family suffers from an emotional illness or to gauge the extent of emotional damages in litigation cases.

To answer questions about tests, you must understand the concepts presented in this book, such as reliability, validity, item analysis, and test constructions. Although a mastery of these concepts will require careful study and a knowledge of basic statistics, your efforts will be richly rewarded.

Basic Concepts

You are probably already familiar with some of the elementary concepts of psychological testing. For the sake of clarity, however, we shall begin with definitions of the most basic terms so that you will know how they are used in this textbook.

What a Test Is

Everyone has had experience with tests. A **test** is a measurement device or technique used to quantify behavior or aid in the understanding and prediction of behavior. A spelling test, for example, measures how well someone spells or the extent to which someone has mastered or learned to spell a specific list of words. At some time during the next few weeks, your instructor will likely want to measure the extent to which you have mastered the material of this book. To accomplish this, your instructor may give you a test.

As you well know, the test your instructor gives may not measure your full understanding of the material. This is because a test measures only a sample of behavior, and error is always associated with a sampling process. Test scores are not perfect measures of a behavior or characteristic, but they do add significantly to the prediction process, as you will see.

An **item** is a specific stimulus to which a person responds overtly; this response can be scored or evaluated (for example, classified, graded on a scale, or counted). Because psychological and educational tests are made up of items, the data they produce are explicit and hence subject to scientific inquiry.

In simple terms, items are the specific questions or problems that make up a test. The problems presented at the beginning of this chapter are examples of test items. The overt response would be to fill in or blacken one of the spaces:

A **psychological test** or educational test is a set of items designed to measure characteristics of human beings that pertain to behavior. There are many types of behavior. Overt behavior is an individual's observable activity. Some psychological tests attempt to measure the extent to which someone might engage in or "emit" a particular overt behavior or not. Other tests measure the extent to which a person has previously engaged in some overt behavior. Behavior can also be covert—that is, it takes place within an individual and cannot be directly observed. For example, your feelings and thoughts are types of covert behavior. Some tests attempt to measure such behavior. Psychological and educational tests thus measure past or present behavior. Some also attempt to predict future behavior, such as success in college or whether you will complete an advanced degree program in law or medicine.

What does it mean when someone gets a score of 75 items correct on a 100-item test? One thing it means, of course, is that 75% of the items were answered correctly. In many situations, however, knowing the percentage of correct items a person obtained can be misleading. Consider two extreme examples. In one case, out of 100 students who took the exam, 99 obtained scores of 90% correct or higher, and one got 75% correct. In another case, 99 of the 100 students obtained scores of 25% or lower, while one had 75% correct. The meaning of the scores can change dramatically, depending on how a well-defined sample of individuals score on a test. To deal with such problems of interpretation, psychologists make use of scales, which relate raw scores on test items to some defined theoretical or empirical distribution. Later in the book you will learn about such distributions.

Scores on tests may be related to traits, which are enduring characteristics or tendencies to respond in a certain manner. Determination, sometimes seen as stubbornness, is an example of a trait; shyness is another. Tests scores may also be related to the state, or the specific condition or status, of an individual. A determined individual after many setbacks may, for instance, be in a weak-

FIGURE 1-3
*Photo of an
individual
administration.*
(*Ann Chwatsky/
Jeroboam.*)

ened state and therefore less inclined than usual to manifest determination. Tests measure many types of behavior.

Types of Tests

Just as there are many types of behavior, so there are many types of tests. Those that can be given to only one person at a time are known as **individual tests** (see Figure 1-3). The situation involved in an individual test is similar to that in individual psychotherapy. The examiner or **test administrator** (the person giving the test) gives the test to only one person at a time, the same way psychotherapists see only one person at a time. A **group test,** by contrast, can be administered to more than one person at a time by a single examiner, such as when your instructor gives everyone in the class a test at the same time.

One can also categorize tests according to the type of behavior they measure. **Ability tests** contain items that can be scored in terms of speed, accuracy, or both. On an ability test, the faster or the more accurate one's responses, the better one scores on a particular characteristic. The more algebra problems you can correctly solve in a given amount of time, the higher you score in the ability to solve such problems.

Historically, experts have distinguished among achievement, aptitude, and intelligence as different types of ability. **Achievement** refers to previous learning. A test that measures or evaluates how many words you can spell correctly is called a spelling achievement test. **Aptitude,** by contrast, refers to the potential for learning or acquiring a specific skill. A spelling aptitude test measures how many words you might be able to spell given a certain amount of training, education, and experience. Your music aptitude refers in part to how well you might be able to learn to play a musical instrument given a certain number of lessons. Traditionally distinguished from achievement and aptitude, **intelligence** refers to a person's general potential to solve problems, adapt to changing circumstances, think abstractly, and profit from experience, independent of prior learning. When you say a person is "smart," you are probably referring to intelligence. When a father scolds his daughter because she has not done as well in school as she is capable of doing, presumably he is saying that she has not used her intelligence (potential) to achieve (that is, acquire new knowledge).

The distinctions among achievement, aptitude, and intelligence, however, are not always so cut-and-dried, for all three are highly interrelated. Attempts to separate prior learning from potential for learning, for example, have not been successful. There is a considerable overlap among achievement, aptitude, and intelligence tests. In view of this overlap, all three concepts are encompassed by the term **human ability.**

There is a clear-cut distinction between ability tests and personality tests. Whereas ability tests are related to capacity or potential, **personality tests** are related to the overt and covert dispositions of the individual—for example, the tendency of a person to show a particular behavior or response in a given situation. Remaining isolated from others, for instance, does not require any special skill or ability, but some people typically prefer or are disposed to remain thus isolated. Personality tests measure typical behavior.

There are several types of personality tests. In Chapter 15 you will learn about structured (that is, objective) personality tests. **Structured personality tests** provide a statement, usually of the "self-report" variety, and require the subject to choose between two or more alternative responses such as "True" or "False" (see Figure 1-4).

In contrast to structured personality tests, projective personality tests are unstructured. In a **projective personality test,** the stimulus (test materials) and the required response or both are ambiguous. For example, in the Rorschach inkblot test, the stimulus is an inkblot. Furthermore, rather than being

FIGURE 1-4
Self-report test items.

	True	False
1. I like heavy metal music.	☐	☐
2. I believe that honesty is the best policy.	☐	☐
3. I am in good health.	☐	☐
4. I am easily fatigued.	☐	☐
5. I sleep well at night.	☐	☐

TABLE 1-1
Types of Tests

I.	Ability tests: Measure skills in terms of speed, accuracy, or both.
	A. Achievement: Measures previous learning.
	B. Aptitude: Measures potential for acquiring a specific skill.
	C. Intelligence: Measures potential to solve problems, adapt to changing circumstances, and profit from experiences.
II.	Personality tests: Measure typical behavior—traits, temperaments, and dispositions.
	A. Structured (objective): Provides a self-report statement to which the person responds "True" or "False," "Yes" or "No."
	B. Projective: Provides an ambiguous test stimulus; response requirements are unclear.

asked to choose among alternative responses, as in structured personality tests, the individual is asked to provide a spontaneous response. The inkblot is presented to the subject, who is asked, "What might this be?" Projective tests assume that a person's interpretation of an ambiguous stimulus will reflect his or her unique characteristics (see Chapter 16).

See Table 1-1 for a summary of ability and personality tests.

Psychological Testing and Individual Differences

Psychological testing refers to all the possible uses, applications, and underlying concepts of psychological and educational tests. The main use of these tests, though, is to evaluate *individual differences,* or variations among individuals. Such tests measure individual differences in ability and personality and assume that the differences shown on the test reflect actual differences among individuals. For instance, individuals who score high on an IQ test are assumed to have a higher degree of intelligence than those who obtain low scores.

Plan for the Book

This book is divided into three parts: *Principles, Applications,* and *Issues.* Together, these parts provide an extensive coverage of psychological testing from the most basic ideas to some of the most complex. Basic ideas and events are introduced early and stressed throughout to reinforce newly acquired knowledge. In covering principles, applications, and issues, we intend to provide not only the *who's* of psychological testing but also the *how's* and *why's* of major developments in the field. We also address an important concern of many students—relevance—by examining the diverse uses of tests and the resulting data.

Principles of Psychological Testing

By *principles of psychological testing* we mean the basic concepts and fundamental ideas that underlie all psychological and educational tests, covered in Part I. Some statistical concepts, for example, that provide the foundation for understanding tests are presented in Chapters 2 and 3. Chapters 4 and 5 cover two of the most fundamental concepts in testing: reliability and validity. **Reliability** refers to the accuracy, dependability, consistency, or repeatability of test results. In more technical terms, reliability refers to the degree to which test scores are free of measurement errors. As you will learn, there are many ways a test can be reliable. For example, test results may be reliable over time, which means that when the same test is given twice within any given time interval, the results tend to be the same or highly similar. **Validity** refers to the meaning and usefulness of test results. More specifically, validity refers to the degree to which a certain inference or interpretation based on a test is appropriate. When one asks the question, "What does this psychological test measure?" one is essentially asking "For what inference is this test valid?"

Another principle of psychological testing concerns how a test is created or constructed. In Chapter 6, we present the principles of test construction. Chapter 7 covers the selection of psychological tests and presents the basic knowledge one needs to select tests for specific purposes. The act of giving a test is known as **test administration.** Though some tests are easy to administer, others must be administered in a highly specific way. The final chapter of Part I covers the fundamentals of administering a psychological test.

Applications of Psychological Testing

Whereas Part I focuses on the principles of testing, Part II focuses on applications. Here we provide a detailed analysis of many of the most popular tests and how they are used or applied. Part II begins with an overview of the essential terms and concepts that relate to the application of tests. After this overview, Chapter 9 discusses interview techniques. An **interview** is a method of gathering information through conversations or direct questions. Not only has the interview traditionally served as a major technique of gathering psychological information in general, but interview data also provide an important complement to test results.

Chapters 10, 11, and 12 cover individual tests of human ability. As you will learn, a wide variety of fine human ability tests exist. In Chapter 13, we present group tests of human ability. Chapter 14 examines interests tests, which measure behavior relevant to such factors as occupational preferences. Chapter 15 covers structured personality tests, and Chapter 16 covers projective personality tests. In Chapter 17, we discuss many recent alternatives to the more traditional tests. We also consider the important influence of cognitive psychology on testing.

Taken together, Chapters 14–17 provide in-depth coverage of the most widely used and newly developed personality and interest tests. These chapters not only provide descriptive information but also delve into the ideas underlying the various tests.

Chapter 18 reviews the research on measures of stress and anxiety. Then, in Chapter 19, the relatively new area of medical testing—for brain damage and health status—is covered.

Issues of Psychological Testing

Beyond principles and applications, many social and theoretical issues accompany testing, such as the controversial topic of racial differences in ability. Part III, the last section of the book, covers many of these issues. To compromise between breadth and depth of coverage, we decided to focus on a comprehensive discussion of those issues that have particular importance in the current professional, social, and political environment.

Chapter 20 examines the issue of test bias, one of the most volatile issues in the field today (National Commission on Testing and Public Policy, 1990). Because psychological tests have been accused of being discriminatory or biased against certain groups, this chapter takes a careful look at both sides of the argument. Because of charges of bias and other problems, psychological testing is increasingly coming under the scrutiny of the law (Saccuzzo & Johnson, 1995). Thus, Chapter 21 examines test bias as related to legal issues. In Chapter 22, you will find a general overview of other major issues presently shaping the future of psychological testing in the United States. From our review of the issues, we speculate on what the future holds for psychological testing.

Historical Perspective

Having given you an overview of the book, we shall now briefly provide the historical context of psychological testing. This historical discussion will touch on some of the material presented earlier in this chapter.

Early Antecedents

It is common to think of testing as both a recent and an American development. Most of the major developments in testing have occurred in this century, many of them in the United States. The origins of testing, however, are neither recent nor American. Historians have obtained evidence that the Chinese had a relatively sophisticated civil service testing program more than 4000 years ago (DuBois, 1970, 1972). Oral examinations were given every third year in China, and their results were used for work evaluations and promotion decisions.

By the Han Dynasty (206 B.C. to A.D. 220), the use of test batteries (two or more tests used in conjunction) was quite common. These early tests related to such diverse topics as civil law, military affairs, agriculture, revenue, and geography. Tests had become quite well developed by the Ming Dynasty (A.D. 1368–1644). During this period, a national multistage testing program involved local and regional testing centers equipped with special testing booths. Those who had done well on the tests at the local level went on to provincial capitals for more extensive essay examinations. After this second testing, those with the highest test scores (best results) went on to the nation's capital for a final round of examinations. Only those who passed this third set of tests were eligible for public office.

The Western world most likely learned about testing programs through the Chinese. Reports by British missionaries and diplomats encouraged the English East India Company to copy the Chinese system in 1832 as a method for selecting employees for overseas duty. Because testing programs worked well for the company, the British government adopted a similar system of testing for its civil service in 1855. After the British endorsement of a civil service testing system, the French and German governments followed suit. In 1883, the U.S. government established the American Civil Service Commission, which developed and administered competitive examinations for certain government jobs. The impetus of the testing movement in the Western world grew rapidly around this time (Parkinson, 1957; J. S. Wiggins, 1973).

Charles Darwin and Individual Differences

Perhaps the most basic concept underlying psychological and educational testing pertains to individual differences. No two snowflakes are identical, no two fingerprints the same. Similarly, no two people are exactly alike in ability and typical behavior. As we have noted, tests are specifically designed to measure these individual differences in ability and personality among people.

Although human beings realized long ago that individuals differ, developing tools for measuring such differences, as you will see, was no easy matter. To develop a measuring device, we must understand what we want to measure. An important step toward understanding individual differences came with the publication of Charles Darwin's highly influential book, *The Origin of Species,* in 1859. According to Darwin's theory, higher forms of life evolved on this planet partially because of differences among individual forms of life within a species. Given that individual members of a species differ, some possess characteristics that are more adaptive or successful in a given environment. Darwin also believed that those with the best or most adaptive characteristics survive at the expense of those who are less fit, and that the survivors then pass their characteristics on to the next generation. Through this process, he argued, life has evolved to its presently complex and incredibly intelligent levels.

A relative of Darwin, Sir Francis Galton (see Figure 1-5), soon began applying Darwin's theories to the study of human beings. Given the concepts of survival of the fittest and individual differences, Galton set out to show that some people possessed characteristics that made them more fit than others, a theory he articulated in his book, *Hereditary Genius,* published in 1869. Galton (1883) subsequently began a series of experimental studies to document the validity of his position. He concentrated on demonstrating that individual differences exist in human sensory and motor functioning, such as reaction time, visual acuity, and physical strength. In so doing, Galton initiated a search for knowledge concerning human individual differences, which is now one of the most important domains of scientific psychology.

Galton's work was extended by the American psychologist James McKeen Cattell, who coined the term *mental test* (J. M. Cattell, 1890). Cattell's doctoral

FIGURE 1-5
*Sir Francis
Galton.*
(From the National
Library of Medicine.)

dissertation was based on Galton's work on individual differences in reaction time. As such, Cattell perpetuated and stimulated the forces that ultimately led to the development of modern tests. Galton's influence is clearly revealed in Cattell's statement that Galton was "the greatest man whom I have ever known" (J. M. Cattell, 1930, p. 116).

Experimental Psychology and Psychophysical Measurement

A second major foundation of testing can be found in experimental psychology and early attempts to unlock the mysteries of human consciousness through the scientific method. Prior to the development of psychology as a science, there were mathematical models, in particular those of J. F. Herbart, who eventually used these models as the basis for educational theories that strongly influenced 19th-century educational practices. E. H. Weber followed Herbart and attempted to demonstrate the existence of a psychological threshold, the minimum amount of stimulus energy necessary to activate a sensory system. Weber originated the famous law expressing the relationship between the strength of a stimulus and the increase necessary to produce a noticeable difference:

$$\frac{\Delta I}{I} = C$$

where ΔI = the increment in stimulus intensity – the just noticeable difference
$\quad I$ = the intensity of the original stimulus (that is, a standard stimulus)
$\quad C$ = a constant within but not between the various senses

Following Weber's tradition, G. T. Fechner devised the law that the strength of a sensation grows as the logarithm of the stimulus intensity:

$$S = k \log I$$

where S = subjective, or perceived, magnitude

I = stimulus intensity, and

k = a constant.

Wilhelm Wundt, who set up a laboratory at the University of Leipzig in 1879, is credited with founding the science of psychology, following in the tradition of Weber and Fechner (Hearst, 1979). Wundt was succeeded by E. B. Titchner, whose student, G. Whipple, recruited L. L. Thurstone at the Carnegie Institute of Technology. Whipple provided the basis for immense changes in the field of testing by conducting a seminar at the Carnegie Institute in 1919 attended by Thurstone, E. Strong, and other early prominent American psychologists. From this seminar came the Carnegie Interest Inventory and later the Strong Vocational Interest Blank. Further in this book, we will discuss in greater detail the contributions of these early pioneers to the testing field as well as the tests they helped develop.

Thus, psychological testing derives from two branches: one based on the work of Darwin, Galton, and Cattell on the measurement of individual differences and the other (more theoretically relevant and probably stronger) based on the work of German psychophysicists Herbart, Weber, Fechner, and Wundt. Experimental psychology developed from the latter branch. From this branch also came the idea that testing is like an experiment and requires rigorous experimental control. Such control, as you will see, comes from administering tests under highly standardized conditions.

The efforts of these researchers, however necessary, did not alone result in the creation of modern psychological tests. Such tests arose in response to important needs. One such need was to classify and identify the mentally and emotionally handicapped. One of the earliest tests resembling present-day procedures, the Seguin Form Board (Seguin, 1866/1907), was developed in an effort to educate and evaluate the mentally disabled. Similarly, Kraepelin (1912) devised a series of examinations or tests for evaluating emotionally impaired people.

An important breakthrough in the creation of modern tests came at the turn of the 20th century. The French minister of public instruction appointed a commission to study ways of identifying intellectually subnormal individuals to provide them with appropriate educational experiences. One member of that commission was Alfred Binet. Working in conjunction with the French physician T. Simon, Binet developed the first major general intelligence test, which contained 30 items of increasing difficulty. Binet's early effort launched the first systematic attempt to evaluate individual differences in human intelligence (see Chapter 10).

The Evolution of Intelligence and Standardized Achievement Tests

The history and evolution of Binet's intelligence test are instructive. The first version of the test, known as the Binet-Simon scale, was published in 1905. As stated, this instrument contained 30 items of increasing difficulty and was designed to identify intellectually subnormal individuals. Like all well-constructed tests, the Binet-Simon scale of 1905 was augmented by a comparison or standardization sample. Binet's standardization sample consisted of 50 children who had been given the test under *standard conditions*—that is, with precisely the same instructions and format. In obtaining this standardization sample, the authors of the Binet test had norms with which they could compare the results from any new subject. Without such norms, the meaning of scores would have been difficult, if not impossible, to evaluate. However, by knowing such things as the average number of correct responses found in the standardization sample, one could at least state whether a new subject was below or above it.

It is easy to understand the importance of a standardization sample. However, the importance of obtaining a standardization sample that represents the population for which a test will be used has sometimes been ignored or overlooked by test users. For example, if the standardization sample consisted of 50 white men from wealthy families, then the meaning of the score of an African-American girl from a poverty-stricken family could not be easily or fairly evaluated. Nevertheless, comparisons of this kind are sometimes made. Clearly, it is not appropriate to compare a person to a group that does represent the individual.

Binet was aware of the importance of a standardization sample. Indeed, one facet in the evolution of the Binet test has been an attempt to increase the size and representativeness of the standardization or comparison sample. A **representative sample** is one that comprises individuals similar to those for whom the test is to be used. When the test is used for the general population, a representative sample must reflect all segments of the population in proportion to their actual numbers.

By 1908, the Binet-Simon scale had been substantially improved. It was revised to include nearly twice as many items (59) as the 1905 scale. Even more significantly, the size of the standardization sample was increased to more than 200. The 1908 Binet-Simon scale also introduced the historically significant concept of mental age. The test determined a child's mental age. In simplified terms, you might think of **mental age** as a measurement of a child's performance on the test relative to other children of that particular age group. If a child's test performance equaled that of the average 8-year-old, for example, then his or her mental age would be 8. That is, in terms of the abilities measured by the test, this child could be viewed as having a similar level of ability as the average 8-year-old. The actual, or chronological, age of the child might be 4 or 12, but in terms of test performance, the child functioned at the same level as the average 8-year-old. The mental age concept was one of the most important contributions of the revised 1908 Binet-Simon scale.

Though the Binet-Simon scale was revised again in 1911, that revision contained only minor improvements. By this time, however, the idea of intelligence testing had swept across the world and was especially entrenched in the

United States. By 1916, L. M. Terman of Stanford University had revised the Binet test for use in the United States. (The earlier American versions will be discussed in Chapter 10.) Terman's revision, known as the Stanford-Binet Intelligence Scale (Terman, 1916), was the only American version of the Binet test that flourished. It also characterizes one of the most important trends in testing—the drive toward better and better tests.

Terman's 1916 revision of the Binet-Simon scale contained numerous improvements. The standardization sample was increased to include 1000 people, original items were revised, and many new items were added. Terman's 1916 Stanford-Binet Intelligence Scale added respectability and momentum to the newly developing testing movement, which began in the United States around World War I in response to the demand for a quick, efficient way of evaluating the emotional and intellectual functioning of thousands of military recruits.

The Binet test was an individual test. World War I, however, created a demand for large-scale group testing, because relatively few trained personnel could evaluate the huge influx of military recruits. Therefore, shortly after the United States became actively involved in World War I, the Army requested the assistance of Robert Yerkes, who was then president of the American Psychological Association (see Yerkes, 1921). Yerkes headed a committee of distinguished psychologists who soon developed group tests of human abilities: the Army Alpha and the Army Beta. The Army Alpha was a structured ability test that required reading ability. The Army Beta, by contrast, was designed to measure the intelligence of illiterate adults.

World War I saw the widespread development of group tests. Also about this time, the scope of testing broadened to include tests of achievement, aptitude, interest, and personality. As previously indicated, however, achievement, aptitude, and intelligence tests overlapped considerably; the distinctions proved to be more illusory than real. It is noteworthy, however, that the 1916 Stanford-Binet Intelligence Scale appeared at a time of strong demand and high optimism for the potential of measuring human behavior through tests. World War I and the creation of group tests then added momentum to the testing movement. Shortly after the appearance of the 1916 Stanford-Binet Intelligence Scale and the Army Alpha test, schools, colleges, and industry began using tests. It appeared to many that this new phenomenon, the psychological test, held the key to the solution of the problems emerging from the rapid expansion of technology and population growth characteristic of modern societies.

Among the most important developments following World War I was the development of standardized achievement tests. In contrast to essay tests, standardized achievement tests provide multiple-choice questions standardized on a large sample to produce norms against which the results of new examinees can be compared.

Standardized achievement tests caught on quickly because of the relative ease of administration and scoring and the lack of subjectivity or favoritism that can occur in essay or other written tests. Through the use of standardized achievement tests in school settings, one could subject a large number of children to identical testing conditions and scoring standards. Such tests also allowed a broader coverage of content and were less expensive and more efficient than essays. In 1923, the development of standardized achievement tests culminated in the publication of the Stanford Achievement Test by T. L. Kelley, G. M. Ruch, and L. M. Terman.

By the 1930s, it was widely held that these new standardized tests were clearly superior to essay tests in their objectivity and reliability. Their use proliferated widely. Interestingly, as you will see later in the book, teachers of today appear to have come full circle. In the 1990s, there has been an emphasis on the use of written tests and work samples (portfolios) over standardized achievement tests as the best way to evaluate children (Corbett & Wilson, 1995; Swanson, Norman, & Linn, 1995).

For every movement there is a countermovement, and the testing movement in the United States in the 1930s was no exception. Critics soon became vocal enough to dampen enthusiasm and to make even the most optimistic advocates of tests defensive. Researchers, who demanded nothing short of the highest possible standards, little by little noted the limitations, weaknesses, and problems with existing tests. One of the most systematic, persistent, and organized attacks on tests by psychologists was directed at the existing structured personality tests. However, no test was safe from criticism, not even the Stanford-Binet, which had been a landmark in the testing field. Although tests were used between the two world wars and many new tests were developed, the accuracy and utility of tests remained under heavy fire.

Just before the outbreak of World War II in Europe in 1939, however, tests began to receive a renewed level of respectability. New, improved tests reflected the knowledge and experience of the previous two decades. By 1937 the Stanford-Binet had been revised again. Among the many improvements was the inclusion of a standardization sample of more than 3000 individuals. No other individual intelligence test before or since has had a larger standardization sample. Only the group tests, such as the Scholastic Aptitude Test (SAT), which can be administered on a mass scale, have larger samples.

A mere two years after the 1937 revision of the Stanford-Binet test, David Wechsler published the first version of the Wechsler intelligence scales (see Chapter 11), the Wechsler-Bellevue Intelligence Scale (W-B) (Wechsler, 1939). The Wechsler-Bellevue scale contained several interesting innovations in intelligence testing. Unlike the Stanford-Binet test, which produced only a single score (the so-called IQ, or intelligence quotient), Wechsler's test yielded several scores, permitting an analysis of an individual's pattern or combination of abilities. Among the various scores produced by the Wechsler test was the performance IQ. As you will see, performance tests do not require a verbal response.

With a performance test, intelligence can be evaluated in a context as free as possible from verbal or language skills. The Stanford-Binet test had long been criticized because of its emphasis on language and verbal skills, making it inappropriate for many individuals (especially those who are nonverbal or illiterate). In addition, few people, if any, believe that language or verbal skills play an exclusive role in human intelligence. Wechsler's inclusion of a nonverbal (performance) scale thus helped overcome some of the weaknesses of the Binet test. The Binet test was drastically revised in 1986 to include performance subtests. (Performance scales and other important concepts in intelligence testing will be formally defined in Chapter 11, which covers the various forms of the Wechsler intelligence scales.)

Personality Tests: 1920–1940

Just before and after World War II, personality tests began to blossom. Whereas intelligence tests attempted to measure ability or potential, personality tests attempted to measure presumably stable characteristics or traits that theoretically underlie behavior. **Traits** can be defined as relatively enduring dispositions (tendencies to act, think, or feel in a certain manner in any given circumstance) that distinguish one individual from another. For example, it can be argued that some people are optimistic and some pessimistic. Optimistic people remain so regardless of whether or not things are going well. A pessimist, by contrast, always looks at the negative side of things. Optimism and pessimism can thus be viewed as traits—relatively enduring characteristics of an individual that manifest themselves in a wide variety of situations. They are characteristics of the individual that are brought to a situation. One of the basic goals of traditional personality tests is to measure traits. As you will learn, however, the notion of traits has important limitations.

The earliest personality tests were structured paper-and-pencil group tests. These tests provided multiple-choice and true/false questions that could be mass (group) administered. Because they provide a high degree of structure (that is, a definite stimulus and specific alternative responses that can be unequivocally scored), these paper-and-pencil group personality tests are often referred to as *objective* or *structured personality tests*. The first structured personality test, the Woodworth Personal Data Sheet, was developed during World War I and was published in final form just after the war (see Figure 1-6).

As indicated earlier, the motivation underlying the development of the first personality test was the need to screen military recruits. History indicates that tests such as the Binet and Woodworth were created by necessity to meet unique challenges. Like the early ability tests, however, the first structured personality test was simple by today's standards. Interpretation of results from the Woodworth test depended on the now-discredited assumption that the content of an item could be accepted at face value. If the person marked "False" to the statement "I wet the bed," then it was assumed that he or she had not wet the bed. As logical as this assumption seems, experience has shown that it is often false. In addition to problems with honesty, the person responding to the question may not interpret the meaning of "wet the bed" in the same way as the test administrator. (Other problems with tests like the Woodworth are discussed in Chapter 15.)

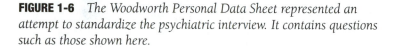

	Yes	No
1. I wet the bed.	☐	☐
2. I drink a quart of whiskey each day.	☐	☐
3. I am afraid of closed spaces.	☐	☐
4. I believe I am being followed.	☐	☐
5. People are out to get me.	☐	☐
6. Sometimes I see or hear things that other people do not hear or see.	☐	☐

FIGURE 1-6   *The Woodworth Personal Data Sheet represented an attempt to standardize the psychiatric interview. It contains questions such as those shown here.*

The introduction of the Woodworth test was enthusiastically followed by the creation of a variety of structured personality tests, all of which assumed the accuracy of test responses. However, researchers scrutinized, analyzed, and criticized the early structured personality tests, just as they had the ability tests. Indeed the criticism of structured personality tests that relied on face value alone became so intense that they were nearly driven out of existence. The development of new tests based on more modern concepts followed, revitalizing the use of structured personality tests (see Chapter 15). Thus, after an initial surge of interest and optimism during most of the 1920s, structured personality tests declined in use by the late 1930s and into the early 1940s. Following World War II, however, personality tests based on fewer or different assumptions were introduced, thereby rescuing the structured personality test concept.

During the brief but dramatic rise and fall of the first structured personality tests, interest in projective tests began to grow. In contrast to structured personality tests, which in general provide a relatively unambiguous test stimulus and specific alternative responses, projective personality tests provide an ambiguous stimulus and unclear response requirements. Furthermore, the scoring of projective tests is often subjective.

Unlike the early structured personality tests, interest in the projective Rorschach inkblot test grew slowly (see Figure 1-7). The rationale for the Rorschach test was first published by Herman Rorschach of Switzerland in 1921. However, several years passed before the Rorschach was introduced in the United States by David Levy. The first Rorschach doctoral dissertation written in a U.S. university was not completed until 1932, when Sam Beck, Levy's student, decided to investigate the properties of the Rorschach test scientifically. Although initial interest in the Rorschach test was lukewarm at best, its attractiveness progressed rapidly following Beck's work, despite suspicion, doubt, and criticism from the scientific community.

FIGURE 1-7

Card I of the Rorschach inkblot test, a projective personality test. Such tests provide an ambiguous stimulus to which a subject is asked to make some response.

Adding to the momentum for the acceptance and use of projective tests was the development of the Thematic Apperception Test (TAT) by Henry Murray and Christina Morgan in 1935. Whereas the Rorschach test contained completely ambiguous inkblot stimuli, the TAT was more structured. Its stimuli consisted of ambiguous pictures depicting a variety of scenes and situations, such as a boy sitting in front of a table with a violin on it. Unlike the Rorschach test, which asked the subject to explain what the inkblot might be, the TAT required the subject to make up a story about the ambiguous scene. The TAT purported to measure human needs and thus to ascertain individual differences in motivation. (In Chapter 16 you will learn more about projective tests in general and about the Rorschach and the TAT in particular.)

The Emergence of New Approaches to Personality Testing

The popularity of the two most important projective personality tests, the Rorschach and TAT, grew rapidly by the late 1930s and early 1940s, perhaps because of disillusionment with structured personality tests (Dahlstrom, 1969a). However, because many psychologists seem to have a deeply ingrained suspicion of projective tests, especially the Rorschach, projective tests are far from universally accepted.

In 1943 the development of the Minnesota Multiphasic Personality Inventory (MMPI) began a new era for structured personality tests. The idea behind the MMPI, though not new, helped revolutionize structured personality tests. The problem with early structured personality tests, such as the Woodworth, was that they made far too many assumptions that subsequent scientific investigations failed to substantiate. The authors of the MMPI, by contrast, argued that the meaning of a test response must be determined by empirical research. The MMPI, along with its updated companion the MMPI-2 (J. N. Butcher, 1989, 1990), is currently the most widely used and referenced personality test in existence. Its emphasis on the need for empirical data in determining the meaning of test results has stimulated the development of a wide body of knowledge (see Ben-Porath & Butcher, 1991).

Like other major tests introduced in the 20th century, the MMPI was met with initial enthusiasm followed by disillusionment as weaknesses became glaringly apparent. However, because of the large number of research studies that provide insight to the meaning of its scores, the MMPI has enjoyed substantial popularity and support from the scientific as well as the professional community. Recently, the MMPI has been revitalized by exceptionally rigorous methods. In 1957 the California Psychological Inventory (CPI) was developed within the context of the same commitment to empirical research. As you will see in Chapter 15, both the original MMPI and the original CPI contain significant problems. However, with the restandardization of the MMPI that took place in 1986 and the revision of the CPI in 1987, many of the problems have been corrected.

Just about the time the MMPI appeared, personality tests based on the statistical procedure called *factor analysis* began to emerge. **Factor analysis** is a method for finding the minimum number of dimensions (characteristics, attributes), called *factors,* to account for a large number of variables. We may say a person is outgoing, is gregarious, seeks company, is talkative, and enjoys relating to others. However, these descriptive adjectives contain a certain amount of redundancy, or overlap. A factor analysis can identify the extent of this overlap. For example, a factor analysis of the given characteristics might reveal that they all can be accounted for or subsumed under a single dimension (or factor): extroversion.

The first serious attempt to use factor analytic techniques in the development of a structured personality test was made by J. P. Guilford in the early 1940s. By the end of that decade, R. B. Cattell had introduced the Sixteen Personality Factor Questionnaire (16PF), which remains to this day one of the most well-constructed structured personality tests and an important example of a test developed with the aid of factor analysis. (Factor analytic personality tests will also be discussed in Chapter 15.) See Table 1-2 for a summary of personality tests.

The Period of Rapid Changes in the Status of Testing

The 1940s saw not only the emergence of a whole new technology in psychological testing but also the growth of applied aspects of psychology. The role and significance of tests used in World War I were reaffirmed in World War II. By this time the U.S. government had become interested in encouraging the continued development of applied psychological technology. As a result, considerable federal funding was funneled through the Veterans Administration to provide paid, supervised training experiences for clinically oriented psychologists. By 1949 formal university training standards were developed and accepted, and clinical psychology was born. Other applied branches of psychology—such as industrial, counseling, educational, and school psychology—soon began to blossom.

TABLE 1-2
Summary of
Personality Tests

Woodworth Personal Data Sheet: An early structured personality test that assumed that a test response can be taken at face value.

The Rorschach Inkblot Test: A projective test that provided an ambiguous stimulus (an inkblot) and asked the subject what it might be.

The Thematic Apperception Test (TAT): A projective test that provided ambiguous pictures and asked subjects to make up a story.

The Minnesota Multiphasic Personality Inventory (MMPI): A structured personality test that made no assumptions about the meaning of a test response. Such meaning was to be determined by empirical research.

The California Psychological Inventory (CPI): A structured personality test developed according to the same principles as the MMPI.

The Sixteen Personality Factor Questionnaire (16PF): A structured personality test based on the statistical procedure of factor analysis.

One of the major functions of the applied psychologist was psychological testing. The Shakow et al. (1947) report, which provided the foundation for the formal training standards in clinical psychology, specified that psychological testing was a unique function of the clinical psychologist and recommended that testing methods be taught to only doctoral psychology students. A position paper of the American Psychological Association published about seven years later (APA, 1954) affirmed that testing belongs to the clinical psychologist; it formally declared that the psychologist would conduct psychotherapy only in "true" collaboration with physicians. Thus, psychologists could conduct testing, but not psychotherapy, independently. Indeed, as long as psychologists assumed the role of testers, they played a complementary, but often secondary or subservient, role vis-à-vis medical practitioners. Though the medical profession could have made clinical psychology's emergence difficult, it did not because as tester the psychologist could aid the physician. Therefore, the late 1940s and early 1950s saw the use of tests as the major function of the clinical psychologist (L. Shaffer, 1953).

For better or worse, depending on one's perspective, the government's efforts to stimulate the development of applied aspects of psychology, especially clinical psychology, were extremely successful. Hundreds of highly talented and creative young people were attracted to clinical and other applied areas of psychology. These individuals, who would use tests and other psychological techniques to solve practical human problems, were uniquely trained as practitioners of the principles, empirical foundations, and applications of the science of psychology.

Many of these early clinical practitioners, armed with powerful knowledge from scientific psychology, must have felt like second-rate citizens when compared with physicians (see Saccuzzo & Kaplan, 1984). Unable to engage independently in the practice of psychotherapy, some psychologists perhaps felt like technicians serving the medical profession. The highly talented group of post–World War II psychologists quickly began to reject this secondary role (Lewandowski & Saccuzzo, 1976).

Because many psychologists, furthermore, associated tests with this secondary relationship, they rejected tests (Lewandowski & Saccuzzo, 1976). At the same time, the potentially intrusive nature of tests and fears of misuse began to create public suspicion, distrust, and contempt for tests. Attacks on testing came from within and without the profession of psychology. These attacks intensified and multiplied so fast that many psychologists jettisoned all ties to the traditional tests developed during the first half of this century. Testing therefore underwent another sharp decline in status in the late 1950s that persisted into the 1970s (see Holt, 1967).

The Current Environment

Most things seem to go through cycles; psychological testing is no exception. Although the attacks and efforts to impose restrictions on tests continue unabated, interest in psychological testing remains strong. Traditional tests continue to be used, and new procedures are developed each year. As in the past, psychological testing remains one of the most important yet controversial topics in psychology.

As a student, no matter what your major, you will find the thorough, up-to-date material in this text invaluable. If you are among those interested in using psychological techniques in an applied setting, then this information will be even more significant. Deep in the historical roots of psychology and through to the present, psychological tests have remained among the most important instruments of the psychologist in general and of those who apply psychology in particular.

Testing is indeed one of the essential elements of psychology. Though not all psychologists use tests and some psychologists are opposed to tests, all areas of psychology depend on knowledge gained in research studies that in turn rely on measurements. The meaning and dependability of these measurements necessarily stand among the most important foundations of psychological research. To study any area of human behavior effectively, one must understand the basic principles of measurement (see Matarazzo, 1990, 1991).

The use of specific psychological tests is one of the basic skills of the applied psychologist. In clinical settings, for example, testing is the unique function of the psychologist. Psychotherapy is often performed by psychiatrists, social workers, nurses, and even untrained volunteers. It is the psychologists, however, who administer and evaluate the results of psychological tests. Thus, training in testing is one of the psychologist's most distinguishing marks. In industrial and educational psychology, knowledge of psychological testing is one of the most important distinguishing skills the psychologist brings to the job.

In today's complex society, the relevance of the principles, applications, and issues of psychological testing extends far beyond the field of psychology. Even if you do not plan to become a psychologist, you are very likely to encounter psychological tests. Attorneys, physicians, social workers, business managers, educators, and many other professionals are frequently confronted with reports based on psychological tests. To make adequate use of such information, one needs the kinds of knowledge presented in this book. Thus, even if you enter a profession or occupation with little relevance to psychological testing, the principles, applications, and issues of psychological testing will be of interest to you.

The lives of you and your family, furthermore, will likely be touched by psychological tests. The more you know about psychological tests, the better able you will be to ensure that your encounters with them are positive. Given the attacks on tests and threats to prohibit or greatly limit their use, you have a responsibility to yourself and to society to know as much as you can about psychological tests. The future of testing may very well depend on you and people like you. A thorough knowledge of testing will allow you to base your decisions on facts and to ensure that tests are used for the most beneficial and constructive purposes.

Tests have probably never been as important as they are in contemporary society. For example, consider just one type of testing—academic aptitude. Every year more than 2.5 million individuals take tests designed to give schools some evidence of their academic suitability, and the testing process begins early in students' lives. Prestigious presecondary schools require a test that is taken by more than 16,000 children each year. When these students become adolescents and want to get into college preparatory schools, about 20,000 take a screening examination. Very few students who want to go to a four-year college can avoid taking a college entrance test. The Scholastic Aptitude Test alone is given to more than 1.8 million high school students each year. Another 100,000 high school seniors take other tests in order to gain advanced placement in college.

These figures do not include the 75,000 people who take a special test for admission to business school or the 120,000 who take a law school admission test. We have not even mentioned tests for graduate school, medical school, dental school, the military, and others. Millions of tests are given each year. As sources of information about human characteristics, the results of these tests affect critical life decisions.

Summary

The history of testing in America has been brief but intense. Although tests have always been available, psychological testing is very much a product of modern society with its unprecedented technology, population growth, and unique problems. By helping to solve the challenges posed by modern developments, tests have played a role in recent U.S. history. You should realize, however, that despite advances in the theory and technique of psychological testing, many unsolved technical problems and hotly debated social, political, and economic issues remain. Nevertheless, the prevalence of tests, despite strong opposition, indicates that although far from perfect, psychological tests must fulfill some important need in the decision-making processes permeating all facets of society. Because decisions must be made, with or without the aid of psychological tests, such tests will flourish until a better or more objective way of making decisions emerges.

Modern history shows that psychological tests have evolved in a complicated environment where hostile and facilitative forces have produced a balance characterized by innovation and a continuous quest for better methods. One interesting thing about tests is that people never seem to remain neutral about them. If you are not in favor of tests, then you probably have some strong reservations about them. We ask that you maintain a flexible, open mind before forming an opinion. No matter what your attitude toward psychological tests, however, studying them can be a most rewarding educational experience. If you know enough to form an independent judgment of psychological testing after reading this book, then we have accomplished our goal.

CHAPTER 2

Norms and Basic Statistics for Testing

LEARNING OBJECTIVES

When you have completed this chapter, you should be able to:

□ Discuss three properties of scales of measurement

□ Determine why properties of scales are important in the field of measurement

□ Tell why methods are available for displaying distributions of scores

□ Describe the mean and the standard deviation

□ Define a Z score and explain how it is used

□ Relate the concepts of mean, standard deviation, and Z score to the concept of a standard normal distribution

□ Define quartiles, deciles, and stanines and explain how they are used

□ Tell how norms are created

□ Relate the notion of tracking to the establishment of norms

We all use numbers as a basic way of communicating: Our money system requires us to understand and manipulate numbers, we estimate how long it will take to do things, we count, we express evaluations on scales, and so on. Think about how many times you use numbers in an average day. There is no way to avoid them.

One advantage of number systems is that they allow us to manipulate information. Through sets of well-defined rules, we can use numbers to learn more about the world. Tests are devices used to translate observations into numbers. Because the outcome of a test is almost always represented as a score, much of this book is about what scores mean. This chapter reviews some of the basic rules used to evaluate number systems. These rules and number systems are the psychologist's partners in learning about human behavior.

If you have had a course in psychological statistics, this chapter will reinforce the basic concepts. If you need additional review, reread your introductory statistics book. Most such books cover the information in this chapter. If you have not had a course in statistics, this chapter will provide some of the information needed for understanding other chapters in this book.

Why We Need Statistics

Through its commitment to the scientific method, modern psychology has advanced beyond centuries of speculation about human nature. Scientific study requires systematic observations and an estimation of the extent to which observations could have been influenced by chance alone. Statistical methods serve two important purposes in the quest for scientific understanding.

First, statistics are used to describe. Numbers provide convenient summaries and allow us to evaluate some observations relative to others. For example, if you get a score of 54 on a psychology examination, you probably want to know what the 54 means. Is it lower than the average score, or is it about the same? Knowing the answer can make the feedback you get from your examination more meaningful. If you discover that the 54 puts you in the top 5% of the class, you might assume you have a good chance for an *A.* If it puts you in the bottom 5%, you will feel differently.

Second, we can use statistics to make **inferences,** which are logical deductions about events that cannot be observed directly. For example, you do not know how many people watched a particular television movie unless you ask everyone. However, in using scientific sample surveys, you can make an inference about the percentage of people who saw the film. Data gathering and analysis might be considered analogous to criminal investigation and prosecution (Tukey, 1977, Brillinger, 1994). The first step is the detective work of gathering and displaying clues, or what Princeton statistician John Tukey calls *exploratory data analysis.* Then comes a period of *confirmatory data analysis,* when the clues are evaluated against rigid statistical rules. This latter phase is like the work done by judges and juries.

Some students have an aversion to numbers and anything mathematical. If you find yourself among them, you are not alone. Feeling uneasy about statistics is common not only among students but also among some professional psychologists. However, it is widely believed that statistics and the basic principles of measurement lie at the center of the modern science of psychology. Scientific statements are usually based on careful study, and such systematic study requires some numerical analysis.

This chapter will review both descriptive and inferential statistics. **Descriptive statistics** are methods used to provide a concise description of a collection of quantitative information. **Inferential statistics** are methods used to make inferences from observations of a small group of people known as a *sample* to a larger group of individuals known as a *population.* Typically the psychologist wants to make statements about the larger group but cannot possibly make all the necessary observations. Instead, he or she observes a relatively small group of subjects (sample) and uses inferential statistics to estimate the characteristics of the larger group.

The topics covered in this chapter include scales of measurement, the frequency distribution, the percentile distribution, the mean, the standard deviation, and norms.

Scales of Measurement

One may define *measurement* as the application of rules for assigning numbers to objects. The rules are the specific procedures used to transform qualities of attributes into numbers (Nunnally & Bernstein, 1994). For example, to rate the quality of wines, wine tasters must use a specific set of rules. They might rate the wine on a 10-point scale in which 1 means extremely bad and 10 means extremely good. For a taster to assign the numbers, the system of rules must be clearly defined. The basic feature of such systems is the scale of measurement. For example, to measure the height of your classmates, you might use the scale of inches; to measure their weight, you might use the scale of pounds.

Psychology does not have clearly acknowledged and widely accepted scales of measurement. Nevertheless, numerous systems exist by which we assign numbers. Indeed, the study of measurement systems is what this book is about. Before we consider any specific scale of measurement, however, we should consider the general properties of measurement scales.

Properties of Scales

Three important properties make scales of measurement different from one another: magnitude, equal intervals, and an absolute 0.

Magnitude. Magnitude is the property of "moreness." A scale has the property of magnitude if we can say that a particular instance of the attribute represents

FIGURE 2-1

Hypothetical relationship between ratings of artwork and manual dexterity. In some ranges of the scale, the relationship is more direct than it is in others.

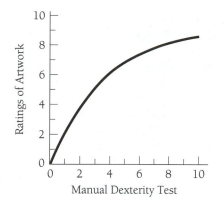

more, less, or equal amounts of the given quantity than another instance (McCall, 1994). On a scale of height, for example, if we can say that John is taller than Fred, then the scale has the property of magnitude. A scale that does not have this property arises, for example, when a gym coach assigns numbers to teams in a league for identification (team 1, team 2, and so forth). Because the numbers only label the teams, the property of magnitude is not achieved. If the coach were to rank the teams by the number of games they have won, then the new numbering system (games won) would have the property of magnitude.

Equal intervals. The concept of equal intervals is a little more complex. A scale has the property of equal intervals if the difference between two points at any place on the scale has the same meaning as the difference between two other points that differ by the same number of scale units. For example, the difference between inch 2 and inch 4 on a ruler means the same as the difference between inch 10 and inch 12. The difference is exactly 2 inches in each case.

As simple as this concept seems, rarely is there good evidence that a psychological test has the property of equal intervals. For example, the difference between IQs of 45 and 50 does not mean the same thing as the difference between IQs of 105 and 110. Although each of these differences is 5 points ($50 - 45 = 5$ and $110 - 105 = 5$), the 5 points at one level do not mean the same thing as 5 points at a higher level. When a scale has the property of equal intervals, the relationship between the measured units and some outcome can be described by a straight line or a linear equation in the form $Y = a + bX$. This equation shows that as one increases in equal units on a given scale, there are equal increases in the meaningful correlates of units. For example, Figure 2-1 shows the hypothetical relationship between scores on a test of manual dexterity and ratings of artwork. Notice that the relationship is not a straight line. By examining the points on the figure, you can see that at some points the relationship is approximately linear: Increases in manual dexterity are associated with increases in ratings of artwork. Then the relationship becomes nonlinear. The figure shows that after a manual dexterity score of about 5, greater increases in dexterity are needed to produce smaller increases in ratings of the quality of the artwork.

Absolute 0. An absolute 0 is obtained when nothing of the property being measured exists. For example, if you are measuring heart rate and observe that your patient has a rate of 0 and has died, you would conclude that there is no heart rate at all. For many psychological qualities, it is extremely difficult, if not impossible, to define an absolute 0 point. For example, if one measures shyness on a scale from 0 through 10, it is hard to say that 0 means the person is not shy at all (McCall, 1994).

Table 2-1 defines four scales of measurement based on the properties we have just discussed.

Types of Scales

Table 2-1 shows that a nominal scale does not have the property of magnitude, equal intervals, or an absolute 0. **Nominal scales** are really not scales at all; their only purpose is to name objects. For example, the numbers on the backs of football players' uniforms are nominal. Nominal scales are used when the information is qualitative rather than quantitative. Social science researchers commonly label groups in sample surveys with numbers (such as 1 = white, 2 = black, and 3 = Mexican-American). When these numbers have been attached to categories, however, some statistical procedures applied to numbers themselves are not advisable. On the scale for ethnic groups, a mean of 1.87 would have no meaning.[1]

A scale with the property of magnitude but not equal intervals or an absolute 0 is an **ordinal scale.** This scale allows one to rank individuals or objects but not to say anything about the meaning of the differences between the ranks. If you were to rank the members of your class in terms of their

---

[1]This is not to say that sophisticated statistical analysis is not possible when the data are nominal. Indeed, several new and exciting developments in data analysis allow extensive and detailed inquiry with nominal data (see Daniel, 1990; Siegel & Castellan, 1988).

TABLE 2-1
Scales of Measurement and Their Properties

	Property		
Type of Scale	**Magnitude**	**Equal Intervals**	**Absolute 0**
Nominal	No	No	No
Ordinal	Yes	No	No
Interval	Yes	Yes	No
Ratio	Yes	Yes	Yes

height, you would have an ordinal scale. Note that you would do this without concern for the differences among the ranks. For example, if Fred was the tallest, Susan the second tallest, and George the third tallest, you would assign them the ranks 1, 2, and 3, respectively. You would not give any consideration to the fact that Fred is 8 inches taller than Susan, but Susan is only 2 inches taller than George.

For most problems in psychology, the precision to measure the exact differences between intervals does not exist. So, most often one must use ordinal scales of measurement. For example, IQ tests (see Chapter 10) do not have the property of equal intervals or an absolute 0, but they do have the property of magnitude. If they had the property of equal intervals, the difference between an IQ of 70 and one of 90 should have the same meaning as the difference between an IQ of 125 and one of 145. Because it does not, the scale can only be considered ordinal. Furthermore, there is no point on the scale that represents no intelligence at all. Thus, the scale does not have the property of an absolute 0.

When a scale has the property of magnitude and equal intervals but not an absolute 0, we refer to it as an **interval scale.** The most common example of an interval scale is the measurement of temperature in degrees Fahrenheit. This temperature scale clearly has the property of magnitude, because 35°F is warmer than 32°F, 65°F is warmer than 64°F, and so on. Also, the difference between 90°F and 80°F is equal to a similar difference of 10 degrees at any point on the scale. However, on the Fahrenheit scale, temperature does not have the property of absolute 0. If it did, the 0 point would be more meaningful. As it is, 0 on the Fahrenheit scale does not have a particular meaning. Water freezes at 32°F and boils at 212°F. Because the scale does not have an absolute 0, it is not possible to make statements in terms of ratios. A temperature of 22°F is not twice as hot as 11°F, and a temperature of 70°F is not twice as hot as one of 35°F.

The Celsius scale of temperature is also an interval rather than a ratio scale. Although 0 represents freezing on the Celsius scale, it is not an absolute 0. Remember that an absolute 0 is a point at which nothing of the property being measured exists. Even on the Celsius scale of temperature, there is still plenty of room on the thermometer below 0. When the temperature goes below freezing, some aspect of heat is still being measured.

A scale that has all three properties (magnitude, equal intervals, and an absolute 0) is called a **ratio scale.** To continue our example with the scales of temperature, a ratio scale is one that has the properties of the Fahrenheit scale and the Celsius scale but also includes a meaningful 0 point. Physicists and chemists agree on a point at which all molecular activity ceases, or point of absolute 0. Because the Kelvin scale of temperature is based on the absolute 0 point, it provides an example of a ratio scale. Examples of ratio scales also appear in the numbers we see on a regular basis. For example, consider the number of yards gained by running backs on football teams. Zero yards actually means that the player has gained no yards at all. If one player has gained

1000 yards and another has gained only 500, then we can say that the first athlete has gained twice as many yards as the second.

Another example is the speed of travel. For instance, 0 mph (miles per hour) is the point at which there is no speed at all. If you are driving onto a highway at 30 mph and you increase your speed to 60 when you merge, you have doubled your speed.

Permissible Operations

Level of measurement is important because it defines which mathematical operations can be performed using the number. For nominal data, each observation can be placed in only one mutually exclusive category. For example, you are a member of only one gender. One can use nominal data to create frequency distributions (see next section), but no mathematical manipulations of the data are permissible. Ordinal measurements can be manipulated using arithmetic; however, the result is often difficult to interpret because it reflects neither the magnitudes of the manipulated observations nor the true amounts of the property that have been measured. For example, if the heights of 15 children are rank ordered, knowing a given child's rank does not reveal how tall he or she stands. Averages of these ranks are equally uninformative about height.

For interval data, one can apply any arithmetic operation to the differences between scores. The results can be interpreted in relation to the magnitudes of the underlying property. However, interval data cannot be used to make statements about ratios. For example, if IQ is measured on an interval scale, one cannot say that an IQ of 160 is twice as high as an IQ of 80. This mathematical operation is reserved for ratio scales, for which any mathematical operation is permissible.

Frequency Distributions

A single test score means more if one relates it to other test scores. A distribution of scores summarizes the scores for a group of individuals. In testing, there are many ways to record a distribution of scores.

A simple way of displaying data from tests, the **frequency distribution** is a technique for systematically displaying scores on a variable or a measure to reflect how frequently each value was obtained. With a frequency distribution, one defines all the possible scores and determines how many people obtained each of these scores. Usually, scores are arranged on the horizontal axis from the lowest to the highest value. The vertical axis reflects how many times each of the values on the horizontal axis was observed. For most distributions of test scores, the frequency distribution is approximately bell shaped, with the greatest frequency of scores toward the center of the distribution and decreas-

FIGURE 2-2

Frequency distribution approximating a normal distribution of 1000 observations.

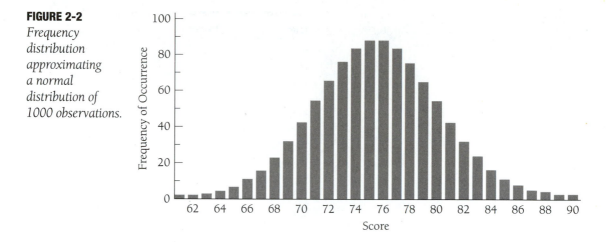

ing scores as the values become greater or less than the value in the center of the distribution.

Figure 2-2 shows a frequency distribution of 1000 observations that takes on values between 61 and 90. Notice that the most frequent observations fall toward the center of the distribution, around 75 and 76. As you look toward the extremes of the distribution, you will find a systematic decline in the frequency with which the scores occur. For example, the score of 71 is observed less frequently than the score of 72, which is observed less frequently than the score of 73, and so on. Similarly, the score of 78 is observed more frequently than the score of 79, which is noted more often than the score of 80, and so forth.

Though this neat symmetric relationship does not characterize all sets of scores, it occurs frequently enough in practice for us to devote special attention to it. In the section on the normal distribution, we will explain this concept in a little more detail.

Table 2-2 lists the rainfall amounts in San Diego, California, between the years 1967 and 1995. Figure 2-3 is a histogram from the observations. Looking at the figure, you will find a distribution that is slightly skewed, or asymmetrical. Figure 2-3 has a positive skew because the tail goes off toward the higher or positive side of the *x* axis.

One can also present this same set of rainfall data as a frequency polygon (see Figure 2-4). Here the amount of rainfall is placed on the graph as a point representing the frequencies with which each interval occurs. Then, lines are drawn to connect these points.

Whenever you draw a frequency distribution or a frequency polygon, you must decide on the width of the class interval. The **class interval** for inches of rainfall is the unit for the horizontal axis. For example, in Figures 2-3 and 2-4, the class interval is 2 inches—that is, the demarcations along the *x* axis increase in 2-inch intervals. This interval is used here because of convenience; the choice of 2 inches is arbitrary.

TABLE 2-2
Inches of Rainfall in San Diego, 1967–1995

Year	Inches
1967	11.04
1968	8.04
1969	11.68
1970	6.48
1971	8.20
1972	6.24
1973	11.16
1974	6.68
1975	10.80
1976	9.24
1977	9.32
1978	17.56
1979	15.52
1980	15.72
1981	7.48
1982	12.04
1983	18.76
1984	5.44
1985	9.76
1986	15.20
1987	9.44
1988	12.64
1989	5.96
1990	7.76
1991	12.20
1992	12.48
1993	18.23
1994	9.92
1995	17.08
Sum	322.07
Mean	11.11
Variance	15.32
Standard deviation	3.91

Percentile Ranks

Percentile ranks replace simple ranks when one wants to adjust for the number of scores in a group. A **percentile rank** answers the question "What percent of the scores fall below a particular score (X_i)?" To calculate a percentile rank, you need only follow these simple steps:

1. Determine how many cases are below the score of interest.
2. Determine how many cases are in the group.

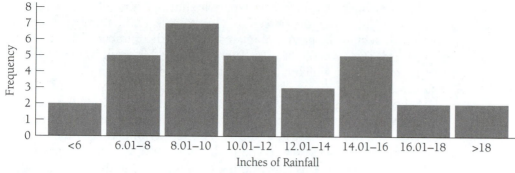

FIGURE 2-3   *Histogram for San Diego rainfall: 1967–1995.*

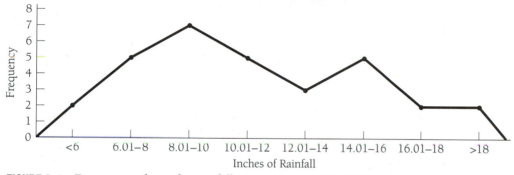

FIGURE 2-4   *Frequency polygon for rainfall in San Diego, 1967–1995.*

3. Divide the number of cases below the score of interest (Step 1) by the total number of cases in the group (Step 2).

4. Multiply the result of Step 3 by 100.

The formula is

$$P_r = \frac{B}{N} \times 100 = \text{percentile rank of } X_i$$

where P_r = percentile rank
 $\quad X_i$ = the score of interest
 $\quad B$ = the number of scores below X_i
 $\quad N$ = the total number of scores

This means that you form a ratio of the number of cases below the score of interest and the total number of scores. Because there will always be either the same or fewer cases in the numerator (top half) of the equation than there are in the denominator (bottom half), this ratio will always be less than or equal to 1. To get rid of the decimal points, multiply by 100.

As an example, consider the runner who finishes 62nd out of 63 racers in a gym class. To obtain the percentile rank, divide 1 (the number of people who finish behind the person of interest) by 63 (the number of scores in the group). This gives you 63, or .016. Then, multiply this result by 100 to obtain the percentile rank, which is 1.6. This rank tells you the runner is below the 2nd percentile.

Now consider the Bay to Breakers race, which attracts 50,000 runners to San Francisco. If you had finished 62nd out of 50,000, then the number of people who were behind you would be 49,938. Dividing this by the number of entrants gives .9988. When you multiply by 100, you get the percentile rank, which is 99.88. This tells you that finishing 62nd in the Bay to Breakers race is exceptionally good, because it places you in the 99.88th percentile.

Technical Box 2-1 presents the calculation of percentile ranks for the infant mortality rates from selected countries. Infant mortality is defined as the number of babies born alive who die before their first birthday per 1000 births. Before proceeding, we should point out that the meaning of this calculation depends on which countries are used in the comparison.

In this example, the calculation of the percentile rank is broken down into five steps and uses the raw data in the table. In Step 1 we arrange the data points in descending order. Japan has the lowest infant mortality rate of 4, Sweden is next with 5 years, and Mozambique has the highest rate at 162.

In Step 2 we determine the number of cases with worse rates than the case of interest. In this example, the case of interest is the United States. Therefore, we count the number of cases with a worse rate than that of the United States (9)—eight countries (Colombia, Saudi Arabia, Turkey, Morocco, Bolivia, Zambia, Ethiopia, Mozambique) have an infant mortality rate greater than 9.

In Step 3 we determine the total number of cases (16).

In Step 4 we divide the number of scores worse than the score of interest by the total number of scores:

$$\frac{8}{16} = .50$$

Technically, the percentile rank is a percentage. Step 4 gives a proportion. Therefore, in Step 5 you transform this into a whole number by multiplying by 100:

$$.50 \times 100 = 50$$

Thus, the United States is in the 50th percentile.

The percentile rank depends absolutely on the cases used for comparison. In this example, you calculated that the United States is in the 50th percentile for infant mortality within this group of countries. If all the countries in the world had been included, the ranking of the United States might have been different.

TECHNICAL BOX 2-1

Infant Mortality in Selected Countries, 1994

Country	Infant Mortality Rate per 1000 Live Births
Australia	7
Bolivia	82
Colombia	21
Ethiopia	122
France	7
Israel	9
Italy	8
Japan	4
Morocco	57
Mozambique	162
Saudi Arabia	28
Spain	8
Sweden	5
Turkey	54
United States	9
Zambia	107

Data from World Development Report, 1994,
World Development Indicators, Oxford
University Press, International Bank, 1994.

To calculate the percentile rank of infant mortality in the United States in comparison to that in selected countries, use the following formula:

$$P_r = \frac{B}{N} \times 100$$

where P_r = the percentile rank
B = the number of cases with worse rates than the case of interest
N = the total number of cases

Steps

1. Arrange data in ascending order—the lowest score first, second lowest score second, and so on.

    $N = 16$, mean = 43.13, standard deviation = 49.91

Continued

Continued

	Infant Mortality Rate
Country	per 1000 Live Births
Japan	4
Sweden	5
Australia	7
France	7
Italy	8
Spain	8
Israel	9
United States	9
Colombia	21
Saudi Arabia	28
Turkey	54
Morocco	57
Bolivia	82
Zambia	107
Ethiopia	122
Mozambique	162

2. Determine the number of cases with worse rates than the score of interest. There are eight countries in this sample with infant mortality rates greater than that in the United States. Note that an equal score (in this case, Israel) is not counted.
3. Determine the number of cases in the sample (16).
4. Divide the number of scores worse than the score of interest (Step 2) by the total number of scores (Step 3):
$$\frac{8}{16} = .50$$
5. Multiply by 100:
$$.50 \times 100 = 50\text{th percentile rank}$$

Using this procedure, try to calculate the percentile rank for Bolivia. The calculation is the same except that there are three countries with worse rates than Bolivia (as opposed to eight worse than the United States). Thus, the percentile rank for Bolivia is

$$\frac{3}{16} = .19 \times 100 = 19$$

or the 19th percentile. Now try Australia. You should get a percentile rank of 75.

Percentiles

Percentiles are the specific scores or points within a distribution. Percentiles divide the total frequency for a set of observations into hundredths. Instead of indicating what percent of scores fall below a particular score, as percentile ranks do, percentiles indicate the particular score, below which a defined percent of scores falls.

Try to calculate the percentile and percentile rank for some of the data in Technical Box 2-1. As an example, look at Italy. The infant mortality rate in Italy is 8/1000. When calculating the percentile rank, you exclude the score of interest and count those below (in other words, Italy is not included in the count). In addition, Spain is excluded because it has the same score as Italy. There are 10 countries in this sample with infant mortality rates worse than Italy's. To calculate the percentile rank, divide this number of countries by the total number of cases and multiply by 100:

$$Pr = \frac{B}{N} \times 100 = \frac{10}{16} \times 100 = .63 \times 100 = 63$$

Thus, Italy is in the 63rd percentile rank, or the 63rd percentile in this example is 8/1000 live births.

Now take the example of Israel. Notice that it has the same infant mortality rate as the United States. The calculation of percentile rank requires looking at the number of cases below the case of interest. In this example, there are eight countries in this group with infant mortality rates worse than Israel's (Colombia, Saudi Arabia, Turkey, Morocco, Bolivia, Zambia, Ethiopia and Mozambique). Thus, the percentile rank for Israel is $8/16 \times 100 = 50$. The 50th percentile corresponds with the point or score 9 (of 9/1000 live births).

In summary, the percentile and the percentile rank are similar. The percentile gives the point in a distribution below which a specified percentage of cases fall (8/1000 for Italy). The percentile is in raw score units. The percentile rank gives the proportion of cases below the percentile; in this example the percentile rank is 63.

When reporting percentiles and percentile ranks, you must carefully specify the population you are working with. Remember that a percentile rank is a measure of relative performance. When interpreting a percentile rank, you should always ask the question "Relative to what?" Suppose, for instance, that you finished in the 17th percentile in a swimming race (or fifth in a heat of six competitors). Does this mean that you are a slow swimmer? Not necessarily. It may be that this was a heat in the Olympic games, and the participants were the fastest swimmers in the world. An Olympic swimmer competing against a random sample of all people in the world would probably finish in the 99.99th percentile. The example for infant mortality rates depends on which countries in the world were selected for comparison. The United States actually does quite poorly when compared to European countries. However, the U.S. infant mortality rate looks much better in comparison to countries in the developing world.

Describing Distributions

Mean

Statistics are used to summarize data. If you consider a set of scores, the mass of information may be too much to interpret all at once. That is why we need certain numerical conveniences to help summarize the information. An example of a set of scores that can be summarized is shown in Table 2-2. These scores are the amounts of rainfall in San Diego in the years 1967–1995. We signify the variable as X. A variable is a score that takes on different values. The amount of rain is a variable because different amounts of rain fell in different years.

The arithmetic average score in a distribution is called the **mean**. To calculate the mean, we total the scores and divide the sum by the number of cases. Usually we signify the number of cases by N. The capital Greek letter sigma (Σ) means summation. Thus, the formula for the mean, which we signify as $\overline{X}$, is

$$\overline{X} = \frac{\Sigma X}{N}$$

In words, this formula says to total the scores and divide the sum by the number of cases. Using the information in Table 2-2, we find the mean by following these steps:

1. Obtain ΣX, or the sum of the scores:
   $11.04 + 8.04 + 11.68 + \cdots + 9.92 + 17.08 = 322.07$
2. Find N, or the number of scores:
   $N = 29$
3. Divide ΣX by N:
   $332.07/29 = 11.11$

Technical Box 2-2 summarizes common symbols used in basic statistics.

TECHNICAL BOX 2-2

Common Symbols

It is important that you understand and learn to recognize the symbols used throughout this book. $\overline{X}$ is the mean; it is pronounced "X bar." Σ is the summation sign. It means sum, or add, scores together and is the capital Greek letter sigma. X is a variable that takes on different values. Each value of X_i represents a raw score, also called an obtained score.

Standard Deviation

The standard deviation is an approximation of the average deviation around the mean. It will be described in more detail in the next section. The standard deviation for the amount of rainfall in San Diego is 3.91. To understand rainfall in San Diego, you need to consider at least two dimensions: first, the amount of rain that falls in a particular year; second, the degree of variation from year to year in the amount of rain that falls. The calculation suggests that, on the average, the variation around the mean is about 3.91 inches.

However informative it is to know the mean of a group of scores, it does not give you all the desired information about the group of scores. As an illustration, look at the following sets of numbers.

Set 1	Set 2	Set 3
4	5	8
4	5	8
4	4	6
4	4	2
4	3	0
4	3	0

Calculate the mean of the first set. You should get 4. Now what is the mean of the second set? If you calculate correctly, you should get 4 again. Next, find the mean for Set 3. It is also 4. The three distributions of scores that appear very different have the same mean. Therefore, it is important to consider other characteristics of the distribution of scores besides the mean. The difference between Set 1, Set 2, and Set 3 lies in variability. There is no variability in Set 1, a small amount in Set 2, and a lot in Set 3.

The variation we would like to consider here is similar to the average deviation around the mean. One way to do this is to subtract the mean from each score $(X - \overline{X})$. Statisticians often signify this with a lowercase x $[x = (X - \overline{X})]$. Then total the deviations. Try this for the data in Table 2-2. Did you get 0? You should have, and this is not an unusual example. In fact, the sum of the deviations around the mean will always equal 0. However, you do have an alternative: You can square all the deviations around the mean in order to get rid of any negative signs. Then you can obtain the average squared deviation around the mean, known as the **variance.** The formula for the variance is

$$\sigma^2 = \frac{\Sigma(X - \overline{X})^2}{N}$$

where $(X - \overline{X})$ is the deviation of a score from the mean. The symbol σ is the lowercase Greek sigma; σ^2 is used as a standard description of the variance.

Though the variance is a very useful statistic commonly used in data analysis, it shows the variable in squared deviations around the mean rather than in deviations around the mean. In words, the variance is the average squared deviation around the mean. To get it back into the units that will make sense to us, we need to take the square root of the variance. The square root of the variance is the standard deviation (σ), and it is represented by the following formula:

$$\sigma = \sqrt{\frac{\Sigma(X - \overline{X})^2}{N}}$$

The **standard deviation** is thus the square root of the average squared deviation around the mean. Although the standard deviation is not an average deviation, it gives a useful approximation of how much a typical score is above or below the average score.

Because of their mathematical properties, the variance and the standard deviation have many advantages. For example, knowing the standard deviation of a normally distributed batch of data allows one to make precise statements about the distribution. The formulas just presented are for computing the variance and the standard deviation of a population. That is why we use the lower-case Greek sigma (σ and σ^2). Technical Box 2-3 summarizes when you should use Greek and Roman letters. Most often we use the standard deviation for a sample to estimate the standard deviation for a population. When we talk about a sample, we replace the Greek σ with a Roman letter S. Also, we divide by $N - 1$ rather than N: Dividing by $N - 1$ compensates for S of a sample underestimating the variance of the population.

$$S = \sqrt{\frac{\Sigma(X - \overline{X})^2}{N - 1}}$$

TECHNICAL BOX 2-3

Terms and Symbols Used to Describe Populations and Samples

	Population	Sample
Definition	All elements with the same definition	A subset of the population, usually drawn to represent it in an unbiased fashion
Descriptive characteristics	Parameters	Statistics
Symbols used to describe	Greek	Roman
Symbol for mean	μ	$\overline{X}$
Symbol for standard deviation	σ	S

In calculating the standard deviation, it is often easier to use the raw score equivalent formula, which is

$$S = \sqrt{\frac{\Sigma X^2 - \frac{(\Sigma X)^2}{N}}{N - 1}}$$

This calculation can also be done automatically by some minicalculators.

In reading the formula, you may be confused by a few points. In particular, be careful not to confuse ΣX^2 and $(\Sigma X)^2$. To get ΣX^2, each individual score is squared and the values are summed. For the scores 3, 5, 7, and 8, ΣX^2 would be $3^2 + 5^2 + 7^2 + 8^2 = 9 + 25 + 49 + 64 = 147$. To obtain $(\Sigma X)^2$, the scores are first summed and the total is squared. Using the example, $(\Sigma X)^2 = (3 + 5 + 7 + 8)^2 = 23^2 = 529$.

Z Score

One of the problems with means and standard deviations is that their interpretations are not clear. For example, if the mean of some set of scores is 57.6, it does not convey all of the information one would like. Other metrics are designed for a more exact interpretation. The Z score transforms data into standardized units that are easier to interpret. A Z score is the difference between a score and the mean, divided by the standard deviation:

$$Z = \frac{X - \overline{X}}{S}$$

In other words, a Z score is the deviation of a score X from the mean $\overline{X}$ in standard deviation units. If a score is equal to the mean, its Z score is 0. For example, suppose the score and the mean are both 6; then $6 - 6 = 0$. Zero divided by anything is still 0. If the score is greater than the mean, the Z score is positive; if the score is less than the mean, the Z score is negative.

Let's try an example. Suppose that $X = 6$, the mean $\overline{X} = 3$, and the standard deviation $S = 3$. Plugging these values into the formula, we get

$$Z = \frac{6 - 3}{3} = \frac{3}{3} = 1$$

Let's try another example. Suppose $X = 4$, $\overline{X} = 5.75$, and $S = 2.11$. What is the Z score? It is $-.83$:

$$Z = \frac{4 - 5.75}{2.11} = \frac{-1.74}{2.11} = -.83$$

This means that the score we observed (4) is .83 standard deviation below the average score, or that the score is below the mean but its difference from the mean is slightly less than the average deviation.

Center for Epidemiologic Studies Depression Scale (CES-D)

Instructions: Circle the number for each statement that best describes how often you felt or behaved this way DURING THE PAST WEEK.

		Rarely or none of the time (less than 1 day)	Some or a little of the time (1–2 days)	Occasionally or a moderate amount of the time (3–4 days)	Most or all of the time (5–7 days)
	1. I was bothered by things that usually don't bother me.	0	1	2	3
	2. I did not feel like eating.	0	1	2	3
	3. I felt that I could not shake off the blues even with help from my family or friends.	0	1	2	3
R	**4.** I felt that I was just as good as other people.	0	1	2	3
	5. I had trouble keeping my mind on what I was doing.	0	1	2	3
	6. I felt depressed.	0	1	2	3
	7. I felt that everything I did was an effort.	0	1	2	3
R	**8.** I felt hopeful about the future.	0	1	2	3
	9. I thought my life had been a failure.	0	1	2	3
	10. I felt fearful.	0	1	2	3
	11. My sleep was restless.	0	1	2	3
R	**12.** I was happy.	0	1	2	3
	13. I talked less than usual.	0	1	2	3
	14. I felt lonely.	0	1	2	3
	15. People were unfriendly.	0	1	2	3
R	**16.** I enjoyed life.	0	1	2	3
	17. I had crying spells.	0	1	2	3
	18. I felt sad.	0	1	2	3
	19. I felt that people disliked me.	0	1	2	3
	20. I could not get "going."	0	1	2	3

Example of depression in medical students—Center for Epidemiologic Studies Depression Scale (CES-D). The CES-D is a general measure of depression that has been used extensively in epidemiologic studies. The scale includes 20 items and taps dimensions of depressed mood, hopelessness, appetite loss, sleep disturbance, and energy level. Each year, students at the University of California, San Diego School of Medicine, are asked to report how often they experienced a particular symptom during the first week of school on a four-point scale ranging from rarely or none of the time [0 to 1 days (0)] to most or all of the time [5 to 7 days (3)]. Items 4, 8, 12, and 16 on the CES-D are reverse scored. For these items, 0 is scored as 3, 1 is scored as 2, 2 as 1, and 3 as 0. The CES-D score is obtained by summing the circled numbers. Scores on the CES-D range from 0 to 60, with scores greater than 16 indicating clinically significant levels of depressive symptomatology in adults.

Feel free to take the CES-D measure yourself. Calculate your score by summing the numbers you have circled. However, you must first reverse the scores on items 4, 8, 12, and 16. As you will see in Chapter 5, the CES-D does not have high validity for determining clinical depression. If your score is less than 16, the evidence suggests that you are not clinically depressed. If your score is high, though, this does not mean that you have a clinical depression problem. However, you may want to talk with your college counselor if you are feeling depressed.

Table 2-3 (on page 48) shows CES-D scores for a selected sample of medical students. You can use these data to practice calculating means, standard deviations, and Z scores.

Figure 2-5 provides a frequency distribution for the CES-D scores of medical students using a class interval of 5.

Standard Normal Deviation

Now we consider the standard normal distribution because it is central to statistics and psychological testing. First, though, you should participate in a short exercise. Take any coin and flip it 10 times. Now repeat this exercise of 10 coin flips 25 times. Record the number of heads you observe in each group of 10 flips. When you are done, make a frequency distribution showing how many times you observed 1 head in your 10 flips, 2 heads, 3 heads, and so on.

FIGURE 2-5

Frequency distribution of CES-D scores for medical students using a class interval of 5.

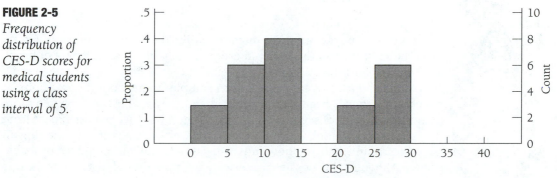

TABLE 2-3

The Calculation of Mean, Standard Deviation, and Z Scores for CES-D Scores

Name	Test Score (X)	X²	Z Score
John	14	196	.42
Carla	10	100	−.15
Fred	8	64	−.44
Monica	8	64	−.44
Eng	26	676	2.13
Fritz	0	0	−1.58
Mary	14	196	.42
Susan	3	9	−1.15
Debbie	9	81	−.29
Elizabeth	10	100	−.15
Sarah	7	49	−.58
Marcel	12	144	.14
Robin	10	100	−.15
Mike	25	625	1.99
Carl	9	81	−.29
Phyllis	12	144	.14
Jennie	23	529	1.70
Richard	7	49	−.58
Tyler	13	169	.28
Frank	1	1	−1.43
	$\Sigma X = 221$	$\Sigma X^2 = 3377$	

$$\bar{X} = \frac{\Sigma X}{N} = \frac{221}{20} = 11.05$$

$$S = \sqrt{\frac{\Sigma X^2 - \frac{(\Sigma X)^2}{N}}{N-1}} = \sqrt{\frac{3377 - \frac{(221)^2}{20}}{20-1}} = 7.01$$

$$\text{Monica's } Z \text{ score} = \frac{X - \bar{X}}{S} = \frac{8 - 11.05}{7.01} = -.44$$

$$\text{Marcel's } Z \text{ score} = \frac{X - \bar{X}}{S} = \frac{12 - 11.05}{7.01} = -.14$$

$$\text{Jennie's } Z \text{ score} = \frac{X - \bar{X}}{S} = \frac{23 - 11.05}{7.01} = 1.70$$

Your frequency distribution might look like the example shown in Figure 2-6. The most frequently observed events are about equal numbers of heads and tails. Toward the 10 heads and 0 tails or the 10 tails and 0 heads, events are observed with less frequency. For example, there were no occasions in which fewer than 2 heads were observed and only 1 occasion in which more than 8 heads were observed. This is very much what we would expect from the laws of probability. On the average, we would expect half of the flips to show heads and half to show tails if heads and tails are equally probable events. Although it is possible to observe a long string of heads or tails, it is improbable. In other words, we will sometimes see the coin come up heads in

FIGURE 2-6
*Frequency
distribution of the
number of heads
in 25 sets of 10
flips.*

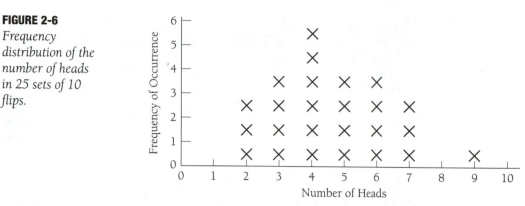

9 out of 10 flips. The likelihood that this will happen, however, is quite small.

Figure 2-7 shows the theoretical distribution of heads in an infinite number of flips of the coin. This figure might look a little like the distribution from your coin flipping exercise or the distribution shown in Figure 2-6. Actually this is a normal distribution, or what is known as a *symmetrical binomial probability distribution.*

On most occasions we refer to units on the *x* (or horizontal) axis of the normal distribution in *Z* score units. Any variable transformed into *Z* score units takes on special properties. First, *Z* scores have a mean of 0 and a standard deviation of 1.0. If you think about this for a minute, you should be able to figure out why this is true. Recall that the sum of the deviations around the mean is always equal to 0. The numerator of the *Z* score equation is the deviation around the mean, while the denominator is a constant. Thus, the mean of *Z* scores can be expressed as

$$\frac{\Sigma(X - \overline{X})/S}{N} \quad \text{or} \quad \frac{\Sigma Z}{N}$$

Because $\Sigma(X - \overline{X})$ will always equal 0, the mean of *Z* scores will always be 0. In Figure 2-7 the standardized, or *Z* score, units are marked on the *x* axis.

The numbers under the curve are the proportions of cases (in decimal form) we would expect to observe in each area. Multiplying these proportions

FIGURE 2-7
*The theoretical
distribution of the
number of heads
in an infinite
number of
coin flips.*

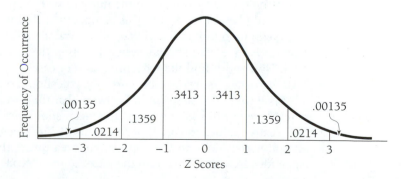

by 100 yields percentages. For example, we see that 34.13% or .3413 of the cases fall between the mean and 1 standard deviation above the mean. Do not forget that 50% of the cases fall below the mean. Putting these two bits of information together, we can conclude that if a score is 1 standard deviation above the mean, then it is at about the 84th percentile rank (50 + 34.13 = 84.13 to be exact). A score that is 1 standard deviation below the mean would be about the 16th percentile rank (50 − 34.13 = 15.87). Thus, you can use what you have learned about means, standard deviations, Z scores, and the normal curve to transform raw scores, which have very little meaning, into percentile scores, which are easier to interpret. These methods can be used only when the distribution of scores is normal or approximately normal. Methods for nonnormal distributions are discussed in most statistics books under "nonparametric statistics."

Percentiles and *Z* scores. Appendix 1 contains two tables that relate Z scores to proportions. Part I of the table gives percentile ranks associated with various Z scores. These percentile ranks are the percentage of scores that fall below the observed Z score. For example, the Z score −1.6 is associated with the percentile rank of 5.48. The Z score 1.0 (third column) is associated with the percentile rank of 84.13.

Part I of Appendix 1 is a simplified table. For more advanced use of Z scores, you will need to use Part II, which gives the areas between the mean and various Z scores. Standard scored values are listed in the "Z" column. To find the proportion of the distribution between the mean of the distribution and a given Z score, you must locate the entry indicated by a specific Z score. Z scores are carried to a second decimal place in the columns that go across the table. First, consider the second column of the table because it is similar to Part I of Appendix 1. Take the Z score of 1.0. The second column is labeled .00, which means that the second decimal place is also 0. The number listed in the table is .3413. Since this is a positive number, it is above the mean. Because the area below the mean is .5, the total area below a Z score of 1.0 is .5 + .3413 = .8413. To make this into a percentile (as shown in Part I of the appendix), multiply by 100 to get 84.13. Now try the example of a Z score of 1.64. To locate this value, find 1.6 in the first column. Then move your hand across the row until you get to the number below the heading .04. The number should be .4495. Again, this is a positive Z score, so you must add the observed proportion to the .5 that falls below the mean. The proportion below 1.64 is .9495. Stated another way, 94.95% of the cases fall below a Z score of 1.64. Now try to find the percentile rank of cases that fall below a Z score of 1.10. If you are using the table correctly, you should obtain 86.43.

Now try −.75. You should be aware that this is a negative Z score, so the percentage of cases falling below the mean should be less than 50. There are no negative values in Part II of Appendix 1. For a negative Z score, there are several ways to obtain the appropriate area under the curve. The tables in Appendix 1 give the area from the mean to the Z score. For a Z score of −.75, the area between the mean and the Z score is .2734. You can find this by entering the table in the row labeled .7 and then moving across the row until you get to the figure in that row below the heading .05. There you should find the number .2734. We know that .5 of the cases fall below the mean. Thus, for a negative Z score, we can obtain the proportion of cases falling below the score by subtracting .2734, the tabled value listed in the appendix, from .5. In this case, the result is

$$.5 - .2734 = .2266$$

Because finding the percentile ranks associated with negative Z scores can be tricky, you might want to use Part I of Appendix 1 to see if you are in the right ballpark. This table gives both negative and positive Z scores but does not give the detail associated with the second decimal place. Look up −.7 in Part I. The percentile rank is 24.20. Now consider a Z score of .8. That percentile rank is 21.19. Thus, you know that a Z score of −.75 should be associated with a percentile rank between 21.19 and 24.20. In fact, we have calculated that the actual percentile rank is 22.66.

Practice with Appendix 1 until you are confident you understand how it works. Do not hesitate to ask your professor or teaching assistant if you are confused. This is a very important concept that you will need throughout the rest of the book.

Look at one more example from Table 2-2 (the table of rainfall amounts in San Diego). California had a dry year in 1990. The newscasters frequently commented that it was a very unusual year. The question is whether or not the amount of rainfall received in 1990 was unusual given what we know about rainfall in general. To evaluate this, calculate the Z score for rainfall. According to Table 2-2, there were 7.76 inches of rainfall in 1990. The mean for rainfall is 11.11 inches and the standard deviation is 3.91. Thus, the Z score is

$$\frac{7.76 - 11.11}{3.91} = -.86$$

Next, determine where a Z score of −.86 falls within the Z distribution. According to Appendix 1, a Z score of −.86 is equal to the 19.49th percentile (50 − 30.51). Thus, the low rainfall year in 1990 was unusual—given all years, it was in about the 19th percentile. However, it was not *that* unusual. You can estimate that there would be less rainfall in approximately 19% of all years.

You can also turn the process around. Instead of using Z scores to find the percentile ranks, you can use the percentile ranks to find the corresponding Z scores. To do this, look in Part II of Appendix 1 under percentiles and find the corresponding Z score. For example, suppose you wish to find the Z score associated with the 90th percentile. When you enter Part II of Appendix 1, look for the value closest to the 90th percentile. This can be a little tricky because of the way the table is structured. Because the 90th percentile is associated with a positive Z score, you are actually looking for the area above the 50th percentile. So, you should look for the entry closest to .4000 (.5000 +

.4000 = .9000). The closest value to .4000 is .3997, which is found in the row labeled 1.2 and the column labeled .8. This tells you that a person who obtains a Z score of 1.28 is at about the 90th percentile in the distribution.

Now return to the example of CES-D scores for medical students. Monica had a Z score on the CES-D of −.44. Using Appendix 1, you can see that she was in the 33rd percentile (obtained as .50 − .1700 =.33 × 100 = 33). Marcel, with his Z score of .14, was in the 56th percentile, and Jennie, with a Z score of 1.70, was in the 96th percentile. You might have few worries about Monica and Marcel. However, it appears that Jennie is more depressed than 96% of her classmates and may need to talk to someone.

An example close to home. One of the difficulties in grading students is that performance is usually rated in terms of raw scores, such as the number of items a person gets correct on an examination. You are probably familiar with the experience of having a test returned to you with some number that makes little sense to you. For instance, the professor comes into class and hands you your test with a 72 on it. You must then wait patiently while he or she draws the distribution on the board and tries to put your 72 into some category that you understand, such as *B+*.

An alternative way of doing things would be to give you a Z score as feedback about your performance. To do this, your professor would subtract the average score (mean) from your score and divide by the standard deviation. If your Z score was positive, you would immediately know that your score was above average; if it was negative, you would know your performance was below average.

Suppose that your professor tells you in advance that you will be graded on a curve system according to the following rigid criteria. If you are in the top 15% of the class, you will get an *A* (85th percentile or above); between the 60th and the 84th percentiles, a *B*; between the 20th and the 59th percentiles, a *C*; between the 6th and the 19th percentiles, a *D*; and in the 5th percentile or below, an *F*. Using Appendix 1, you should be able to find the Z scores associated with each of these cutoff points for normal distributions of scores. Try it on your own, then consult Table 2-4 to see if you are correct. Looking at Table 2-4, you should be able to determine what your grade would be in this class on the basis of your Z score. If your Z score is 1.04 or greater, you would

TABLE 2-4

Z Score Cutoffs for a Grading System

Grade	Percentiles	Z Score Cutoff
A	85–100	1.04
B	60–84	.25
C	20–59	−.84
D	6–19	−1.56
F	0–5	<−1.56

receive an *A*; if it were greater than .25 but less than 1.04, you would get a *B*; and so on. This system assumes that the scores are normally distributed.

Now try an example that puts a few of the concepts together. Suppose you get a 60 on a social psychology examination. You learned in class that the mean for the test was 55.70 and that the standard deviation was 6.08. If your professor uses the grading system that was just described, what would your grade be?

To solve this problem, first find your *Z* score. The formula for a *Z* score is

$$Z = \frac{X - \overline{X}}{S}$$

So your *Z* score would be

$$Z = \frac{60 - 55.70}{6.08} = \frac{4.30}{6.08} = .707$$

Looking at Table 2-4, you see that .707 is greater than .25 (the cutoff for a *B*) but less than 1.04 (the cutoff for an *A*). Now, find your exact standing in the class. To do this, look again at Appendix 1. Because the table gives *Z* scores only to the second decimal, round .707 to .71. Looking at the appendix, you will find that 76.11% of the scores fall below a *Z* score of .71. This means that you would be in approximately the 76th percentile, or you would have performed better on this examination than approximately 76 out of every 100 students.

McCall's T

There are a variety of other systems by which one can transform raw scores to give them more intuitive meaning. One system was established in 1939 by W. A. McCall, who originally intended to develop a system to derive equal units on mental quantities. He suggested that a random sample of 12-year-olds be tested and that the distribution of their scores be obtained. Then percentile equivalents were to be assigned to each raw score, showing the percentile rank in the group for the people who had obtained that raw score. After this had been accomplished, the mean of the distribution would be set at 50, to correspond with the 50th percentile. In McCall's system, called **McCall's T**, the standard deviation was set at 10.

In effect, what McCall generated was a system that is exactly the same as standard scores (*Z* scores), except that the mean in McCall's system is 50 rather than 0 and the standard deviation is 10 rather than 1. Indeed, a *Z* score can be transformed to a **T score** by applying the linear transformation

$$T = 10Z + 50$$

You can thus get from a *Z* score to McCall's *T* by multiplying the *Z* score by 10 and adding 50. It should be noted that McCall did not originally intend to create an alternative to the *Z* score. He wanted to obtain one set of scores that could then be applied in other situations without standardizing the entire set of numbers.

There is nothing magical about the mean of 50 and the standard deviation of 10. It is a simple matter to create systems such as standard scores with any mean and standard deviation you like. If you want to say that you got a score 1000 points higher than a person who was 1 standard deviation below you, you could devise a system with a mean of 100,000 and a standard deviation of 1000. If you had calculated Z scores for this distribution, you would obtain this with the transformation

$$NS \text{ (for new score)} = 1000Z + 100,000$$

In fact, you can create any system you desire. To do so, just multiply the Z score by whatever you would like the standard deviation of your distribution to be and then add the number you would like the mean of your new distribution to be.

An example of a test developed using standardized scores is the Scholastic Aptitude Test (SAT). When this test was created in 1941, the developers decided to make the mean score 500 and the standard deviation 100. Thus, they multiplied the Z scores for those who took the test by 100 and added 500. For a long time, the basic scoring system was used and the 1941 norms were applied. That is, if the average score of test takers was below the 1941 reference point, the mean for any year could be less than or more than 500. However, in 1995, the test was changed so that the mean each year would be 500 and the standard deviation would be 100. In other words, the test is recalibrated each year.

It is important to make the distinction between standardization and normalization. McCall's T and the other methods described in this section standardize scores by applying a linear transformation. These transformations do not change the characteristics of the distributions. If a distribution of scores is skewed prior to applying the transformation, it will also be skewed after the transformation has been used. In other words, transformations standardize but do not normalize.

Quartiles and Deciles

The terms *quartiles* and *deciles* are frequently used when tests and test results are discussed. The two terms refer to divisions of the percentile scale into groups. The quartile system divides the percentage scale into four groups, whereas the decile system divides the scale into ten groups.

Quartiles are points that divide the frequency distribution into equal fourths. The first quartile is the 25th percentile; the second quartile is the median, or 50th, percentile; and the third quartile is the 75th percentile. These are abbreviated Q1, Q2, and Q3, respectively. One-fourth of the cases will fall below Q1, one-half will fall below Q2, and three-fourths will fall below Q3. The **interquartile range** is the interval of scores bounded by the 25th and

Chapter 2 Norms and Basic Statistics for Testing 55

75th percentiles. In other words, the interquartile range is bounded by the range of scores that represents the middle 50% of the distribution.

Deciles are similar to quartiles except that they use points that mark 10% rather than 25% intervals. Thus, the top decile, or D9, is the point below which 90% of the cases fall. The next decile (D8) marks the 80th percentile, and so forth.

Another system developed in the U.S. Air Force during World War II is knows as the **stanine system.** This system converts any set of scores into a transformed scale, which ranges from 1 to 9. Actually the term *stanine* comes from "standard nine." The scale is standardized to have a mean of 5 and a standard deviation of approximately 2. It has been suggested that stanines had computational advantages because they require only one column on a computer card (Anastasi, 1976). Today computer cards are no longer used, so this advantage is questionable. Table 2-5 shows how percentile scores are converted into stanines.

As you can see in Table 2-5, for every 100 scores, the lowest 4 (or bottom 4% of the cases) fall into the first stanine. The next 7 (of 7% of the cases) fall into the second stanine, and so on. Finally, the top 4 cases fall into the top stanine. Using what you have learned about Z scores and the standard normal distribution, you should be able to figure out the stanine for a score if you know the mean and the standard deviation of the distribution the score comes from. For example, suppose that Igor received a 48 on his normally distributed chemistry midterm. The mean in Igor's class was 42.6, and the standard deviation was 3.6. First you must find Igor's Z score. Do this by using the formula

$$Z = \frac{X - \overline{X}}{S} \quad \text{so} \quad Z = \frac{48 - 42.6}{3.6} = 1.5$$

Now you need to transform Igor's Z score into his percentile rank. To do this, use Appendix 1. Part I shows that a Z score of 1.5 is in approximately the 93rd percentile (middle column) and falls into the 8th stanine.

Actually you would rarely go through all these steps to find a stanine. There are easier ways of doing this, as well as computer programs that do it

TABLE 2-5

Transformation of Percentile Scores into Stanines

Percentage of Cases	Percentiles	Stanines
4	1–4	1 Top 4 percent
7	5–11	2
12	12–23	3
17	24–40	4
20	41–60	5
17	61–77	6
12	78–89	7
7	90–96	8
4	97–100	9 Bottom 4 percent

automatically. However, working out stanines the long way will help you become familiar with a variety of concepts covered in this chapter, including (1) standard scores, (2) means, (3) standard deviations, and (4) percentiles. First, review the five steps to go from raw scores to stanines:

1. Find the mean of the raw scores.
2. Find the standard deviation of the raw scores.
3. Transform the raw scores to Z scores.
4. Transform the Z scores to percentiles (using Appendix 1).
5. Use Table 2-5 to convert percentiles into stanines.

An alternative method is to calculate the percentile rank for each score and use Table 2-5 to obtain the stanines. Remember, in practice you probably would use a computer program to obtain the stanines. Although stanines are not used much in the modern computer era, you can still find them in popular educational tests such as the Stanford Achievement Test.

Norms

Norms refer to the performance by a defined group on a particular test. There are many ways to express norms, and we have discussed some of these under the headings of Z scores, percentiles, and means. The norms for a test are based on the distribution of scores obtained by some defined sample of individuals. The mean is a norm, and the 50th percentile is a norm. Norms are used to give information about performance relative to what has been observed in a standardization sample.

Much has been written about norms and their inadequacies. We shall discuss this material in later chapters in relation to particular tests. In this section, though, we shall cover only the highlights. Whenever you see a norm for a test, you should ask how it was established. Norms are obtained by administering the test to a sample of people and obtaining the distribution of scores for that group.

For example, you might develop a measure of anxiety associated with taking tests in college. After establishing some psychometric properties for the test, you administer the test to normative groups of college students. The scores for these groups of students might then serve as the norms. For example, it might be found that for the normative groups of students, the average score was 19. Then, when your friend Alice comes to take the test and obtains a score of 24, the psychologist using the test might conclude that Alice is above average in test anxiety.

The SAT, as indicated earlier, has norms. The test was administered to millions of high-school seniors from all over the United States. With distributions of scores for this normative group, one could obtain a distribution to provide meaning for particular categories of scores. For example, in the 1941 national sample, a person who scored 650 on the verbal portion of the SAT was at the

93rd percentile of high-school seniors. However, if you took the test before 1995 and scored 650, it did not mean that you were in the 93rd percentile of the people who took the test when you did. Rather, it meant that you would have been at the 93rd percentile if you had been in the group the test had been standardized on. However, if the normative group was a representative sample of the group to which you belonged (and there is every reason to believe it was), then you could reasonably assume that you were in approximately the 93rd percentile of your own group.[2] After 1995 an SAT score of 650 would place you in the 93rd percentile of the people who took the test during the year you completed it. Some controversies surrounding norms are discussed in Technical Box 2-4.

---

[2]Based on the American Testing Program Guide for 1989–1991, College Board of the Educational Testing Service, Princeton, New Jersey.

TECHNICAL BOX 2-4

Within-Group Norming Controversy

One of the most troubling issues in psychological testing is that different racial and ethnic groups do not have the same average level of performance on many tests (see Chapters 20–21). When tests are used to select employees, a higher percentage of majority applicants are typically selected in comparison with their representation in the general population. For example, employers who use general aptitude tests consistently overselect white applicants and underselect African Americans and Hispanics. Overselection is defined as selecting a higher percentage from a particular group than would be expected on the basis of the representation of that group in the applicant pool. If 60% of the applicants are white and 75% of those hired are white, overselection has occurred.

The United States Department of Labor uses the General Aptitude Test Battery (GATB) to refer job applicants to employers. Studies demonstrated, however, that the GATB adversely affected the hiring of African Americans and Hispanics. To remedy this problem, the department created separate norms for different groups. In other words, to obtain a standardized score, each applicant was compared only with members of his or her own racial or ethnic group. As a result, overselection based on test scores was eliminated. However, this provoked other problems. For example, consider two applicants, one white and one African-American, who are in the 70th percentile on the GATB. Although they receive the same score, they are compared against different normative groups. The raw score for the white applicant would be 327 while that for the African American would be 283 (D. C. Brown, 1994).

The problem of within-group norming is highlighted by opposing opinions from different prestigious groups. The National Academy of Sciences, the most elite group

Continued

Continued

of scholars in the United States, reviewed the issue. After review, the Academy concluded that separate norms were appropriate. Specifically, they argued that minority workers at a given level of expected job performance are less likely to be hired than are majority group members. The use of separate norms was therefore required in order to avoid adverse impact in hiring decisions (Gottfredson, 1994; Hartigan & Wigdor, 1989).

In contrast to this conclusion, legislation has led to different policies. The Civil Rights Act of 1991 is very specific about separate test norms (see Chapter 21). Specifically, section 106 of the act made it illegal to use separate norms. The act states that it is unlawful for employers

> In connection with the selection or referral of applicants or candidates for employment or promotion to adjust the scores of, use different cut-offs for, or otherwise alter the results of employment-related tests on the basis of race, color, religion, sex, or national origin.

Employers may have a variety of different objectives when making employment decisions. One goal may be to enhance the ethnic and racial diversity of their work force. Another goal may be to hire those with the best individual profiles. Often, these goals compete. The law may now prohibit employers from attempting to balance these competing objectives (Sackett & Wilk, 1994).

Age-Related Norms

Certain tests have different normative groups for particular age groups. Most IQ tests are of this sort (see Chapter 10). When the Stanford-Binet IQ test was originally created, distributions of the performance of random samples of children were obtained for various age groups. When applying an IQ test, the tester's task is to determine the mental age of the person being tested. This is accomplished through various exercises that help locate the age-level norm at which a child is performing.

Tracking

One of the most common uses of age-related norms is for growth charts used by pediatricians. Consider the question "Is my son tall or short?" The answer will usually depend on a comparison of your son to other boys of the same age. Your son would be very tall if he were 5 feet at age 8 but very short if he were only 5 feet at age 18. Thus the comparison is usually with people of the same age.

Beyond this rather obvious type of age-related comparison, child experts have discovered that children at the same age level tend to go through different growth patterns. Children who are small infants often remain small and continue to grow at a slower pace than others. Pediatricians must therefore know more than a child's age; they must also know the child's percentile within a given age group. For a variety of physical characteristics, children tend to stay at about their same percentile level relative to other children in their age group as they grow older. This tendency to stay at about the same level relative to one's peers is known as **tracking.** Height and weight are good examples of physical characteristics that track. Figures 2-8 and 2-9 show the expected rates of growth for boys and girls in terms of height and weight. Notice that the children who were the largest babies are expected to remain the largest as they get older.

A pediatrician would use the charts to determine the expected course of growth for a child. For example, if a 3-month-old boy came into the office and weighed 13.2 pounds (6 kilograms), the doctor would locate the child on the center line on the bottom half of Figure 2-8. By age 36 months, the child would be expected to weigh just under 33 pounds. The tracking charts are very useful to doctors because they help determine whether the child is going through some unusual growth pattern. A boy who weighed 13 pounds at age 3 months might come under scrutiny if at age 36 months he weighed only 28 pounds. This might be normal for 3-year-olds in a different track, but the doctor might want to examine a child who started out larger to determine why the child did not stay in his track.

Figure 2-10 shows an example of a child going out of her track. There is some concern that children who are fed a fat-restricted diet experience stunted growth (Kaplan & Toshima, 1992). The consequences of a slightly restricted vegetarian diet are mild if they exist at all. However, very restricted diets may affect growth. For instance, Pugliese et al. (1983) studied 24 adolescents who had voluntarily undergone severe caloric restrictions because they wanted to lose weight. Though they did not have anorexia nervosa, they consumed only a small percentage of the calories recommended for their age. Figure 2-10 shows the growth pattern for one of these children. As the figure suggests, the child grew normally until age 9. At that point, very restricted dieting began. Within a few years, growth was interrupted. The arrow in the figure shows the point at which psychotherapy began. After this point, normal feeding resumed, and growth started once again. However, at age 18, the child was still below the 5th percentile in height and weight. Given normal tracking, this child should have been between the 25th and the 50th percentile.

Although the tracking system has worked well for medicine, it has stirred considerable controversy as applied to education. Some people believe there is an analogy between the rates of physical growth and the rates of intellectual growth. Just as there are some slow growers who eventually will be shorter than average adults, some researchers believe that there are slow learners who will eventually know less as adults. Furthermore, some suggest that children learn at different rates. Children are therefore separated early in their educational careers and placed in classrooms that correspond with these different tracks. Many educators have attacked the tracking system because it discriminates against some children. Because people use psychological tests to place

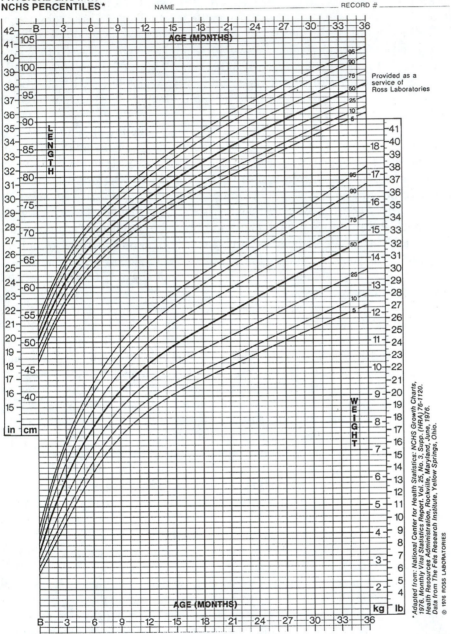

BOYS: BIRTH TO 36 MONTHS
PHYSICAL GROWTH
NCHS PERCENTILES*

FIGURE 2-8 *Tracking chart for boys' physical growth from birth to 36 months.*

(Adapted from the National Center for Health Statistics: NCHS Growth Charts. Health Resources Administration, Rockville, Maryland, June 1976.)

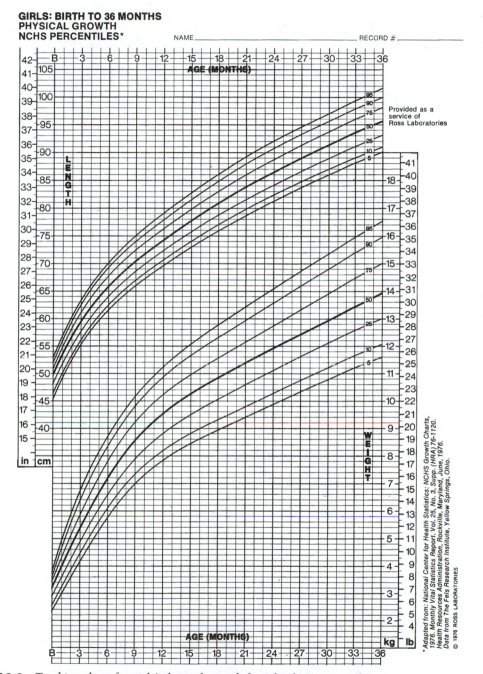

FIGURE 2-9 *Tracking chart for girls' physical growth from birth to 36 months.*
(From the National Center for Health Statistics: NCHS Growth Charts. Health Resources Administration, Rockville, Maryland, June, 1976.)

FIGURE 2-10

Growth description with severe dietary restriction. The scales represent percentile standards for height and weight, and the plotted values are for the clinical case.

(From Pugliese et al., 1983, p. 514; reprinted by permission of The New England Journal of Medicine, 309, 513–518, 1983.)

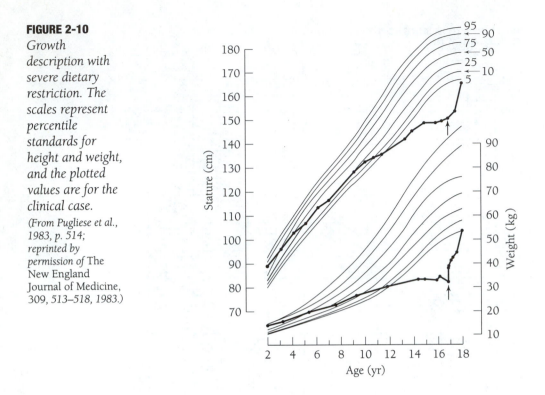

children in these tracks, some tests have come under severe scrutiny and attack. We shall return to this controversy in Chapter 20.

Criterion-Referenced Tests

The purpose of establishing norms for a test is to determine how a test taker compares with others. A **norm-referenced test** compares each person to a norm. Many have objected to this use of tests because it forces competition among people. Young children exposed to many norm-referenced tests in elementary school can get caught up in a never-ending battle to perform better than average. In addition to ranking people according to performance, however, tests can play an important role in identifying problems and suggesting new directions for individualized programs of instruction. During the last two decades interest has grown in tests applied to determine whether students know specific information. These tests do not compare students with one another; they compare each student's performance with a criterion or an expected level of performance (Linn, 1980).

A **criterion-referenced test** describes the specific types of skills, tasks, or knowledge that the test taker can demonstrate, such as mathematical skills. The results of such a test might demonstrate that a particular child can add, subtract, and multiply but has difficulty with both long and short division.

The results of the test would not be used to make comparisons between the child and other members of his or her class. Instead, they would be employed to design an individualized program of instruction that focuses on division. Thus, the criterion-referenced testing movement emphasizes the diagnostic use of tests, in that one can use them to identify problems that can be remedied.

Summary

In this chapter we discussed some basic rules for translating observations of behavior and of mental processes into numbers. The use of number systems is important for precision in all scientific exercises. Measures of psychological processes are represented by one of four types of scales. A *nominal scale* simply assigns numbers to categories. This type of scale has none of the properties of a numbered scale. An *ordinal scale* has the property of magnitude and allows us to rank objects, but it does not have the property of equal intervals or an absolute 0. An *interval scale* can describe the distances between objects because it has the property of equal intervals in addition to the property of magnitude. The *ratio scale* has an absolute 0 in addition to equal intervals and magnitude. Any mathematical operation is permissible with a ratio scale.

To make sense out of test scores, we have to examine the score for an individual relative to the scores of others. To do this requires creating a distribution of test scores. There are several ways to display the distribution of scores, including frequency distributions and frequency polygons. We also need statistics to describe the distribution. The *mean* is the average score, the *variance* is the averaged squared deviation around the mean, and the *standard deviation* is the square root of the variance. Using these statistics, we can tell a lot about a particular score by relating it to characteristics of a well-known probability distribution known as the standard normal distribution.

Norms are used to relate a score to a particular distribution for a subgroup of a population. For example, norms are used to describe where a child is on some measure relative to other children of the same age. In contrast, *criterion-referenced tests* are used to document specific skills rather than to compare people.

In summary, this chapter reviewed basic statistical methods for describing scores on one variable. In Chapter 3, we will discuss statistical methods for showing the relationship between two or more variables.

Correlation and Regression

LEARNING OBJECTIVES

When you have completed this chapter,[1] you should be able to:

- ☐ Express the extent to which two measures are associated

- ☐ Explain what a scatter diagram is and how it is used

- ☐ Define a positive correlation and a negative correlation

- ☐ Discuss some of the differences between correlation and regression

- ☐ Tell how a regression line describes the relationship between two variables

- ☐ Discuss under which circumstances you would use the point biserial correlation, the phi coefficient, and the tetrachoric correlation

- ☐ Outline the procedure you would use to predict one score from the linear combination of several scores

- ☐ Explain factor analysis and how it is used

---

[1]Portions of this chapter are taken from *Basic Statistics for the Behavioral Sciences* by R. M. Kaplan (Newton, MA: Allyn & Bacon, 1987).

A banner headline in an issue of the *National Enquirer* read, "FOOD CAUSES MOST MARRIAGE PROBLEMS." The article talked about "Startling Results of Studies by Doctors and Marriage Counselors." Actually the headline was not based on any systematic study. Rather, it used the opinions of some physicians and marriage counselors who felt that high levels of blood sugar are related to low energy levels, which in turn cause marital unhappiness.

Unfortunately, the *National Enquirer* did not report enough data for us to evaluate the hypothesis. We feel comfortable concluding that an association between diet and divorce has not been established. Before we are willing to accept the magazine's conclusion, we must ask many questions. This chapter focuses on one of the many issues raised in the report—the level of association between variables.[2]

The *Enquirer* tells us that diet and unhappiness are associated, but not to what extent. Is the association greater than we would expect by chance? Is it a strong or weak association?

Lots of things seem to be related. For example, life stress is associated with heart disease, training is associated with good performance in athletics, overeating is associated with indigestion. People are always telling us that things are associated. For some events the association is obvious. For example, the angle of the sun in the sky and the time of day are associated in a very predictable way. This is because time was originally defined by the angle of the sun in the sky. Other associations are less obvious, such as the association between performing well on the SAT and obtaining good grades in college.

Sometimes we do not know whether events are meaningfully associated with one another. If we do conclude that events are associated in some fundamental way, it is important to have a precise index of the degree. This chapter discusses statistical procedures that allow us to make precise estimates of the degree to which variables are associated. These methods are very important; we shall refer to them frequently in the remainder of this book. The indexes of association used most frequently in testing are correlation, regression, and multiple regression.

The Scatter Diagram

Before presenting the measures of association, we will look at visual displays of the relationships between variables. In Chapter 2, we concentrated on univariate distributions of scores, which involve only one variable—each person has only one score. This chapter considers statistical methods for studying bivari-

---

[2]There were many other problems with the *National Enquirer* report. The observation was based on the clinical experiences of some health practitioners who found that many couples who came in for counseling had poor diets. One major oversight was that there was no control group of people who were not having marriage problems. We do not know from the study whether couples with problems have poor diets in

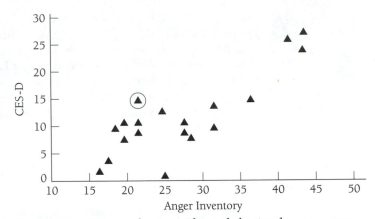

FIGURE 3-1 *A scatter diagram. The circled point shows a person who had a score of 21 on X and 14 on Y (see the text).*

ate distributions, which have two scores for each individual. For example, when we study the relationship between test scores and classroom performance, we are dealing with a bivariate distribution. Each person has a score on the test and a score for classroom performance. We must examine the scores of all the individuals to know whether these two variables are associated.

A **scatter diagram** is a picture of the relationship between two variables. An example of a scatter diagram is shown in Figure 3-1, which relates scores on a measure of anger for medical students to scores on the CES-D. The axes in the figure represent the scales for two variables. Values of X for the anger inventory are shown on the horizontal axis and values of Y for the CES-D on the vertical axis. Each point on the scatter diagram shows where a particular individual scored on both X and Y. For example, one person had a score of 14 on the CES-D and a score of 21 on the anger inventory. This point is circled in the figure. You can locate it by finding 21 on the X axis and then going straight up to the level of 14 on the Y axis. Each point indicates the scores for X and Y for one individual. As you can see, the figure presents a lot of information. Each point represents the performance of one person who has been assessed on two measures.

The next sections present methods for summarizing the information in a scatter diagram by finding the straight line that comes closest to more points

greater proportions than people in general. Another problem is that neither diet nor marital happiness was measured in a systematic way. Thus, we are left with subjective opinions about the levels of these variables. Finally, we do not know the direction of the causation: Does poor diet cause unhappiness, or does unhappiness cause poor diet? Another possibility is that some other problem (such as stress) may cause both poor diet and unhappiness.

FIGURE 3-2

A scatter diagram showing a nonlinear relationship. (From R. M. Kaplan & Grant, 1995.)

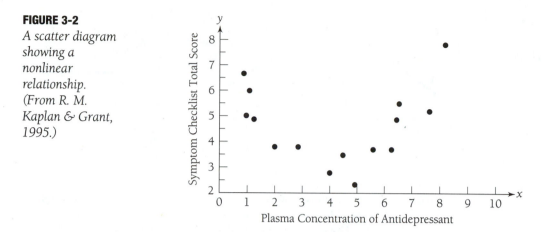

than any other line. One of the reasons that it is important to examine the scatter diagram is that the relationships between *X* and *Y* are not always best described by a straight line. For example, Figure 3-2 shows the hypothetical relationship between levels of antidepressant medication in the blood of depressed patients and the number of symptoms they report. However, the relationship is systematic. Patients who have too little or too much medication experience more symptoms than those who get an intermediate amount. The methods of linear correlation or linear regression to be presented in this chapter are not appropriate for describing nonlinear relationships such as this.

Correlation

In correlational analysis, we ask whether two variables covary. In other words, does *Y* get larger as *X* gets larger? For example, does the patient feel dizzier when the doctor increases the dose of a drug? Do people get more diseases when they are under more stress? Correlational analysis is designed primarily to examine linear relationships between variables. Although one can use correlational techniques to study nonlinear relationships, doing so lies beyond the scope of this book.[3]

A **correlation coefficient** is a mathematical index that describes the direction and magnitude of a relationship. Figure 3-3 shows three different types of relationships between variables. Part (a) of the figure demonstrates a *positive correlation*. This means that high scores on *Y* are associated with high scores on *X*, and low scores on *Y* correspond to low scores on *X*. Part (b) shows *negative correlation*. When there is a negative correlation, higher scores on *Y* are associ-

---

[3]Readers interested in methods for studying nonlinear relationships should review Pedhazur (1991).

FIGURE 3-3
Three hypothetical relationships: (a) positive correlation, (b) negative correlation, (c) no correlation.

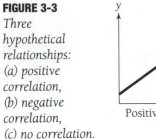 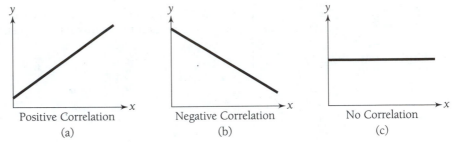

ated with lower scores on *X*, and lower scores on *Y* are associated with higher scores on *X*. This might describe the relationship between barbiturate use and amount of activity: The higher the drug dose, the less active patients are. Part (c) of Figure 3-3 shows no correlation, or a situation in which the variables are not related. Here, scores on *X* do not give us information about scores on *Y*. An example of this sort of relationship is the lack of correlation between shoe size and IQ.

There are many ways to calculate a correlation coefficient. All involve pairs of observations: For each observation on one variable, there is an observation on one other variable for the same person.[4] Appendix 3-1 offers an example of the calculation of a correlation and regression. Table 3-5 in Appendix 3-1 (see page 95) shows a set of observations on two variables. The first set of observations includes the numbers of games won by the 30 teams in the National Football League. Each of these teams plays 16 games during the season. The second set of observations contains the average salaries for players on the teams. It is widely speculated that a systematic relationship exists between the amount that football owners will pay for exceptional athletes and the number of games their franchise teams win. All methods of calculating a correlation coefficient are mathematically equivalent. Before we present methods for calculating the correlation coefficient, however, we shall discuss regression, the method on which correlation is based.

Regression

The Regression Line

We use correlation when we are interested in assessing the magnitude and direction of a relationship. A related technique, known as *regression*, is used to make predictions about scores on one variable from knowledge of scores on another variable. These predictions are obtained from the **regression line.** The regression line is the best-fitting straight line through a set of points in a scat-

---

[4]The pairs of scores do not always need to be for a person. They might also be for a group, an institution, a team, and so on.

ter diagram. It is found by using the principle of least squares, which minimizes the squared deviation around the regression line. Let us explain.

The mean is the point of least squares for any single variable. This means that the sum of the squared deviations around the mean will be less than it is around any value other than the mean. For example, consider the scores 5, 4, 3, 2, and 1. The mean is $\Sigma X/N = 15/5 = 3$. The squared deviation of each score around the mean can be found. For the score 5, the squared deviation is $(5 - 3)^2 = 4$. For the score 4, it is $(4 - 3)^2 = 1$. The score 3 is equal to the mean, so the squared deviation around the mean will be $(3 - 3)^2 = 0$. By definition, the mean will always be the point of least squares.

The regression line is the running mean or the line of least squares in two dimensions or in the space created by two variables. Consider the situation shown in the scatter diagram in Figure 3-1. For each level of X (or point on the X scale) there is a distribution of scores on Y. In other words, we could find a mean of Y when X is 3, another mean of Y when X is 4, and so on. The least squares method in regression finds the straight line that comes as close to as many of these Y means as possible. In other words, it is the line for which the squared deviations around the line are at a minimum.

To use the regression equation, we must define some of the terms. The term on the left of the equation is Y'. This is the predicted value of Y. When we create the equation, we use observed values of Y and X. The equation is the result of the least squares procedure and shows the best linear relationship between X and Y. When the equation is available, we can take a score on X and plug it into the formula. What results is a predicted value of Y or Y'.

The most important term in the equation is the *regression coefficient,* or b, which is the slope of the regression line. The regression coefficient can be expressed as the ratio of the sums of squares for the covariance to the sums of squares for X. Sums of squares are defined as the sum of the squared deviations around the mean. For X, this is the sum of the squared deviations around the X variable. Covariance is used to express how much two measures covary, or vary together. To understand covariance, let's look at the extreme case of the relationship between two identical sets of scores. In this case there will be a perfect association. We know that we can create a new score that exactly repeats the scores on any one variable. If we created this new twin variable, it would covary perfectly with the original variable. Regression analysis attempts to determine how similar the variance between two variables is by dividing the covariance by the average variance of each variable. The covariance is calculated from the cross products, products of variations around each mean. Symbolically, this is

$$\Sigma XY = \Sigma(X - \overline{X})(Y - \overline{Y})$$

The regression coefficient can be defined by the following formula:

$$b = \frac{N(\Sigma XY) - (\Sigma X)(\Sigma Y)}{N\Sigma X^2 - (\Sigma X)^2}$$

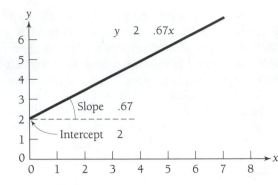

FIGURE 3-4
The regression equation. The slope is the amount of increase on the y axis divided by the range of scores on the x axis. The intercept is value of Y when X is 0.

The **slope** describes how much change is expected in Y each time X increases by one unit. For example, Figure 3-4 shows a regression line with a slope of .67. In this figure, the difference between 1 and 2 in units of X is associated with an expected difference of .67 in units of Y (for $X = 1$, $Y = 2.67$ and for $X = 2$, $Y = 3.34$; $3.34 - 2.67 = .67$). The regression coefficient is sometimes expressed in different notation. For example, the Greek β is often used for a population estimate of the regression coefficient.

The **intercept,** *a,* is the value of Y when X is 0. In other words, it is the point at which the regression line crosses the Y axis. This is shown in Figure 3-4. It is easy to find the intercept when we know the regression coefficient. The intercept is found by using the following formula:

$$a = \overline{Y} - b\overline{X}$$

The Best-Fitting Line

Correlational methods require finding the best-fitting line through a series of data points. In Figure 3-4, a regression line is shown, which is based on a series of observations for particular individuals. Each individual had actually obtained a score on X and on Y. Take the example of someone who obtained a score of 4 on X and 6 on Y. The regression equation gives a predicted value for Y, denoted as Y'. Using the regression equation, we can calculate Y' for this person. It is

$$Y' = 2 + .67X$$

so

$$\begin{aligned} Y' &= 2 + .67(4) \\ &= 4.68 \end{aligned}$$

If that person received a score of 4 on Y, the regression equation predicts that he or she would have a score of 4.68. The difference between the observed and predicted score ($Y - Y'$) is called the **residual.** The best-fitting line keeps residuals to a minimum. In other words, it minimizes the deviation between observed and predicted Y scores. Since residuals can be positive or negative and will cancel to 0 if averaged, the best-fitting line is most appropriately found by squaring each residual. Thus, the best-fitting line is obtained by keeping these squared residuals as small as possible. This is known as the *principle of least squares*. Formally, it is stated as

$$\Sigma(Y - Y')^2 \qquad \text{is at a minimum}$$

An example showing how to calculate a regression equation is given in Appendix 3-1. Whether or not you become proficient at calculating regression equations, you should learn to interpret them in order to be a good consumer of research information.

An example of a regression problem is summarized in Table 3-1 and Figure 3-5. The data come from international studies on the relationship between price per pack of cigarettes and the number of cigarettes consumed per capita. There is considerable variability in the price per pack of cigarettes among European countries. The differences between countries is primarily defined by the level of taxation. Some countries, such as Norway, have very high taxes on tobacco. Therefore, the price per pack for cigarettes is much higher. Figure 3-5 shows the scatter diagram relating price to number of cigarettes consumed.

TABLE 3-1

Relationship of Cigarette Price and Consumption

	Country	Average Cigarettes/Year	Price per Pack ($)
1.	Belgium	1990	1.540
2.	Czechoslovakia	2520	1.90
3.	Denmark	2110	3.60
4.	Finland	1720	2.50
5.	France	2400	0.80
6.	GFR	2380	2.90
7.	GDR	2340	1.78
8.	Greece	3640	0.48
9.	Hungary	3260	0.36
10.	Iceland	3100	3.51
11.	Ireland	2560	2.77
12.	Italy	2460	1.21
13.	Netherlands	1690	1.65
14.	Norway	710	4.17
15.	Portugal	1730	0.72
16.	Romania	2110	0.37
17.	Spain	2740	0.55
18.	Sweden	1660	2.30
19.	Switzerland	2960	1.84
20.	Turkey	3000	0.54
21.	USSR	2170	0.80
22.	UK	2120	2.45

FIGURE 3-5

Scatter diagram relating price to number of cigarettes consumed

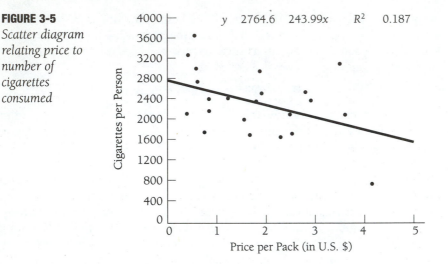

Although the relationship is not strong, there is a negative trend, which is defined by the regression equation. The intercept in this equation is 2764.6. This means the line intersects the y axis at 2764.6. The intercept provides an estimate of the number of cigarettes that would be consumed if cigarettes were free. The regression coefficient for this model is $b = -243.99$. The regression coefficient tells how much cigarette consumption should decline for each dollar that is added to the price of a pack of cigarettes. In other words, this equation suggests that on average, people will smoke 244 fewer cigarettes per year for each dollar added to the price of cigarettes. Thus, according to this simple model, adding a $2.00 tax to cigarettes would decrease consumption on average by about 488 cigarettes per year (Kaplan et al., 1995).

Correlation is a special case of regression in which the scores for both variables are in standardized, or Z, units. Having the scores in Z units is a nice convenience because it eliminates the need to find the intercept. In correlation, the intercept is always 0. Furthermore, the slope in correlation is easier to interpret because it is in a standardized unit. An example of how to calculate a correlation coefficient is given in Appendix 3-1. In the calculation of the correlation coefficient, we can bypass the step of changing all the scores into Z units. This gets done as part of the calculation process. You may notice that Steps 1–13 are identical for calculating regression (Appendix 3-1) and correlation (Appendix 3-2). Technical Box 3-1 gives a theoretical discussion of correlation and regression.

The **Pearson product moment correlation coefficient** is a ratio used to determine the degree of variation in one variable that can be estimated from knowledge about variation in the other variable. The correlation coefficient can take on any value from -1.0 to 1.0.

Table 3-2 gives the raw data for CES-D and anger inventory scores for medical students. Try to find the regression of anger upon CES-D and the correlation between these two measures. The correct answer is $r = .82$.

TABLE 3-2

*CES-D
Correlation
Example*

X, Anger Inventory	Y, CES-D	X²	Y²	XY	Predicted	Residual
21	14	441	196	294	7.31	6.69
21	10	441	100	210	7.31	2.69
21	8	441	64	168	7.31	.69
27	8	729	64	216	11.35	−3.35
43	26	1849	676	1118	22.14	3.86
24	0	576	0	0	9.33	−9.33
36	14	1296	196	504	17.42	−3.42
17	3	289	9	51	4.61	1.61
31	9	961	81	279	14.05	−5.05
19	10	361	100	190	5.96	4.04
19	7	361	49	133	5.96	1.04
24	12	576	144	288	9.33	2.67
27	10	729	100	270	11.35	−1.35
41	25	1681	625	1025	20.79	4.21
18	9	324	81	162	5.29	3.71
24	12	576	144	288	9.33	2.67
43	23	1849	529	989	22.14	.86
28	7	784	49	196	12.03	−5.03
31	13	961	169	403	14.05	−1.05
16	1	256	1	16	3.94	−2.94

See Appendix 3-1, pages 96–97, for definitions of steps.

Step 1: $N = 20$

Step 2: $\Sigma X = 531$

Step 3: $\Sigma Y = 221$

Step 4: $\Sigma X^2 = 15,481$

Step 5: $\Sigma Y^2 = 3377$

Step 6: $\Sigma XY = 6800$

Step 7: 281,961

Step 8: 48,841

Steps 9, 10, 11: $20(6800) - (531)(221) = 18,649$

Steps 12, 13: $20(15,481) - (531)(531) = 27,659$

Step 14: $b = .67$

Step 15: $\bar{X} = 26.55$

Step 16: $\bar{Y} = 11.05$

Steps 17, 18: $a = 6.85$

Step 19: CES-D $= -6.85 + .67$(anger)

For correlation:

Step 16: 22,741.93

Step 17 correlation: .82

As you will see from Appendix 3-1, calculations of the correlation coefficient and the regression can be long and difficult. You may be able to avoid the
many computational steps by using a calculator. Many inexpensive pocket calculators are preprogrammed for correlation and regression. When you buy a
calculator, choose one with these functions.

TECHNICAL BOX 3-1

A More Theoretical Discussion of Correlation and Regression

The difference between correlation and regression is analogous to the difference between standardized scores and raw scores. In correlation we look at the relationship between variables when each one is transformed into standardized scores. In Chapter 2, standardized, or Z, scores were defined as $(X - \overline{X})/S$. In correlation, both variables are in Z scores, so they both have a mean of 0. In other words, the mean for the two variables will always be the same. As a result of this convenience, the intercept will always be 0 (when X is 0, Y is also 0) and will drop out of the equation. The resulting equation for translating X into Y then becomes $Y = rX$. The correlation coefficient (r) is equal to the regression coefficient when both X and Y are measured in standardized units. In other words, the predicted value of Y equals X times the correlation between X and Y. If the correlation between X and Y is .80 and the standardized (Z) score for the X variable is 1.0, the predicted value of Y will be .80. Unless there is a perfect correlation (1.0 or -1.0), scores on Y will be predicted to be closer to the Y mean than scores on X. A correlation of .80 means that the prediction for Y is 80% as far from the mean as the observation for X. A correlation of .50 means that the predicted distance between the mean of Y and the predicted Y is half of the distance between the associated X and the mean of X.

One benefit of using the correlation coefficient is that it has a reciprocal nature. The correlation between X and Y will always be the same as the correlation between Y and X. For example, if the correlation between drug dose and activity is .68, the correlation between activity and drug dose is .68. Regression is used to transform scores on one variable into estimated scores on the other. We often use regression to predict raw scores on Y on the basis of raw scores on X. For instance, we might seek an equation to predict a student's grade point average on the basis of his or her SAT score. Because regression uses the raw units of the variables, the reciprocal property does not hold. The coefficient describing the regression of X on Y is usually not the same as the coefficient describing the regression of Y on X.

The term *regression* was first used in 1885 by an extraordinary British intellectual named Sir Francis Galton. Fond of describing social and political changes that occur over successive generations, Galton noted that extraordinarily tall men tended to have sons who were a little shorter than they and that unusually small men tended to have sons closer to the average height (but still shorter than average). Over time, individuals with all sorts of unusual characteristics tended to produce offspring who were closer to the average. Galton thought of this as regression toward mediocrity, an idea that became the basis for a statistical procedure describing how scores tend to regress toward the mean. If a person had been extreme on X, regression would predict that he or she would be less extreme on Y. Karl Pearson developed the first statistical models of correlation and regression in the late 19th century.

Statistical Definition of Regression

Regression analysis is used to show how change in one variable is related to change in another variable. In psychological testing, we often use regression to determine whether changes in test scores are related to changes in performance. Do people who score higher on tests of manual dexterity perform better in dental school? Can IQ scores measured during high school predict monetary income 20 years later? Regression analysis and related correlational methods reveal the degree to which these variables are linearly related. In addition, they offer an equation that estimates scores on a criterion (such as dental-school grades) on the basis of scores on a predictor (such as manual dexterity).

In Chapter 2, we introduced the concept of variance. You might remember that *variance* was defined as the average squared deviation around the mean. We used the term *sum of squares* for the sum of squared deviations around the mean. Symbolically, this is

$$\Sigma(X - \overline{X})^2$$

The variance is the sum of squares divided by $N - 1$. The formula for this is

$$S_X^2 = \frac{\Sigma(X - \overline{X})^2}{N - 1}$$

We also gave some formulas for the variance of raw scores. The variance of X can be calculated from raw scores using the formula

$$S_X^2 = \frac{\Sigma X^2 - \frac{(\Sigma X)^2}{N}}{N - 1}$$

If there is another variable, Y, we can calculate the variance using a similar formula:

$$S_Y^2 = \frac{\Sigma Y^2 - \frac{(\Sigma Y)^2}{N}}{N - 1}$$

To calculate regression we need a term for the *covariance*. This tells us how much two measures covary, or vary together. To understand covariance, let's look at the extreme case of the relationship between two identical sets of scores. In this case, there will be a perfect association. We know that we can create a new score that exactly repeats the scores on any one variable. If we create this new twin variable, it will covary perfectly with the original variable. Regression analysis attempts to determine how similar the variance between two variables is by dividing the covariance by the average variance from each variable.

To calculate the covariance, we need to find the sum of cross products, which is defined as

$$\Sigma XY = \Sigma(X - \overline{X})(Y - \overline{Y})$$

and the raw score formula, which is often used for calculation, is

$$\Sigma XY - \frac{(\Sigma X)(\Sigma Y)}{N}$$

The covariance is the sum of cross products divided by $N - 1$.

Continued

Continued

Now look at the similarity of the formula for the covariance and the formula for the variance:

$$S_{XY}^2 = \frac{\Sigma XY - \dfrac{(\Sigma X)(\Sigma Y)}{N}}{N - 1}$$

$$S_X^2 = \frac{\Sigma X^2 - \dfrac{(\Sigma X)^2}{N}}{N - 1}$$

Try substituting X for Y in the formula for the covariance. You should get

$$\frac{\Sigma XX - \dfrac{(\Sigma X)(\Sigma X)}{N}}{N - 1}$$

If you replace ΣXX with ΣX^2 and $(\Sigma X)(\Sigma X)$ with $(\Sigma X)^2$, you will see the relationship between variance and covariance:

$$\frac{\Sigma X^2 - \dfrac{(\Sigma X)^2}{N}}{N - 1}$$

In regression analysis we examine the ratio of the covariance to the average of the variances for the two separate measures. This gives us an estimate of how much variance in one variable we can determine by knowing about the variation in the other variable.

Testing the Statistical Significance of a Correlation Coefficient

One of the most important questions in evaluating a correlation is whether it is larger than one would expect by chance. We begin with the null hypothesis that there is no relationship between variables. The null hypothesis is rejected if there is evidence that the association between two variables is significantly different from 0. Correlation coefficients can be tested for statistical significance using the t distribution. The t distribution is not a single distribution (such as the Z distribution), but a family of distributions each with its own degrees of freedom. The *degrees of freedom* (df) are defined as the sample size minus one, or $N - 1$. The formula for calculating the t value is

$$t = r\sqrt{\frac{N - 2}{1 - r^2}}$$

The significance of the t value, where df $= N - 2$ and N is the number of pairs, can then be obtained by using Appendix 4.

Let's take one example of a correlation of .37 based on 50 pairs of observations. Using the formula, we obtain

$$t = .37\sqrt{\frac{48}{.86}}$$
$$= .37(7.47)$$
$$= 2.76$$

Now, suppose we had stated the null hypothesis that the population association between these two variables is 0. Test statistics are used to estimate whether the observed correlation based on samples is significantly different from 0. This would be tested against the alternative hypothesis that the association between the two measures is significantly different from 0 in a two-tailed test. A significance level of .05 is used. Formally, then, the hypothesis and alternative hypothesis are

$$H_0: \quad r = 0$$
$$H_1: \quad r \neq 0$$

Using the formula, we obtain a t value of 2.76 with 48 degrees of freedom. According to Appendix 4, this t value is sufficient to reject the null hypothesis. Thus, we conclude that the association between these two variables was not due to chance.

There are also statistical tables that give the critical values for r. One of these tables is included as Appendix 4. The table lists critical values of r for both the .05 and the .01 alpha levels according to degrees of freedom. For the correlation coefficient, df = $N - 2$. Suppose, for example, that you want to determine whether a correlation coefficient of .45 is statistically significant for a sample of 20 subjects. The degrees of freedom would be 18 ($20 - 2 = 18$). According to Appendix 4, the critical value for the .05 level is .444 with 18 df. Since .45 exceeds .444, you would conclude that the chances of finding a correlation as large as the one observed by chance alone would be less than 5 in 100. However, the observed correlation is less than the criterion value for the .01 level (that would require .561 with 18 df).

How to Interpret a Regression Plot

Regression plots are pictures that show the relationship between variables. A common use of correlation is to determine the **criterion validity** of a test, or the relationship between a test score and some well-defined criterion. The association between a test of job aptitude and the criterion of actual performance on the job is an example of criterion validity. The problems dealt with in studies of criterion validity require one to predict some criterion score on the basis of a predictor or test score. Suppose that you want to build a test to predict how enjoyable someone will turn out to be as a date. If you selected your dates randomly, with no information about them in advance, you might be best off just using normative information.

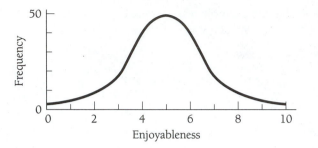

FIGURE 3-6

Hypothetical distribution of the enjoyableness of dates. Few dates are extremely enjoyable or extremely unenjoyable. The greatest number fall about in the middle.

You might expect that the distribution of enjoyableness of dates is normal. Some people are just not fun for you to go out with, whereas others are exceptionally enjoyable. However, the great majority of the people are some fun but not excessively so and thus fall between these two extremes. Figure 3-6 shows what a frequency distribution for enjoyableness of dates might look like. As you can see, the highest point, which shows where dates are most frequently classified, is the location of the average date.

If you had no other way of predicting how much you would like your dates, the safest prediction would be to pick this middle level of enjoyableness because it is one observed most frequently. This is called *normative* because it uses information gained from representative groups. Knowing nothing else about an individual, you can make an educated guess that a person will be average in enjoyableness because past experience has demonstrated that the mean, or average, score is also the one observed most frequently. In other words, knowing about the average date gives you some information about what to expect from a particular date. But it is doubtful that you would really want to choose dates this way. You probably would rather use other information such as the person's educational background, attitudes, and hobbies to predict whether that person would be enjoyable on a date with you.

Most people do use some system to help them make important personal choices. These systems, however, are never perfect. Thus, you are left with something that is not perfect but is still better than using just normative information. In regression studies, researchers develop equations that help them describe more precisely where tests fall between being perfect predictors and being no better than just using the normative information. This is done by graphing the relationship between test scores and the criterion. Then a mathematical procedure is used to find the straight line that comes as close to as many of the points as possible. (You may want to review the section on the regression line, earlier in this chapter.)

Figure 3-7 shows the points on hypothetical scales of dating desirability and the enjoyableness of dates. The line through the points is the one that minimizes the squared distance between the line and the data points. In other words, the line is the one straight line that summarizes more about the relationship between dating desirability and enjoyableness than any other straight line.

Figure 3-8 shows the hypothetical relationship between a test score and a criterion. Using this figure, you should be able to find the predicted value on the criterion variable by knowing the score on the test or the predictor. Here is

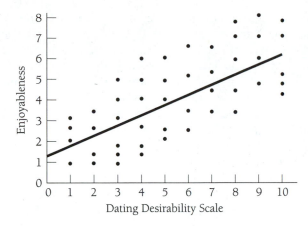

FIGURE 3-7

Hypothetical relationship between dating desirability and the enjoyableness of dates. Each point summarizes the dating desirability score and the enjoyableness rating for a single subject. The line was derived from a mathematical procedure to come as close to as many points as possible.

how you read the graph. First pick a particular score on the test, say 8. Find 8 on the axis of the graph with the label "Test Score" (horizontal axis). Now draw a line straight up until you hit the slanted line on the graph. This is the regression line. Now make a 90-degree left turn and draw another line until it hits the other axis of the graph, which is labeled "Criterion Score." The dashed line in Figure 3-8 shows the course you should take. Now read the number on the criterion axis where your line has stopped. On the basis of information you gained by using the test, you would thus expect to obtain 7.4 as the criterion variable.

Notice that the line in Figure 3-8 is not at a 45° angle and that the two variables are measured in the same units. If it were at a 45° angle, the test would be a perfect (or close to perfect) forecaster of the criterion. However, this is almost never the case in practice. Now do the same exercise you did for the test score of 8 with test scores from the extremes of the distributions. Try the scores 0 and 10. You will find that the score of 10 for the test gives a crite-

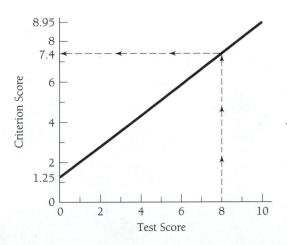

FIGURE 3-8

Predicted relationship between a test score and a criterion. The dotted line shows how you should have obtained a predicted criterion score of 7.4 from the test score of 8.

rion score of 8.95, and the test score of 0 gives a criterion score of 1.25. Notice how far apart 0 and 10 are on the test. Now look at how far apart 1.25 and 8.95 are on the criterion. You can see that using the test as a predictor is not as good as perfect prediction, but it is still better than using the normative information. If you had used only the normative information, you would have predicted that all scores would be the average score on the criterion. And if there were perfect prediction, the distance between 1.25 and 8.95 on the criterion would be the same as the distance between 0 and 10 on the test.

Figure 3-9 shows a variety of different regression slopes. Notice that the higher the standardized regression coefficient (b), the steeper the line. Now look at the regression line with a slope of 0. It is parallel to the axis for the test score and perpendicular to the line for the criterion. A regression line like this shows that the test score tells us nothing about the criterion beyond the normative information. Whatever test score you choose, the criterion score will be the same, the average score on the criterion. The slope of 0 tells you that the test and the criterion are unrelated and that your best bet under these circumstances is to predict the average score on the criterion.

Take some time and try finding the predicted score on the criterion for test scores of 11 and 3 for several of the different slopes shown in Figure 3-9. Notice that the steeper the slope of the regression line, the farther apart the predicted scores on the criterion. Table 3-3 shows the predicted scores for all the different slopes. You can use it to check your answers.

When the regression lines have slopes of 0 or nearly 0, it is best not to take any chances in forecasting the criterion. Instead you should depend on the normative information and guess the mean of Y. As the slope becomes steeper, it makes more sense to take some chances and estimate that there will be differences in criterion scores.

FIGURE 3-9

Regression lines with different standardized slopes.

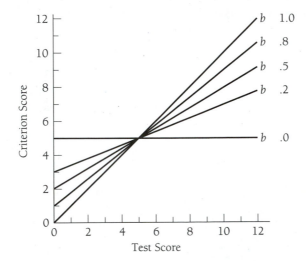

TABLE 3-3

Expected Criterion Scores for Two Test Scores when Predicted from Regression Lines with Different Slopes

Test Score	Slope	Predicted Criterion Score
11	1.0	11.00
3	1.0	3.00
11	.8	9.90
3	.8	3.50
11	.5	8.25
3	.5	4.25
11	.2	6.60
3	.2	5.00
11	.0	5.50
3	.0	5.50

Figure 3-9 is also instructive regarding psychological tests. For example, if SAT scores have a slope of .5 for predicting grades in college, this means that the SAT-performance relationship is defined by the "b = .5" line. Using this sort of information, college administrators can infer that SAT scores may predict differences in college performance. However, because the slope is not steep, those predictions are not far from what they would get if they used the consensus information.

Other Correlation Coefficients

The Pearson product moment correlation is only one of many types of correlation coefficient. It is the one most commonly used because most often we want to find the correlation between two continuous variables. Continuous variables, such as height, weight, and intelligence, can take on any values over a range of values. However, there are situations in which we want to find the correlations between variables scaled in other ways.

Spearman's rho is a method of correlation for finding the association between two sets of ranks. The rho coefficient (ρ) is easy to calculate and is often used when the individuals in a sample can be ranked on two variables but their actual scores are not known or have a very nonnormal distribution.

There is a whole family of correlation coefficients that involve dichotomous variables. Dichotomous variables have only two levels. Examples are yes/no, correct/incorrect, and male/female. Some dichotomous variables are called *true dichotomous* because they naturally form two categories. For example, gender is a true dichotomous variable. Other dichotomous variables are called *artificial dichotomous* because they reflect an underlying continuous scale forced into a dichotomy. Passing or failing a bar examination is an example of such an artificial dichotomy; although many scores can be obtained, the examiners consider only pass and fail. The types of correlation coefficients used to

TABLE 3-4

Appropriate Correlation Coefficients for Relationships Between Dichotomous and Continuous Variables*

Variable *Y*	Continuous	Variable *X* Artificial Dichotomous	True Dichotomous
Continuous	Pearson *r*	Biserial *r*	Point biserial *r*
Artificial dichotomous	Biserial *r*	Tetrachoric *r*	Phi
True dichotomous	Point biserial *r*	Phi	Phi

*The entries in the table suggest which type of correlation coefficient is appropriate given the characteristics of the two variables. For example, if variable *Y* is continuous and variable *X* is true dichotomous, you would use the point biserial correlation.

find the relationship between dichotomous and continuous variables are shown in Table 3-4.

The **biserial correlation** expresses the relationship between a continuous variable and an artificial dichotomous variable. For example, the biserial correlation might be used to assess the relationship between passing or failing the bar examination (artificial dichotomous variable) and grade point average in law school (continuous variable). If the dichotomous variable had been "true" (such as gender), we would use the *point biserial correlation*. For instance, the point biserial correlation would be used to find the relationship between gender and grade point average. When both variables are dichotomous and at least one of the dichotomies is "true," the association between them can be estimated using the *phi coefficient*. For example, the relationship between passing or failing the bar examination and gender could be estimated using the phi coefficient. If both dichotomous variables are artificial, we might use a special correlation coefficient known as the *tetrachoric correlation*. Among these special correlation coefficients, the point biserial, phi, and Spearman's rho coefficients are probably used most often. The formulas for calculating these correlations are given in Technical Box 3-2.

TECHNICAL BOX 3-2

Formulas for Spearman's Rho, the Point Biserial Correlation, and the Phi Coefficient

$$\text{Spearman's rho formula: } \rho = 1 - \frac{6\Sigma d_i^2}{N^3 - 3}$$

where ρ = Spearman's rho coefficient

d_i = a subject's rank order on variable 2 minus his or her rank order on variable 1

N = the number of paired ranks

When used: To find the association between pairs of observations, each expressed in ranks.

Point biserial correlation formula: $r_{pbis} = \left[\dfrac{\overline{Y}_1 - \overline{Y}}{S_y} \right] \sqrt{\dfrac{P_x}{1 - P_x}}$

where r_{pbis} = the point biserial correlation coefficient
X = a true dichotomous (two-choice) variable
Y = a continuous (multilevel) variable
Y_1 = the mean of Y for subjects having a "plus" score on X
P = the mean of Y for all subjects
S_y = the standard deviation for Y scores
P_x = the proportion of subjects giving a "plus" score on X

When used: To find the association between a dichotomous (two-choice) variable and a continuous variable. For the true dichotomous variable, one of the two choices is arbitrarily designated as a "plus" response.

Phi coefficient formula: $\phi = \dfrac{P_c - P_x P_y}{P_x(1 - P_x)P_y(1 - P_y)}$

where ϕ = the phi coefficient
P_c = the proportion in the "plus" category for both variables
P_x = the proportion in the "plus" category for the first variable
P_y = the proportion in the "plus" category for the second variable

When used: To find the association between two dichotomous (two-category) variables. A dichotomous variable might be yes/no or on/off. In each case, one of the two choices is arbitrarily chosen as a "plus" response. When you use phi, one of the variables must be "true" dichotomy (if both were "artificial," the tetrachoric correlation would be more appropriate).

Terms and Issues in the Use of Correlation

When you use correlation or read studies that report correlational analysis, you will need to know the terminology. Some of the terms and issues you should be familiar with are *residual, standard error of estimate, coefficient of determination, coefficient of alienation, shrinkage, cross validation, correlation-causation problem,* and *third variable*. Brief discussions of these terms and concepts follow.

Residual. A regression equation gives a predicted value of Y' for each value of X. In addition to these predicted values, there are observed values of Y. The difference between the predicted and the observed values is called the **residual**. Symbolically, the residual is defined as $Y - Y'$.

Consider the example of the CES-D. Earlier we calculated the regression equation that predicted CES-D scores from scores on the anger inventory. The equation suggested that predicted CES-D = $-6.85 + .67 \times$ anger score. Let's take the example of a person who had an anger score of 19 and an observed CES-D score of 7. The predicted CES-D score is

$$-6.85 + (.67 \times 19) = 5.88$$

In other words, the person had an observed score of 7 and a predicted score of 5.88. The residual is[5]

$$7 - 5.88 = 1.12$$

In regression analysis the residuals have certain properties. One important property is that the sum of the residuals always equals 0 $[\Sigma(Y - Y') = 0]$. In addition, the sum of the squared residuals is the smallest value according to the principle of least squares $[\Sigma(Y - Y')^2 = \text{smallest value}]$.

Standard error of estimate. Once we have obtained the residuals, we can find their standard deviation. However, in creating the regression equation, we have found two constants (a and b). Thus, we must use two degrees of freedom rather than one, as is usually the case in finding the standard deviation. The standard deviation of the residuals is known as the **standard error of estimate**, which is defined as

$$S_{yx} = \sqrt{\frac{\Sigma(Y - Y')^2}{N - 2}}$$

The standard error of estimate is a measure of the accuracy of prediction. Prediction is most accurate when the standard error of estimate is relatively small. As it becomes larger, the prediction becomes less accurate.

Coefficient of determination. The square of the correlation coefficient is known as the **coefficient of determination**. This value tells us the proportion of the total variation in scores on Y that we know as a function of information about X. For example, if the correlation between the SAT score and performance in the first year of college is .40, the coefficient of determination is .16. This means that we can explain 16% of the variation in first-year college performance by knowing SAT scores. In the CES-D and anger example, the correlation is .82. Therefore, the coefficient of determination is .67, suggesting that 67% of the variance in CES-D can be accounted for by the anger score.

Coefficient of alienation. The **coefficient of alienation** is a measure of nonassociation between two variables. This is calculated as $\sqrt{1 - r^2}$, where r^2 is the coefficient of determination. For the SAT example, the coefficient of alienation is $\sqrt{1 - .16} = \sqrt{.84} = .92$. This means that there is a high degree of nonassociation between SAT scores and college performance. In the CES-D and anger example, the coefficient of alienation is $\sqrt{1 - .67} = .57$.

---

[5]Note: There is a small discrepancy between 1.12 and the 1.04 for the example in Table 3-2. The difference is due to rounding error.

Shrinkage. Many times a regression equation is created on one group of subjects and then used to predict the performance of another group. One problem with regression analysis is that it takes advantage of chance relationships within a particular sample of subjects. Thus, there is a tendency to overestimate the relationship, particularly if the sample of subjects is small. **Shrinkage** is the amount of decrease observed when a regression equation is created for one population and then applied to another. Formulas are available to estimate the amount of shrinkage to expect given the characteristics of variance, covariance, and sample size (Brennan, 1994; Jaccard & Wan, 1995; F. M. Lord, 1950; Q. McNemar, 1969).

An example of shrinkage is when a regression equation is developed to predict first-year college grade point average on the basis of Scholastic Aptitude Test scores. Although the proportion of variance in grade point average might be fairly high for the original group, we can expect to account for a smaller proportion of the variance when the equation is used to predict grade point average in the next year's class. This decrease in the proportion of variance accounted for is the shrinkage.

Cross validation. The best way to ensure that proper references are being made is to use the regression equation to predict performance in a group of subjects other than the ones on which the equation was created. Then a standard error of estimate can be obtained for the relationship between the values predicted by the equation and those observed. This process is known as **cross validation.**

The correlation-causation problem. Just because two variables are correlated does not necessarily imply that one has caused the other (see Focused Example 3-1). For example, a correlation between the number of hours spent viewing television and aggressive behavior does not mean that excessive viewing of television causes aggression. This relationship could mean that an aggressive child might prefer to watch a lot of television.

Third variable explanation. There are other possible explanations for the observed relationship between television viewing and aggressive behavior. One is that some third variable causes both excessive viewing of television and aggressive behavior. For example, poor social adjustment might explain both. Thus, the apparent relationship between viewing and aggression actually might be the result of some variable not included in the analysis. We usually refer to this external influence as a **third variable.**

Multivariate Analysis (Optional)

Multivariate analysis considers the relationship among combinations of three or more variables. For example, the prediction of success in the first year of college from the linear combination of SAT verbal and SAT quantitative scores is a problem for multivariate analysis. However, because the field of multivariate analysis requires an understanding of linear and matrix algebra, a detailed discussion of it lies beyond the scope of this book.

On the other hand, you should have at least a general idea of what the different common testing methods entail. This section will familiarize you with some of the multivariate analysis terminology. It should help you identify the situations in which some of the different multivariate methods are used. Several references are available in case you would like to learn more about the

---

Focused Example 3-1

THE DANGER OF INFERRING CAUSATION FROM CORRELATION

A recent newspaper article discussed the stressfulness of a variety of occupations. It rated 130 job categories for stressfulness by examining Tennessee hospital and death records for evidence of stress-related diseases such as heart attacks, ulcers, arthritis, and mental disorders. The 12 highest and the 12 lowest jobs are listed in the table to the right.

The article advises readers who want to remain healthy to avoid the "most stressful" job categories. The evidence, however, may not warrant the advice offered in the article. Although certain diseases may be associated with particular occupations, holding these jobs does not necessarily cause the illnesses. Other explanations abound. For example, people with a propensity for heart attacks and ulcers might tend to select jobs as unskilled laborers or secretaries. Thus, the direction of causation might be that a health condition causes job selection rather than the reverse. Another possibility involves a third variable, some other factor that might cause the apparent relationship between job and health. For example, a certain income level might cause both stress and illness. Finally, wealthy people tend to have better health than poor people. Impoverished conditions may cause a person to accept certain jobs and also to have more diseases.

These three possible explanations are diagrammed in the right-hand column. An arrow indicates a causal connection.

In this example we are *not* ruling out the possibility that jobs cause illness. In fact, it is quite plausible. However, because the nature of the evidence

Most Stressful	Least Stressful
1. Unskilled laborer	1. Clothing sewer
2. Secretary	2. Garment checker
3. Assembly-line inspector	3. Stock clerk
4. Clinical lab technician	4. Skilled craftsperson
5. Office manager	5. Housekeeper
6. Foreperson	6. Farm laborer
7. Manager/ administrator	7. Heavy-equipment operator
8. Waiter	8. Freight handler
9. Factory machine operator	9. Child-care worker
10. Farm owner	10. Factory package wrapper
11. Miner	11. College professor
12. House painter	12. Personnel worker

Job $\rightarrow$ Illness	Illness $\rightarrow$ Job	Economic Status
		$\swarrow \quad \searrow$
		Job Illness
Job causes illness	Tendency toward illness causes people to choose certain jobs	Economic status (third variable) causes job selection and illness

is correlational, we cannot say with certainty that job causes illness.

technical details (Cliff, 1987; Grim & Yarnold, 1995; Tabachnick & Fidell, 1989).

General Approach

The correlational techniques we presented thus far in the chapter describe the relationship between only two variables, such as stress and illness. To understand more fully the causes of illness, we need to consider many potential factors in addition to stress. Multivariate analysis allows one to study the relationship between many predictors and an outcome, as well as the relationship among the predictors.

Multivariate methods differ in the number and kind of predictor variables they use. All these methods transform groups of variables into linear combinations. A *linear combination* of variables is a weighted composite of the original variables. The weighting system combines the variables in order to achieve some goal. Multivariate techniques differ according to the goal they are trying to achieve.

A linear combination of variables looks like this:

$$Y' = a + b_1X_1 + b_2X_2 + b_3X_3 + \ldots + b_kX_k$$

where Y' is the predicted value of Y, a is a constant, X_1 to X_k are variables and there are k such variables, and the b's are regression coefficients. If you feel anxious about such a complex-looking equation, there is no need to panic. Actually, this equation describes something similar to what was presented in the section on regression. The difference is that instead of relating Y to X, we are now dealing with a linear combination of X's. The whole right side of the equation creates a new composite variable by transforming a set of predictor variables.

An Example Using Multiple Regression

Suppose we want to predict success in law school from three variables: undergraduate grade point average (GPA), rating by former professors, and age. This type of multivariate analysis is called **multiple regression,** and the goal of the analysis is to find the linear combination of the three variables that provides the best prediction of law school success. We find the correlation between the criterion (law school GPA) and some composite of the predictors (undergraduate GPA plus professor rating plus age). The combination of the three predictors, however, is not just the sum of the three scores. Instead, we program the computer to find a specific way of adding the predictors together that will make the correlation between the composite and the criterion as high as possible. A weighted composite might look something like this:

law school GPA = .80(Z scores of undergraduate GPA)
+ .24(Z scores of professor ratings)
+ .03(Z scores for age)

This example suggests that undergraduate GPA is given more weight in the prediction of law school GPA than the other variables. The undergraduate GPA is multiplied by .80, whereas the other variables are multiplied by much smaller coefficients. Age is multiplied by only .03, which is very close to no contribution. This is because .03 times any Z score for age will give a number that is nearly 0 and, in effect, we would just be adding 0 to the composite.

The reason for using Z scores for the three predictors is that the coefficients in the linear composite are greatly affected by the range of values taken on by the variables. GPA is measured on a scale from 0 to 4.0, whereas the range in age might be 21 to 70. To compare the coefficients to one another, we need to transform all the variables into similar units. This is accomplished by using Z scores (see Chapter 2). When the variables are expressed in Z units, the coefficients, or weights for the variables, are known as standardized regression coefficients (sometimes called *B*'s and betas). There are also some cases in which we would want to use the variables in their natural units. For example, we sometimes want to find an equation we can use to estimate someone's predicted level of success on the basis of personal characteristics, and we do not want to bother changing these characteristics into Z units. When we do this, the weights in the model are called *raw regression coefficients* (sometimes called *b*'s).

Before moving on, we should caution you about interpreting regression coefficients. Besides reflecting the relationship between a particular variable and the criterion, the coefficients are affected by the relationship among the predictor variables. You need to be very careful when the predictor variables are highly correlated with one another. Two predictor variables that are highly correlated with the criterion will not both have large regression coefficients if they are highly correlated with one another. For example, suppose that undergraduate GPA and the professors' rating are both highly correlated with law school GPA. However, these two predictors also are highly correlated with each other. In effect, the two measures seem to be of the same thing (which would not be surprising, because the professors assigned the grades). So professors' rating may get a lower regression coefficient because some of its predictive power is already taken into consideration through its association with undergraduate GPA. We can only interpret regression coefficients confidently when the predictor variables do not overlap. They may do so when the predictors are uncorrelated.

Discriminant Analysis

Multiple regression is appropriate when the criterion variable is continuous (not nominal). However, there are many cases in testing where the criterion is a set of categories. For example, we often want to know the linear combination of variables that differentiates passing from failing. When the task is to find the linear combination of variables that provides a maximum discrimination between categories, the appropriate multivariate method is **discriminant analysis.** An example of discriminant analysis involves attempts to determine whether a set of measures predicts success or failure on a particular performance evaluation. Many tests had been given previously, and discriminant analysis is used to find the linear combination of these tests that best separates success from failure. Sometimes we want to determine the categorization in more than two categories. To accomplish this we use *multiple discriminant analysis*.

Discriminant analysis has many advantages in the field of test construction. For example, one approach to test construction is to identify two groups of people who represent two distinct categories of some trait. For example, two groups of children might be classified as "language disabled" and "normal." Then a variety of items would be presented, and discriminant analysis would be used to find the linear combination of items that best accounts for differences between the two groups. With the use of this information, new tests could be developed to help diagnose language impairment. Furthermore, learning about the differences between impaired and nonimpaired children might provide insight into the nature of the problem and eventually lead to better treatments.

Factor Analysis

Discriminant analysis and multiple regression analysis are techniques that find linear combinations of variables that maximize the prediction of some criterion. Factor analysis is used to study the interrelationships among a set of variables without reference to a criterion. You might think of factor analysis as a data reduction technique. When we have responses to a large number of items or a large number of tests, we often want to reduce all this information to more manageable chunks. In Figure 3-1 we presented a two-dimensional scatter diagram. The task in correlation is to find the best-fitting line through the space created by these two dimensions. As we add more variables in multivariate analysis, we increase the number of dimensions. For example, a three-dimensional plot is shown in Figure 3-10. You can use your imagination to visualize what a larger set of dimensions would look like. Some people claim they can visualize more than three dimensions, while others feel they cannot.

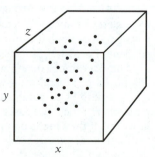

FIGURE 3-10

A three-dimensional scatter plot might be represented by this box. In addition to plotting points on the x and y axes, we must locate them in relation to a third z axis. Although it is hard to show more than two dimensions on a flat page, you can think of a three-dimensional figure as a box.

In any case, consider that points are plotted in the space created in these many dimensions.

In factor analysis, we first create a matrix that shows the correlation between every variable and every other variable. Then we find the linear combinations of the variables that describe as much of the interrelationships

---

Focused Example 3-2

THE FACTORS OF TRUST

Rotter (1967) described a scale for the measurement of interpersonal trust. Trust was defined as "an expectancy held by an individual or a group that the word, promise, verbal or written statement of another individual or group can be relied upon" (p. 651). However, since the publication of the original trust article, several authors have reported that trust seems to be composed of several independent factors (Chun & Campbell, 1974; R. M. Kaplan, 1973; Wright & Tedeschi, 1975). The method used to draw these conclusions was factor analysis. In each case, the items were given to a large group of people, and the results were subjected to factor analysis. This procedure reduced the many items down to a smaller number of factors. The factors are linear combinations of the original items. Then item loadings, which are the correlations of the original items with the factors, were studied in order to name the factors. The table that follows shows the loadings of the items on three of the factors (from R. M. Kaplan, 1973).

Once they have obtained the factor loadings, the researchers must attempt to name the factors by examining which items load highly on them. In this case, an item was used to help interpret a factor if its item loading on the factor was greater than .35 or less than −.35. Three factors of trust were found.

Factor I: Institutional trust. This represented trust toward major social agents in society. It included items regarding the competence of politicians, such as "This country has a dark future unless we can attract better people into politics" (−.67). Many of the items conveyed the idea of misrepresentation of public events by either the government or the mass media. For example, some items with high loadings were "Most people would be horrified if they knew how much news the public hears and sees is distorted" (−.69) and "Even though we have reports in newspapers, radio, and TV, it is hard to get objective accounts of public events" (−.67).

Factor II: Sincerity. Items loading highly on sincerity tended to focus on the perceived sincerity of others. These items included "Most idealists are sincere and usually practice what they preach" (.62) and "Most people answer public opinion polls honestly" (.58). Nearly all the items with high loadings on the second factor began with the word "most." Because of this loose wording, it would be possible for people to agree with the items because they believe in the sincerity of most people in a given group but still feel little trust for the group because of a few "rotten eggs." Thus, a woman could believe most car repairers are sincere but still service her car herself because she fears being overcharged.

Factor III: Caution. This contained items that expressed fear that some people will take advantage of others. For example, items stated that "In dealing with strangers, one is better off being cautious until they have provided evidence that they are trustworthy" (.74) and "In these competitive times you have to be alert or someone is likely to take advantage of you" (.53). Note that caution appears to be independent of perceived sincerity.

The data imply that generalized trust may be composed of several dimensions. The trust scale may prove to be a valuable tool for clinicians and researchers. Their purposes may be better served, however, if they focus on specific components of trust rather than the generalized case.

Item number	Item	Loading factor I	II	III
A. *Items with high loadings on institutional factor*				
4.	This country has a dark future unless we can attract better people into politics.	−.67	−.12	−.06
5.	Fear of social disgrace or punishment rather than conscience prevents most people from breaking the law.	−.54	.02	−.06
13.	The United Nations will never be an effective force in keeping world peace.	−.41	.09	−.21
16.	The judiciary is a place where we can all get unbiased treatment.	.37	.23	.00
19.	Most people would be horrified if they knew how much news the public hears and sees is distorted.	−.69	.18	.28
21.	Most elected public officials are really sincere in their campaign promises.	.44	.17	−.02
24.	Even though we have reports in newspapers, radio, and TV, it is hard to get objective accounts of public events.	−.67	−.08	.00
28.	If we really knew what was going on in international politics, the public would have more reason to be more frightened than it now seems to be.	−.49	.01	.24
33.	Many major national sports contests are fixed in one way or another.	−.55	−.04	.28
B. *Items with high loadings on sincerity factor*				
1.	Hypocrisy is on the increase in our society.	.09	−.52	.08
12.	Most students in school would not cheat even if they were sure of getting away with it.	.29	.45	.07
27.	Most experts can be relied upon to tell the truth about the limits of their knowledge.	.20	.66	.20
34.	Most idealists are sincere and usually practice what they preach.	.12	.62	−.20
38.	Most repair persons will not overcharge even if they think you are ignorant of their specialty.	.11	.48	−.35
44.	Most people answer public opinion polls honestly.	.04	.58	.16
C. *Items with high loadings on caution factor*				
2.	In dealing with strangers, one is better off being cautious until they have provided evidence that they are trustworthy.	−.22	−.03	.74
7.	Using the honor system of *not* having a teacher present during examinations would probably result in increased cheating.	.13	.08	.45
32.	In these competitive times you have to be alert or someone is likely to take advantage of you.	−.12	−.01	.53
42.	A large share of the accident claims filed against insurance companies are phony.	−.07	−.14	.57

Adapted from Rotter (1967).

between the variables as possible. These linear combinations of the variables are called *principal components,* and the goal in creating them is to describe as much of the association between the variables as possible. We can find as many principal components as there are variables. However, each principal component is extracted according to mathematical rules that make it independent of or uncorrelated with the other principal components. The first component will be the most successful in describing the variation among the variables, with each succeeding component somewhat less successful. Thus, we often decide to examine only a few components that account for larger proportions of the variation. Technically, principal components analysis and true factor analysis differ in how the correlation matrix is created. Even so, principal components are often called factors.

Once the linear combinations or principal components have been found, we can find the correlation between the original items and the factors. These correlations are called *factor loadings.* The expression "item 7 loaded highly on factor I" means there is a high correlation between item 7 and the first principal component. By examining which variables load highly on each factor, we can help determine the meaning for the factors. Focused Example 3-2 shows how the meanings of various factors in a scale on interpersonal trust are evaluated.

Factor analysis is a complex and technical method with many options the user must learn about. For example, users frequently use methods that help them get a clearer picture of the meaning of the components by transforming the variables in a way that pushes the factor loadings toward the high or the low extreme. Because these transformation methods involve rotating the axes in the space created by the factors, they have been labeled *methods of rotation.* There are many options for methods of rotation, as well as other options about the characteristics of the matrix originally entered into the analysis. If you are interested, several books discuss factor analysis methods in great detail (Bryant & Yarnold, 1995; P. Kline, 1994).

Summary

This chapter began with a discussion of a claim made in the *National Enquirer* that poor diet causes marital problems. Actually there was no specific evidence that diet *causes* the problems—only that diet and marital difficulties are associated. However, the *Enquirer* failed to specify the exact strength of the association. The rest of the chapter was designed to help you be more specific than the *Enquirer* by learning to specify associations with precise mathematical indexes known as *correlation coefficients.*

First, we presented pictures of the association between two variables, which are called *scatter diagrams.* Second, we presented a method for finding a linear equation to describe the relationship between two variables. This regression method uses the data in raw units. The results of regression analysis are two constants: a *slope* describing the degree of relatedness between the variables and an *intercept* giving the value of the Y variable when the X variable is 0. When both of the variables are in standardized or Z units, the intercept is always 0 and it drops out of the equation. In this unique situation, we solve for only one constant, which is *r,* or the *correlation coefficient.*

When using correlational methods, you must take many things into consideration. For example, correlation does not mean the same thing as causation. In the case of the *National Enquirer* article, the observed correlation between diet and problems in marriage may mean that diet causes the personal difficulties. However, it may also mean that marriage problems cause poor eating habits or that some *third variable* causes both diet habits and marital problems. In addition to the difficulties associated with causation, you must always consider the strength of the correlational relationship. The *coefficient of determination* describes the percentage of variation in one variable that is known on the basis of its association with another variable. The *coefficient of alienation* is an index of what is not known from information about the other variable.

A *regression line* is the best-fitting straight line through a set of points in a scatter diagram. The regression line is described by a mathematical index known as the regression equation. The *regression coefficient* is the ratio of covariance to variance and is also known as the slope of the regression line. The regression coefficient describes how much change is expected in the *Y* variable each time the *X* variable increases by one unit. Other concepts discussed were the *intercept,* the *residual* (the difference between the predicted value given by a regression equation and the observed value), and the *standard error of estimate* (the standard deviation of the residuals obtained from the regression equation).

The field of *multivariate analysis* involves a complicated but important set of methods for studying the relationships among many variables. *Multiple regression* is a multivariate method for studying the relationship between one criterion variable and two or more predictor variables. A similar method known as *discriminant analysis* is used to study the relationship between a categorical criterion and two or more predictors. *Factor analysis* is another multivariate method for reducing a large set of variables down to a smaller set of composite variables.

Correlational methods are the most commonly used statistical techniques in the testing field. The concepts presented in this overview will be referred to throughout the rest of this book.

Appendix 3-1: Calculation of a Regression Equation and a Correlation Coefficient

The example in Appendix 3-1 considers the relationship between payroll for teams in the National Football League and team performance. Data for the example were taken from the 1995–1996 season and are available on the Internet. Payroll is measured in millions of dollars spent per team while performance is measured in terms of the number of games won. The data for the example are shown in Table 3-5 and are summarized in Figure 3-11. Each dot

FIGURE 3-11
Regression of payroll and team performance: NFL, 1995–1996.

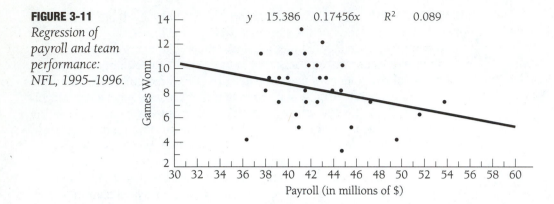

on the figure represents one team. In the example created in the mid-1980s (for the third edition of this book), there was a positive relationship between payroll and performance. In other words, teams with higher payrolls had better performance. As you will see, in the current example there is a negative relationship. In other words, each increase in expenditure is associated with a decrease in performance. The regression coefficient (-0.17) suggests that for each million dollars spent, the team's performance decreases by an average of .17 games per season. Overall, the relationship is not strong and the best explanation is that there is little association between payroll and performance.

Calculation of a Regression Equation (Data from Table 3-5)

Formulas: $b = \dfrac{N(\Sigma XY) - (\Sigma X)(\Sigma Y)}{N\Sigma X^2 - (\Sigma X)^2}$

$\qquad\quad a = \overline{Y} - b\overline{X}$

Steps

1. Find N by counting the number of pairs of observations.
   $N = 30$
2. Find ΣX by summing the X scores.
   $53.4 + 51.2 + 49.1 + \cdots + 35.8 = 1269.3$
3. Find ΣY by summing the Y scores.
   $7 + 6 + 4 + \cdots + 4 = 240$
4. Find ΣX^2. Square each X score and then sum them.
   $(53.4)^2 + (51.2)^2 + (49.1)^2 + \cdots + (35.8)^2 = 54212.21$
5. Find ΣY^2. Square each Y score and then sum them.
   $(7)^2 + (6)^2 + (4)^2 + \cdots + (4)^2 = 2094$
6. Find ΣXY. For each pair of observations multiply X by Y. Then sum the products.

TABLE 3-5

Games Won and Average Salaries for Teams in the National Football League

Team	X Payroll (Millions)	Y Games Won	X²	Y²	XY
Carolina	53.4	7	2851.56	49	373.8
Washington	51.2	6	2621.44	36	307.2
Jacksonville	49.1	4	2410.81	16	196.4
Houston	48.3	7	2332.89	49	338.1
St. Louis	46.7	7	2180.89	49	326.9
N.Y. Giants	45.1	5	2034.01	25	225.5
Buffalo	44.3	10	1962.49	100	443
N.Y. Jets	44.3	3	1962.49	9	132.9
Denver	44	8	1936	64	352
Oakland	43.6	8	1900.96	64	348.8
Chicago	42.7	9	1823.29	81	384.3
Dallas	42.5	12	1806.25	144	510
Miami	42.4	9	1797.76	81	381.6
Tampa Bay	41.9	7	1755.61	49	293.3
Detroit	41.8	10	1747.24	100	418
Philadelphia	41.3	10	1705.69	100	413
Cincinnati	40.9	7	1672.81	49	286.3
Minnesota	40.8	8	1664.64	64	326.4
San Francisco	40.7	11	1656.49	121	447.7
Kansas City	40.6	13	1648.36	169	527.8
Cleveland	40.3	5	1624.09	25	201.5
New England	39.9	6	1592.01	36	239.4
Pittsburgh	39.6	11	1568.16	121	435.6
Indianapolis	39.2	9	1536.64	81	352.8
New Orleans	38.4	7	1474.56	49	268.8
Atlanta	38.3	9	1466.89	81	344.7
San Diego	37.8	9	1428.84	81	340.2
Seattle	37.3	8	1391.29	64	298.4
Green Bay	37.1	11	1376.41	121	408.1
Arizona	35.8	4	1281.64	16	143.2
	ΣX 1269.3	ΣY 240	ΣX^2 54,212.21	ΣY^2 2094	ΣXY 10,065.7
	42.31	8			

Summary

ΣX	1269.3	$b = -0.17456266$
ΣY	240	$a = 15.3857461$
ΣXY	10065.7	$r = -0.2983066$
ΣX^2	54212.21	
ΣY^2	2094	
N	30	
$\overline{X}$	42.31	
$\overline{Y}$	8	

$$(53.4 \times 7) + (51.2 \times 6) + (49.1 \times 4) + \cdots + (35.8 \times 4)$$
$$= 373.8 + 307.2 + 196.4 + \cdots + 143.2 = 10{,}065.7$$

7. Find $(\Sigma X)^2$ by squaring the results of Step 2.
   $(1269.3)^2 = 1{,}611{,}122.49$

8. Find $(\Sigma Y)^2$ by squaring the results of Step 3.
   $(240)^2 = 57{,}600$

9. Find $N\Sigma XY$ by multiplying the results of Step 1 by Step 6.
   $30 \times 10{,}065.7 = 301{,}971$

10. Find $(\Sigma X)(\Sigma Y)$ by multiplying the results of Steps 2 and 3.
    $1269.3 \times 240 = 304{,}632$

11. Find $(N\Sigma XY) - (\Sigma X)(\Sigma Y)$ by subtracting the results of Step 10 from the result of Step 9.
    $301{,}971 - 304{,}632 = -2661$

12. Find $N\Sigma X^2$ by multiplying the results of Steps 1 and 4.
    $30 \times 54{,}212.21 = 1{,}626{,}366.3$

13. Find $N\Sigma X^2 - (\Sigma X)^2$ by subtracting the result of Step 7 from that of Step 12.
    $1{,}626{,}366.3 - 1{,}611{,}122.49 = 15243.81$

14. Find b by dividing the result of Step 11 by that of Step 13.
    $-2{,}661/15{,}243.81 = -.1745$

15. Find the mean of X by dividing the result of Step 2 by that of Step 1.
    $1269.3/30 = 42.31$

16. Find the mean of Y by dividing the result of Step 3 by that of Step 1.
    $240/30 = 8$

17. Find $b\overline{X}$ by multiplying the results of Steps 14 and 15.
    $-.1745 \times 42.31 = -7.386$

18. Find a by subtracting the results of Step 17 from Step 15.
    $8 - (-7.386) = 15.386$

19. The resultant regression equation is
    $Y = a + bX$
    $Y = 15.386 + -.1745(X)$

Calculation of a Correlation Coefficient (Data from Table 3-5)

Formula: $r = \dfrac{N\Sigma XY - (\Sigma X)(\Sigma Y)}{\sqrt{[N\Sigma X^2 - (\Sigma X)^2][N\Sigma Y^2 - (\Sigma Y)^2]}}$

Steps

1. Find N by counting the number of pairs of observations.
   $N = 30$

2. Find ΣX by summing the X scores.
   $53.4 + 51.2 + 49.1 + \cdots + 35.8 = 1269.3$

3. Find ΣY by summing the Y scores.
   $7 + 6 + 4 + \cdots + 4 = 240$

4. Find ΣX^2. Square each X score and then sum them.
   $(53.4)^2 + (51.2)^2 + (49.1)^2 + \cdots + (35.8)^2 = 54,212.21$

5. Find ΣY^2. Square each Y score and then sum them.
   $(7)^2 + (6)^2 + (4)^2 + \cdots + (4)^2 = 2,094$

6. Find ΣXY. For each pair of observations multiple X by Y. Then sum the products.
   $(53.4 \times 7) + (51.2 \times 6) + (49.1 \times 4) + \cdots + (35.8 \times 4)$
   $= 373.8 + 307.2 + 196.4 + \cdots + 143.2 = 10,065.7$

7. Find $(\Sigma X)^2$ by squaring the results of Step 2.
   $(1269.3)^2 = 1,611,122.49$

8. Find $(\Sigma Y)^2$ by squaring the results of Step 3.
   $(240)^2 = 57,600$

9. Find $N\Sigma XY$ by multiplying the results of Step 1 by Step 6.
   $30 \times 10,065.7 = 301,971$

10. Find $(\Sigma X)(\Sigma Y)$ by multiplying the results of Steps 2 and 3.
    $1269.3 \times 240 = 304,632$

11. Find $(N\Sigma XY) - (\Sigma X)(\Sigma Y)$ by subtracting the result of Step 10 from that of Step 9.
    $301,971 - 304,632 = -2,661$

12. Find $N\Sigma X^2$ by multiplying the results of Steps 1 and 4.
    $30 \times 54,212.21 = 1,626,366.3$

13. Find $N\Sigma X^2 - (\Sigma X)^2$ by subtracting the result of Step 7 from that of Step 12.
    $1,626,366.3 - 1,611,122.49 = 15,243.81$

14. Find $N\Sigma Y^2$ by multiplying the results of Steps 1 and 5.
    $30 \times 2094 = 62,820$

15. Find $N\Sigma Y^2 - (\Sigma Y)^2$ by subtracting the result of Step 8 from that of Step 14.
    $62,820 - 57,600 = 5220$

16. Find $\sqrt{[N\Sigma X^2 - (\Sigma X)^2][N\Sigma Y^2 - (\Sigma Y)^2]}$ by multiplying the results of Steps 13 and 15 and taking the square root of the product.
    $15,243.81 \times 5220 = 7,957,2688.2$
    $\sqrt{79,572,688.2} = 8920.35$

17. Find $r = \dfrac{N\Sigma XY - (\Sigma X)(\Sigma Y)}{\sqrt{[N\Sigma X^2 - (\Sigma X^2)][N\Sigma Y^2 - (\Sigma Y)^2]}}$ by dividing the result of Step 1 by that of Step 16.
    $-2661/8920.35$
    $r = -0.2983$

CHAPTER 4

Reliability

LEARNING OBJECTIVES

When you have completed this chapter, you should be able to:

☐ Tell what measurement error is and how it interferes with scientific studies in psychology

☐ Given that reliability is the ratio of true variability to observed variability, explain what this tells us about a test with a reliability of .30, .60, or .90

☐ Describe how test-retest reliability is assessed

☐ Explain the difference between test-retest reliability estimates and split-half reliability estimates

☐ Discuss how the split-half method underestimates the reliability of a short test and what can be done to correct this problem

☐ Know the easiest way to find the average reliability

☐ Define coefficient alpha and tell how it differs from other methods of estimating reliability

☐ Discuss how high a reliability coefficient must be before you would be willing to say the test is "reliable enough"

☐ Explain what can be done to increase the reliability of a test

☐ Tell how the reliability of behavioral observations is assessed

*I*n the gymnastics competition at an international meet, a young Romanian woman received an 8.9 for the first portion of her routine. As she reappeared for the second portion, the television commentator said, "The 8.9 rating for her first routine does not accurately represent her ability. This young woman is clearly a 9.5 performer." With this remark, the commentator indicated a discrepancy between the gymnast's score for the first routine and her true ability, a common occurrence in the measurement of many different human abilities. For example, after an examination students sometimes feel that the actual questions did not allow them to display their real knowledge. And actors sometimes complain that the five-minute sample of their performance in an audition is not an adequate measure of their talents.

Discrepancies between true ability and measurement of ability constitute errors of measurement. In psychological testing, the word *error* does not imply that a mistake has been made. Rather than a negative connotation, error implies that there always will be some inaccuracy or error in one's measurements. One's task is to find the magnitude of this error and to develop ways to minimize it. This chapter discusses the conceptualization and assessment of measurement error. We call the chapter "Reliability" because tests that are relatively free of measurement error are deemed to be reliable. Tests that have relatively greater measurement error are considered unreliable.

History and Theory of Reliability

Conceptualization of Error

Students who major in physical science have chosen to study phenomena that are relatively easy to measure quite precisely. If you want to measure the width of this book, for example, you need only apply a ruler and record the number of inches or centimeters.

In psychology, many problems make the measurement task more difficult. First, rarely are researchers interested in measuring simple qualities such as width. Instead, they usually pursue more complex traits such as intelligence or aggressiveness, which one can neither see nor touch. Furthermore, with no rigid yardsticks available to measure such characteristics, testers must use "rubber yardsticks," which may stretch to overestimate some measurements and shrink to underestimate others (Nunnally & Bernstein, 1994). Psychologists must assess their measuring instruments to determine how much rubber is in them. A psychologist attempting to understand human behavior on the basis of unreliable tests is like a carpenter trying to build a house with a rubber measuring tape that never records the same length for the same piece of board.

As you will learn from this chapter, the theory of measurement error is well developed within psychology. This is not to say that measurement error is unique to psychology. In fact, serious measurement error occurs in most physical, social, and biological sciences. For example, measures of the gross national product (economics) and blood pressure (medicine) are known to be less reliable than well-constructed psychological tests. However, the concern with reliability has been a particular obsession for psychologists and provides evidence of the advanced scientific status of the field.

Spearman's Early Studies

Psychology owes its advanced development of reliability assessment to the early work of the British psychologist Charles Spearman. The basic notion of sampling error was introduced in 1733 by DeMoivre (cited in J. C. Stanley, 1971), and the product moment correlation (see Chapter 3) was developed by Karl Pearson and published in 1896 (Pearson, 1896). Reliability theory puts these two concepts together in the context of measurement. A contemporary of Pearson, Spearman actually worked out most of the basics of contemporary reliability theory and published his work in a 1904 article entitled "The Proof and Measurement of Association Between Two Things." Because the *British Journal of Psychology* did not begin until 1907, Spearman published his work in the *American Journal of Psychology*. Spearman's work was absorbed quickly in the United States. The article came to the attention of measurement pioneer Edward L. Thorndike, who was then writing the first edition of *An Introduction to the Theory of Mental and Social Measurements* (1904).

Thorndike's book is remarkably sophisticated, even by contemporary standards. Since 1904, many developments on both sides of the Atlantic Ocean have led to further refinements in the assessment of reliability. Most important among these is a 1937 article by Kuder and Richardson, in which several new reliability coefficients were introduced. Later Cronbach and his colleagues (Cronbach, 1989, 1995; Cronbach et al., 1972) made a major advance by developing methods for evaluating many sources of error in behavioral research. Reliability theory continues to evolve. In recent years, sophisticated mathematical models have been developed to quantify "latent" variables based on multiple measures (P. M. Bentler, 1990, 1991, 1994).

Basics of Test Score Theory

Classical test score theory assumes that each person has a true score that would be obtained if there were no errors in measurement. However, because measuring instruments are imperfect, the score observed for each person may differ from the person's true ability or characteristic. The difference between the **true score** and the observed score results from **measurement error.** In symbolic representation, the observed score (X) has two components; a true score (T) and an error component (E):

$$X \quad = \quad T \quad + \quad E$$

Observed score $\quad$ True score $\quad$ Error

Or we can say that the difference between the score we obtain and the score we are really interested in equals the error of measurement:

$$X - T = E$$

A major assumption in classical test theory is that errors of measurement are random. Although systematic errors are acknowledged in most measurement problems, they are less likely than other errors to force an investigator to make the wrong conclusions. A carpenter who always misreads a tape measure by 2 inches (or makes a systematic error of 2 inches) would still be able to cut boards the same length. Using the rubber-yardstick analogy, we would say that this carpenter works with a ruler that is always 2 inches too long. Classical test theory deals with rubber-yardstick problems in which the ruler stretches and contracts in a random way.

Using a rubber yardstick, we would not get the same score on each measurement. Instead, we would get a distribution of scores like that shown in Figure 4-1. Each observed score in the distribution is made up of two components: a true score component (T) and an error component (E). Basic sampling theory tells us that the distribution of random errors is bell shaped. Thus, the center of the distribution should represent the true score, and the dispersion around the mean of the distribution should display the distribution of sampling errors. Though any one application of the rubber yardstick may or may not tell us the true score, we can estimate the true score by finding the mean of the observations from repeated applications.

Figure 4-2 shows three different distributions. In the left-hand distribution, there is a great dispersion around the true score. In this case, you might not want to depend on a single observation because it might fall far from the true score. The right-hand distribution displays a very small dispersion around the true score. In this case, most of the observations actually are very close to the true score, and it might be more accurate to draw conclusions on the basis of fewer observations.

The dispersions or distributions around the true score in Figures 4-1 and 4-2 tell us how much error there is in the measure. Classical test theory

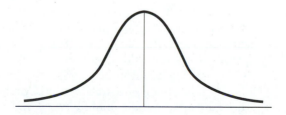

FIGURE 4-1 *Distribution of observed scores for repeated testing of the same person. The mean of the distribution is the estimated true score, and the dispersion represents the distribution of random errors.*

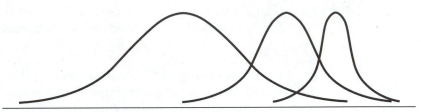

FIGURE 4-2   *Three distributions of observed scores. The left distribution reflects the greatest error, and the right distribution the least.*

assumes that the true score for an individual will not change with repeated applications of the same test. Because of random error, however, repeated applications of the same test can produce different scores. Random error is responsible for the distribution of scores shown in Figures 4-1 and 4-2. Theoretically, the standard deviation of the distribution of errors for each person tells us about the magnitude of measurement error. Because we usually assume that the distribution of random errors will be the same for all people, classical test theory uses the standard deviation of errors as the basic measure of error. Usually this is called the **standard error of measurement**:

$$\sigma_{\text{meas}}$$

The rubber-yardstick analogy may help you understand this concept. Suppose you have a table that is 30 inches high. If you measured the height of the table using a steel yardstick, you would probably always find it to be the same height: 30 inches. However, now you try to measure the table with the rubber yardstick. The first time you try, the stick has stretched and you record 28 inches. The next time, you discover the stick has shrunk, and it gives you 32 inches for the height of the table. Now you are in trouble, because repeated applications of the yardstick do not always give you the same information about the height of the table.

There is one way out of this situation. If we assume that the yardstick stretches and shrinks randomly, then you can say that the distribution of scores given by the yardstick will be normal. Most scores will be close to the actual or true score; scores that greatly differ from the true score occur less frequently. Thus, it would be rare to observe a score as low as 5 inches or as high as 53 inches. The mean of the distribution of scores from repeated applications of the rubber yardstick would be an estimate of the table's true height. The standard deviation would be the standard error of measurement. Remember from Chapter 3 that the standard deviation tells us something about the average deviation around the mean. The standard error of measurement tells us, on the average, how much a score varies from the true score. In practice, the standard deviation of the observed score and the reliability of the test are used to estimate the standard error of measurement. We will return to this concept after reviewing methods for estimating reliability.

Models of Reliability

Federal government guidelines require that a test be reliable before one can use it to make employment decisions. In this section we hope to justify the need for high standards of reliability. Most reliability coefficients are correlations; however, it is sometimes more useful to define reliability as its mathematically equivalent ratio. The reliability coefficient is the ratio of the variance of the true scores on a test to the variance of the observed scores:

$$r = \frac{\sigma^2_T}{\sigma^2_X}$$

where r = the theoretical reliability of the test

σ^2_T = the variance of the true scores

σ^2_X = the variance of the observed scores

We have used the Greek σ^2 instead of S^2 to symbolize the variance, because the equation describes theoretical values in a population rather than those actually obtained from a sample. The ratio of true score variance to observed score variance can be thought of as a percentage. In this case, it is the percentage of the observed variation (σ^2_X) that is attributable to variation in the true score. If we subtract this ratio from 1.0, we will have the percentage of variation attributable to random error.

Consider the situation in which the reliability is estimated to be .60; that is, 60% of the variation is associated with true variation among people who took the test. The remaining 40% of the variation is random. Suppose you are given a test that will be used to select people for a particular job, and the reliability of the test is .40. When the employer gets the test back and begins comparing applicants, 40% of the variation or difference among the people will be explained by real differences among people, and 60% must be ascribed to random or chance factors. Now you can see why the government needs to insist on high standards of reliability.

Sources of Error

An observed score may differ from a true score for many reasons. There may be situational factors such as loud noises in the room while the test is being administered. The room may be too hot, or it may be too cold. The health status of the test takers also could affect test scores. For example, you may know how hard it is to do well on an examination when you have a cold or are feeling depressed. Reliability assessment deals with these factors indirectly by using time sampling. The test is given at different times, and each test administration is considered an independent sample. The most common use of time sampling is for **test-retest reliability**. With this method the same group of people is tested at two different times with the same test. Then the correlation between these two samples is used as an estimate of reliability. Though the test-retest method is best suited to time-related sources of error, it does not help evaluate errors internal to the test. Studies that evaluate internal problems are best understood in terms of a domain sampling model (see the section on The Domain Sampling Model). Methods are available to assess each of these types of errors.

Time Sampling: Test-Retest Method

As you know, test-retest reliability estimates are used to evaluate the error associated with administering a test at two different times. This type of analysis is of value only when one measures "traits" or characteristics that do not change over time. For instance, we usually assume that an intelligence test measures a consistent general ability. As such, if an IQ test administered at two points in time produces different scores, we might conclude that the lack of correspondence is due to random measurement error. Usually we do not assume that a person got smarter or less so.

Some tests might not be appropriate for test-retest evaluation because they measure some constantly changing characteristic. In Chapter 16, we will discuss the Rorschach inkblot test and note that its value seems to be to tell the clinician how the client is functioning at a particular time. Thus, differences between Rorschach scores at two times could reflect one of two things: (1) a change in the true score being measured or (2) measurement error. This tells us that the test-retest method applies only to measures of stable traits.

Test-retest reliability is relatively easy to evaluate. All you need to do is administer the same test on two well-specified occasions and then find the correlation between scores from the two administrations using the methods presented in Chapter 3.

However, you need to consider many other details besides the methods for calculating the test-retest reliability coefficient. Understanding and using the information gained from these mechanical exercises requires some careful thought. One thing you always should consider is the possibility of a carryover effect. This effect occurs when the first testing session influences scores from the second session. This happens when test takers remember their answers from the first time they took the test. Suppose we ask someone the trivia question "Who was the next door neighbor in the television program *Home Improvement*"? Then we ask the same question two days later. Response on the second occasion might be influenced by hearing the question only two days earlier. When there are carryover effects, the test-retest correlation usually overestimates the true reliability.[1]

Practice effects are one important type of carryover effect. Some skills improve with practice. Thus, when a test is given a second time, test takers

---

[1]Carryover problems are of concern only when the changes over time are random. In cases where the changes are systematic, carryover effects do not harm the reliability. An example of a systematic carryover is when everyone's score improves exactly five points. In this case, no new variability occurs. Random carryover effects occur when the changes are not predictable from earlier scores or when something affects some but not all test takers.

score better because they have sharpened their skills by having taken the test the first time. Asking people trivia questions about old television programs might stimulate them to think more about the old shows or may actually give them some of the information. This sometimes happens on tests of manual dexterity: Experience taking the test can improve dexterity skills. As a result, scores on the second administration are usually higher than they were on the first. Practice may affect test takers in different ways, so the changes are not constant across a group.

Because of these problems, the time interval between testing sessions must be selected and evaluated carefully. If the two administrations of the test are very close in time, there is a relatively great risk of carryover and practice effects. However, as the time between testing sessions increases, many other factors can intervene to affect scores. For example, if a test is given to children at ages 4 and 5, and the scores from the two administrations of the test corre-late at .43, we are left with alternative explanations. The low correlation might mean that (1) the test has poor reliability, (2) children change on this charac-teristic between ages 4 and 5, or (3) some combination of low reliability and change in the children is responsible for the .43 correlation. Most test-retest evaluations do not allow one to choose among these alternatives.

When you find a test-retest correlation in a test manual, you should pay careful attention to the interval between the two testing sessions. A well-evalu-ated test will have many retest correlations associated with different time inter-vals between testing sessions. Most often you want to be assured that the test is reliable over the time interval of your own study. You also should consider what events occur between the original testing and the retest. For example, activities such as reading a book, participating in a course of study, or watch-ing a TV documentary can alter the test-retest reliability estimate.

Of course, sometimes poor test-retest correlations do not mean that a test is unreliable; instead, they suggest that the characteristic under study has changed. One of the problems with classical test theory is that it assumes that behavioral dispositions are constant over time. For example, if you are an aggressive person, it is assumed that you will be aggressive all the time. How-ever, some authors have suggested that important behavioral characteristics, such as motivation, fluctuate over time. In fact, important variables such as health status are expected to vary (Guyatt, Feeney & Patrick, 1993; Kaplan et al., 1995). In classical test theory these variations are assumed to be error. However, advanced theories of motivation predict these variations, so that test theorists have been challenged to develop models to account for these system-atic variations (J. W. Atkinson, 1981; McClelland, 1994; Pattishall, 1992).

Error Associated with the Use of Particular Items

Another concern in building a reliable test is that the test scores not represent any one particular set of items. If you are making a test for some particular characteristic, you might choose many different items to represent this construct. For example, if you are developing a test to determine spelling ability, many different words could be chosen for inclusion in the spelling test. One form of reliability analysis is to determine the error variance attributable to the selection of one particular set of items.

Parallel forms reliability compares two equivalent forms of a test that measure the same attribute. The two forms use different items; however, the rules used to select items of a particular difficulty level are the same.

When two forms of the test are available, one can compare performance on one form versus the other. Some textbooks refer to this process as *equivalent forms reliability,* whereas others call it simply *parallel forms.* Sometimes the two forms are administered to the same group of people on the same day. The Pearson product moment correlation coefficient (see Chapter 3) is used as an estimate of the reliability. When both forms of the test are given on the same day, the only sources of variation are random error and the difference between the forms of the test. (The order of administration is usually counterbalanced to avoid practice effects.) Sometimes the two forms of the test are given at different times. In these cases, error associated with time sampling is also included in the estimate of reliability.

The use of parallel forms provides one of the most rigorous assessments of reliability commonly in use. Unfortunately, the use of parallel forms occurs in practice less often than is desirable. Often test developers find it burdensome to develop two forms of the same test, and practical constraints make it difficult to retest the same group of individuals. Instead, many test developers prefer to estimate the reliability based on a single form of the same test.

The Domain Sampling Model

The domain sampling model considers the problems of using a limited number of items to represent some larger domain. For example, suppose we want to evaluate your spelling ability. The best technique would be to go systematically through a dictionary, have you spell each word, and determine the percentage you spelled correctly. However, it is unlikely that you would have time for this. Instead, we need to find a way to evaluate your spelling without having you spell every word. To accomplish this evaluation, we use a sample of words. Remember that what we are really attempting to evaluate is how well you can spell, which would be determined by your percentage correct if you had been given all the words in the English language. This percentage would be your "true score." Our task in reliability analysis would be to estimate how much error we would make by using the score from the shorter test as an estimate of your true ability.

Theoretically, this model conceptualizes reliability as the ratio of the variance of the observed score on the shorter test and the variance of the long-run true score. The measurement considered in the domain sampling model is the error introduced by using a sample of items (or words in this case) rather than the entire domain.[2] As the sample gets larger, it increasingly represents the domain. As a result, the greater the number of items, the higher the reliability. We will show you exactly how a larger number of items increases reliability in a later section of this chapter.

When tests are constructed, each item is a sample of the ability or behavior under study. Long tests have many such samples, and short tests have very few. However, each item should equally represent the studied ability.

Reliability can be estimated from the correlation of the observed test score with the true score.[3] This would be easy to find if one could obtain true scores. However, finding the true scores is not practical and is rarely possible. In the example just presented, finding the true score would involve testing people on all of the words in the English language.

Because true scores are not available, our only alternative is to estimate what they would be. Given that items are randomly drawn from a given domain, each test or group of items should yield an unbiased estimate of the true score. Because of sampling error, however, different random samples of items might give different estimates of the true score. The distribution of these estimates should be random and normally distributed. If we create many tests by sampling from the same domain, we should get a normal distribution of unbiased estimates of the true score. To estimate reliability, we can create many randomly parallel tests by drawing repeated random samples of items from the same domain. In the spelling test example, we would draw several different lists of words randomly from the dictionary and consider each of these samples to be an unbiased test of spelling ability. Then we would find the correlation between each of these tests and each of the other tests. The correlations then would be averaged.[4]

In practice psychologists rarely develop randomly parallel tests because test items are seldom selected at random. In fact, the items usually are selected for a particular purpose. However, the same general strategy is often used to select items for the different parallel forms of the test. Selecting the items by this nonrandom process does not greatly affect estimates of reliability. Another problem is that it is uncommon in practice to have more than two forms of a test. Instead of evaluating the average correlation between a test and all of its randomly parallel forms, psychologists typically evaluate the correlation between the test and the one other form they have created. As a result, the estimates of reliability used in practice may be less dependable than desired.

---

[2]The term *domain* is used to describe a very large collection of items. Some authors prefer the term *universe* or *population* to describe the same concept (Nunnally & Bernstein, 1994).

[3]As Allen and Yen (1979) point out, there are at least six alternative interpretations of the reliability coefficient. The interpretation we offer here is the one most commonly used.

[4]Technically, it is inappropriate to average correlation coefficients. The appropriate method is to use Fisher's r to Z' transformation to convert the correlations into approximate Z scores. Then the Z' scores are averaged, and the mean Z' is transformed back into a correlation (Silver & Dunlap, 1987).

Technical Box 4-1 considers one of the technical issues in estimating true reliability.

In practice, psychologists do not always have two forms of a test. More often they have only one test form and must estimate the reliability for this single group of items. You can assess the different sources of variation within a single test in many ways. One method is to evaluate the internal consistency of the test by dividing it into subcomponents. The test-retest method involves examining the error variance that might be introduced by readministering the test at different points in time (see the section on Time Sampling: Test-Related Method).

Internal consistency: split-half method. In **split-half reliability,** a test is given and divided into halves that are scored separately. The results of one half of the test are then compared with the results of the other. The two halves of the test can be created in a variety of ways. If the test is long, the best method is to divide the items randomly into two halves. For ease in computing scores for the different halves, however, some people prefer to calculate a score for the first half of the items and another score for the second half. Although conve-

---

TECHNICAL BOX 4-1

The Unbiased Estimate of Reliability

Theorists have demonstrated mathematically that an unbiased estimate of a test's reliability is given by the square root of the average correlation between a test and all other randomly parallel tests from the domain. Symbolically,

$$r_{1t} = \sqrt{\bar{r}_{1j}}$$

where 1 = scores on test 1
  t = the true score for the ability of interest
  r_{1j} = the average correlation between test 1 and all other randomly parallel tests

As you learned in Chapter 3, product moment correlation coefficients always take on values between -1 and 1. When we estimate reliability, the correlation will always be positive. When a number is less than 1.0, its square root will always be larger than itself. Thus, the correlation between two randomly parallel tests will be smaller than the estimated correlation between one of the tests and the true score according to the formula. For example, if the correlation between two randomly parallel tests is .64, the estimated reliability of the test will be $\sqrt{.64} = .80$. This is built into the estimation of reliability because it would be impossible for a test to correlate more highly with any other test than it would correlate with its own true score. Thus, the correlation between two randomly parallel tests would be expected to be less than the correlation of either test with the true score.

nient, this method can cause problems when items on the second half of the test are more difficult than items on the first half. If the items get progressively more difficult, you might be better advised to use the odd-even system, whereby one subscore is obtained for the odd-numbered items in the test and another for the even-numbered items.

To estimate the reliability of the test, you could find the correlation between the two halves. However, this would be an underestimate because each subtest is only half as long as the full test. As we discussed earlier, test scores gain reliability as the number of items increases. An estimate of reliability based on two half-tests would be deflated because each half would be less reliable than the whole test. The correlation between the two halves of the test would be a reasonable estimate of the reliability of half the test. To correct for half-length, you can apply the Spearman-Brown formula, which allows you to estimate what the correlation between the two halves would have been if each half had been the length of the whole test:

$$r = \frac{2r}{1 + r}$$

where r is the estimated correlation between the two halves of the test if each had had the total number of items, and r is the correlation between the two halves of the test.[5] For example, when the CES-D is divided into two equal parts, the correlation between the two halves of the test (for medical students) is .78. According to the formula, the estimated reliability would be

$$r = \frac{2(.78)}{1 + .78} = \frac{1.56}{1.78} = .876$$

Using the Spearman-Brown formula increases the estimate of reliability. The left-hand column in Table 4-1 shows several estimates of reliability that are not corrected using the Spearman-Brown procedure. The middle column

TABLE 4-1

Estimates of Split-Half Reliability Before and After Correction for Half-Length Using the Spearman-Brown Formula

Before Correction	After Correction	Amount of Change
.05	.09	.04
.15	.26	.11
.25	.40	.15
.35	.52	.17
.45	.62	.17
.55	.71	.16
.65	.79	.14
.75	.86	.11
.85	.92	.07
.95	.97	.02

[5]There are different forms of the estimation formula, as you will see later in the chapter.

shows the same values after they have been corrected. The right-hand column shows the amount of change the correction introduces. As you can see, the Spearman-Brown procedure has a substantial effect, particularly in the middle ranges of the scale.

There are some circumstances in which the Spearman-Brown correction is not advisable. One of these is when the two halves of the test have unequal variances. When the halves do not appear to be equivalent, Cronbach's (1951) coefficient alpha (α) can be used. This general reliability coefficient provides the lowest estimate of reliability that one can expect. If alpha is very high, you might assume that the reliability of the test is acceptable because the lowest boundary of reliability is still very high; the reliability will not drop below alpha. A low alpha level, on the other hand, gives you less information. Because the alpha coefficient marks only the lower bound for the reliability, the actual reliability may still be high. Thus, if the variances for the two halves of the test are unequal, coefficient alpha can confirm that a test has substantial reliability; however, it cannot tell you that a test is unreliable. (Appendix 4-1 provides an example.) The formula for coefficient alpha is

$$\alpha = \frac{2[\sigma_x^2 - (\sigma_{y1}^2 \sigma_{y2}^2)]}{\sigma_x^2}$$

where α = the coefficient alpha for estimating split-half reliability
σ_x^2 = the variance for scores on the whole test
$\sigma_{y1}^2 \, \sigma_{y2}^2$ = the variances for the two separate halves of the test

When the variances for the two halves of the test are equal, the Spearman-Brown coefficient and coefficient alpha give the same results. Under other specific circumstances, both procedures may underestimate the true reliability (see Allen & Yen, 1979).

General measures of internal consistency. In addition to the split-half technique, there are many other methods for estimating the internal consistency of a test. Many years ago, Kuder and Richardson (1937) greatly advanced reliability assessment by developing methods for evaluating reliability within a single administration of a test.

Their approach does not depend on some arbitrary splitting of the test into halves. Decisions about how to split tests into halves cause many potential problems for split-half reliability. The two halves may have different variances. The split-half method also requires that each half be scored separately, possibly creating additional work. Because it is a general method that simultaneously considers all possible ways of splitting the items, the Kuder-Richardson technique avoids these problems.

KR_{20}.   The formula for calculating the reliability of a test in which the items are dichotomous, scored 0 or 1 (usually for right or wrong), is known as the **Kuder-Richardson 20**, or KR_{20} or $KR\ 20$. The formula came to be labeled this way because it was the 20th formula presented in the famous article by Kuder and Richardson (the *K* and *R* are the authors' initials).

The formula is

$$KR_{20} = r = \frac{N}{N-1}\left(\frac{S^2 - \Sigma_{pq}}{S^2}\right)$$

where KR_{20} = the reliability estimate (r)
   N = the number of items on the test
   S^2 = the variance of the total test score
   p = the proportion of people getting each item correct (this is found separately for each individual item)
   q = the proportion of people getting each item incorrect. For each item, q equals $1 - p$.
   Σ_{pq} = the sum of the products of p times q for each item on the test

Although we will not go through the mathematical derivations of the KR_{20}, studying the components of the formula may give you a better understanding of how it works. First, you will recognize the term S^2 from Chapter 2. This is the variance of the test scores. The variance term appears twice in the formula: once on the top of the right portion in the equation and once on the bottom of the right portion. The other term in the right portion is Σ_{pq}. This is the sum of the product of the proportion of people passing each item times the proportion of people failing each. The product pq is the variance for an individual item. Thus Σ_{pq} is the sum of the individual item variances.

Now think about conditions that would make the term on the right side of the equation either large or small. First, consider the situation in which the variance (S^2) is equal to the sum of the variances of the individual items. Symbolically, this would be $S^2 = \Sigma_{pq}$. In this case, the right-hand term in the formula would be 0 and, as a result, the estimate of reliability would be 0. This tells us that to have nonzero reliability, the variance for the total test score must be greater than the sum of the variances for the individual items. This will happen only when the items are measuring the same thing.

The only situation that will make the sum of the item variance less than the total test score variance is when there is covariance between the items. Covariance occurs when the items are correlated with one another. The greater the covariance, the smaller the Σ_{pq} term will be. When the items covary, they can be assumed to measure the same general trait, and the reliability for the test will be high. As Σ_{pq} approaches 0, the right side of the equation approaches 1.0. The other factor in the formula is an adjustment for the number of items in the test. This will allow the estimate of reliability to be higher for longer tests. (Appendix 4-2 provides an example.)

In addition to the KR_{20}, Kuder and Richardson presented Formula 21, or KR_{21}, a special case of the reliability formula that does not require the calculation of the p's and q's for every item. Instead, the KR_{21} uses an approximation of the sum of the pq products—the mean test score. The KR_{21} procedure rests on several important assumptions. The most important is that all the items are of equal difficulty, or that the average difficulty level is 50%. *Difficulty* is defined as the percentage of test takers who pass the item. In practice, these assumptions are rarely met, and it is usually found that the KR_{21} formula underestimates the split-half reliability:

$$KR_{21} = \frac{N}{N-1}\left[1 - \frac{\overline{X}\left(1 - \frac{\overline{X}}{N}\right)}{S^2}\right]$$

where all terms are as previously defined.

Alpha.   Mathematical proofs have demonstrated that the KR_{20} formula gives the same estimate of reliability that you would get if you took the mean of the split-half reliability estimates obtained by dividing the test in all possible ways (Cronbach, 1951). You can see that because the Kuder-Richardson procedure is general, it is usually more valuable than a split-half estimate of internal consistency.

The KR_{20} formula, however, is not appropriate for evaluating internal consistency of some cases. The KR_{20} formula requires that you find the proportion of people who got each item "correct." There are many types of tests, though, for which there are no right or wrong answers, such as many personality and attitude scales. For example, on an attitude questionnaire, you might be presented with a statement such as "I believe extramarital sexual intercourse is immoral." You must indicate whether you strongly disagree, disagree, are neutral, agree, or strongly agree. None of these choices is incorrect, and none is correct. Rather, your response indicates where you stand on the continuum between agreement and disagreement. To use the Kuder-Richardson method with this sort of item, Cronbach developed a formula that estimates the internal consistency of tests in which the items are not scored as 0 or 1 (right or wrong). In doing so, Cronbach developed a more general reliability estimate, which he called **coefficient alpha,** or α. The formula for coefficient alpha is[6]

$$r = \alpha = \left(\frac{N}{N-1}\right)\left(\frac{S^2 - \Sigma S^2{}_i}{S^2}\right)$$

As you may notice, this looks very similar to the KR_{20} formula. The only difference is that Σpq has been replaced by ΣS_i^2. This new term, S_i^2, is for the variance of the individual items (i). The summation sign informs us that we are to sum the individual item variances. S^2 is for the variance of the total test score. The only real difference is the way the variance of the items is expressed. Actually, coefficient alpha is a more general reliability coefficient than KR_{20} because S_i^2 can describe the variance of items whether or not they are in a right/wrong

---

[6]Although this formula appears different from the formula for coefficient alpha from the section "Internal consistency: split-half method," the equations are mathematically equivalent.

format. Thus, coefficient alpha is the most general case of internal consistency reliability.

All the measures of internal consistency evaluate the extent to which the different items on a test measure the same ability or trait. They will all give low estimates of reliability if the test is designed to measure several traits. Using the domain sampling model, we define a domain that represents a single trait or characteristic, and each item is an individual sample of this general characteristic. When the items do not measure the same characteristic, the test will not be internally consistent.

One popular method for dealing with the situation in which a test apparently measures several different characteristics is to perform factor analysis (see Chapter 3). This can be used to divide the items into subgroups, each internally consistent; however, the subgroups of items will not be related to one another. Factor analysis can help a test constructor build a test that has submeasures for several different traits. When factor analysis is used correctly, these subtests will be internally consistent (highly reliable) and independent of one another. For example, you might use factor analysis to divide a group of items on interpersonal communication into two subgroups, perhaps assertiveness items and aggressiveness items. The reliability of the aggressiveness and the assertiveness subscales might be quite high; however, the correlation between assertiveness and aggressiveness scores would be quite low. The nature of the factor analysis method ensures these characteristics. Thus, factor analysis is of great value in the process of test construction.

Reliability of a Difference Score

Some applications of psychological testing require a difference score, created by subtracting one test score from another. This might be the difference between performances at two points in time—for example, when you test a group of children before and after they have experienced a special training program. Or it may be the difference between measures of two different abilities, such as whether a child is doing better in reading than in math. Whenever comparisons between two different attributes are being made, one must make the comparison in *Z*, or standardized, units (see Chapter 2).

Difference scores create a host of problems that make them more difficult to work with than single scores. To understand the problems, you must refer back to the definition of an observed score as composed of both true score (T) and error (E). In a difference score, the E, or error portion, is expected to be larger than either score because it absorbs error from both of the scores used to create the difference score. Furthermore, the T, or true score portion, might be expected to be smaller because whatever is common to both measures is canceled out when the difference score is created. As a result of these two factors, the reliability of a difference score is expected to be lower than the reliability of either score on which it is based. If two tests measure exactly the same trait, the score representing the difference between them is expected to have a reliability of 0.

As we have previously mentioned, it is most convenient to find difference scores by first creating Z scores for each measure and then finding the difference between them (score 2 − score 1). The reliability of scores that represent the difference between two standard scores (or Z scores) is given by the formula

$$r = \frac{\frac{1}{2}(r_{11} + r_{22}) - r_{12}}{1 = r12}$$

where r_{11} = the reliability of the first measure
r_{22} = the reliability of the second measure
r_{12} = the correlation between the first and the second measures

Using this formula, you can calculate the reliability of a difference score for any two tests for which the reliabilities and the correlation between them are known. For example, suppose that the correlation between two measures is .70 and the reliabilities of the two measures are .90 and .70, respectively. The reliability of the difference between these two measures is

$$r = \frac{\frac{1}{2}(.90 + .70) = .70}{1 = .70}$$
$$= \frac{.10}{.30}$$
$$= .33$$

As this example demonstrates, the reliability of the difference score between tests with reliabilities as high as .90 and .70 is only .33. The situation in which the reliability of the difference score is lower than the average reliabilities of the two initial measures is not unusual. In fact, it occurs in all cases except when the correlation between the two tests is 0.

The low reliability of a difference score should concern the practicing psychologist and education researcher. Because of their poor reliabilities, difference scores cannot be depended on for interpreting patterns.

For example, it may be difficult to draw the conclusion that a patient is more depressed than schizophrenic on the basis of an MMPI (see Chapter 15) profile that shows a lower depression than schizophrenia score. Any differences between these two scales must be interpreted cautiously because the reliability of the score that represents the difference between the two scales can be expected to be low. The difficulties associated with using difference scores have been well studied. In a widely cited article, Cronbach and Furby (1970) demonstrated that there are many pitfalls associated with using difference scores to measure change. For example, it appears impossible to make a meaningful interpretation of the difference between scores on the same children that are taken at the beginning and at the end of a school year. Measuring the "change" that occurred during that school year requires the use of sophisticated experimental designs in which children are randomly assigned to experimental and control conditions.

Although reliability is often difficult to calculate, computer programs that do much of the work are now available. Technical Box 4-2 describes one such program.

Reliability in Behavioral Observation Studies

Psychologists with behavioral orientations usually prefer not to use psychological tests. Instead, they favor the direct observation of behavior. To measure aggression, for example, they would record the number of times a child hits or kicks another child. Observers would tabulate the number of observable responses in each category. Thus, there would be a score for "hits," another score for "kicks," and so on.

Some people feel that behavioral observation systems are so simple that they are free from psychometric problems. Unfortunately, this is not the case. In practice, behavioral observation systems are frequently unreliable because of discrepancies between true scores and the scores recorded by the observer.

TECHNICAL BOX 4-2

Reliability is difficult to calculate by hand: However, you can efficiently calculate reliability using computers. One of the most common statistical programs for calculating reliability is part of the Statistical Package for the Social Sciences (SPSS, 1995). The SPSS program calculates several different types of reliability. A summary of an analysis performed by SPSS is given here. The data for this analysis come from the CES-D example. However, instead of using the subsample of 20 medical students as in Chapter 3, we used an entire class of 117 medical students. The first column in the table gives the item number. The second column lists the mean of the CES-D if an item was deleted. Unfortunately, the program is unable to make the adjustment for the CES-D, in which 20 points are subtracted from each score. This adjustment has no impact on the statistical properties of the CES-D (i.e., it does not affect the correlation with other variables); however, it does affect the mean. The table tells us that if the first item of the CES-D was eliminated, the mean score for the CES-D would be 28.5983; with the 20-point adjustment, the mean is 8.5983. The second column in the table shows that the mean CES-D score is relatively unaffected by the elimination of any particular item. The third column in the table gives the scale variance if the item was deleted. We will not attempt to interpret that in this exercise. The fourth column gives the corrected item-total correlation. This column describes the correlation between any particular item and the total test score minus the item. Notice that the item-test correlation for item 2 is relatively low (.1689), meaning that item 2 is a relatively poor item because it is unrelated to the total test score. Item 2 is "I did not feel like eating: my appetite was poor." Item 18, on the other hand, had a high correlation with the

Continued

total score. Item 18 is "I enjoy life," and it was scored in the reverse direction. This item is conceptually close to the total score of the CES-D.

The column labeled "Squared Multiple Correlation" gives the proportion of variance in each item that can be explained by the other items. For example, about 35% of the variance in item 1 (.3520) can be explained by its relationship to the other items on the scale. For item 20, about 51% of the variance (.5096) can be explained through its associations with other items. These values are obtained by performing a multiple regression analysis in which each item is predicted from the combination of all the other items.

The final column in the table is the alpha for the total test if the particular item was deleted. As the numbers suggest, the alpha for the scale remains approximately the same if any single item is left out.

The computer summary also provides summary statistics for different methods of calculating reliabilities. It gives the alpha coefficient and a more complex standardized item alpha. The program is also capable of calculating different types of reliability. For example, the program was asked to calculate the split-half reliability. The printout shows that the correlation between the two halves of the test is .7807. The Spearman-Brown correction adjusts this reliability to .8768. Another method of split-half reliability that performs the correction automatically is called the Guttman split-half method, which gives a reliability of .8760. This program also calculates the alpha coefficient for the first and the second halves of the tests separately.

```
          R E L I A B I L I T Y   A N A L Y S I S  -  S C A L E   (C E S - D)

ITEM-TOTAL STATISTICS

             SCALE          SCALE         CORRECTED
             MEAN           VARIANCE      ITEM-          SQUARED        ALPHA
             IF ITEM        IF ITEM       TOTAL          MULTIPLE       IF ITEM
             DELETED*       DELETED       CORRELATION    CORRELATION    DELETED

1            28.5983        48.3286        .4884          .3520          .8671
2            28.9145        51.9237        .1689          .2528          .8773
3            28.7521        48.0329        .5290          .4813          .8655
4            28.8547        49.0908        .3800          .3736          .8715
5            28.4957        48.9073        .3793          .2736          .8718
6            28.4872        46.1830        .7330          .6876          .8577
7            28.6581        47.9338        .5768          .5180          .8639
8            28.8974        49.2825        .5321          .4468          .8661
9            29.1368        52.3604        .2585          .2270          .8734
10           28.6325        49.4241        .3896          .3216          .8707
11           28.6752        50.4626        .2880          .2533          .8743
12           28.6496        47.6089        .6275          .5927          .8622
13           28.6325        49.4586        .3781          .3367          .8712
14           28.2991        46.5735        .5958          .5930          .8628
15           28.8205        49.7175        .4466          .3494          .8685
16           28.7778        47.7605        .6068          .5635          .8629
17           28.9145        50.8375        .3372          .2737          .8717
18           28.6154        47.5663        .6525          .5671          .8615
19           28.8718        49.5610        .5209          .4631          .8666
20           28.7009        48.1080        .6074          .5096          .8632

Alpha Method

RELIABILITY COEFFICIENTS    20 ITEMS
```

```
ALPHA =   .8734    STANDARDIZED ITEM ALPHA = .8739

Split-Half Method

RELIABILITY COEFFICIENTS    20 ITEMS

CORRELATION BETWEEN FORMS =.7807    EQUAL LENGTH SPEARMAN-BROWN =      .8768

GUTTMAN SPLIT-HALF =        .8760    UNEQUAL-LENGTH SPEARMAN-BROWN =    .8768

ALPHA FOR PART 1 = .7424    ALPHA FOR PART 2 =        .8031

10 ITEMS IN PART I          10 ITEMS IN PART 2
```

*NOTE—The CES-D uses a correction in which 20 is subtracted from each score. This correction is not reflected in the computer program. So, for example, the mean if item 1 was deleted would be 8.5983, not 28.5983.

For example, there may be a difference between the actual number of times a child hits or kicks and the number of behaviors the observer reports for these categories. For instance, errors commonly occur when an observer misses certain events. Also, because psychologists cannot always monitor behavior continuously, they often take samples of behavior at certain time intervals. Under these circumstances, sampling error must be considered (C. Kaplan, 1993).

Sources of error introduced by time sampling are similar to those with sampling items from a large domain. When each time sample is thought of as an "item," these problems can be handled using sampling theory and methods such as alpha reliability.

The problem of error associated with different observers, however, presents some unique difficulties. To assess these problems, one needs to estimate the reliability of the observers (Cordes, 1994). There are at least three different ways to do this. The most common method is to record the percentage of times that two or more observers agree. Unfortunately, this method is not the best one, for at least two reasons. First, percentage agreement does not take into consideration the level of agreement that would be expected by chance alone. For instance, if two observers are recording whether a particular behavior either occurred or did not occur, they would have a 50% likelihood of agreeing by chance alone. A method for assessing such reliability should include an adjustment for the level of agreement to be expected by chance. Second, percentages should not be mathematically manipulated. For example, it is not technically appropriate to average percentages. Indexes such as standardized, or *Z,* scores are manipulable and thus better suited for the task of reliability assessment.

After reviewing several approaches, Shrout, Spitzer, and Fleiss (1987) concluded that the kappa statistic is best suited for assessing the level of agreement among several observers. The kappa statistic was introduced by J. Cohen (1960) as a measure of agreement between two judges who each rate a set of objects using nominal scales. Fleiss (1971) extended the method to consider the agreement between any number of observers. The calculation of kappa is beyond the scope of this presentation; interested readers can find the procedures in Fleiss (1971) and Shrout, Spitzer, and Fleiss (1987). An approximation of the coefficient for the agreement between two observers is also given by the phi coefficient, which was discussed in Chapter 3.

Connecting Sources of Error with Reliability Assessment Method

Table 4-2 relates sources of measurement error to the methods used to assess reliability. Remember that *reliability* is a generic term. Psychologists use different methods of reliability assessment to describe different sources of measurement error. Each of these has a different meaning. As Table 4-2 suggests, one source of measurement error is time sampling. The same test given at different points in time may produce different scores, even if given to the same test takers. This source of error is typically assessed using the test-retest method. Another source of error is item sampling. The same construct or attribute may be assessed using a wide pool of items. For example, no one item is used to assess human intelligence. Yet, different items used to measure this general construct may not always give the same reflection of the true ability. This sort of error is assessed using alternate forms or parallel forms reliability. Typically, the correlation between two forms of a test is created by randomly sampling a large pool of items believed to assess a particular construct. This correlation is used as an estimate of this type of reliability.

The internal consistency of a test refers to the intercorrelations among items within the same test. If the test is designed to measure a single construct and all items are equally good candidates to measure that attribute, then there should be a high correspondence between the items. This internal consistency is evalu-

TABLE 4-2

Sources of Measurement Error and Methods of Reliability Assessment

Source of Error	Example	Method	How Assessed
Time sampling	Same test given at two points in time (item sampling)	Test-retest	Correlation between scores obtained on the two occasions
Item sampling	Different items used to assess the same attribute	Alternate forms/ parallel forms	Correlation between equivalent forms of the test that have different items
Internal consistency	Consistency of items within the same test	1. Split-half	1. Corrected correlation between two halves of the test
		2. KR_{20}	2. See Appendix 4-1
		3. Alpha	3. See Appendix 4-2
Observer differences	Different observers recording	Adjusted agreement	Kappa statistic

ated using split-half reliability, the KR_{20} method, or coefficient alpha. Another source of measurement error occurs when different observers record the same behavior. Even though they have the same instructions, different judges observing the same event may record different numbers. This source of error is evaluated using an adjusted index of agreement, such as the kappa statistic.

As you can see, the term *reliability* refers to several different methods used to assess different sources of error. Sometimes different sources of error occur in the same situation—for example, error associated with item sampling and additional error linked to time sampling. When evaluating reliability information, you should take into consideration all potential sources of error. A joint committee of the American Education Research Association, the American Psychological Association, and the National Council on Measurement in Education (1985) proposed standards for manuals describing educational or psychological tests. A summary of the standards for reporting information about reliability is presented in Focused Example 4-1.

Using Reliability Information

Now that you have learned about reliability theory and methods, you will benefit from reviewing some practical aspects of reliability assessment. Different situations call for different levels of reliability.

Standard Errors of Measurement and the Rubber Yardstick

Earlier in this chapter, we used the rubber yardstick to introduce the concept of the standard error of measurement. Remember that psychologists working with unreliable tests are like carpenters working with rubber yardsticks that stretch or contract and misrepresent the true length of a board. However, as all rubber yardsticks are not equally inaccurate, all psychological tests are not equally inaccurate. The standard error of measurement allows us to estimate the degree to which a test provides inaccurate readings; that is, it tells us how much "rubber" there is in a measurement. The larger the standard error of measurement, the less certain we can be about the accuracy with which an attribute is measured. Conversely, small standard errors of measurement tell us that an individual score is probably close to the measured value. Some textbooks refer to the standard error of measurement as the standard error of a score. To calculate the standard error of measurement, we need to use the standard deviation and the reliability coefficient. The formula for this calculation is

$$S_m = S\sqrt{1 - r}$$

where S_m = the standard error for the measurement

S = the standard deviation of the scores
r = the reliability coefficient

For example, suppose that an IQ test has a mean of 100 for a particular sample, with a standard deviation of 14. You are particularly interested in a person with a score of 106. The reliability of the test is .89. Plugging these values into the formula, you find

$$S_m = 14\sqrt{1 - .89} = 4.64$$

Standard errors of measurement are used to create confidence intervals around specific observed scores. You may want to review the concept of a con-

---

Focused Example 4-1

SUMMARY OF GUIDELINES FOR RELIABILITY

 The American Psychological Association, American Educational Research Association, and National Council on Measurement in Education suggest several standards for reliability.* Some of these standards are summarized as follows:

Primary Standards

1. Reliability estimates should be provided for each score, subscore, or combination of scores.
2. The procedures used in the study from which the reliability estimate was obtained should be described in detail. This should include the exact numbers of participants and statistical descriptions of these people.
3. The exact statistical methods for obtaining the reliability estimate should be reported.
4. If statistical adjustments are made in the calculation of a reliability coefficient, both the adjusted and unadjusted coefficients should be reported.
5. When alternate forms of a test are given to the same sample of individuals on two separate occasions, the order of administration and the interval between test administrations should be reported. In addition, the rationale for choosing that interval should be described. Means and standard deviations for both forms should be reported, along with standard errors of measurement and the estimate of alternative forms of reliability.
6. Estimates of the internal consistency of a test obtained with measures such as KR_{20} or alpha

should not be interpreted as substitutes for alternative form reliability or estimates of stability of a measure over the course of time.

7. Some measures yield inflated estimates of reliability. For example, split-half coefficients used on speeded tests often overestimate their reliability and should therefore not be used on such tests.
8. In some tests, the judgmental process may affect the scores—for example, when judges rate the performance of a worker. When these judgments can affect a score, the interrater or interobserver agreement should be reported.

Conditional and Secondary Standards

9. When different populations are likely to have different reliabilities, separate reliability estimates should be reported for each of these groups (for example, if one expects the reliability to differ between men and women, blacks and whites, and so on). A reliability coefficient for each separate group should be given.
10. When tests are used in a decision process and there is a cut score, or a score at which those below fail or are not selected, the standard error of measurement at that critical score should be reported.
11. When a test is used to divide people into two groups (pass/fail or accept/reject), the percentage of test takers who are classified in the same way on two different occasions or with alternate forms of the test should be reported.

---

* Standards not applicable to basic psychometrics are not listed here.

Adapted from American Education Research Association et al. (1985, pp. 13–18).

fidence interval in your introductory statistics textbook. Briefly, we never know whether an observed score is the "true" score. However, we can form intervals around an observed score and use statistical procedures to estimate the probability that the true score falls within a certain interval. Common intervals used in testing are the 68% interval, the 95% interval, and the 99% interval. These intervals are created using Z scores (see Chapter 2). Let's suppose that we wish to create the 95% confidence interval for this specific IQ test. The 95% confidence interval is associated with the Z score of 1.96. The upper bound of the confidence interval is equal to the mean plus $1.96(S_m)$, or, in this example,

$$106 + 1.96(4.64) = 115.09$$

The lower bound of the interval is equal to the mean minus

$$1.96 \times S_m$$

So, in this example, the lower bound would be

$$106 - 1.96(4.64) = 96.91$$

Although we do not know the true score for a person who received the mean score of 106, we can be 95% confident that the true score falls between 96.9 and 115.1. As you can see, however, the scores of 96 and 115 on an IQ test (see Chapters 11 and 12) are quite different. Tests with more measurement error include more "rubber." In other words, the larger the standard error of measurement, the larger the confidence interval. When confidence intervals are very wide, our ability to make precise statements is greatly diminished.

How Reliable Is Reliable?

People often ask how high a reliability coefficient must be before it is "high enough." The answer depends on the use of the test. It has been suggested that reliability estimates in the range of .70 and .80 are good enough for most purposes in basic research. In many studies, researchers attempt to gain only approximate estimates of how two variables are related. For research, it may be appropriate to estimate what the correlation between two variables would have been if the measures had been more reliable. Promising results can justify spending the extra time and money necessary to make the research instruments more reliable. It even has been argued that it would be a waste of time and effort to refine research instruments beyond a reliability of .90. Although the higher reliability is desirable, it may not be worth the added burden and costs (Nunnally & Bernstein, 1994).

In clinical settings, high reliability is extremely important. When tests are used to make important decisions about someone's future, you must be certain to minimize any error in classification. Thus, a test with a reliability of .90 might not be good enough. For a test used to make a decision that affects some person's future, you should attempt to find a test with a reliability greater than .95.

What to Do About Low Reliability

Often, test constructors want their tests to be used in applied settings, but analysis reveals inadequate test reliability. Fortunately, psychometric theory offers some options. Two of the most common approaches are to increase the length of the test and to throw out items that run down the reliability. Another procedure is to estimate what the true correlation would have been if the test did not have measurement error.

Increase the number of items. According to the domain sampling model, each item in a test is an independent sample of the trait or ability being measured. The larger the sample, the more likely that the test will represent the true characteristic. In the domain sampling model, the reliability of a test increases as the number of items increases.

A medical example will help clarify why longer tests are more reliable. Suppose that you go to the doctor with indigestion. It is in your best interest for the doctor to make a reliable judgment about the etiology of your problem. How comfortable would you feel if the doctor asked only one question before making a diagnosis? You probably would feel more comfortable if the doctor asked numerous questions. In general, people feel that the more information a doctor obtains by asking questions and performing tests, the more reliable the diagnosis will be. This same principle applies to psychological tests.

A decision to increase the number of items in a test might result in a long and costly process. With new items added, the test must be reevaluated; it may turn out to fall below an acceptable level of reliability. In addition, adding new items can be costly and can make a test so long that few people would be able to sit through it. Fortunately, by applying the Spearman-Brown prophecy formula, one can estimate how many items will have to be added in order to bring a test to an acceptable level of reliability.

The **prophecy formula** for estimating how long a test must be in order to achieve a desired level of reliability is another case of the general Spearman-Brown method for estimating reliability. Algebraic manipulations of the general formula allow one to solve it for the length needed for any desired level of reliability:

$$N = \frac{r_d(1 - r_o)}{r_o(1 - r_d)}$$

where N = the number of tests of the current version's length that would be needed to have a test of the desired level of reliability

r_d = the desired level of reliability

r_o = the observed level of reliability based on the current version of the test

Consider the example of the 20-item CES-D test that had a reliability for medical students of .87. We would like to bring the reliability up to .95. Putting these numbers into the prophecy formula, we get

$$N = \frac{.95(1 - .87)}{.87(1 - .95)} = \frac{.124}{.044} = 2.82$$

These calculations tell us that we would need 2.82 tests the length of the current 20-item test to bring the reliability up to the desired level. To find the number of items required, we must multiply the number of items on the current test by N from the preceding formula. In the example, this would give 20 $\times$ 2.82 = 56.4. So the test would have to be expanded from 20 to about 56 items to achieve the desired reliability, assuming that the added items come from the same pool as the original items and that they have the same psychometric properties.

The decision to expand a test from 20 to 56 items must depend on economic and practical considerations. The test developer must first ask whether the increase in reliability is worth the extra time, effort, and expense required to achieve this goal. If the test is to be used for personnel decisions, it may be dangerous to ignore any effort that will enhance the reliability of the test. On the other hand, if the test is to be used only to see if two variables are associated, the expense of extending it may not be worth the effort and cost.

When the prophecy formula is used, certain assumptions are made that may or may not be valid. One of these assumptions is that the probability of error in items added to the test is the same as that for the original items in the test. However, adding many items may bring about new sources of error, such as fatigue associated with taking a very long test.

As an example of a situation in which increasing the reliability of a test may not be worthwhile, consider a 40-item test with a reliability of .50. We would like to bring the reliability up to .90. Using the prophecy formula, we get

$$N = \frac{.90(1 - .50)}{.50(1 - .90)} = \frac{.90(.50)}{.50(.10)} = \frac{.45}{.05} = 9$$

These figures tell us that the test would have to be nine times its present length to have a projected reliability of .90. This is calculated as 9 $\times$ 40 = 360 items long. Creating a test 360 items long would be very expensive, and validating it would require a considerable investment of time for both test constructors and test takers. Beyond these problems, new sources of error might arise in the 360-item test that would not have been a problem for the shorter measure. For example, many errors may occur on the longer test simply because people get tired and bored during the long process of answering 360 questions. There is no way to take these factors into account using the prophecy formula.

Factor and item analysis. The reliability of a test depends on all the items measuring the same underlying characteristic. Although psychologists always intend to create tests this way, often some items do not measure the given construct. Leaving these items in the test reduces its reliability. To ensure that the items measure the same thing, two approaches are suggested. One is to perform factor analysis (see Chapter 3 and also Fidell & Tabachnick, 1989; Grim & Yarnold, 1995; Pedhazer, 1991). Tests are most reliable if they are unidimensional. This means that one factor should account for considerably more of the variance than any other factor. Items that do not load on this factor might be considered for elimination.

Another approach is to examine the correlation between each item and the total score for the test. This form of item analysis (see Chapter 6) is often called **discriminability** analysis. When the correlation between the performance on a single item and the total test score is low, the item is probably measuring something different from the other items on the test. It also might mean that the item is so easy or so hard that people do not differ in their response to it. In either case, the low correlation indicates that the item drags down the estimate of reliability and that one should exclude it.

Correction for attenuation. Low reliability is a real problem in psychological research and practice because it reduces the chances of finding significant correlations between measures. If a test is unreliable, information obtained with it is of little or no value. Thus, we say that potential correlations are attenuated, or diminished, by measurement error.

Fortunately, measurement theory does allow one to estimate what the correlation between two measures would have been if they had not been measured with error. These methods "correct" for the attenuation in the correlations caused by the measurement error. To use the methods, one needs to know only the reliabilities of two tests and the correlation between them. The **correction for attenuation** is

$$\hat{r}_{12} = \frac{r_{12}}{\sqrt{r_{11}r_{22}}}$$

where $\hat{r}_{12}$ = the estimated true correlation between tests 1 and 2
  r_{12} = the observed correlation between tests 1 and 2
  r_{11} = the reliability of test 1
  r_{22} = the reliability of test 2

Suppose, for example, that the correlation between the CES-D and ratings of clinical skill was .34; the reliabilities of the tests were .87 and .70 for the CES-D and the clinical skill tests, respectively. The estimated true correlation between depression and clinical skill would be

$$\frac{.34}{\sqrt{(.87)(.70)}} = \frac{.34}{\sqrt{.609}} = \frac{.34}{.78} = .44$$

As the example shows, the estimated correlation increases from .34 to .44 when the correction is used.

Sometimes one measure meets an acceptable standard of reliability but the other one does not. In this case, we would want to correct for the attenuation caused only by the one unreliable test. To do this we use the formula

$$\hat{r}_{12} = \frac{r_{12}}{\sqrt{r_{11}}}$$

where $\hat{r}_{12}$ = the estimated true correlation
r_{12} = the observed correlation
r_{11} = the reliability of the variable that does not meet our standard of reliability

For example, suppose we want to estimate the correlation between the CES-D score and grade point average in medical school. The reliability of the CES-D test is .75, which is not quite as good as we would like, but medical school GPA is assumed to be measured without error. Using the fallible depression test, we observe the correlation to be .53. Plugging these numbers into the formula, we get

$$\frac{.53}{\sqrt{.75}} = \frac{.53}{.87} = .61$$

This informs us that correcting for the attenuation caused by the CES-D test would increase our observed correlation from .53 to .61.

Summary

Measurement error is common in all fields of science. Psychological and educational specialists, however, have devoted a great deal of time and study to measurement error and its effects. Tests that are relatively free of measurement error are considered to be reliable, and tests that contain relatively large measurement error are considered unreliable. In the early part of the 20th century, Charles Spearman worked out the basics of contemporary theories and methods of reliability. Test score and reliability theories have gone through continual refinements.

When we evaluate *reliability*, we must first specify the source of measurement error we are trying to evaluate. If concerned about errors that result from the test's being given at different times, we might consider the *test-retest method*, in which test scores obtained at two different points in time are correlated. On other occasions, we may be concerned about errors that arise because we have selected a small sample of items to represent a larger conceptual domain. To evaluate this type of measurement error, we would use a method that assesses the internal consistency of the test, such as the *split-half method*. The KR_{20} and alpha methods are general methods for estimating the internal consistency of a test.

The standard of reliability for a test depends on the situation in which the test will be used. In some research settings, it may not be worth the extra time and money required to bring a test up to an exceptionally high level of reliability. On the other hand, very strict standards for reliability are required for a test used to make decisions that will affect people's lives. When a test has unacceptably low reliability, the test constructor might wish to boost the reliability by increasing the test length or by using factor analysis to divide the test into homogeneous subgroups of items. In research settings, one can sometimes deal with the problem of low reliability by estimating what the correlation between tests would have been if there had been no measurement error. This procedure is called *correction for attenuation*.

Recently, interest has increased in evaluating the reliability of behavioral observations. The percentage of items observers agree on is not the best index of reliability for these studies, because it does not take into consideration how much agreement is to be expected by chance alone. Correlationlike indexes such as kappa or phi are better suited to estimate reliability in these behavioral studies.

Reliability is one of the basic foundations of behavioral research. If a test is not reliable, one cannot demonstrate that it has any meaning. In the next chapter, we will focus on how the meaning of tests is defined.

Appendix 4-1: Using Coefficient Alpha to Estimate Split-Half Reliability when the Variances for the Two Halves of the Test Are Unequal

Formula:
$$\alpha = \frac{2[S_x^2 - (S_{y1}^2 + S_{y2}^2)]}{S_x^2}$$

Data:
$S_x^2 = 11.5$
$S_{y1}^2 = 4.5$
$S_{y2}^2 = 3.2$

Steps

1. Find the variance for the whole test.

   $S_x^2 = 11.5$

2. Add together the variances for the two halves of the test.

   $S_{y1}^2 = 4.5$ $S_{y2}^2 = 3.2$ $4.5 + 3.2 = 7.7$

3. Find $S_x^2 - (S_{y1}^2 + S_{y2}^2)$ by subtracting the result of Step 2 from that of Step 1.

   $11.5 - 7.7 = 3.8$

4. Find $2[S_x^2 - (S_{y1}^2 + S_{y2}^2)]$ by multiplying the result of Step 3 times 2.

   $2(3.8) = 7.6$

5. Find alpha by dividing the result of Step 4 by that of Step 1.

   $\dfrac{7.6}{11.5} = .66$

Appendix 4-2: The Calculation of Reliability Using KR_{20}

Formula: $KR_{20} = \dfrac{N}{N-1}\left(\dfrac{S^2 - \Sigma pq}{S^2}\right)$

Data: NS = number of test takers = 50
N = number of items = 6
S^2 = variance (Step 6) = 2.8

Item	Number of Test Takers Responding Correctly	p (from Step 2)	q (from Step 3)	pq (from Step 4)
1	12	.24	.76	.18
2	41	.82	.18	.15
3	18	.36	.64	.23
4	29	.58	.42	.24
5	30	.60	.40	.24
6	47	.94	.06	.06
				$\Sigma pq = 1.10$ (from Step 5)

Steps

1. Determine the number of test takers NS.

   $NS = 50$

2. Find p by dividing the number of people responding correctly to each item by the number of people taking the test (Step 1). This is the level of difficulty.
   $\dfrac{12}{50} = .24 \quad \dfrac{41}{50} = .82 \cdots$

3. Find q for each item by subtracting p (the result of Step 2) from 1.0. This gives the proportion responding incorrectly to each item.

   $1.0 - .24 = .76 \quad 1.0 - .82 = .18 \cdots$

4. Find pq for each item by multiplying the results of Steps 2 and 3.

   $(.24)(.76) = .18 \quad (.82)(.18) = .15 \cdots$

5. Find Σpq by summing the results of Step 4 over the N items.

   $.18 + .15 + .23 + .24 + .24 + .06 = 1.1$

6. Find S^2, which is the variance for the test sources. To do this you need the scores for each individual in the group. The formula for the variance is

$$S^2 = \frac{\Sigma X^2 - \left[\dfrac{\Sigma X^2}{NS}\right]}{NS - 1}$$

In this example $S^2 = 2.8$.

7. Find $S^2 - \Sigma pq$ by subtracting the result of Step 5 from that of Step 6.

   $2.8 - 1.1 = 1.7$

8. Find $(S^2 - \Sigma pq)/S2$ by dividing the result of Step 7 by that of Step 6.

   $\dfrac{1.7}{2.8} = .607$

9. Find N or the number of items.

   $N = 6$

10. Find $N/(N - 1)$ by dividing the result of Step 9 by Step 9 minus 1.

    $\dfrac{6}{5} = 1.2$

11. Find KR_{20} by multiplying the results of Steps 8 and 9.

    $(1.2)(.607) = .73$

CHAPTER 5

Validity

LEARNING OBJECTIVES

When you have completed this chapter, you should be able to:

☐ Determine the relationship between establishing test validity and the use of the scientific method

☐ Explain why it is inappropriate to refer to so-called face validity as a form of validity

☐ List the categories of validity recognized in the booklet *Standards for Educational and Psychological Testing*

☐ Tell how the strategy for establishing content validity differs from that used to obtain evidence for other types of validity

☐ Discuss the difference between predictive and concurrent criterion validity

☐ Relate the concept of the coefficient of determination (from Chapter 3) to the interpretation of the validity coefficient in criterion validity

☐ Tell how to interpret the results of a test that, for example, had a validity coefficient of .35 for predicting success on a particular job

☐ List some of the issues to take into consideration when you interpret a validity coefficient

☐ Know when construct validation is appropriate

☐ Select some hypothetical construct and describe how you would go about developing a measure for it

The case of Willie Griggs was argued before the U.S. Supreme Court in October 1970. Griggs and 12 other black laborers were employees of the Dan River Steam Station of the Duke Power Company in Draper, North Carolina. The company classified Griggs and the other complainants as laborers, whose primary work assignment was sweeping and cleaning. The men would have preferred to be promoted to the next higher classification level, which was coal handler. However, the company required a passing score on a general intelligence test for that promotion. Of the 95 employees at the power station, 14 were black. Among the 14 black workers, 13 were assigned to sweeping and cleaning duties. The major obstacle for the men who wanted to move up in the company was their performance on the test.

Because the test appeared to render ineligible a much higher proportion of black employees than white ones, the power company was sued for engaging in discriminatory employment practice. The lawsuit centered on the meaning of the test scores. The power company managers argued that using the test "would improve the overall quality of the work force." They suggested that they did not intend to discriminate on the basis of race and that the test helped them find the employees who were the most capable.

In the course of the court battle, the power company was required to show why the test had meaning for the particular jobs within their establishment. In other words, the company had to prove that the test had a specific meaning for particular jobs such as laborer or coal handler. On hearing the arguments, the Supreme Court decided that the tests were unrelated to measuring job capability. They ruled that the tests served as "built-in head winds" for minority groups and had no meaning for the purpose of hiring or promoting workers to the classification of coal handler. The decision has been reaffirmed and eventually became the basis of the Civil Rights Bill of 1991 (see Chapter 21).

As a result of the *Griggs* v. *Duke Power* decision, employers have been forced to provide evidence that a test used for the selection of employees or for promotion purposes has a specific meaning. In the field of testing, we refer to this meaning as validity. The meaning of a test is defined by specific evidence, and one uses specific methods to acquire this information. The meaning of a test is established by this evidence and not by the word of a psychologist. As in a legal court proceeding, a psychologist must obey specific rules of evidence in establishing that a test has a particular meaning for a specific purpose. In this chapter, we will review the rules of evidence most frequently employed. Some court cases similar to the one involving Willie Griggs will be discussed in Chapter 21.

Learning to Ask About the Validity Evidence

Psychologists and other professionals continually attempt to convince the public that their discipline is meaningful. Regarding psychological tests, certain segments of the public may have become too trusting. After you read this chapter, we hope that you can determine when test results are meaningful and when questionable.

The Definition of Validity

Validity can be defined as the agreement between a test score or measure and the quality it is believed to measure. Over the years, psychologists created many subcategories of validity, and definitions of validity blossomed. In time, it became hard to determine whether psychologists who referred to different types of validity were really talking about different things. Though validity defined the meaning of tests and measures, the term itself was beginning to lose its meaning. In 1985, a joint committee of the American Education Research Association, the American Psychological Association, and the National Council on Measurement in Education published a booklet entitled *Standards for Educational and Psychological Testing.* We shall refer to this booklet frequently because it provides a sensible set of guidelines for psychological tests that have won approval by major professional groups.

The joint committee set aside numerous possible definitions of validity by suggesting the following: Validity is the evidence for inferences made about a test score. There are three types of evidence: (1) construct-related, (2) criterion-related, and (3) content-related. Though other textbooks may use other headings for validity, these headings can all be subsumed under the three categories suggested by the joint committee. For example, what have been called *concurrent* validity and *predictive* validity are really subcategories of criterion validity. *Empirical* validity and *statistical* validity also are synonyms for criterion validity. *Convergent* validity and *discriminant* validity are really types of evidence for construct validity. Finally, *trait* validity and *factorial* validity can also be considered synonyms of construct validity.

Though categories for grouping different types of validity are convenient, the use of categories does not imply that there are distinct forms of validity. Sometimes psychologists have been overly rigorous about making distinctions among categories when, indeed, different categories conceptually overlap (Anastasi, 1995).

Nature of Evidence

Obtaining data in validity studies is like gathering evidence for a court trial. For instance, psychologists always begin by assuming that there is no reason to believe a measure is valid. Evidence for validity comes from showing the association between the test and other variables. The rules strictly forbid saying there is a relationship without some proof, similar to the legal notion of innocent until proven guilty. Proof of guilt must be persuasive. In a similar manner, one must have convincing proof that there is a relationship between two variables before one justifiably touts the connection.

Types of Validity

In this section, we shall discuss each type of the committee's three types of validity evidence. In addition, we will comment on what some call *face validity.* The joint committee refused to recognize face validity as a legitimate category because it is not technically a form of validity. However, the term needs to be mentioned because it is commonly used in the testing literature.

Face Validity

Face validity is the mere appearance that a measure has validity. Sometimes psychologists report exactly what they observe and do not try to generalize. When they do, they depend on face validity. They assume that the measures have meaning themselves, and that no other generalizations are necessary. In many behavioral studies, this type of validity works well. For example, if you are interested in bar-pressing behavior in rats and observe the bar press, no generalizations are necessary. The observed bar-press response is exactly what you want to talk about. Indeed, the face validity is all that you need to make your point. On the other hand, implying that the bar-press response means something—for instance, that it can predict later feeding behavior—requires some evidence that feeding is really predictable from bar pressing. In other words, you are now using bar pressing as a real basis for inference, and so you need real validity evidence.

We are not suggesting that face validity is unimportant. In many settings, it is crucial to have a test that "looks like" it is valid. These appearances can help motivate test takers because they can see that the test is relevant. For example, suppose you had developed a test to screen applicants for a training program in accounting. Items that ask about balance sheets and ledgers might make applicants more motivated than items about fuel consumption. However, both types of items might be testing the same arithmetic reasoning skill. We often say a test has face validity if the items are reasonably related to the perceived purpose of the test.

Content-Related Validity

How many times have you studied for an examination and known almost everything, yet the professor comes up with some strange items that do not seem to represent the content of the course? If this has happened, you may have encountered a test with poor content validity. A test or measure possesses **content validity** to the extent that it provides an adequate representation of the conceptual domain it is designed to cover. For example, if you are being tested on the first six chapters of this book, the test you take is content valid to the extent that the items on the test adequately represent the information in the chapters.

Traditionally, content validity has been of greatest concern in educational testing. The score on your history test should represent your comprehension of the history you are expected to know. Many factors can limit performance on history tests, though, therefore making the professor's inferences about your knowledge less valid. These factors could include characteristics of the items (such as vocabulary some students do not understand) and the sampling of items (such as the selection of items that do not represent the information the test is supposed to evaluate).

It is difficult to separate content validity from other types of validity. In fact, many psychologists have commented that the boundaries between content and other forms of validity are not clearly defined (Anastasi, 1993, 1995; Cronbach, 1989, 1995; Landy, 1986; Lawshe, 1985; Messick, 1994; Tenopyr, 1993). However, the content validation strategy offers some unique features. Aside from face validity, content validity is the only type of validity for which the evidence is logical rather than statistical. Actually, content validation involves inferences about the test scores (Tenopyr, 1984). In content validation, one attempts to determine whether the test has been constructed adequately. (See Focused Example 5-1.) For example, one asks whether the items were chosen to be a fair sample of the content area. Establishing the content validity of a test requires good logic, intuitive skills, and perseverance. The test constructor must be careful and willing to revise the items continually.

Often, test scores reflect many factors besides what the test supposedly measures. For example, your professor may assume that your score on a psychology examination represents the proportion of items you know how to answer correctly. However, it may be that you knew how to answer many more of the items correctly but that other factors interfered. For example, many students do poorly on tests because of anxiety (see Chapter 18) or reading problems. A slow reader may get a low score on an examination because he or she did not have adequate time to read through all the questions. Thus,

---

Focused Example 5-1

CHALLENGING THE PROFESSOR

 Most professors have had the content validity of their tests challenged at some time or other. A student may complain, "Your test did not give me an opportunity to demonstrate what I know" or "You assigned Chapters 1 through 5, but nearly all of the items came from Chapters 1 and 2—how can you evaluate whether we know anything about the other material we were supposed to read?" In the process of creating good and fair tests, professors should continually face this sort of questioning and attempt to create tests that will not evoke legitimate criticism. Good judgment is always required in test development: We can never get around the need for careful planning (Ebel, 1977).

content validity must consider *all* factors that might influence performance. Only in this way can one make accurate generalizations about what the test score really means. Chapter 8 will present a more detailed discussion of this problem.

Criterion-Related Validity

Folklore includes stories about fortune tellers who can look into crystal balls and see the future. Much to our dismay, we do not believe that anyone has been able to manufacture a crystal ball that tells exactly what the future will hold. Instead of turning to fortune tellers with crystal balls, people who need to know about the future have frequently turned to psychologists. We want to know how well someone will do on a job or which students we should select for our graduate program or who is most likely to get a serious disease. We depend on psychological testing to forecast behavior and inclinations.

Criterion validity tells us just how well a test predicts. A measure achieves **criterion validity** to the extent that it corresponds to an accurate measure of interest. The reason for assessing criterion validity is that the test or measure is to serve as a "stand-in" for the measure we are really interested in.

Predictive and concurrent validity. The forecasting function of tests is actually a type or form of criterion validity known as **predictive validity.** One uses predictive validity to forecast. For example, the SAT has predictive validity as a college admissions test if it accurately forecasts how well high school students will do in their college studies. The SAT, including its quantitative and verbal subtests, is the predictor variable, and the college grade point average is the criterion. The purpose of the test is to predict the likelihood of succeeding on the criterion—that is, achieving a high grade point average in college. A valid test for this purpose would make the task of college admissions committees much easier because they would have some feeling in advance about which students would succeed. Unfortunately, many tests do not have exceptionally impressive prediction records, and we must search continually for better ways to predict outcomes.

Another type of criterion validity is concurrent validity. Studies of **concurrent validity** assess the simultaneous relationship between the test and the criterion, as between a learning disability test and school performance. Here, the measures and criterion measures are actually taken at the same time because the test is designed to explain why the person is now having difficulty in school. The test may give diagnostic information that can help guide the development of individualized learning programs. Concurrent validity applies when the test and the criterion can be measured at the same time.

Job samples provide a good example of the use of concurrent validity (Triandis et al., 1994) . Industrial psychologists often have to select employees on the basis of limited information. One method that has recently gained popularity is to test potential employees on a sample of behaviors that represent the tasks to be required of them. For example, Campion (1972) found that the most effective ways to select maintenance mechanics was to obtain samples of their mechanical work. Because these samples were shown to correlate well with performance on the job, the samples alone could be used for the selection and screening of applicants. Impressive results support the use of work samples for selecting employees in a variety of areas, including motor skills (Asher & Sciarrino, 1974) and work in the petroleum industry (Dunnette, 1972).

According to current standards for equal employment opportunity, employers must demonstrate that tasks used to test potential new employees relate to actual job performance. Thompson and Thompson (1982) reviewed 26 federal court decisions in which the validity of tests used to screen employees had been challenged. The judgments in the various cases show that the job-related test must focus on tasks, should be in a written form, and must include several data sources with large samples. In other words, the courts require good scientific evidence that a test used to screen employees is valid inferring how job candidates will perform if employed (Zedeck & Cascio, 1984). See Focused Example 5-2 for a closer look at this process.

Another use of concurrent validity occurs when a person might not know how he or she would respond to the criterion measure. For example, the Strong-Campbell Interest Inventory (SCII) uses as criteria patterns of interest among people satisfied with their careers (Campbell, 1977). Then the patterns of interest for people taking the tests are matched to patterns of interest in various occupations.

Validity coefficient. The relationship between a test and a criterion is usually expressed as a correlation called a *validity coefficient*. This coefficient tells the extent to which the test is valid for making statements about the criterion.

There are no hard-and-fast rules about how large a validity coefficient must be to be meaningful. In practice, one rarely sees a validity coefficient larger than .60, and validity coefficients in the range of .30 to .40 are commonly considered high. A coefficient is statistically significant if the chances of obtaining its value by chance alone are quite small: usually less than 5 in 100. For example, suppose that the SAT had a validity coefficient of .40 for predicting grade point average at a particular West Coast university. Because this coefficient is likely to be statistically significant, we can say that the SAT score tells us more about how well people will do in college than we would know by chance.

College students differ in their academic performance for many reasons. You probably could easily list a dozen. Because there are so many factors that contribute to college performance, it would be too much to expect the SAT to explain all the variation. The question we must ask is "How much of the variation in college performance will we be able to predict on the basis of SAT scores?"

The validity coefficient squared is the percentage of variation in the criterion that we can expect to know in advance because of our knowledge of the test scores. Thus, we will know .40 squared, or 16%, of the variation in college performance because of the information we have from the SAT test. This is the coefficient of determination that was discussed in Chapter 2. The remainder of the variation in college performance is actually the greater proportion: 84% of the total variation is still unexplained. In other words, when students arrive at college, most of the reasons they perform differently will still be a mystery to college administrators and professors. (See Focused Example 5-3 on pp. 138–139.)

Focused Example 5-2

VALIDATION OF A SELF-REPORT MEASURE OF DEPRESSION

 In Chapters 2, 3, and 4, we offered some data on depression based on the Center for Epidemiologic Studies Depression Scale (CES-D). The CES-D is a general measure of depressive symptoms that has been used extensively in epidemiologic studies (M. M. Weissman et al., 1977). The scale includes 20 items and taps dimensions of depressed mood, feelings of guilt and worthlessness, appetite loss, sleep disturbance, and energy level. These items are assumed to represent all the major components of depressive symptomatology. Sixteen of the items are worded negatively, whereas the other four are worded positively to avoid the possibility of patterned responses. The respondents are asked to report how often they experienced a particular "symptom" during the past week on a four-point scale: 0 (rarely or none of the time—less than 1 day), 1 (some or a little of the time—1 to 2 days), 2 (occasionally or a moderate amount of the time—3 or 4 days), and 3 (most or all of the time—5 to 7 days). The responses to the four positive items are reverse scored. Scores on the CES-D scale can range from 0 to 60, with scores greater than 18 suggesting clinically significant levels of depression.

Validity studies have demonstrated that the CES-D is highly correlated with other measures of depression. For example, one validity study demonstrated significant correlations with the more complete Beck Depression Inventory. The CES-D, however, was designed for studies of nonpsychiatric populations (Gottlib & Cine, 1989). A series of studies have demonstrated that the CES-D is associated with clinical diagnoses of depression; however, the CES-D is a better screening instrument than diagnostic tool. Lewinsohn and Teri (1982) demonstrated that scores of less than 16 on the CES-D were highly associated with clinical judgments of nondepression. Conversely, scores of 17 or greater had only a moderate association with psychiatric diagnoses of depression.

Since the CES-D has only moderate validity for the evaluation of clinical depression, one needs more-complex methods for such evaluations. It has been suggested that as many as 3% of the population experience major depressive problems at any given time. The *American Psychiatric Association, in its Diagnostic and Statistical Manual of Mental Disorders,* fourth edition (DSM-IV) (APA, 1995), suggests that the diagnosis of major depressive disorder involves three components:

1. A clinician identifies a series of specific symptoms.
2. The symptoms persist for at least two weeks.
3. The diagnosis is not ruled out for another reason.

These judgments require the active involvement of a trained psychiatrist or psychologist. Most measures of depression do not provide enough information for one to make these complex judgments.

M. Zimmerman and Coryell (1987) have offered a 22-item self-report scale that can be used

In many circumstances, using a test is not worth the effort because it contributes only a few percentage points to the understanding of variation in a criterion. However, low validity coefficients (.30 to .40) can sometimes be very useful even though they may explain only about 10% of the variation in the criterion. For example, Dunnette (1967) demonstrated how a simple questionnaire used for military screening could save taxpayers $4 million every month even though the validity was not remarkably high. (And this analysis

---

to diagnose major depressive disorder. They suggest that the scale may give an accurate estimate of the prevalence of these problems in the general population. Thus, researchers can estimate the proportion of the general population that suffers from depression without the expense of having a psychiatrist or psychologist interview large samples. Zimmerman and Coryell call their measure the Inventory to Diagnose Depression (IDD). The IDD includes 22 items. For each item, the person records a score of 0, which represents no disturbance, through 4, which indicates that the symptom is present. The numbers 1, 2, and 3 suggest different gradations of the symptom. For example, the IDD item about insomnia includes the following choices:

0 = I am not sleeping less than usual.
1 = I occasionally have slight difficulty sleeping.
2 = I clearly don't sleep as well as usual.
3 = I sleep about half my normal amount of time.
4 = I sleep less than two hours per night.

The IDD also considers whether the symptoms have been present for less than or more than two weeks. Some of the depressive symptoms considered by the IDD are decreased energy, decreased interest in sex, guilt, weight gain, anxiety, irritability, and weight loss.

Although the IDD seems to measure the concept of depression (face validity), systematic evidence obtained in validity studies is required. In other words, we need to ask, "What is the evidence that self-reports on this scale actually measure depression?"

The first step in establishing the validity of the IDD was to demonstrate that it was related to other measures designed to assess depression. For example, it was shown to be significantly correlated with the Hamilton Rating Scale for Depression in 234 adults ($r = .80$), the Beck Depression Inventory in 234 adults ($r = .87$), and the Carroll Depression Scale in 105 adults ($r = .81$). In addition, reports of the experience of specific symptoms on the IDD were systematically related to clinicians' judgments of individual symptoms for the same patients.

In another study, first-degree relatives of patients with psychiatric disorders were interviewed using a highly structured system known as the *diagnostic interview schedule*. The system uses a computer program to generate diagnoses for specific disorders. In the study of 394 cases, the IDD gave the same diagnostic classification of depression as the more complex interview in 97.2% of the cases. Though the detailed interview identified some cases not detected by the IDD, the estimates of the rates of major depression assessed with the IDD come quite close to those found in major studies of the general population.

Many other measures of depression exist in addition to the IDD. However, most of these are not designed to make the specific diagnosis of major depressive disorder. Discriminant evidence for validity demonstrates the advantage of the IDD in comparison with other approaches. In particular, other measures do not feed directly into the DSM-IV classification system.

was done before the days of high inflation. If it had been done today, the estimated savings would be far more!) Landy, Farr, and Jacobs (1982) found that a performance evaluation and feedback system with a validity of .30 could translate into increased earnings of $5.3 million in one year. In some circumstances, though, a validity coefficient of .30 or .40 means almost nothing. In Chapter 7, we will show how validity coefficients are translated into specific decision models and how industrial psychologists use information about test validity to save money (Landy & Shankster, 1994). Focused Example 5-4 on pp. 140–141 discusses the validity of tests used in the medical field.

Evaluating validity coefficients. To be an informed consumer of testing information, you should learn to review carefully any information offered by a test developer. Because not all validity coefficients of .40 have the same meaning, you should watch for several things in evaluating this information. We will cover some of these issues here and go into more depth in Chapter 7.

In its booklet *Standards for Educational and Psychological Testing,* the joint committee of the American Education Research Association, the American Psychological Association, and the National Council on Measurement in Education (1985) lists several issues to be concerned about when interpreting validity coefficients. Here are some of its recommendations.

Look for changes in the cause of relationships.   You should always be aware that the conditions of a validity study are never exactly reproduced. For exam-

---

Focused Example 5-3

NADER'S RAID ON THE EDUCATIONAL TESTING SERVICE

Ralph Nader, an aggressive attorney and consumer advocate, has earned a solid reputation over the years for his attacks on giant corporations, including automobile manufacturers and food producers. Nader "exposes" the misdeeds of the corporations to the public. Early in 1980, Nader released the results of his six-year investigation of the Educational Testing Service (ETS)—America's largest test producer. At a press conference he exclaimed, "What this report makes clear is that ETS's claims to measure aptitude and predict success are false and unsubstantiated and can be described as a specialized kind of fraud" (R. M. Kaplan, 1982).

What Nader disputed was the predictive validity of ETS tests such as the SAT and the Graduate Record Examination (GRE). The data used by Nader and his team of researchers were no different from those used by ETS officials; however, the way Nader chose to interpret the data was very different. ETS has consistently reported that the SAT, for example, accounts for a small but significant percentage of the variance in first-year college grade point averages. Nader did not interpret the results in terms of percentage of variance as typically explained in the field of psychometrics. Instead, he reported the percentage of cases the test successfully predicted according to his own criteria. On the basis of this approach, he concluded that the test predicted successfully in only 12% of the cases; however, Nader's calculations were not based on an appropriate statistical model (Kaplan, 1982, 1985d).

ple, if you take the GRE in order to gain admission to graduate school, the conditions under which you take the test may not be exactly the same as those in the studies that established the validity of the GRE. Many things may change, including the way grades are assigned in graduate school and the population taking the test.

The logic of criterion validation presumes that the causes of the relationship between the test and the criterion will still exist when the test is in use. Though this presumption is true for the most part, there may be circumstances in which the relationship changes. For example, a test might be used and shown to be valid for selecting supervisors in industry; however, the validity study may have been done at a time when all the employees were men, making the test valid for selecting supervisors for male employees. If the company hires female employees, the test may no longer be valid for selecting supervisors because it may not take into consideration the abilities necessary to supervise a sexually mixed group of employees.

What does the criterion mean? Another element to watch for when you evaluate validity coefficients is the meaning of the criterion. Criterion validity studies mean nothing at all unless the criterion is valid and reliable. Some test constructors attempt to correlate their tests with other tests that have unknown validity. A meaningless group of items that correlates well with another meaningless group remains meaningless.

For applied research, the criterion should relate specifically to the use of the test. Because the SAT attempts to predict performance in college, the

---

On the basis of his interpretation, Nader suggested that there should be more regulation of the testing industry. Referring to ETS, he explained, "They have assumed a rare kind of corporate power, the power to change the way people think about their own potential, and through the passive acceptance of their test scores by admissions officers, to decide who will be granted and who will be denied access to education and career opportunities" (from *APA Monitor,* 1980, *11*(2), 1–7).

Though Nader uncovered an important problem, it is not certain that the Educational Testing Service deserves all of the blame. ETS puts out its own guidelines for the use of the SAT and other tests. Designed to be read by college admissions officers, these booklets clearly acknowledge the limitations of the tests. For example, college administrators are told that the test accounts for a small but significant percentage of the variation in college performance, and

they are advised to look at other criteria in addition to test scores. Thus, much of the problem lies with admissions committees and with college administrators who passively accept SAT scores as the ultimate predictor of college performance.

Those administrators who know how to interpret the evidence for predictive validity do not make the sort of error Nader warned about. However, if school officials have used the SAT to select students, they have done so to learn about the 16% of the variation among students that could be predicted before any students were admitted. It is important to realize that accounting for small percentages of the variance in some criterion under different circumstances is very useful for people making decisions. Obviously, college administrators feel that the small bit of information they get from SAT scores aids them in selecting the right students for their institutions.

appropriate criterion is grade point average, a measure of college performance. Any other inferences made on the basis of the SAT require additional evidence. For example, if you want to say that the SAT tells you something about adaptability, you must obtain evidence on the relationship between the SAT and some measure of adaptability.

Review the subject population in the validity study. Another reason to be cautious of validity coefficients is that the validity study might have been done on a population that does not represent the group to which inferences will be made. For example, some have debated whether or not validity coefficients for intelligence and personnel tests that are based primarily on white samples are accurate when used to test African-American students (Educational Testing Service, 1991; Gottfredson, 1994; Herrnstein & Murray, 1994; Oakland & Parmelee, 1985; Sackett & Wilk, 1994; Sattler, 1992). We will review this problem in detail in Chapter 20.

In industrial settings, attrition can seriously jeopardize validity studies. Those who do poorly on the job drop out or get fired and thus cannot be studied when it comes time to do the job assessment. If there was a group that did well on the test but failed on the job, it might not be represented and could be

---

Focused Example 5-4

THE CHOLESTEROL TEST: PREDICTIVE VALIDITY

The concept of predictive validity applies to medical tests as well as to psychological measures. One of the major issues in contemporary public health is the relationship between cholesterol levels and death from heart disease. Systematic studies have demonstrated that high levels of cholesterol in the blood can help predict early death from heart disease and stroke. To learn more about these problems, physicians take samples of blood and examine the cholesterol level. To evaluate this information, they must consider the relationship between the test (blood cholesterol level) and the criterion (premature death). Although this relationship has been established in many studies, the level of association is actually quite low. Some studies show the relationship to fall near .1, or to account for about 1% of the variance in mortality. Furthermore, those with high levels of blood cholesterol are advised to eat foods low in saturated fats and cholesterol.

However, some systematic studies have failed to find strong, statistically significant relationships between these dietary habits and mortality rates (Stallones, 1983). These low validity coefficients suggest that these measures tell us very little about what can be predicted for a particular individual. However, heart disease is a very serious problem for the general population. Each year, more than 600,000 Americans die of these problems. Thus, even weak associations help explain a significant number of cases. As a society, if we reduce blood cholesterol levels, there will be a significant reduction in the number of deaths. The low correlation between these cholesterol tests and heart disease suggests that we will not be able to say precisely which specific individuals will benefit. However, the small but significant statistical relationship tells us that there is some important predictive value in cholesterol tests (R. M. Kaplan, 1990; Verschuren et al., 1995).

systematically eliminated from the study because the workers were already off the job by the time the assessment came around.

Be sure the sample size was adequate.   Another problem to look for is a validity coefficient based on a small number of cases. Sometimes a proper validity study cannot be done because there are too few people to study. A common practice is to do a small validity study with the people one has around. Unfortunately, such a study can be quite misleading. You cannot depend on a correlation obtained from a small sample, particularly for multiple correlation and multiple regression. The smaller the sample, the more likely chance variation in the data will affect the correlation. Thus, a validity coefficient based on a small sample tends to be artificially inflated.

A good validity study will present some evidence for cross validation. A cross-validation study assesses how well the test actually forecasts for an independent group of subjects. In other words, the initial validity study assesses the relationship between the test and the criterion, whereas a cross-validation study checks how well this relationship holds for an independent group of subjects. The larger the sample size in the initial study, the better the likelihood that the relationship will cross validate.[1]

Never confuse the criterion with the predictor.   At the university where we work, one department requires students to meet a certain cutoff score on the GRE before they could be admitted to the program. Occasionally, the department admits a student who did not get the cutoff score, but it still requires the student to meet the minimum GRE score before it confers a degree. The logic behind this policy represents a clear misunderstanding of the test and its purpose.

In this case, the GRE is the predictor, and success in graduate school is the criterion. The only reason for using the test in the first place is to help select students who have the highest probability of success in the program. By completing the program, the students have already succeeded on the criterion (success in the program). Before the university would acknowledge that the students indeed had succeeded, they had to go back and demonstrate that they would have been predicted to do well on the criterion. This reflects a clear confusion between predictor and criterion.

This example also demonstrates that the GRE is not a valid predictor of success among those provisionally accepted into this program. Indeed, most of the students provisionally admitted because of low GRE scores succeeded by completing the program. The only reason for using the test is to forecast who is likely to finish. When the students succeed in completing the requirements

---

[1]Correct cross-validation methodology requires that the raw score weights from the original sample be applied to the validation sample. The use of standard score or standardized weights is not appropriate, because the means and standard deviations for the validation sample may differ from those in the original sample (Dorans & Drasgow, 1980).

for their degrees, there is no longer any need for the test. This calls into question the rationale for using the test at all.

Check for restricted range on both predictor and criterion. A variable has a "restricted range" if all scores for that variable fall very close together. For example, the grade point averages of graduate students in Ph.D. programs tend to fall within a limited range of the scale—usually above 3.5 (on a 4-point scale). The problem this creates is that correlation depends on variability. If all the people in your class have a grade point average of 4.0, you cannot predict variability in graduate-school grade point average. Correlation requires that there be variability in both the predictor and the criterion.

One of the major problems with the GRE is that it does not correlate well with graduate-school grade point average. Ingram (1980) did a detailed review of studies on the value of the GRE as a predictor of success in graduate school. He found that among all the published studies, the verbal portion of the GRE significantly predicted graduate-school grade point average in only 25% of the studies and the quantitative portion predicted this same criterion in only 12.5% of the studies. The Educational Testing Service now disputes these findings. However, according to their documents, the average correlation between GRE verbal and first-year psychology graduate school GPA is .28. The correlation between GRE quantitative and first-year grade point average is .29. The validity coefficient for the analytic portion of the GRE is .38 (*GRE Guide,* 1990).

There are at least three explanations for Ingram's findings. First, the GRE may not be a valid test for selecting graduate students. Second, those students who are admitted to graduate school represent such a restricted range of ability that it is not possible to find significant correlations. Those students with low GRE scores are never admitted to graduate school and, therefore, never get into the study. Third, grades in graduate school often represent a restricted range. Once admitted, students in graduate programs usually receive A's and B's. A grade of C is usually considered a failing grade.

Review evidence for validity generalization. Criterion-related validity evidence obtained in one situation may not be generalized to other similar situations. *Generalizability* refers to the evidence that the findings obtained in one situation can be generalized or applied to other situations. Rather than a matter of judgment, this is an issue of empirical study. In other words, one must prove that the results obtained in a validity study are not situation specific. There are many reasons why results may not be generalized. For example, differences may exist in the way the predictor construct is measured or in the type of job or curriculum involved—in the actual criterion measure—between the groups of people who take the test; differences may also exist in the time period—year or month—when the test is administered. Because of these problems, we cannot always be certain that the validity coefficient reported by a test developer will be the same for our particular situation. An employer, for example, might use a work sample test based on information reported in the manual, yet the situation in which he or she uses the test may differ from the situations of the original validation studies. When using the test, the employer might be using different demographic groups or different criterion measures or else predicting performance on a similar but different task. Generalizations from the original validity studies to these other situations should be made only on the basis of new evidence.

Consider differential prediction.   Predictive relationships may not be the same for all demographic groups. The validity for men could differ in some circumstances from the validity for women. Or the validity of the test may be questionable because it is used for a group whose native language is different from English, even though the test was validated for those who always spoke only English. Under these circumstances, separate validity studies for different groups may be necessary. This issue will be discussed in more detail in Chapter 20.

Although criterion validity is very common in psychological and educational research, there are some instances in which it simply does not apply. By definition, the criterion must be the most accurate measure of the phenomenon if it is to serve as the "gold standard." If a criterion exists, only greater practicality or less expense justifies the use of concurrent measures as proxies or substitutes for the criterion. If the criterion is not a superior measure, then failure of correspondence by any new measure may reveal a defect in the criterion itself. For example, studies on the validity of measures of general health have been hindered because a clear criterion of health has never been defined (Kaplan et al., 1995). The development of a health index helped define the meaning of the term *health*. Often, work on a psychological test involves the simultaneous development of a concept and the instrumentation to measure the concept. This cannot be accomplished by criterion validity studies. Instead, we need a more involved approach known as *construct validation.*

Construct-Related Validity

Before 1950, most social scientists considered only criterion and content forms of validity. By the mid-1950s, investigators concluded that no clear criteria existed for most of the social and psychological characteristics they wanted to measure. Developing a measure of intelligence, for example, was difficult because no one could say for certain what intelligence was. Criterion validity studies would require that a specific criterion of intelligence be established against which tests could be compared. However, there was no criterion for intelligence, a hypothetical construct we cannot touch or feel. A *construct* is defined as something constructed by mental synthesis.

Contemporary psychologists often want to measure intelligence, love, curiosity, or mental health. None of these constructs are clearly defined, and there is no established criterion against which psychologists can compare the accuracy of their tests. These are the truly challenging problems in measurement.

Construct validity is established through a series of activities in which a researcher simultaneously defines some construct and develops the instrumentation to measure it. This process is required when "no criterion or universe of content is accepted as entirely adequate to define the quality to be measured" (Cronbach & Meehl, 1955, p. 282). Construct validation involves assembling evidence about what a test really means. This is done by showing the relationship between a test and other tests and measures. Each time a relationship is demonstrated, one additional bit of meaning can be attached to the

---

Focused Example 5-5

THE MEANING OF LOVE

An interesting example of construct validation comes from the work of Zick Rubin (1970, 1973), who noted that love has been one of the most discussed issues of all time. Throughout history, men and women have written and sung about love more than any other topic. The index to Bartlett's *Familiar Quotations* shows that references to love are second only to citations to "man" (with "love" cited 769 times and "man" cited 843 times). All this preoccupation with love, however, has not led to a better understanding of its true meaning. Perhaps it is something we can feel but not necessarily understand well enough to describe in a definite way.

In the mid-1970s, there was a famous trial in Los Angeles in which the singer Mischelle Triola Marvin sued actor Lee Marvin for half his earnings while the couple lived together. A major issue in the trial was the couple's unmarried status during the period in which the earnings occurred. During the trial, Lee's attorney questioned the actor about the extent to which he loved Mischelle while they lived together. Unfortunately, there is no scale on which the actor could rate his love. If he had been asked his height, he could have used the scale of inches. But love? How could he put that into a number? However, the actor did resort to a gas-tank analogy. He said his love for the singer was like when you are driving your car and you look over at your gas gauge and find it "about half full." That is about how much he loved Mischelle—about half a tank. If there had been a measure of love, he would not have needed to use such a vague analogy (Rubin, 1979).

In developing his love scale, Rubin first had to create a list of items that represented all the different things people might call love. This was not an easy task because we all have different ideals. To create a measure of love, Rubin had to condense conventional wisdom about loving and liking into sets of statements to which people could respond on a scale. The scale presented statements, and subjects could respond by indicating the extent to which they agreed or disagreed on a 5-point scale (where 1 is for strong disagreement and 5 is for strong agreement).

Collecting the statements or any other original set of items for construct validation is not easy because we never know which items eventually will be relevant to the construct we are attempting to measure. Building the love scale was particularly difficult in this regard. To prepare his measure, Rubin read extensively about love.

Elizabeth Barrett Browning wrote, "How do I love thee? Let me count the ways." Indeed, after reading the many diverse views of love, Rubin hardly knew where to begin counting. Because this was a study in construct validity, however, it was important that Rubin considered counting. Construct validity requires that there be content validity. Content validity in turn requires that the items fully represent the domain of inference (in this case, love). All the ways that love is defined by different people must be included in this collection.

Rubin began his study with his sets of statements that people could respond to on a scale ranging from disagreement to agreement. Some of the items were intended to measure love, whereas others were supposed to tap liking. Next he gave the

test. Over a series of studies, the meaning of the test gradually begins to take shape. Construct validation is an ongoing process, similar to amassing support for a complex scientific theory. Though no single set of observations provides crucial or critical evidence, many observations over time gradually clarify what the test means. An example of construct validation is given in Focused Example 5-5.

---

pool of items to 198 students from the University of Michigan. Each of the items had a blank in which a name could be filled in. The students responded to the questions twice, one time filling in the name of their lover and another time filling in the name of a friend. Then the items were subjected to factor analysis. This is a method for reducing a large number of items or variables into smaller and more manageable composites of items called factors, as you will recall from Chapter 3.

In the love scale, three factors were obtained: attachment, caring, and intimacy. The items on the attachment scale emphasized desire to be with the loved person, or to seek him or her out if lonely. The caring scale included items about empathy and concern for the loved person's welfare. The intimacy scale considered exclusive aspects of the relationship; for example, the willingness to confide in him or her about intimate personal problems. The items on the liking scale focused on favorable aspects of the other person along such dimensions as adjustment, maturity, good judgment, and intelligence.

The data from these scales were subjected to several statistical procedures that helped discriminate between the responses of lovers and friends and eventually led to the establishment of two measures: a love scale and a liking scale. With these measures of liking and loving in hand, Rubin next had to determine whether they were really measuring what they were supposed to. One study using dating couples suggested that loving and liking were not necessarily related. There was a modest relationship between scores on the two scales, which was weaker for women than for men. This suggested, especially for women, that it is possible to love someone whom you may not particularly like.

There are several indications that the love scale really was measuring "love." For example, men and women scored higher on the love scale when they filled in the names of their lovers than when they filled in the name of a same-sex friend (all were assumed to be heterosexual). There also was a substantial correlation between love scale scores and estimates of the likelihood of marriage. The greater the love score, the more probable marriage was considered to be.

Finally, some of the dating couples were separated into strong love (high love scores) and weak love (low love scores) groups. From behind a one-way mirror, the researchers noted how much eye contact the lovers had with one another. Strong lovers, it was observed, spent more time simply gazing into one another's eyes than did weak lovers. When paired with a strong opposite-sex lover from another couple, strong lovers made no more mutual eye contact than did weak lovers.

In summary, Rubin began his study of love with neither a clear definition of love nor a method of measuring it. Through a series of structured exercises, he gradually came to have a better grasp of the construct. For example, he discovered that lovers mark some items differently than couples who are just friends. He also discovered that "love" may have at least three independent components. Once the basic scale was developed, each new application defined a new meaning. For instance, one study showed that the scale predicts how much time lovers will spend gazing into each other's eyes. Thus, in future applications of the love scale, we would expect couples who score as strong lovers (for one another) to spend much time in mutual gaze.

Years ago, Campbell and Fiske (1959) introduced an important set of logical considerations for developing tests with construct validity. They distinguished between two types of evidence essential for a meaningful test: convergent and discriminant. To argue that a test has meaning, a test constructor must be armed with as much evidence as possible for these two types of validity. We will present the basic logic of the Campbell and Fiske approach here. For those who desire a more detailed presentation, we recommend the 1959 reference.

Convergent evidence. When a measure correlates well with other tests believed to measure the same construct, **convergent evidence** for validity is obtained. This sort of evidence shows that measures of the same construct "converge," or narrow in, on the same thing. In many ways, convergent evidence for construct validity is like criterion validity. In each case, scores on the test are related to scores on some other measure. In the case of convergent evidence for construct validity, however, there is no criterion to define what we are attempting to measure. Criterion validity is fine for situations in which we are attempting to predict performance on a particular variable, such as success in graduate school. Here the task is well defined, and all we need to do is find the items that are good predictors of this graduate-school criterion. Because there is no well-defined criterion in construct validity, the meaning of the test comes to be defined by the variables it can be shown to be associated with.

An example of the need to obtain construct validation evidence comes from studies by R. M. Kaplan, Bush, and Berry (1976), who attempted to define and measure the construct *health,* a complex concept. Because of this complexity, no single measure can serve as the criterion against which a measure of health can be assessed. This situation requires studies in construct validation. Some of the construct validation studies were used to demonstrate the convergent validity of the measure of health the authors called a *health index.*

Convergent evidence is obtained in one of two ways. In the first, one shows that a test measures the same things as other tests used for the same purpose. In the second, one demonstrates specific relationships that could be expected if the test is really doing its job. The studies on the health index included both types of evidence. In demonstrating the meaning of the health index, the authors continually asked themselves, "If we were really measuring health, which relationships would we expect to observe between the health index and other measures?" The simplest relationship, between health index scores and the way people rate their own health status, was strong and clearly showed that the index captured some of the same information individuals used to evaluate their own health. However, a good measure must go beyond this simple bit of validity evidence because self-ratings are unreliable. If they were not, we would use self-perceived health status as the index of health because it is easier than using the health index.

In construct validity, no single variable can serve as the criterion. Thus, other studies were used to show a variety of other relationships. For example, people who scored as less healthy on the health index also tended to report more symptoms and chronic medical conditions. The authors also hypothesized that health status would be related to age, and they observed that these two variables were indeed systematically related. Older persons in the sample tended to have a lower health status.

The researchers also evaluated specific hypotheses based on certain theoretical notions about the construct. In the health index studies, the authors reasoned, "If the index really measures health, then we would expect that people who score low on the measure should visit doctors more often." A study confirming that they should provided evidence for one more inference. Also, certain groups (such as disabled persons) should have lower average scores on the index than other groups (such as nondisabled persons). Again, a study confirmed this hypothesis (R. M. Kaplan, 1994a).

In another series of studies, investigators argued that a health index should correlate with specific physiological measures representing disease states. In one study, for example, patients with chronic lung diseases took measures of lung function. These measures were more strongly correlated with the general health index than they were with a variety of other physiological and social variables (R. M. Kaplan & Ries, 1996). Other studies demonstrated that the measures were related to clinical indicators of arthritis, AIDS, and cystic fibrosis (R. M. Kaplan et al., 1989; R. M. Kaplan et al., 1995). If a health index really measures health, then treatments designed to improve health should be reflected by changes in the measure. In one study, patients with arthritis underwent a new treatment believed to remedy their condition. The general health index demonstrated the significant improvements caused by the treatment (Bombardier et al., 1986). Other studies showed the measure was related to improvements in conditions such as Alzheimer's disease (Kerner et al., 1995), schizophrenia (T. Patterson et al., 1996), and several other conditions (R. M. Kaplan, 1993).

Thus, a series of studies expanded the number of meanings that could be given to the health index. Yet, convergent validity does not constitute all the evidence necessary to argue for the meaning or construct validity of a psychological test or measure. We also must have discriminant evidence for such validity.

Discriminant evidence. Science can be very conservative. It confronts scientists with difficult questions such as "Why should we believe your theory if we already have a theory that seems to say about the same thing?" An eager scientist may answer this question by arguing that his or her theory is distinctive and better. In testing, psychologists face a similar dilemma. Why should they create a new test if there is already one available to do the job? Thus, one type of evidence a person needs in test validation is proof that the test measures something unique. For example, if a health index measures the same thing as self-rated health, number of symptoms, and number of chronic medical conditions, why do we need it in addition to all these other measures? The answer is that the measure taps something other than the tests used in the convergent validity studies. This demonstration of uniqueness is called **discriminant evidence.** Some authors call this same evidence *divergent validation.* To demonstrate discriminant validity, a test should have low correlations with measures of unrelated constructs, or evidence for what the test does not measure.

By providing evidence that a test measures something different from other tests, we also provide evidence that we are measuring some unique construct. Calling an old construct by a new name always should be avoided. Discriminant evidence indicates that the measure does not represent a construct other than the one for which it was devised.

As this discussion implies, construct validity actually subsumes all the activities used in other types of validation studies. In construct validation, for example, content validation is an essential step. Furthermore, convergent and discriminant studies actually correlate the tests with many different criteria. Thus, there is a similarity between construct and criterion validity. Some psychologists argue that construct validity actually is the only major category of validity that need concern us and that others might be thought of as subcategories of construct validity (Anastasi, 1993, 1995; Cronbach, 1989, 1995; Landy, 1986; Lawshe, 1985; Messick, 1994; Tenopyr, 1993). According to the testing pioneer Lee Cronbach, it may not be appropriate to continue to divide validity into three parts. Cronbach maintains, "All validation is one, and in a sense all is construct validation" (1980, p. 99).

Criterion-referenced tests. The procedures for establishing the validity of a criterion-referenced test resemble those for studying the validity of any other test. As you may recall from Chapter 2, criterion-referenced tests have items designed to match certain specific instructional objectives. For example, if the objective of some educational program is for children to be able to list 75% of the countries in Europe, the criterion-referenced test could ask that the countries be listed. Children who listed 75% of the countries would pass the test. They would be evaluated against this specific criterion rather than on the basis of how they perform relative to other students. Validity studies for the criterion-referenced tests would compare scores on the test to scores on other measures that are believed to be related to the test. Some specific procedures for evaluating the validity of a criterion-referenced test have been discussed in more technical articles (see Forsyth, 1991; Hambleton, 1994; Popham, 1994).

Relationship Between Reliability and Validity

Attempting to define the validity of a test will be a futile effort if the test is not reliable. Theoretically, a test should not correlate more highly with any other variable than it correlates with itself. The maximum validity coefficient (R_{12max}) between two variables is equal to the square root of the product of their reliabilities, or $R_{12max} = \sqrt{R_{11}R_{22}}$, where R_{11} and R_{22} are the reliabilities for the two variables.

Because validity coefficients are not usually expected to be exceptionally high, a modest correlation between the true scores on two traits may be missed if the test for each of the traits was not highly reliable. Table 5-1 shows the maximum validity you would expect to find given various levels of reliability for two tests. Sometimes one cannot demonstrate that a reliable test has meaning. In other words, one can have reliability without validity. However, it is logically impossible to demonstrate that an unreliable test is valid.

Reliability and validity are related concepts. Figure 5-1 divides the total

TABLE 5-1
*How Reliability
Affects Validity**

Reliability of Test	Reliability of Criterion	Maximum Validity (Correlation)
1.0	1.0	1.00
.8	1.0	.89
.6	1.0	.77
.4	1.0	.63
.2	1.0	.45
.0	1.0	.00
1.0	.5	.71
.8	.5	.63
.6	.5	.55
.4	.5	.45
.2	.5	.32
.0	.5	.00
1.0	.0	.00
.8	.0	.00
.6	.0	.00
.4	.0	.00
.2	.0	.00
.0	.0	.00

* The first column shows the reliability of the test. The second column displays the reliability of the validity criterion. The numbers in the third column are the maximum theoretical correlations between tests, given the reliability of the measures.

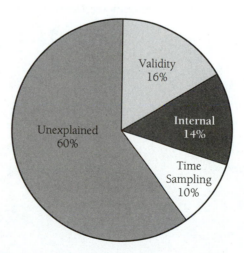

FIGURE 5-1 *Division of total variation on a performance measure as a function of validity and reliability. Many sources of variation are reflected in a test score. Most of the variance in scores remains unexplained (60%). Internal error (14%) and time-sampling error (10%) are two types of reliability that reduce the validity of the test. Validity accounts for about 16% of the total variance in this example.*

variation of a test score into different parts. The example used is a test with a validity coefficient of .40. If we consider the total variability on some measure, such as college performance, about 16% of the variation might be explained by performance on a predictor test. There is also variation in the score, part of which is explained by measurement error. As noted in Chapter 4, this error might be related to time sampling, internal consistency, item sampling, and so forth. The figure hypothetically shows these relationships. Finally, some of the variability is "unexplained" or explained by factors of which we are unaware.

Summary

Validity is a basic idea in measurement and in the science of psychology Although we have emphasized the validity of psychological tests, the ideas we discussed apply equally to all measures. To make any inference, a good scientist must have substantiating data.

Once a test is "validated," many psychologists mistakenly think it can be used for all purposes. The mistake is that tests are appropriately used to support many different inferences. Actually, there should be as many validity studies as there are inferences about the scores (Cronbach, 1995). Anytime we claim that a test score means something different, we need a new validity study. Validity really refers to the things that are said on the basis of the test scores and not to the tests themselves (Landy, 1986).

Thus, acquiring evidence about the meaning of tests should be an ongoing process. The more a test or a measure is used, the more we learn about what it means. According to two well-known applied psychologists, "Test users should never feel that they know enough about the behavioral meaning of their selection methods" (Dunnette & Borman, 1979, p. 484).

CHAPTER 6

Building a Test

LEARNING OBJECTIVES

When you have completed this chapter, you should be able to:

- Describe two types of item formats commonly used in objective classroom examinations

- Know whether or not you should guess on a multiple-choice examination when you are not sure of the correct answer

- Explain the types of measurement problems the Likert format is used for

- Discuss what sorts of problems you might encounter if you used a 10-point category scale to rate the abilities of a group of similar individuals

- Set the level of item difficulty needed for a test that discriminates well among individuals

- Describe the process of assessing item discriminability

- Define an item characteristic curve and tell how it is used

- Draw an item characteristic curve for an item that discriminates well at high levels of performance but not at low levels

- Explain how item characteristic curves can be used to find items that are unfair to students who "overstudied"

- Discuss some of the limitations of item analysis for tests designed to find specific learning problems

At this point in your studies, you have had much experience taking tests. Most of these have been classroom exercises; however, you also have been exposed to standardized tests such as the SAT or the Iowa Test of Basic Skills.

As a seasoned test taker, you also may have become an experienced test critic. After taking a test, most students are willing to render an opinion: to judge whether it was a fair or good test. When you feel that the test was bad, you might ask yourself, "How could the test have been better?" In this chapter, we offer some of the basics for creating test items. In the next chapter, we will discuss how to choose and use published tests.

Item Writing

When a professor announces that there will be a test, one of the first questions is "What kind of test?" Will it be true/false, multiple-choice, essay, or fill-in-the-blank? As you will learn in Part II of this book, personality and intelligence tests require all sorts of different responses. After defining the objectives and purpose of the test, the test constructor must determine the type of response he or she wants to require. In part this choice stems from the purpose of the test. For example, if the test requires right or wrong answers, the task will usually be true/false, multiple choice, matching, or essay.

Writing items can be difficult. DeVellis (1991) provided several simple guidelines for item writing. Some of these suggestions are as follows:

1. Define clearly what you want to measure. To do this, use substantive theory as a guide and try to make items as specific as possible.

2. Generate an item pool. Theoretically, all items are randomly chosen from a universe of item content. In practice, however, care in selecting and developing items is valuable. Avoid redundant items. In the initial phases, you may want to write three or four items for each one that will eventually be used on the test or scale.

3. Avoid exceptionally long items, which are rarely good.

4. Keep the level of reading difficulty appropriate for those who will complete the scale.

5. Avoid "double barreled" items, which convey two or more ideas at the same time. For example, consider an item that asks the respondent to agree or disagree with the statement, "I vote Democratic because I support social programs." There are two different statements with which the person could agree: "I vote Democratic" and "I support social programs."

6. Consider mixing positively and negatively worded items. Sometimes, respondents develop the acquiescence response set. This means that the respondents will tend to agree with most items. To avoid this bias, you can include some items worded in the opposite direction. For example, in ask-

ing about depression, the CES-D (see Chapter 2) uses mostly negatively worded items (such as "I felt depressed"). However, the CESD also includes items worded in the opposite direction ("I felt hopeful about the future").

Item Formats

The type of test you probably have experienced most in the classroom is one in which you receive credit for a specific response, or selection of the single "correct" alternative for each test item. True/false and multiple-choice examinations use this system. Similar formats are used for many other purposes, such as evaluating attitudes, determining knowledge about traffic laws, or deciding whether someone has characteristics associated with a particular health condition. The simplest test of this type uses a dichotomous format.

The dichotomous format. The **dichotomous format** offers two alternatives for each item. Usually a point is given for the selection of one of the alternatives. The most common example of this format is the true/false examination. This test presents students with a series of statements. The student's task is to determine which statements are true and which are false. There are many virtues of the true/false test, including ease of construction and ease of scoring, but the method has also become popular because a teacher can easily construct a test by copying lines out of a textbook. The lines that are copied verbatim are designated as "true." Other statements are altered so that they are no longer true.

The advantages of true/false items include their obvious simplicity, ease of administration, and quick scoring. However, there are also disadvantages. For example, true/false items encourage students to memorize material, making it possible for students to perform well on a test that covers materials they do not really understand. Also, the mere chance of getting any item correct is 50%. Thus, for a true/false test to be reliable, it requires many items.

The dichotomous format does not appear only as true/false or educational tests. Many personality tests require responses in a true/false or some other two-choice format, such as yes/no. Personality test constructors often prefer this type of format because it requires absolute judgment. For example, in response to an item such as "I often worry about my sexual performance," people cannot be ambivalent—they must respond "True" or "False." Dichotomous items have many advantages for personality tests with many subscales. One is that they make the scoring of the subscales easy. All that one need do is count the number of items a person endorses from each subscale.

Although the true/false format is popular in educational tests, it is not used as frequently as the multiple-choice test, which represents the polytomous format.

The polytomous format. The **polytomous format** (sometimes called polychotomous) resembles the dichotomous format except that each item has more than two alternatives. Typically, a point is given for the selection of one of the alternatives, and no point is given for selecting any other choice. Because it is a popular method of measuring academic performance in large classes, the multiple-choice examination is the polytomous format you have encountered most often. Multiple-choice tests are easy to score, and the probability of obtaining a correct response by chance is lower than it is for true/false items. A major advantage of this format is that it takes very little time for test takers to respond to a particular item because they do not have to write. Thus, the test can cover a large amount of information in a relatively short time.

When taking a multiple-choice examination, you must determine which of several alternatives is "correct." Incorrect choices are called distractors. As we will demonstrate in the section on item analysis, the choice of distractors is very important.

Because most students are familiar with multiple-choice tests and related formats such as matching, there is no need to elaborate on their description. However, it is worthwhile to consider some of the issues in the construction and scoring of multiple-choice tests. One question is "How many distractors should a test have?"

Psychometric theory suggests that adding more distractors should increase the reliability of the items. However, in practice, adding distractors may not actually increase the reliability because it is difficult to find good ones. The reliability of an item is not enhanced by distractors that are never selected. Studies have shown that it is rare to find items for which more than three or four distractors operate efficiently. Ineffective distractors actually may hurt the reliability of the test because they are time consuming to read and can limit the number of items that can be included in a test. After a careful review of the distractor problem, Wesman (1971) concluded that item writers should try to find three or four good distractors for each item. Well-chosen distractors are an essential ingredient of good items.

Sometimes, psychometric analysis can pave the way toward the development of simpler tests. For example, most multiple-choice tests have followed Wesman's suggestion of four or five alternatives. However, this traditional practice may not be the best use of resources. In one evaluation of tests for entry-level police officers, applicants completed a test battery with either five alternative multiple-choice items or three alternative items. Psychometric analysis showed that the validity and reliability were about equal for the two types of tests. This result suggests that three alternative multiple-choice items may be better than five alternative items because they retain the psychometric value but take less time to administer (Sidick, Barrett, & Boverspike, 1994).

Another issue concerns the scoring of multiple-choice examinations. Suppose you bring your roommate to your sociology test, and he or she fills out an answer sheet without reading the items. Will your roommate get any items correct? The answer is yes—by chance alone. If each test item has four choices, the test taker would be expected to get 25% correct. If the test items had three choices, a 33.33% rate of success would be expected. Because test takers get some "correct" answers simply by the luck of guessing, a correction for guessing is sometimes used. The formula to correct for guessing on a test is

$$\text{corrected score} = R - \frac{W}{n - 1}$$

where R = the number of right responses
W = the number of wrong responses
n = the number of choices for each item

Omitted responses are not included; they provide neither credit nor penalty. For example, suppose that your roommate randomly filled out the answer sheet to your sociology test. The test had 100 items, each with four choices. By chance, his or her expected score would be 25 correct. Let's assume that he or she got exactly that (if the test was filled out randomly, we might not get exactly 25, which is the average random score). The expected score corrected for guessing would be

$$R - \frac{W}{n - 1} = 25 - \frac{75}{4 - 1} = 25 - \frac{75}{3} = 25 - 25 = 0$$

In other words, when the correction for guessing is applied, the expected score is 0.

A question frequently asked by students is "Should I guess on multiple-choice items when I don't know the answer?" The answer depends on how the test will be scored. If a correction for guessing is not used, the best advice is "guess away." By guessing, you have a chance of getting the item correct. You do not have this chance if you do not attempt the item. However, if a correction for guessing is used, random guessing will do you no good. Some speeded tests are scored so that the correction for the guessing formula includes only the items that were attempted—that is, those that were not attempted are not counted either right or wrong. In this case, random guessing and leaving the items blank have the same expected effect.

How about cases when you don't know the right answer but are able to eliminate one or two of the alternatives? How many times have you had it down to two alternatives but couldn't figure out which of the two was correct? In this case, we advise you to guess. The correction formula assumes that you are equally likely to respond to each of the four categories. For a four-choice item, it would estimate your chance of getting the item correct by chance alone to be one in four. However, if you can eliminate two alternatives, the chances are actually one in two. This gives you a slight advantage over the correction formula. Recently, new mathematical methods have been introduced to summarize information in multiple-choice tests. These methods summarize the mean, the reliability as calculated from the binomial distribution, and a guessing threshold. The guessing threshold describes the chances that a low-ability testing taker will obtain each score. These newer methods are highly technical and are beyond the scope of this text. In summary, the techniques are derived from the first three moments of the test score distribution. Mathematically inclined readers interested in the methods should consult Carlin and Rubin (1991).

As you have seen, true/false and multiple-choice formats are common to educational and achievement tests. Similar formats are found on personality tests. For example, frequently used personality inventories such as the Minnesota Multiphasic Personality Inventory (MMPI) or the California Psychological Inventory (CPI) present subjects with a long list of statements to which one responds either "True" or "False" (see Chapter 14).

Other personality and attitude measures do not deem any response "right." Rather, they attempt to quantify characteristics of the response. These formats include the Likert format, the category scale, and the Q-sort. Some of these formats will be discussed in more detail in Chapter 14. We should also mention the essay format. This is commonly used in classroom evaluation. Furthermore, the Educational Testing Service now uses a writing sample as a component of its testing programs. Essay exams can be evaluated using the same principles as structured tests. For example, the validity of the test can be established through correlations with other tests. The reliability of the scoring procedure should be assessed by determining the association between two scores provided by independent scorers. In practice, however, the psychometric properties of essay exams are rarely evaluated.

The Likert format. One popular format for attitude and personality scales requires that a respondent indicate the degree of agreement with a particular attitudinal question. This technique is called the **Likert format** because it was used as part of Likert's (1932) method of attitude scale construction. A scale using the Likert format consists of a series of items such as "I am afraid of heights." Instead of asking for a yes/no reply, five alternatives are offered: strongly disagree, disagree, neutral, agree, and strongly agree. In some applications, six options are used to avoid allowing the respondent to be neutral. The six responses might be: strongly disagree, moderately disagree, mildly disagree, mildly agree, moderately agree, and strongly agree. Scoring requires that any negatively worded items be reverse scored and the responses then be summed. This format is especially popular in attitude measurement. For example, it is possible to determine the extent to which people endorse statements such as "The government should not regulate private business."

Because responses in Likert format can be subjected to factor analysis, one can find groups of items that go together. A similar technique that uses an even greater number of choices is the category format.

The category scale. Measures in which people rate items on a 10-point scale have become commonplace. The scale need not have exactly 10 points; it can have either more or fewer categories. Rating scales of this sort have a **category format.**

Although the 10-point scale is very common in psychological research and everyday conversation, controversy exists regarding when and how it should be used. We recently encountered a college basketball coach who rates the quality of upcoming high-school players on a 10-point rating scale. It is assumed that this rating provides a reliable estimate of the players' abilities. However, experiments have shown that responses to items on 10-point scales are affected by the groupings of the items being rated. For example, if coaches are asked to rate the abilities of a group of 20 very talented players, they may tend to make fine distinctions among them and use many of the categories on the 10-point scale. A particular player rated as a 6 when he was on a team with many outstanding players might be rated as a 9 if he were judged with a group of poorly coordinated players (Parducci, 1968, 1995). When given a group of objects to rate, subjects have a tendency to spread their responses evenly across the 10 categories (Stevens, 1966).

Experiments have shown that this problem can be avoided if the endpoints of the scale are clearly defined and the subjects are frequently reminded of the definitions of the endpoints. For example, instead of asking coaches to rate the ability of basketball players on a 10-point scale, testers might show them films depicting the performance of a player rated as 10 and other films showing what was meant by 1. Under these circumstances, the subjects are less likely to offer a response affected by other stimuli in the group (R. M. Kaplan & Ernst, 1983).

People often ask, "Why use a 10-point scale instead of a 13-point or a 43-point scale?" As it turns out, this has been a matter of considerable study. Some have argued that the optimal number of points is around seven (Symonds, 1924), whereas others have suggested that the optimal number of categories should be three times this number (Champney & Marshall, 1939). As is often the case, the number of categories required depends on the fineness of the discrimination subjects are willing to make. If the subjects are unconcerned about something, they will not make fine discriminations, and a scale with just a few categories will do about as well as a scale that has many. However, when people are very involved with some issue, they will tend to use a greater number of categories. For most rating tasks, however, a 10-point scale seems to provide enough discrimination. N. H. Anderson (1991) has found that a 10-point scale provides substantial discrimination among objects for a wide variety of stimuli.

Checklists and Q-sorts. One format common in personality measurement is the adjective checklist (Gough, 1960). With this method, a subject is given a long list of adjectives and asked to indicate whether each one is characteristic of himself or herself. Adjective checklists can be used for describing either oneself or someone else. (See Focused Example 6-1.) For example, in one study at the University of California at Berkeley, raters checked the traits they thought characterized a group of 40 graduate students. Half these students had been designated by their instructors as exceptional in originality, and the other half low in originality. The results demonstrated that the adjectives chosen to describe members of these two groups differed. The highly original students were described most often by the traits "adventurous," "alert," "curious," "quiet," "imaginative," and "fair-minded." In contrast, the low-originality students were seen as "confused," "conventional," "defensive," "polished," "prejudiced," and "suggestible."

The adjective checklist requires subjects either to endorse such adjectives or not, allowing only these two choices. A similar technique known as the *Q-sort* increases the number of categories. The Q-sort can be used to describe oneself or to provide ratings of others (Stephenson, 1953). With this technique, a subject is given statements and asked to sort them into nine piles. For example, Block (1961) gave observers 100 statements about personal characteristics. The statements were sorted into piles indicating the degree to which they appeared to accurately describe a given person. If you were using this method, you might be asked to rate your roommate. You would receive a set of 100 cards, each with a statement on it such as the following:

Has a wide range of interests.

Is productive; gets things done.

Is self-dramatizing, is histrionic.

Focused Example 6-1

THE EFFECT OF CONTEXT ON VALUE RATINGS

The numbers we assign when using rating scales are sometimes influenced by the context or the background against which objects are rated. In one experiment, college students were asked to rate how immoral they believed certain acts to be. The students were divided into two groups. One group rated the items that typically represented "mild" actions (List 1), and the other group rated items that typically represented more severe actions (List 2). The numbers on the right represent average ratings by a large number of college students. The six items included on both lists are marked with asterisks. These items are judged more leniently when included in List 2 than when in List 1. This experiment shows that the numbers we assign when using rating scales are affected by context (Parducci, 1968).

List 1

Registering in a hotel under a false name.	1.68
Bawling out servants publicly.*	2.64

Contributing money to a cause in which you do not believe in order to escape criticism.	3.03
Keeping a dime you find in a telephone booth.	1.08
Publishing under your own name an investigation originated and carried out without remuneration by a graduate student working under you.*	3.95
Failing to pay your bus fare when the conductor overlooks you.	2.36
Playing poker on Sunday.	1.17
Failing to put back in the water lobsters shorter than the legal limit.*	2.22
Cheating at solitaire.	1.53
Fishing without a license.	2.27
Habitually borrowing small sums of money from friends and failing to return them.*	2.93
Stealing towels from a hotel.	2.58
Stealing a loaf of bread from a store when you are starving.	1.79

Is overreactive to minor frustrations; is irritable.

Seeks reassurance from others.

Appears to have a high degree of intellectual capacity.

Is basically anxious.

If a statement really hit home, you would place it in pile 9. Those that were not at all descriptive would be placed in pile 1. Most of the cards are usually placed in piles 4, 5, and 6. The frequency of items placed in each of the categories usually looks like a bell-shaped curve (see Figure 6-1). The items that end up in the extreme categories usually say something interesting about the person.

Other Possibilities

We have discussed only a few of many item formats. If you are interested in learning more about item writing and item formats, you might check some classic references (A. L. Edwards, 1957; Guilford, 1954; Torgerson, 1958).

Poisoning a neighbor's dog whose barking bothers you.*	4.19
Lying about your whereabouts to protect a friend's reputation.	1.60
Wearing shorts on the street where it is illegal.	1.59
Pocketing the tip the previous customer left for the waitress.*	3.32
Getting your own way by playing on people's sympathies.	2.90

List 2

Using guns on striking workers.	3.82
Bawling out servants publicly.*	2.39
Stealing ten dollars from an impecunious acquaintance.	3.79
Selling to a hospital milk from diseased cattle.	4.51
Publishing under your own name an investigation originated and carried out without remuneration by a graduate student working under you.*	3.47
Spreading rumors that an acquaintance is a sexual pervert.	3.91

Having a sane person committed to a mental hospital in order to get rid of him.	4.46
Failing to put back in the water lobsters that are shorter than the legal limit.*	1.82
Having sexual relations with a sibling (brother or sister).	3.72
Putting your deformed child in the circus.	3.81
Habitually borrowing small sums of money from friends and failing to return them.*	2.37
Having incestuous relations with your parent.	3.88
Murdering your mother without justification or provocation.	4.79
Poisoning a neighbor's dog whose barking bothers you.*	3.65
Testifying falsely against someone for pay.	4.07
Teaching adolescents to become dope addicts.	4.51
Pocketing the tip the previous customer left for the waitress.*	2.46
Sending another person to take a civil service exam for you.	3.39

*Items followed by an asterisk appear on both lists.

From Parducci (1968). Reprinted by permission.

FIGURE 6-1

The California Q-sort. The numbers of items distributed in the nine piles of the California Q-sort approach a normal distribution.

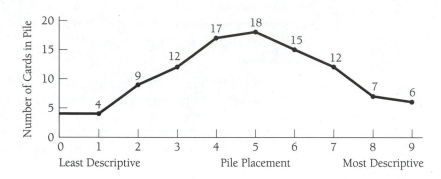

Unfortunately, there is no simple recipe for item writing. Several people have studied the issue carefully and have contributed many useful suggestions (see DeVellis, 1991). If you need to write test items, you should consult these sources. However, writing good items remains an art rather than a science. There is no substitute for using precise language, knowing the subject matter, being familiar with the level of examinees, and using your imagination (Wesman, 1971). Once the items are written and have been administered, you can use item analysis techniques to evaluate them.

Item Analysis

A good test has good items. But what are good items? How many times have you been in a class in which students launched a full-scale battle over particular items in a multiple-choice test? Tests with good items are hard to create. Good test making requires careful attention to the principles of test construction. Item analysis, a general term for a set of methods used to evaluate test items, is one of the most important aspects of test construction. The basic methods involve assessment of item difficulty and item discriminability.

Item Difficulty

For a test that measures achievement or ability, item difficulty is defined by the number of people who get a particular item correct. For example, if 84% of the people taking a particular test get item 24 correct, then the difficulty level for that item is .84. Some people have suggested that these proportions do not really indicate item "difficulty" but item "easiness." The higher the proportion of people who get the item correct, the easier the item (M. J. Allen & Yen, 1979).

How hard should items be in a good test? This depends on the uses of the test and the types of items. The first thing a test constructor needs to determine is the probability that an item could be answered correctly by chance alone. A true/false item could be answered correctly half the time if people just guessed randomly. Thus, a true/false item with a difficulty level of .50 would not be a good item. A multiple-choice item with four alternatives could be answered correctly 25% of the time. Therefore, we would require difficulty greater than 25% for an item to be reasonable in this context. Other obvious limits are the extremes of the scale. An item that is answered correctly by 100% of the respondents offers little value because it does not discriminate among individuals.

The optimum difficulty level for items is usually about halfway between 100% of the respondents getting the item correct and the level of success expected by chance alone. Thus, the optimum difficulty level for a four-choice multiple-choice item is about .625. To arrive at this value, we take the 100% success level (1.00) and subtract from it the chance performance level (.25). Then we divide the result by 2 to find the halfway point and add this value to the expected chance level. The steps are outlined here.

Step 1. Find half of the difference between 100% success and chance performance.

$$\frac{100. - .25}{2} = \frac{.75}{2} = .375$$

Step 2. Add this value to the probability of performing correctly by chance.

$$
\begin{array}{c}
\text{Chance} \\
\text{performance} \\
\downarrow \\
.375 + .25 = .625 \\
\swarrow \qquad\qquad \searrow \\
\text{Midway} \qquad \text{Optimum item} \\
\text{point} \qquad\quad \text{difficulty}
\end{array}
$$

A simpler method for obtaining the same result is to add 1.00 to chance performance and divide by 2.0. For this example, the result would be

$$\frac{.25 + 1.0}{2.00} = .625$$

In most tests, all the items should not have equal difficulty but should represent a variety of difficulty levels. This is important because a good test discriminates at a variety of levels. For example, a professor who wants to determine how much his or her students have studied might like to discriminate between students who have not studied at all and those who have studied just a little. Furthermore, the professor might want to discriminate between students who have studied just a little and those who have studied a fair amount. Finally, he or she might want to distinguish those students who have studied more than average from those who have worked and studied exceptionally hard. In other words, the professor needs to make many discriminations. To accomplish this, he or she requires items at many different levels of difficulty.

For most tests, items in the difficulty range of .30 to .70 tend to maximize information about the differences among individuals. However, some tests require a concentration of more-difficult items. For example, if a test is to be used to select medical students and only a small number of qualified applicants can be accepted, a test with more difficult items will make finer discriminations. Conversely, a test used to select students for educable mentally challenged classes should have a greater concentration of easier items to make fine discriminations among individuals who ordinarily do not perform well on tests (M. J. Allen & Yen, 1979). In constructing a good test, one also must give some consideration to human factors. For example, though items answered correctly by all students will have poor psychometric qualities, they may help the morale of the students who take the test. A few easier items may help keep test anxiety in check, which in turn adds to the reliability of the test. Although we have discussed item analysis in relation to achievement tests, the same methods can be used to evaluate other measures. For example, instead of considering an item as right or wrong, one could set it up to indicate whether it is or is not associated with a particular diagnosis, group membership, etc.

Item difficulty is only one way to evaluate test items. Another way is to examine the relationship between performance on particular items and performance on the whole test. This is known as **discriminability**.

Discriminability

In the previous section, we discussed the analysis of item difficulty. These procedures are used to determine the proportion of people who succeed on a particular item. Another way to examine the value of items is to ask, "Who gets this item correct?" Assessment of **item discriminability** is used to determine whether the people who have done well on particular items have also done well on the whole test. One can evaluate the discriminability of test items in many ways.

The extreme group method. This method compares people who have done very well and those who have done very poorly on a test. For example, you might find the students with test scores in the top third and those in the bottom third of the class. Then you can find the proportions of people in each group who got each item correct. The difference between these proportions is the discrimination index. Technical Box 6-1 demonstrates this method.

The point biserial method. Another way to examine the discriminability of items is to find the correlation between performance on the item and performance on the total test. You might remember from Chapter 3 that the correlation between a dichotomous (two-category) variable and a continuous variable is called a *point biserial correlation*. The point biserial correlation between an item and a total test score is

$$r_{pbis} = \left[\frac{\overline{Y}_1 - \overline{Y}}{S_y} \right] \sqrt{\frac{P_x}{1 - P_x}}$$

where r_{pbis} = the point biserial correlation or index of discriminability

$\overline{Y}_1$ = the mean score on the test for those who got item 1 correct

$\overline{Y}$ = the mean score on the test for all persons

S_y = the standard deviation of the exam scores for all persons

P_x = the proportion of persons getting the item correct (from Allen & Yen, 1979)

For example, suppose that 58% of the students in a psychology class gave the correct response to item 15 on their midterm exam. The mean score on the

---

TECHNICAL BOX 6-1

Finding the Item Discrimination Index by Using the Extreme Group Method

Step 1. Identify a group of students who have done well on the test—for example, those in the 67th percentile and above. Also identify a group who have done poorly—for example, those in the 33rd percentile and below.

Step 2. Find the proportion of students in the high group and the proportion of students in the low group who got each item correct.

Step 3. For each item, subtract the proportion of correct responses for the low group from the proportion of correct responses for the high group. This gives the item discrimination index (d_i).

Example

Item Number	Proportion Correct for Students in the Top Third of Class (P_t)	Proportion Correct for Students in the Bottom Third of Class (P_b)	Discriminability Index ($d_i = P_t - P_b$)
1	.89	.34	.55
2	.76	.36	.40
3	.97	.45	.52
4	.98	.95	.03
5	.56	.74	−.18

In this example, items 1, 2, and 3 appear to discriminate reasonably well. Item 4 does not discriminate well, because the level of success is high for both groups; it must be too easy. Item 5 appears to be a bad item because it is a "negative discriminator." This sometimes happens on multiple-choice examinations when overprepared students find some reason to disqualify the response keyed as "correct."

whole test for these students who got item 15 correct was 57.6, and the mean score for the entire class was 54.3. The standard deviation on the test was 9.7. To calculate the discriminability of item 15 by the point biserial method, you would enter this information into the formula:

$$\left(\frac{57.6 - 54.3}{9.7}\right)\sqrt{\frac{.58}{.42}} = .34 \times \sqrt{1.38} = (.34)(1.17) = .40$$

In other words, the correlation between succeeding on item 15 and total test performance is .40.

On tests with only a few items, using the point biserial correlation is problematic, because performance on the item contributes to the total test score. For example, if a test has six items, there is bound to be a positive correlation between getting a particular item correct and the total test score because one sixth of the total score is performance on that item. To compensate for this problem, it is sometimes advisable to exclude the item from the total test score. For the six-item test, we might look at the point biserial correlation between passing item 1 and the test score derived from items 2 through 6.

The point biserial correlation (r_{pbis}) between an item and the total test score is evaluated in very much the same way as the extreme group discriminability index. If this value is negative or low, the item should be eliminated from the test. The closer the value of the index is to 1.0, the better the item. Note that very easy items, such as those answered correctly by 90% or more, usually do not appear to be good items on the discriminability index. If 90% of test takers get an item correct, there is too little variability in performance for a substantial correlation with the total test score.

Pictures of Item Characteristics

A valuable way to learn about items is to graph their characteristics, which you can do with the **item characteristic curve.** A graph can be prepared for particular items in which the total test score is plotted on the *x*, or horizontal, axis and the proportion of examinees who get the items correct is plotted on the *y*, or vertical, axis. The total test score is used as an estimate of the amount of the "trait" possessed by individuals. Because we can never measure traits directly, the total test score is the best approximation we have. Thus, the relationship between performance on the item and performance on the test gives some information about how well the item is tapping the information we are interested in.

Drawing the item characteristic curve. To draw the item characteristic curve, you need to define discrete categories of test performance. If the test has been given to many people, you can have a category for each test score (65, 66, 67, and so on). However, if the test has been given to a smaller group, you might use a smaller number of class intervals (such as 66–68, 69–71). Once you have arrived at these categories, you need to determine what proportion of the people within each category got each item correct. For example, you must determine what proportion of the people with a total test score of 65 got item 34 correct, what proportion of the people with a total test score of 66 got item 34 correct, and so on. Once this series of breakdowns has been obtained, a plot of the proportions of correct responses to an item by total test scores is created. Examples of these graphs are shown in Figures 6-2 to 6-6.

Figure 6-2 shows the item characteristic curve for a "good" test item. The gradual positive slope of the line demonstrates that the proportion of people who pass the item gradually increases as test scores increase. This means that the item successfully discriminates at all levels of test performance. The curve shown in Figure 6-3 illustrates an item that discriminates very well between people at the lower level of performance. However, because all the people who scored above average on the test got this item correct, it did not provide much discrimination in the higher ranges of performance.

Figure 6-4 shows a variety of item characteristic curves. The items shown in the figure are each sensitive in a particular range. Figures 6-5 and 6-6 show item characteristic curves for poor items. The flat curve in Figure 6-5 indicates that test takers at all levels of ability were equally likely to get the item correct. Figure 6-6 demonstrates a particularly troublesome problem. The item characteristic curve gradually rises, showing that the item is sensitive to most levels

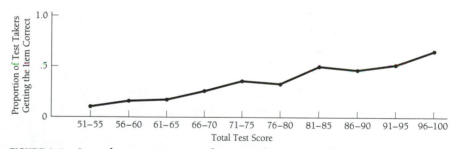

FIGURE 6-2   *Item characteristic curve for a "good" test item. The proportion of test takers who get the item correct increases as a function of the total test score.*

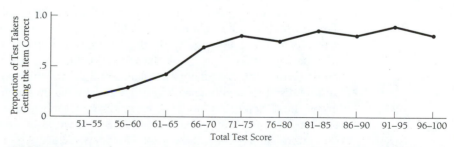

FIGURE 6-3   *Item characteristic curve for a test item that discriminates well at low levels of performance but not at higher levels.*

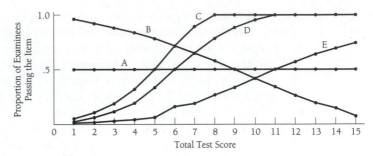

FIGURE 6-4 *Item characteristic curves for several items.*
(From Allen and Yen, 1979.)

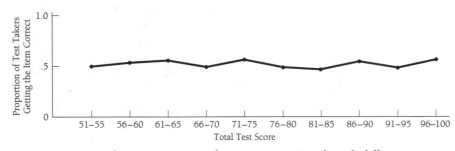

FIGURE 6-5 *Item characteristic curve for a poor item. People with different test scores were equally likely to get the item correct.*

of performance. Then it turns down for people at the highest levels of performance, suggesting that those with the best overall performance on the test did not have the best chances of getting the item correct. This can happen on multiple-choice examinations when one of the alternatives is "none of the above." Students who are exceptionally knowledgeable in the subject area can sometimes rule out all the choices even though one of the alternatives had actually been designated as correct.

Another convenient picture of item characteristics is shown in Figure 6-7. This graph plots the item numbers within the space created by difficulty on one axis and discriminability (in this case point biserial correlation between item passage and test score) on the other axis. Item 12 has been circled on the graph so that you can identify it. Of all respondents, 46% got this item correct, and its discriminability level is .60. Thus, item 12 on the graph is adjacent to 46 on the difficulty axis and .60 on the discriminability axis. Earlier in the discussion we noted that "good" items usually fall within the range of .30 and .70 on item difficulty. Thus, these boundaries represent the region with acceptable levels of difficulty and discriminability. The shaded region within these boundaries represents the region in which acceptable levels of difficulty and discrim-

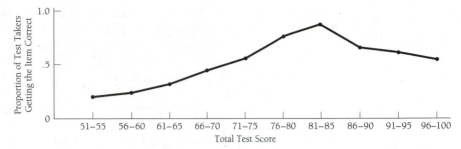

FIGURE 6-6 *Another example of a problem item. Sometimes test takers who "know too much" will rule out the alternative designated as correct.*

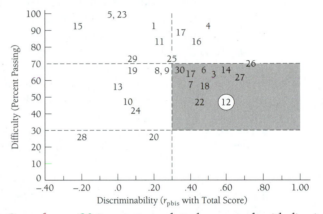

FIGURE 6-7 *Items from a 30-item test are plotted on a graph with discriminability on one axis and difficulty on the other. Each number on the graph represents a test item: 1 is for item 1 and so on. The shaded area represents items above a discriminability level of .30 and between 30% and 70% in difficulty level. These items would be the best candidates to include in the final version of the test. Item 12 (circled) was passed by 46% of the respondents and was correlated .60 with total test score. Thus, it should be retained.*

inability are achieved. Thus, items for the final version of the test should be selected from this area.

Item response theory. The new approaches to item analysis have generated a new model of psychological testing. According to classical test theory, a score is derived from the sum of an individual's responses to various items, which are sampled from a larger domain representing a specific trait or ability. Newer approaches to testing based on item analysis consider the chances of getting particular items right or wrong. These approaches, now known as *item response theory* (IRT), make extensive use of item analysis (Cascio, 1987; Steinberg & Thissen, 1995). According to these approaches, each item on a test has its own item characteristic curve that describes the probability of getting each particular item right or wrong given the ability of the test takers. With the computer, items can be sampled, and the specific range of items where the test taker begins to have difficulty can be identified. In this way, testers can make an ability judgment without subjecting the test taker to all the test items.

There are various approaches to the construction of tests using item response theory. Some of the approaches use the two dimensions shown in Figure 6-7: difficulty and discriminability. Other approaches add a third dimension for the probability of test takers with very low levels of ability getting a correct response. Still other approaches use only the difficulty parameter. All the approaches grade items in relation to the probability that those who do well or poorly on the exam will have different levels of performance. One can average item characteristic curves to create a test characteristic curve, which gives the proportion of responses expected to be correct for each level of ability (Guion & Ironson, 1983).

Perhaps the most attractive advantage of tests based on item response theory is that one can easily adapt them for computer administration. The computer can rapidly identify the specific items required to assess a particular ability level. With this approach, test takers do not have to suffer the embarrassment of attempting multiple items beyond their level of ability. Conversely, they do not need to waste their time and effort on items far below their capability. In addition, each test taker may get different items to answer, greatly reducing the chances of cheating. It has been suggested that computer-adapted testing will increase efficiency by 50% or more by reducing the amount of time each test taker spends responding to items (Weiss, 1985; Weiss & Yoes, 1991).

Figure 6-8 shows the measurement precision associated with conventional and computer-adapted tests. Most conventional tests have the majority of their

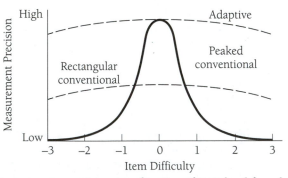

FIGURE 6-8 *Measurement precision as a function of trait level for adaptive, peaked, and rectangular conventional tests. Adaptive tests based on item response theory (IRT) have higher precision across the range of ability levels.*
(From Weiss, 1985.)

items at or near an average level of difficulty, represented by the "peaked conventional" portion of the figure. Though the precision of the test is very good for those at average ability levels, those with very low or very high ability levels are not well assessed by this type of test. An alternative approach, labeled "rectangular conventional" in Figure 6-8, requires that test items be selected to create a wide range in level of difficulty. These items are pretested and selected to cover evenly the span from very easy to very difficult. The problem with this approach is that only a few items of the test are appropriate for individuals at each ability level; that is, many test takers spend much of their time responding to items either considerably below their ability level or too difficult to solve. As a result, measurement precision is constant across the range of test-taker abilities but relatively low for all people, as shown in Figure 6-8.

The supporters of item response theory believe the solution to this problem lies in computer-adaptive testing. The computer samples items and determines the range on the ability continuum that best represents each test taker. Then testing time is spent focusing on the specific range that challenges the respondent, specifically, items that have a 50% probability of a correct response (assuming no guessing) for each individual. This results in a measurement instrument of equally high precision for all test takers.

Many critics have asserted that computer-adaptive testing using item response theory is not feasible. However, a variety of computer-adaptive tests are now available, and there is growing enthusiasm for this approach (Weiss, 1985). Presently, computers are used in many different aspects of psychological testing (Fowler, 1985).

External criteria. Item analysis has been persistently plagued by the continued dependence on internal criteria against which to evaluate items. By *internal criteria* we mean total test score. The examples we have just given demonstrate how to compare performance on an item with performance on the total test. You can use similar procedures to compare performance on an item with performance on an external criterion. For example, if you were building a test to select airplane pilots, you might want to evaluate how well individual items predict success in pilot training or flying performance. The advantages of using external rather than internal criteria against which to validate items were outlined by Guttman (1950) more than 45 years ago. Nevertheless, external criteria are rarely used in practice (Linn, 1994a, 1994b).

Items for Criterion-Referenced Tests

In Chapter 2, we briefly mentioned the concept of criterion-referenced testing. The traditional use of tests requires that we determine how well someone has done on a test by comparing the person's performance to that of others. For example, the meaning of Jeff's 67 on a geography test is interpreted by his percentile rank in the geography class. Another way of evaluating Jeff's performance is to ask how much he learned in comparison to how much he "should

FIGURE 6-9
Frequency polygon used to evaluate a criterion-referenced test.

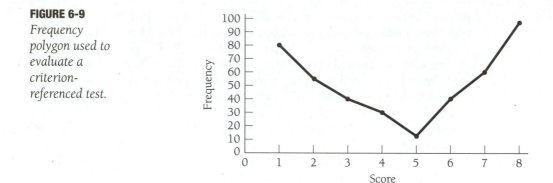

have" learned. Jeff is no longer in competition with everyone else. Instead, we have defined what Jeff must do to be considered knowledgeable about a certain unit. How much Jeff knows rather than whether or not he knows more than someone else determines his grade.

A *criterion-referenced test* compares performance with some clearly defined criterion for mastery. This approach is popular in individualized instruction programs. For each student, a set of objectives is defined that state exactly what the student should be able to do after an educational experience. For example, an objective for a junior-high algebra student might be to solve linear equations with two unknowns. The criterion-referenced test would be used to determine whether this objective had been achieved. After demonstrating this knowledge, the student could move ahead to another objective. Many educators regard criterion-referenced tests as diagnostic instruments. When a student does poorly on some items, the teacher knows that the individualized education program needs more focus in a particular area.

Many problems arise in the development of criterion-referenced tests. The first step involves clearly specifying the objectives by writing clear and precise statements about what the learning program is attempting to achieve. These statements are usually stated in terms of something the student will be able to do. For example, a unit in high-school civics might aim at getting students to understand the operation of municipal government. Test items that assess the attainment of this objective might ask about the taxation powers of local governments, the relation of municipal to state government, and so on.

To evaluate the items in the criterion-referenced test, one should give the test to two groups of students—one that has been exposed to the learning unit and one that has not. Figure 6-9 shows what the distribution of scores would look like. The frequency polygon looks like a V. The scores on the left side of the V are probably those from students who have not experienced the unit. Scores on the right represent those who have been exposed to the unit. The bottom of the V is the *antimode,* or the least frequent score. This point divides those who have been exposed to the unit from those who have not been exposed and is usually taken as the cutting point. When people get scores higher than the antimode, we assume that they have met the objective of the test. When they get lower scores, we assume they have not. In Figure 6-9 the cutting score is 5.

Criterion-referenced tests offer many advantages for newer approaches to education such as computer-assisted instruction. For example, a large program created by the American Institutes for Research and the Westinghouse Learning Corporation involves students obtaining much of their education by interacting with a computer terminal. Each student works at his or her own pace on an individualized program of instruction, after which a criterion-referenced test is used to evaluate progress. Students who pass the test can move on to the next unit. Students who do not pass can repeat some of the instruction until they pass. Some people feel this approach to education maximizes individual potential (J. C. Flanagan, 1971).

Limitations of Item Analysis

The growing interest in criterion-referenced tests has posed new questions about the adequacy of item analysis procedures. The main problem is this: Though statistical methods for item analysis tell the test constructor which items do a good job of separating students, they do not help the students learn. Young children do not care as much about how many items they missed as they do about what they are doing wrong (Davis, 1979). Many times a child will make very specific errors and will continue to make them until discovering why he or she is making the mistakes.

For example, an achievement test might ask a fourth-grade student to add .40 and .30. One of the multiple-choice alternatives would be .07 because item analysis had demonstrated that this was a good distractor. The child who selected .07 would not receive a point on the item and also might continue to make similar errors. Although the data are available to give the child feedback on the "bug" in his or her thinking, nothing in the testing procedure initiates this guidance (Linn, 1994a). One study involving 1300 fourth-, fifth-, and sixth-graders found that 40% of the children made the same type of error when given problems of a particular kind (J. S. Brown & Burton, 1978). Some researchers in educational measurement now appear to be moving toward testing programs that diagnose as well as assess (Linn, 1994a, 1994b, Linn & Burton, 1994). Tests can have different purposes. In the past, many have placed too much emphasis on ranking students and not enough on discovering specific weaknesses or gaps in knowledge.

Summary

There is an art and a science to test construction. Writing good items is a complex and demanding task. The first step involves deciding what sort of information you are trying to obtain. True/false items may be used if you are attempting to evaluate absolute judgment. A similar format used to evaluate whether or not test takers know "the right information" is multiple-choice, in which a correct choice must be selected among several alternatives. With these types of formats, the test constructor always must consider the probability that someone will get an answer correct by chance.

Many formats are available for tests that do not have right or wrong answers. The Likert format is popular for attitude scales. In this format, respondents check on a 5-point scale the degree to which they agree or disagree with the given statements. Similarly, in the category-scaling method, ratings are obtained on a scale with defined endpoints. The familiar 10-point scale is an example of a category scale. Unfortunately, category scales are subject to some bias when the endpoints are not clearly defined. Checklists and Q-sorts number among the many item formats used in personality research. These methods require people to make judgments about whether certain items describe themselves or others.

Once you have created test items, you can administer them to groups of individuals and systematically assess the values of the items. One method of item analysis requires evaluation of item difficulty, usually assessed by examining the number of people who get each item correct. In addition to difficulty analysis, test constructors usually examine the correlation between getting any item correct and the total test score. This correlation is used as an index of *discriminability*.

Another way to learn about the value of items is to draw a picture of the *item characteristic curve*. For example, the proportion of people who get an item correct can be plotted as a function of the total test score. The best items are those for which the probability of getting the item correct is highest among those with the highest test scores.

Criterion-referenced tests require a different approach to test construction. With such tests, a person's knowledge is evaluated against what he or she is expected to know rather than against what others know. To evaluate items in criterion-referenced tests, one compares performance for those who would be expected to know the material with performance of others who would not be expected to have mastered the information.

CHAPTER 7

Selection and Decision Analysis

LEARNING OBJECTIVES

When you have completed this chapter, you should be able to:

- Discuss the proper methods for selecting a meaningful test

- Identify the first consideration in determining whether it is worthwhile to administer a test

- Explain the meaning of base rates in personnel selection

- Identify three methods for estimating the amount of information a test gives beyond what is known by chance

- Define incremental validity

- Discuss the significance of utility and decision theory

- Explain the problem with utility theory equations

- List several sources that contain valuable information about psychological tests

O f the literally thousands of psychological tests, some are valuable, others are useless. As a student of psychology, you will need to learn how to be a good consumer of testing materials.

Table 7-1 presents two sets of items from two "tests." One set is from the Experiential World Inventory, the other from the writings of the columnist and humorist Art Buchwald. Though both sets seem ridiculous, one set claims to have a purpose beyond providing humor. Can you tell which test is which?

Just because the promoters of a personality test known as the Experiential World Inventory argue that their measure is valuable, you do not have to accept their opinion. Instead, you must carefully evaluate it yourself. Do items that ask about drinking blood have more meaning than those that ask about being bored by thoughts of death? The answer depends on the evidence the test constructors have to support the meaning of their test. In this case, the Experiential World Inventory offers little reason to believe that scores on this test are more meaningful than the scores on a purely humorous test created by Art Buchwald.

This chapter will review methods for selecting a meaningful test. These methods assess whether the test results will provide useful information.

The Test Manual

Before you use a test, you must consider many things. Tests are categorized as proprietary and nonproprietary. A *proprietary* test is owned by a test developer or a publishing company and is protected by copyright laws; thus, a user must pay to use it. The items on proprietary tests are protected and generally kept restricted. For example, unless you are a professional psychologist, you probably would not have access to the items from widely used tests such as the Minnesota Multiphasic Personality Inventory or the Stanford-Binet intelligence scales. *Nonproprietary* tests are not protected by copyright in the same way. Most often they are distributed by the test developer or are published in jour-

TABLE 7-1

Items from Two Personality Scales

Set 1	Set 2
The sight of blood no longer excites me.	Animals often try to fool me.
It makes me furious to see an innocent man escape the chair.	I feel like killing untidy people.
When I was a child, I was an imaginary playmate.	I sometimes taste sound.
I am bored by thoughts of death.	Someone is making copies of me.
I become homicidal when people try to reason with me.	I sometimes think other people's thoughts.
I don't like it when somebody is rotten.	I am afraid somebody may cut off my nose.
Most of the time I go to sleep without saying goodbye.	Old men are indecent.
Frantic screams make me nervous.	I am someone else.
	I would like to drink blood
	I feel that my ideas may turn into insects.

From "Objective Personality Tests and Measures" by L. R. Goldberg. Reproduced, with permission, from the *Annual Review of Psychology*, Vol. 25. © 1974 by Annual Reviews, Inc. (Set 1 is from Art Buchwald's column, and set 2 is from the Experiential World Inventory.)

nals. For example, the Internal-External Locus of Control Scale (Rotter, 1966), one of the most widely used measures in personality research, was published in an academic journal. Most users of this scale simply copy the items from the article and pay no royalty. Even so, before you use test items in a written publication, you should check with the publisher. The June/July 1981 *APA Monitor* reported that *Boston Magazine* was required to pay psychologist Zick Rubin $5000 for using his love questionnaire without permission (Foltz, 1981).

Testing is a large and profitable business that has not been controlled. In many ways, the use of psychological tests resembles the use of prescription drugs. Although there are no toxic effects from the tests, people could be unnecessarily hurt if the tests classified them improperly. For a new drug to get on the market, it must meet the standards of the Food and Drug Administration (FDA). No equivalent agency monitors the standards for psychological tests. In place of a federal bureau responsible for overseeing psychological tests, a joint committee of the American Education Research Association, the American Psychological Association, and the National Council for Measurement in Education (1985) created standards and published them in *Standards for Educational and Psychological Testing.* The short booklet provides a clear set of standards for test developers and users and defines the minimum information necessary for a test manual. Proprietary tests are protected by copyright. Often, the holder of the copyright charges a fee for their use. In order to protect consumers, the testing community emphasizes that proprietary tests should meet at least a minimum standard

Many psychologists find proprietary tests best suited for their purposes. To use this kind of test, you need to be a qualified test administrator, one with appropriate training and experience. To decide whether the test was suited for your purpose, you would need to consult the test manual.

The test manual should give all the basic information needed to administer a test, to score it, and to make sense out of the results. If a test manual is constructed according to the *Standards* defined by the joint committee, it will answer most of the questions you have about validity, reliability, and norms. Because we covered these topics in earlier chapters, you should have a good feel for the meaning of norms and the minimum standards for reliability and validity. When evaluating a test, you should ask a series of questions; these are summarized in Table 7-2.

For many industrial applications, other factors also must be considered, such as the amount of information the test gives beyond what is known without it. This can be derived from an analysis of base and hit rates.

Base Rates and Hit Rates

Tests must be evaluated in terms of how much they contribute beyond what would be known without them. Often, tests are used to place individuals into one of two categories. For example, on the basis of an employment test, a can-

TABLE 7-2

Checklist of Questions the Test Manual Should Answer

Standardization Sample

1. How many subjects were used to establish the reliability, validity, and norms for the test?
2. What were the demographic and personal characteristics of these subjects? Are they similar to those of the group you will give the test to?

Reliability

1. What methods were used to estimate the reliability of the test?
2. Is the reliability high enough for your purposes (usually .90 or above for tests used to make decisions about individuals and .70 or above for research purposes)?

Validity

1. Is there evidence that the test is meaningful for *your* purposes?
2. What specific criteria was the test validated against?

Scoring

1. Are scoring keys available?
2. If the test can be scored by machine, how much does it cost and what sort of report is offered?

Practical Considerations

1. How long does it take to administer the test?
2. Does the test require reading? If so, is it at the right level for the people you will test?
3. How much training is required for the test administrator? How can the training be obtained?

didate can be deemed acceptable or unacceptable. In a medical setting, a test may determine whether or not a person has a tumor in a certain area of the brain. Because tests vary in their accuracy, one must examine the possibility of erroneously assigning someone to a category.

If a test is used to make a dichotomous (two-choice) decision, a cutoff score usually is used. Values above this score might go into the plus category, with values below it into the minus category. The plus category might indicate that the person is suitable for the job or that he or she has the tumor. The score marking the point of decision is called the *cutting score*. Establishing a cutting score, though, does not insure correct decisions. For example, suppose that a person scores above the cutting score for an employment test but later fails on the job. This suggests that the test has not done its job.

Tests can be evaluated by how well they sort people into the right categories. For example, in a test that determines which people to hire for a particular job, those who score above the cutting score might be labeled "acceptable" and those below it "unacceptable." In addition to the scores on the test, one must have some data on how people really do on the job. To do this, the employer must define some criterion for deciding whether job performance has been acceptable or unacceptable. Using these two sets of categories, we can construct a chart such as that shown in Table 7-3. There are four cells in this table. Two of the four cells are labeled "Hit" because the test has made the correct prediction. *Hits* occur when (1) the test predicts that the person will be unacceptable and he or she does fail, or (2) the test indicates that the person is

TABLE 7-3

Hits and Misses for Predicting a Dichotomous Outcome Using a Cutting Score

	Decision on the Basis of Cutting Score	
Performance on the Job	**Acceptable**	**Unacceptable**
Success	Hit	Miss
Failure	Miss	Hit

acceptable and he or she does succeed. *Misses* occur when the test makes an inaccurate prediction. The **hit rate** is the percent of cases in which a test accurately predicts success or failure.

Often, a test does not need a good hit rate, because the rate of predicting success on the job is high without the test. For example, admissions officers might predict who will do well in law school on the basis of information other than scores on the Law School Admissions Test (LSAT). They might use college grades. Success on the criterion in this case might be passing the bar examination on the first attempt. The pass rate not using the LSAT would be called the **base rate.** The real value of a test comes from a comparison of the hit rate with the base rate. In other words, the hit rate must tell us how much information a test contributes to the prediction of success beyond what we would know by just examining the proportion of people who succeed.

For example, suppose the LSAT has a hit rate of 76% for predicting who will pass the bar examination in a certain state. However, 85% of the people who take the test for the first time in that state pass. The LSAT in this case tells us less than the available information. In other cases, you could imagine a low hit rate and an even lower base rate. For example, suppose you need to select people for a position that will involve world-class competition. Under the circumstances, very few people could be expected to do well—say only 3% would be expected to succeed. If a test could be developed that had a 10% hit rate, it might be considered valuable.

Another problem to consider with regard to hit and miss rates is relative cost. Medical situations provide good examples of costly misses. Consider the cost of concluding on the basis of a test that a tumor is benign (not cancerous) when it is really malignant (cancerous). The cost of this sort of miss is that the life of the patient is seriously endangered. In a psychological application, concluding that someone is not suicidal because he or she is below the cutoff score when, in fact, there is suicide potential may allow a preventable suicide. These cases are **false negatives.** If the cost of a false negative is high, you might lower the cutting score. With a lower cutting score, the test will make more but safer errors.

The other type of miss is the **false positive.** For example, say someone is selected for a job on the basis of a test. Once on the job, the person does poorly and gets fired. High costs sometimes accompany this type of error. For instance, time and money might be invested to train a person who cannot really do the job. In addition, job failure can deal a blow to the person's self-esteem and self-confidence. If the costs of a false positive are high, you may want to raise the cutting score.

A few examples may help clarify the concepts of hits and misses for different base rates. Table 7-4 presents a medical example in which a test indicates whether or not a patient has brain damage. In a validation study, an expensive radiological procedure is used to confirm whether the patient actually has brain damage. The radiological test suggests that 23 of 100 patients have brain damage, while the other 77 are normal. The table also shows the actual number of patients who have brain damage or are normal. In reality, 10 of the 100 have damage, while 90 are normal.

There are two types of hits in Table 7-4. For the 10 patients who actually have brain damage, 8 are detected by the tests. In other words, the test has a detection rate of 80%. In addition, the test says that 75 individuals are normal who, it is confirmed, are actually normal. Both of these cases are hits because the test produces the correct result. There are 83 cases in 100 when the test produces an accurate conclusion; that is, the test has 83% accuracy.

There are also two types of misses. In two cases, the test suggests that a person is normal when he or she actually has brain damage. Those are false negatives. In addition, there are 15 false positives, or cases in which the test suggests that a person has a problem when in fact he or she is normal.

The cells in Table 7-4 are labeled A, B, C, and D. Cells A and D are hit cells. The sum of these cells divided by the sum of all cells (A + B + C + D) is the accuracy rate. Cell B is a false negative, cell C a false positive. Cell A divided by the sum of A and B is the detection rate.

TABLE 7-4

Hypothetical Example of Hits and Misses, with 83% Accuracy and 80% Detection*

		Test Result		
		Brain Damage	**Normal**	**Total**
	Brain Damage	A 8	B 2	10
Actual	**Normal**	C 15	D 75	90
	Total	23	77	100

A = hit   A + B = base rate
B = false negative
C = false positive
D = hit
A/(A + B) = detection rate (sensitivity)
D/(C + D) = specificity
(A + D)/(A + B + C + D) = accuracy rate

* We are grateful to Dr. Frank M. Rosekrans, Eastern Washington University, for suggesting this example.

The example in Table 7-4 suggests that the test is relatively good at detecting brain damage. One of the reasons the test works well in this situation is that the base rate for brain damage is relatively low. In actuality, only 10% of the patients have this problem, and the test detects 80% of the cases.

Now consider the example in Table 7-5. In this case, a test is used on a population with a very high base rate for brain damage (90%). The test suggests that 50 of 100 people have brain damage when, in fact, 90 of 100 people have the problem. The test is accurate in 44% (40/90 = .44) of the cases. In this example, there are only 10 false positives. The test, however, has a high false-negative rate. Finally, the table suggests that the test never concludes that someone is normal when he or she does not have a problem.

False negatives and false positives may have different meanings, depending on their context. For example, a variety of methods have been developed to predict antisocial behavior in children. Childhood aggression is a good predictor of later aggressive behavior (Dishion, Andrews, & Crosby, 1995). However, measures of childhood aggression will identify some children as potentially dangerous who turn out not to be aggressive when they are older (O'Donnell, Hawkins, & Abbott, 1995). These are false positives. In fact, up to half the cases may be false positives (Lochman, 1995). A program that identifies and treats high-risk youth may subject many to unnecessary treatment. On one extreme, some people believe high-risk youth should be under police surveillance. Because of false positives, these programs would unjustly deprive some youth of their rights.

TABLE 7-5

Hypothetical Example of Hits and Misses, with 40% Accuracy and 44% Detection*

		Test Result		
		Brain Damage	**Normal**	**Total**
	Brain Damage	A 40	B 50	90
Actual	**Normal**	C 10	D 0	10
	Total	50	50	100

A = hit   A + B = base rate

B = false negative

C = false positive

D = hit

A/(A + B) = detection rate (sensitivity)

D/(C + D) = specificity

(A + D)/(A + B + C + D) = accuracy rate

* We are grateful to Dr. Frank M. Rosekrans, Eastern Washington University, for suggesting this example.

Using cutting scores to find hits and misses involves criterion validity (see Chapter 5). Many years ago, H. C. Taylor and J. T. Russell (1939) demonstrated how to relate validity coefficients to accuracy rates in selection.

Taylor-Russell Tables

The decision to use a test must depend on what the test offers. In Chapter 5, we showed that tests with significant predictive or concurrent validity coefficients did better than chance in forecasting performance on a criterion. However, knowing that a test is better than chance is not good enough for making choices about whether it will serve in some applications. In the previous section, we noted that a worthwhile test must provide more information than do the base rates alone.

In 1939, Taylor and Russell developed a method for evaluating the validity of a test in relation to the amount of information it contributes beyond the base rates. This method is neatly summarized in a series of tables known as the **Taylor-Russell tables.** To use them, you must have the following information:

1. *Definition of success.* For each situation in which the test is to be used, success on the outcome must be defined. This could be that the patient lived, that the person succeeded on the job, or that the student did well in college. One must define success clearly by dichotomizing some outcome variable. For example, first-year grade point averages above 2.3 might be defined as success in college and those below might be defined as failures. Or salespersons who achieve average monthly sales over $5000 might be deemed successful, and those who sell less than $5000 might be thought of as unsuccessful.

2. *Determination of base rate.* The percentage of people who would succeed if there were no testing or screening procedure must be determined.

3. *Definition of selection ratio.* The **selection ratio** must be defined. This is the percentage of applicants selected or admitted.

4. *Determination of validity coefficient.* Finally, a validity coefficient for the test, usually the correlation of the test with the criterion, is required.

The Taylor-Russell tables give the likelihood that a person selected on the basis of the test score will actually succeed. There is a different table for each base rate. Table 7-6 is a Taylor-Russell table for a base rate of .60.

To use the table, find the row representing the validity of the test that would be used for selection. Then find the column associated with the proportion of people who can be selected. The number in the body of the table associated with a particular row and a particular column gives you an estimate of the percentage of people who could be expected to succeed when they are selected on the basis of the test.

For example, suppose that you are put in charge of deciding who will be admitted to a program to train secondary-education teachers. The first thing

Focused Example 7-1

THE MAMMOGRAPHY CONTROVERSY

 Medical tests resemble psychological tests in that they both have validity and reliability and can be assessed in relation to their hit rates and miss rates. One interesting controversy involves the use of mammography to screen women for breast cancer. Mammography has clearly been shown to be a valuable medical test for women age 50 and older. Some controversy, however, surrounds its use for younger women. The reason for this controversy is related to the base rates and the rates of false positives and false negatives.

Breast cancer is very much related to age. Although the American Cancer Society argues that one in nine women will develop breast cancer, these tumors are much more common among older women than among younger ones (see Figure 7-1). For women in their 20s, breast cancer is an extremely rare disease. In fact, 100,000 mammograms would have to be performed to find one such woman with breast cancer. This suggests that for younger women the base rate for breast cancer is very low (1/100,000). This has become somewhat of a controversy because the popular media have launched a campaign attempting to increase the use of mammography for all women. If we pay for

mammography from public funds, and the cost of a mammogram is $100, it would cost about $10 million to detect one case. Of course, any investment would be valuable if it saved lives. However, analyses of studies of breast cancer suggest that the rare case of breast cancer detected in young women results in no better chance of survival than a case left undetected. Even so, this remains a matter of considerable debate in the medical community.

The related concern for performing mammography in younger women is that breast tissue in young women is denser than it is in older women. As a result, there is a significant number of false positives in younger women. It has been estimated that one younger woman in three who gets repeated mammograms will have a false positive that requires further medical tests or biopsies (A. B. Miller, 1991).

What does this tell us? Clearly, mammography has been shown to be a valuable medical test for older women, but for younger women, those in their 20s and early 30s, the picture may be different. There is a very low base rate for the problem, and there is a significant risk of false-positive results. Of course, women with risk factors for breast cancer, such as a strong family history of the condition, may still benefit from routine screening.

FIGURE 7-1

Relationship of age to breast cancer. [Data from National Cancer Institute, Cancer Statistics Review 1973–1988 (Bethesda, MD: July 1991, Table II-40).]

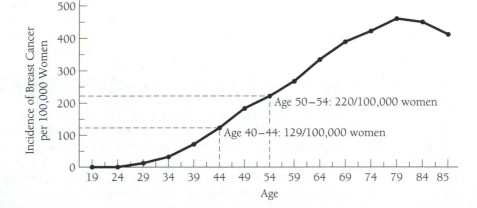

TABLE 7-6

Taylor-Russell Table for a Base Rate of .60

Validity (ρ_{xy})	Selection Ratio										
	.05	.10	.20	.30	.40	.50	.60	.70	.80	.90	.95
.00	.60	.60	.60	.60	.60	.60	.60	.60	.60	.60	.60
.05	.64	.63	.63	.62	.62	.62	.61	.61	.61	.60	.60
.10	.68	.67	.65	.64	.64	.63	.63	.62	.61	.61	.60
.15	.71	.70	.68	.67	.66	.65	.64	.63	.62	.61	.61
.20	.75	.73	.71	.69	.67	.66	.65	.64	.63	.62	.61
.25	.78	.76	.73	.71	.69	.68	.66	.65	.63	.62	.61
.30	.82	.79	.76	.73	.71	.69	.68	.66	.64	.62	.61
.35	.85	.82	.78	.75	.73	.71	.69	.67	.65	.63	.62
.40	.88	.85	.81	.78	.75	.73	.70	.68	.66	.63	.62
.45	.90	.87	.83	.80	.77	.74	.72	.69	.66	.64	.62
.50	.93	.90	.86	.82	.79	.76	.73	.70	.67	.64	.62
.55	.95	.92	.88	.84	.81	.78	.75	.71	.68	.64	.62
.60	.96	.94	.90	.87	.83	.80	.76	.73	.69	.65	.63
.65	.98	.96	.92	.89	.85	.82	.78	.74	.70	.65	.63
.70	.99	.97	.94	.91	.87	.84	.80	.75	.71	.66	.63
.75	.99	.99	.96	.93	.90	.86	.81	.77	.71	.66	.63
.80	1.00	.99	.98	.95	.92	.88	.83	.78	.72	.66	.63
.85	1.00	1.00	.99	.97	.95	.91	.86	.80	.73	.66	.63
.90	1.00	1.00	1.00	.99	.97	.94	.88	.82	.74	.67	.63
.95	1.00	1.00	1.00	1.00	.99	.97	.92	.84	.75	.67	.63
1.00	1.00	1.00	1.00	1.00	1.00	1.00	1.00	.86	.75	.67	.63

From "The Relationship of Validity Coefficients to the Practical Effectiveness of Tests in Selection: Discussion and Tables" by H. C. Taylor and J. T. Russell. *Journal of Applied Psychology,* 1939, *23,* 565–578. Copyright 1939 by the American Psychological Association.

you must do is decide on a definition of success. After meeting with a committee, you may decide that success will be defined as completing the program and obtaining a satisfactory performance evaluation in student teaching. By studying records, you determine that when no selection procedure was used, 60% of the applicants to the program succeeded on this task. Thus, the base rate would be 60%, and the Taylor-Russell table for a base rate of .60 would be used. You then consider using the Graduate Record Examination (GRE) to select people for your program, because you can accept only 70% of the applicants. A study is done, determining that the correlation between GRE scores and success (completing the program and obtaining a satisfactory evaluation in student teaching) is .30. This is the validity of the test for predicting the criterion.

To estimate how many people would be expected to succeed if they are selected on the basis of GRE scores, we must use the Taylor-Russell table (Table 7-6) for a base rate of .60. Find the row associated with the .30 validity and move across the table until you are in the column for a selection ratio of .70 (the percentage of applicants you can admit to your program). You should arrive at the number .66, which is the proportion of applicants you would expect to be successful if the selection was based on the GRE. This analysis tells you that 66% of those selected on the basis of GRE scores can be expected to be successful and 60% of those selected at random can be. Should the GRE be required for admittance to your program? To answer this question, you must decide whether the increment of 6% associated with the use of the test is worth the extra effort and expense of requiring it.

Looking at Table 7-6, you can see that tests will be more valuable in some situations than in others. For example, a test is most useful when the validity of the test is high and the selection ratio is low, as the lower left-hand portion of Table 7-6 shows. Conversely, when the validity is low and the selection ratio is high (the upper right-hand portion of the table), the test will be of little value. When the test has no validity (the first row of the table), using the test will be no better than selecting applicants by chance. Similarly, when nearly everyone is selected (last column), there is little reason to use a test.

Whenever a selection procedure is used, always remember that some qualified applicants will be turned away. The use of rational selection procedures should help make the system more fair by decreasing the number of qualified applicants not selected. One way to evaluate the selection procedure is to show the ratio of people selected by the test who then succeed and the ratio of those who would have succeeded but were not selected.

Suppose that you are the personnel manager for a company and that you can choose 30 of 100 applicants for a job. To make this decision, you have the results of a test with a validity of .70. You also know that the base rate for success on the job is .60. Using the Taylor-Russell table for a base rate of .60, you find that 91% of those selected on the basis of the test would be expected to succeed on the job. Because you can select 30 people, the table implies that approximately 27 of them will succeed and 3 fail (91% of 30 = 27.3).

When you decide to hire 30 of the applicants, you also are deciding not to hire 70 people. It is important to realize that not all of the 70 people would fail if they were selected. In fact, many of them will be capable people whom the testing procedure has "misdiagnosed." To justify your use of the test, it would be your responsibility to explain why your selection procedure is worthwhile even though it turns down some people who would have succeeded and selects some who fail.

Table 7-7 shows what would happen to all the applicants. Of 100, 30 would be accepted and 70 rejected (the selection ratio equals .30). However, because the base rate for success is .60, 60 of the 100 applicants would have succeeded on the job and 40 would have failed. As you have seen, the Taylor-Russell table shows that 91% of those selected on the basis of the test will succeed, or 27 of the 30 selected (.9 × 30 = 27.3), with only about 3 of the 30 to fail.

Among the 60 people who would have succeeded, only 27 could be selected. This means that 33 people who would have been good choices were

TABLE 7-7
*What Would
Happen to 100
Applicants If 30
People Were
Selected on the
Basis of a Test
with a Validity of
.70 for a Job with
a 60% Base
Success Rate?*

	Decision		
Performance	**Select**	**Reject**	**Total**
Success*	27	33	60
Failure	3	37	40
Total	30	70	100

*Success ratio given selection = 27/30 = .90 (actually .91
without rounding, see Table 7-6). Success ratio given rejection
= 33/70 = .47.

rejected. However, among the 40 people who would have failed, an estimated 37 would be in the rejected group. Using Table 7-7, we also can calculate the proportion of those rejected on the basis of the test who would be expected to succeed: 33/70 = .47. Although the procedure leads to the rejection of many capable applicants, it can be defended as rational because the proportion of those succeeding is much higher among those who are selected by the procedure than among those rejected by the procedure.

A common argument is that increased minority hiring will result in lower average job performance because some applicants with lower test scores will be hired. However, systematic study of this issue has not always supported these arguments. For example, increased minority hiring in some industries has resulted in only a small loss in job performance. There may be circumstances in which average job performance declines with an overselection of low-scoring job applicants, but the data from these studies are typically complex (Silva & Jacobs, 1993).

The Taylor-Russell tables can also help one show the futility of certain types of assessment procedures. For example, McDaniel (1989) suggested that routine background information may be useful in predicting employee success. In his study, McDaniel used information on school suspension, drug use, quitting school, participation in social clubs, school grades, contacts with the legal system, and socioeconomic status to predict success in the military service. The criterion for success was to keep from being discharged for being unsuitable. The study demonstrated that though most of the background variables predicted unsuitability discharges, the validity coefficients were very low. The highest validity coefficient was about .15. Let us assume that the selection ratio for the armed services is about .9. In other words, 9 out of every 10 applicants are admitted to the military service. Let us also assume the base rate of success of 60%. (Actually, in the McDaniel study the base rate was about 85%, but assuming 60% allows us to do this exercise with Table 7-6.) When we use the Taylor-Russell table for a validity of .15 and a selection ratio of .90, we find that the proportion who succeed in military service goes to .61. Using only base-rate information, we would have predicted that 60% succeed. The information on dropping out of school improves this prediction by only 1%! The low validity for the background information is the reason for this negligible improvement. Although background information may be useful, it may provide only a minimum of information about future success.

Utility Theory and Decision Analysis

The use of Taylor-Russell tables requires that the criterion be a dichotomous variable. However, success usually is measured on a more refined numerical scale. By considering success as only a dichotomous variable, one ignores much of the information available to the analyst. For example, it seems more reasonable to use a continuum of job performance as the criterion than to consider merely whether or not someone failed on a job. Developments since the publication of the Taylor-Russell tables have attempted to define levels besides success and failure. These formulations are based on utility theory (Brennan, 1994; Broaden, 1946, 1949; Cronbach & Gleser, 1965; Schmidt & Rothstein, 1994).

Although the use of decision and utility theory greatly serves the industrial psychologist, the equations used to calculate the value of test information are quite complex. Furthermore, the equations require certain information that is hard to estimate. For example, to use the equations, you must estimate the dollar value associated with different levels of performance on the job, an estimation difficult for most jobs (Dunnette & Borman, 1979). Schmidt and Hunter (1983) demonstrated that 40% of the average salary can be used as a rough estimate of the standard deviation of the output. They presented mathematical arguments showing that the 40% rule produces reasonable estimates in most cases. Several other approaches have been suggested to resolve this problem, although progress has been slow (Cascio & Ramos, 1986; Eaton, Wing, & Mitchell, 1985). Raju and co-workers (1993) developed a new approach to utility assessment that did not require an estimate of the dollar value for performance. They proposed that the value of each individual can be estimated from the total value of his or her compensation package. This approach simplifies the calculations and produces results similar to other methods; however, the Raju method may shift the subjective judgment of the standard deviation of the criterion to estimating the coefficient of variation of the criterion. In other words, the estimation problem has not been solved (Judiesch, Schmidt, and Hunter, 1993). In summary, the utility methods hold great promise for making rational personnel decisions, yet the difficulty in applying utility formulations has prevented their widespread use. Even so, studies do demonstrate financial advantages for companies that select employees on the basis of these formal models (Burke & Doran, 1989). Further, the methodology for utility analysis continues to improve (Schmidt et al., 1993). An example of utility calculations is given in Focused Example 7-2.

Incremental Validity

Validity defines the inferences that one can make on the basis of a score or measure (see Chapter 5). Evidence that a test is valid for particular inferences does not necessarily mean that the test is valuable. Though a test may be reliable and valid, the decision to use it depends on additional considerations. For example, does the test give you more information than would be expected if it were not used? What information can the test provide beyond what is already known? This added bit of information gained through using the test is known as *incremental validity*.

The sections on base and hit rates and on Taylor-Russell tables considered problems in incremental validity. We presented methods for evaluating what a

---

Focused Example 7-2

HOW MUCH MONEY CAN BE SAVED THROUGH VALID SELECTION?

A major issue in business and industrial psychology is how to get the most productivity out of employees. Employers often use tests to select employees who have the greatest chance of being productive. Some industrial psychologists, however, may have failed to realize just how much economic value can be gained from effective selection procedures. Although Cronbach and Gleser (1965) developed methods for evaluating the cost-effectiveness of testing many years ago, their technique was not frequently used, because it required estimating the standard deviation of the dollar value of employee performance. However, newer methods developed to estimate this quantity allow one to determine how much money one saves by using a valid selection procedure.

One study on the use of these decision models concerned the selection of computer programmers using the Programmer Aptitude Test (PAT). A fairly good predictor of the job performance of programmers, the PAT has a validity coefficient of .76. A series of analyses showed that the use of the PAT, in place of less-valid selection procedures, saves considerable money. For example, the U.S. government employs about 17,000 computer programmers. Researchers compared the dollars saved using the PAT and those saved using an alternative procedure with a validity of only .20. Twenty percent of the applicants could be selected. The analysis demonstrated that the savings to the government could be $1.2 billion. Expanded to the economy as a whole, the impact of using the PAT for one year would be $10.78 billion. According to this analysis, the gains in productivity associated with using a valid selection procedure are much greater than previously realized (Schmidt et al., 1979).

Although this analysis is very encouraging, there is at least one problem with the application to programmers. At present, there are more jobs for programmers than there are trained people to fill them. Thus, for the entire economy, the selection ratio cannot be 20%. In fact, nearly 100% of the qualified programmers find work. Gains realized by those who employ the best qualified programmers are offset by losses to those who employ those less qualified.

In another analysis, Hunter and Hunter (1984) considered the consequences of substituting less-valid predictors for the selection of employees for entry-level government jobs. They argued that the most valid predictors of performance on the job were ability and work sample tests, which have validities of .53. If a good but less valid predictor involving job tryouts (validity of .44) was used, losses in productivity would be $3.12 billion per year. However, selecting employees on the basis of age, which has only a low correlation with job performance ($r = -.01$), would result in losses of $15.89 billion per year. Of course, employers need to take into consideration many factors when making employment decisions. For example, selection on the basis of test performance alone may have adverse consequences for minority groups.

test contributed beyond what was known from base rates. The assessment of incremental validity is not necessarily limited to comparisons with base rates, though. A particularly important aspect of incremental validity is the determination of how much information a test contributes beyond some simpler method for making the same prediction.

Most of the examples given in the preceding sections concerned tests used for selection purposes. However, the same rules and methods apply for tests used for the evaluation of personality or in the practice of clinical psychology.

Recent research on the prediction of behavior in particular situations has yielded some simple but startling results. Although it is difficult to predict behavior on the basis of reports by trained clinical psychologists (Meehl, 1995), people are remarkably good at predicting their own behavior (Bandura, 1994; Funder et al., 1993). We can learn a lot about whether a person will be able to perform a particular behavior by simply asking him or her.

Frequently, expensive and time-consuming psychological tests are given in order to make predictions about future behavior. Before exerting this effort, one should ask what the tests might reveal beyond information obtained in some simpler manner. For example, a simple self-rating of health predicts functioning and life expectancy for lung patients about as well as a complex set of medical tests. Detailed interviews and tests give little information beyond the simple patient self-report (Kaplan et al., 1994).

Other studies have attempted to determine, on the basis of a variety of tests and self-ratings, how a person will be rated by peers. The results often demonstrate that simple self-ratings are as good at predicting how someone will be rated by peers as complex personality tests that make inferences about underlying traits (Hase & Goldberg, 1967). Alternatively, work supervisors are known not to be accurate raters. One variable that may affect ratings is the supervisor's own level of security. For example, studies have demonstrated that supervisors who have conflict over their own roles give relatively higher ratings of the performance of their subordinates (Fried & Tiegs, 1995). Self-predictions are also not always accurate. Even so, they no less accurately predict who will go under a hypnotic trance than complex hypnotizability scales (Melei & Hilgard, 1964). On the other hand, personality tests have been of little value in predicting whether snake phobics will learn to approach a snake after therapy; however, self-predictions have been found to be very accurate (Bandura, 1994).

A variety of investigations have considered the validity of employment interviews. The most comprehensive summary of these studies, reported by McDaniel and associates (1994), combined results from a variety of other investigations, involving 86,331 individuals. The analysis suggested that the validity of interview information depends on many variables. Situational interviews had higher validity than job-related interviews. Psychologically based interviews had the lowest validity of all the categories studied. Structured interviews had higher validity than unstructured ones. Other studies have demonstrated that biographical information used for employment decisions is often unreliable (Schmidt & Rothstein, 1994). There is some hope for improving ratings. Studies have shown that rating accuracy can improve with specific cognitive training (Day & Sulsky, 1995).

Often, the predictive validity of selection tests is modest. For example, one investigation attempted to predict who would be the best support-persons for insurance agencies. A battery of tests involving cognitive ability, personality, and biographical data was administered to 357 subjects. Among these, 337 were eventually hired and rated by their immediate supervisor for job performance. The range of the validity coefficients was .17 to .28. In other words, the extensive testing battery explains only about 4% to 9% of the variance in job performance (Bosshardt et al., 1992). Another study evaluated applicants for eight telecommunications companies. Using structural behavioral interviews to estimate job performance yielded criterion validity estimates of about .22 (Motowidlo et al., 1992).

We do not offer these examples to convince you that personality tests are meaningless. As you will see in Chapters 14–17, personality measures make many important contributions. However, test users always should ask themselves whether they can gain the same information with a simpler or less expensive method or with one that will cause less strain for the subject. Tests should be used when they provide significantly more information over that which simpler methods would obtain. To ensure that testing is a worthwhile use of time and resources, one must carefully select one's testing materials.

Locating Information About Published Tests

When choosing a test for a particular purpose, you should carefully research your options. Many reference books provide information about tests and refer you to other journal articles that summarize specific evaluations of a given test. To get a general overview of a test, you will find seven references particularly valuable: *Tests in Print IV* (Murphy, Conoley, & Impara, 1994); *The Mental Measurements Yearbook* (Kramer & Conoley, 1992); *Tests: A Comprehensive Reference for Assessment in Psychology, Education, and Business* (Sweetland & Keyser, 1991); *Test Critiques* (Keyser & Sweetland, 1985); *Measures of Personality and Social Psychological Attitudes* (Robinson, Shaver, & Wrightsman, 1991); *Unpublished Experimental Mental Measures* (B. A. Goldman & Osbourne, 1985); and the *International Assessment of Health-Related Quality of Life* (Shumaker & Berzon, 1995).

Tests in Print IV

This exhaustive reference book summarizes information on most of the tests in the English language. The book lists the following information: the title of the test, whom the test is designed for, when the test was developed (copyright date), the acronym for the test (or the set of letters the test is often called by, such as SAT), available subtests, whether or not there is a test manual, problems in updating the test materials, the authors and publisher of the test, the country of publication, and cross references to *The Mental Measurements Yearbook* and *Personality Tests and Reviews* along with references to relevant journal articles. If you do not know the name of a test, you can locate it by content using this source.

The Mental Measurements Yearbook

A classic collection of test reviews, this book was begun in 1938 by Oscar K. Buros (1978). After his death in 1978, the University of Nebraska Press took over the series and has been publishing it since 1985. The MMY, as it is often called, provides comprehensive reviews of testing materials by hundreds of noted psychologists and education specialists. Each review comments on the evidence for the validity and reliability of a test. Often, the reviews are quite critical. The reviewer also critiques the meaning of the available data. More than 1880 references for journal articles reviewing the tests are also given. Several sourcebooks made up of selected subsections of the MMY include *Vocational Tests and Reviews* (Buros, 1975c), which consists of the vocational sections of the seventh MMY and *Tests in Print IV. Personality Tests and Reviews* (Buros, 1975b) comprises the sections on personality tests, and *Intelligence Tests and Reviews* (Buros, 1975a) includes the intelligence testing sections.

The 11th edition of the *Mental Measurements Yearbook,* published in 1992, includes a bibliography of commercially available tests and reviews of tests by well-qualified measurement experts, as well as bibliographies and references about the specific tests, their construction, validity, and so forth. This edition focuses on new tests or those revised after 1989. The book includes a test title index with extensive cross-referencing, a classified subject index, a directory of publishers with information on how to obtain tests, and other indexes that allow the search for test information by author names, test names, test acronyms, and types of score. In addition, the 11th edition includes the *Mental Measurement Database,* which is an on-line computer service.

The most common type of test reviewed in the *Mental Measurements Yearbook* is the vocation test (25%). The next most common is the personality test. Table 7-8 summarizes the major types of test classifications in 16 major categories.

The MMY also helps identify which tests are cited most frequently. Table 7-9 provides this summary. Among all tests, the Wide Range Achievement Test—Revised (see Chapter 12) is the most commonly cited.

Tests: A Comprehensive Reference for Assessment in Psychology, Education, and Business

The excellent tradition begun by Buros has continued in a series of new volumes. *Tests: A Comprehensive Reference for Assessment in Psychology, Education, and Business* (Sweetland & Keyser, 1991) provides descriptive information on

TABLE 7-8

Tests by Major Classifications, from the Mental Measurements Yearbook, 10th Edition

Classification	Number	Percentage
Vocations	100	25.3
Personality	72	18.2
Miscellaneous	43	10.9
Developmental	31	7.8
Intelligence and scholastic aptitude	28	7.1
English	24	6.1
Reading	24	6.1
Speech and hearing	22	5.6
Education	20	5.1
Achievement	12	3.0
Mathematics	9	2.2
Social studies	3	.8
Fine arts	2	.5
Foreign languages	2	.5
Sensory-motor	2	.5
Neuropsychological	2	.5
Total	396	100.00

From Conoley & Kramer (1989, p. x).

TABLE 7-9

Number of References for the Ten Most Frequently Cited Tests

Name of Test	Number of References
Wide Range Achievement Test—Revised	161
Stanford-Binet Intelligence Scale, 4th Edition	89
Multiple Affect Adjective Check List, Revised	84
Bayley Scales of Infant Development	80
California Achievement Tests, Forms E and F	68
Personality Research Form, 3rd Edition	68
Iowa Tests of Basic Skills, Forms G and H	45
Metropolitan Achievement Tests, 6th Edition	45
Myers-Briggs Type Indicator	42
Woodcock Reading Mastery Tests—Revised	38

From Conoley & Kramer (1989, p. xii).

more than 3500 tests from 467 publishers. These tests are divided into three categories: psychology, education, and business. The volume describes the format for tests; provides a statement of purpose for each; and describes the relevant information on cost, available data, and scoring. Information is also provided on computer scoring, and indexes allow the easy location of the author, publisher, and other relevant information.

Test Critiques

In 1985, a new volume by Keyser and Sweetland was published to supplement their comprehensive reference for tests (Sweetland & Keyser, 1983), which had omitted important psychometric information on reliability, validity, and normative development. As we noted in Chapters 4 and 5, it is difficult to evaluate the merits of a test without knowing this information. *Test Critiques* (Keyser & Sweetland, 1985) provides detailed reviews on different topic areas. For example, experts critique tests of achievement and aptitude, educational development, gerontology, intelligence, and so on. Some critiques focus on specific tests, while others cover broader areas such as attitude survey tests.

Measures of Personality and Social Psychological Attitudes

This reference is particularly valuable for people interested in measures of personality and social attitudes. Edited by Robinson, Shaver, and Wrightsman (1991), the reference includes 12 edited chapters that cover a wide range of measures of personality, depression, coping, and other psychological processes. The book provides evaluative information about the measures and establishes criteria for a good measure. It also gives samples of the items for some measures.

Unpublished Experimental Mental Measures

Not all measures are published. *Unpublished Experimental Mental Measures* (Goldman & Osbourne, 1985) describes such measures, in four volumes covering several thousand measures. Each entry is accompanied by a brief summary of research relevant to the measure. Unfortunately, the volumes did not get wide circulation and are difficult to find in some college libraries.

International Assessment of Health-Related Quality of Life

In recent years, medical and health-care researchers have begun using behavioral measures as their primary outcomes. As a result, a wide variety of psychological and functional measures have been developed. These measures are used on a very large scale to determine the health status of populations and to assess the effectiveness of treatment. Some of these measures are reviewed in more detail in Chapter 19.

The many measures of health-related quality of life have been reviewed in several publications (Spilker, 1990a, 1996). One recent review of measures entitled, *The International Assessment of Health-Related Quality of Life Theory, Translation, Measurement and Analysis,* summarizes many measures and actually includes them along with a detailed analysis of theory. The book also presents translations of the measures into several different languages (Shumaker & Berzon, 1995).

Summary

Making a selection among the many published tests has become a technical skill. One of your first considerations should always be whether it is worthwhile to administer a given test. How much information does the test promise beyond what is known without the test? In personnel selection, the *base rate* is the probability of succeeding without any selection procedure. A variety of methods have been developed to estimate the amount of information a test gives beyond what is known by chance. This estimate depends on the validity of the test, the percentage of people being selected, and the proportion of people expected to succeed if no selection test is used. *Taylor-Russell tables* can be used for outcomes defined in terms of success and failure. You can use utility and decision theories for some outcomes involving more than these two levels. However, the application of the utility theory equations is fairly difficult in most circumstances.

Because there are so many tests available, a wise consumer will carefully review published information on a test before making a decision about using it. Valuable sourcebooks on testing information include *Tests in Print III; The Mental Measurements Yearbook; Tests: A Comprehensive Reference for Assessment in Psychology, Education, and Business; Test Critiques; Measures for Psychological Assessment; Measures of Personality and Social Psychological Attitudes; Unpublished Experimental Mental Measures;* and the *International Assessment of Health-Related Quality of Life.*

CHAPTER 8

Test Administration

LEARNING OBJECTIVES

When you have completed this chapter, you should be able to:

☐ Know whether the majority of the research evidence shows that white examiners impede the intelligence test performance of African-American children

☐ Discuss how the relationship between the examiner and the test taker can have an impact on test scores

☐ Discuss an expectancy effect and how it might affect a test score

☐ Examine the relationship between reinforcing particular responses and test performance

☐ Outline some of the advantages of computer-assisted test administration

☐ List what characteristics of the state of the subject should be considered when evaluating a test score

☐ Know what problems you would need to consider in training your observers if you were in charge of a behavioral observation study

*I*n the last six chapters, we discussed many topics related to test construction. Now you are ready to make the transition to using psychological tests. Before you move on to the section on applications, however, one final methodological issue needs to be covered: the administration of tests.

Many factors influence test scores. We have a tendency to think that an observed score really represents the true ability or trait we are trying to measure. In Chapter 4, we reviewed the concept of reliability and introduced measurement error, or the difference between the true score and the observed score. Reliability theory is primarily concerned with random sources of error. In the actual application of tests, we must consider many other potential sources of error, including the testing situation, tester characteristics, and test taker characteristics.

The Examiner and the Subject

The Race of the Tester

Because of concern about bias, the effects of the tester's race have generated considerable attention. Some groups feel that their children should not be tested by anyone except a member of their own race. For example, some claim that African-American children receive lower test scores when tested by white examiners rather than examiners of the same race. Although the effects of racial bias in test administration are discussed frequently, relatively few experimental studies have examined the exact impact of these effects. Sattler has reviewed such effects on several occasions (1970, 1973a, 1973b, 1973c, 1982, 1988). After careful consideration of the problem and occasional reanalysis of the data, Sattler concluded that there is little evidence that the race of the examiner significantly affects intelligence test scores.

The most common finding in studies of this type is that the race of the examiner has nonsignificant effects on test performance for both African-American and white children. These results occurred for both the Stanford-Binet scale and the Peabody Picture Vocabulary Test (J. Costello & Dickie, 1970; J. O. Miller & Phillips, 1966). A similar study with older children (African-American sixth-graders) failed to show differences between the children when they were given the Stanford-Binet by an African-American examiner and by a white one (Caldwell & Knight, 1970).

This same result also has been obtained for group intelligence tests. Scores of African-American and white fourth-, fifth-, and sixth-graders were not found to be significantly influenced by having a trained African-American or white examiner give the Lorge-Thorndike Group Intelligence Test (S. Lipsitz, 1969). Only a few studies have shown an effect attributed to the race of the examiner; in fact, these effects have been found in only 4 of 29 studies (Sattler, 1979a). Sattler and Gwynne (1982) have referred to the belief that white examiners impede the test performance of African-American children as a myth widely held but unsupported by scientific studies.

One of the reasons so few studies show effects of the examiner's race on the results of IQ tests is that the procedures for properly administering an IQ test are so specific. Anyone who gives the test should do so according to a strict procedure. In other words, well-trained African-American and white test administrators should act almost identically. Deviation from this procedure might produce differences in performance associated with the race of the examiner. For example, in the next sections we will show how very subtle (nonverbal) cues can affect test scores. Even though most standardized tests require a strict administration procedure, the examiner can still communicate a hostile or friendly atmosphere, a hurried or relaxed manner, or an inquisitorial or therapeutic role. Rather than race, these effects may reflect individual or cultural differences.

Sattler (1973c) has shown that the race of the examiner affects test scores in some situations. Examiner effects tend to increase when examiners are given more discretion about the use of the tests. In one study in which a small effect of the examiner's race was found, the examiners were paraprofessionals rather than psychologists. In this study, white examiners obtained higher scores from white than African-American children, whereas scores for both groups of children were comparable when tested by African-American examiners (T. Abramson, 1969). However, after a detailed review of the literature, Sattler (1988) concluded that the effects of administrators' race are negligible.

The Examiner/Test-Taker Relationship

Both the behavior of the examiner and his or her relationship to the test taker can affect test scores. In one study, first- through seventh-grade children were given the Wechsler Intelligence Scale for Children (or WISC; see Chapter 11) under one of two conditions. Half the children were given the test under enhanced rapport conditions, in which the examiner used friendly conversation and verbal reinforcement during the test administration. The other children took the test under a neutral rapport condition: The examiner neither initiated conversation nor used reinforcement (Feldman & Sullivan, 1960). The examiner's rapport had little effect on the scores of the younger children (through third grade). However, average IQ scores for the fifth- through ninth-grade students were higher for those who had received the test under the enhanced rapport condition (mean IQ = 122) than for those with a neutral administrator (mean IQ = 109). This difference (122 − 109) is almost a full standard deviation.

Another study compared scores obtained by examiners who made approving comments (such as "good" or "fine") with those obtained by examiners who used disapproving comments ("I thought you could do better than that") or neutral ones. Children who took the test under a disapproving examiner received lower scores than children exposed to a neutral or an approving examiner (Witmer, Bernstein, & Dunham, 1971). For younger children, a familiar examiner may make a difference. In one study, 137 children took a reading test, half with a familiar proctor, half with an unfamiliar proctor. Reading scores were significantly lower when the proctor was unfamiliar (DeRosa & Patalano, 1991).

Enough studies have accumulated on examiner/test-taker relationships that a quantitative review of the literature has been performed. Fuchs and Fuchs (1986) reviewed 22 different studies that involved 1489 children. Averaging across the studies, they found that test performance was about .28 standard deviation, or about 4 IQ points, higher when the examiner was familiar with the test taker than when not. In those studies involving children from lower socioeconomic classes, familiarity accounted for about 7.6 IQ points. The review raises some important concerns because it demonstrates that familiarity with the test taker, and perhaps preexisting notions about the test taker's ability, can either positively or negatively bias test results.

In most testing situations, examiners should not strive for a particular rapport with different test takers. They should also keep in mind that rapport might be influenced by very subtle processes such as the level of performance expected by the examiner.

Training of Test Administrators

There are no standardized protocols for training people to administer complicated tests such as the Wechsler Adult Intelligence Scale-Revised (WAIS-R; see Chapter 11). Many training programs have students complete only four practice administrations of the WAIS-R. In one study of 22 graduate students, there were numerous errors in scoring the test, with no improvement over five practice administrations. The error rate went down only after about ten administrations, suggesting that students need at least ten practice sessions to begin gaining competence with the WAIS-R (M. Patterson, et al. 1995).

Expectancy Effects

A well-known line of research in psychology has shown that data sometimes can be affected by what an experimenter expects to find. Robert Rosenthal and his colleagues at Harvard University conducted many experiments on such **expectancy effects,** often called the **Rosenthal effect.** In a typical experiment, Rosenthal employed a large number of student experimenters to help collect data on a task such as rating human faces for success or failure. Half the student experimenters were led to believe that the average response would fall toward the success side of the scale, and the other half that the average response would fall on the failure side. The results of these experiments have consistently demonstrated that the subjects actually provide data that confirm the experimenter's expectancies. However, the magnitude of the effects is small—about a 1-point difference on a 20-point scale (Rosenthal, 1966).

The experimenter's influence is not limited to human subjects. Other experiments have demonstrated that rats expected to be "maze bright" will learn to run through a maze more quickly than rats expected to be "maze dull." All the rats are from the same litter, but the experimenter is told to expect a difference (Rosenthal & Fode, 1963).

Several authors have challenged the Rosenthal experiments, claiming that they are based on unsound statistical procedures or faulty design (Barber & Silver, 1968; Elashoff & Snow, 1971; R. L. Thorndike, 1968). Rosenthal has acknowledged some problems in his early work and has greatly improved his own skills as a methodologist (Rosenthal & Rosnow, 1991). Other questions have been raised about the expectancy effect. For example, in one study from Israel, women supervisors were told that some women officer cadets offered exceptional potential. This selection was made randomly instead of on the basis of any evidence. The study failed to show any expectancy effect. In a follow-up study, expectancy information was given to men and women who were leaders with regard to men and women who were subjects. The results replicated the effect of expectancy for men when they were supervised by a man and for women when they were led by a man, but failed to replicate the results when women were led by women (Dvir, Eden, & Banjo, 1995). After reviewing many studies, we conclude that an expectancy effect exists in some, but not all, situations.

Two aspects of the expectancy effect relate to the use of standardized tests. First, the expectancy effects observed in Rosenthal's experiments were obtained when all the experimenters followed a standardized script. Although gross forms of bias are possible, Rosenthal argued that the expectancy effect results from very subtle uses of nonverbal communication between the experimenter and the subject. The experimenter may not even be aware of his or her role in the process. Second, the expectancy effect has a very small, subtle effect on scores and occurs in some situations but not in others. Determining whether expectancy affects test scores requires careful studies for the particular tests being used.

The expectancy effect can impact intelligence testing in many ways, such as scoring. In a series of experiments, graduate students with some training in intelligence testing were asked to score ambiguous responses from certain intelligence tests. Sometimes they were told that the responses had been given by persons who were "bright," and other times the responses were attributed to "dull" persons. The students tended to give more credit to responses purportedly from bright test takers (Sattler, Hillix, & Neher, 1970; Sattler & Winget, 1970). Other studies have demonstrated that the expectancy effect can occur even if the responses are not ambiguous (Egeland, 1969; W. E. Simon, 1969).

A variety of interpersonal and cognitive process variables have been shown to affect one's judgment of others (Arkes, 1991). These biases may also affect test scoring. For example, Donahue and Sattler (1971) demonstrated that students who scored the WAIS would most likely give credit for selected items to examinees they liked or perceived to be warm. Thus, examiners must remain aware that their relationships with examinees can affect their objectivity about certain types of tests.

Studies of expectancies in test administrators (who give rather than just score tests) have yielded somewhat inconsistent results. Some have shown a significant effect (Hersh, 1971; Larrabee & Kleinsaser, 1967; Schroeder & Kleinsaser, 1972), whereas others have not demonstrated an expectancy effect (Dangel, 1970; Ekren, 1962; Gillingham, 1970; Saunders & Vitro, 1971).

Many studies have attempted to find subtle variables that affect test responses. For example, Rappaport and McAnulty (1985) presented tape-recorded responses to people scoring IQ tests. Though the children on the recording gave the same response with or without an accent, no difference between these two conditions surfaced.

In reviewing these studies, Sattler (1988) noted that those that showed an expectancy effect tended to have an administrator test only two children (one under a high and one under a low expectancy condition). The studies that did not find an expectancy effect tended to have more subjects tested by each test administrator. The studies that used more samples of each tester's behavior should produce more reliable estimates of the expectancy effect; therefore, the studies that failed to show an expectancy effect may be more credible than those that showed it.

In spite of these inconsistent results, you should pay careful attention to the potentially biasing effect of expectancy. Even Rosenthal's harshest critics do not deny the possible biasing effect of expectancy. Thus, it is always important to do as much as you can to eliminate this possibility.

Effects of Reinforcing Responses

Because we know that reinforcement affects behavior, we should always administer tests under controlled conditions. Sattler and Theye (1967) reviewed the literature on procedural and situational variables in testing and found that an inconsistent use of feedback can damage the reliability and validity of test scores.

Several studies have shown that reward can significantly affect test performance. For example, incentives can help improve performance on IQ tests for specific subgroups of children. In one study, 6- to 13-year-olds received tokens they could exchange for money each time they gave a correct response on the WISC verbal scale. This incentive improved performance for lower-class white children but not for middle-class children or lower-class African-American children (Sweet, 1969).

Many studies have shown that children will work very hard to obtain praise such as "You are doing well" (Eisenberger, 1970, 1972). Several studies have shown that the effects of verbal reinforcement or praise are about as strong as monetary rewards or candy (I. Cohen, 1970; Quay, 1971; Sattler, 1992; Tiber & Kennedy, 1964). The results of these studies, however, are sometimes complicated. For instance, one study found that girls increased their accuracy on the WISC block design subtest when given any type of reinforcement for a correct response. Boys increased their accuracy only when given chips that could be exchanged for money. However, girls decreased in speed when given reinforcement, and boys increased in speed only when given verbal praise (A. Bergan, McManis, & Melchert, 1971).

Some evidence suggests that African-American children do not respond as well to verbal reinforcers as they do to tangible rewards such as money or candy (Schultz & Sherman, 1976). However, Terrell and his colleagues (Terrell, Taylor, & Terrell, 1978) suggested that this is because the verbal reinforcement often given to the African-American children is not culturally relevant. To demonstrate their point, they administered the WISC-R intelligence test to lower-class African-American second-graders and gave one of four types of feedback for each correct response. One-quarter of the children received no feedback at all about whether or not they had made a correct response. One group received verbal praise; another group, candy. The final group was given culturally relevant verbal praise. For example, after each correct response, the African-American test administrator remarked "Nice job, Blood" or "Nice job, little Brother." Culturally relevant feedback boosted IQ a remarkable 17.6 points, whereas other feedback had very little effect (about 3 points). Tangible rewards boosted performance about 11 points. This result is most unusual in light of several previous studies that show only minor reinforcement effects. Certainly, the effects of culturally relevant rewards deserve more attention.

Some of the most potent effects of reinforcement arise in attitudinal studies. In survey research, the answer given by a respondent is not necessarily right or wrong but rather an expression of how someone feels about something. Repeated studies have demonstrated that the way an interviewer responds affects the content of responses in interview studies (Cannell & Henson, 1974). In one of the most interesting of these, respondents in a household survey were asked if they suffered from certain physical symptoms. For half the subjects, the interviewer gave an approving nod each time a symptom was reported. For the other half, the interviewer remained expressionless. The number of symptoms reported increased significantly with such approval. In a similar study, two symptoms that no one should report were added to the list: "Are your intestines too long?" and "Do the ends of your hair itch?" More people reported these symptoms if they had been reinforced for reporting other symptoms than if they had not.

Reinforcement and feedback guide the examinee toward a preferred response. Another way to demonstrate the potency of reinforcement involves misguiding the subject. A variety of studies have demonstrated that random reinforcement destroys the accuracy of performance and decreases the motivation to respond (Eisenberger, Kaplan, & Singer, 1974; Koller & Kaplan, 1978). Consider how you might feel if the grades you received were totally random. The effects of random feedback are rather severe, causing low motivation for responding, depression, and inability to solve problems. This condition is known as *learned helplessness* (Abramson, Metalsky, & Alloy, 1995).

Reinforcement's potency requires strict control over the use of feedback by test administrators (see Technical Box 8-1). Because different test takers make different responses, one cannot ensure that advantages due to reinforcement will be the same for all people. As a result, most test manuals and interviewer guides insist that no feedback be given.

Testing also requires standardized conditions because situational variables can affect test scores. The *Standards for Educational and Psychological Testing* published by the American Psychological Association and other professional groups (1985) emphasizes that a test manual should clearly spell out the directions for administration. These directions should be sufficiently detailed to be duplicated in all situations in which the test is given. A good test manual will give the test examiner instructions that include the exact words to be read to the test takers. Furthermore, it should spell out which questions one should expect and how one should answer them.

Inexperienced test administrators often do not fully appreciate the importance of standardization in administration. Whether you give tests or supervise others who do, you must consider that the test may not remain reliable or valid if you deviate from the specified instructions.

A few occasions do require deviation from standardized testing procedures. Sattler (1988) acknowledges that the blind need special considerations, and O. J. Kaplan (1979) discusses the testing needs of the aged. However,

---

TECHNICAL BOX 8-1

The Incentive Scoreboard

As noted in the text, because most psychologists agree that reinforcement can affect test performance, methods are usually implemented to standardize reinforcement during testing procedures. However, as in most areas of psychology, there is some inconsistency in the literature. J. M. Sattler (1988) reviewed 34 studies that evaluated the effect of incentives, which included praise, candy, and money as well as social reinforcement and reinforcement with tokens. The subjects in these experiments included normal and handicapped children of various ethnic groups. By tallying the results of these studies, Sattler observed that 14 studies found that incentives or feedback did not affect performance, 13 studies found mixed results, and 7 studies found clear evidence that reinforcement either improved or hindered performance.

There appeared to be no clear and consistent difference between the studies that showed a positive and those that showed a negative effect of token and social reinforcement. One issue raised by research on incentive effects concerns what the results imply for test interpretation. If a child's IQ score of 110 can be boosted to 120 with reinforcement for correct responses, does this mean the child is likely to do well in school? The validity of the test is based on a standardized administration procedure, so it is not clear that enhancing IQ scores with reinforcement would enhance the validity of the test.

many widely used tests have now developed special standardized methods for testing particular populations. To assure that tests are given under standardized conditions, some examiners prefer to give instructions through a tape recorder. Others have opted for computer-assisted test administration.

Computer-Assisted Test Administration

Computer technology impacts many fields, including testing and test administration. Today most colleges and many elementary and secondary schools enjoy interactive computer capabilities. Easy access to computers allows the administration of a test through interaction with a computer.

Interactive testing involves the presentation of test items through a computer terminal or personal computer and the automatic recording of test responses. The computer also can be programmed to instruct the test taker and to provide some instruction when parts of the testing procedure are not clear. As early as 1970, Cronbach recognized the value of computers as test administrators. Here are some advantages computers offer:

Excellence of standardization

Individually tailored sequential administration

Precision of timing responses

Release of human testers for other duties

Patience (test taker not rushed)

Control of bias

Since the publication of the first edition of this book in 1982, computer technology has bloomed in testing. Today, many of the major psychological tests are available for use on a personal computer. Further, the computer is playing an increasingly important role in test administration. Some people, though, feel uneasy interacting with computers, or suffer from "keyboard phobia." Newer technologies use bar codes or other procedures to reduce resistance to computers (Pfister, 1995). The computer offers many advantages in test administration, scoring, and interpretation (Britton and Tidwell, 1995), including ease of application of complicated psychometric issues and the integration of testing and cognitive psychology (DiBello, Stout, & Roussos, 1995).

Computer-assisted test administration does not necessarily depend on a structured order of test items. Indeed, one advantage of this approach is that the items can be given in any order or in a unique random order for every test taker. Computers are objective and cost-effective. Furthermore, they allow more experimental control. For example, if you want a precise limit on the amount of time any one item can be studied, the computer can easily be programmed to flash the items on the screen for specific durations. The computer-assisted method also prevents test takers from looking ahead at other sections of the test or going back to sections already completed (Groth-Marnat & Shumaker, 1989; Lautenschlager & Flaherty, 1990). Comparisons of test scores obtained have not tended to show large differences between computer-assisted and paper-and-pencil tests (Ward et al., 1989), yet the computer method ensures standardization and control and also reduces scoring errors. It was once thought that people would rebel against interactions with machines. However, newer evidence suggests test takers actually find interactions with computers more enjoyable than paper-and-pencil tests (Rosenfeld et al., 1989).

One of the most interesting findings concerns the use of computers to obtain sensitive information. In one study, 162 college students were assessed on the MMPI and questionnaires concerning drinking and other personal information. The information was obtained in one of three ways: computer, questionnaire, or interview. The results suggested that students were less likely to disclose socially undesirable information during a personal interview. In fact, students may be more honest when tested by a computer than by a person. Further, the students had the most positive experience with the computer (Locke & Gilbert, 1995).

Not all observers endorse the rapid development of computerized test administration. For example, Matarazzo (1986) suggested that computer-generated test reports in the hands of an inexperienced psychologist cannot replace clinical judgment. In such cases, computerized reports may actually cause harm if misinterpreted. Other problems include computerized scoring routines that have errors or are poorly validated; such problems are often difficult to detect within the software. Hartman (1986b) speculated that consumer liability cases involving software products will emerge. Groth-Marnat and Schumaker (1989) outlined a number of problems caused by faulty computerized testing systems. For example, some programs have untested claims of validity, and computerized reports might be based on an obsolete database. A clinical psychologist who lets the computer do too much of the thinking may misinterpret test responses. With the growth in computerized testing, the industry may need new guidelines.

Subject Variables

A final variable that may be a serious source of error is the state of the subject. It is well known that motivation and anxiety can greatly affect test scores. For example, studies have shown that many college students suffer from a serious debilitating condition known as **test anxiety.** Such students often have difficulty focusing attention on the test items and might be distracted by other thoughts such as "I am not doing well" or "I am running out of time." Because test anxiety is an important problem, we shall cover this topic in detail in Chapter 18.

It may seem obvious that illness affects test scores. When you have a cold or the flu, you might not perform as well as when you are feeling well. Many variations in health status affect performance in behavior and in thinking (R. M. Kaplan, 1995). In fact, medical drugs are now evaluated according to their effects on the cognitive process (Spilker, 1996). Some populations need special consideration. For example, the elderly may do better with individual testing sessions, even for tests that can be administered to groups (Martin et al., 1994). The measurement of the effects of health status on functioning will be discussed in more detail in Chapter 19.

Some have debated whether or not normal hormonal variations affect test performance. For instance, healthy women experience variations in their perceptual and motor performance as a function of menstrual cycle. In the middle of each monthly cycle, women may perform better on tests of speeded motor coordination than during menstruation. However, these same women may perform more poorly on tests of perceptual and spatial abilities during midcycle than during menses (Hampson & Kimura, 1988). Studies reported by Kimura at the 1991 neurosciences meetings suggest that men also vary in test performance as a function of variations in male sex hormones.

Behavioral Assessment Methodology

Measurement goes beyond the application of psychological tests. Many assessment procedures involve the observation of behavior. For example, personnel psychologists often obtain work samples to estimate job performance. These samples require the performance of tasks in environments similar to the actual work setting. During this performance, they make systematic observations of behavior. Some applied psychologists believe that work samples provide the most valid indication of actual work performance (D. F. Green & Wing, 1988). Behavioral observation methods are also becoming increasingly important in clinical psychology (Bellack & Hersen, 1988; Hersen, Kazdin, & Bellack, 1991; Tryon, 1991). Many new problems, though, have accompanied the increasing use of behavioral observation methods. As you have seen in this chapter, minor variations in standard test administration procedures can affect test scores. However, one can overcome most of these problems by adhering closely to standard test administration procedures. In behavioral observation studies, the observer plays a more active role in recording the data and, therefore, is much more likely to make errors. Some of the problems include reactivity, drift, and expectancies (Kazdin, 1977).

Reactivity

The reliability of observers in behavioral observation studies is usually assessed in selected sessions, during which an experimenter "observes the observers." In other words, someone looks over the observer's shoulder to determine whether he or she is recording properly. Studies have shown that reliability and accuracy are highest when someone is checking on the observers. This increase in reliability is called **reactivity** because it is a reaction to being checked. In one study, observers rated behavior recorded on a videotape under one of two conditions. First, the observers were told that their ratings would be checked against a standard for accuracy. Later, the observers were told there was no standard. In both cases, there actually was a standard against which the accuracy of each was checked. The data demonstrated that accuracy dropped by 25% when the observers were led to believe their observations would not be evaluated (Reid, 1970). Indeed, many studies have demonstrated that accuracy and interrater agreement decrease when observers believe their work is not being checked (F. C. Harris & Lahey, 1982; R. N. Kent et al., 1977; Taplin & Reid, 1973).

To deal with this problem, some experimenters resort to covert operations. For example, the experimenter might randomly check on the performance of the observers without their knowledge. In general, you should always use caution in interpreting reports on interrater reliability. Often, the estimate of rater reliability is based on assessment during training. When observers are not observed (when they are actually collecting data), their accuracy will likely drop.

Drift

When trained in behavioral observation methods, observers receive extensive feedback and coaching. After they leave the training sessions, though, observers have a tendency to **drift** away from the strict rules they followed in training and to adopt idiosyncratic definitions of behavior (O'Leary & Kent, 1973; J. B. Reid & DeMaster, 1972). One of the most common problems, the *contrast effect,* is the tendency to rate the same behavior differently when observations are repeated in the same context. Further, standards may shift, resulting in biased ratings of behavior. This bias can affect performance ratings or ratings of potential employees in interviews (Maurer & Alexander, 1991). The drift may not always stem from an individual observer. Sometimes when many observers work together on the same job, they seem to drift away from the original definitions of the behavior, but as a group (O'Leary & Kent, 1973). Observer drift and contrast effects suggest that observers should be periodically retrained. Observers should participate in frequent meetings to discuss methods; these meetings can eliminate some of the difficulties (Bellack & Hersen, 1988).

Expectancies

The literature on observer expectancies resembles that on examiner expectancies. As noted earlier, Rosenthal has accumulated some evidence that the expectancies of experimenters can affect the results of behavioral experiments. Some of the Rosenthal experiments show the effects of such expectancies, whereas others do not. Similarly, some studies show that administrator expectancies can affect scores on individual IQ tests, whereas other studies do not (Sattler, 1988).

The same sort of inconsistent picture appears for studies on behavioral observation. Some studies have shown that behavioral observers will observe the behavior they expect (Azrin et al., 1961; Scott, Burton, & Yarrow, 1967). On the other hand, some very thorough studies do not support an expectancy effect (R. N. Kent et al., 1974; Redfield & Paul, 1976). Expectancies more consistently cause bias in the behavioral observation when observers receive reinforcement for recording a particular behavior than when they do not (O'Leary, Kent, & Kanowitz, 1975).

The impact of expectancy is subtle. It probably has some minor biasing effect on behavioral data. The finding that expectancy bias occurs significantly in some studies but not others is consistent with the notion that expectancy produces a minor but potentially damaging effect. To avoid this sort of bias, observers should not know what behavior to expect.

Problems in Rating Accuracy

Most people feel confident they can accurately judge other people. For example, people often feel they can figure out whether someone else is lying. Different people use different cues in their attempts to catch a liar. For example, when U.S. Supreme Court Justice Clarence Thomas was up for confirmation by the U. S. Senate, he was accused of sexually harassing a former employee. Both Thomas and his accuser were interviewed by a congressional committee, and the hearings were broadcast to the American public. Though Thomas denied the allegations, people disagreed on whether he or his accuser was lying. A few years later a similar event occurred during the murder trial of O. J. Simpson. A police detective named Mark Furman was asked on the witness stand if he had used the racist term *nigger* during the last 10 years. When he said no, media commentators agreed that his response was very convincing. However, a few months later the defense lawyers produced tape-recorded interviews in which the officer used the racial slur repeatedly.

Systematic studies show that most people do a remarkably poor job in detecting a liar. Many of these studies use videotapes in which someone is either lying or telling the truth. Not only do average people poorly detect deception, but so do people in professions that obligate them to detect these problems. For example, one study evaluated U.S. Secret Service agents, Central Intelligence Agency (CIA) agents, Federal Bureau of Investigation (FBI) investigators, employees of the National Security Agency, employees of the Drug Enforcement Agency, police officers, judges, and psychiatrists. Evaluation of the data suggested that only Secret Service agents performed better than chance in spotting deception (Ekman & O'Sullivan, 1991).

The detection of lying and honesty has become a major industry. For example, despite substantial evidence questioning their value, lie detector tests are commonly given. In addition, a new industry of "psychological services" has created commercial tests to evaluate the honesty and integrity of prospective employees. One of the current controversies in personnel testing concerns the use of integrity tests, which are used to predict integrity. These tests supposedly estimate who would likely steal cash or merchandise. Several groups have reviewed the issue of integrity tests. The United States Congress Office of Technology Assessment did so to decide whether preemployment integrity tests should be banned. Lie detectors are prohibited under the Employee Polygraph Protection Act of 1988. Although integrity tests are widely used, their validity is questionable. For example, the correlation between scores on honesty tests and documented thefts is about .13. In other words, the tests account for about 1% of the variance in actual thefts. Among those who fail the test, the Office of Technology Assessment estimated that 95.6% would be false positives, or incorrectly labeled as dishonest. Projected to a national scale, this would mean that more than one million U.S. workers would be falsely accused of being dishonest each year (Rieke and Guastello, 1995). In an important statement on this topic, Camara and Schneider (1994) suggested that the use of integrity tests did not meet APA's ethical principles of psychologists and their Code of Conduct.

In rebuttal, Ones, Viswesvaran, and Schmidt (1995) argued that integrity tests are valid and useful for employment decisions. They compiled over 650 criterion-related validity coefficients using a meta-analysis over a half million participants. The review suggested that integrity tests, on average, are good predictors of overall supervisor ratings of job performance. The mean validity coefficient was .41. In addition, integrity tests were also correlated with measures of counter-productive behavior. Thus, they argued that integrity tests measure a broad construct relevant to job performance instead of the narrowly focused concern about honesty. Clearly, continuing scrutiny of integrity tests is important (Lilienfeld, Alliger, & Mitchell, 1995).

Statistical Control of Rating Errors

Many efforts to improve the accuracy of raters have produced discouraging results. Attempts to increase rater reliability through extended training have been particularly frustrating for many researchers and applied psychologists because training is expensive and time consuming. Some psychologists have argued that halo or leniency errors can be controlled statistically. (The halo effect is the tendency to ascribe positive attributes independently of the observed behavior.) This is accomplished through *partial correlation,* in which the correlation between two variables is found while variability in a third variable is controlled.

For example, one study evaluated 537 supervisory ratings of middle-level managers. Each manager was rated on 15 specific attributes and 1 overall performance rating. Then the variance associated with the overall performance rating was separated from the other ratings. By using this method, the variance attributable to the halo effect was reduced and the discriminant validity of the method for rating performance was improved (Landy et al., 1980). Rater characteristics may play an important role in the accuracy of evaluations. Raters with greater cognitive abilities and higher spatial aptitudes may make more accurate ratings. Sometimes, more critical raters tend to produce scores that are more accurate. However, we need more research on factors associated with rater accuracy, because accurate performance evaluations provide the basis for employee selection and advancement (Borman & Hallman, 1991).

Summary

Standardized test administration procedures are necessary. Extensive research in social psychology has clearly demonstrated that situational factors can affect scores on mental and behavioral tasks. These effects, however, can be subtle and may not be observed in all studies. For example, a few studies have shown that the race of the examiner affects scores on standardized intelligence tests; however, the majority of the studies do not find this to be so. Similarly, the examiner's rapport and expectancies may influence scores on some but not all occasions. Direct reinforcement of specific responses (something that should not be done in most testing situations) does have an acknowledged impact.

Toward reducing some of the effects of the examiner, interest has increased in computer-assisted test administration. Computers can administer and score most tests with great precision and with minimum bias. This mode of test administration is expected to become more common in the near future. Other issues relevant to test administration are provided in recent overviews for personality testing (Beutler & Berren, 1995; Hurt, Reznikoff, & Clarkin, 1995).

The state of the subject also affects test scores. For example, some students suffer from debilitating test anxiety, which seriously interferes with performance.

The use of behavioral observation raises some of the same problems as test administration. In such observation, an observer records the responses of others, whereas in traditional test taking the subject records his or her own behavior. A common problem in behavioral observation is *reactivity,* in which the observer is most accurate only when he or she thinks someone is checking the work. A second problem is *drift,* in which observers gradually come to ignore the procedure they were taught and adopt their own observation method. A third problem is *expectancy,* or the tendency for observations to be affected by what the observer expects to observe. Though the magnitude of these effects is probably small, the potential bias they introduce is serious enough to recommend precautions.

Applications

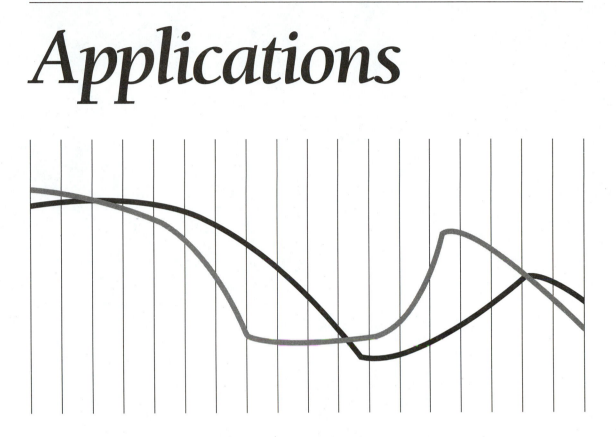

Applications

Although psychology began as a strictly scientific discipline, today applications of psychology abound, as evidenced by the employment announcements in the *APA Monitor*. Indeed, many students associate psychology more with its applications in clinical, counseling, educational, and industrial settings than with its scientific base. Furthermore, an apparently increasing number of students enter applied psychology. Perhaps this interest reflects a need to find relevance in the educational process. Nevertheless, because applied psychology depends on psychology's scientific base, a thorough knowledge of scientific principles is essential for a good understanding of any applied branch of psychology, including psychological tests.

In Chapters 2–8, we stressed scientific knowledge and the principles underlying psychological tests. Part II on applications continues the emphasis on scientific findings, major principles, and basic concepts. However, consistent with current interest, Part II also provides an in-depth discussion of applied aspects of testing. Our decision to present this material is based primarily on student interest. It also serves the increasing numbers of nonpsychologists who make use of tests. Thus, the application section provides an overview of many of the most important and highly used psychological tests and represents a good introduction for those who may directly or indirectly make use of tests in professional activities.

In the first eight chapters, certain key terms and distinctions were introduced and subsequently reviewed to facilitate learning and offer you the opportunity to study the material from many perspectives. In this section, we will not only introduce some new terms and distinctions but also review some of the previously presented concepts. Success in mastering the application of psychological testing depends on attaining a firm understanding of several basic ideas and distinctions. Through repetition and presentation of these basic concepts in a variety of contexts, we hope to establish them in your long-term store of knowledge.

The Issue of Test Use

A little knowledge can be a dangerous thing. Without a proper perspective, you can misuse or improperly apply certain facts. Because psychological and educational tests can be extremely powerful tools, the danger of their misuse is great. Therefore, in learning about the application of tests, one has a responsibility to be cautious and to remain within the boundaries of one's training and experience. Indeed, of all the issues involving tests, the use of tests is perhaps the most critical from an ethical and moral standpoint.

In society, especially as it functions today, decisions are constantly made that affect the lives of countless individuals. Most people eventually find themselves grouped, categorized, selected, or rejected (for example, for college or a job). This decision process is neither good nor bad; it is simply a reality of contemporary life. By now you are well aware that tests often are used in this decision process. One important issue facing both professionals and the public is whether tests should play a role in this process.

Given that psychological and educational tests are imperfect instruments, what role do you feel tests should play in decision making? The American Education Research Association, American Psychological Association, and National Council on Measurement in Education (1985) noted in their *Standards for Educational and Psychological Testing* that some people believe that because tests may be biased or lack accuracy, no test should be used until alternative tests are developed. In defense of tests, the committee argued that the basic issue is not so much test quality as test use (see also APA, 1974). We agree.

Any test can be misused regardless of its fairness, lack of bias, and psychometric adequacy. As previously indicated, decisions will be made with or without tests. Thus, it seems most relevant to ask whether tests can be fairly and appropriately used. The elimination of tests will not solve the problems inherent in the decision-making process. Bias or potential bias would not be eliminated, because people can be just as biased, if not more so, as tests. Thus, in solving the problems of the decision process, we must look beyond tests per se (Cicchetti, 1994; Geisinger, 1994).

Testing continues to flourish despite heavy attacks from both the public and professionals. This seems to indicate that many decision makers consider tests useful. Again, how the tests are used matters most. Tests themselves are neither good nor bad, but unless properly used, they can greatly harm individuals as well as society. Thus, the real problem for test users and the public is to ensure that tests are *properly used* (for example, see Lancaster & Drasgow, 1994).

To make proper use of a test, a tester must have a complete understanding of it. This involves knowledge of the **standardization sample** and the procedures for administering the test. According to the *Standards for Educational and Psychological Testing* (1985), a test manual must describe these two things. The procedure outlined in the test manual, when followed, is known as a **standard administration** of the test. If the test is not administered according to this procedure, one cannot compare the resulting test data to the standardization sample, which received a standard administration (Cicchetti, 1994; L. D. Nelson, 1994). Furthermore, the importance of comparing a test result to an appropriate standardization sample cannot be overemphasized. If the standardization sample is made up of exclusively middle-class, white Americans, then the validity of the test for other populations is highly questionable

(Geisinger, 1994). Thus, the validity of such tests for other populations cannot be assumed.

In Chapters 4 and 5, you learned about the different types of reliability and validity. To use tests properly, however, you must ask more than "Is this test reliable?" or "Is this test valid?" A test may have an extremely high level of internal consistency, as indicated by high split-half reliability coefficients, which provide support for the test. However, an internally consistent test is not necessarily reliable over time. Thus, in making appropriate use of a test, you cannot feel comfortable just because the test manual reports that the test is "highly reliable" or "highly valid." You also must know whether the test has the type of reliability and the type of validity appropriate for your purposes. If you need results that are stable across time, for example, you would expect to find evidence of test-retest reliability. Test users therefore must ask, "Does this test have the type of reliability and validity I need to use it?" If the answer is "No," then the test should not be used.

To understand a test means to know (1) the characteristics of its standardization sample, (2) the types and quality of its reliability and validity, (3) the reliability and validity of comparable tests, (4) its scoring procedures, (5) its method of administration, (6) its limitations, and (7) its strengths. The test manual should offer information on all these areas. Testers also should know the basic concepts covered in this book.

Even if you understand a test completely, you can still misuse it unless you have training in its proper use and experience with the test, preferably under supervision. In the absence of such experience, you should state the limitations of the results and caution anyone who might use the test score.

State licensing laws and professional ethical codes serve to protect the public from abuses that result from test misuse. Licensing laws attempt to prevent tests from being used by unqualified people. Ethical codes of such organizations as the American Medical Association and American Psychological Association go further, prohibiting even highly trained specialists from using procedures beyond their competency. Despite these safeguards, the responsibility for proper tests rests on all concerned. Teachers, counselors, and others who do not actually administer tests but do make use of test results have a responsibility to understand the appropriate uses and limitations of any test they use. In the absence of such knowledge, one should view test results cautiously. For example, if a high-school counselor encounters a result based on a new test, the result should not be used until all the necessary information about the test has been obtained. The counselor must be satisfied that the result can be appropriately applied to the person for whom it is being used.

In addition, the public or consumer of tests must share the burden of ensuring that tests are properly used. This means that we should become as informed as possible about any tests used in decisions affecting our lives. One major intent of this book is to provide test consumers as well as users with sufficient information to become responsible, informed participants in the pervasive field of testing.

Concepts and Distinctions

To properly use tests, you should know some important concepts, definitions, and distinctions. We now discuss a test battery, then make a distinction between testing and assessment.

A Test Battery

In reading Part II, you no doubt will quickly conclude that although they are useful in applied settings, even the best available tests leave much to be desired in terms of scientific, or *psychometric,* adequacy. However, as in medicine, psychological practitioners must daily base decisions on existing technology. Because of the need for psychological services, practitioners do not have the luxury of waiting until conclusive evidence is published before applying existing technology. On the other hand, all psychologists are rooted to a scientific perspective. Those who use psychological tests, therefore, usually have a scientific orientation. Though acutely aware of the limitations of the existing technology, they often find themselves forced to use the best of what is available.

To deal with their need for tests that are both useful and sound, psychologists have come up with better ways of using the existing tools. One method involves the concept of a test battery. In a **test battery,** the scores of two or more tests are used together, to appraise an individual. In using a test battery, the practitioner refuses to accept the validity of a bit of isolated information. Instead, he or she draws on a variety of data sources. These sources may include an interview, direct observations, input from others such as the person's peers or relatives, and records of past performance. In using a test battery and other sources of information, the test user integrates a wide variety of findings. This helps to reduce potential errors and avoid the pitfalls that can occur when only isolated bits of information are used.

Testing versus Assessment

Often, people confuse the terms *testing* and *assessment.* The goal of **assessment** is to evaluate an individual in terms of current and future functioning. Psychological assessment involves classifying behavior into categories measured against a normative standard. Tests are used in the assessment process; not all assessment procedures are tests. In the strictest sense, an assessment procedure is called a *test* only when its procedures for administration, scoring, and interpretation are standardized; there is a standardization sample; and evidence supports its reliability and validity.

Many psychologists have concluded that certain so-called tests would be more appropriately labeled assessment tools because, although useful in evaluating an individual's functioning, they do not meet the requirements of a test. In Part II, we call many procedures tests that others might prefer to call assessment techniques. Thus, where we use the term *test* to describe a particular procedure, your instructor might prefer a term such as technique or *assessment tool.*

Summary

In this brief transition to Part II, we have provided an introduction to the *applications* of psychological tests and have discussed the use of test results. Consistent with the *Standards for Educational and Psychological Testing* and with expert opinion, we believe that the main problem today with tests is not their quality or soundness but the way test results are used (Snyderman & Rothman, 1987). Although new and better tests are most welcome, the real challenge is to ensure that the available tests are used properly.

One important way of making appropriate use of psychological tests is to use them in a battery. A *test battery* does not rely on a single bit of information; rather, data from two or more tests are combined with other sources of information, such as an interview. In the next chapter, you will be exposed to major concepts underlying several types of interviews, including employment and clinical. Because the interview plays such an important role in so many decisions and complements standard tests so well, the importance of an interview as an adjunct to the testing process cannot be overemphasized.

CHAPTER 9

Interviewing Techniques

LEARNING OBJECTIVES

When you have completed this chapter, you should be able to

- Explain the difference between a structured and an unstructured interview
- Discuss the importance of setting the proper tone for the interview
- Describe the role of the interviewer's attitude in the interviewing process
- Identify some of the characteristics of effective interviewing
- List which types of statements tend to keep the interaction flowing or elicit self-exploration in the interviewee
- Explain the effects of empathy statements on interviewee responses
- Identify the various sources of error in the interview
- Appreciate the role of cultural, ethnic, and socioeconomic factors in the interview process
- Explain how interview skills are acquired and developed

*J*ohn was being considered for a high-level public relations position with the computer firm he worked for. The job duties would require him to interact with a wide variety of people, ranging from heads of state and corporation presidents to rank-and-file employees and union officials. In addition, the position would involve making formal policy statements for the press. Any poorly phrased statement or inappropriate reaction on his part could result in adverse publicity, which could cost the firm millions of dollars. The application process therefore involved an elaborate testing procedure, including two lengthy interviews. The first was with the firm's personnel selection officer, the second with the firm's clinical psychologist. (See Figure 9-1).

Knowing the importance of first impressions (Dougherty, Turban, & Callender, 1994; Lyman, Hatlelid, & Macundy, 1981), John took care to appear neat and well groomed. In his first interview, the personnel officer read from a form as she conducted the interview, which went something like this:

Officer: I've read your application form and have gone over your qualifications. Would you now please outline your educational experiences, beginning with high school?

John: I graduated from high school in June 1984 with a major in history and social studies. I began attending college in September 1985. I graduated in June 1989 with a major in psychology and minor in business management. I then entered the university's graduate program in business. I obtained my master's degree in business administration in 1991.

Officer: What is your work history? Begin with your first full-time employment.

John described his work history. The personnel officer then continued a series of questions, which John systematically answered. The questions went something like this:

How do your education and experience relate to the job for which you are applying?

What educational experiences have you had that might help you function in the job for which you are applying?

What employment experiences have you had that might help you function in the job for which you are applying?

Identify any deficiencies in your educational and work experiences.

What educational and work experiences have you had that might impair your ability to function in the job for which you are applying?

The interview continued in a similar manner. With each question, the personnel officer attempted to relate John's educational and work experiences to the particular job duties he hoped to assume. For her final question, the personnel officer asked, "Why do you believe you would make a good candidate for this position?"

John felt good about his interview with the personnel officer. He thought the questions were clear and straightforward, and he was pleased by his

FIGURE 9-1
An interview.

answers. The next day he appeared for his interview with the clinical psychologist. Unlike the personnel officer, the psychologist conducted the interview without using written interview questions. This second interview, quite different from the first, went something like this:

Psychologist: John, why don't you tell me a little bit about yourself.

John: Where do you want me to begin?

Psychologist: Oh, it doesn't matter. Just tell me about yourself.

John: I graduated from high school in June of 1984. I majored in history and social studies.

Psychologist: Yes, I see.

John: I then attended college and finally finished graduate school in 1991. My master's degree should help me to assume the duties of the new position.

Psychologist: You feel that your master's degree is a useful asset in your application.

John: Yes, my graduate experiences taught me how to work with others.

Psychologist: With these graduate experiences, you learned the art of working with other people.

John: Well, I guess I didn't learn it all in graduate school. I've always managed to get along well with others.

Psychologist: As far as you can tell, you work pretty well with people.

John:	That's right. As the oldest of three children, I've always had the responsibility for supervising others. You know what I mean?
Psychologist:	Being the oldest, you were given extra responsibilities as a child.
John:	Not that I resented it. Well, maybe sometimes. It's just that I never had much time for myself.
Psychologist:	And having time for yourself is important to you.
John:	Yes, of course it is. I guess everybody needs some time alone.
Psychologist:	As a person who deals with others all day long, you must treasure those few moments you have to yourself.
John:	I really do. Whenever I get a chance I like to drive up to the lake all by myself and just think.
Psychologist:	Those moments are precious to you.

The interview continued like this for about an hour. After it was over, John wasn't sure how he had done. Think about the two interviews. In what ways were they alike? How did they differ? As you contemplate your answers, you will soon realize that there is more than one type of interview and that interviews can differ considerably.

The first interview with the personnel officer was highly structured. The interviewer read from a printed set of questions, using a **standardized interview.** Thus, all applicants for the position were asked the same questions in the same sequence. By contrast, the second was an **unstructured interview** and therefore unstandardized. The clinical psychologist didn't appear to have any specific or particular questions in mind, and the sequence of questions followed from John's statements. Each applicant, no doubt, would be asked different questions, depending on his or her responses.

Can you identify other differences between the two interviews? The first was narrow and restricted. It focused on two specific areas: John's education and work experiences. The second was broad and unrestricted. It touched on a variety of areas, although the interview clearly focused on John himself. The first interview was *directive*. The personnel officer directed, guided, and controlled the course of the interview. The second interview was *nondirective*. The clinical psychologist let John determine the direction of the interview. When John talked about his master's degree, the psychologist discussed it. When John talked about being the oldest of three children, this became the focus of the psychologist's response. Furthermore, unlike the personnel officer, the psychologist rarely asked questions. Instead, the psychologist tended to comment or reflect on John's previous statement. Last, but perhaps most important, John's interview with the personnel officer can best be described as an **employment** (selection) **interview,** designed to elicit information pertaining to John's qualifications and capabilities for particular employment duties. The second interview, on the other hand, can best be described as a **diagnostic**

TABLE 9-1

Similarities Between an Interview and a Test

Method for gathering data
Used to make predictions
Evaluated in terms of reliability
Evaluated in terms of validity
Group or individual
Structured or unstructured

interview, designed to elicit information concerning John's emotional functioning. His qualifications were clearly not an issue in the second interview. Rather, in conducting a diagnostic interview, the clinical psychologist was interested in John's feelings, thoughts, attitudes, and the like, which might impede or facilitate John's ability to function competently.

The Interview as a Test

In many respects, an interview resembles a test (see Table 9-1). Like any psychological or educational test, an interview is a method for gathering data or information about an individual. This information is then used to describe the individual, make future predictions, or both. Like tests, interviews can be evaluated in terms of standard psychometric qualities such as reliability and validity. Furthermore, there are several types of interview procedures, depending on the type of information sought and the interviewer's goals.

Like any test, the interview involves the interaction of two or more people. Some interviews proceed like individually administered tests, the interviewer interacting with a single individual at a time. In others, such as the family interview, a single interviewer works with two or more individuals at the same time, just as in a group test. Like all tests, an interview has a defined purpose. Furthermore, just as the person who gives a test must take responsibility for the test administration process, so the interviewer must assume responsibility for the conduct of the interview.

Many tests, such as the Thematic Apperception Test (TAT), cannot be properly used without adequate interview data. The interview, on the other hand, is often the only or most important source of data. Good interviewing skills may be one of the most important tools for functioning in today's society. Further, interviewing is the chief method of collecting data in clinical psychiatry (J. G. Allen & Smith, 1993; D. Shaffer, 1994). It is also used in all health-related professions, including general medicine and nursing. Interviewing is an essential testing tool in subspecialties such as clinical, industrial, counseling, school, and correctional psychology.

Such fields as social work, vocational and guidance counseling, and marriage and family counseling use interviewing. Parole boards conduct parole interviews. The researcher also depends on interviewing. Business people and managers use it to evaluate employees as well as potential clients, and it is a primary tool of the courtroom attorney. Indeed, interview skills are important in most professions involving people. Contractors or architects must possess such skills to determine exactly what their customers want them to do. Interviewing also plays a role in everyday life, such as when a parent questions a group of children to find out whose home run broke the window. To begin new relationships on a positive note, one must possess a degree of interviewing skill. Given such a broad application, no introductory text on psychological tests could be complete without reference to the interview.

Reciprocal Nature of Interviewing

Although there are many types and purposes of interviews, all share certain factors. First, all interviews involve mutual or shared interaction (Wiens, 1976). The participants are interdependent and influence each other (Heller, 1971, pp. 145–148). A study by Heller, Davis, and Myers (1966) illustrates the transactional or reciprocal nature of the interview process. They found that if one of the participants in the interview increased his or her activity level, the activity of the other participant also increased. Similarly, a reduction in activity by one triggered reduction in the other. Matarazzo and colleagues (1968) reported a similar finding. Thus, the participants in an interview profoundly affect each other.

In addition to influencing each other's activity, they also affect each other's mood. Heller (1971), for example, reported that when professional actors responded with anger (hostility) to highly trained, experienced interviewers, the interviewers responded in kind; that is, they became angry themselves and directed this back toward the actors. The phenomenon observed by Heller, or **social facilitation** (see Bandura, 1986), means we tend to act like the models around us. If the interviewer is tense, anxious, defensive, and aloof, the interviewee tends to respond in kind. Thus, if the interviewer wishes to create conditions of openness, warmth, acceptance, comfort, calmness, and support, he or she must exhibit these qualities.

Social facilitation is one of the most important concepts underlying the interview process. Because the participants in an interview influence each other, the good interviewer must provide a relaxed and safe atmosphere. Through social facilitation, the interviewee eventually begins to feel relaxed and safe. However, although both parties influence each other, the good interviewer remains in control and sets the tone. If he or she reacts to the interviewee's tension and anxiety with more tension and anxiety, then these feelings will mount. By remaining relaxed, confident, and self-assured, the interviewer has a calming effect on the interviewee. In our experience, even potentially violent prison inmates or disturbed psychotic people become manageable when the interviewer sets the proper tone.

Principles of Effective Interviewing

Naturally, specific interview techniques and approaches vary, depending on such factors as the type of interview (for example, employment versus diagnostic) and the goals of the interviewer (for example, description versus prediction). Thus, there are no set rules that apply to all interview situations. However, some principles facilitate the conduct of almost any interview. We present these principles because they will increase your understanding of the factors and processes that underlie the interview. Knowledge of these principles should also help you acquire interview skills of your own.

The Proper Attitudes

As Tyler (1969) noted, good interviewing is actually more a matter of attitude than skill. Experiments in social psychology have shown that interpersonal influence (that is, the degree to which one person can influence another) is related to interpersonal attraction (that is, the degree to which people share a feeling of understanding, mutual respect, similarity, and the like) (B. L. Green & Kenrick, 1994; Hensley, 1994). Attitudes related to good interviewing skills include warmth, genuineness, acceptance, understanding, openness, honesty, and fairness. Saccuzzo (1975), for example, studied the initial psychotherapeutic interviews of first-year clinical psychology graduate students. Patients and therapists both responded to a questionnaire. Their task was to rate the quality of the interview and indicate the topics, concerns, problems, and feelings of the patient as well as the feelings of the therapist.

Although the patients' feelings and concerns were important, the most important factor in the patients' evaluations of the quality of the interview was their perceptions of the interviewer's feelings. The session received a good evaluation by both participants when the patient saw the interviewer as warm, open, concerned, involved, committed, and interested, regardless of subject matter or the type or severity of the problem. On the other hand, independent of all other factors, when the interviewer was seen as cold, defensive, uninterested, uninvolved, aloof, and bored, the session was rated poorly. To appear effective and establish rapport, the interviewer must display the proper attitudes.

Responses to Avoid

In a "stress interview" the interviewer may deliberately induce discomfort or anxiety in the interviewee. As a rule, however, making interviewees feel uncomfortable tends to place them on guard, and guarded or anxious interviewees tend to reveal little information about themselves. However, one purpose of the stress interview is to determine how well an individual functions in a stressful, uncomfortable, or demanding situation. Thus, the purpose of the interview dictates the type of responses to use or avoid. If the goal is to elicit as much information as possible, or if one wishes the interview to be considered satisfactory by the interviewee, then one should avoid certain responses, including *judgmental or evaluative statements, probing statements, hostility,* and *false reassurance.*

Judgmental or evaluative statements are particularly likely to inhibit the interviewee. Being judgmental means evaluating the thoughts, feelings, or actions of another. When we use such terms as *good, bad, excellent, terrible, disgusting, disgraceful,* and *stupid,* we make **evaluative statements.** By judging the other person, we put the person on guard because we communicate, "I don't approve of this aspect of you." In placing the person on guard, we limit his or her ease in revealing important information. Thus, unless the goal of the interview is to determine how a person responds to being evaluated or to apply stress by responding with strong disapproval or displeasure, evaluative or judgmental statements should usually be avoided in good interview behavior.

Also to be avoided, unless necessary for a specific purpose or type of interview, are **probing statements.** These demand more information than the interviewee wishes to provide voluntarily. The most common way to phrase a probing statement is to ask a question that begins with "Why?" Asking "Why?" tends to place the person on the defensive. When we ask "Why?" as in "Why did you stay out so late?" we are demanding that the person explain his or her behavior. Such a demand obviously has a judgmental quality. Furthermore, in probing we may induce the interviewee to reveal something he or she is not yet ready to reveal. If this happens, the interviewee will probably feel anxious and thus not very well disposed to revealing additional information.

In some circumstances, probes are appropriate and necessary. With children, for instance, one often needs to ask questions to elicit meaningful information. Highly anxious or withdrawn individuals may also need a probe to get beyond a superficial interchange. In such circumstances, one must use the probe wisely, avoiding "Why?" statements and replacing them with "Tell me" or "How?" statements, as illustrated in Table 9-2.

The **hostile statement** directs anger toward the interviewee. Clearly, one should avoid such responses unless one has a specific purpose, such as determining how an interviewee responds to anger.

TABLE 9-2
Effective Probing Statements

Poor	Better
Why did you yell at him?	1. Tell me more about what happened.
	2. How did you happen to yell at him?
	3. What led up to the situation?
Why did you say that?	1. Can you tell me what you mean?
	2. I'm not sure I understand.
	3. How did you happen to say that?
Why can't you sleep?	1. Tell me more about your sleeping problem.
	2. Can you identify what prevents you from sleeping?
	3. How is it that you are unable to sleep?

FIGURE 9-2

Responses to avoid in an unstructured interview.

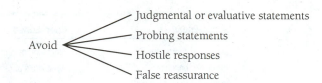

The **reassuring statement** attempts to comfort or support the interviewee: "Don't worry. Everything will be all right." Though reassurance is sometimes appropriate, you should almost always avoid false reassurance. For example, imagine a friend of yours flunks out of college, loses her job, and gets kicked out of her home by her parents. You are lying to this person when you say, "Don't worry; no problem; it's okay." This false reassurance does nothing to help your friend except perhaps make her realize that you are not going to help her. What has happened to your friend is terrible and will require specific action on her part to prevent even more disastrous developments. Naturally, you should not overwhelm your friend with all the facts at once, but she needs to come to grips with the situation in manageable doses before taking the necessary steps to constructively solve the problem. The person who gives false reassurance usually know he or she is doing it, as does the person who receives it. (See Figure 9-2.)

Effective Responses

Knowing what types of responses to avoid, how does one go about conducting an effective interview? One major principle of effective interviewing is keeping the interaction flowing. The interview is a two-way process; first one person speaks, then the other, and so on. Furthermore, the interviewer usually exerts a minimum amount of effort to keep the interaction flowing. As long as the interviewee's verbalizations relate to the purpose of the interview, the interviewer listens with interest by maintaining face-to-face contact.

Except in structured interviews or for a particular purpose, one can effectively initiate the interview process by using an **open-ended question.** This is one that usually cannot be answered specifically, as opposed to a **closed-ended question,** which can. Examples of open-ended questions are "Tell me a little bit about yourself," "Tell me about what interests you," and "What is it that brings you here to see me?" Examples of closed-ended questions are "Do you like sports?" "Are you married?" and "How old are you?"

A closed-ended question brings the interview to a dead halt, thus violating the principle of keeping the interaction flowing. In the example at the beginning of this chapter, even the personnel officer's opening statement was sufficiently open-ended to permit a variety of responses, depending on the interviewee. Where one individual might provide every minute detail of his or her education, a second might simply include major events. In degree, however, the clinical psychologist's opening statement—"Why don't you tell me a little bit about yourself?"—was even more open-ended. John could have replied with just about anything.

TABLE 9-3
*Open- and
Closed-Ended
Questions*

Closed-Ended	Open-Ended
Do you like sports cars?	What kind of cars do you like?
Do you like baseball?	What kinds of recreational activities do you prefer?
Are you having a problem?	Tell me about your problems.
Is your father strict?	Describe your father.
Would you like to vacation in Hawaii?	What are your favorite vacation spots?

Open-ended questions give the interviewee wide latitude in choosing the topics he or she feels are important. Except for highly specific structured interviews, we usually can learn a lot more about people when they tell us what they think is important than when we try to guess by asking a series of closed-ended questions. The open-ended question requires the interviewee to produce something spontaneously; the closed-ended question, to recall something. Table 9-3 presents some closed-ended questions along with corresponding open-ended ones.

Conducting an interview requires flexibility. If not structured, most interviews cannot be conducted in precisely the same way. In therapeutic or diagnostic interviews, the interviewer usually follows only general guidelines in conducting the interview. Their goal is to get to know the interviewees as well as possible to understand them and predict their behavior.

Responses to Keep the Interaction Flowing

After asking the open-ended question, the interviewer as a rule lets the interviewee respond without interruption; that is, the interviewer remains quiet and listens. Unless the interview is structured, once the interviewee's response dies down, the interviewer usually responds in a way that will keep the interaction flowing. A closed-ended question at this point would naturally bring the interview to a halt. Instead, the interviewer should use minimum effort to maintain the flow. After the initial response to the open-ended question has been completed, the interviewer could use a transitional phrase such as "Yes," "I see," or "And." These transitional phrases imply that the interviewee should continue on the same topic. In John's interview with the clinical psychologist, for example, John stated, "I graduated from high school in June 1984. I majored in history and social studies." The clinical psychologist simply responded with the transition, "Yes, I see." John then elaborated.

Sometimes the transitional phrase fails to have the desired effect. When this occurs, the interviewer should make a response relevant to what has just been communicated. In other words, the interview is thematic; it does not jump from one unrelated topic to another as it might if the interviewer asked a series of questions. The theme in John's interview with the clinical psychologist was John. Although the topics changed from John's education to his feeling about being the oldest of three, John himself remained the central focus. The psychologist accomplished this by making statements relevant to what John was saying.

To make such a response, the interviewer may use any of the following types of statements: verbatim playback, paraphrasing, restatement, summarizing, clarifying, and understanding. You can view these statements on a continuum ranging from being totally interchangeable with the interviewee's response to adding to or going beyond it.

In a verbatim playback, the interviewer simply repeats the interviewee's last response. For example, in his interview with the clinical psychologist, John stated, "I majored in history and social studies." The psychologist replied with the transitional phrase "Yes, I see." A verbatim playback, "You majored in history and social studies," would have been equally effective. In either case, John most likely would continue to elaborate on his previous response. Thus, like the transitional phrase, the verbatim playback generally leads to an elaboration of the interviewee's previous response.

Closely related to the verbatim playback in terms of eliciting elaborations, paraphrasing and restatement responses are both interchangeable with the interviewee's response. A paraphrase tends to be more similar to the interviewee's response than the restatement, but both capture the meaning of the interviewee's response. When John said, "My master's degree should help me assume the duties of the new position," the psychologist replied, "You feel that your master's degree is a useful asset in your application," a restatement. A paraphrase might have taken the form "You feel that your master's degree will be an important aid in tackling the responsibilities of the new position." In his restatement, the psychologist introduced "useful asset" to restate John's attitude toward his master's degree. The paraphrase, on the other hand, simply replaced "important aid" to "help" and "tackling the responsibilities" for "assuming the duties." Neither statement, however, added anything to John's.

Summarizing and clarification statements go just beyond the interviewee's response. In summarizing, the interviewer pulls together the meaning of several interviewee responses. To John's last statement in the example, the psychologist could have replied with a summarizing statement such as "As a youth you never had much time to yourself because you were responsible for taking care of the two younger children. Today you enjoy those few moments you have to be alone. Whenever you get a chance to be alone you drive to the lake all by yourself and just think." Notice that this summarizing statement involves verbatim playback, paraphrasing, and restating. With these three types of statements, the psychologist summarizes an entire sequence of responses.

The clarification statement, as its name implies, serves to clarify the interviewee's response. When John stated, "Not that I resented it. Well, maybe sometimes. It's just that I never had much time for myself," the psychologist attempted to clarify what John was trying to say. It was not that John resented the extra responsibilities; rather, he simply wanted some time to be alone. Thus, the psychologist clarified John's statement by saying, "And having time for yourself is important to you."

The clarification statement—like summarizing, paraphrasing, restatement, and verbatim playback—remains very close to the meaning of the intervie-

TABLE 9-4

Responses to Keep the Interaction Flowing

Response	Definition or Example
Transitional phrase	"Yes," "I see," "Go on"
Verbatim playback	Repeats interviewee's exact words
Paraphrasing and restatement	Repeats interviewee's response using different words
Summarizing	Pulls together the meaning of several responses
Clarification	Clarifies the interviewee's response
Empathy/Understanding	Communicates understanding

wee's response. These responses are either interchangeable with the interviewee's own response or add slightly to it. Each of these responses communicates or facilitates a degree of understanding. At the lowest level, the verbatim playback communicates that the interviewer at least heard the communication. The restatement, paraphrase, and summarizing responses go a bit further by communicating that the interviewer has a good idea of what the interviewee is trying to communicate.

Even more powerful is the **empathy** or **understanding response.** This response communicates that the interviewer understands how the interviewee must feel. When the psychologist stated, "These moments are precious to you," he did not simply paraphrase or restate. Instead, he communicated that he understood how John felt about having time to himself. (See Table 9-4 for a summary of responses that keep the interview flowing.)

Many students find it difficult to see the value of statements that stay close to the interviewee's response. Some students consider such statements artificial and weak because of their noncommittal quality. However, the rationale for such responses is based on the well-known and well-documented finding that when we show people we understand, they will talk about or explore themselves at deeper and deeper levels (Beutler, Crago, & Arizmendi, 1986; Rogers, 1980). Accurate empathy elicits self-exploration. Consider the following example:

Psychologist: What's been happening today, Bill? *(open-ended question)*

Bill: My physics teacher yelled at me in front of the whole class.

Psychologist: That's embarrassing. *(understanding)*

Bill: Not only that, she seems to pick on me all the time.

Psychologist: That must make you angry. *(understanding)*

Bill: Yeah, I guess so. It seems like she's always finding fault with my work. No matter what I do, she just doesn't like it.

Psychologist: That is really frustrating, Bill. You just can't seem to please her. *(understanding)*

Bill: The other day we had an exam and I got an F. I checked my answers with Tom, and mine were the same as his. Yet I got an F and Tom got a B.

Psychologist:	Hey, that doesn't seem fair. *(clarification and understanding)*
Bill:	You bet it isn't fair. But when I tried to talk to her about it, she refused to listen.
Psychologist:	That's scary. *(understanding)*
Bill:	It sure is. I get one more *F,* I'll be kicked out of school.
Psychologist:	This is really serious. *(clarification)*
Bill:	Yeah, If I got kicked out of school, I couldn't face my parents or friends.
Psychologist:	This whole thing has really got you upset. *(understanding)*

Certainly, the psychologist's responses are not the only ones that would work. However, you should note how the psychologist, in providing a series of understanding responses, could "uncover" the real source of Bill's anguish. The feelings Bill expressed moved from embarrassment to anger to fear of being kicked out of school and finally to fear of how his friends and family would view his failure.

Let's consider other possible responses to Bill's initial statement, "My physics teacher yelled at me in front of the whole class." The psychologist could have replied the following: (1) "Why did she do that?" With this probing statement, Bill would have to defend himself or explain why it happened. He would have to go over the circumstances that preceded the incident, actually leading away from Bill's real feelings and concerns. (2) "Why did you let her do that to you? That wasn't very smart of you." This evaluative statement places Bill on the defensive, criticizes him, and possibly hurts his feelings. Given this type of reaction from the psychologist, Bill would not feel safe exploring his real feelings. (3) "That woman is always yelling at somebody. You should report her to the chairperson." With this off-the-cuff advice, the psychologist again removes himself from Bill's real concerns. The two might spend the rest of their time together weighing the pros and cons of reporting Bill's physics teacher. Still worse, Bill might impulsively follow the advice and get into real trouble if he cannot substantiate his claims. (4) "Don't worry. That physics teacher yells at everyone. It doesn't mean a thing." With this false reassurance, Bill no longer is free to express his real concern. The psychologist has already dismissed the whole matter as insignificant.

In short, understanding responses that stay close to the content and underlying feeling provided by interviewees permit them to explore their situations out loud and at deeper and deeper levels. In general, unstructured interviewing is an uncovering process. Questions, evaluations, reassurances, and the like—unless specifically called for, as in a structured interview—generally allow only superficial understanding of an individual.

As a rule, the interviewing centers on obtaining verbal information from the interviewee. One good way to accomplish this involves facilitative statements. The facilitative interview provides a positive atmosphere. It begins with an open-ended question followed by understanding statements that capture

FIGURE 9-3
Exercise in keeping the interaction flowing.

Directions: Below is a list of statements, each followed by two possible replies. Select the one that would tend to keep the interaction flowing.

1. I hate school.
☐   a. It sounds like you're fed up with school.
☐   b. What's wrong with school?

2. My dad is a jerk.
☐   a. Why don't you just tell him to "chill out"?
☐   b. You're angry with your dad.

3. Most people are liars.
☐   a. Don't be so negative.
☐   b. You feel that most people can't be trusted.

4. We were ahead until the last minute of the game.
☐   a. That's disappointing.
☐   b. Why didn't you win?

5. She stood me up again.
☐   a. If I were you, I wouldn't ask her out again.
☐   b. It hurts to be treated like that.

6. I hope I passed the test.
☐   a. You're worried about how you did on the test.
☐   b. Don't worry. I'm sure you passed.

Answers: 1. a; 2. b; 3. b; 4. a; 5. b; 6. a

Notes:
1b is a probing statement.
2a is advice.
3a is advice.
4b is a probing statement.
5a is advice.
6b is false reassurance.

the meaning and feeling of the interviewee's communication. See Figure 9-3 for an exercise in keeping the interaction flowing.

Measuring Understanding

One can further appreciate understanding statements by analyzing measures of understanding. Attempts to measure understanding or empathy originated with Carl Rogers's research into the effects of client-centered therapy (Rogers, 1959a, 1961b; A. M. Walker, Rablen, & Rogers, 1960). It culminated in a five-point scoring system (Truax & Carkhuff, 1967, pp. 46–58), subsequently revised (Carkhuff & Berenson, 1967). Each level in this system represents a degree of empathy. They range from a response that bears little or no relation-ship to the previous statement to a response that captures the precise meaning and feeling of the statement. The highest degree of empathy, level five, is rele-vant primarily for therapeutic interviews. Levels four and three represent vari-ous degrees of true empathy or understanding and may be used in all types of unstructured or semistructured (that is, partially structured) interviews. The lowest levels, one and two, have no place in a professional interview and should be avoided. Low-level responses, however, occur frequently in every-day conversations. We discuss these levels to illustrate how one can measure understanding.

Level-one responses. Level-one responses bear little or no relationship to the interviewee's response. According to Carkhuff and Berenson (1967), these responses do not attend to or detract significantly from the interviewee's responses. A level-one conversation might proceed as follows:

Jennifer: Jason, look at my new dress.

Jason: I sure hope it doesn't rain today.

Jennifer: See, it's red with blue stripes.

Jason: If it rains, my baseball game might get canceled.

Jennifer: I really love this dress, it's my favorite.

Jason: It's sure going to tick me off if that game gets canceled.

The two might as well be talking to themselves.

Level-two responses. The level-two response communicates a superficial aware-ness of the meaning of a statement. The individual who makes a level-two response never quite goes beyond his or her own limited perspective. Level-two responses subtract from the communication. For example,

Jennifer: Boy, I feel good. I just got a beautiful new dress.

Jason: I feel bad. It's probably going to rain.

Jennifer: I'll wear this dress to your baseball game.

Jason: If it rains, there won't be a game.

Here the conversation is related, but only superficially. Neither person really responds to what is going on in the other.

Level-three responses. A level-three response is interchangeable with the inter-viewee's statement. According to Carkhuff and Berenson (1967), level three is the minimum level of responding that can help the interviewee. Clearly nonfa-cilitative, responses at levels one and two can actually harm a person in need of help.

Level-four and level-five responses. Level-four and level-five responses not only provide accurate empathy but also go beyond the statement given. In a level-four response, the interviewer adds "noticeably" to the interviewee's response. In a level-five response, the interviewer adds "significantly" to the response (Carkhuff & Berenson, 1967). We recommend that beginning interviewers learn to respond at levels three and four to maximize self-exploration and the uncovering process in unstructured and semistructured interviews. In the example with Jennifer and Jason, a level-four interchange might proceed as follows:

> Jennifer: I just got a new dress.
>
> Jason: You feel glad because you like new clothes.
>
> Jennifer: This one is beautiful; it has red and blue stripes.
>
> Jason: You really love that new dress. It is a nice addition to your wardrobe.

Active listening. An impressive array of research has accumulated documenting the power of the understanding response (C. H. Patterson, 1974; Rogers, 1980; Truax & Mitchell, 1971). This type of responding, sometimes called *active listening,* is the foundation of good interviewing skills for many different types of interviews.

Types of Interviews

The previously discussed guides provide a general format for conducting an interview. The specifics vary, however, depending on the interviewer's goal, purpose, and theoretical orientation. We can distinguish, for example, among five types of interviews: the evaluation interview, the structured clinical interview, the case history interview, the mental status examination, and the employment or selection interview.

Evaluation Interview

Maloney and Ward's (1976) conception of an evaluation interview suggests guides similar to those presented in this chapter for effective interviewing. This similarity is not surprising, for both methods stem from the research-based principle that accurate understanding leads to self-exploration. Thus, Maloney and Ward recommend beginning with an open-ended question, with the interviewer "listening, facilitating, and clarifying" during the initial phases of the interview. In addition, they recommend that the powerful tool of confrontation be included in the process.

Though the confrontation response is usually most appropriate in therapeutic interviews, experienced interviewers should have this technique at their disposal. A **confrontation** is a statement that points out a discrepancy or inconsistency. Carkhuff (1969) distinguishes among three types: (1) a discrepancy between what the person is and what he or she wants to become, (2) a discrepancy between what the person says about himself or herself and what he or she does, and (3) a discrepancy between the person's perception of himself or herself and the interviewer's experience of the person.

Confrontation may induce anxiety by bringing conflicts or inconsistencies into a person's awareness when he or she is not ready to handle them. We therefore strongly recommend that the beginning student leave confrontation for the more experienced practitioner.

Direct questions can be used toward the end of the interview to fill in any needed details or gaps in the interviewer's knowledge. For unstructured or semistructured interviews, we advocate the use of direct questions whenever (1) the data can be obtained in no other way, (2) time is limited and the interviewer needs specific information, or (3) the interviewee cannot or will not cooperate with the interviewer. The open-ended, facilitative technique does not work well for nonverbal, intellectually limited, and uncooperative subjects. It also doesn't work well with children, who require direct questioning and careful observation (D. Shaffer, 1994; D. J. Wood, 1982). With these subjects, it is exceedingly difficult to get the interview off the ground. Thus, direct questioning becomes necessary.

Structured Clinical Interviews

Recently, structured clinical interviews have proliferated (F. Allen, 1994; K. Hodges, 1994; Knauper & Wittchen, 1994). Structured interviews, as we have indicated, provide a specific set of questions presented in a particular order. In addition, there is usually a carefully specified set of rules for probing so that, as in a standardized test, all interviewees are handled in the same manner. Structured interviews lend themselves to scoring procedures so that norms can be developed and applied. Typically, cutoff scores are used so that a particular score indicates the presence or absence of a given condition.

The development of structured clinical interviews followed the evolution of the *Diagnostic and Statistical Manual of Mental Disorders* (DSM). First published in 1952, revised in 1968, 1980, 1987, and 1995, the DSM attempts to classify mental disorders into specific, definable categories. Before the 1980 DSM-III however, mental disorders were poorly defined. The result was a very low reliability in psychiatric diagnosis.

The DSM-III attempted to overcome this lack of reliability by providing a specific set of criteria for each category of mental disorder. Table 9-5, for example, shows the diagnostic criteria for an obsessive-compulsive disorder from the DSM-IV (American Psychiatric Association [APA], 1995).

With specifiable criteria for mental disorders, one could develop a specific set of questions to determine whether or not a person met the criteria. For example, Spitzer and colleagues developed a comprehensive interview specifically for making diagnoses from the DSM-III-R, called the Structural Clinical Interview for the DSM-III-R, or the SCID (Spitzer et al., 1990a). Table 9-6 pro-

TABLE 9-5

Diagnostic Criteria for an Obsessive-Compulsive Disorder

A. Either obsessions or compulsions

Obsessions

1. Recurrent and persistent thoughts, impulses, or images that are experienced as intrusive and inappropriate and that cause marked anxiety or distress.

2. The thoughts, impulses, or images are not simply excessive worries about real-life problems.

3. The person attempts to ignore or suppress such thoughts, impulses, or images or to neutralize them with some other thought or action.

4. The person recognizes that the obsessions, impulses, or images are the product of his or her own mind.

Compulsions

1. Repetitive behaviors (e.g., hand washing, ordering, checking) or mental acts (e.g., praying, counting, repeating words silently) that the person feels driven to perform in response to an obsession, or according to rules that must be applied rigidly.

2. The behavior or mental acts are aimed at preventing or reducing distress or preventing some dreaded event or situation; however, these behaviors or mental acts either are not connected in a realistic way with what they are designed to neutralize or prevent or are clearly excessive.

From *Diagnostic and Statistical Manual of Mental Disorders, Fourth Edition, Revised* (DSM-IV). Washington, DC: American Psychiatric Association, 1995.

vides an example of the SCID used to diagnose obsessive-compulsive disorder. Notice that the interview formula is quite specific, allows for a specific scoring system, and makes clear-cut provisions for unclear responses.

Today there are countless structured interviews for just about every imaginable problem. Interviews are available to assess disorders in children: the Diagnostic Interview Schedule for Children and various revisions, or DISC, DISC-R, and DISC-2 (K. Hodges, 1994; D. Shaffer, 1994), and the Child Assessment Schedule, or CAS (F. Allen, 1994; Hodges, 1985); to assess personality disorders: the Structured Clinical Interview for DSM-III-R—Personality Disorders, or SCID-II (Spitzer et al., 1990b); and to do preliminary screening of mental illness in jails: the Referral Decision Scale, or RDS (Teplin & Schwartz, 1989).

As we have emphasized, structured interviews offer reliability but sacrifice flexibility. They can especially help researchers document and define a specific group. For example, if you plan to study obsessive-compulsive disorder, then you need subjects who fall into this category, and there is no better way to document such subjects than to conduct a structured clinical interview. Of course, if you don't know what you're looking for, a structured interview that covers more than 20 diagnoses could become quite a lengthy task. Such interviews require the cooperation of the interviewee, which is not always easy to obtain when the interviewee is a disturbed mental patient or in acute distress.

A major limitation of the structured interview is that it relies exclusively on the respondent. It assumes that the respondent is honest and capable of accurate self-observation and that the respondent will provide frank, candid answers, even to embarrassing questions. As we discuss in Chapter 15, such assumptions cannot always be considered valid. Particularly in forensic settings, one often should not accept the validity of an interviewee's response at face value. After all, if a person facing a death sentences pleads insanity, we

TABLE 9-6
SCID 9/1/89 Version Obsessive-Compulsive Disorder Anxiety Disorders

Obsessive-Compulsive Disorder	Obsessive-Compulsive Disorder Criteria				

A. Either obsessions or compulsions:

		?	1	2	3
Now I would like to ask you if you have ever been bothered by thoughts that didn't make any sense and kept coming back to you even when you tried not to have them? (What were they?)	Obsessions: (1), (2), (3), and (4):	?	1	2	3
	(1) Recurrent and persistent ideas, thoughts, impulses, or images that are experienced, at least initially, as intrusive and senseless, e.g., a parent's having repeated impulses to hurt a loved child, a religious person's having recurrent blasphemous thoughts				
(What about awful thoughts, like actually hurting someone even though you didn't want to, or being contaminated by germs or dirt?)	NOTE: DO NOT INCLUDE BROODING ABOUT PROBLEMS (SUCH AS HAVING A PANIC ATTACK) OR ANXIOUS RUMINATIONS ABOUT REALISTIC DANGERS.				
When you had these thoughts, did you try hard to get them out of your head? (What would you try to do?)	(2) The person attempts to ignore or suppress such thoughts or to neutralize them with some other thoughts or action	?	1	2	3
IF UNCLEAR: Where did you think these thoughts were coming from?	(3) The person recognizes that the obsessions are the product of his or her own mind, not imposed from without (as in thought insertion)	?	1	2	3
	(4) If another Axis I disorder is present, the content of the obsession is unrelated to it, i.e., the ideas, thoughts, impulses, or images are not about food in the presence of an Eating Disorder, about drugs in the presence of a Psychoactive Substance Use Disorder, or guilty thoughts in the presence of a Major Depression	?	1	2	3

OBSES-SIONS

DESCRIBE:

		?	1	2	3
Was there ever anything that you had to do over and over again and couldn't resist doing, like washing your hands again and again, or checking something several times to make sure you'd done it right?	Compulsions: (1), (2), and (3):	?	1	2	3
	(1) Repetitive, purposeful, and intentional behaviors that are performed in response to an obsession, or according to certain rules, or in a stereotyped fashion				
IF YES: What did you have to do? (What were you afraid would happen if you didn't do it?) (How many times did you have to _____? How much time did you spend each day _____?)	(2) The behavior is designed to neutralize or prevent discomfort or some dreaded event or situation; however, either the activity is not connected in a realistic way with what it is designed to neutralize or prevent, or it is clearly excessive	?	1	2	3
IF UNCLEAR: Do you think that you (DO COMPULSIVE BEHAVIOR) more than you should? (Do you think [COMPULSION] makes sense?)	(3) The person recognizes that the behavior is excessive or unreasonable (this may no longer be true for people whose obsessions have evolved into overvalued ideas)	?	1	2	3

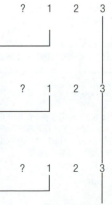

Continued

TABLE 9-6
Continued

Obsessive-Compulsive Disorder	Obsessive-Compulsive Disorder Criteria

COMPULSIONS

DESCRIBE:

IF NEITHER OBSESSIONS NOR COMPULSIONS, CHECK HERE AND GO TO *GENERALIZED ANXIETY DISORDER* _____.

What effect did this (OBSESSION OR COMPULSION) have on your life? (Did _____ bother you a lot?)

(How much time do you spend [OBSESSION OR COMPULSION])?

(Did anyone in your family, or your friends, have to go out of their way because of your [OBSESSION OR COMPULSION]?)

B. The obsessions or compulsions cause marked distress, are time-consuming (take more than an hour a day), or significantly interfere with the person's normal routine, occupational functioning, or usual social activities or relationships with others

?   1   2   3

GO TO *GAD,*

DESCRIBE:

OBSESSIVE COMPULSIVE DISORDER CRITERIA A AND B ARE CODED "3"

1   3

GO TO *GAD,*

OBSES-SIVE COMPUL-SIVE DISORDER

CHRONOLOGY

IF UNCLEAR: During the past month, did the (OBSESSIONS OR COMPULSIONS) have any effect on your life or bother you a lot?

Has met criteria for Obsessive Compulsive Disorder during past month (criteria A and B)

?   1   3

When were you last bothered by (ANY OBSESSIONS OR COMPULSIONS)?

Number of months prior to interview when last had symptoms of Obsessive-Compulsive Disorder

___ ___ ___

PAST FIVE YEARS

During the past five years, how much of the time have (ANY OBSESSIONS OR COMPULSIONS) had an effect on your life or bothered you a lot?

Would you say . . . [CODE DESCRIPTIONS]?

Approximate percentage of time during past five years that any symptoms of Obsessive-Compulsive Disorder were present

1   Not at all (0%)

2   Rarely (e.g., 5–10%)

3   A significant minority of the time (e.g., 20–30%)

4   About half the time

5   A significant majority of the time (e.g., 70–80%)

6   Almost all the time (e.g., 90–100%)

7   Unknown

How old were you when the (OBSESSIONS OR COMPULSIONS) first had any effect on your life or bothered you a lot?	Age at onset of Obsessive-Compulsive Disorder (criteria A and B) (CODE 99 IF UNKNOWN) ____ ____

? = inadequate information   1 = absent or false   2 = subthreshold   3 = threshold or true
From Spitzer et al. (1990a).

may not believe his or her response, "Yes, I hear voices all the time." On a less obvious level, an interviewee may simply be trying to impress the interviewer or dramatize his or her plight by endorsing symptoms that aren't really present. Thus, although structured interviews may be a valuable source of information, you should interpret the results from such procedures cautiously.

Case History Interview

An interview that begins with an open-ended question followed by level-three and level-four responses can yield a wealth of data about an individual. The interviewer obtains an in-depth description of those factors most important to the interviewee. However, case history data may or may not be revealed, depending on their relevance to central issues in the interviewee's life. To obtain a complete *case history*—that is, a biographical sketch—one often needs to ask specific questions. Case history data may include a chronology of major events in the person's life, a work history, a medical history, and a family history. A family history should include a complete listing of the ages and genders of each member of the immediate family. One should also note whether any family members—including parents, grandparents, uncles, aunts, and siblings—have experienced difficulties similar to those experienced by the interviewee. Many conditions occur more frequently in families than in the general population (F. Allen, 1994).

In obtaining the history, the interviewer often takes a developmental approach, examining an individual's entire life, beginning with infancy. For example, the interviewer may say, "Tell me about your work record." After the work history is clarified, another category such as medical history can be explored.

The purpose of obtaining a case history is understanding individuals' backgrounds. Only with this understanding can one interpret a test score. To this end, one should attempt to uncover information pertaining to religious preference, premarital and marital experiences, hobbies, education, accomplishments, and habits. Life-style information such as smoking behavior, use of alcohol, exercise patterns, and current stressors can also be useful. If a child is

TABLE 9-7

Part of a Branching Algorithm for a Computerized Interview

1. Have you ever used tobacco?

   If No, go to 2.

   If Yes, answer *a–d.*

   a. At what age did you first start smoking?

   b. About how many cigarettes did you smoke on the average?

   c. Have you ever tried to quit?

      If No, go to *d.*

      If Yes, answer *i–iii.*

      i.   When was the first time you tried to quit?

      ii. To what extent were you able to reduce the number of cigarettes you smoked each day?

      iii. How many times have you tried to quit?

   d. Identify any stressors that seem to cause you to smoke more.

2. Have you ever used alcohol?

   If No, go to 3.

   If Yes, answer *a–e.*

the focus of the interview, then information about the parent as well as the child should be obtained.

Case history interviews are relatively easy to present on a computer rather than by a person (Nurius, 1990). Naturally, such interviews are highly structured. They do, however, possess some flexibility through structured branching, in which algorithms make questions contingent on an examinee's responses. For example, the interviewee may be asked, "Do you smoke?" If the answer is "no," the program goes to the next main question. If the answer is "yes," however, the questioning branches into a number of other questions about smoking, such as "How many cigarettes do you smoke per day?" "How long have you been smoking?" and "Have you ever tried to quit?" Still another branch may relate to previous efforts to quit, such as "How many times have you tried to quit?" See Table 9-7 for an example of part of a branching algorithm.

Computerized interviews have the advantage of nearly perfect interviewer reliability. However, unlike a human interviewer, the computer cannot respond to facial expressions and similar nonverbal cues, so in some situations valuable information is lost.

Mental Status Examination

An important tool in psychiatric and neurological examinations, the mental status examination is used primarily to diagnose psychosis, brain damage, and other major mental health problems. Its purpose is to evaluate a person suspected of having neurological or emotional problems in terms of variables known to be related to these problems.

The areas covered in the mental status examination include the person's appearance, attitudes, and general behavior. The interviewer is also alert to the interviewee's emotions. For example, is there one dominant emotion that fluctuates little? Is there an absence of emotion (that is, a flat affect)? Are the emotions appropriate? Do the emotions fluctuate widely? The person's thought processes are also evaluated. Intelligence can be evaluated by such factors as speed and accuracy of thinking, richness of thought content, memory, judgment, and ability to interpret proverbs. Especially important in the assessment of schizophrenia, a major form of psychosis involving loss of contact with reality, is the quality of the person's thought processes. This can be assessed through an analysis of thought content. For example, is there anything unusual or peculiar about the person's thoughts? Is the person preoccupied with any particular idea? Are the person's ideas realistic?

Other important areas evaluated in the mental status examination include the person's ability to direct and deploy attention. Is the person distracted? Can he or she stick to a task as long as needed to complete it? Sensory factors also are considered. Is the person seeing things that aren't there? What is the accuracy of the person's perceptions? A number of guides for conducting mental status exams are available (see, for example, MacKinnon, 1980; Sands, 1972).

Keep in mind that to make proper use of the mental status examination, you must have a broad understanding of the major mental disorders and the various forms of brain damage. There is no room for amateurs or self-appointed practitioners when a mental status examination is needed. However, knowledge of those areas covered in the mental status examination can be useful to interviewers interested in knowing the important variables in observing and evaluating another human being.

Employment Interview

The employment interview helps people make selection and promotion decisions in business and industry. A number of important articles and books are exclusively devoted to the employment (selection) interview.

The first extensive review of the employment interview was provided by R. Wagner (1949), who reviewed about 100 studies. He severely criticized most of the studies, however, emphasizing that much of the literature consisted of contradicting opinions and how-to formulas. Following Wagner's call for more and better studies, E. C. Webster (1964) presented a series of important experimental investigations into the nature of the employment interview. Two independent reviews of the literature on the employment interview were subsequently published in the mid-1960s (Mayfield, 1964; Ulrich & Trumbo, 1965). Both reviews began where R. Wagner (1949) had left off. O. R. Wright (1969) then reviewed the literature between 1964 and 1969. Subsequent literature has been examined by Schmitt (1976), Arvey and Campion (1982), and Zedeck, Tziner, and Middlestadt (1983) (also see Dougherty, Ebert, & Callender, 1986). More recent approaches have emphasized the importance of combining interview data with other sources of information (Dalessio & Silverhart, 1994).

These reviews have revealed some extremely valuable information about interviews in general and the employment interview in particular. Interestingly, the reviewers almost unanimously recommended a structured format for the employment interview. A number of studies clearly pointed to the superiority of structured interviews for enabling interviewers to reach agreement concerning their employment decisions. Thus, the loss of flexibility in structured interviews can be balanced by increases in reliability. A meta-analytic investigation of the literature found that structured interviews produced mean validity coefficients twice as high as did unstructured interviews (Wiesner & Cronshaw, 1988). As you will see later, when we discuss sources of error in the interview, researchers who have studied the employment interview have often found less than satisfactory results (Balzer, Rohrbaugh, & Murphy, 1983; Schuler, 1993; Zedeck, Tziner, & Middlestadt, 1983). In this section, we briefly touch on what interviewers look for in employment interviews and on methods of presenting oneself in an interview.

It has long been known that the employment interview often involves a search for negative or unfavorable rather than favorable evidence about a person (E. C. Webster, 1964). If a negative is found, the person probably will not be hired unless there is a high demand for workers and few individuals available to fill open positions. In one study reported by E. C. Webster (1964), it was noted that as few as one unfavorable impression was followed by final rejection in 90% of the cases. This rejection rate, however, dropped to 25% when early impressions were favorable. Webster and others caution employment interviewers against forming an early bias that might result in rejecting a competent individual. Despite widespread knowledge of Webster's cautions, interviewers continue to make basic errors when formulating personnel decisions (Dreher, Ash, & Hancock, 1988).

Negative factors that commonly lead to the rejection of candidates include poor communication skills, lack of confidence or poise, low enthusiasm, nervousness, and failure to make eye contact (Nykodym & Ruud, 1985; Nykodym & Simonetti, 1981). Positive factors include the ability to express oneself, self-confidence and poise, enthusiasm, the ability to sell oneself, and aggressiveness (Baehr, 1987).

Can you increase your chances of presenting yourself favorably in a job interview? With the tightening of the job market in many sectors of the economy, this is not an idle question. And, as Heimberg, Keller, and Peca-Baker (1986) noted, competent performance in job interviews is widely regarded as one of the most important factors in obtaining employment. Thus, a number of approaches have been recommended for prospective employees who wish to tip the balance in their favor (Baron, 1986; Larkin & Pines, 1994).

A good first impression is one of the most important factors in a successful job interview (Dougherty, Turban, & Callender, 1994). To make a good first impression, research has revealed the value of a professional style of dress and good grooming (Cash, 1985; Dipboye, Arvey, & Terpstra, 1977), projecting an aura of competence and expertise (Baron, 1986; Price & Garland, 1983), and transmitting an impression of friendliness or personal warmth through nonverbal cues (Imada & Hakel, 1977). But going too far with these tactics can sometimes backfire.

Baron (1986) had female confederates pose as applicants for an entry-level management position. Some wore perfume, others did not. In addition, some attempted to convey friendliness through nonverbal behaviors including a high level of eye contact with the interviewer; an informal, friendly posture (such as leaning forward at predetermined points); and frequent smiling. Interviewees in the neutral cue condition refrained from these nonverbal behaviors. The results revealed that when used alone, either perfume or positive nonverbal behaviors produced enhanced ratings for the applicants. When used together, however, these tactics produced negative reactions among interviewers, probably because they caused the applicant to be perceived as manipulative (Baron, 1986). Thus, while it is important to put your best foot forward in an interview, you must be careful not to overdo it.

Developing Interviewing Skills

One controversy in the field of interviewing concerns whether or not interviewing skills can be learned and acquired (Wiens, 1976). The general consensus is that interviewing skills can be acquired (Latham, 1987). To obtain such skills, you should familiarize yourself with research and theory on the interview. By understanding the principles and underlying variables in the interview, you will have taken the first step toward acquired interviewing skills.

A second factor in learning such skills is supervised practice. Experience truly is the best teacher. No amount of book learning can compare with having one's taped interview analyzed by an expert.

A third factor has to do with the principles for learning such skills. As a student, you must make a conscious effort to apply the principles learned from books and supervisors. For example, you must continuously try to apply the principles involved in keeping the interaction flowing. In addition, you must continually ask yourself questions such as "What does this person mean? Am I communicating that I understand? Is the person exploring at deeper levels? What is being communicated nonverbally?"

In the initial phase of learning any new skill, it seems as though you must attend to a hundred things at once—an impossible task. However, if you make a persistent effort, you will eventually respond appropriately by habit. Thus, experienced interviewers automatically attend to the person's appearance, nonverbal communications, emotional tone, and so on. They do so not because they are endowed with special abilities, but because they trained themselves to do so. With practice, many interviewing behaviors can be completed almost automatically.

Sources of Error in the Interview

To make appropriate use of the interview, you must develop an awareness of the various sources of error or potential bias in data from interviews. Then, you can try to compensate for their negative effects. Furthermore, in acquiring this knowledge you will develop a better awareness of the limitations inherent in judging human beings on the basis of the interview.

Interview Validity

Many sources of interview error come from the extreme difficulty we have in making accurate, logical observations and judgments (Schuler, 1993). Suppose, for example, in his first day of teaching a fifth-grade class, a teacher observes that one child follows all the rules and directions, but a second child just cannot seem to stay out of trouble. If that teacher is not careful, he might develop a bias. He might see the first child as good even if she breaks the rules for several weeks in a row. On the other hand, he might see the second child as bad even if she follows the rules for the rest of the school term. Similarly, a child may turn in a composition replete with grammatical and spelling errors. This child may have just had a bad day. However, even if his or her next paper is relatively free of errors, the teacher will have a tendency to look for them and to view the child as weak in grammar. Furthermore, the teacher may see the child as weak in other areas just on the basis of his early impression of the child's grammatical skills.

E. L. Thorndike (1920) labeled this tendency to judge specific traits on the basis of a general impression the *halo effect*. Thorndike became aware of this effect when he noticed that ratings of behavioral tendencies (that is, traits) based on interview data tended to correlate more highly than one should reasonably expect.

People apparently tend to generalize judgments from a single, limited experience (W. H. Cooper, 1981). In the interview, halo effects occur when the interviewer forms a favorable or unfavorable early impression. The early impression then biases the remainder of the judgment process. Thus, with an early favorable impression or positive halo, the interviewer will have difficulty seeing the negatives. Similarly, with an early negative halo, the interviewer will have difficulty seeing the positives. In short, halo effects impair objectivity and must be consciously avoided.

Similarly, people tend to judge on the basis of one outstanding characteristic. Hollingworth (1922) first called this error *general standoutishness*. One prominent characteristic can bias the interviewer's judgments and prevent an objective evaluation. In an early paper, Burtt (1926) noted the tendency of interviewers to make unwarranted inferences from personal appearance. A well-groomed, attractive individual might be rated higher in intelligence than a poorly groomed, unattractive individual, even though the latter is more intelligent than the former. It remains widely recognized that physical appear-

TABLE 9-8

Suggestions for Handling Cross-Ethnic, Cross-Cultural, and Cross-Class Interviews

- **Increase Cultural Awareness**
  Try to become sensitive to cultural, social class, and ethnic differences. Study the culture, language, and traditions of groups you are likely to have contact with as an interviewer.

- **Know Yourself**
  Examine your own stereotypes and prejudices. What are your preconceived notions about individuals from races, cultures, and socioeconomic groups other than your own?

- **Be Flexible**
  Try to suspend your preconceived notions. Be willing to accept a perspective other than your own.

- **Look Beyond Yourself**
  Try to appreciate the interviewee's perspective. Put yourself in the interviewee's shoes. Look for ways to circumvent potential difficulties.

Based on Sattler (1988, p. 462).

ance can play a major role in how a job applicant is perceived and rated (Gilmore, Beehr, & Love, 1986).

Another potential source of error in the interview can be found in cross-ethnic, cross-cultural, and cross-class interviewing (Sattler, 1970, 1973b, 1977). In the international business community, ignorance of cultural differences is becoming increasingly apparent. Japanese and Arabs consider direct eye contact a sign of aggression. The Japanese person avoids eye contact as a sign of deference and respect. In middle-class America, by contrast, direct eye contact is expected as a sign of honesty and sincerity. Unless we understand and take cultural differences into account, it is easy to send the wrong message or misinterpret the intentions of others. Even within the United States there are cultural differences that, if not understood, may lead to bias in the interview process. For example, whereas middle-class whites generally look at a speaker while listening, many African Americans tend to look away while listening. These differences in style may lead a white interviewer to believe she is not being listened to, or an African American to feel like he is being unduly scrutinized (Sattler, 1988, p. 461). Although reviews of the literature have failed to provide a framework from which to understand bias in the personnel selection process (Nevo & Jager, 1993; Ralston, 1988), Sattler (1988) has offered a number of suggestions for handling cross-ethnic, cross-cultural, and cross-class interviews. Table 9-8 summarizes some of these suggestions.

Sources of error such as cultural distortions can reduce the validity of interview data. Recall that validity tells us about the meaning of test scores. Errors that reduce the objectivity of the interviewer produce inaccurate judgments, thus biasing the validity of the evaluation. These tendencies perhaps explain why the predictive validity of interview data varies so widely. R. Wagner (1949), for example, reported studies that attempted to correlate judgments from interview data with such factors as grades, intelligence, and performance on standardized tests. The correlations ranged from .09 to .94, with a median of .19. Studies reviewed by Ulrich and Trumbo (1965) revealed a similar range of predictive validity coefficients, with correlations as low as −.05 and as high as .72 when ratings based on interview data were correlated with a variety of indices such as job performance. Carlson and colleagues

(1971) reported similar findings, as have Arvey and Campion (1982). Other reviews have suggested higher and more consistent coefficients in the .70s, especially when structured interviews are used (M. M. Harris, 1989).

Although one can question the validity of interview data, the interview does provide a wealth of unique data. The safest approach is to consider interview data as tentative: a hypothesis or a set of hypotheses to be confirmed by other sources of data. Interview data may have dubious value without the support of more standardized procedures. Results from standardized tests, on the other hand, are often meaningless if not placed in the context of case history or other interview data. The two go together, each complementing the other, each essential in the process of evaluating human beings (Dalessio & Silverhart, 1994).

Interview Reliability

Recall that reliability refers to the stability, dependability, or consistency of test results. For interview data, the critical questions about reliability have centered on interinterviewer agreement (agreement between two or more interviewers). As with the validity studies, reliability coefficients for interinterviewer agreement vary widely. For example, R. Wagner (1949) found a range of reliability coefficients from .23 to .97 (median .57) for ratings of traits. The range of coefficients for ratings of overall ability was even wider (−.20 to .85; median .53). Ulrich and Trumbo's (1965) review reported similar findings.

Again, reliability runs twice as high for structured as for unstructured interviews (M. M. Harris, 1989; Schwab-Stone et al., 1994). E. C. Webster (1964) argued that one reason for fluctuations in interview reliability is that different interviewers look for different things, an argument echoed by others (Schmitt, 1976; Zedeck, Tziner, & Middlestadt, 1983). Thus, whereas one interviewer might focus on strengths, another might focus on weaknesses. The two interviewers would disagree because their judgments are based on different aspects of the individual. To enhance interrater reliability in interviewer behavior, Callender and Dougherty (1983) recommended that interviewers be trained to evaluate very specific dimensions. Such an approach has, in fact, been shown to have merit (Dougherty, Ebert, & Callender, 1986; Dreher, Ash, & Hancock, 1988).

As we have noted, agreement among interviewers varies for different types of interviews. The research suggests that a highly structured interview in which specific questions are asked in a specific order can produce highly stable results (M. M. Harris, 1989). For example, if we ask a person his or her name, date of birth, and parents' names, as well as the addresses of all residences within a particular time span, and then ask the same questions a year later, results should be nearly identical. Reliability would be limited only by the memory and honesty of the interviewee and the clerical capabilities of the interviewer. Although extreme, this example should make it clear that highly structured interviews should produce fairly dependable results. The problem is that such structure can limit the content of the interview, thus defeating the purpose of providing a broad range of data.

Unstructured or semistructured interviews frequently provide data that other sources cannot provide. However, the dependability of such results is clearly limited. The same question may not be asked twice, or it may be asked in different ways. Thus, interviewers readily acknowledge the limited reliability of interview data.

Summary

In a *structured interview,* the interviewer asks a specific set of questions. In the structured *standardized* interview, these questions are printed. The interviewer reads the questions in a specific order or sequence. In the *unstructured interview,* there are no specific questions or guidelines for the interviewer to follow. Thus, each unstructured interview is unique. Such interviews provide considerable flexibility at the expense of data stability.

An *interview* is an interactive process. The participants (interviewer and interviewee) influence each other. Good interviewers set the tone of the interview by maintaining a warm, open, confident atmosphere.

Good interviewing is a matter of attitude. A study by Saccuzzo (1975) showed that interviewees give positive evaluations to interviewers when the interviewer is seen as warm, genuine, accepting, understanding, open, committed, and involved. Poor evaluations come forth when interviewers exhibit the opposite attitudes and feelings. Good interview behavior involves developing the proper attitudes and displaying them during the interview.

Good interviewing also involves avoiding statements that are judgmental, probing, evaluative, or hostile. An unstructured interview should begin with an *open-ended question*—that is, one that cannot be answered "Yes" or "No" or with a short, specific response. The process of interviewing then involves facilitating the flow of communication. *Closed-ended questions,* which can be answered with a "Yes" or "No" or a specific response, usually bring the interview to a halt and typically should be reserved for instances where less directive procedures fail to produce the desired information.

Transitional phrases such as "I see" help keep the interview flowing. Statements that communicate understanding or are interchangeable with the interviewee's responses tend to elicit self-exploration at increasingly deeper levels. These responses include verbatim playback, paraphrasing, restatement, summarizing, clarification, and understanding.

Efforts to assess the quality of understanding or empathetic statements have led to a five-point scale system developed by Truax, Carkhuff, and coworkers. A large body of knowledge has shown that understanding statements are extremely powerful in helping the interviewee uncover and explore underlying feelings. Types of interview include the evaluation or assessment interview, the structured clinical interview, the case history interview, the mental status examination, and the employment interview.

There are two primary sources of error in the interview: those pertaining to the validity or meaning of data and those pertaining to its dependability or reliability. Tendencies to draw general conclusions about an individual based on just the data of a first impression limit the meaning and accuracy of interview data. Such tendencies have been labeled the *halo effect* and *standoutishness*. Cultural distortions can also bias interview data and lead to inaccurate conclusions. Furthermore, predictive validity coefficients for interview data vary widely. The reliability of interview data has been measured primarily in terms of agreement among interviewers on variables such as intelligence, overall ability, and traits. The more structured the interview, the more interviewers agree. Thus, like predictive validity coefficients, reliability coefficients for interview data vary widely. Training tends to enhance reliability.

One develops interviewing skills through knowledge about good interview behavior and principles, supervised practice, and a conscious effort to form the right habits. However, the interview is fallible. Interview data can best be seen as the complement of other data sources.

CHAPTER 10

Tests of Mental Ability: The Binet Scale

LEARNING OBJECTIVES

When you have completed this chapter, you should be able to:

☐ Explain how Binet and other psychologists have defined *intelligence*

☐ Identify Binet's two guiding principles of test construction

☐ Describe the concept of age differentiation

☐ Describe the concept of mental age (MA)

☐ Describe the intelligence quotient (IQ) concept

☐ Define deviation IQ

☐ Discuss the fourth edition of the Stanford-Binet Intelligence Scale

Three 8-year-old children, Fred, Maria, and Dale, were being evaluated for a special program for the gifted in a magnet school. Those who qualify are placed in a special, accelerated program where the student-teacher ratio is 15 to 1 rather than the usual 25 to 1. The gifted program also has special funds for enrichment programs such as field trips and hands-on exposure to computers. To qualify, a child must score three standard deviations above the mean on the Stanford-Binet Intelligence Scale: Fourth Edition (R. L. Thorndike, Hagen, & Sattler, 1986).

Since the Stanford-Binet is standardized, all three children were exposed to identical conditions. The test began with a set of vocabulary items. On the first item, each child was asked to name a pictured object. Then each was asked to define words such as *quarter, sailor,* and *borrow* at the lower end of difficulty and *predilection* at the upper end. In fact, there were some 14 different tasks, including one that required the children to reproduce bead patterns by finding them in photographs (bead memory) and others that asked them to predict the next two numbers in a series such as 9, 8, 7, -, -.

As it turned out, only Dale scored high enough on the test to be placed in the gifted program. Now, given that all children were exposed to the same set of tasks, can we rest assured that the procedure was fair and that Dale was indeed the most intelligent of the three? As a critical thinker, you of course cannot give an unqualified "Yes" to the question. You need much more information.

To say that one person is more intelligent than a second, one must be prepared to define *intelligence*. Unfortunately, of all the major concepts in the field of testing, intelligence is among the most elusive.

Alfred Binet, one of the original authors of the test that bears his name, defined intelligence as "the tendency to take and maintain a definite direction; the capacity to make adaptations for the purpose of attaining a desired end, and the power of autocriticism" (cited in Terman, 1916, p. 45). Later in the chapter we will look more closely at this definition of intelligence. Spearman (1923), by contrast, defined intelligence as the ability to educe either relations or correlates. According to Freeman (1955), intelligence is "adjustment or adaptation of the individual to his total environment," "the adaptation of the individual to his total environment," "the ability to learn," and "the ability to carry on abstract thinking" (pp. 60–61). And Das (1973) defined intelligence as "the ability to plan and structure one's behavior with an end in view" (p. 27). H. Gardner (1983) defined intelligence in terms of the ability "to resolve genuine problems or difficulties as they are encountered" (p. 60); while Sternberg (1986, 1988) defined intelligence in terms of "mental activities involved in purposive adaptation to, shaping of, and selection of real-world environments relevant to one's life" (1986, p. 33).

As you can surmise, a test that examines one's ability to define words and remember bead patterns certainly does not meet the standards of all or even most definitions. But assume for the purpose of argument that the Stanford-Binet scale is a valid measure of intelligence, however defined. Can you then safely say that the evaluation procedure for Fred, Maria, and Dale was fair? Again, you cannot answer unequivocally.

Maria, a Mexican American, had Spanish-speaking parents, neither of whom finished high school. Her father spent most of his life working as a tomato picker. Fred, an African American, came from a family of ten children. As with Maria, neither of Fred's parents completed high school. Although Fred's father worked long, hard hours as a machine operator on an assembly line, the family was very poor. Dale's parents, by contrast, had a combined income of $180,000 per year and were well educated. His mother was a clinical psychologist, his father a prominent attorney.

There is a correlation between socioeconomic background and scores on standardized intelligence tests such as the Stanford-Binet. Examination of the test manual for the fourth edition of the Stanford-Binet shows that the average score for children of college graduates is more than 10 points above the mean, whereas that for children of parents with less than high-school educations is about 6 points below the mean. Similar differences occur depending on the occupation of the parents. Thus, many have charged that intelligence tests are biased, especially against ethnic minorities and the poor. Ironically, as you will see, intelligence tests were initially developed to eliminate subjectivity in the evaluation of children's ability.

What do you think of when someone mentions intelligence testing? For many people, the topic arouses strong feelings and sometimes strong personal biases, even among experts (Snyderman & Rothman, 1987). Proponents hold that intelligence tests provide a universal and objective standard of competence and potential (Brim, 1965; E. W. Jackson, 1980). Critics charge that intelligence tests not only are biased against certain racial and economic groups but also are used by those in power to maintain the status quo (Gould, 1981; Owen, 1985). In fact, intelligence tests have been under attack almost from their inception (Haney, 1981; Snyderman & Rothman, 1987).

Intelligence testing began with the decision of a French minister of public instruction around the turn of the century. Some today might criticize the minister's decision to create a procedure for identifying intellectually limited individuals so they could be removed from the regular classroom and receive special educational experiences. This decision provided the force behind the development of modern intelligence tests and the heated controversy presently associated with them.

In 1904, the French minister officially appointed a commission, to which he gave a definite assignment: to recommend a procedure for identifying so-called subnormal (intellectually limited) children. One member of this commission, Alfred Binet, had demonstrated his qualifications for the job by his earlier research on human abilities (Binet, 1890a, 1890b). The task of the commission was indeed formidable. No one doubted that human beings were capable of incredible accomplishments, which obviously reflected intelligence. Nor was there much doubt that differences existed among individuals in their level of intelligence. But how was one to define intelligence?

Binet had few guideposts. A study by Wissler (1901) indicated that simple functions such as reaction time, sensory acuity, and the like failed to discriminate well among individuals of high and low scholastic ability. Therefore, Binet looked for complex processes in his struggle to understand human intelligence. However, unlike today, there were few available definitions of intelligence. Binet's first problem was to decide what he wanted to measure—that is, to define intelligence. Beginning with this definition, Binet and his colleagues developed the world's first intelligence test.

In this chapter, we examine the test that Binet and his colleagues developed, as well as its many subsequent revisions. In its present form, the Binet scale bears little resemblance to the original. Because the principles used to construct the various versions of the test illustrate the main approaches to intelligence tests, our discussion will cover much of what comprised the past scales as well as the new scale. We will highlight various changes that took place in the evolution of the Binet scale, examine the most recent version, and finally consider some basic issues pertaining to the nature of human intelligence.

Binet's Principles of Test Construction

In choosing a definition, Binet took the necessary first step in developing a measure of intelligence. However, he still faced the problem of deciding exactly what he wanted to measure. Binet believed that intelligence, as he defined it, expressed itself through the judgmental, attentional, and reasoning facilities of the individual (Binet & Simon, 1905). He therefore decided to concentrate on finding tasks related to these three facilities.

In developing tasks to measure judgment, attention, and reasoning, Binet used trial and error as well as experimentation and hypothesis-testing procedures. He was guided by two major concepts that to this day underlie the Binet scale and its many revisions and offshoots: age differentiation and general mental ability. These principles, which perhaps represent Binet's most profound contribution to the study of human intelligence, provided the foundation for subsequent generations of human ability tests.

Principle 1: Age Differentiation

Age differentiation refers to the simple fact that one can differentiate older children from younger children by the former's greater capabilities. For example, whereas most 9-year-olds can tell that a 50-cent coin is worth more than a quarter, a quarter is worth more than a dime, and so on, most 5-year-olds cannot. In employing the principle of age differentiation, Binet searched for tasks that could be completed by between 66.67% and 75% of the children of a particular age group and also by a smaller proportion of younger children but a larger proportion of older ones. Thus, Binet eventually assembled a set of tasks that an increasing proportion of children could complete as a function of increase in age.

Using these tasks, he could estimate the mental ability of a child in terms of his or her completion of the tasks designed for the average child of a particular age, regardless of the child's actual or chronological age. A particular 5-year-old child might be able to complete tasks that the average 8-year-old could complete. On the other hand, another 5-year-old might not be capable of completing even those tasks that the average 3-year-old could complete. With the principle of age differentiation, one could determine the equivalent age capabilities of a child independent of his or her chronological age. This equivalent age capability was eventually called mental age. If a 6-year-old completed tasks appropriate for the average 9-year-old, then the 6-year-old had demonstrated that he or she had capabilities equivalent to those of the average 9-year-old, or a mental age of 9.

Principle 2: The Concept of General Mental Ability

Binet was also guided in his selection of tasks by his decision to measure only the total product of the various separate and distinct elements of intelligence, that is, "general mental ability." With the concept of general mental ability, Binet freed himself from the burden of identifying each element or independent aspect of intelligence. He also was freed from finding the relation of each element to the whole. Binet's decision to measure general mental ability was based on practical considerations. He could restrict the search for tasks to anything related to the total or the final product of intelligence. He could judge the value of any particular task in terms of its correlation with the combined result (total score) of all other tasks. Tasks with low correlations could be eliminated, and tasks with high correlations retained.

The notion of general mental ability was previously propounded by F. Galton (1869) in his classic work, *Hereditary Genius: An Inquiry into Its Laws and Consequences* (see Chapter 1). And independently of Binet, in Great Britain, Charles Spearman (1904a, 1927) advanced the notion of a general mental ability factor underlying all intelligent behavior (see R. M. Thorndike, 1990a, 1990b). According to Spearman's theory, intelligence consists of one general factor (g) plus a large number of specific factors (see Figure 10-1). Spearman's notion of general mental ability, which he referred to as psychometric g (or simply g), was based on his observation, and the well-documented phenomenon, that when a set of diverse ability tests are administered to large, unbiased samples of the population, almost all the correlations are positive. This phenomenon is called *positive manifold,* which according to Spearman was due to the fact that all tests, no matter how diverse, are influenced by g. For Spearman, g could best be conceptualized in terms of mental energy.

To understand how a single general factor can underlie all intelligent behavior, consider the analogy of a central power station for a large metropolitan city. The same station provides the power for lights of all sizes and types.

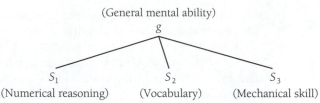

FIGURE 10-1   *Spearman's model of intelligence. According to the model, intelligence can be viewed in terms of one general underlying factor (g) and a large number of specific factors ($S_1, S_2, \cdots, S_n$). Thus, intelligence can be viewed in terms of g (general mental ability) and S (specific factors). Spearman's theory was consistent with Binet's approach to constructing the first general intelligence test.*

Although some lights may be brighter or better than others, all depend on power from the central power source. Reducing the output from the central source affects all the lights.

To support the notion of *g*, Spearman developed a statistical technique called *factor analysis*. Factor analysis is a method for reducing a set of variables or scores to a smaller number of hypothetical variables called *factors*. Through factor analysis, one can determine how much variance a set of tests or scores has in common. This common variance represents the g factor. The g in a factor analysis of any set of mental ability tasks can be represented in the first unrotated factor in a principal components analysis (Saccuzzo, Johnson, & Guertin, 1994). Spearman found that as a general rule, about half the variance in a set of diverse mental ability tests is represented in the g factor.

The concept of general intelligence implies that a person's intelligence can best be represented by a single score, *g*, that presumably reflects the shared variance underlying performance on a diverse set of tests. True, performance on any given individual task can be attributed to g as well as to some specific or unique variance (just as the luminance of a light depends on the central power source as well as the individual qualities of the light). However, if the set of tasks is large and broad enough, the role of any given task can be reduced to a minimum. Differences in unique ability stemming from the specific task tend to cancel each other, and overall performance comes to depend most heavily on the general factor. Such reasoning underlay the development of the Binet scale as well as all its subsequent revisions.

The Early Binet Scales

Using the principles of age differentiation and general mental ability, Binet and another appointee of the French minister of public instruction, T. Simon, collaborated to develop the first version of what would eventually be called the Stanford-Binet Intelligence Scale. The first version, the 1905 Binet-Simon

Scale, was limited compared to current applications of intelligence tests. Its purpose was restricted to identifying mentally defective children in the Paris school system.

Nature of the 1905 Binet-Simon Scale

The 1905 Binet-Simon Scale was an individual intelligence test consisting of 30 items presented in an increasing order of difficulty. Item 4, for example, tested the subject's ability to recognize food (for example, to discriminate between chocolate and wood). Item 14 required subjects to define familiar objects such as a fork. The most difficult item, 30, required subjects to define and distinguish between paired abstract terms (for example, *sad* and *bored*). Binet proposed that item 9, which required subjects to name designated objects in a picture, was the approximate limit of the average 3-year-old.

In Binet's time, three levels of intellectual deficiency were designated by terms no longer in use today because of the derogatory connotations they have acquired. *Idiot* described the most severe form of intellectual impairment, *imbecile* moderate levels of impairment, and *moron* the mildest level of impairment. Binet believed that the ability to follow simple directions and imitate simple gestures (item 6 on the 1905 scale) was the upper limit of adult idiots. The ability to identify parts of the body or simple objects (item 8) would rule out the most severe intellectual impairment in an adult. The upper limit for adult imbeciles was item 16, which required the subject to state the differences between two common objects such as wood and glass.

A scientific breakthrough, the collection of 30 tasks of increasing difficulty in the Binet-Simon scale provided the first major measure of human intelligence. Binet had solved two major problems of test construction: He determined exactly what he wanted to measure, and he developed items for this purpose. He fell short, however, in several other areas. The 1905 Binet-Simon Scale lacked an adequate measuring unit to express results; it also lacked adequate normative data and evidence to support its validity. The classifications Binet used (idiot, imbecile, and moron) can hardly be considered sufficient for expressing results and, as Binet himself knew, little had been done to document the scale's validity. Furthermore, norms for the 1905 scale were based on only 50 children who had been considered normal based on average school performance. (See Figure 10-2.)

The 1908 Scale

Binet wanted to produce a sound scientific instrument rather than defend his position at the expense of progress. He therefore strove to deal with the limitations of the 1905 scale in his second major revision. In the 1908 scale, Binet and Simon retained the principle of age differentiation. Indeed, the 1908 scale was an age scale, which means items were grouped according to age level rather than simply increasing difficulty, as in the 1905 scale (see Table 10-1).

FIGURE 10-2
Schematic summary of the evolution of the Binet scale: 1905 scale.

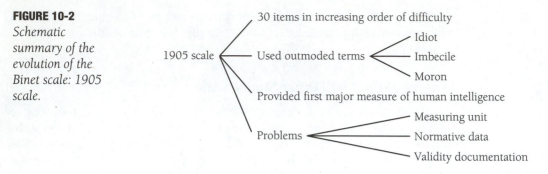

30 items in increasing order of difficulty

1905 scale

Used outmoded terms — Idiot, Imbecile, Moron

Provided first major measure of human intelligence

Problems — Measuring unit, Normative data, Validity documentation

The age scale provided a model for innumerable tests still used in educational settings. However, the age scale format also presented a serious limitation. When items are grouped according to age level, it is difficult, if not impossible, to compare a child's performance on different kinds of tasks. For example, does the child perform exceptionally well on quantitative items? The limitations of the age scale format were considered so great that the most recent revision of the Binet scale excludes it (Thorndike, Hagen, & Sattler, 1986).

Despite its limitations, the 1908 Binet scale clearly reflected improvement over the 1905 scale. However, Binet had done little to meet one persistent criticism: the verbal/language emphasis of the scale. The scale provided many tasks in a variety of areas. As an individual test, it required 30 to 85 minutes of professional time to administer to a single person. Yet, for all this time and

TABLE 10-1
Sample Items from the 1908 Binet-Simon Scale

Age Level 3 (Five items)
1. Point to various parts of face.
2. Repeat two digits forward.

Age Level 4 (Four Items)
1. Name familiar objects.
2. Repeat three digits forward.

Age Level 5 (Five Items)
1. Copy a square.
2. Repeat a sentence containing ten syllables.

Age Level 6 (Seven Items)
1. State age.
2. Repeat a sentence containing 16 syllables.

Age Level 7 (Eight Items)
1. Copy a diamond.
2. Repeat five digits forward.

Age Level 8 (Six Items)
1. Recall two items from a passage.
2. State the differences between two objects.

Age Level 9 (Six Items)
1. Recall six items from a passage.
2. Recite the days of the week.

Age Level 10 (Five Items)
1. Given three common words, construct a sentence.
2. Recite the months of the year in order.

Age Level 11 (Five Items)
1. Define abstract words (for example, justice).
2. Determine what is wrong with absurd statements.

Age Level 12 (Five Items)
1. Repeat seven digits forward.
2. Provide the meaning of pictures.

Age Level 13 (Three Items)
1. State the differences between pairs of abstract terms.

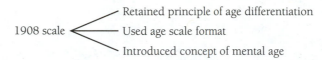

FIGURE 10-3   *Schematic summary of the evolution of the Binet scale: 1908 scale.*

effort, the scale produced only one score, almost exclusively related to verbal, language, and reading ability. Binet claimed that a single score was consistent with the notion of general mental ability, and therefore appropriate. Unfortunately, Binet made little effort to diversify the range of abilities tapped. As a result, the scale remained heavily weighted on language, reading, and verbal skills at the expense of other factors such as the integration of visual and motor functioning (for example, eye-hand coordination). Not until the 1986 revision were these problems seriously addressed.

Perhaps the main improvement in the 1908 scale was the introduction of the concept of mental age. Here Binet attempted to solve the problem of expressing the results in adequate units. A subject's mental age was based on his or her performance compared with the average performance of individuals in a specific chronological age group. In simple terms, if a 6-year-old can perform the tasks that can be done by two-thirds to three-fourths of the representative group of 8-year-old children, then this child has a mental age of 8. A 10-year-old who can do no more than pass items that two-thirds to three-fourths of the representative group of 5-year-olds can pass is said to have a mental age of 5.

To summarize, the 1908 Binet-Simon scale introduced two major concepts: the age scale format and the concept of mental age. However, even though both concepts were eventually abandoned, they found widespread use and application in a host of new tests as well as in subsequent revisions of the Binet. (See Figure 10-3.)

Terman's Stanford-Binet Intelligence Scale

Though Binet and Simon again revised their intelligence scale in 1911, this third version contained only minor improvements. By this time, the potential utility of the Binet scale had been recognized throughout Europe and in the United States. For example, in the United States, H. H. Goddard published a translation of the 1905 Binet-Simon scale in 1908, and the 1908 scale in 1911 (Hernstein, 1981). Other Americans subsequently published many versions of the scale. These included R. M. Yerkes's 1915 and 1923 versions, J. P. Herring's 1922 version, and F. Kuhlmann's 1912, 1922, and 1930 versions. However, it was the 1916 Stanford-Binet version, developed under the direction of L. M. Terman, that flourished and served for quite some time, as the dominant intelligence scale in the world.

In this section, we continue our analysis of the Binet scale evolution. First, we examine Terman's 1916 version of the scale and see how he incorporated

FIGURE 10-4
*Schematic
summary of the
evolution of the
Binet scale: 1916
scale.*

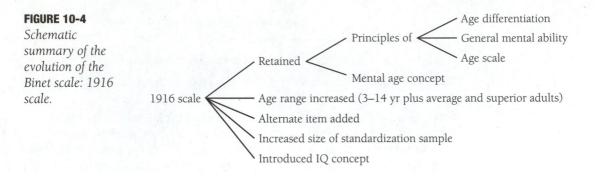

the concept of mental age into the intelligence quotient (IQ) concept. Then we look at the 1937 and 1960 revisions before we move on to the modern Binet.

The 1916 Stanford-Binet Intelligence Scale

In developing the 1916 Stanford-Binet version, Terman relied heavily on Binet's earlier work. The principles of age differentiation, general mental ability, and the age scale were retained. The mental age concept also was retained. (See Figure 10-4.)

Terman's 1916 revision increased the size of the standardization sample. Unfortunately, the entire standardization sample of the 1916 revision consisted exclusively of white native Californian children. Thus, although the standardization sample was markedly increased, it was far from representative. In fact, given that geographic location may affect test performance (Lewandowski & Saccuzzo, 1976; Saccuzzo & Lewandowski, 1976), this sample cannot even be considered to represent white native-born Americans. Nevertheless, the increased sample size clearly marked an improvement over the meager 50 and 203 individuals of the 1905 and 1908 Binet-Simon versions.

The Intelligence Quotient (IQ)

The 1916 scale provided the first significant application of the now outdated **intelligence quotient (IQ)** concept. As Hernstein (1981) noted, the IQ concept recommended by Stern (1912) used a subject's mental age in conjunction with his or her chronological age to obtain a ratio score. This ratio score presumably reflects the subject's rate of mental development. Table 10-2 illustrates how IQ is determined.

In calculating IQ, the first step is to determine the subject's chronological age. To obtain this, we need only know his or her birthday. In the second step, the subject's mental age is determined by his or her score on the scale. Finally, to obtain the IQ, the chronological age (*CA*) is divided into the mental age (*MA*) and the result multiplied by 100 to eliminate fractions:

$$IQ = \frac{MA}{CA} \times 100$$

As you can see in Table 10-2, when MA is less than CA, the IQ is below 100. In this case, the subject was said to have slower than average mental development. When MA exceeded CA, the subject was said to have faster than average mental development.

The IQ score altered the nature of the measuring unit used to express the results. However, as you will see, the method may have actually been a step backward; the MA/CA method of calculating IQ scores was ultimately abandoned. The 1916 scale had a maximum possible mental age of 19.5 years; that is, if every group of items was passed, this score would result. Given this limitation, anyone older than 19.5 would have an IQ of less than 100 even if all items were passed. Therefore, a maximum limit on the chronological age had to be set. Because it was believed in 1916 that mental age ceased to improve after 16 years of age, 16 was used as the maximum chronological age.

The 1937 Scale

The 1937 scale extended the age range down to the 2-year-old level. Also, by adding new tasks, developers increased the maximum possible mental age to 22 years, 10 months. Scoring standards and instructions were improved to reduce ambiguities, enhance the standardization of administration, and increase interscorer reliability. Furthermore, a number of performance items, which required the subject to do things such as copy designs, were added to decrease the scale's emphasis on verbal skills.

TABLE 10-2

The Intelligence Quotient Concept

Child 1:

Chronological age (*CA*): 6 years

Mental age (*MA*): 6 years

$$IQ = \frac{MA}{CA} \times 100 = \frac{6}{6} \times 100 = 100$$

Child 2:

Chronological age (*CA*): 6 years

Mental age (*MA*): 3 years

$$IQ = \frac{MA}{CA} \times 100 = \frac{3}{6} \times 100 = 50$$

Child 3:

$CA = 6;\ MA = 12;\ IQ = 200$

Adult 1:

$CA = 50;\ MA = 16$

$$IQ = \frac{16}{16} \times 100 = 100$$
$\leftarrow$ (the maximum *CA*)

The standardization sample was markedly improved. Whereas the 1916 norms were restricted to Californians, the new subjects for the 1937 Stanford-Binet standardization sample came from 11 states representing a variety of regions in the United States. Subjects were selected according to their fathers' occupations. In addition, the standardization sample was substantially increased. Unfortunately, the sample included only whites and an excess of urban versus rural subjects (Terman & Merrill, 1937). Nevertheless, this improved sample represented a desirable trend. The 3184 individuals included in the 1937 standardization sample represented more than a three-fold increase from the 1916 scale and was more than 63 times larger than the original sample of the 1905 scale.

Perhaps the most important improvement in the 1937 version was the inclusion of an alternate equivalent form. Forms L and M were designed to be equivalent in terms of both difficulty and content. With two such forms, the psychometric properties of the scale could be readily examined.

Psychometric Properties of the 1937 Scale

Subjects in the 1937 standardization sample were tested on the second form within one day to one week after the initial testing. Results were extremely impressive, with a correlation of greater than .91 for unselected cases (Terman & Merrill, 1937). As Q. McNemar (1942) noted, however, reliability coefficients were higher for older subjects. Thus, results for younger individuals were not as stable as those for older ones. Reliability figures also varied as a function of IQ level, with higher reliabilities in the lower IQ ranges (that is, less than 70) and poorer ones in the higher ranges. The lowest reliabilities occurred in the youngest age groups in the highest IQ ranges. These findings apply generally to all modern intelligence tests: Scores are most unstable for young children in high IQ ranges.

Along with the differing reliabilities, each age group in the standardization sample produced a unique standard deviation of IQ scores. This differential variability in IQ scores as a function of age created the single most important problem in the 1937 scale. More specifically, despite the great care taken in selecting the standardization sample, different age groups showed significant differences in the standard deviation of IQ scores. As reported by Terman and Merrill (1937), for example, the standard deviation in the IQ scores at age 6 was approximately 12.5. The standard deviations at ages 2½ and 12, on the other hand, were 20.6 and 20.0, respectively. Because of these discrepancies, IQs at one age level were not equivalent to IQs at another. This concept is elaborated on in Focused Example 10-1.

Despite some problems related to reliability, the validity of the 1937 scale was strongly supported. Clearly, the scale had content validity. The 1937 Stanford-Binet scale also had well-documented predictive validity. In one sense, however, the scale's high level of predictive validity was a mixed blessing. The high correlations between the 1937 scale and school success (Terman & Mer-

FIGURE 10-5
Schematic summary of the evolution of the Binet scale: 1937 scale.

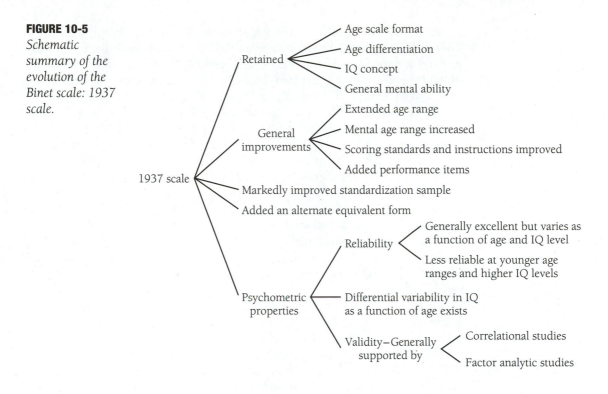

rill, 1953; R. I. Watson, 1951) suggested that the scale measured mostly scholastic aptitude, academic achievement, verbal ability, and reading skills. Other evidence, however, supported the scale. Biserial correlational analysis revealed a sizable correlation between each item and the total test score (Terman & Merrill, 1937). That is, each item contributed substantially to the total test score, just as the concept of general mental ability demanded. Because more items were passed with increasing age, the concept of age differentiation and thus the construct validity of the scale also were supported. Finally, factor analytic studies supported the validity of the scale. (See Figure 10-5.)

The 1960 Stanford-Binet Revision

The developers of the 1960 revision tried to create a single instrument by selecting the best from the two forms of the 1937 scale. Tasks that showed an increase in the percentage passing with an increase in age—the main criterion and guiding principle for all versions of the Binet scale—received the highest priority, as did tasks that correlated highly with scores as a whole—the second guiding principle of the Binet scale. In addition, instructions for scoring and test administration were improved, and IQ tables were extended from age 16 to 18 (Terman & Merrill, 1960). Perhaps most important, the problem of differential variation in IQs was solved by the deviation IQ concept.

As used in the Stanford-Binet scale, the deviation IQ is simply a standard score with a mean of 100 and a standard deviation of 16. With the mean set at 100 and assigned to scores at the 50th percentile, the deviation IQ was ascertained by evaluating the standard deviation of mental age for a representative sample at each age level. New IQ tables were then constructed that corrected for differences in variability at the various age levels. By correcting for these differences in variability, the 1960 IQ tables produced IQs comparable from one age level to another (Terman & Merrill, 1960). With the deviation IQ, scores finally could be directly compared across age groups. Thus, scores could be interpreted in terms of standard deviations and percentiles with the assurance that IQ scores for every age group corresponded to the same percentile. Today, the deviation IQ method is considered the most precise way of expressing the results of an intelligence test. (See Figure 10-6.)

The 1960s revision did not include a new normative sample or restandardization. The investigators argued that psychometric data accumulated on the 1937 scale could be transformed to the 1960 scale (Terman & Merrill, 1960).

Criticisms of the 1960 revision were met by positive action rather than by defensive arguments. By 1972, a new standardization group consisting of a representative sample of 2100 children (about 100 at each Stanford-Binet age level) had been obtained for use with the 1960 revision (R. L. Thorndike, 1973). Unlike all previous norms, the 1972 norms included nonwhites. For many, however, the general improvements in the 1960 revision, even with the new 1972 norms, did not suffice. In 1986, a new and drastically revised version of the Binet scale was published (R. L. Thorndike, Hagen, & Sattler, 1986).

Focused Example 10-1

DIFFERENTIAL VARIABILITY IN IQ SCORES

 Recall our discussion of standard deviations and percentiles in Chapter 2. A score that is two standard deviations above the mean is approximately at the 98th percentile. Therefore, if the mean IQ is 100, a 6-year-old, where the standard deviation is 12.5, would need an IQ of 125 to be two standard deviations above the mean, or the 98th percentile. However, at 12 years of age, where the standard deviation is 20, the same child would need an IQ of 140 to be two standard deviations above the mean and in the 98th percentile. Say a child at age 6 with an IQ of 125 obtained an IQ of 125 at age 12. He or she would then be only 1.25 standard deviations above the mean (because the standard deviation at age 12 is 20) and thus at only about the 89th percentile. You can see that in the 1937 scale, an IQ at one age range was not comparable to an IQ at another age range in terms of percentiles.

FIGURE 10-6
Schematic summary of the evolution of the Binet scale: 1960 scale.

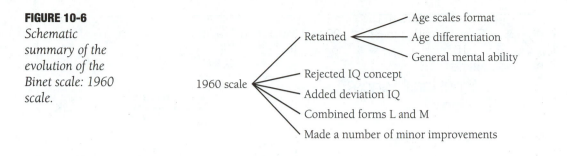

The Modern Binet Scale

Our discussion of the evolution of the Binet scale has illustrated many of the concepts that have dominated intelligence testing from its inception to the present. The modern fourth edition of the Stanford-Binet scale continues this tradition of innovation and incorporation of central psychometric and theoretical concepts. In this section, we examine the modern Binet scale, which its authors developed because of cultural and social changes and new research in cognitive psychology. First, we consider the basic model that guided this development. Next, we compare the modern Binet to its predecessors and look at what was retained, what was changed, and what was added. Then we consider the test itself—the various subtests, summary scores, and procedures for administration. We also examine the scale's psychometric properties. Finally, we attempt a tentative evaluation of this latest edition in the long, distinguished line of Binet scales. (See Figure 10-7.)

Model of the Modern (1986) Binet Scale

The model for the modern Binet is far more elaborate than the Spearman model that best characterized the original versions of the scale. It is based on the three-level hierarchical model shown in Figure 10-8. At the top of the hierarchy is *g*—general intelligence, which reflects the common variability of all tasks. At the next level are three group factors. *Crystallized abilities* reflect learning—the overlay of experience on original potential. *Fluid-analytic abilities* represent original potential, or the basic capabilities used to acquire crystallized abilities (Horn & Cattell, 1966). *Short-term memory* refers to one's memory during short intervals—the amount of information one can retain briefly after a single, short presentation. In addition, crystallized ability has two subcategories: verbal reasoning and quantitative reasoning. By referring to Figure 10-9, you can discern which subtests are associated with each of the four major content areas.

The model of the modern Binet represents an attempt to place an evaluation of *g* in the context of a multidimensional model from which one can evaluate specific abilities. The impetus for a multidimensional model stemmed from the work of Thurstone (1938). He argued that, contrary to Spearman's

9-74534

STANFORD-BINET INTELLIGENCE SCALE

RECORD BOOKLET

Stanford-Binet Intelligence Scale: Fourth Edition

Name _____

_____ Sex _____

Ethnicity   NA   H   B   W/NH   O/AA   PI   Other _____

	YEAR	MONTH	DAY
Date of Testing			
Birth Date			
Age			

School _____

Grade _____

Examiner _____

Father's Occupation: _____

Mother's Occupation: _____

FACTORS AFFECTING TEST PERFORMANCE
Overall Rating of Conditions

Optimal	Good	Average	Detrimental	Seriously detrimental

	RAW SCORE	STANDARD AGE SCORE
Verbal Reasoning		
1 Vocabulary		
6 Comprehension		
7 Absurdities		
14 Verbal Relations		
Sum of Subtest SAS's		
Verbal Reasoning SAS		
Abstract/Visual Reasoning		
5 Pattern Analysis		
9 Copying		
11 Matrices		
13 Paper Folding & Cutting		
Sum of Subtest SAS's		
Abstract/Visual Reasoning SAS		
Quantitative Reasoning		
3 Quantitative		
12 Number Series		
15 Equation Building		
Sum of Subtest SAS's		
Quantitative Reasoning SAS		
Short-Term Memory		
2 Bead Memory		
4 Memory For Sentences		
8 Memory For Digits		
10 Memory For Objects		
Sum of Subtest SAS's		
Short-Term Memory SAS		
Sum of Area SAS's		

		COMPOSITE SCORE
Test Composite		
Partial Composite		
Partial Composite based on _____		

	1	2	3	4	5	
Attention						
a) Absorbed by task						Easily distracted
Reactions During Test Performance						
a) Normal activity level						Abnormal activity level
b) Initiates activity						Waits to be told
c) Quick to respond						Urging needed
Emotional Independence						
a) Socially confident						Insecure
b) Realistically self-confident						Distrusts own ability
c) Comfortable in adult company						Ill-at-ease
d) Assured						Anxious
Problem-Solving Behavior						
a) Persistent						Gives up easily
b) Reacts to failure realistically						Reacts to failure unrealistically
c) Eager to continue						Seeks to terminate
d) Challenged by hard tasks						Prefers only easy tasks
Independence of Examiner Support						
a) Needs minimum of commendation						Needs constant praise and encouragement
Expressive Language						
a) Excellent articulation						Very poor articulation
Receptive Language						
a) Excellent sound discrimination						Very poor sound discrimination

Was it difficult to establish rapport with this person?

Easy | | | | | | Difficult

The Riverside Publishing Company

Robert L. Thorndike
Elizabeth P. Hagen
Jerome M. Sattler

FIGURE 10-7 *Cover page of Stanford-Binet Intelligence Scale.*
(Courtesy of The Riverside Publishing Company.)

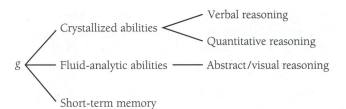

FIGURE 10-8 *Three-level hierarchical model of the modern Binet.*
(Adapted from Figure 2.1 in Thorndike, Hagen & Sattler, 1986, p. 9.)

FIGURE 10-9
The four major content areas of the modern Binet and associated tests.

1. Verbal reasoning
   - Vocabulary test
   - Comprehension test
   - Absurdities test
   - Verbal relations test

2. Abstract/visual reasoning
   - Pattern analysis test
   - Copying test
   - Matrices test
   - Paper-folding and -cutting test

3. Quantitative reasoning
   - Quantitative test
   - Number series test
   - Equation-building test

4. Short-term memory
   - Bead memory
   - Memory for sentences
   - Memory for digits
   - Memory for objects

notion of intelligence as a single process, intelligence could best be conceptualized as independent factors, or "primary mental abilities." Years of painstaking work ultimately revealed evidence for group abilities factors that were relatively, but not totally, independent. The group factors were correlated, and from them a *g* factor could be extracted, as in the hierarchical model of the modern Binet.

Characteristics of the 1986 Revision

The 1986 revision attempted to retain all the strengths of the earlier revisions while eliminating the weaknesses. This was no easy task. To continue to provide a measure of general mental ability, the authors of the 1986 revision decided to retain the wide variety of content and task characteristics of earlier versions. However, to avoid having this wide content unevenly distributed across age groups, the age scale format was eliminated. In place of the age scale, items with the same content were placed together into any one of 15 separate tests. For example, all vocabulary items were placed together in one test; all matrices items placed together in a second. (See Table 10-3 for a list of tests.)

Placing together items of similar content permits the calculation of specific scores for each of the 15 tests. Thus, in addition to an overall score that presumably reflects *g*, one can obtain scores related to each specific content area. In addition, each of the specific 15 tests can be grouped into one of four content areas, as illustrated in Figure 10-9.

In administering the modern Binet, one must determine where to begin each specific test. One does this by using the individual's score on the vocabulary test in conjunction with the person's chronological age. Since the scale purports to measure intelligence in individuals aged 2 years through adult, obviously all items in any given test will not be appropriate for all subjects. The test format is *adaptive:* Each individual is tested with a range of tasks best suited to his or her ability (R. L. Thorndike, Hagen, & Sattler, 1986). What one must do is establish a **basal age** for each test: the lowest level or point where two consecutive items of approximately equal difficulty are passed. Testing then proceeds within each test until a **ceiling** is reached: the point at which at least three out of four items are missed. The concept of age differentiation is retained, in that within each test, items are presented in order of increasing difficulty roughly according to their ability to discriminate different age groups.

The modern Binet scale retains the use of standard scores. Raw scores on each of the 15 tests can be converted to a *standard age score* with a mean of 50 and a standard deviation of 8. The grouping of individual tests into content areas permits one to calculate four area-content scores, each with a mean of 100 and standard deviation of 16. A composite score that reflects general mental ability and that is based on the tests given to an individual is also calculated. The mean of this composite is also 100 (SD = 16) as in the deviation IQ of the 1960 version. (See Figure 10-10.)

Psychometric Properties of the Modern Binet

The modern Binet was constructed with exceptional diligence. It continues the tradition of its predecessors in providing a state-of-the-art model for intelligence tests in terms of its psychometric standards, theoretical foundation, and empirical support. Items were subjected to two separate field trials, each followed by careful revision and fine-tuning. Items were also extensively reviewed for fairness and to identify and eliminate sources of bias or imbalance in ethnic or gender representation.

The standardization sample consisted of more than 5000 subjects in 47 states and the District of Columbia. The sample was stratified on the basis of

TABLE 10-3

The 15 Tests of the Modern Binet

1. *Vocabulary (46 items)*

   For the first 14 items, a picture of an object is presented and the subject must name the object. Each of 32 words is then presented orally, and the subject is asked to provide a definition. Words similar to those used on the actual tests are *truck* and *cryptic.*

2. *Bead memory (42 items)*

   The subject is asked to reproduce a pattern of beads on a stick or by locating them in a photograph.

3. *Quantitative (40 items)*

   The subject is asked to solve quantitative problems such as "What is the area of a rectangle that is 3 feet by 5 feet?"

4. *Memory for sentences (42 items)*

   The subject must repeat orally presented sentences of increasing length.

5. *Pattern analysis (42 items)*

   The subject must reproduce with blocks a design drawn on a card.

6. *Comprehension (42 items)*

   The subject must answer questions dealing with social situations or involving judgment; for example, "Why do we limit the president's term of office?"

7. *Absurdities (32 items)*

   The subject must identify a problem or incongruity in a picture, such as someone trying to drive a car without a steering wheel.

8. *Memory for digits (26 items)*

   The subject must repeat strings of digits forward and backward (e.g., repeat 3, 6, 9, 8, 1).

9. *Copying (28 items)*

   The subject must copy geometric designs (e.g., line, circle, triangle) shown on a card.

10. *Memory for objects (14 items)*

    The subject must recall a series of pictured objects in the order in which they were presented.

11. *Matrices (26 items)*

    The subject must complete the pattern in a matrix, such as

A	B
C	

    DEFGH

12. *Number series (26 items)*

    The subject must predict which two numbers appear next in a series, such as

    $$\frac{1}{3}, \frac{1}{4}, \frac{1}{5}, \underline{\quad}, \underline{\quad}$$

13. *Paper folding and cutting (18 items)*

    The subject must choose among five alternatives to match how a folded, cut piece of paper looks when unfolded.

14. *Verbal relations*

    The subject must indicate how the first three items are alike and how they differ from a fourth item; for example, "How are a peach, banana, and plum alike and different from a loaf of bread?"

15. *Equation building*

    The subject must arrange numbers and mathematical symbols (e.g., $+$, $\times$, $\div$, $=$) into an equation; for example $4 = \underline{\quad} \times 2$.

FIGURE 10-10
*Characteristics of
the modern
(1986) Binet.*

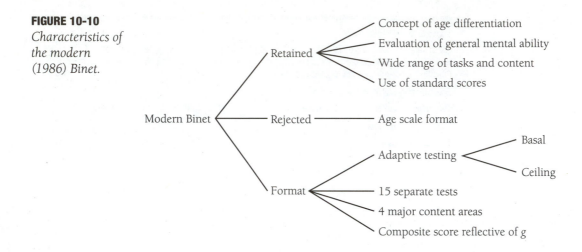

geographic region, community size, ethnic group, age, and gender (based on the 1980 census).

Overall, the reliability of the modern Binet is quite good. Data on the internal consistency as well as test-retest reliabilities are reported in the manual as a function of age range. Internal consistency estimates are based on the Kuder-Richardson formula, KR_{20}, which calculates the highest reliability from all possible half-splittings of the data. To use this formula, the authors assumed that all items below the basal were passed and all items above the ceiling failed. As the authors of the manual note, this procedure is not very conservative and most likely leads to slightly inflated (at best, the upper bounds of) reliability.

Table 10-4 shows the median reliability coefficients across age groups for individual tests, area scores, and the composite. Examination of the table reveals that the reliabilities of area scores and the composite are well above the .90 minimum that most experts believe a test should have if it is to be used to make decisions about individuals. Coefficients for individual tests, however, often fall below this minimum or are right on the borderline. Given that these coefficients represent the upper bounds of reliability, the need for caution in using individual test scores is evident.

Test-retest reliability data were obtained from a sample of 57 5-year-olds and 55 8-year-olds. The average interval between the two testings was about 16 weeks. The figures were somewhat disappointing except for the composite, which yielded reliabilities of .91 and .90 for the 5- and 8-year-olds, respectively. Although most of the coefficients for individual tests were in the low .80s or high .70s, a few low coefficients emerged. For instance, test-retest reliabilities for the quantitative and copying tests in the 8-year-old group were .28 and .46, respectively.

The technical manual reports three types of evidence that support the validity of the modern Binet: (1) the intercorrelations and factor structure of

TABLE 10-4

Median Reliabilities (KR$_{20}$) of the Modern Binet Across Age Groups

	Median Reliability, KR$_{20}$
Verbal reasoning area	.97*
Vocabulary	.87
Comprehension	.89
Absurdities	.87
Verbal relations	.91
Abstract/visual reasoning area	.96*
Pattern analysis	.92
Copying	.87
Matrices	.90
Paper folding and cutting	.94
Quantitative reasoning area	.96*
Quantitative	.88
Number series	.90
Equation building	.91
Short-term memory area	.93*
Bead memory	.87
Memory for sentences	.89
Memory for digits	.83
Memory for objects	.73
Composite	.98

Based on Table 5.2 in R. L. Thorndike, Hagen, & Sattler (1986, p. 41).
*All area scores are based on the maximum number of tests for any given area.

the 15 specific tests, (2) the correlation of test scores with other measures purporting to measure intelligence, and (3) the performance of children designated as intellectually gifted or intellectually dull by other measures. We briefly discuss each type of evidence.

Correlational and factor analytic procedures reported in the test manual generally supported the validity of the modern Binet. Each of the 15 tests received substantial loadings (i.e., correlations between the variable and the factor) on the *g* factor (range of .79 for number series to .51 for memory for objects). In addition, four group factors corresponding to the four area composites emerged from a factor analysis of the intercorrelation matrix, thus supporting the general model on which the modern Binet is based.

The modern Binet correlates well with other intelligence measures. Illustrative correlations of the composite score of the modern Binet with other tests reported in the technical manual are as follows: Stanford-Binet Form L-M (1972)—.81; Wechsler, Intelligence Scale for Children, Revised (WISC-R), full-scale IQ—.83; Wechsler Preschool and Primary Scale of Intelligence (WPPSI), full-scale IQ—.80; Wechsler Adult Intelligence Scale, Revised

(WAIS-R), full-scale IQ—.91; and Kaufman Assessment Battery for Children (K-ABC), standard scores—.82–.89. The relatively low correlation between the modern Binet and Form L-M is attributable to the high verbal emphasis of the latter. As the technical manual notes, students with exceptional verbal skills but only above-average skills in other cognitive areas receive a bonus on Form L-M that they would not get with the modern (fourth edition) Binet (R. L. Thorndike, Hagen, & Sattler, 1986). For samples of learning-disabled children, the modern Binet composite correlates .79 with Form L-M; .87 with the Wechsler Intelligence Scale for Children, full-scale IQ; and .66 with the Kaufman Assessment Battery for Children.

Table 10-5 shows the correlations of the composite score of the modern Binet with more established measures of intelligence. The correlations are quite high.

Research on the Modern Binet

To date, of the relatively few published studies about the modern Binet, many have examined the factor structure. Boyle (1989), for example, noted the several inconsistent factor loadings that had not been accounted for. Using different techniques of factor analysis, Boyle (1989, 1990) and R. M. Thorndike (1990) found that the initially reported inconsistent factor loadings were essentially artifacts of the particular factor analytic procedures used, thus supporting the validity of the modern Binet. Nevertheless, the four-factor hierarchical model underlying the Binet has yet to be fully confirmed empirically (Glutting, 1989; R. B. Kline, 1989). Determining whether the four-factor theory is viable or in need of modification is a major topic of investigation (McCallum, 1990).

Other studies on the modern Binet have correlated it with more-established standardized intelligence tests such as the Wechsler Intelligence Scales (McCrowell & Nagle, 1994; Sakolfske et al., 1994). In general, the conclusions have supported the results provided in the manual. Carvajal and Weyand (1986) reported a correlation of .78 between the composite score of the modern Binet and the full-scale IQ Wechsler Intelligence Scale for Children, Revised. For the Wechsler Preschool and Primary Scale of Intelligence, Carvajal, Hardy, et al., (1988) reported a correlation of .587 between the overall composite of the modern Binet and full-scale IQ. Both studies are limited, however, because they are based on small samples, of 20 or less. A study comparing the modern Binet composite and the full-scale IQ of the WAIS-R for 15 adults found that the mean WAIS-R score was 13.8 points lower than that of the Stanford-Binet composite (Templer, Schmitz, & Corgiat, 1985). This may be because the WAIS-R has an entire performance scale. Similar results are found when the Binet is correlated with the most recent version of the Wechsler Intelligence Scale for Children, the WISC-III (Prewett & Matavich, 1994). (For more on the Wechsler intelligence scales, see Chapter 11.) The composite score of the Binet has correlated in the .50s to .70s for a variety of other stan-

TABLE 10-5

Correlation of the Composite of the Modern (1986) Binet with Established Measures of Intelligence

Measure	Correlation
Stanford-Binet Form L-M (1972)	.81
Wechsler Intelligence Scale for Children, Revised	
Verbal IQ	.78
Performance IQ	.73
Full-scale IQ	.83
Wechsler Preschool and Primary Scale of Intelligence	
Verbal IQ	.78
Performance IQ	.71
Full-scale IQ	.80
Wechsler Adult Intelligence Scale, Revised	
Verbal IQ	.90
Performance IQ	.85
Full-scale IQ	.91
Kaufman Assessment Battery for Children	
Sequential processing	.84
Simultaneous processing	.82
Mental processing composite	.89
Achievement	.89

Based on data from R. L. Thorndike, Hagen & Sattler (1986, pp. 60–68).

dardized tests such as the Peabody Picture Vocabulary Test, Revised; Columbia Mental Maturity Scales; and McCarthy Scales of Children's Abilities (see Chapter 12) (Carvajal, Hardy, Harmon, et al., 1987; Carvajal, Karr, et al., 1988).

A few studies have attempted to compare the modern Binet with other tests such as the Matrix Analogies Test—Short Form (Prewett & Farhney, 1994). A survey of 856 school psychologists by Chattin and Bracken (1989) is an example of this work. They surveyed the membership of the National Association of School Psychologists about four commonly used individual IQ tests: the Kaufman Assessment Battery for Children (see Chapter 12), the McCarthy Scales for Children's Abilities (see Chapter 12), the Wechsler Intelligence Scale for Children, Revised (see Chapter 11), and the modern fourth edition of the Stanford-Binet. The school psychologists were asked to rate each of the tests in terms of ease of administration, interpretation, and usefulness. The WISC-R was by far the most favorably rated on all dimensions. Unfortunately, the modern Binet consistently received the lowest ratings. The authors attribute these ratings to both its newness and its relative complexity and difficulty of administration (Chattin & Bracken, 1989). They are quick to point out, however, that all four of the measures surveyed are well constructed and useful.

Evaluation of the Modern Binet

It has been said that a camel is a horse made by committee; the modern Binet may be such an animal. In many ways, it is cumbersome. From the standpoint of test administration, it's a nightmare. One must obtain basals and ceilings for all 15 tests. The examiner must estimate where to begin each test by using the vocabulary and age of the subject. The value of having specific test scores is somewhat lessened by the borderline or less than satisfactory reliabilities these tests yield.

Although items have been evaluated for fairness and possible bias, a consistent trend persists: The mean scores increase as the educational level of the parents increases. Thus, Binet scores remain tied to socioeconomic factors. Moreover, three ethnic groups—Hispanics, Asian Americans, and African Americans—have distinctive patterns of mean scores, indicating that race affects performance on the modern Binet.

On the positive side, the area and composite scores possess more than adequate reliability. Together, these scores provide a wealth of knowledge concerning general intelligence as well as four specific areas of considerable interest in the evaluation of giftedness, learning disability, and mental retardation. Overall, the modern Binet is a well-constructed instrument. Though far from perfect, it meets the highest standards for a modern psychological test.

Summary

Binet defined *intelligence* as the capacity (1) to find and maintain a definite direction or purpose, (2) to make necessary adaptations—that is, strategy adjustments—to achieve that purpose, and (3) for self-criticism so that necessary adjustments in strategy can be made.

Binet's two principles of test construction were age differentiation and general mental ability. *Age differentiation* refers to the fact that with increasing age, children develop their abilities. Thus, older children have greater abilities than younger ones.

Mental age is a unit of measurement for expressing the results of intelligence tests. The concept was introduced in the second revision of the Binet scale in 1908. A subject's mental age is based on his or her performance compared to the average performance of individuals in a specific chronological age group. For example, if a 6-year-old child can perform tasks that the average 8-year-old can do, then the 6-year-old child is said to have a mental age of 8.

Like mental age, the *intelligence quotient* (IQ) is a unit of measure for expressing the results of intelligence tests. Introduced in the Terman 1916 Stanford-Binet revision of the Binet scale, the IQ is a ratio score. Specifically, the IQ is the ratio of a subject's mental age (as determined by his or her performance on the intelligence scale) and chronological age. This ratio is then multiplied by 100 to eliminate fractions.

The deviation IQ, as used in the Stanford-Binet scale, is a standard score with a mean of 100 and a standard deviation of 16.

The most recent revision of the Binet scale, the fourth edition, was released in 1986. The modern Binet consists of 15 individual tests, each of which falls into one of four major content areas.

CHAPTER 11

The Wechsler Intelligence Scales

LEARNING OBJECTIVES

When you have completed this chapter, you should be able to:

☐ Identify the major motivation for the development of the Wechsler scales

☐ Briefly describe the point and performance scale concepts

☐ Distinguish between verbal and performance subtests

☐ Explain the concept of a declining age standard

☐ Tell how IQ scores are determined on the Wechsler Scales

☐ Describe the reliability of the Wechsler Scales

☐ Describe the validity of the Wechsler Scales

☐ Identify some of the major advantages and disadvantages of the Wechsler scales

Susan's family had just moved from a small rural town to a large city on the East Coast. At age 9, she remained shy around strangers and lacked confidence. Her attempt to adjust to a new school was a disaster. Because she started in the middle of the school term, all the other children seemed way ahead of her; she felt hopelessly behind. To make matters worse, she had an unusually strong fear of failure. Rather than make an error, she would remain silent even if she knew an answer. With all her negative experiences in the new school, she began to develop a poor attitude toward school tasks and therefore avoided them. Eventually, her teacher referred her to the school psychologist for testing. To Susan, this referral was the school's way of punishing her for not doing her homework. Fearful, upset, and angry, she made up her mind not to cooperate with the psychologist.

When the time finally came for her appointment, Susan began to cry. The principal was called in to accompany her to the psychologist's office. All the psychologist's attempts to comfort Susan did little to reduce her fear and anxiety. Finally, the psychologist decided to begin the testing. He started with a relatively simple task that required Susan to repeat digits. The psychologist stated, "I'm going to say some numbers. Listen, because when I'm through, I want you to say them as I do." He began the first set of digits and stated in a soft, clear voice, "Six, one, three." Susan did not even respond. She had been staring blankly at the walls and had not heard what the psychologist had said. The psychologist attracted her attention and said, "Now say what I say: four, two, seven." This time Susan heard, but again she remained silent.

Now think for a moment. How many different factors were involved in the psychologist's ostensibly simple request to repeat three digits forward? To comply with this request, Susan would have had to direct her attention to the words of the psychologist, possess adequate hearing, and understand the instructions. She would also have had to cooperate, make an effort, and be capable of repeating what she had heard. Certainly her familiarity with numerals—that is, her previous learning and experience—could influence her performance. If the children in her new school had more exposure to numerals than she, then they would have an advantage over her in this regard. Furthermore, her lack of confidence, negative attitude toward school, fear of failure, and shyness all played a role in her performance. A more confident, less fearful child with positive attitudes toward school would have a clear advantage over Susan. Thus, in addition to memory, many nonintellective factors (for example, attitude, experience, and emotional functioning) play an extremely important role in a person's ability to perform a task even as "simple" as repeating three digits forward.

Though both Binet and Terman considered the influence of nonintellective factors on results from intelligence tests, David Wechsler has been perhaps one of the most influential advocates of the role of nonintellective factors in these tests. In the fourth edition of his book *The Measurement and Appraisal of Adult Intelligence,* Wechsler stated, "Factors other than intellectual ability, for example, those of drive and incentive, are involved in intelligent behavior" (1958, pp. vii–viii).

In the highly influential fifth revision of Wechsler's (1958) book, Matarazzo added, "Although the IQ is the best single measure of intelligence, it is neither the only nor a complete measure of it. It [IQ] is a function of other factors besides sheer intellectual ability" (1972, p. 132). Wechsler (1981) subsequently reasserted the importance of nonintellective factors but warned that "no amount of drive will develop a dullard into a mathematician" (p. 8).

The Wechsler Intelligence Scales

The role of nonintellective factors is apparent in the Wechsler intelligence scales. Just two years after the Binet scale's monumental 1937 revision, the Wechsler-Bellevue Intelligence Scale challenged its supremacy as a measure of human intelligence. With so many different and varied abilities associated with intelligence, Wechsler objected to the single score offered by the 1937 Binet scale. In addition, although Wechsler's test did not directly measure nonintellective factors, it took these factors into careful account in its underlying theory. In constructing his own intelligence test, Wechsler deviated considerably from many of the Binet scale's central concepts.

Wechsler (1939) capitalized on the inappropriateness of the Binet scale as a measure of the intelligence of adults. Because the Binet scale items were selected for use with children, Wechsler concluded that these items lacked validity when answered by adults. Further, examiner-subject rapport was often impaired when adults were tested with the Binet scale. Wechsler (1939) also noted that the Binet scale's emphasis on speed, with timed tasks scattered throughout the scale, tended to unduly handicap older adults. Furthermore, mental age norms clearly did not apply to adults. Finally, Wechsler criticized the Binet scale because it did not consider the possible deterioration of intellectual performance with increasing age.

Advances in Intelligence Testing:
Point and Performance Scale Concepts

Many of the differences between the Wechsler and the 1937 Binet scales are profound. Two of the most critical differences are (1) Wechsler's use of the point scale concept rather than an age scale and (2) Wechsler's inclusion of a performance scale.

The point scale concept. Recall that from 1908 to 1972, the Binet scale grouped items by age level. Each age level included a group of tasks that could be passed by two-thirds to three-fourths of the individuals at that age level. In an **age scale** format, the arrangement of items has nothing to do with their content. At a particular year level, there might be one task related to memory, a second to reasoning, and a third to skill in using numerical data. Another level might also include a task related to memory but then include other tasks related to concentration or language skills. Thus, various types of content are scattered throughout the scale. Furthermore, subjects do not receive a specific amount of points or credit for each task completed. For example, if a Binet scale subject is required to pass three out of four tasks in order to receive credit for a particular test, then passing only two tasks would produce no credit at all for that test.

In a **point scale**, credits or points are assigned to each item. An individual receives a specific amount of credit for each item passed. The Binet scale has never afforded such credit. For example, on the modern Binet, a basal may be reached whether the individual is correct on three out of four or on all four items at two consecutive levels. The individual who gets three items correct obtains the same basal score as the one who gets all four correct. Thus, although the modern Binet abandoned the age scale concept (see Chapter 10), it did not go so far as to adopt the point scale concept.

The point scale offers an inherent advantage. This scale makes it easy to group items of a particular content together, which is exactly what Wechsler did. The effect of such groupings was so powerful that a similar concept was used in the revision of the 1986 modern Binet scale. By arranging items according to content and assigning a specific number of points to each item, Wechsler constructed an intelligence test that yielded not only a total overall score, as the 1937 Binet did, but also scores for each content area. Thus, the point scale concept allowed Wechsler to devise a test that permitted an analysis of the individual's ability in a variety of content areas (for example, judgment, vocabulary, and range of general knowledge).

The performance scale concept. The 1937 Binet scale has been persistently and consistently criticized for its emphasis on language/verbal skills. To deal with this problem, Wechsler included an entire scale that provided a measure of nonverbal intelligence: a **performance scale.** In addition to measuring adults and yielding separate scores, Wechsler's approach thus offered a third major advantage over the Binet scale. The performance scale consists of tasks that require a subject to do something (for example, copy symbols or point to a missing detail) rather than merely to answer questions. (See Figure 11-1.)

Although the 1937 Binet scale contained some performance tasks, these tended to be concentrated at the early age levels. Furthermore, the results of a subject's response to a performance task on the Binet scale were extremely difficult to separate from the results of verbal tasks. Thus, one could not determine the precise extent to which a subject's response to a performance task increased or decreased the total score. The Wechsler scale, however, included two separate scales. The verbal scale provided a measure of verbal intelligence, the performance scale a measure of nonverbal intelligence.

The concept of a performance scale was far from new. Before the Wechsler scale, several performance tests served as supplements or alternatives to the verbally weighted Binet scale (such as the Leiter International Performance Scale, discussed in Chapter 12). However, Wechsler's new scale first offered

FIGURE 11-1
*Advantages of
Wechsler's scale.*

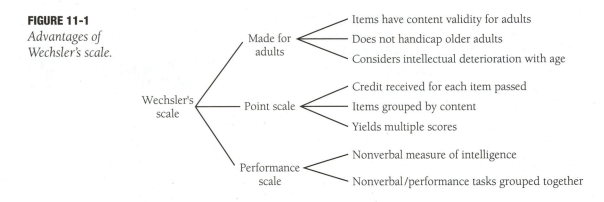

the possibility of directly comparing an individual's verbal and nonverbal intelligence. That is, both verbal and performance scales were standardized on the same sample, and results for both scales were expressed in comparable units.

A performance scale attempts to overcome (to the extent possible) biases caused by language, culture, and education. Furthermore, if verbal tasks provide a useful context in which to observe problem solving, then tasks that require the subject to do something can offer an even richer and more varied context. Indeed, performance tasks tend to require a longer interval of sustained effort, concentration, and attention than most verbal tasks. Therefore, despite their relative insensitivity to language, educational, and cultural factors, performance tasks are generally more vulnerable to emotional disorders (Rapaport, Gill, & Schafer, 1968). Even so, Wechsler went a long way toward resolving one of the major problems in the 1937 Binet scale. (See Figure 11-2.)

From the Wechsler-Bellevue Intelligence Scale to the WAIS-III

Despite his conceptual improvements, Wechsler's first effort to measure adult intelligence, the Wechsler-Bellevue scale (Wechsler, 1939), was poorly standardized. Its normative sample consisted of a nonrepresentative sample of 1081 whites from the eastern United States (primarily New York residents). By 1955, however, Wechsler had revised the Wechsler-Bellevue scale into its modern form, the Wechsler Adult Intelligence Scale (WAIS), which was revised in 1981 (the WAIS-R) and again in 1997 (the WAIS-III).

Scales and Subtests of the Wechsler Scales

Like Binet, Wechsler defined intelligence as the capacity to act purposefully and to adapt to the environment. Intelligence is, he stated, "the aggregate or global capacity of the individual to act purposefully, to think rationally and to deal effectively with his environment" (Wechsler, 1958, p. 7). Wechsler

NAME _____ AGE _____ SEX _____

MARITAL STATUS _____ HANDEDNESS _____

OCCUPATION _____ EDUCATION _____

PLACE OF TESTING _____

TESTED BY _____

REFERRED BY _____

REASON FOR REFERRAL _____

WAIS-R® EXPANDED RECORD FORM

	Year	Month	Day
Date Tested	____	____	____
Date of Birth	____	____	____
Age	____	____	____

SUMMARY

	Raw Score	Scaled Score	Age-Scaled Score[1]
VERBAL SUBTESTS			
Information	____	____	____
Digit Span	____	____	____
Vocabulary	____	____	____
Arithmetic	____	____	____
Comprehension	____	____	____
Similarities	____	____	____
Verbal Score		____	
PERFORMANCE SUBTESTS			
Picture Completion	____	____	____
Picture Arrangement	____	____	____
Block Design	____	____	____
Object Assembly	____	____	____
Digit Symbol	____	____	____
Performance Score		____	

[1]Scaled score equivalents of raw scores for a specific age range(see Manual, Table 21). Not to be used for determination of IQ.

TABLE OF SCALED SCORE EQUIVALENTS*

Scaled Score	VERBAL SUBTESTS						PERFORMANCE SUBTESTS					Scaled Score
	Information	Digit Span	Vocabulary	Arithmetic	Comprehension	Similarities	Picture Completion	Picture Arrangement	Block Design	Object Assembly	Digit Symbol	
19	—	28	70	—	32	—	—	—	51	—	93	19
18	29	27	69	—	31	28	—	—	—	41	91-92	18
17	—	26	68	19	—	—	20	20	50	—	89-90	17
16	28	25	66-67	—	30	27	—	—	49	40	84-88	16
15	27	24	65	18	29	26	—	19	47-48	39	79-83	15
14	26	22-23	63-64	17	27-28	25	19	—	44-46	38	75-78	14
13	25	20-21	60-62	16	26	24	—	18	42-43	37	70-74	13
12	23-24	18-19	55-59	15	25	23	18	17	38-41	35-36	66-69	12
11	22	17	52-54	13-14	23-24	22	17	15-16	35-37	34	62-65	11
10	19-21	15-16	47-51	12	21-22	20-21	16	14	31-34	32-33	57-61	10
9	17-18	14	43-46	11	19-20	18-19	15	13	27-30	30-31	53-56	9
8	15-16	12-13	37-42	10	17-18	16-17	14	11-12	23-26	28-29	48-52	8
7	13-14	11	29-36	8-9	14-16	14-15	13	8-10	20-22	24-27	44-47	7
6	9-12	9-10	20-28	6-7	11-13	11-13	11-12	5-7	14-19	21-23	37-43	6
5	6-8	8	14-19	5	8-10	7-10	8-10	3-4	8-13	16-20	30-36	5
4	5	7	11-13	4	6-7	5-6	5-7	2	3-7	13-15	23-29	4
3	4	6	9-10	3	4-5	2-4	3-4	—	2	9-12	16-22	3
2	3	3-5	6-8	1-2	2-3	1	2	1	1	6-8	8-15	2
1	0-2	0-2	0-5	0	0-1	0	0-1	0	0	0-5	0-7	1

*Clinicians who wish to draw a profile may do so by locating the examinee's raw scores on the table above and drawing a line to connect them. See Chapter 4 in the Manual for a discussion of the significance of differences between scores on the subtests.

	Scaled Score	IQ	Percentile Rank	Classification
Verbal Score	____†	____	____	____
Performance Score	____‡	____	____	____
Full Scale Score	____	____	____	____

†Prorated from 5 subtests, if necessary.
‡Prorated from 4 subtests, if necessary.

FIGURE 11-2 *WAIS-R Expanded Record Form.*

(Wechsler Adult Intelligence Scale—Revised. Copyright © 1981, 1955 by The Psychological Corporation. Reproduced by permission. All rights reserved.)

TABLE 11-1
Wechsler Subtests

Subtest	Major Function Measured
Verbal Scales	
Information	Range of knowledge
Comprehension	Judgment
Arithmetic	Concentration
Similarities	Abstract thinking
Digit span	Immediate memory, anxiety
Vocabulary	Vocabulary level
Performance Scales	
Digit symbol	Visual-motor functioning
Picture completion	Alertness to details
Picture arrangement	Planning ability
Block design	Nonverbal reasoning
Object assembly	Analysis of part-whole relationships

believed that intelligence comprised specific elements that one could individually define and measure; however, these elements were interrelated—that is, not entirely independent. This is why he used the terms *global* and *aggregate*. Wechsler's definition implies that intelligence comprises a number of specific interrelated functions or elements and that general intelligence results from the interplay of these elements. Theoretically, by measuring each of the elements, one can measure general intelligence by summing the individual's capacities on each element. Thus, Wechsler tried to measure separate abilities, which Binet had avoided in adopting the concept of general mental ability. For his adult intelligence scales, Wechsler identified 11 elements or functions, 6 related to verbal intelligence and 5 to nonverbal intelligence. Table 11-1 lists these 11 subtests and the basic function they purportedly measure (Rapaport, Gill, & Schafer, 1968; Sattler, 1982; Wechsler, 1958; Zimmerman, Woo-Sam, & Glasser, 1973).

The Verbal Subtests

The six verbal subtests are (1) information, (2) comprehension, (3) arithmetic, (4) similarities, (5) digit span, and (6) vocabulary. Each of these is briefly discussed as follows.

The information subtest. College students typically find the information subtest relatively easy and fun. As in all Wechsler subtests, items appear in order of increasing difficulty. Item 6 asks something like, "Name four famous U.S. presidents." In all, there are about 30 items. Item 22 asks something like, "How many members are there in the U.S. Congress?" Like all Wechsler subtests, the information subtest involves both intellective and nonintellective components, including several abilities to comprehend instructions, follow directions, and

FIGURE 11-3

Information subtest: intellective and nonintellective components. (Based on factor analytic and logical analyses of intellective and nonintellective components in the information subtest.)

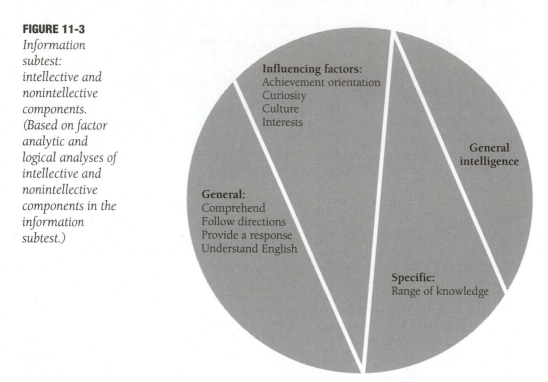

Influencing factors:
Achievement orientation
Curiosity
Culture
Interests

General intelligence

General:
Comprehend
Follow directions
Provide a response
Understand English

Specific:
Range of knowledge

provide a response. Although purportedly a measure of the subject's range of knowledge, nonintellective factors such as curiosity and interest in the acquisition of knowledge tend to influence test scores. Figure 11-3 illustrates how one can parcel a score on the information subtest.

The comprehension subtest. As in the information subtest, examiners give no specific instructions before the comprehension subtest. They simply read each question and wait for the response. The comprehension subtest has three types of questions. The first asks the subject what should be done in a given situation. For example, a person might be asked something like, "What should you do if you find an injured person lying in the street?" The second type of question asks the subject to provide a logical explanation for some rule or phenomenon, as in "Why do we bury the dead?" The third type asks the subject to define proverbs such as "A stitch in time saves nine." Previous learning and scholastic aptitude play a far smaller role in the comprehension than in the information subtest; generally, the former measures judgment in everyday practical situations, or common sense. In addition, emotional difficulties frequently reveal themselves on this subtest and lower the person's score. For example, to the question concerning what to do if you find an injured person, a psychopathic individual might respond, "Tell them I didn't do it." A phobic neurotic might respond, "Make sure I don't get any blood on myself." A schiz-

FIGURE 11-4
Arithmetic subtest: intellective and nonintellective components.

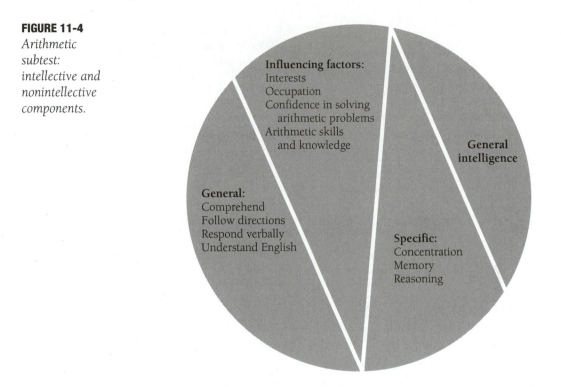

ophrenic might say, "Run!" In each case, the person's emotional disturbance interferes with his or her judgment and results in an inappropriate response.

The arithmetic subtest. The arithmetic subtest contains about 15 relatively simple problems. The ninth most difficult item is as easy as this: "A person with $17.50 spends $7. How much does he have left?" Obviously, you need not be a mathematician to figure this one out; however, you must be able to retain the figures in memory while manipulating them. In a few cases, such as in mentally handicapped or educationally deprived subjects, arithmetic skills can play a significant role. Generally, however, concentration, motivation, and memory are the main factors underlying performance. Figure 11-4 illustrates some of the intellective and nonintellective components of the arithmetic subtest as revealed by factor analytic and logical analyses.

The similarities subtest. The similarities subtest consists of about 15 paired items of increasing difficulty. The subject must identify the similarity between the items in each pair. The examiner may ask, for example, "In what way are a horse and a cow alike?" Many of the early, easier items are so well known that responses simply reflect previously learned associations (Zimmerman, Woo-Sam, & Glasser, 1973). However, the more difficult items—for example, "In what way are an ant and a rose alike?"—definitely require the subject to think abstractly. This subtest measures the subject's ability to see the similarity between apparently dissimilar objects or things.

The character of a person's thought processes can be seen in many cases. For example, schizophrenic people tend to give concepts that have meaning only to them—that is, idiosyncratic concepts. Such a response to the horse and cow item might be "Both are places to hide." Such a response has meaning only to the schizophrenic person, who may further explain, "My favorite hiding place is on my uncle's farm." Brain-injured and mentally handicapped individuals tend to find thinking abstractly difficult. The character of their thought processes is concrete. A concrete response is highly specific, such as "A cow and a horse both have four legs."

The digit span subtest. The digit span subtest requires the subject to repeat digits, given at the rate of one per second, forward and backward. In terms of intellective factors, the digit span subtest measures short-term auditory memory. As with other Wechsler subtests, however, nonintellective factors (for example, attention) often influence the results. For example, a large body of literature has shown that anxiety in the test situation impairs performance on the digit span subtest (Boor & Schill, 1968; G. A. Edwards, 1966; W. Hodges & Spielberger, 1969).

The vocabulary subtest. The ability to define words is not only one of the best single measures of intelligence but also the most stable and least deteriorating aspect of intelligence (Rapaport, Gill, & Schafer, 1968). Vocabulary tests appear on nearly every individual test involving verbal intelligence. The relative stability of the vocabulary scale is one of its most important features. If an individual has shown deterioration (that is, lowered performance compared with a previously higher level) because of emotional factors or brain damage, for example, vocabulary is one of the last subtests to be affected. For example, the poor concentration of schizophrenic people lowers their performance on arithmetic or digit span tasks long before vocabulary. Whereas mild concentration difficulties lower optimal performance on arithmetic and digit span tasks, such difficulties generally do not affect vocabulary until they become quite severe. Because the vocabulary subtest provides a relatively stable estimate of general verbal intelligence, one can use it to evaluate baseline intelligence (that is, what a person's intellectual capacity probably was prior to an emotional illness, brain injury, or trauma).

Raw Scores, Scaled Scores, and the Verbal IQ

The six verbal subtests make up the verbal scale. Each subtest produces a raw score—that is, a total number of points—and has a different maximum total.

To deal with the raw scores' lack of comparability for the individual subtests, the raw scores for each subtest are converted to a standard or **scaled score** with a mean of 10 and a standard deviation of 3. On the WAIS-R, for example, a raw score for any given subtest yields the same scaled score regardless of age, because norms for WAIS-R scaled scores were based on a reference sample of 500 cases ranging between 20 and 34 years of age selected from the standardization sample. For a given subject, the scaled score on one subtest can be directly compared with any other score. For example, a scaled score of 10 is at the 50th percentile for all subtests. Thus, a person's relative strength on any subtest can be directly compared to his or her strength on any other. This feature opens the possibility of pattern analysis, in which one can examine a person's pattern of weaknesses and strengths for particular problems (Crawford & Allan, 1994; Schinka, Vanderploeg, & Curtiss, 1994).

To obtain the verbal IQ, the scaled scores on each of the six verbal subtests are summed. This sum is then compared to the standardization sample of the person's age group. The same sum produces different IQs, depending on age. For example, a sum of 60 yields a verbal IQ of 97 in the 25–34 age group, but a verbal IQ of 109 in the 70–74 age group for the WAIS-R. Focused Example 11-1 discusses the reason older subjects require a lower scaled score sum to produce the same IQ as middle-aged subjects. Given people's ages and summed scaled scores, you can look up their IQs in tables the manuals provide (WAIS-R and WAIS-III). The verbal IQ for each age level is a deviation IQ with a mean of 100 and a standard deviation of 15. In considering the concept of a declining age standard (Focused Example 11-1), you should keep in mind that the IQ and intercorrelations of cognitive abilities remain stable through adulthood (Ivnik et al., 1995).

The Performance Subtests

The five performance subtests of the Wechsler Adult tests are digit symbol, picture completion, block design, picture arrangement, and object assembly. We shall discuss each, as follows.

The digit symbol subtest. The digit symbol subtest requires the subject to copy symbols. In the upper part of the standard WAIS-III response form, the numbers 1 through 9 are each paired with a symbol (see Figure 11-5). After completing a short practice sample, the subject has 90 seconds to copy as many symbols as possible. The subtest measures such factors as ability to learn an unfamiliar task, visual-motor dexterity, degree of persistence, and speed of performance (Zimmerman, Woo-Sam & Glasser, 1973). Naturally, the subject must have adequate visual acuity and appropriate motor capabilities to complete this subtest successfully.

The picture completion subtest. In the picture completion subtest, the subject is shown a picture in which some important detail is missing, such as a horse without a tail. Asked to tell which part is missing (Wechsler, 1955), the subject can obtain credit by simply pointing to the missing part. As in other WAIS-III performance subtests, picture completion is timed. As simple as this task seems from an administrative standpoint, the importance of an experienced examiner becomes clear with close examination. If, for example, the subject points, the examiner must ascertain that the right detail has been identified. An experienced examiner also knows that it is unwise to force a subject to struggle over a picture when he or she clearly has no idea of the answer. One needs discretion in giving this, as well as other, WAIS-III performance subtests.

Focused Example 11-1

THE DECLINING AGE STANDARD

One of the important debates within psychology has centered on the question "Does intelligence decrease in the later years of life?" Analysis of the 1955 WAIS standardization indicated that scores rise until a person's late 20s or 30s, then decline until about age 60, which marks a relatively sharp decline in intelligence (Doppelt & Wallace, 1955). However, the WAIS was standardized cross-sectionally. This means a different sample of subjects was tested at each age level. In contrast to the cross-sectional method, the longitudinal method requires testing the same subjects at various points in time. Obviously, the longitudinal method provides far greater control over important variables than the cross-sectional one.

When the same individuals are tested several times over a long period of time (longitudinal method), testers can account for educational opportunities (more colleges available today than 40 years ago), cultural experiences, technological advances (availability of home computers), and a host of other factors. Furthermore, a longitudinal study eliminates the effects of inadvertently having unusually bright (or limited) individuals at one particular age group, which would otherwise bias the results. However, a longitudinal study requires many years to complete. In standardizing the WAIS, Wechsler could not afford to take the same group of adults and test them over 50 years. However, relatively recent evidence from longitudinal studies has indicated that intelligence actually does not decline as dramatically as indicated by an analysis of Wechsler's cross-sectional normative sample (Mortenson & Kleven, 1993). In fact, the evidence indicates that, except in certain abnormal conditions and just prior to death, when there is a "terminal drop" in IQ (Rinn, 1988), intelligence remains fairly stable throughout the life span. In one longitudinal study of the WAIS, Mortensen & Kleven (1993) tested 141 subjects, born in 1914, at ages 50, 60, and 70. They reported only slight declines between successive testings. The investigators also reported a strikingly high test-retest reliability coefficient over a 20-year period ($r = 0.90$) for the Full-Scale IQ as well as additional support for the terminal drop hypothesis (i.e., sharp IQ declines just before death).

The reason for the dramatic differences between the verbal IQ for a scaled score sum of 60 in the 25–34 age group (IQ = 97) and the verbal IQ for a sum of 60 in the 70–74 age group (IQ = 109) is that norms for the Wechsler Adult Scales (WAIS, WAIS-R, and WAIS-III) are based on cross-sectional data. The decline in intelligence in the later years of life indicated by the cross-sectional data is reflected in the IQ conversions for a particular age group. For example, the average sum of the verbal subtest scaled scores in the WAIS cross-sectional standardization sample was about 48 in the 70–74 age range. The average sum in the 25–34 age range, however, was 61. Therefore, to obtain a verbal IQ of 100, someone in the 70–74 age range would need a sum of 48, whereas someone in the 25–34 age range would need a sum of 61. This phenomenon is known as the *declining age standard.*

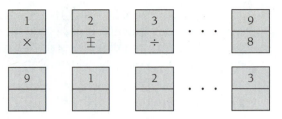

FIGURE 11-5   *Digit symbol: an illustrative example. The top row contains divided boxes with a number in the upper half and a mark underneath. The bottom row contains divided boxes with numbers on top but no marks. The subject must supply the appropriate mark in the lower half of the bottom row.*

The block design subtest. Block design tasks have long been included in non-verbal measures of intelligence (G. Arthur, 1930; Kohs, 1923). Materials for the design subtest include nine blocks. Some sides are all red, some are all white, and others are red on one half and white on the other. The materials also include a booklet with pictures of the blocks arranged according to a specific design or configuration. The subject must arrange the blocks into increasingly difficult designs. This subtest requires the subject to reason, analyze spatial relationships, and integrate visual and motor functions. The input information (that is, pictures of designs) is visual, but the response (output) is motor. The subtest provides an excellent measure of nonverbal concept formation, or abstract thinking (Rapaport, Gill, & Schafer, 1968).

The picture arrangement subtest. The picture arrangement subtest also requires the subject to notice relevant details. In addition, the subject must be able to plan adequately and notice cause-effect relationships (Zimmerman, Woo-Sam, & Glasser, 1973). The subtest consists of about 10 items, each of which contains a series of related pictures like those found in most comic strips. The subject must put the misarranged pictures in the right order to tell a story. Because the individual must find the logical sequence of events, the subtest taps nonverbal reasoning ability. Because some of the items involve social or interpersonal content, some say the subtest also taps the ability to interpret social situations accurately (Sattler, 1982; Zimmerman, Woo-Sam, & Glasser, 1973).

The object assembly subtest. Object assembly consists of puzzles (cut-up objects) that the subject is asked to put together as quickly as possible. This subtest measures the subject's ability to see part-whole relationships and involves "visual analysis and its coordination with simple assembly skills" (Zimmerman, Woo-Sam, & Glasser, 1973, p. 63).

Performance IQs

As with the verbal subtests, the raw scores for each of the five performance subtests are converted to scaled scores. The mean and standard deviation are the same as for the verbal subtests—10 and 3, respectively. The performance IQ is obtained by summing the scaled scores on the performance subtests and comparing this score with the appropriate age group. Like the verbal IQ, the performance IQ is a deviation IQ with a mean of 100 and a standard deviation of 15.

Full-Scale IQs

The full-scale IQ follows the same principles of the verbal and performance IQs. It is obtained by summing the scaled scores of the verbal subtests with the performance subtests and comparing the subject to his or her appropriate age group. Again, a deviation IQ with a mean of 100 and a standard deviation of 15 is obtained. Table 11-2 shows the conversions of IQ to percentile ranks for the verbal, performance, and full-scale IQs. As you can see, IQs between 45 and 67 are all in the 1st percentile. An IQ of 80 is at the 9th percentile, an IQ of 110 at the 75th percentile, and so on.

Interpretive Features of the Wechsler Tests

The Wechsler tests, such as the WAIS-R and WAIS-III, provide a rich source of data that often furnishes significant cues in the diagnosis of evaluation of emotionally disordered states. The comparison verbal and performance IQs and analysis of the pattern of subtest scores are particularly helpful in evaluating people in disordered states (Crawford & Allan, 1994; Ryan, Paolo, & Van Fleet, 1994).

Verbal-Performance IQ Comparisons

In providing a measure of nonverbal intelligence in conjunction with a verbal IQ, the WAIS-III offers an extremely useful opportunity not offered by the early Binet scales. First, the performance IQ aids in the interpretation of the verbal IQ (Sattler, 1988). Assume, for example, that a subject obtains a verbal IQ (VIQ) in the low ranges (such as VIQ = 60). If the performance IQ is also approximately 60, then results with the verbal IQ have been confirmed, and we have a good indication that the individual is, in fact, intellectually retarded. Remember, however, that a diagnosis of mental retardation should not be made on the basis of IQ alone. The individual must show significant deficits in adaptive functioning as well as a full-scale IQ below 70. Suppose, however, that the performance IQ exceeded 100, but the verbal IQ was 55. In this case, the individual is at least average in his or her nonverbal skills but three standard deviations below the mean in the verbal area. Even though the full-scale IQ might still fall within the retarded range, it is quite unlikely that such a person is mentally retarded. Instead, language, cultural, or educational factors might account for the differences in the two IQs.

TABLE 11-2

Percentile Rank (PR) Equivalents for Verbal, Performance, and Full-Scale IQs*

IQ	PR	IQ	PR	IQ	PR
45	1	80	9	115	84
46	1	81	10	116	86
47	1	82	12	117	87
48	1	83	13	118	88
49	1	84	14	119	90
50	1	85	16	120	91
51	1	86	18	121	92
52	1	87	19	122	93
53	1	88	21	123	94
54	1	89	23	124	95
55	1	90	25	125	95
56	1	91	27	126	96
57	1	92	30	127	96
58	1	93	32	128	97
59	1	94	34	129	97
60	1	95	37	130	98
61	1	96	40	131	98
62	1	97	42	132	98
63	1	98	45	133	99
64	1	99	47	134	99
65	1	100	50	135	99
66	1	101	53	136	99
67	1	102	55	137	99
68	2	103	58	138	99
69	2	104	61	139	99
70	2	105	63	140	99
71	3	106	66	141	99
72	3	107	68	142	99
73	4	108	70	143	99
74	4	109	73	144	99
75	5	110	75	145	99
76	5	111	77	146	99
77	6	112	79	147	99
78	7	113	81	148	99
79	8	114	82	149	99
				150	99

*Wechsler Adult Intelligence Scale—Revised, 1981.

In one study of verbal versus performance IQs, Saccuzzo, Johnson, and Russell (1992) examined approximately 5000 gifted children from four ethnic backgrounds: African-American, Caucasian, Filipino, and Hispanic. Results showed that even though all children had IQs of 125 or greater, the nature of the verbal-performance discrepancy, if any, depended on ethnic background. The African-American and Caucasian groups had higher verbal than performance IQs. The reverse was found for the Filipinos, who had significantly higher performance IQs. No differences were found between the verbal and performance IQs for the Hispanics. Results such as these indicate that it is not appropriate to make sweeping generalizations about the meaning of a verbal and performance IQ discrepancy. When considering any test sign, you must take the ethnic background of the individual into account.

Pattern Analysis

The separate subtest scores of the WAIS-III offer an opportunity for pattern analysis. In such analysis, one evaluates relatively large differences between subtest scaled scores. Wechsler (1958) believed that certain patterns of scores might be related to certain types of emotional problems. He reasoned that different types of emotional problems might have differential effects on the subtests. For example, hysterics (people with conversion disorders) use denial and repression—that is, put things out of awareness as a defense mechanism. Therefore, they should show lapses in their long-term store of knowledge, which might produce a relatively low score on the information subtest. Schizophrenia involves poor concentration and impaired judgment, which might turn up as relatively low scores on arithmetic and comprehension. Wechsler (1958) provided a host of patterns tentatively proposed as diagnostically significant.

Following Wechsler's (1958) proposed patterns, many investigators empirically studied the potential validity of pattern analysis (Guertin, Ladd, et al., 1966, 1971; Guertin, Rabin, et al., 1962). The results were inconclusive and contradictory. Indeed, G. H. Frank (1970) surveyed the literature relevant to the diagnostic and personality implications of the WAIS. He concluded that the available research was so poorly controlled that the best thing to do would be to forget the work that had been done and start again from scratch.

Following Frank's criticisms of the literature and all but dismissal of pattern analysis, Lewandowski and Saccuzzo (1975, 1976) and Saccuzzo and Lewandowski (1976) listed a number of methodological considerations that one must follow to answer fairly the questions concerning the validity of pattern analysis. Specifically, they tried to illustrate how these considerations might be applied to validate a given Wechsler intelligence scale pattern for a particular disordered state. These authors failed to confirm many of Wechsler's (1958) hypotheses concerning the meaning of certain subtest patterns, which had been based on his examination of the standardization sample. However, they associated a definite, reliable pattern of subtest scores with individuals incarcerated for delinquency. This work was subsequently cross-validated and confirmed by Wickham (1978).

Although the issue of pattern analysis validity has yet to be resolved, clinical practitioners continue to interpret Wechsler subtest patterns. The hypothetical cases that follow illustrate what the various Wechsler subtest scores might mean to a clinician.

Hypothetical Case Studies

Consider the following example of a 16-year-old high-school junior with a *D* average despite a previously stable *B* average. Standard achievement tests found

TABLE 11-3
Scaled Scores

Verbal Scales	Performance Scales
Information: 11	Digit symbol: 4
Comprehension: 9	Picture completion: 10
Arithmetic: 7	Book design: 5
Similarities: 11	Picture arrangement: 11
Digit span: 5	Object assembly: 6
Vocabulary: 11	
Scaled score sum: 54	Scaled score sum: 36
Verbal IQ: 104*	Performance IQ: 83*
Sum of scaled scores for verbal and performance scales: 90	
Full-scale IQ: 93*	

*According to Table 20 provided in the WAIS-R manual (*Wechsler, 1981, pp. 92–93).

his reading and arithmetic grades appropriate. His scaled scores are as shown in Table 11-3 (remember, the mean is 10 and the standard deviation is 3).

The previously stable *B* average indicates that this individual is probably of at least average intelligence. The rapid decline in his grades, however, suggests some dramatic change or shift in functioning. His scaled score of 11 on vocabulary is above the mean. Because vocabulary is a relatively stable measure of IQ, the scaled score of 11 also indicates this individual's IQ of 93 is most likely an underestimate of his intelligence. Assuming that this individual's typical scaled score performance would be about 11, as reflected in his scaled score on vocabulary and confirmed by his scaled scores on information and similarities, we find evidence for deterioration in his judgment (comprehension), concentration (arithmetic), and immediate memory (digit span) in the verbal areas. We also find deterioration in his visual-motor speed and integration (digit symbol), nonverbal reasoning (block design), and ability to see part-whole relationships (object assembly) in the performance areas.

When we consider all the areas of impairment, as indicated by relatively low-scaled scores, we must hypothesize the possibility of some type of brain injury or tumor, because these impair performance on all the subtests in which the subject has shown evidence of deterioration (e.g., Lincoln et al., 1994; Ryan, Paolo, & Van Fleet, 1994). With the possibility of a brain tumor, both a medical examination and additional tests are necessary.

With no evidence to the contrary, the clinician would strongly suspect that the subject's shift in grades may be due to a brain injury or tumor. However, the clinician would consider other possibilities as well. Environmental or situational factors could lead to impairment on the various WAIS-R and WAIS-III subtests. For example, because the subject may have become involved with drugs, this possibility must be examined. Furthermore, schizophrenia may cause similar decrements in performance. Therefore, signs of peculiar behavior or other symptoms of schizophrenia should be ruled out by an interview and perhaps a projective test (see Chapter 16). Ruling out situational, environmental, or schizophrenic factors, the examiner might interview to determine whether the subject has suffered a recent blow to the head. If these possibilities prove to be negative, the subject should be immediately referred for a neurological examination.

As you no doubt have observed, this analysis resulted in several speculations, and the clinician exercised the usual caution in using the results. For the next example, we present a pattern very much like the one that Saccuzzo and Lewandowski (1976) and Wickham (1978) found in acting-out youths.

In this example, we have the scaled scores of a 16-year-old girl with chronic school problems. Identified as a slow learner in the earlier grades, she reads far below her grade level. Her scores are shown in Table 11-4.

The subject is nearly one standard deviation above the mean in her performance IQ; all her subtests in the performance area are at or greater than the mean. Clearly, she does not lack intellectual potential. Thus, her verbal IQ of 89 most likely underestimates her intellectual capacity. Furthermore, she obtains an above-average score on similarities, a noneducationally related measure of abstract thinking skills. Her major weaknesses arise in the subtests related to academic achievement, information, and arithmetic. In addition, she shows some impairment in her judgment. Her verbal IQ thus appears to be lowered because of her lack of motivation for academic achievement and her poor judgment. Her pattern of subtest scores is one typically found in poor readers and delinquents.

In considering these illustrations, remember that the validity of pattern analysis is still questionable. Saccuzzo and Lewandowski (1976) found a pattern for acting-out behavior that Wickham later substantiated (1978). However, evidence supporting the validity of most patterns, for reasons we shall discuss more fully, is still questionable (Alexander et al., 1994; J. D. Lipsitz, Dworkin, & Erlenmeyer-Kimling, 1993). Our illustrations are designed to give you a flavor of the approach that is taken by many practicing psychologists.

TABLE 11-4
Scaled Scores for a Slow Learner

Verbal Scales	Performance Scales
Information: 3	Digit symbol: 12
Comprehension: 7	Picture completion: 11
Arithmetic: 4	Block design: 13
Similarities: 11	Picture arrangement: 10
Digit span: 10	Object assembly: 12
Vocabulary: 8	
Scaled score sum: 43	Scaled score sum: 58
Verbal IQ: 89	Performance IQ: 112
Sum of scaled scores for verbal and performance scales: 101	
Full-scale IQ: 99	

Most real-life examples, however, are nowhere nearly as clear-cut as our hypothetical example.

Psychometric Properties of the Wechsler Adult Scales

The Wechsler adult scales (WAIS, WAIS-R, and WAIS-III) do well in both reliability and validity. Here is a summary of these qualities based on the WAIS-R. The figures for the WAIS and WAIS-III are very similar to those of the WAIS-R.

Reliability

The impressive reliability coefficients for the Wechsler adult scales attest to the internal and temporal reliability of the verbal, performance, and full-scale IQs. When the split-half method is used for all subtests except digit span[1] and digit symbol,[2] the average coefficients across age levels are .97 for the full-scale IQ and the verbal IQ and .93 for the performance IQ (Wechsler, 1981). Test-retest coefficients reported in the manual are only slightly lower.

The Wechsler (1981) manual reports an overall standard error of measurement of 2.53 for the full-scale IQ, 2.74 for the verbal IQ, and 4.14 for the performance IQ. As you may recall from our discussion of correlation and reliability (see Chapter 4), all tests possess a certain degree of measurement error. The standard error of measurement (SEM) is the standard deviation of the distribution of error scores. Theoretically, an error score is the difference between the score one would obtain by giving the test and the individual's true score given a perfect measuring instrument. In practice, the SEM is based on the reliability coefficient, given by the formula

$$\text{SEM} = S\sqrt{1 - r_{xx}}$$

where S is the standard deviation of the test scores and r_{xx} is the reliability coefficient.

In practice, the SEM can be used to form a confidence interval within which an individual's true score is likely to fall. More specifically, we can determine the probability that an individual's true score will fall within a certain range a given percentage of the time. To be roughly at the 68% level, an obtained score must fall within the range of one SEM. The 95% confidence interval is approximately two SEMs.

Using this information, we can see that the smaller SEM for the verbal and full-scale IQs means that we can have considerably more confidence that an obtained score represents an individual's true score than we can for the performance IQ. Thus, given a full-scale IQ of 110, we can assume that 95% of the

---

[1]For digit span, digits forward are compared with digits backward.
[2]For digit symbol, a parallel form is used to estimate reliability.

time the subject's true score would fall at ±5.06 (two SEMs) of the true score. In other words, 95% of subjects with a score of 110 have a true score between 105 and 115 and only 5% don't.

Test-retest reliability coefficients for the 11 subtests have tended to vary widely. For data presented by Wechsler (1981), coefficients for most subtests run in the low .90s or high .80s. However, some are in the .60s. These relatively low coefficients again indicate the potential hazards of pattern analysis. Unstable subtests would produce unstable patterns, thus limiting the potential validity of pattern interpretation.

Perhaps you can now understand why the validity of pattern analysis is questionable and difficult to document. The dependability of pattern analysis depends on subtest intercorrelation as well as the separate reliabilities of the subtests. As the subtest intercorrelations increase and the reliabilities of individual subtests decrease, pattern analysis becomes increasingly dubious (Saccuzzo, Braff, et al., 1981).

Validity

The validity of the WAIS-III rests primarily on studies done with earlier versions of the test, the Wechsler-Bellevue (1939), WAIS (1955), and the WAIS-R (1981). About 80% of the WAIS-III items on the traditional 11 subtests originated from the WAIS and WAIS-R, because the test authors wanted to maintain continuity in the meaning of the IQ score across all revisions of the test from the WAIS. In general, the WAIS and WAIS-R have been shown to correlate at between .40 and .80 with a host of other measures that purport to measure intelligence.

Table 11-5 shows the correlations between the WAIS-R and the WAIS as well as the Wechsler Intelligence Scale for Children—Revised (WISC-R). Inspection of the table reveals an extremely high degree of shared variability

TABLE 11-5

Correlations of the WAIS-R with the WAIS and the WISC-R*

Scale	N	r_{12}
WAIS	72	
Verbal IQ		.91
Performance IQ		.79
Full-scale IQ		.88
WISC-R	80	
Verbal IQ		.89
Performance IQ		.76
Full-scale IQ		.88

Data from Tables 17 and 18 of the WAIS-R manual (Wechsler, 1981).
*For groups of individuals tested with both scales.

FIGURE 11-6 *Idealized factor analysis of the WAIS-III. Verbal IQ consists primarily of information, comprehension, similarities, vocabulary, and arithmetic. Performance IQ consists primarily of the five performance subtests. Memory consists primarily of digit span and arithmetic.*

between the WAIS-R and both the WAIS and WISC-R. Data for the WAIS-III are quite comparable.

The concurrent validity of the WAIS-R has also been supported by numerous studies correlating scores on the WAIS-R with those from other tests of ability (Fowles & Tunick, 1986; Retzlaff, Sligner, & Gibertini, 1986), tests of achievement (Ryan & Rosenberg, 1983), and formal education (Matarazzo & Herman, 1984). In general, the correlations range from .43 to .94 (see Sattler, 1988, p. 224), with a median coefficient in the high .60s.

Factor analytic studies have supported the construct validity of Wechsler's intelligence scales. What typically emerges is a general second-order factor corresponding to g and two or three group factors corresponding to the verbal IQ, the performance IQ, and memory, sometimes called *freedom from distractibility* (Anastopoulos, Spisto, & Maher, 1994; J. Cohen, 1957). (See Figure 11-6.)

Evaluation of the Wechsler Adult Scales

The Wechsler adult scales are extensively used as measures of adult intelligence. These scales are well constructed and their primary measures—the verbal, performance, and full-scale IQs—are highly reliable. As with the modern Binet, the reliability of the individual subtests makes analysis of subtest patterns dubious, if not hazardous, for the purpose of making decisions about individuals. Yet, making such conclusions is commonplace. As we have noted, though such analysis may be useful for generating hypotheses, it calls for extreme caution.

The strong correlations among the WAIS-III, WAIS-R, WAIS, and the original Wechsler-Bellevue are somewhat of a mixed blessing. Clearly, the WAIS-III is much the same test as the original Wechsler-Bellevue of 1939. Thus, the WAIS-III relies heavily on the theories and data of the 1920s and 1930s. It does little to incorporate the notions of intellectual functioning in the mushrooming area of cognitive psychology. Moreover, the WAIS-III does not allow for the idea of multiple intelligences, an important concept. According to one modern theory, there are at least seven distinct and independent intelligences—linguistic, body-kinesthetic, spatial, logical-mathematical, musical, intrapersonal, and interpersonal (H. Gardner, 1983). The older view of intelligence reflected in the WAIS-III leaves little room for such ideas.

The WAIS-III also does not measure extreme IQs well. The lowest possible IQ one can obtain ranges from 45 to 50, depending on age. A 65-year-old who fails every single item would obtain a verbal IQ of 53, a performance IQ of 60, and a full-scale IQ of 50.

In evaluating the WAIS-III, one must also consider the issue of bias. Is the WAIS-III fair to racial and cultural minorities? We will discuss this concern in greater detail by looking at the WISC-III.

Downward Extensions of the WAIS-III: The WISC-III and WPPSI-R

Most of the basic ideas of the WAIS-III apply to its downward extension, the WISC-III, first published in 1949, revised in 1974, and most recently revised in 1991. The WISC-III measures intelligence from ages 6 through 16 years, 11 months, 30 days. The basic ideas of the WAIS-III also apply to the Wechsler Preschool and Primary Scale of Intelligence—Revised (WPPSI-R). The WPPSI-R, first published in 1967 and revised in 1989, measures intelligence in children from 4 to 6½ years old. Basic ideas that apply to all Wechsler scales will not be discussed again here, nor will the details previously provided on the WAIS-R and WAIS-III. If you understand the WAIS-III, then you should have little difficulty with the WISC-III and WPPSI-R. We present only the major distinguishing features of these Wechsler scales.

The WISC-III

The Wechsler Intelligence Scale for Children—Third Edition (WISC-III) is the latest version of this scale. The original form of the WISC-III is based on Form II of the Wechsler-Bellevue scale, which provided a point scale measure of intelligence for children between the ages of 6 years and 16 years, 11 months. The WISC-III contains 13 subtests, three of which are supplementary. Within the WISC-III verbal scale are information, comprehension, arithmetic, similarities, and vocabulary subtests. Digit span is a supplementary subtest. Within the WISC-III performance scale are picture completion, picture arrangement, block design, object assembly, and coding (which parallels digit symbol on the WAIS-III) subtests. The supplementary tests are a series of mazes, through which the child must traverse with a pencil, and a symbol search consisting of paired groups of symbols. In this latter subtest, each pair contains a target group and a search group. The child scans the two groups and indicates whether or not a target symbol appears in the search group. These subtests, with the exception of mazes and symbol search, parallel the corresponding WAIS-III subtests in content and functions measured. Items are arranged in order of difficulty and are grouped by content. (See Figure 11-7.)

One of the major differences between the WAIS-III and WISC-III concerns termination of subtest administration. In general, the WISC-III terminates a subtest administration after a fewer number of consecutive errors than does the WAIS-III. This is to prevent subjects from experiencing too many failures and to reduce administration time, which usually takes about an hour.

The verbal scales of the WISC-III. The information subtest of the WISC-III contains items such as "Who was the first president of the United States?" Some items, however, are more difficult, such as "Who was the first person who sailed around the world?" As in the WAIS-III, the WISC-III comprehension subtest puts the subject in a situation or asks a question that requires common sense in order to measure judgment. A WISC-III comprehension item might ask, "What should you do if you were the first person to see a house on fire?" As in the WAIS-III, the early items of the arithmetic subtest are fairly simple. Later items, however, can be difficult even for adults, such as "27 is three-fourths of what number?" Also as in the WAIS-III, the similarities subtest contains items that require the subject to state the similarity between two objects or things, such as brick and wood. The vocabulary and digit span subtests are identical in format to their counterparts in the WAIS-III.

The performance scales of the WISC-III. As in the verbal subtests, the regular performance subtests of the WISC-III parallel those of the WAIS-III. Indeed, the formats for picture completion, picture arrangement, block design, object assembly, and coding (called digit symbol on the WAIS-III) are nearly identical. The major difference between the WAIS-III and WISC-III on the performance scale is the content, geared toward children on the latter. As you will recall, the only WISC-III subtests not included on the WAIS-III are mazes, which measure planning ability and perhaps general intelligence, and symbol search.

Standardization of the WISC-III. The WISC-III standardization sample consisted of 2200 children selected to represent the 1988 U.S. census. The sample was stratified using age, gender, race (black, Hispanic, white, other), geographic region, parental occupation, and urban-rural residence as variables. It contained 100 boys and 100 girls at each age from 6 through 16 years. (See Figure 11-8.)

Raw scores and scaled scores. In scoring the WISC-III, scaled scores are calculated from raw scores on the basis of norms at each age level. This procedure differs from that for the WAIS-III, in which scaled scores are obtained from a representative sample at only one age level. However, as for the WAIS-III, the mean scaled score is set at 10 and the standard deviation at 3. Scaled scores are summed for verbal, performance, and full-scale IQs. These totals are then compared against a single table of standard scores with a mean of 100 and a standard deviation of 15 for each of the three IQs—verbal, performance, and full-scale.

Information (30 questions)

How many legs do you have?
What must you do to make water freeze?
Who discovered the North Pole?
What is the capital of France?

Similarities (17 questions)

In what way are pencil and crayon alike?
In what way are tea and coffee alike?
In what way are inch and mile alike?
In what way are binoculars and microscope alike?

Arithmetic (18 questions)

If I have one piece of candy and get another one, how
  many pieces will I have?
At 12 cents each, how much will 4 bars of soap cost?
If a suit sells for 1/2 of the ticket price, what is the cost of
  a $120 suit?

Vocabulary (32 words)

ball   poem
summer   obstreperous

Comprehension (17 questions)

Why do we wear shoes?
What is the thing to do if you see someone dropping his
  packages?
In what two ways is a lamp better than a candle?
Why are we tried by a jury of our peers?

Digit Span

Digits Forward contains seven series of digits, 3 to 9
  digits in length (Example: 1-8-9).
Digits Backward contains seven series of digits, 2 to 8
  digits in length (Example: 5-8-1-9).

Picture Completion (26 items)

The task is to identify the essential missing part of the
picture.
A picture of a car without a wheel.
A picture of a dog without a leg.
A picture of a telephone without numbers on the dial.
An example of a Picture Completion task is shown below.

Picture Arrangement (12 items)

The task is to arrange a series of pictures into a meaningful sequence.

Block Design (11 items)

The task is to reproduce stimulus designs using four or
nine blocks. An example of a Block Design item is shown
below.

Object Assembly (4 items)

The task is to arrange pieces into a meaningful object. An
example of an Object Assembly item is shown below.

Coding

The task is to copy symbols from a key (see below).

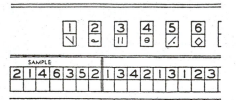

Mazes

The task is to complete a series of mazes.

Note. The questions resemble those that appear on the WISC-R
but are not actually from the test. Chapter 7 describes each subtest in more detail.

FIGURE 11-7   *WISC-III–like items.*

*(Simulated items similar to those in the Wechsler Intelligence Scales for Adults and Children. Copyright 1949,
1955, 1974, 1981 and 1989 by The Psychological Corporation. Reproduced by permission. All rights
reserved.)*

WISC-III™   *Characteristics of the Standardization Sample*

■ Percentage of the population based on the 1988 U.S. Census.

■ Percentage in the WISC-III norm sample.

These graphs show demographic characteristics of the WISC-III norm sample compared with those of the U.S. population. The total number sampled was 2,200 children between ages 6 and 16, with equal numbers of males and females.

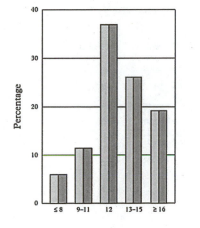
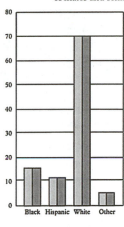
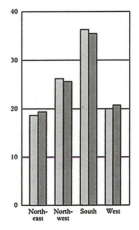

FIGURE 11-8   *Characteristics of the WISC-III standardization sample.*
(Wechsler, 1989)

Interpretation: Hypothetical case studies. Interpretation of the WISC-III also parallels that of the WAIS-III. Consider the following example. A 7-year-old, white, English-speaking boy having school problems obtains the scaled scores shown in Table 11-6. This child shows deficiencies in all areas measured by the WISC-III. In no case has he obtained a scaled score as high as even one standard deviation below the mean. Because this child is consistently impaired in all areas, his full-scale IQ of 54, more than two standard deviations below the mean, clearly indicates mental retardation. Thus, the WISC-III is consistent with this conclusion. However, additional data (for example, a medical examination and a history of social functioning) would be necessary for one to make a diagnosis of mental retardation (Malgady et al., 1980).

Consider another example, of a 9-year-old, white, English-speaking girl who is having school difficulties (see Table 11-7). Although this child has verbal and full-scale IQs that are both two standard deviations below the mean and thus in the mentally retarded range according to the WISC-III manual, analysis of her profile pattern indicates average or better performance in three areas: information, picture completion, and coding. Her average or better abilities in these areas would make a diagnosis of mental retardation highly suspect and premature. However, the wide variability in subtests, known as **subtest scatter,** indicates her performance is below what she might have

TABLE 11-6

Scaled Scores for a Boy Having School Problems

Verbal Scales	Performance Scales
Information: 4	Picture completion: 5
Comprehension: 5	Picture arrangement: 2
Arithmetic: 3	Block design: 6
Similarities: 0	Object assembly: 6
Vocabulary: 1	Coding: 4
Scaled score sum: 13	Scaled score sum: 23
Verbal IQ: 53	Performance IQ: 62
Sum of scaled scores for verbal and performance scales: 36	
Full-scale IQ: 54	

TABLE 11-7

Scaled Scores for a Girl Having School Problems

Verbal Scales	Performance Scales
Information: 10	Picture completion: 11
Comprehension: 1	Picture arrangement: 3
Arithmetic: 2	Block design: 9
Similarities: 5	Object assembly: 1
Vocabulary: 8	Coding: 10
Scaled score sum: 26	Scaled score sum: 34
Verbal IQ: 70	Performance IQ: 78
Sum of scaled scores for verbal and performance scales: 60	
Full-scale IQ: 71	

accomplished at some previous time. This lowered performance from previous levels suggests deterioration. Her main areas of weakness in the verbal areas are judgment (comprehension subtest), concentration (arithmetic subtest), and abstract thinking (similarities subtest). Her adequate scores on coding and block design, however, indicate no apparent brain damage or visual motor difficulties. One possible hypothesis in this case is that emotional difficulties are responsible for this child's school problems.

Reliability of the WISC-III. When the WISC-III was revised in 1991, developers intended to maintain the general properties of its predecessors, most recently WISC-R. Indeed, the psychometric properties of the former are quite similar to those of the latter. Reliability coefficients for the WISC-III and the WISC-R were obtained as for the WAIS-R and WAIS-III subtests. Split-half reliabilities for the WISC-III's full-scale, verbal, and performance IQs average .96, .95, and .91, respectively; standard errors of measurement average 3.20, 3.53, and 4.54, respectively. Test-retest reliability coefficients are only slightly below those obtained using the split-half method.

Reliability coefficients for individual subtests are somewhat less impressive, with most in the .70s and .80s. As with the Binet scales, reliability coefficients are poorest for the youngest groups. Test-retest coefficients tend to run in the high .80s to low .90s for the three IQs.

WISC-III validity. The correlation between the WISC-III and other Wechsler scales is rather good. Because the WISC-III overlaps with both the WAIS-R for 16-year-olds and the downward extension of the WISC-III (the WPPSI-R for 6-year-olds), the WISC-III could be correlated with both the WAIS-R and the WPPSI-R. All coefficients were in the .70s and .80s. The manual also reported correlations with the WISC-III and the Stanford-Binet scale, with the majority of coefficients in the .60s and .70s for individual subtests and in the .80s to low .90s for the three IQs.

Evaluation of the WISC-III

Though the WISC-III shares many strengths with the WAIS-III, it also suffers from the same weaknesses. These include its underlying model of intelligence, its poor treatment validity for academically impaired children, and possible problems of selection bias toward certain cultural and racial groups (Saccuzzo & Johnson, 1995). We shall touch briefly on each of these problems.

As with the WAIS-III, the WISC-III's model of intelligence does not reflect recent developments in cognitive science and theories of multiple intelligences. Cognitive science has emphasized analysis in terms of components of information processing (E. Hunt, 1980) and abilities such as executive processes (Sternberg, 1984), organizing skills (Das, 1987), and metacognition (see Sternberg, 1985; Sternberg & Gardner, 1982). The WISC-III's only attempt to incorporate any of these concepts is the supplemental symbol search subtest. In fact, the changes that have been made in the various revisions of this test have been disappointingly minimal.

Another problem with the WISC-III is its questionable usefulness for enhancing remedial intervention for children who show specific academic deficiencies. Like the WISC-R, it lacks treatment validity (Witt & Gresham, 1985). Specific deficits on the WISC-III do not necessarily suggest specific treatments. Further, although the WISC-III predicts school achievement for children regardless of ethnic background, the issue of the clear superiority in IQ scores for whites when compared with culturally different groups has not been confronted in the most recent 1991 revision. The result is a selection bias. African-American children are overselected for mentally retarded classes and underselected for gifted programs. The issue of test bias is as controversial as it is complex. Because of the selection bias of standardized intelligence tests such as the WISC, standardized tests were banned in California as a means of determining mental retardation and special education placement for African-American children. The existence of a selection bias does not necessarily mean the WISC-III is defective (see Saccuzzo & Johnson, 1995), but it does raise some important issues that we further discuss in Chapter 20.

The WPPSI-R

In 1967, Wechsler published a scale for children 4 to 6½ years of age, the Wechsler Preschool and Primary Scale of Intelligence (WPPSI). Revised in 1985, this test became the WPPSI-R. It parallels the WAIS-III and WISC-III in format, in the method of determining reliabilities, and in subtests. Only three unique subtests are included: (1) animal pegs, an optional test that is timed and requires the child to place a colored cylinder into an appropriate hole in front of the picture of an animal; (2) geometric design, a perceptual motor task in which the child must select a matching design from four choices or, for the more advanced items, copy a geometric design shown on a printed card; and (3) sentences, a second optional test of immediate recall in which the child is asked to repeat sentences presented orally by the examiner. (See Figure 11-9.) Reliability coeffi-

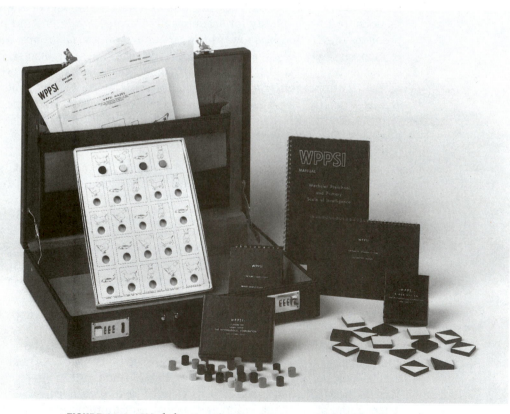

FIGURE 11-9 *Wechsler Preschool and Primary Scale of Intelligence.*
(Courtesy of The Psychological Corporation.)

cients are comparable to those obtained with the other Wechsler scales except for the performance IQ at the 7-year-old level. The manual reports validity studies, however, with a rather wide range of correlation coefficients for a variety of measures, from the Stanford-Binet scale (.92) to motor scales (.07).

Most of the support for the WPPSI-R is based on earlier studies with the WPPSI. The manual reports coefficients of .82, .85, and .87 for the performance, verbal, and full-scale IQs, respectively, when the WPPSI and WPPSI-R are correlated. Factor analyses of the WPPSI-R subtests reported in the manual have resulted in a two-factor solution, supporting an interpretation in terms of separate performance and verbal abilities (Webster, 1989). Independent analyses have confirmed and supported the two-factor solution for the WPPSI-R (Gyurke, Stone, & Beyer, 1990; LoBello & Gulgoz, 1991).

A major advantage of the WPPSI-R over many other tests of very young children is that it measures the same abilities that will be appraised later on, assuming, of course, that the WISC-III and WAIS-III will be used at the later date. Typically, as you will see in Chapter 12, a low correlation exists between tests given at very young ages and those given to the same children at school age. In large part, one can attribute this low correlation to the fact that the tests used at earlier ages do not measure the same functions as those emphasized later on.

The WPPSI-R was standardized on a stratified sample, which means that individuals were selected in proportion to their numbers in the population based on the 1980 census and using the following variables: age, gender, geographic region, urban-rural, color (white/nonwhite), and parental occupation. The standardization sample included 1700 children. Overall, the WPPSI-R is a very well constructed test. Its strengths and weaknesses resemble those of the WAIS-III and WISC-III.

Summary

Motivation for the development of the Wechsler scales began with the search for a more appropriate measure of adult intelligence than that provided by the 1937 Binet scale. The first product of this effort was the Wechsler-Bellevue scale.

In a *point scale,* a specific number of credits or points is assigned to each item. A *performance scale* measures nonlanguage intelligence, as opposed to a *verbal scale,* which measures language/verbal intelligence. On a performance scale, the subject is required to do something other than answer questions.

The six standard verbal subtests of the WAIS-III and the functions they purportedly measure are as follows:

1. Information: range of knowledge
2. Comprehension: judgment
3. Arithmetic: concentration
4. Similarities: abstract thinking
5. Digit span: immediate memory, anxiety
6. Vocabulary: vocabulary level

The five standard performance subtests of the WAIS-III and the functions they purportedly measure are as follows:

1. Digit symbol: visual-motor functioning
2. Picture completion: alertness to details
3. Picture arrangement: planning ability
4. Block design: nonverbal reasoning
5. Object assembly: analysis of part-whole relationships

The WAIS-III uses a declining age standard. This means that elderly subjects must obtain fewer correct responses in order to achieve the same IQs as young adults. The declining age standard resulted from the cross-sectional nature of the standardization sample. This sample, which involved testing different subjects of differing ages at about the same time, suggested that intelligence declined with age. However, longitudinal studies, which test the same subjects at varying intervals over time, have indicated that intelligence remains relatively stable over the life span. They imply that the norms must be periodically revised, as they were in 1981 with the WAIS-R and again in 1997 with the WAIS-III.

Three IQ scores can be obtained from the WAIS-III: verbal IQ, performance IQ, and full-scale IQ. The verbal and performance IQs are obtained by converting the raw score of each subtest to a standard score of 10 with a standard deviation of 3. The *scaled scores* are then summed separately for the verbal and performance IQs. Each of the IQs can be determined from a table that converts the summed scaled scores to a standard score with a mean of 100 and a standard deviation of 15. To obtain the full-scale IQ, the scaled scores for the verbal and performance IQs are summed. This sum is again brought to a table of norms, which converts it to a standard score (mean 100; SD = 15).

The reliability coefficients of the Wechsler adult scales such as the WAIS-R and WAIS-III are excellent for verbal, performance, and full-scale IQs, in terms of both temporal stability and internal consistency. Reliabilities for the individual subtests, however, vary widely. Evidence for the validity of the WAIS-III comes from a variety of sources.

This test offers several advantages. The WAIS-III (1) is appropriate for adults, (2) uses deviation IQs, (3) has strong evidence of reliability and validity, (4) uses a point scale, (5) includes a performance scale, and (6) offers the possibility of pattern analysis.

The disadvantages of the WAIS-III include the following: (1) It has poor reliability for the individual subtests, (2) It is a poor measure of extreme (high and low) levels of intelligence, and (3) It does not take into account recent empirical and theoretical advances, especially those in cognitive science.

The WISC-III is a downward extension of the WAIS-III for measuring children's intelligence. First published in 1949, the WISC was revised in 1974. The latest revision, the WISC-III, was done in 1991.

The WPPSI-R is a downward extension of the WISC-III for measuring intelligence in very young children (4 to 6½ years). It was published in 1967 and revised in 1989.

CHAPTER 12

Other Individual Tests of Ability

LEARNING OBJECTIVES

When you have completed this chapter, you should be able to:

- Identify the advantages and disadvantages of the alternative individual ability tests compared with the Binet and Wechsler scales

- List six differences among the alternative individual ability tests

- Discuss the strengths and weaknesses of the Bayley Scales of Infant Development compared with other measures of infant intelligence

- Identify some of the purposes of the Columbia Mental Maturity Scale

- Explain the major theory behind tests of learning disability

- Explain the main idea behind testing for brain damage

- List three possible reasons for errors on the Bender Visual Motor Gestalt Test

- Describe the general reaction among reviewers to the Torrance Tests of Creative Thinking

- Identify a major problem with the Wide Range Achievement Test, Revised

For assessing general intelligence in relatively normal individuals, the Binet and Wechsler scales are exceptionally good instruments. As we have noted, however, both scales have limitations. For instance, the standardization samples do not include individuals with sensory, physical, or language handicaps. How, then, can one fairly evaluate the performance on the Binet scale of someone who has been blind for life? What about individuals who cannot speak? Clearly, numerous circumstances arise where a score on the major scales would be either impossible to obtain or seriously biased against the individual. Thus, a number of individual tests have been created to meet special problems, measure specific abilities, or address the limitations of the Binet and Wechsler scales.

General Features of Alternative Individual Ability Tests

Before beginning our discussion of specific tests, some general comments are in order. As you will see, there is quite an array of individual ability tests; however, most were designed primarily to provide an alternative to the Binet and Wechsler scales. We shall therefore compare the general features of the alternative individual tests with those of the Binet and Wechsler scales.

Alternative Individual Ability Tests Compared with the Binet and Wechsler Scales

Recalling the information in Chapters 10 and 11 on the Binet and Wechsler scales, you may find it instructive to consider individual ability tests, particularly individual intelligence tests, as they compare with these two important scales. That most individual intelligence tests are newer and less well established than the Binet and Wechsler scales does not alone explain why no other individual intelligence test is used as much as these two major scales. Despite the limitations of the Binet and Wechsler scales, none of the alternatives is clearly superior from a psychometric standpoint. Some of the alternative individual intelligence tests are weaker in terms of the representativeness or quality of the standardization sample. Some are less stable, and most are more limited in their documented validity. Some have inadequacies in the test manual, such as unclear or poorly standardized administration instructions, and others provide insufficient information about psychometric adequacy, appropriate uses, and limitations. Indeed, some of the alternatives compare poorly on all counts. Except for some specific advantages, perhaps none of the alternatives can be considered better than the two major scales when one considers all relevant factors.

Though usually weaker in psychometric properties, many of the alternatives to the major scales do not rely on a verbal response as much as the Binet and Wechsler verbal scales do. Many require the subject only to point or to make any response indicating "Yes" or "No" and thus do not depend as much on the complex integration of visual and motor functioning. Like the Wechsler scales, most of the alternatives contain a performance scale or subscale. Indeed, the dearth of performance tasks in the Binet scale helped to stimulate the development of many alternative individual tests of ability.

In providing a performance component (many alternatives are exclusively performance scales), alternatives to the Binet scale (and to the Wechsler in some cases) have particular relevance for special populations. In many respects, the alternatives to the major intelligence scales were developed to fill the gaps in the applicability of the major scales. Some were designed for special populations, such as individuals with sensory limitations (for example, deaf people) or physical limitations (for example, people who are paralyzed or partially paralyzed). Others were designed to evaluate those with language limitations, such as culturally deprived persons, certain brain-damaged individuals, and foreign-born or non-English-speaking individuals. Still others were designed to assess learning disabilities.

Because the tests were designed for special populations or purposes, the existence of alternatives is justifiable. However, their specificity often limits the range of functions or abilities that they can measure. Thus, one may consider the greater specificity of some alternatives a weakness as well as a strength. Although the alternatives may be much more suitable for special populations than the major scales would be, an IQ score based on one of the alternatives, with rare exceptions, cannot be used interchangeably with a score from one of the major scales. The alternatives are generally most appropriate when used for their own purposes. In addition, the alternatives are often useful as a supplement for results obtained with one of the major scales, such as for screening purposes, for follow-up or reevaluations, or when insufficient time is available to administer one of the major scales.

Because they are designed for special populations, some alternatives can be administered totally without verbal instructions (for example, through pantomime or chalkboard instructions). One can administer and score a few of the alternatives without speaking a single word. Furthermore, most are less related than the Binet scale to reading ability, and a few are almost totally independent of reading ability. As a consequence, the scores from many alternatives contain less variability because of scholastic achievement than either the Binet or the Wechsler scale, both of which correlate strongly with scholastic achievement. See Table 12-1 for a summary of alternative tests versus the major scales.

Alternatives Compared with One Another

To construct and publish a useful test, one must develop a better method than is currently available. One may develop a test to measure some factor not tapped by any existing measure or provide a test for a particular group for whom existing procedures have not worked. If a new test offers no specific advantages, most examiners would probably stay with a more established test.

TABLE 12-1

*Comparison of
General Features
of Alternatives
with the Wechsler
and Binet Scales*

Disadvantages of Alternatives

Weaker standardization sample

Less stable

Less documentation on validity

Limitations in test manual

Not as psychometrically sound

IQ scores not interchangeable with Binet or Wechsler

Advantages of Alternatives

Can be used for specific populations and special purposes:

Sensory limitations

Physical limitations

Language limitations

Culturally deprived people

Foreign-born individuals

Non-English-speaking people

Not as reliant on verbal responses

Not as dependent on complex visual motor integration

Useful for screening, supplement, and reevaluations

Can be administered nonverbally

Less variability due to scholastic achievement

Given a choice between a more established test in which they have experience and an equally sound new test for the same purpose, they will probably choose the former. Therefore, most alternatives tend to differ from one another in some important way. Alternatives to the major scales that do no more than attempt to measure abilities in the same way, only better, have met with little success.

In comparing individual intelligence tests other than the Binet and Wechsler scales, we find that some apply to only very young children, others to older children and adolescents, and still others to both children and adults. Thus, the alternatives to the major scales differ in their targeted age ranges. A second important difference concerns what is measured. Some of the alternatives attempt to measure language or vocabulary skills through nonverbal techniques, some to measure nonverbal or nonlanguage intelligence, and others to measure perceptual-motor skills. Alternatives also differ in the type of score they produce. Some give only a single score, as in the older Binet scales. Others, however, produce several scores, as in the Wechsler scales. The alternatives differ also in the type of response required of subjects. As previously indicated, whereas some present the items in a multiple-choice format, requiring that the subject choose or point to a correct alternative, others simply require the subject to indicate "Yes" or "No" by whatever means possible.

Other important differences mark the alternative individual tests of human ability. Some require simple motor skills, whereas others demand more complex motor behavior. A few sample a wide range of abilities, but most are quite narrow in this range. Still another difference concerns the target population (for example, deaf, blind, physically handicapped, learning-disabled, language-impaired, and foreign-born people). Furthermore, some provide timed tasks, whereas others do not. Some claim to have significance for personality and clinical diagnoses; others are exclusively related to an ability.

Another difference is the amount of examiner skill and experience necessary for administration. Whereas some tests require as much skill and experience as the Binet or Wechsler scales, others require only minimal examiner skill and could probably be administered by a trained paraprofessional under supervision. To avoid confusing the various tests in this chapter, you should compare the various alternatives with the Binet and Wechsler scales; you should also compare them to each other in terms of their main distinguishing features, as summarized in Table 12-2.

Specific Individual Ability Tests

The earliest individual ability tests were typically designed for specific purposes or populations. One of the first, the Seguin Form Board Test (Seguin, 1866, 1907), actually preceded the Binet. This test, of the performance variety, produced only a single score. It consisted of a simple form board with objects of various shapes placed in appropriately shaped holes (such as squares or circles). The Seguin Form Board Test was used primarily to evaluate mentally retarded adults and emphasized speed of performance. A version of this test is still available. Quite a while after the development of the Seguin test, the Healy-Fernald Test (1911) was developed as an exclusively nonverbal test for adolescent delinquents. Although it produced only a single score, the Healy-Fernald Test provided several types of tasks, rather than just one as in the Seguin Form Board Test, and there was less emphasis on speed. Then Knox (1914) developed a battery of performance tests for non-English-speaking adult immigrants to the United States. The test was one of the first that could be administered without language. Speed was not emphasized.

TABLE 12-2

Summary of Differences Among Individual Ability Tests Other Than the Binet and Wechsler Scales

Difference	Definition or Example
Age range	Different tests are designed for specific age groups
What is measured	Verbal intelligence, nonverbal intelligence, and so on
Type of score	Single score versus multiple scores
Type of skill required	Simple motor, complex motor, and so on
Range of abilities sampled	Single specific ability versus a wide range of abilities
Target population	Deaf, blind, learning-disabled, and so on
Timing	Some are timed; others are not
Personality versus ability	Some relevant for personality and clinical diagnoses, others for ability
Examiner skill and experience	Some require far less examiner skill and experience to administer and interpret than others

In sum, early individual ability tests other than the Binet scale were designed for specific populations, produced a single score, and had nonverbal performance scales. The emphasis on speed gradually decreased from the earliest to the more recent tests. These early procedures demonstrated the feasibility of constructing individual nonverbal performance tests that could provide an alternative to the verbally dependent Binet scale, could be administered without visual instructions, and could be used with children as well as adults.

Infant Scales

An important category of individual tests of ability attempts to measure intelligence in infants and young children. Four such tests are discussed here.

Brazelton Neonatal Assessment Scale (BNAS). The BNAS is an individual test for infants between 3 days and 4 weeks of age (Brazelton, 1973, 1984). It purportedly provides an index of a newborn's competence. Developed by a Harvard pediatrician, the Brazelton scale produces 47 scores—27 behavioral items and 20 elicited responses (Buros, 1978). These scores are obtained in a variety of areas, including neurological, social, and behavioral aspects of a newborn infant's functioning. Factors such as reflexes, responses to stress, startle reactions, cuddliness, motor maturity, ability to habituate to sensory stimuli, and hand-mouth coordination are all assessed. Reviews of the Brazelton scale have been favorable (Britt & Myers, 1994). As Sostek (1978) stated, the Brazelton has "the greatest breadth of the available neonatal examinations" (p. 208). The Brazelton also has a considerable research base (e.g., Gauvain, 1994; see also Bornstein, 1993; Field, 1993; Kappelman, 1993).

The Brazelton scale has found wide use as a research tool and as a diagnostic tool for special purposes (Beal, 1991). For example, the scale has been used to assess the characteristics of drug-addicted neonates (Strauss et al., 1975) and to evaluate the effects of low birth weight on premature infants (Als, Tronick, Lester, et al., 1976). Researchers have used it to study the effects of cocaine use in pregnancy (Chasnoff, Burns, & Burns, 1987), prenatal alcohol exposure (Coles, Smith, & Falek, 1987), and environmental agents (Tronic, 1987). Others have used the scale to study parent-infant attachment (Beal, 1991) and high-risk neonates (Emory, Tynan, & Dave, 1989). Reviews of the relevant literature have been highly enthusiastic (Als, 1984; Als, Tronick, Lester, et al., 1979; Gauvain, 1994).

Despite the enthusiasm for the scale, it has a number of significant drawbacks. No norms are available. Thus, although examiners and researchers can state that one infant scored higher than another in a particular area, there is no standard sample against which to compare test results. In addition, more research is needed concerning the meaning and implication of scores. The scale purportedly helps one assess the infant's role in the mother-infant social relationship, and, presumably, high scores are associated with high levels of intelligence (Brazelton, 1993). Like most infant intelligence measures, how-

FIGURE 12-1

Schematic summary of the Brazelton Neonatal Assessment Scale.

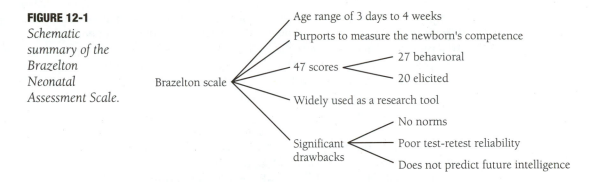

ever, the Brazelton scale has poorly documented predictive and construct validity. The scale has not been shown to be of value in predicting later intelligence (Tronick & Brazelton, 1975). Furthermore, despite relatively good inter-rater reliability for trained examiners, with coefficients ranging from .85 to .90 (Sostek, 1978), the test-retest reliability (that is, reliability over time) leaves much to be desired. As for all measures of intelligence when development is rapid and uneven, prior to age 8, test-retest reliability coefficients for the Brazelton scale are typically poor and unstable. (See Figure 12-1.)

In conclusion, although the Brazelton scale may offer much as a research tool, as an individual test of infant intelligence it leaves much to be desired. Its lack of norms is a serious shortcoming, and its failure to predict future intelligence leaves us wondering what the scale is really measuring. In fairness to the Brazelton, the scale is extremely well constructed. Moreover, as you will see, all infant ability tests based on sensorimotor functioning have proven ineffective in predicting later intelligence except in the lowest ranges (Fagan, 1985; McCall, Hogarty, & Hurlburt, 1972).

Gesell Developmental Schedules (GDS). The Gesell Developmental Schedules—also known as the Gesell Maturity Scale, the Gesell Norms of Development, and the Yale Tests of Child Development (see Buros, 1974)—are one of the oldest and most established infant intelligence measures. First published in 1925 (Gesell, 1925), the Gesell scale has been subjected to extensive research and refinement (Banerji, 1992a; Williamson et al., 1990). One of the leading infant intelligence measures from the 1930s through the 1960s, the Gesell scale continues to be used by those interested in assessing infant intelligence (Banerji, 1992b; Bernheimer & Keogh, 1988). However, because the Gesell scale suffers from a number of psychometric weaknesses, interest in and use of the scale has fallen considerably.

The Gesell Developmental Schedules claim to provide an appraisal of the developmental status of children from 2½ to 6 years of age. The scale is based on normative data from a carefully conducted longitudinal study of early human development (see Gesell et al., 1940). The idea behind procedures based on developmental data is that human development unfolds in stages or in sequences over time. Gesell and colleagues obtained normative data concerning these various stages in maturation. With data on when specific developmental milestones manifest themselves (for example, when the infant first rolls from back to stomach unassisted, when the child first utters words, or when the child learns to walk), one can compare the rate of development of any infant or young child with established norms. If the child shows behavior or responses associated with a more mature level of development than typically found for his or her chronological age, then one can assume that the child is ahead in development compared with others of the same age. Accelerated development can be related to high intelligence.

In the Gesell scale, an individual's **developmental quotient (DQ)** is determined according to a test score, which is evaluated by assessing the presence or absence of behavior associated with maturation. The DQ score concept parallels the mental age (MA) concept. Thus, the Gesell produces an intelligence quotient (IQ) score similar to that of the Binet scale. The formula for IQ in the Gesell scale is as follows:

$$IQ = \frac{developmental\ quotient}{chronological\ age} \times 100$$

or more simply,

$$IQ = \frac{DQ}{CA} \times 100$$

Normative data for the Gesell scale were obtained from a sample of 107 American-born Caucasian infants (49 boys, 58 girls), judged to be normal and whose parents were of northern European descent. You should readily and immediately recognize the lack of representativeness of this sample. Even so, these infants were carefully studied. Beginning at 4 weeks of age, they were examined at 2-week intervals until the 8th week of life. From the 8th through the 56th weeks, they were examined at 4-week intervals (12th, 16th, 20th, and so on). The sample was examined again at $1\frac{1}{2}$ and 2 years of age and also at yearly intervals between ages 2 and 6.

Despite years of extensive use and some updating, the Gesell scale continues to fall short of acceptable psychometric standards. As previously indicated, the standardization sample is inadequate. Despite efforts to add to the original 107 subjects (Knobloch & Pasamanick, 1974), the sample consists predominantly of individuals of northern European descent living in the northeastern part of the United States. The manual and book that come with the test offer no evidence of reliability or validity. The test directions are vague, the scoring procedures questionable (Naglieri, 1985). As with all sensorimotor infant tests, the Gesell does not predict later intelligence except at the low end of scores. (See Figure 12-2.)

In conclusion, Gesell's concept of empirically determining developmental sequence norms in evaluating infants and young children is logical and

FIGURE 12-2
Schematic summary of the Gesell Developmental Schedules.

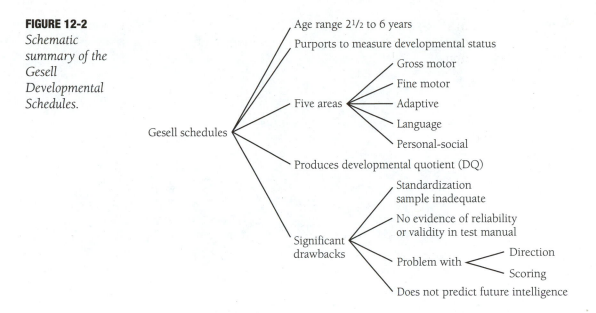

promising. When first constructed, the Gesell scale was nothing short of a breakthrough in infant ability testing. The use of a nonrepresentative sample in its initial development, furthermore, was not at all unusual. However, since its early construction, little has been done to improve the Gesell scale according to today's more rigorous standards for standardization samples. By providing a standard format for observing behavior, the Gesell scale may be of value to the highly trained and experienced examiner. Even so, the available empirical data indicate that it is not highly accurate for predictive purposes except at the low ranges. The scale does appear to help uncover subtle deficits in infants (Williamson et al., 1990).

Bayley Scales of Infant Development (BSID). As with many infant tests, the underlying idea of the Bayley Scales of Infant Development is the same as that for the Gesell scale. The Bayley bases its assessments on normative maturational developmental data. Published only four years before the Brazelton scale, the Bayley scale was the product of 40 years of study (Bayley, 1969). It was designed for infants between 2 and 30 months of age; it produces two main scores (mental and motor) and 30 ratings of behavior. To assess mental functions, the Bayley scale uses measures such as the infant's response to a bell, the ability to follow an object with the eyes, and, in older infants, the ability to follow oral instructions. The heart of the Bayley scale is the motor scale, because it assumes that later mental functions depend on motor development (Bayley, 1969). (See Figure 12-3.)

Unlike the Gesell and Brazelton scales, the Bayley scale has an excellent standardization. With a normative sample of 1262 infants between 2 and 30 months of age divided into subgroups by gender, race, socioeconomic status,

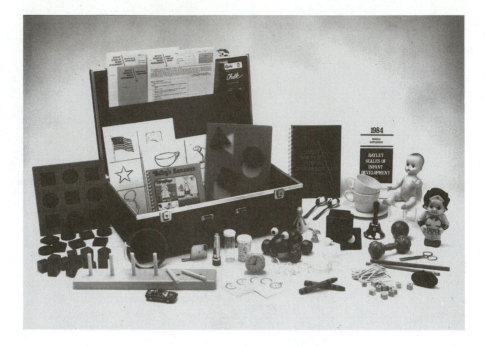

rural versus urban area, and geographic region, the Bayley scale is currently the best standardized test of its kind available.

As in the Stanford-Binet scale, raw scores on the Bayley scale are converted to standard scores with a mean of 100 and a standard deviation of 16. Given the care and effort Bayley put into its development, the generally positive reviews of the Bayley scale come as no surprise (Nellis & Gridley, 1994; Pomerleau, Leahey, & Malcuit, 1994). In addition to its exemplary standardization, the median split-half reliability coefficients are about .88 for the mental scale and .84 for the motor scale, with ranges from the low .80s to low .90s for the mental scales and ranges from the high .60s to low .90s for the motor scales (Bayley, 1969).

Research interest in the Bayley scale continues to grow (Kaplanestrin, Jacobson, & Jacobson, 1994; Raggio, Massingale, & Bass, 1994). Nevertheless, more validity studies are needed. In terms of construct validity, Bayley (1969) reported that the performance scale increases with increasing chronological age. However, the manual presents data on neither the validity of the motor scale nor the predictive validity of the mental scale. Moreover, the bulk of available research casts considerable doubt on Bayley's (1969) assumption concerning the relationship between motor behavior and later mental functions. In its favor, the Bayley scale does predict mental retardation (Self & Horowitz, 1979). Infants who score two standard deviations below the mean on the Bayley have a high probability of testing in the retarded ranges later in life (Ames, 1967; A. J. Simon & Bass, 1956). However, for infants who score within the normal ranges, there is no more than low correlation (roughly .10 to .50) between Bay-

FIGURE 12-4
Schematic summary of the Bayley Scales of Infant Development.

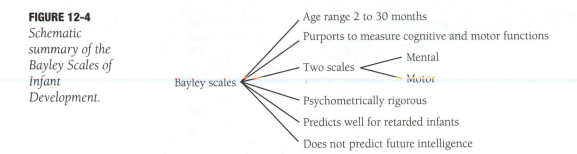

Bayley scales
- Age range 2 to 30 months
- Purports to measure cognitive and motor functions
- Two scales
  - Mental
  - Motor
- Psychometrically rigorous
- Predicts well for retarded infants
- Does not predict future intelligence

ley's scores and those obtained from standard intelligence tests, such as the WISC-R and Binet scale (Bayley, 1949; Hindley, 1965; McCall, 1979). Like the Brazelton, the Bayley is widely used in research (L. Atkinson, 1990a; Sloman, Bellinger, & Krentzel, 1990). A major research use is to assess infants of drug-using mothers (e.g., van Baar, 1990) and other at-risk infants (Gerken, Eliason, & Arthur, 1994; Wasik et al., 1990). (See Figure 12-4.)

In conclusion, the Bayley is the most psychometrically sound test of its kind (Self & Horowitz, 1979). The question remains as to whether tests of this type can predict future intelligence. Available research indicates that although the Bayley may be a good predictor for handicapped populations, it does not predict well within the normal ranges.

Cattell Infant Intelligence Scale (CIIS). Another noteworthy infant ability test is the Cattell Infant Intelligence Scale (CIIS), which is also based on normative developmental data. Designed as a downward extension of the Stanford-Binet scale for infants and preschoolers between 2 and 30 months of age, the Cattell scale purports to measure intelligence in infants and young children (Cattell, 1940). Patterned after the 1937 Binet in an age scale format, the Cattell scale contains five test items for each month between 2 and 12 months of age and five items for each two-month interval between 12 and 36 months of age. The items are similar to those on other infant tests such as the Gesell scale. Tasks for infants include attending to a voice and following objects with his or her eyes. Tasks for young children involve using a form board and manipulating common objects. The ability to follow oral instructions becomes more and more important as age increases.

For examiners who require a Gesell-type developmental infant test with a standardization more adequate than that of the Gesell, the Cattell Infant Intelligence Scale is among the most popular options (Damarin, 1978b; Hooper, Conner, & Umansky, 1986). In fact, in his review of the Cattell scale, Damarin found little difference between the types of tasks used in the Bayley scale and those in the Cattell scale. Further, though the Cattell scale was copyrighted nearly three decades before the Bayley scale, being an older, more established instrument offers no advantage. Normative data for the Cattell scale compare unfavorably with those of the Bayley scale in several respects. In addition to being outdated and more than four times smaller, the Cattell scale sample is

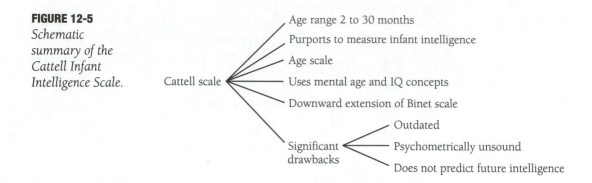

based primarily on children of parents from the lower and middle classes and therefore does not represent the general population.

Because the Cattell scale's normative data are considerably weaker than those of the Bayley scale, one should ask whether the CIIS presents *any* advantages over its more recent competitor, the Bayley scale. Evidence in support of the reliability and validity of the two instruments is similar. If time is limited, the Cattell scale may be preferable because it takes only about half as long to administer. However, it produces only a single score rather than the two scores and 30 observations of the Bayley scale. Thus, its shorter administration time is balanced by more limited results. Furthermore, as a downward extension of the Stanford-Binet scale, the Cattell scale seems to need updating in that the former no longer uses the intelligence quotient for calculating scores. Thus, IQ scores from the Cattell scale may not be comparable to deviation IQs on the Binet scale. Moreover, the modern Binet scale differs drastically from the form on which the Cattell is based. In one of the few recently published studies comparing the Cattell scale with the Bayley, scores derived from the Bayley predicted Stanford-Binet IQs better than the Cattell scores did (L. Atkinson, 1990b). (See Figure 12-5.)

In sum, the Cattell scale has remained relatively unchanged for almost 60 years. It is psychometrically unsatisfactory. Reliability coefficients vary widely, with many being less than acceptable (see Hooper, Conner, & Umansky, 1986). Moreover, what the scale measures is unclear; it does not predict future intelligence for infants in the normal ranges.

See Table 12-3 for a summary of the properties of infant scales.

Recent developments in infant intelligence testing. Recent efforts to evaluate infant intelligence have attempted to look beyond indices of sensorimotor development (Bendell-Estroff et al., 1989). Fagan (1985), for example, has cogently argued for attempting to evaluate skills such as memory and abstraction, because intelligence tests given later will evaluate them. The work of Fagan and colleagues has shown that one can evaluate such skills as early as the first day of life, because from birth infants demonstrate memory skills (for instance, they can recognize which of two targets they have seen before).

TABLE 12-3
*Summary of
Infant Scales*

Scale	Age Range	Standardization Sample	Psychometric Properties
Brazelton	3 days–4 weeks	None	Good interrater reliability, poor test-retest reliability
Gesell	2½–6 years	107 Caucasians	Little evidence, some support for construct validity
Bayley	2–30 months	1262 infants	Very good split-half reliability
Cattell	2–30 months	285 infants	Little evidence, some support for construct validity

General: For children younger than 18 months, these measures do not correlate significantly with IQ later in life. After 18 months, there are significant but small and clinically unhelpful correlations. Correlations tend to increase with the age of the infant at the time of testing.

Major alternative: Tests of memory, particularly visual memory and abstraction. Such tests do correlate with IQs in later life, even for infants tested in the first few days after birth.

Fagan's approach, which stems from his work in cognitive science, currently appears to hold the best promise for developing procedures that some day will be able to predict future intelligence from infant behavior.

In support of Fagan, researchers have found that measures of visual recognition memory help predict IQ in infants. In one study (Bendell-Estroff et al., 1989), a measure of visual recognition memory taken at 3 months of age predicted later IQ, whereas the Bayley scale, taken on the same infants, did not. The future of infant testing appears to rest in the cognitive sciences.

Major Tests for Young Children

In this section we discuss two major individual tests specifically developed to evaluate intelligence in young children: the McCarthy Scales of Children's Abilities (MSCA) and the Kaufman Assessment Battery for Children (K-ABC).

McCarthy Scales of Children's Abilities (MSCA). A product of the early 1970s, the McCarthy Scales of Children's Abilities (MSCA) measure ability in children between 2½ and 8½ years old. It picks up just about where the Bayley scale leaves off. Overall, the McCarthy scale is a carefully constructed individual test of human ability. In fact, were it not for its relatively meager validity data, the McCarthy scale might well have reached the status of the Wechsler scale (WPPSI-R), which overlaps with the McCarthy scale's age range. Indeed, the McCarthy scale seems to offer some advantages over the WPPSI-R and even the Binet scale for the 2½–8½ year age range. Unfortunately, because of McCarthy's death (she died before the test was even published), the task of strengthening the McCarthy scale falls to interested researchers. (See Figure 12-6.)

On the positive side, the McCarthy scale produces a pattern of scores as well as a variety of composite scores. Its battery of 18 tests samples a wide variety of functions long held to be related to human intelligence. Of the 18 scales, 15 are combined into a composite score known as the **general cogni-**

FIGURE 12-6
McCarthy Scales of Children's Abilities.

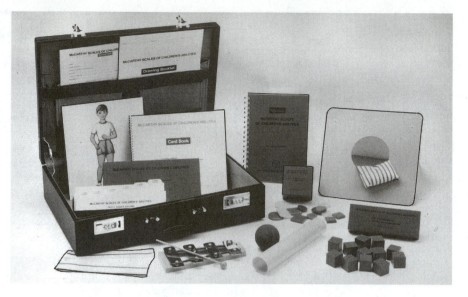

tive index (GCI), a standard score with a mean of 100 and a standard deviation of 16. Presumably, the index reflects how well the child has integrated prior learning experiences and adapted them to the demands of the scales. One can reasonably assume two things: McCarthy believed that the general cognitive index reflected intelligence, and her definition of intelligence must have included something like the ability to integrate past learning and adapt it to solving new problems. Sattler (1978), for example, argued that the definition of McCarthy's general cognitive index resembles definitions of the intelligence quotient (IQ) and most likely was meant as a substitute for the IQ concept. (See Figure 12-7.)

The psychometric properties of the McCarthy scale are relatively good. Reliability coefficients for the general cognitive index tend to run in the low .90s. Validity data are also encouraging. Although concurrent validity data are limited, correlations with the Stanford-Binet scale (Form L-M) and the WPPSI are quite good. The general cognitive index correlates at .81 with the Binet IQ and at .71 with the WPPSI full-scale IQ. The manual and T. V. Hunt (1978) provide additional validity coefficients based on small samples.

The McCarthy scale has been used in a variety of research studies (Gomezbenito & Fornssantacana, 1993; W. G. Mitchell et al., 1991). Wasik and co-workers (1990) used the McCarthy scale to evaluate the effects of early intervention on at-risk children. After six months of intervention, children who had received educational day care and family support had significantly higher scores than the control. Two studies have used the McCarthy scale to document the adverse effects of particular prenatal environments. For example, children of mothers who quit smoking during pregnancy had significantly higher McCarthy scores than children of those who did not (Sexton, Fox, &

FIGURE 12-7

Schematic overview of the general cognitive index of the McCarthy scales.

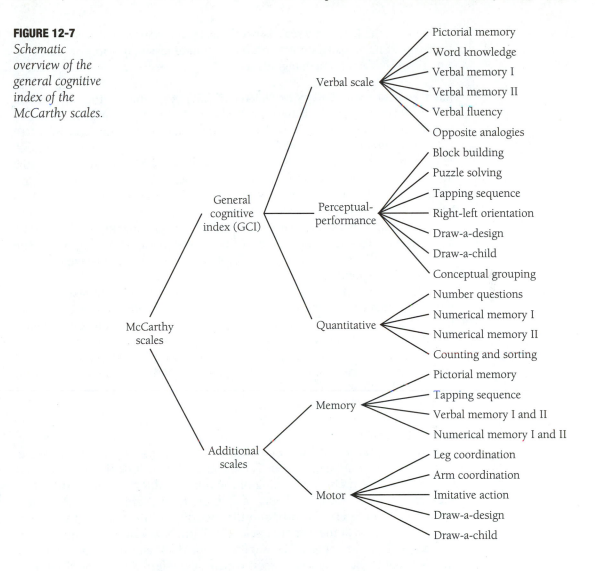

Hebel, 1990). Low-birth-weight children also had lowered scores on the McCarthy scale when compared with normal-weight controls (A. E. Smith & Knight-Jones, 1990). In another study, McMichael and colleagues (1988) attempted to evaluate the effects of environmental exposure to lead on children's abilities. Exposed children were found to suffer deficits in the perceptual-performance and memory areas. Finally, Valencia (1988) reviewed the literature pertaining to the use of the McCarthy scales with Hispanic children. The available studies, including a number of unpublished doctoral dissertations and articles in Spanish, indicated that the McCarthy scale has clear promise as a useful psychoeducational assessment tool for English-speaking Mexican-American children (Valencia, 1988).

In sum, the McCarthy scale is psychometrically sound. The available studies support its validity, and its promise as an assessment tool for Mexican-American children is encouraging.

Kaufman Assessment Battery for Children (K-ABC). A product of the early 1980s, the Kaufman Assessment Battery for Children (K-ABC) is an individual ability test for children between 2½ and 12½ years of age. The K-ABC consists of 16 subtests combined into five global scales called sequential processing, simultaneous processing, mental processing composite (a combination of sequential and simultaneous processing), achievement, and nonverbal. Figure 12-8 presents a schematic overview of the structure of the K-ABC. As the figure shows, the mental processing composite consists of the sequential processing and simultaneous processing scales, each of which has specific subtests. The achievement scale is independent of the mental processing composite. The nonverbal scale consists of those subtests that can be administered in pantomime and responded to physically.

The K-ABC, as its stated purposes and intentions in the test manuals reveal (Kaufman & Kaufman, 1983a, 1983b), is quite ambitious. It is intended for psychological, clinical, minority group, preschool, and neuropsychological assessment as well as research. The test also purports to enable the psychoeducational evaluation of learning disabled and other exceptional children and educational planning and placement. Later, we will examine the extent to which the K-ABC succeeds in meeting such lofty goals, but first we will look at some of its underlying concepts.

The K-ABC measures intelligence through its three mental processing scales: sequential processing, simultaneous processing, and mental processing. Theoretically, the K-ABC is based on the combination of several theoretical approaches (see Kaufman, 1984). These approaches include the neuropsychological model of brain functioning of the renowned Russian neuroscientist, Aleksandr Luria (1966); the theory of split brain functioning of the American Nobelist, Roger Sperry (1968); and the theories of information processing, most notably that of the cognitive scientist, Ulric Neisser (1967). In the work of these and other scientists, the Kaufmans noted a major distinction between two types of higher-brain processes, which they referred to as the *sequential-simultaneous distinction* (Kaufman, 1984). Sequential processing refers to the child's ability "to solve problems by mentally arranging input in sequential or serial order" (Kaufman, Kaufman, & Kaufman, 1985, p. 250). Examples of sequential processing are number and word-order recall. Presented one at a time, items must be dealt with sequentially, rather than all at once. In contrast, simultaneous processing takes place in parallel. It refers to a child's ability to "synthesize information (from mental wholes) in order to solve a problem" (Kaufman, Kaufman, & Kaufman, 1985, p. 250).

The sequential-simultaneous distinction of the K-ABC is one of the test's most distinguishing characteristics (Kamphaus & Reynolds, 1984; Rothlisberg & Dearn, 1989). Kaufman and Kaufman (1983b), however, did not claim to

FIGURE 12-8

Schematic overview of the Kaufman Assessment Battery for Children.

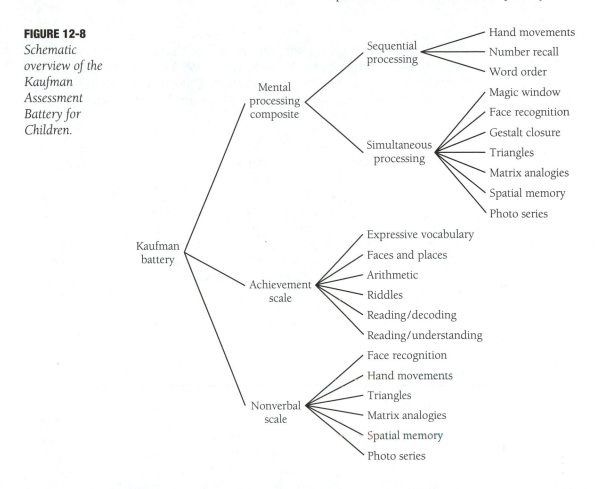

provide a pure measure of either sequential or simultaneous processing with the K-ABC. Instead, they selected tasks that from a rational analysis appeared to distinguish one type of processing from the other.

A major intent of providing separate measures of simultaneous and sequential processing is to identify the child's unique strengths and problem-solving strategies. Such information can presumably help others develop educational and remedial intervention strategies for a child (Gunnison, 1984; Majovski, 1984).

In addition to its sequential-simultaneous distinction, the K-ABC provides an independent achievement score. Offering independent and comparable scores for both intelligence and achievement in the same test is a major advantage of the K-ABC. In addition, the K-ABC's nonverbal scale provides a measure of ability specifically designed to be as fair as possible to children who are linguistically different or handicapped (R. Flanagan, 1995).

The K-ABC is well constructed and psychometrically sound. It was standardized on a sample of 2000 children stratified according to age (100 at each half-year between 2½ and 12½), gender, geographic region, race (black, white, Hispanic, other), parental education, community size, and educational placement (regular or special class) per the 1980 census. The sample also included learning disabled, mentally retarded, and gifted and talented children selected approximately in proportion to their numbers in the general population. Finally, supplementary norms based on 496 black and 119 white children are available.

Raw scores for each of the 16 subtests can be converted to standard scores with a mean of 10 (SD = 3). The global scales can be converted to standard scores (mean = 100, SD = 15), percentiles, and age-equivalent norms.

Split-half reliabilities for the individual subtests are, on the average, slightly lower than those of the individual Wechsler subtests and specific tests of the modern Binet. Coefficients range from .72 (magic window) to .88 (number recall) for preschool children and from .71 (Gestalt closure) to .85 (matrix analogies) for school-age children. Split-half coefficients for the global scales range from .86 (simultaneous processing) to .93 (achievement) for preschool children and from .89 (sequential processing) to .97 (achievement) for school-age children. Thus, as with other major ability tests, reliability is lower for younger children. Test-retest coefficients are just slightly lower than those obtained by the split-half method.

Validity in the K-ABC test manual has received considerable attention. Factor analytic studies support its sequential-simultaneous and mental-processing–achievement distinctions. The K-ABC intelligence estimates also tend to show smaller (about 8 points) black-white differences than either the WISC-R or Binet scales, in which whites typically score about 15 points higher than blacks (see Jensen, 1985). Thus, it tends to be less biased against minorities (Nolan, Watlington, & Willson, 1989). However, the K-ABC also tends to underestimate the scores of gifted children (compared with the Binet Form L-M and the WISC-R); therefore, its validity for evaluating giftedness is questionable (McCallum, Karnes, & Oehier-Stinnett, 1985).

Since its publication in April 1983, the K-ABC has generated considerable interest. Reactions have varied widely, however. In summarizing the strengths of the K-ABC, Kaufman, Kaufman, and Kaufman (1985, p. 268) point to its strong theoretical orientation, separate intelligence and achievement scales, separate nonverbal scale, limited oral instructions, limited verbal responding, colorful and interesting items, inclusion of sociocultural norms, and empirical documentation of smaller black-white, Hispanic-white, and Native American–white differences on the K-ABC compared with other tests. These strengths are acknowledged by independent reviewers (Aiken, 1987; Anastasi, 1984).

Criticism of the K-ABC has been harsh. According to Jensen (1984), one can attribute the smaller white-minority differences on the K-ABC to its poorer predictive validity for school achievement and its less effective measurement of general intelligence than the Binet and WISC-R. Other critics point to the K-ABC's imperfect match with its theoretical foundation and disproportionate contribution of the simultaneous and mental-processing composites (Bracken, 1985). In addition, the K-ABC is highly visual, limiting its use for visually handicapped children, and it does not test the extremes of intelligence well (Aiken, 1987, pp. 225–226). Moreover, the neuropsychological model that underlies the sequential-simultaneous distinction is poorly supported at best and at worst inaccurate and outmoded (Herbert, 1982).

Perhaps the most severe criticism of the K-ABC has come from Sternberg (1984), who charges that the K-ABC manual misrepresents the support for the theory underlying the K-ABC. He also maintains that the test suffers from a noncorrespondence between its definition and its measurement of intelligence. Sternberg found that empirical support for the theory underlying the K-ABC is questionable. Sternberg also noted, as did Jensen (1984), an overemphasis on rote learning at the expense of ability to learn.

Although the criticisms of the K-ABC are largely valid, it is important to see them in perspective. First, many of these criticisms, such as lack of correspondence between definition and measurement of intelligence, also apply to the K-ABC's major competitors. Even the best available instruments have shortcomings and limitations. Although the underlying theory of the K-ABC has yet to be fully established, at least the test has a theoretical structure. As a replacement for the WISC-III and Binet scales, the K-ABC leaves much to be desired, for it does not predict academic achievement as well as these tests. However, the K-ABC is the best alternative or supplement for specific questions and educational assessment to date.

General Individual Ability Tests for Handicapped and Special Populations

In addition to tests for infants and young children, a number of alternatives are specifically designed to provide a more valid measure of intellectual functioning than the Binet and Wechsler scales for cases in which the major scales may be biased or inappropriate. Each of these general individual ability tests for handicapped and special populations contains unique strengths and limitations.

Columbia Mental Maturity Scale—Third Edition (CMMS). A variety of sensory and physical limitations often make a valid administration of the Binet, Wechsler, or even many of the major alternative scales (such as the McCarthy scale) quite impossible. Therefore, for children suffering from physical limitations (such as cerebral palsy), speech impairments, language limitations, or hearing loss, instruments are needed that do not create negative bias. One such instrument is the Columbia Mental Maturity Scale—Third Edition (CMMS), which evaluates ability in normal and variously handicapped children from 3 through 12 years of age. When used for individuals with special needs, the test often provides a more suitable measure of intelligence than do the more established scales (Kamhi, Minor, & Mauer, 1990).

The most recent version of the Columbia scale was revised in the early 1970s (Burgemeister, Blum, & Lorge, 1972). It requires neither a verbal response nor fine motor skills. Presented as a measure of general reasoning ability, the Columbia scale requires the subject to discriminate similarities and differences by indicating which drawing does not belong on a 6-by-9-inch card containing three to five drawings, depending on the level of difficulty. The task, then, is multiple choice.

The 1972 edition of the Columbia scale contains 92 different cards grouped into eight overlapping levels, or scales, according to chronological age. Testing begins at a scale appropriate for the child's age. Advantages of the Columbia scale include its relative independence of reading skills, ease of administration and scoring, and the clarity of its test manual (Egeland, 1978). Because subjects are not timed, pressure is minimal.

Earlier versions of the Columbia scale used a weak standardization sample. However, the 1972 standardization sample is impressive. It consists of 2600 children divided into 13 levels from 3 years, 6 months to 9 years, 11 months. Each level contains 200 children. The sample is stratified according to the U.S. population in terms of variables including gender, race, geographic region, and parental occupation.

Raw scores from the Columbia scale can be converted to a standard score with a mean of 100 and a standard deviation of 16, which is known as the *age deviation score* (ADS). One can express the age deviation score in terms of percentiles. Raw scores can also be converted to mental age equivalents. In this scale, as in the best or most recent tests, the child is compared to his or her own age group in the standardization sample.

The Columbia scale manual contains data on both split-half and test-retest reliability for some age groups in the standardization sample. The scale is internally as well as temporarily consistent for short intervals. Coefficients range between .85 and .90 for both split-half and test-retest reliabilities.

Although we have seen great strides in terms of minimum acceptable normative and reliability requirements in individual tests of ability, validity requirements appear to be weaker than before. The Columbia scale also could benefit greatly from additional validity documentation. The available validity data reported in the manual and elsewhere have been encouraging; however, data sufficient for a complete evaluation do not exist. The highest correlate of the 1972 edition is the 1959 edition of the Columbia scale. Thus, the newer scale overlaps considerably with the older scale, with a correlation of about .84 according to the manual. The Columbia scale's correlation with the Binet scale (Form L-M), as reported in the manual, is .67. Correlations with group ability tests are similar.

All users should know that the Columbia scale is highly vulnerable to random error. A young child can obtain a score of 82 simply on chance alone, and a score in the average ranges can be obtained with just a few lucky guesses (Kaufman, 1978). Theoretically, if 100 apes were administered the lower levels of the Columbia scale, an alarming number might obtain scores in the average ranges for human beings.

In conclusion, the Columbia scale is a well-standardized, reliable instrument useful in assessing ability in many people with sensory, physical, or language handicaps. Because of its multiple-choice nature, however, and consequent vulnerability to chance variance, one should use results with caution. When used with subjects for whom the major scales would be appropriate, the Columbia scale might best be seen as a screening device. The importance and value of the Columbia scale can be found in its relevance to a variety of special populations. Even for these populations, however, the Columbia scale might be more safely used in conjunction with those Wechsler or K-ABC subtests that can be given. If the child can point, for example, Wechsler's picture completion subtest can be given in conjunction with the Columbia scale as an additional check on the accuracy of the results. If the child is physically handicapped but can speak, then some of the Wechsler verbal subtests can be used to support results.

Peabody Picture Vocabulary Test—Revised (PPVT-R). Similar to the Columbia scale in several respects, the Peabody Picture Vocabulary Test, Revised (PPVT-R) was developed by L. M. Dunn (1959, 1965) and L. M. Dunn and Dunn (1981). Although the age range of 2½ through 18 years and adults is considerably wider than the range of the Columbia scale, both are multiple-choice tests that require a subject to indicate only "Yes" or "No" in some manner. Primarily for the physically or language handicapped, the PPVT-R cannot be used with the deaf because the subject must be able to hear the instructions. However, the test has been used in research with the deaf to evaluate their ability to define words (Krinsky, 1990). The test purports to measure hearing or **receptive vocabulary**, presumably providing a nonverbal estimate of verbal intelligence. One can use it as a screening instrument or as a supplement to other measures in evaluating learning problems (McGivern et al., 1991), linguistic problems (Bayles, 1990), and many other special problems (Knotek, Bayles, & Kaszniak, 1990; P. A. Wagner, 1994). Though untimed, the PPVT-R can be administered in 20 minutes or less, and it requires no reading ability. Two forms (L and M) are available. Each form has 175 plates, each containing four numbered pictures. The subject must indicate which of the four pictures best relates to a word read by the examiner. Items are arranged in increasing order of difficulty, and administration entails determination of a basal and ceiling performance, as in the modern Binet scale. The number of incorrect responses is subtracted from the ceiling to produce a total score. This total score can then be converted to a standard score (mean = 100, SD = 15), percentile rank, stanine, or age-equivalent score.

The Peabody test was standardized in 1979 on a national sample of 4200 people, ages 2½ to 18 and 800 adults ages 19 to 40. The sample was stratified by gender, race, parental occupation, geographic location, and community size according to the 1970 census. Reliability coefficients range from .71 to .81 for internal consistency estimates, from .52 to .90 for test-retest estimates, and from .71 to .91 for alternate form estimates. The manual offers no direct evidence of predictive validity, although the PPVT-R does correlate with the older

PPVT (L. M. Dunn, 1959), which has been shown to have correlations with the Binet and Wechsler scales ranging from the low .20s to low .90s. In addition, a number of studies have investigated the validity of the Peabody test for specific uses.

The PPVT-R tends to underestimate Wechsler or Binet IQs for retarded (Prout & Sheldon, 1984) as well as for gifted children (Hayes & Martin, 1986). Research has supported its use for adults referred to the California State Department of Rehabilitation (J. D. Stevenson, 1986) and for adults with developmental handicaps (Groenweg, Conway, & Stan, 1986). However, the manual advises caution when using the test with adults. Moreover, even where its use is supported, the Peabody test tends to underestimate the IQ score (J. D. Stevenson, 1986). Because it evaluates only receptive vocabulary and not problem solving, abstract thinking, and other functions tapped by the major IQ tests, the PPVT-R should never be used as a substitute for a Wechsler or Binet IQ.

In conclusion, the Peabody test has a number of pros and cons. On the positive side are its ease of administration and utility for certain handicapped groups. On the negative side, its tendency to underestimate IQ scores, in conjunction with the problems inherent in the multiple-choice format, indicate that the Peabody test cannot be used in place of the Binet and Wechsler scales. One should use it for general screening purposes and evaluation of receptive vocabulary.

Leiter International Performance Scale (LIPS). Whereas the Columbia and Peabody tests measure verbal aspects of intelligence, the Leiter International Performance Scale (LIPS) is strictly a performance scale. It aims at providing a nonverbal alternative to the Stanford-Binet scale for the age range of 2 to 18 years. (See Figure 12-9.) First developed in the 1930s and last revised in 1948, the Leiter scale has undergone a recent decrease in interest among researchers, although one finds it frequently used in clinical settings. The Leiter scale purports to provide a nonverbal measure of general intelligence by sampling a wide variety of functions, from memory to nonverbal reasoning. One can administer it without using language, and it requires no verbal response from subjects.

Presumably, one can apply it to a large range of handicapped individuals, particularly the deaf and language disabled. Like the Peabody test and the Columbia scale, the Leiter scale is untimed. Patterned after the old Binet scale, the 54 tests of the Leiter scale are arranged in an age scale format at yearly intervals from 2 through 18. Despite its many positive features and utility for subjects who cannot or will not provide a verbal response, the Leiter scale presents some noteworthy problems. Published during a time when test developers commonly left the job of psychometric documentation to users and general researchers, the Leiter manual fails to include information routinely found in modern test manuals. However, the Leiter scale's validity documentation is extremely good, with a range of criterion validity coefficients from .52 to .92 (median .83).

FIGURE 12-9
*Leiter
International
Performance
Scale.*
(Courtesy of Stoelting
Co.)

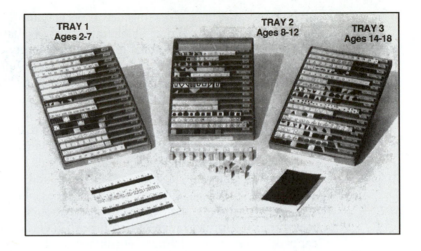

We agree with Sattler (1988) that the Leiter scale merits consideration as an aid to clinical diagnosis in handicapped children. As with other tests discussed in this chapter, however, we must encourage the test user to exercise caution in interpreting Leiter test results, because the meaning of test scores requires more research (Lewis & Lorentz, 1994). We hope that researchers will see the need for additional investigations into the properties of the Leiter scale. In addition, a careful standardization of the Leiter scale would be most welcome.

Broad-Range Individual Ability Tests: Child Through Adult

Whereas the tests discussed in the previous sections tend to apply to a specific population or age group, one can usually use broad-range individual ability tests with people of all ages. In addition, these tests are designed to estimate intelligence in both normal and special populations.

Porteus Maze Test (PMT). A popular but poorly standardized nonverbal performance measure of intelligence is the Porteus Maze Test (PMT). This test has been one of the more important individual ability tests since it was first published at about World War I. As its name implies, the Porteus Maze Test consists of maze problems. Like the Leiter scale, the Porteus test can be administered without verbal instruction and thus can be used for a variety of special populations.

The Porteus test has no manual. Furthermore, its standardization sample is quite old (Doctor, 1972). Despite its problems, however, the Porteus test meets an important need in providing a measure of ability for many groups to whom the Binet and Wechsler scales do not apply. Like many similar tests, a restandardization would greatly improve the quality of the Porteus test.

Other broad-range tests. The widespread use and interest in tests such as the Peabody, Leiter, and Porteus clearly indicate the need for strictly nonverbal or performance measures of intelligence, especially for the handicapped. Therefore, it is unfortunate that so many of the available instruments need restandardization and additional reliability or validity documentation. Other procedures—such as the Columbia scale, the Quick Test (Ammons & Ammons, 1962), the Pictorial Test of Intelligence (French, 1964), and the Slosson Intelligence Test (Slosson, 1963)—may offer some hope, but these also show limitations similar to those of the tests we have just discussed.

Much can be said for the Quick Test, except that standardization sample does not represent the general population. The Slosson Test also works well as a quick measure of intelligence, but it depends heavily on language skills. The Pictorial Test of Intelligence is almost as sound as the Columbia scale and can be used for similar purposes. In general, the Columbia scale and the Pictorial Test of Intelligence are perhaps the most strongly supported general ability measures for a broad range of handicaps. Each of the tests for the handicapped, however, offers unique advantages and disadvantages. All should be interpreted with caution and subjected to additional research investigation. One of the most promising of the broad-range tests, the Raven Progressive Matrices Test, can be administered to other groups or individuals, and is discussed in the next chapter.

Individual Tests of Ability for Specific Purposes

The tests discussed next serve as the best examples, according to our criteria, of individual ability tests for a variety of specific abilities such as learning ability and memory. Though far from complete, our discussion does focus on important or instructive instruments. Students interested in encyclopedic coverage should consult *The Mental Measurements Yearbook* and other source books.

Learning Disabilities

One of the most important areas in education involves the study of specific learning disabilities. A major concept in this field is that a child average in intelligence may fail in school because of a specific deficit or disability that prevents learning (Coplan & Gleason, 1990). Thus, a learning disability is defined in terms of a significant difference between IQ and achievement. In most states, this definition is operationalized in terms of a $1\frac{1}{2}$ to 2 standard deviation difference between a score on an IQ test and one on an achievement test.

Of the major tests designed specifically to assess learning disabilities, none more illustrates the theory of learning disabilities and has generated more interest than the controversial Illinois Test of Psycholinguistic Abilities (ITPA). Based on modern concepts of human information processing, the ITPA assumes that failure to respond correctly to a stimulus can result not only from a defective output (that is, response) system but also from a defective input or information-processing system. Consistent with information-processing theory

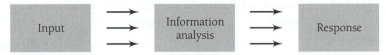

FIGURE 12-10   *Information-Processing Model (Three-Stage Model)*

(for example, see Haber, 1969), the Illinois test assumes that a human response to an outside stimulus can be viewed in terms of discrete stages or processes. In Stage 1, the senses receive input, or incoming environmental information. Thus, the information must first be received by the senses before it can be analyzed. During Stage 2, this information is analyzed or processed. Finally, having processed the information, the individual must make a response—Stage 3. (See Figure 12-10.)

Assuming that a learning disability can occur at any level of processing, the Illinois test theorizes that the child may be impaired in one or more specific sensory modalities. Input may be visual, auditory, or tactile. The Illinois test provides three subtests that measure the individual's ability to receive visual, auditory, or tactile input, independently of processing and output factors. Three additional subtests provide independent measures of processing in each of these three sense modalities, and other subtests provide independent measures of motor and verbal output. (See Table 12.4.)

By providing relatively independent measures for each of these areas, the Illinois test purports to help isolate the specific site of a learning disability. For example, a child may receive age-appropriate scores for all three input and all three processing subtests but may have an unusually low score on motor (but not verbal) output. This result would indicate that, although the child can receive and process information as well as others do, he or she has trouble in motor output. The treatment can therefore focus on enhancing motor skills. Similarly, if the problem involves auditory processing, then this area becomes the focus.

Designed for use with children ages 2 through 10, the Illinois test has found widespread use and interest among educators, psychologists, learning disability specialists, and researchers (Crisco, Dobbs, & Mulhern, 1988). This popularity, however, does not come from its psychometric qualities (Bell, 1990). Not only is the Illinois test one of the most difficult individual ability tests to administer, but the manual presents no reliability or validity data. Although normative data are provided, the exact nature of the normative sample is difficult to ascertain from the manual—a problem that has been severely criticized (Lumsden, 1978). In fact, the Illinois test has been criticized on many grounds, including inadequate validity, excessively low reliabilities for individual subtests, and failure to provide normalized standard scores. Moreover, because it was normed on middle-class children and contains culturally loaded content, the ITPA is not appropriate for use with lower-class children or disadvantaged minority groups. The reviews of both Lumsden (1978) and Wiederholt (1978) conclude that the test should not be used to assess learning disabilities; we concur.

TABLE 12-4

Description of Illinois Test of Psycholinguistic Abilities (ITPA) Subtests

Subtest	Description
Auditory Reception	Measures ability to understand spoken words. Example: "Do chairs eat?"
Visual Reception	Measures ability to gain meaning from familiar pictures. Example: Matching picture stimulus with picture from same category.
Auditory Association	Measures ability to relate concepts presented orally. Example: Verbal-analogies test (e.g., "Grass is green, sugar is _____.").
Visual Association	Measures ability to relate concepts presented visually. Example: Relating a pictorial stimulus to its conceptual counterpart (e.g., bone goes with dog).
Verbal Expression	Measures ability to express concepts verbally. Example: Describing common objects verbally.
Manual Expression	Measures ability to demonstrate knowledge of the use of objects pictured. Example: Express an idea with gestures (e.g., "Show me what to do with a hammer").
Grammatic Closure	Measures ability to use proper grammatical forms to complete statement. Example: "Here is a dog. Here are two _____."
Visual Closure	Measures ability to identify common objects from an incomplete visual presentation. Example: Locating specific objects in a scene filled with distracting stimuli.
Auditory Sequential Memory	Measures ability to reproduce orally a sequence of digits from memory. Example: Repeating digits.
Visual Sequential Memory	Measures ability to reproduce sequences of geometrical forms from memory. Example: Placing geometric shapes in proper sequence from memory.
Auditory Closure	Measures ability to complete a word when only fragments of it are orally presented. Example: "Listen. Tell me who I am talking about. DA / Y. Who is that?"
Sound Blending	Measures ability to synthesize into words syllables spoken at half-second intervals. Example: "What word is D—OG?"

Note. The two supplementary subtests are Auditory Closure and Sound Blending.
Reprinted by permission of Jerome M. Sattler, Publisher, P.O. Box 151677, San Diego, Calif. 92115. Copyright 1988.

A much better test for evaluating learning disabilities is the Woodcock-Johnson Psycho-Educational Battery—Revised (Woodcock & Johnson, 1989). The Woodcock-Johnson was designed as a broad-range individually administered test to be used in educational settings. It assesses cognitive ability, achievement, and interest. By comparing a child's score on cognitive ability with his or her score on achievement, one can evaluate possible learning problems. Such problems are defined in terms of a major discrepancy (usually $1\frac{1}{2}$ to 2 standard deviations) between cognitive ability (intelligence) and achievement. If a child is at the mean for cognitive ability (i.e., 50th percentile) and is two standard deviations below the mean in achievement (i.e., 2.2 percentile), a learning disability can be suspected and it indicates the need for a deeper evaluation.

The Woodcock-Johnson's tests of cognitive ability include picture vocabulary, spatial relations, memory for sentences, concept formation, analogies, and a variety of quantitative problems. The tests of achievement cover letter and word recognition, reading comprehension, proofing, calculation, science, social science, and humanities. Finally, the tests of interest level cover reading interest, math interest, language interest, physical interest, and social interest. Scores can be converted to percentile ranks. These ranks, in turn, can be converted to a standard score with a mean of 100 and a standard deviation of 15.

The Woodcock-Johnson has relatively good psychometric properties. The standardization sample included more than 4700 people representative of the U.S. population in terms of gender, race, occupational status, geographic region, and urban versus rural status. Many of the specific tests have split-half reliabilities in the .80s and .90s, with a range of .57 to .96 when both split-half and test-retest reliabilities are considered. However, factor analytic studies have failed to support the validity of the structure (McGhee, 1993). Factor analysis of the standardization sample yielded only two factors: a verbal factor that accounted for nearly 70% of the variance and a smaller nonverbal/visual-spatial factor (McGrew, 1986).

The Woodcock-Johnson has shown potential for classifying exceptional students (Evans, Carksen, & McGrew, 1993) as well as those with learning disabilities (McGrew, 1993). However, its correlations with Wechsler scales vary widely (Meinhardt et al., 1993).

The field of learning disability assessment is relatively new, and so are tests in this area. As a result, with the possible exception of the K-ABC, new tests of learning disabilities are in the same stage as early intelligence instruments. When judged by modern standards for individual ability tests, especially those that purportedly measure intelligence, these tests compare unfavorably in many respects.

For learning disability tests, three conclusions seem warranted. First, test constructors should attempt to respond to the same criticisms that led to changes in the Binet and Wechsler scales and ultimately to the development of the K-ABC. Second, much more empirical and theoretical research is needed. Finally, users of learning disabilities tests should take great pains to understand the weaknesses of these procedures and not overinterpret results. The ITPA should not be used to make decisions that might affect the future of a child. The Woodcock-Johnson is much more suitable but should also be used carefully.

Visiographic Tests

Visiographic tests require a subject to copy various designs. Such tests have achieved a central position in neuropsychological testing because of their sensitivity to many different kinds of brain damage (Lezak, 1976). In this section we briefly describe three such tests. Then in Chapter 19 we shall discuss neuropsychological testing in greater detail.

Benton Visual Retention Test (BVRT). Tests for brain damage are based on the concept of psychological deficit, in which a poor performance on a specific task is related to or caused by some underlying deficit. By knowing the underlying function or ability measured by a specific psychological test, the test examiner

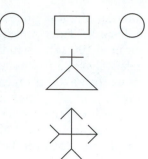

FIGURE 12-11
Designs similar to those on the Benton Visual Retention Test.

can relate a poor performance on that test to this underlying function (Downey et al., 1991). Such is the idea behind the Benton Visual Retention Test (BVRT), which assumes that brain damage easily impairs visual memory ability. Thus, a deficit on a visual memory task is consistent with possible brain damage or brain diseases such as Alzheimer's (Rebok, Brandt, & Folstein, 1990).

Designed for individuals age 8 and older, the Benton test consists of geometric designs briefly presented and then removed (see Figure 12-11). The subject must then reproduce the designs from memory. The responses are scored according to criteria in the manual. The subject loses points for mistakes and omissions and gains points for correct or partially correct responses. Norms are then available to evaluate scores. As the number of errors increases, the subject approaches the organic (brain-damaged) range.

Bender Visual Motor Gestalt Test (BVMGT). Also used in the assessment of brain damage, the Bender Visual Motor Gestalt Test (BVMGT) has a variety of uses and is among the most popular individual tests. It consists of nine geometric figures (such as a circle and a diamond) that the subject is simply asked to copy (see Figure 12-12). With a number of specific errors identified for each design, the Bender test is scored according to the number of errors the subject makes (Bolen et al., 1992). Developmental norms are available that describe the number of errors associated with children ages 5 through 8 (see Koppitz, 1964). By age 9, any child of normal intelligence can copy the figures with only one or two errors. Therefore, anyone over 9 who cannot copy the figures may suffer from some type of deficit.

Research on the Bender test (see Koppitz, 1964) has shown that errors can occur for people whose mental age is less than 9 (for example, because of low intelligence), those with brain damage, and those with emotional problems (Shapiro & Simpson, 1994). Errors associated with brain damage have been identified, and a variety of scoring systems for brain damage are available. However, the reliability of such systems has been questioned (Howell, 1985; Lubin & Sands, 1992; E. E. Wagner & Flamos, 1988).

Memory-for-Designs Test (MFD). Another simple drawing test involving perceptual-motor coordination is the Memory-for-Designs Test (MFD). Requiring

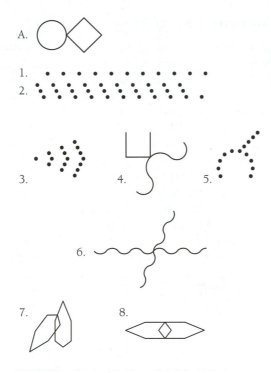

FIGURE 12-12
The figures of the Bender Visual Motor Gestalt Test.

(From The Bender Visual Motor Gestalt Test by L. Bender, 1962. Reprinted with permission from The American Orthopsychiatric Association.)

only a 10-minute administration, the Memory-for-Designs Test can be used for individuals 8½ to 60 years of age. Empirical data have tended to support its use as an indicator of brain injury (Graham & Kendall, 1960) and brain disease (Strauss & Brandt, 1990; Teng et al., 1989). As in the Benton test, the subject attempts to draw a briefly presented design from memory. Drawings are scored from 0 to 3, depending on how they compare with representative drawings from normal controls and people with varying degrees of brain injury. A raw score total based on all 15 drawings can then be corrected for age and intelligence by reference to a table. This corrected score can then be evaluated against a relatively large (825) normative sample.

Reported split-half reliability indices are quite good (.92), and test-retest indices range from .81 to .90 (Graham & Kendall, 1960). Like so many psychological tests, the MFD needs additional validity documentation. Available studies have been quite supportive (Goldstein, Canavan, & Polkey, 1988; Mandes & Gessner, 1988).

Evaluation of individual perceptual motor drawing tests of brain damage. Like all psychological tests of brain damage used in isolation, the Benton, Bender, and MFD have been criticized because of their limitations in reliability and validity documentation. However, all three can be used as screening devices. An excessive number of errors on any of these procedures provides a signal for the examiner that more in-depth testing or a medical evaluation may be necessary.

Creativity: Torrance Tests of Creative Thinking

The 1960s and 1970s saw a growing interest in the assessment of a previously overlooked ability: creativity. One can define creativity as the ability to be original, to combine known facts in new ways, or to find new relationships between known facts. Like learning disability tests, most creativity tests are still in the early stages of development. One of the best, most established, and most popular of these creativity tests is the Torrance Tests of Creative Thinking (TTCT).

The Torrance tests measure aspects of creative thinking such as fluency, originality, and flexibility. In measuring fluency, administrators ask an individual to think of as many different solutions to a problem as possible. The more distinct solutions a person can find, the greater his or her fluency. To evaluate originality, a test maker attempts to evaluate how new or unusual a person's solutions to problems are. Finally, flexibility is measured in terms of an individual's ability to shift directions or try a new approach to problem solving. For example, if your primary study method on exams has not met your goals, you would show flexibility if you tried a new approach. Instead of spending all your time passively rereading, you might try the more active recall method, in which you spend half your study time trying to recall and synthesize what you have learned.

Like many other creativity tests, the Torrance tests fluency, flexibility, and originality. One can obtain scores on the TTCT in each of these areas. However, like individual ability tests for the handicapped and tests of learning disability, the TTCT does not quite meet the Binet and Wechsler scales in terms of standardization, reliability, and validity. Reliability studies have varied widely (for example, correlations of .35 to .73 for a three-year period), and validity studies have tended to be varied as well as inconclusive (Hattie, 1980). Reviewers typically suggest that more work is needed (Baird, 1972; R. L. Thorndike, 1972). Unlike some creativity tests, the TTCT was conservatively presented as a research tool, but little has been done to prevent it from being used in applied settings. On the positive side, a number of research studies have supported the utility of the Torrance tests as an unbiased indicator of giftedness (Esquivel & Lopez, 1988; Torrance, 1970, 1977).

In sum, the Torrance tests are typical of creativity tests. Applied practitioners demand such a tool for their work, and, though inconsistent, available data reflect the tests' merit and fine potential. As with so many other tests, however, more work is needed. One should view results from the new creativity tests as tentative.

Individual Achievement Tests: Wide Range Achievement Test—Revised

We have discussed the widely made distinction between intelligence and achievement. As you know, intelligence tests measure potential ability, whereas achievement tests measure what the person has actually acquired or done with that potential. Although scores from intelligence tests and achievement tests often overlap, discrepancies sometimes arise between intelligence and achievement tests. Such discrepancies may occur if a person of average potential has not made full use of that potential. Such a person would tend to score higher on a general ability test than on a specific achievement test, especially if the general ability test minimizes the effects of learning and the achievement test is highly specific. Similarly, a person may score average on a general intelligence test but, because of a high level of interest, motivation, or special training, score above average on achievement. Thus, despite the overlap of intelligence and ability tests, comparing their data can sometimes be extremely revealing.

Most achievement tests are group tests, to be discussed in the next chapter. Among the most widely used individual achievement test is the Wide Range Achievement Test—Revised (WRAT-R), which purportedly permits an estimate of grade-level functioning in reading, spelling, and arithmetic (Kareken, Gur, & Saykin, 1995). It can be used for children age 5 and older and has two levels for each of the three achievement areas.

Revised in 1984, the Wide Range Achievement Test is easy to administer. It also is highly popular (Wasserman et al., 1991). The WRAT-R has been used to assess the effects of low birth weight (Saigal et al., 1991), diabetes (Hosey et al., 1990), and attention deficit disorder (Ackerman, Dykman, & Gardner, 1990). However, although the test may have research and clinical uses, users must again be cautioned about the many problems of the WRAT-R.

N. Reid (1986) criticizes the WRAT-R on a number of grounds. As Reid notes, there is confusion about what the WRAT-R really measures, because the validity of the test is poorly documented. According to Reid, although the WRAT-R has possible clinical and research applications, it is unsuitable for general use.

Other reviewers are equally pessimistic (Reynolds, 1986). Witt (1986) believes that the WRAT-R contains some of the worst characteristics of the testing industry. According to Witt, using the scores derived from the norms of the WRAT-R as roughly equivalent to a child's academic achievement is like performing inner ear surgery with a chainsaw. This criticism of the WRAT-R norms is well founded. For example, average readers in the 11th grade (50th percentile) score about two years behind when compared with individuals for the test's norms. Such individuals might be inappropriately labeled "reading disabled." Another problem with the reading section is that it measures word recognition rather than reading comprehension. Individuals are merely asked to pronounce words such as "egregious" and "beatitude." If they can pronounce the word they get credit, even if they have no idea what the word means or how to use it in a sentence.

The problems with the WRAT-R underscore our repeated warning for caution in the use of test results. All test users should learn as much as they can about the tests they use. Statements from the test publishers or distributors of tests, and even statements in the test manuals, always must be carefully examined. In Chapter 13, we will discuss a number of sound group achievement tests.

Summary

The number of individual ability tests is almost overwhelming. Most of these tests serve highly specific purposes, and their strength lies in their specificity. Table 12-2 summarizes some of the major differences among the various individual tests of ability. Of the infant and preschool scales, the Bayley Scales of Infant Development are the most psychometrically sound. The McCarthy Scales of Children's Abilities appear to be promising tests for measuring intelligence in young children, but more work is needed. The K-ABC is a relatively new test of considerable value, but it has been strongly criticized. Overall, general ability tests for handicapped and special populations should be used cautiously. Among the tests of ability for the handicapped, the Columbia Mental Maturity Scale—Third Edition is one of the most promising.

Learning disability tests are based on information-processing theory. Because these tests are relatively new, one should view their results with caution. These tests, like creativity tests, have a long way to go if they hope to reach the standards of the Binet and Wechsler scales. A number of useful drawing tests such as the Bender, the Benton, and the Memory-for-Designs are all excellent and economical screening devices for brain damage. These tests attempt to measure an ability related to brain functioning. From a deficit, brain damage is inferred. The Bender Visual Motor Gestalt Test, in addition to being a screening device for brain damage, can be used to measure intellectual and emotional functioning. Finally, although achievement and intelligence tests often overlap, a comparison of the two can be useful. One of the major individual achievement tests is the Wide Range Achievement Test—Revised. This test, however, can lead to incorrect conclusions because of a number of serious problems, including poor norms.

CHAPTER 13

Group Ability Tests: Intelligence, Achievement, and Aptitude

LEARNING OBJECTIVES

When you have completed this chapter, you should be able to:

☐ Compare group and individual ability tests

☐ Identify the major characteristics of group tests

☐ List four general rules for using results from group ability tests

☐ Evaluate the adequacy of the group ability tests used in kindergarten through 12th grade

☐ Identify and evaluate two major group ability tests for college entrance

☐ Identify and evaluate two major group ability tests for graduate-school entrance

☐ Identify some of the advantages of the Goodenough-Harris Drawing Test

☐ Identify some group ability tests widely used in business and industry

With individual tests, a single person can, in effect, be placed under a microscope and analyzed in minute detail. Group tests can place a whole nation under the microscope. Consider, for example, the reading proficiency of 9-year-olds in the United States. According to data collected by the National Assessment of Education Progress (NAEP) and the Educational Testing Service (ETS), only about one in six 9-year-old children in the United States can read well enough to search for specific information, interrelate ideas, and make generalizations (Educational Testing Service, 1991).

Figure 13-1 shows the results of a national testing program to assess academic achievement in the United States. The figure presents a graph of the percentage of 9-year-olds at or above Level 250 on the NAEP reading scale, which evaluates a reader's ability to use intermediate skills and search for, locate, and organize information. As the figure shows, only small changes have occurred between 1971 and 1988 in the percentage of 9-year-old children who can read at Level 250, considered a middle level. A goal of a national education initiative called Goals 2000 is to increase, by the year 2000, the reading skills of all American children regardless of race, gender, or disabilities.

The microscope of national testing programs can also be used to examine racial and ethnic differences in achievement, as well as those pertaining to geographic location and other variables. Consider, for example, Figure 13-2. In 1988 substantial ethnic differences existed in the reading levels of 9-year-olds. In addition, children in the central and in the northeastern United States scored considerably higher than those in the southeast and west. Not surprisingly, reading achievement was correlated with parent education, as illustrated in the bar graph on the far right of Figure 13-2. It will be interesting to see if the hundreds of millions of dollars in grant money awarded by the U.S. Department of Education and other agencies can succeed in narrowing or eliminating achievement differences across racial, gender, and socioeconomic lines.

In this chapter, we examine many of the group tests used on a daily basis in schools, colleges, graduate and professional schools, the civil service, the military, business, and industry. Before discussing specific tests, we compare group and individual tests and also reexamine the distinctions among achievement, aptitude, and intelligence.

Comparison of Group and Individual Ability Tests

Individual tests, you will recall, require a single examiner for a single subject. The examiner provides the instructions according to a standardized procedure stated in the test manual. The subject responds, and the examiner records the response verbatim. The examiner then evaluates and scores the subject's responses. This scoring process usually involves considerable skill. In contrast, a single examiner can administer group tests to more than one person at the same time. The examiner may read the instructions and impose time limits. Subjects record their own responses, which usually are choices between two

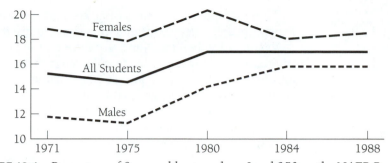

FIGURE 13-1   *Percentage of 9-year-olds at or above Level 250 on the NAEP Reading Scale.*

(From "Performance at the Top: From Elementary Through Graduate School," p. 5. Copyright © 1991 by Educational Testing Service. Reprinted by permission of Educational Testing Service, the copyright holder.)

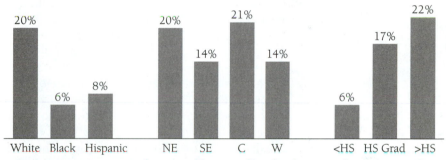

FIGURE 13-2   *Percentage of 9-year-olds at or above level 250 on the NAEP Reading Scale by Race/Ethnicity, Region, and Parental Education, 1988.*

(From "Performance at the Top: From Elementary Through Graduate School," p. 5. Copyright © 1991 by Educational Testing Service. Reprinted by permission of Educational Testing Service, the copyright holder.)

or more alternatives. Scoring is typically objective and requires no skill on the part of the examiner, who simply adds the number of correct responses and in some cases subtracts a certain percentage for incorrect responses.

In addition to differences in whether a single person or a group is tested at once, who records the response (examiner or subject), and the objectivity of scoring, another important difference exists between group and individual tests. In most individual tests, the examiner takes the responsibility for eliciting a maximum performance. If a problem exists that might inhibit a maximum performance—for example, if a subject is frightened, nervous, uncooperative, or unmotivated—the examiner takes responsibility for neutralizing this problem. In an individual test, the examiner may, depending on the standardization procedure, encourage guessing—for example, by saying in a warm, friendly, supportive tone, "Sure you know that; just guess."

Those who use the results of group tests must assume the subject was cooperative and motivated. Subjects are not praised for responding, as they may be on individual tests, and there are no safeguards to prevent a person from receiving a low score for reasons other than low ability, such as lack of motivation, lack of cooperation, or emotional upset. As a result of this lack of safeguards, low scores on group tests are often difficult to interpret. With high scores, especially very high scores, one can logically assume that the subject was motivated and has mental abilities commensurate with the obtained score. Low scores, however, may have been due to low ability, lack of interest, inadequate motivation, clerical errors in recording responses, or a host of other factors. Table 13-1 compares individual and group tests.

Advantages of Individual Tests

Individual tests can provide a wealth of information about a subject above and beyond the test score. Because in these tests the instructions and methods of administration are as identical as possible, the situation in which subjects take an individual test is typically the same. Therefore, differences observed in behavior and attitudes most likely reflect differences in the individuals taking the test. One person may respond quickly and enthusiastically when correct but become hesitant or withdrawn following failure. Another person may react to failure by trying harder and may actually do better in the face of frustration and failure.

After examiners have gained experience with an individual test and know how to use it properly, they have the opportunity to observe different reactions from individuals placed in the same situation. Experienced examiners eventually develop internal norms. They have an idea of how most subjects react to a certain task or situation and can easily identify unusual reactions. The opportunity to observe behavior in a standard situation can be invaluable to an examiner trying to understand the unique attributes of a person and interpret the meaning of a test score.

By providing the opportunity to observe behavior under standardized conditions, individual tests add a whole new dimension to the information one can obtain from an interview. Some subjects will not talk; some cannot talk. How can the examiner gain an understanding of such individuals? Information provided by friends or relatives cannot be relied on because they are rarely objective and usually are not trained in observing human behavior. Simply observing the person in a natural setting may provide some useful information, but then the examiner has nothing with which to compare these observations. Thus, by allowing observations of behavior under standard conditions, individual tests provide an invaluable opportunity for the examiner to get information beyond what he or she can obtain in an interview.

Advantages of Group Tests

Group tests also offer unique advantages. Cost-efficient, group tests minimize professional time needed for administration and scoring; they also involve less

TABLE 13-1
*Individual Versus
Group Tests*

Individual Tests	Group Tests
One subject is tested at a time.	Many subjects are tested at a time.
Examiner records responses.	Subjects record own responses.
Scoring requires considerable skill.	Scoring is straightforward and objective.
Examiner flexibility can elicit maximum performance if permitted by standardization.	There are no safeguards.

expensive materials and usually require less examiner skill and training than individual tests. Scoring for group tests is more objective and hence typically more reliable than the subjective scoring of many individual tests. Group tests can be used with large numbers of individuals. When combined with data from other sources, group test results can yield information as useful and meaningful as that obtained from individual tests.

Whereas individual tests find their greatest application in the assessment and diagnosis of psychological or medical problems, the application of group tests is far broader. Group tests are used in schools at every level—from kindergarten through graduate school. The military, industry, and researchers also use them extensively. Group test results can be used for screening and selection purposes; to assess mental, vocational, or special abilities; to assess mastery of a particular discipline or subject area; and to assess interests and aptitudes for specific occupations or job duties.

If the examiner's purpose does not require the benefits of individual tests, or if many individuals must be tested in a limited time with limited personnel, then group tests, administered and interpreted carefully, can be extremely valuable tools. Table 13-2 lists the advantages of individual and group tests.

General Features of Group Tests

Characteristics of Group Tests

In general, group tests can be characterized as paper-and-pencil or booklet-and-pencil tests because the only materials required are a printed booklet of test items, a test manual, a scoring key, an answer sheet, and a pencil. Most group tests are multiple choice; that is, the subject must select one alternative from as many as eight possible responses. Some group tests also require a free response, such as completing a sentence or design.

Group tests by far outnumber individual tests. Like the latter, group tests vary among themselves in many respects. One major difference is whether the test is primarily verbal (thus requiring reading or language skills), primarily nonverbal, or a combination. Some group tests group items by type (for example, all verbal analogy problems are in the same section, with items arranged in order of increasing difficulty). A test of this kind is ideally suited for producing a variety of scores such as those obtained from the Wechsler scales.

TABLE 13-2

Unique Advantages of Individual and Group Tests

Individual Tests

Provide information beyond the test score

Allow the examiner to observe behavior in a standard setting

Allow individualized interpretation of test scores

Group Tests

Are cost-efficient

Minimize professional time for administration and scoring

Require less examiner skill and training

Have more objective and reliable scoring procedures

Have a very broad application

Other group tests present different tasks arranged in no particular or systematic order. A test of this kind typically produces a single score related to general ability. Group test scores can be converted to a variety of units. Most produce percentiles or some type of standard score, but a few produce ratio or deviation IQs.

Selecting Group Tests

In selecting a group test, one should remember that there are a sufficient number of psychometrically adequate group tests for most purposes. Therefore, the test user need never settle for any tests but those with well-documented psychometric soundness. This is especially true for ability tests used in the schools.

In view of the ready availability of psychometrically sound instruments, we shall not discuss poorly standardized or marginally reliable tests. Our treatment of group tests, however, is not comprehensive. Therefore, tests that are not included in our discussion are not necessarily psychometrically unsound instruments. We gave highest priority to established, highly used tests that continue to generate interest among researchers and practitioners. However, we also include tests that illustrate concepts or meet specific needs. Finally, we include a few recent tests as well as tests of historical value.

Using Group Tests

Overall, the tests included in our discussion are about as reliable and well standardized as the best individual tests. However, as for some individual tests, validity data for some group tests are weak, meager, contradictory, or all three. Therefore, all users of group tests must carefully interpret and make use of test scores. These tests should not be seen as a simple solution to the decision-making process; rather, their main value arises when used in conjunction with other data.

Test use is an especially important issue for group tests because the results from these procedures are probably used by more people than the results from individual tests. Therefore, to the thousands of teachers, educators, school administrators, personnel staff, counselors, and others who routinely access results from group tests, we offer the following suggestions.

Use results with caution. Never consider scores in isolation or as absolutes. Try to include the test score as only one bit of data, tentatively accepted unless not confirmed by other data. Be especially careful in using these tests for prediction, except for predicting relatively limited factors over a brief time. Avoid overinterpreting test scores or attributing to test scores more value than their limitations warrant.

Be especially suspicious of low scores. Users of group tests must of necessity assume that subjects understand the purpose of testing, want to do well and are equally rested and free of emotional problems. Many group tests also require reading ability as well as an interest in solving test problems. Failing to fulfill any of these assumptions and requirements can produce an artificially low score.

Consider wide discrepancies a warning signal. When an individual exhibits wide discrepancies either among test scores or between a test score and other data, all may not be well with the individual (assuming no clerical errors). The discrepancy may reflect emotional problems or severe stress. For example, a child with high test scores may obtain poor grades because of emotional upset. Or a child with good grades may obtain a poor test score because of a crisis, such as a death in the family.

When in doubt, refer. With low scores, wide discrepancies, or sufficient reason to doubt the validity or fairness of a test result, the safest course is to refer the subject for individual testing by a competent professional. Given the reasons for the referral, a professional trained in individual test use can generally ascertain the cause of the problem and provide the unique interpretation called for in such cases. It is often dangerous as well as reckless to take on a responsibility that is appropriate for a trained specialist.

Group Tests in the Schools: Kindergarten Through 12th Grade

The purpose of these tests is to measure educational achievement in school children. Before proceeding to a discussion of the specific tests, we shall review the nature of achievement tests and how they differ from aptitude tests.

Achievement Tests versus Aptitude Tests

Achievement tests attempt to assess what one has learned following a specific course of instruction. As you saw in Chapter 1, the first achievement tests

TABLE 13-3

Achievement Tests versus Aptitude Tests

Achievement Tests
1. Evaluate the effects of a known or controlled set of experiences
2. Evaluate the product of a course of training
3. Rely heavily on content validation procedures

Aptitude Tests
1. Evaluate the effects of an unknown, uncontrolled set of experiences
2. Evaluate the potential to profit from a course of training
3. Rely heavily on predictive criterion validation procedures

used in the schools were of the essay variety. Such tests were rapidly replaced in the 1930s by standardized achievement tests such as the Stanford Achievement Test, still in use today. These tests were more cost-effective than their essay counterparts. The scoring of such tests was also far more objective and reliable. However, like their predecessors, standardized achievement tests had as their goal the evaluation of a student's knowledge after a standard course of training. They represented an endpoint evaluation of performance and helped reveal how much a student had learned. In such tests, validity is determined primarily by content validation procedures. These tests are considered valid if they adequately sample the domain of the construct (e.g., math, science, or history) being assessed.

As you learned in Chapter 1, aptitude tests attempt to evaluate a student's potential for learning rather than how much a student has already learned. Unlike achievement tests, aptitude tests evaluate a wide range of experiences obtained in a variety of ways. They evaluate the effects of unknown and uncontrolled experiences. The validity of an aptitude test is judged primarily on its ability to predict future performance. Thus, such tests rely heavily on criterion-oriented validity studies. Table 13-3 lists contrasting characteristics of achievement and aptitude tests.

A third type of ability test, the intelligence test, measures general ability. Like aptitude tests, intelligence tests attempt to predict future performance. However, such tests predict generally and broadly, as opposed to aptitude tests, which typically predict potential in a specific area such as math, science, or music.

Clearly, as we have stressed, achievement, aptitude, and intelligence are highly interrelated. What one has learned is related to general intelligence, specific aptitude, motivation, and a host of other factors. And what one has learned (achievement) can be used to predict future success, just as an algebra achievement test might be used to predict success (aptitude) in a geometry course.

In our discussion of group tests, we consider all three types, beginning with achievement tests. Then we consider group intelligence tests used in the school system. Finally, we examine tests used to measure scholastic aptitude.

Group Achievement Tests

As previously indicated, the Stanford Achievement Test (SAT) is one of the oldest of the standardized achievement tests widely used in the school system (Gardner et al., 1982). Published by the Psychological Corporation, the Stanford Achievement Test is a well-normed, criterion-referenced test with exemplary psychometric documentation. It evaluates achievement in first through ninth grades in the following areas: spelling, reading comprehension, word study and skills, language arts, social studies, science, mathematics, and listening comprehension. Figure 13-3 shows an example of the scoring output for the Stanford Achievement Test. Two related tests, the Stanford Early School Achievement Tests—Second Edition (SESAT) and the Stanford Test for Academic Skills—Second Edition (TASK), are used to extend the grade range to K through 13th. Together, all three tests are referred to as the Stanford Achievement Series.

Another well-standardized and psychometrically sound group measure of achievement is the Metropolitan Achievement Test (MAT), which measures achievement in reading by evaluating vocabulary, word recognition, and reading comprehension. An example of a reading item follows:

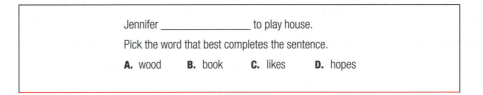

Jennifer _____ to play house.

Pick the word that best completes the sentence.

A. wood   **B.** book   **C.** likes   **D.** hopes

The MAT also measures mathematics by evaluating number concepts (e.g., measurement, decimals, factors, time, money), problem solving (e.g., word problems), and computation (addition, subtraction, multiplication, division). For example, a child might be presented with this item:

Jason had four candy bars. He gave one to Mary and one to Bill. Which number sentence below shows how many candy bars he had left?

A. $4 - 2 = \square$ **B.** $4 + 2 = \square$ **C.** $2 + 2 = \square$ **D.** $2 - 2 = \square$

Spelling is evaluated on the MAT in a normal spelling test format in which the student is asked to spell an orally dictated word presented in a sentence. Language skills are evaluated with a grammar test as well as a measure of alphabetizing skills. Science knowledge is evaluated in items such as the following:

A thermometer is used to measure _____.

(Mark the best answer.)

A. light   **B.** dark   **C.** temperature   **D.** planets

Finally, the MAT has a number of social studies items. Students are tested on their knowledge of geography, economics, history, political science, anthropology, sociology, and psychology, as in the following:

Paris is in _____.

(Mark the best answer.)

A. England   **B.** Spain   **C.** Canada   **D.** France

The most recent version of the MAT was standardized in 1985 on more than 250,000 students. The sample was stratified by school size, public versus nonpublic school affiliation, geographic region, socioeconomic status, and ethnic background. Reliabilities of the total scores run in the high .90s, while those for the five major content areas range from .90 to .96.

The Stanford Achievement Test and Metropolitan Achievement Test are state-of-the-art achievement tests. Their psychometric documentation is outstanding. The tests are reliable and normed on very large samples. They sample a variety of school subjects and cover all grade levels.

Group Tests of Mental Abilities (Intelligence)

In this section, we discuss four group tests of mental abilities: the Kuhlmann-Anderson, the Henmon-Nelson, the Cognitive Abilities Test, and the Developing Cognitive Abilities Test.

Kuhlmann-Anderson Test—Eighth Edition (KAT). The Kuhlmann-Anderson Test (KAT) is a group intelligence test with eight separate levels covering all grades, kindergarten through 12th. Each level of the KAT contains several tests, with a variety of items on each test. As in most multilevel batteries that cover many age or grade ranges, KAT items are primarily nonverbal at lower levels, requiring minimal reading and language ability. However, whereas most multilevel batteries become increasingly verbal with increasing age or grade level, the KAT remains primarily nonverbal throughout. Thus, the KAT is suited not only to young children but also to those who might be handicapped in following verbal procedures.

The results of the most recent (eighth) edition of the KAT can be expressed in verbal, quantitative, and total scores. At some levels, total scores can be expressed as deviation IQs. Scores at other levels can be expressed as percentile

FIGURE 13-3

Example of a score report for the Stanford Achievement Test.

(Reproduced by permission from the Score Report for the Stanford Achievement Test, 7th Edition. Copyright © 1982 by Harcourt Brace Jovanovich, Inc. All rights reserved.)

STANFORD

ACHIEVEMENT TEST SERIES, EIGHTH EDITION
WITH OTIS-LENNON SCHOOL ABILITY TEST, SIXTH EDITION

TEACHER:	CESTERO		1988 NORMS:	STANDARD OLSAT STUDENT SKILLS ANALYSIS
SCHOOL:	NEWTOWN ELEM	GRADE: 04	SPRING	GRADE 04 GRADE 04 FOR
DISTRICT:	NEWTOWN	TEST DATE:	LEVEL:	NATIONAL NATIONAL ANDREW D ARCANGEL
		03/89	FORM:	INTERMED 1 E J 1

TESTS	NO. OF ITEMS	RAW SCORE	SCALED SCORE	NATL PR-S	LOCAL PR-S	GRADE EQUIV	AAC RANGE	NATIONAL GRADE PERCENTILE BANDS 1 10 30 50 70 90 99
Total Reading	94	63	628	52-5	51-5	4.9	MIDDLE	
Vocabulary	40	32	655	75-6	71-6	6.3	HIGH	
Reading Comp.	54	31	611	37-4	33-4	4.0	MIDDLE	
Total Math	118	70	615	42-5	58-5	4.5	MIDDLE	
Concepts of No.	34	20	618	44-5	60-6	4.6	MIDDLE	
Computation	44	21	594	25-4	39-4	3.8	LOW	
Applications	40	29	635	59-5	70-6	5.4	MIDDLE	
Total Language	60	45	627	57-5	63-6	5.4	MIDDLE	
Lang Mechanics	30	20	616	36-4	34-4	4.1	MIDDLE	
Lang Expression	30	25	662	74-6	78-7	8.5	HIGH	
Spelling	40	22	615	37-4	35-4	4.2	MIDDLE	
Study Skills	30	16	606	30-4	38-4	3.3	LOW	
Science	50	36	642	79-7	84-7	7.3	HIGH	
Social Science	50	34	627	63-6	61-6	5.6	MIDDLE	
Listening	45	36	660	90-8	85-7	8.3	HIGH	
Using Information	70	43	619	41-5	46-5	4.3	MIDDLE	
Thinking Skills	101	67	627	61-6	65-6	5.4	MIDDLE	
Basic Battery	387	252	623	49-5	54-5	4.7	MIDDLE	
Complete Battery	487	322	627	54-5	56-5	5.2	MIDDLE	

OTIS-LENNON SCHOOL ABILITY TEST	RAW SCORE	SAI	AGE PR-S	AGE NCE	SCALED SCORE	NATL GRADE PR-S	NATL GRADE NCE	1 10 30 50 70 90 99
Total	72	35	105	62-6	56.4	598	49-5	49.5
Verbal	36	15	102	55-5	52.6	588	36-4	42.5
Nonverbal	36	20	108	69-6	60.4	608	59-5	54.8

AGE   9 YRS   8 MOS

READING GROUP
Comprehension

LANGUAGE ARTS GROUP
Study Skills

MATHEMATICS GROUP
Computation

COMMUNICATIONS GROUP
Reading

CONTENT CLUSTERS	RAW SCORE/ NUMBER OF ITEMS	BELOW AVERAGE	AVERAGE	ABOVE AVERAGE	CONTENT CLUSTERS	RAW SCORE/ NUMBER OF ITEMS	BELOW AVERAGE	AVERAGE	ABOVE AVERAGE
Reading Vocabulary	32/ 40		✓		Language Mechanics	20/ 30		✓	
Synonyms	21/ 24			✓	Capitalization	6/ 7			✓
Context	4/ 8		✓		Punctuation	5/ 11	✓		
Multiple Meanings	7/ 8			✓	Applied Grammar	9/ 12		✓	
Reading Comprehension	31/ 54		✓		Language Expression	25/ 30		✓	
Recreational	14/ 18		✓		Sentence Correctness	16/ 20		✓	
Textual	7/ 18	✓			Sentence Effectiveness	9/ 10		✓	
Functional	10/ 18		✓		Spelling	22/ 40		✓	
Literal	10/ 21		✓		Study Skills	16/ 30		✓	
Inferential	18/ 26		✓		Library/Reference Skills	9/ 17		✓	
Critical	3/ 7		✓		Information Skills	7/ 13		✓	
Concepts of Number	20/ 34		✓		Science	36/ 50			✓
Whole Numbers	8/ 16		✓		Physical Science	11/ 16		✓	
Fractions	1/ 4		✓		Biological Science	13/ 20		✓	
Decimals	3/ 3			✓	Earth/Space Science	12/ 14			✓
Operations and Properties	8/ 11		✓		Social Science	34/ 50		✓	
Mathematics Computation	21/ 44		✓		Geography	10/ 13		✓	
Add and Subtract/Whole Nos	8/ 12		✓		History	6/ 8		✓	
Multiplication/Whole Numbers	6/ 12	✓			Political Science	5/ 10		✓	
Division/Whole Numbers	4/ 10		✓		Economics	7/ 10		✓	
Add and Subtract/Decimals	3/ 6		✓		Psych/Sociol/Anthro	6/ 9		✓	
Add and Subtract/Fractions	0/ 4	✓			Listening	36/ 45			✓
Mathematics Applications	29/ 40		✓		Vocabulary	11/ 15			✓
Problem Solving	16/ 22		✓		Listening Comprehension	25/ 30			✓
Graphs and Charts	4/ 6		✓		Using Information	43/ 70		✓	
Geometry/Measurement	9/ 12		✓		Thinking Skills	67/101		✓	

Scores based on Normative Data Copyright © 1988 by Harcourt Brace Jovanovich, Inc. All rights reserved.
COPY 01   PROCESS NO. 18904271-8909-00038-1

Actual size 8 ½" × 11".
Simulated data.

THE PSYCHOLOGICAL CORPORATION®
HARCOURT BRACE JOVANOVICH, INC.

bands. A **percentile band** is like a confidence interval. It provides the range of percentiles that most likely represent a subject's true score. One creates it by forming an interval one standard error of measurement above and below the obtained score and then converting the resulting values to percentiles.

An overwhelming majority of reviews have praised the KAT for its construction, standardization, and other excellent psychometric qualities. Normative data have been continually improved and are based on more than 10,000 representative subjects. Reliability coefficients are quite good, with split-half coefficients running in the low .90s and test-retest coefficients ranging from the low .80s to the low .90s. Validity is also well documented. The KAT correlates highly with a variety of ability tests and, in particular, has an impressive correlation with the Stanford-Binet (Form L-M). In sum, the KAT is an extremely sound, sophisticated group test. Its nonverbal items make it particularly useful for special purposes. Its impressive validity and reliability also make it one of the most popular group ability tests for all grade levels.

Henmon-Nelson Test (H-NT). A second well-standardized, highly used, and carefully constructed test for all grade levels is the Henmon-Nelson Test (H-NT) of mental abilities. Although it produces only a single score believed to reflect general intelligence, two sets of norms are available. One set is based on raw score distributions by age, the other on raw score distributions by grade. Raw scores can be converted into deviation IQs as well as percentiles. The availability of only a single score has continued to spur controversy. However, a single score is consistent with the purpose of the test, which is to obtain a relatively quick measure of general intelligence (it takes approximately 30 minutes to complete the 90 items).

As in the other tests for school-age individuals, most of the reliability coefficients, both split-half and test-retest, reported in the manual run in the .90s. Furthermore, the H-NT correlates well with a variety of intelligence tests (median .76, range .50–.84) and achievement test scores (median .79, range .64–.85). Correlations with grades, though not as high, are impressive, with a median coefficient of .60.

In sum, the H-NT is an extremely sound instrument. It can help predict future academic success quickly. However, the H-NT has some important limitations when used as the sole screening instrument for selecting giftedness or identifying learning disabilities in minority, culturally diverse, and economically disadvantaged children.

By providing only a single score related to Spearman's g factor, the H-NT does not consider multiple intelligences. When the test was being developed, no special effort was made to check for content bias, either by judges or by statistical analysis. The manual presents no data pertaining to the norms for special racial/ethnic or socioeconomic groups, nor was the test designed to be used for culturally diverse children. Indeed, the manual pointedly calls for caution when using the H-NT for individuals from an educationally disadvan-

taged subculture. It also advises caution when extreme scores (below 80 or above 130) are obtained. Consistent with these cautions, research suggests that the H-NT tends to underestimate Wechsler full-scale IQ scores by 10 to 15 points for certain populations (Watson & Klett, 1975). A major problem with the H-NT is its relatively low ceiling. For example, to achieve an IQ of 130, a ninth-grade child would have to answer about 85 of the items correctly. This leaves only five items to discriminate all those above 130.

Cognitive Abilities Test (COGAT). In terms of its reliability and validity, the Cognitive Abilities Test (COGAT) is comparable to the H-NT. Unlike the H-NT, however, the COGAT provides three separate scores: verbal, quantitative, and nonverbal. Reliabilities (KR_{20}) for the verbal score are in the high .90s; for the quantitative, the low .90s; and for the nonverbal, the high .90s.

The COGAT's item selection is superior to that of the H-NT in terms of selecting minority, culturally diverse, and economically disadvantaged children. Unlike the H-NT, the COGAT was specifically designed for poor readers, the poorly educated, and people for whom English is a second language.

The test authors of the COGAT took special steps to eliminate irrelevant sources of test difficulty, especially those pertaining to cultural bias. All items were scrutinized for content that might be biased for or against any particular group. Statistical tests were then performed to eliminate items that might predict differentially for white and minority students. To eliminate the effect of test-taking skills, the test administration includes extensive practice exercises.

The COGAT offers advantages over the H-NT in evaluating minority, culturally diverse, and economically disadvantaged children. Moreover, research has revealed that the COGAT is a sensitive discriminator for giftedness (Harty, Adkins, & Sherwood, 1984) and a good predictor of future performance (Henry & Bardo, 1990).

On the negative side, each of the three subtests of the COGAT requires 32 to 34 minutes of actual working time, which the manual recommends be spread out over two or three days. The manual claims that the tests are primarily "power tests" but provides no data to support this claim. Despite the apparent strength of the norms, uncertainty remains as to whether they are, in fact, representative. For example, when a selected community declined to participate in the norming process, a second, third, fourth, or, in some cases, fifth choice was needed to find a replacement. No data are provided regarding the frequency and magnitude of this type of sampling bias. A more serious potential drawback can be found in the information presented in the manual regarding ethnic group means. The standard age scores (SAS—normalized standard scores with a mean of 100 and standard deviation of 16) averaged about 15 or more points lower for black students (versus whites) on the verbal battery and quantitative batteries. Hispanic students also tended to score lower than white students across the test batteries and grade levels (see Ansorge, 1985).

Summary of Group Tests in the Schools

The SAT, MAT, KAT, H-NT, and COGAT are all sound, viable instruments. The SAT and MAT provide outstanding measures of achievement. A particular strength of the KAT in evaluating intelligence is its set of nonverbal items. The H-NT provides a quick estimate of g (general intelligence) for most children but is not as valid as the COGAT for assessing minority or culturally diverse children. Each test should be used only by those who know its particular properties, strengths, and limitations.

College Entrance Tests

Three of the most widely used and well-known entrance tests are the Scholastic Assessment Test (formally known as the Scholastic Aptitude Test), the Cooperative School and College Ability Tests, and the American College Test.

The Scholastic Assessment Test

Up until March 1995, the Scholastic Assessment Test (SAT-I) was known as the Scholastic Aptitude Test (SAT). The SAT-I remains the most widely used of the college entrance tests.

In continuous use since 1926, the SAT was given on an annual basis to some 1.5 million students at 5000 test centers around the country. From 1941 through April 1995, norms for the SAT were based on a sample of 10,000 students who took the test in 1941. When compared with these original norms, modern users tended to score about 20 to 80 points lower for each of the two main sections of the test, the SAT-V (Verbal) and the SAT-M (Math). With the original mean at 500 for each of the two sections, national averages in the 1980s and early 1990s tended to run about 420 for the SAT-V and about 480 for the SAT-M. Numerous explanations were advanced to explain the decline, which became somewhat of a national embarrassment (Hanford, 1986).

In June 1994, the test developers announced it would restore the national average to the 500-point level of 1941. They accomplished this by renorming the test on 1.8 million students and converting raw scores to standard scores with a mean of 500 and a standard deviation of 100. The new norms pushed up national SAT averages about 75 points on the Verbal and about 20 points on the Math.

The renorming did not alter the relative standing of test takers to one another in terms of percentile rank. However, some confusion exists in comparing scores from individuals who took the SAT before April 1995 and those who have since taken the SAT. To help matters, the College Board provides a "score converter" for colleges.

The revised SAT showed many changes that the College Board believed reflected educational reform movements of the 1980s and 1990s. The SAT Verbal and Math sections were renamed the SAT-I: Reasoning Tests. In the Ver-

bal sections of the SAT-I, reasoning tests included an increased emphasis on critical reading—for example, a double passage with different points of view. Antonyms were removed, but a number of new questions that measure vocabulary in context were included. The Math section of the SAT-I now offers some questions that require students to produce their own responses (as opposed to selecting from a choice of answers). Students are encouraged to bring calculators. In addition, emphasis on interpretation of data and applied mathematics has increased. The College Board provides a well-written guide for taking the SAT-I. This guide includes tips on how to prepare, simple test-taking strategies, sample questions with explanations, and a practice test. College counselors can read a number of reports and other literature that explain the revision. Such reports can be easily obtained by writing to the College Board (P.O. Box 6200, Princeton, N.J. 08514-6200). Figures 13-4 and 13-5 illustrate differences in the content for the Verbal and Math sections, respectively.

Along with the SAT-I: Reasoning Tests, the College Board released the SAT-II: Subject Tests. The SAT-II includes a direct writing test, new tests in Asian languages, and a new English-as-a-Second-Language Proficiency Test.

It is too early to evaluate the revised SAT. Certainly some confusion will arise during the transition between the new and old versions. However, SAT-I will most likely inherit many of the strengths as well as the weaknesses of the original.

A major weakness of the original SAT as well as other major college entrance tests is relatively poor predictive power regarding the grades of students who score in the middle ranges. It is not uncommon for a student at the mean on the SAT to have a higher college grade point average than a student who scores a standard deviation above the mean on both sections, perhaps because factors such as motivation, determination, personality, emotional stability, and home and social life also influence first-year grades. In other words, test scores and high-school performance records do not alone determine college success. Furthermore, the number of English or math units a student has does not correlate significantly with his or her SAT-V or SAT-M score (Sinha, 1986). This may be due to the effects of coaching—that is, training courses that expose students to questions like those on the actual test and promote good test-taking skills.

Despite its critics, the SAT is a sound instrument, and the SAT-I promises to follow in its footsteps. It can help predict grades during the early years of college when used with other sources of data, such as the high-school record. The psychometric adequacy of the SAT may be the highest possible for any such test, and the SAT-I will likely play a role in college entrance decisions for some time to come.

Cooperative School and College Ability Tests

Second to the SAT in terms of usage is the Cooperative School and College Ability Tests (SCAT), developed in 1955. In addition to the college level, the

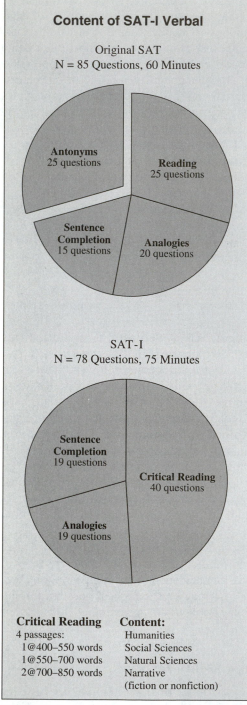

Content of SAT-I Verbal

Original SAT
N = 85 Questions, 60 Minutes

Antonyms
25 questions

Reading
25 questions

Sentence
Completion
15 questions

Analogies
20 questions

SAT-I
N = 78 Questions, 75 Minutes

Sentence
Completion
19 questions

Critical Reading
40 questions

Analogies
19 questions

Critical Reading	Content:
4 passages:	Humanities
1@400–550 words	Social Sciences
1@550–700 words	Natural Sciences
2@700–850 words	Narrative
	(fiction or nonfiction)

SAT-I: Reasoning tests reflect what students experience in today's classrooms.

Consisting of two parts–Verbal Reasoning and Mathematical Reasoning–SAT-I will require three hours of testing time. Exact time limits will be determined after further research, but will approximate:

- **Verbal Reasoning:**   75 minutes
- **Mathematical Reasoning:**   75 minutes
- **Equating or Pretesting:**   30 minutes

Verbal Reasoning puts the emphasis on critical reading.

Much of the content of the SAT-I Verbal Test will remain the same, although antonyms will no longer appear. The test will include questions and reading passages that reflect both what colleges expect of today's students and current instructional theory.

The Verbal section of SAT-I will focus even more than the current test on students' ability to read critically. The SAT-I Verbal Test will include the following new features:

- Approximately half of the questions will be based on reading passages;
- Longer reading passages;
- Reading material that is more accessible and engaging;
- A pair of reading passages on the same or related topics. One of the passages will oppose, support, or in some way complement the point of view expressed in the other;
- Introductory information to give students a context for each reading passage;
- Questions that test students' verbal reasoning skills and knowledge of vocabulary in context.

FIGURE 13-4   *Verbal content of revised SAT (SAT-I) compared with the original.*

SAT-I: Mathematical Reasoning focuses on problem-solving skills important to success in college.

The content of the SAT-I Mathematical Reasoning Test will also remain fundamentally the same as the current SAT Mathematical Test, but with increased emphasis on a student's ability to apply mathematical concepts and interpret data. The current multiple-choice and quantitative comparisons will continue to appear on the test.

Two significant new features also will be introduced:

■ Questions that require students to produce and "grid-in" their own answers–not just select one from a set of multiple-choice alternatives, and
■ It is recommended that students bring calculators.

The introduction of calculator use will parallel the changes occurring nationally in the use of calculators in mathematics instruction.

The policies that govern the use of calculators on SAT-I are supported by the recommendations and standards of the:

■ National Council of Teachers of Mathematics
■ National Council of Supervisors of Mathematics
■ Mathematical Sciences Education Board
■ Mathematical Association of America
■ American Mathematical Society

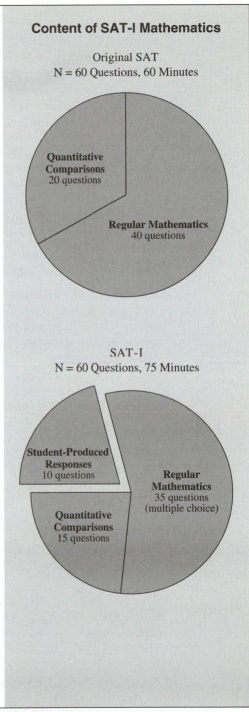

Content of SAT-I Mathematics

Original SAT
N = 60 Questions, 60 Minutes

Quantitative Comparisons
20 questions

Regular Mathematics
40 questions

SAT-I
N = 60 Questions, 75 Minutes

Student-Produced Responses
10 questions

Regular Mathematics
35 questions
(multiple choice)

Quantitative Comparisons
15 questions

FIGURE 13-5   *Math content of revised SAT (SAT-I) compared with the original.*

SCAT covers three precollege levels beginning at the fourth grade. The SCAT purports to measure school-learned abilities as well as an individual's potential to undertake additional schooling.

Although the SCAT is well designed and constructed, H. L. Butcher (1972) questions the representativeness of its standardization sample. Psychometric documentation of the SCAT, furthermore, is neither as strong nor as extensive as that of the SAT. Another problem is that little empirical data support the major assumption that previous success in acquiring school-learned abilities can predict future success in acquiring such abilities. Even if this assumption were accurate—and it probably is—grades, which also reflect school-learned abilities, should provide about as much information as the SCAT, especially at the college level. In view of these considerations, we concur with H. L. Butcher (1972) that additional evidence on the SCAT would be highly desirable. Also, despite its reasonably good correlation with the SAT, we see little advantage of the SCAT over the SAT for predicting college success.

The American College Test

The American College Test (ACT) is another popular and widely used college entrance (aptitude) test. In some states (for instance, Alabama), most students take it. The ACT produces specific content scores and a composite. The content scores are in English, mathematical usage, social studies reading, and natural science reading. In expressing results, the ACT makes use of the Iowa Test of Educational Development (ITED) Scale. Scores on this scale can vary between 1 and 36, with a standard deviation of 5 and a mean of 16 for high-school students and a mean of 19 for college aspirants. Figure 13-6 shows a sample profile report for the ACT.

The ACT compares with the SAT in terms of predicting college GPA alone or in conjunction with high-school GPA. In fact, the correlation between the two tests is quite high—high .80s (Pugh, 1968). However, internal consistency coefficients are not as strong in the ACT, with coefficients in the mid .90s for the composite and in the high .70s to high .80s for the four content scores.

Graduate and Professional School Entrance Tests

If you plan to go to graduate school, then you very likely have to take a graduate school entrance test. The two most widely used are the Graduate Record Examination Aptitude Test and the Miller Analogies Test. Tens of thousands also take entrance tests for professional degree programs such as medical and law school. The Law School Admissions Test (LSAT) serves to illustrate such tests.

Graduate Record Examination Aptitude Test

The Graduate Record Examination Aptitude Test, better known as the GRE, is one of the most commonly used tests for graduate school entrance. Almost

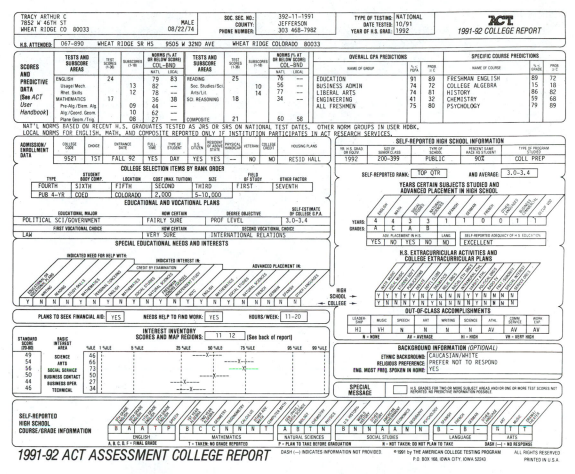

FIGURE 13-6   *A sample student profile from ACT.*

(*Copyright 1991 by The American College Testing Program. All rights reserved. Reproduced with permission.*)

any student who wishes to pursue graduate work in psychology, as well as many other disciplines, will likely have to face the GRE. Offered throughout the year at designated examination centers located mostly at universities and colleges, the GRE purports to measure general scholastic ability. It is most frequently used in conjunction with grade point average, letters of recommendation, and other academic factors in the highly competitive graduate school selection process. The GRE contains a general section that produces verbal (GRE-V), quantitative (GRE-Q), and analytic (GRE-A) scores. In addition to this general test used for all college majors, the GRE contains an advanced section that measures achievement in at least 20 majors, such as psychology, history, and chemistry (see Figures 13-7, 13-8, and 13-9).

With a standard mean score of 500 and a standard deviation of 100, the verbal section covers reasoning, identification of opposites, use of analogies,

FIGURE 13-7

GRE verbal ability sample items.

(GRE test items in Figures 13-7, 13-8, and 13-9 selected from GRE General Test administered December, 1991. Reprinted by permission of Educational Testing Service, the copyright owner.)

Directions: Each sentence below has one or two blanks, each indicating that something has been omitted. Beneath the sentence are five lettered words or sets of words. Choose the word or set of words for each blank that *best* fits the meaning of the sentence as a whole.

1. From observing the —— of those about me during the flag raising, I concluded that patriotism, if not actually on the decline, is at least in a state of ——.

   (A) irreverence..amelioration   (B) absorption..atrophy   (C) lassitude..rampancy
   (D) allegiance..decadence   (E) apathy..dormancy

2. Long before there was a European or American civilization, the Greeks demonstrated the —— of war, fighting chiefly among themselves until their great city-states became the —— of lesser folk.

   (A) imbecility..bane   (B) grandeur..scapegoats   (C) transience..paragons
   (D) futility..prey   (E) profitability..allies

   • • •

Directions: In each of the following questions, a related pair of words or phrases is followed by five lettered pairs of words or phrases. Select the lettered pair that best expresses a relationship similar to that expressed in the original pair.

8. Apprentice:Master::   (A) novice:expert   (B) specimen:scientist
   (C) doctor:psychiatrist   (D) teacher:dean   (E) musician:orchestra

9. Pursuit:Capture::   (A) fight:siege   (B) competition:prize   (C) fugitive:posse
   (D) courtship:ambush   (E) stampede:migration

and paragraph comprehension. The quantitative section covers arithmetic reasoning, algebra, and geometry. However, the normative sample for the GRE is only about one-fifth the size of the SAT sample (about 2000 college seniors tested at 11 colleges in 1952). The psychometric adequacy of the GRE is also less spectacular than that of the SAT, both in the reported coefficients of validity and reliability and in the extensiveness of documentation. Nevertheless, the GRE is a relatively sound instrument.

The stability of the GRE based on Kuder-Richardson and odd-even reliability is adequate, with coefficients only slightly lower than those of the SAT. However, the predictive validity of the GRE is far from convincing. Independent studies of the GRE vary from those that find moderate correlations between the GRE and grade point average to those that find no or even a negative relationship between the two. Although one can say that high GRE scorers tend to complete graduate school more often than low scorers for certain programs, general predictive studies have proved somewhat discouraging.

At this point, those who aspire to enter graduate school might be asking, "With its limitations, why is it that the GRE has such a critical effect on my

Numbers: All numbers used are real numbers.

Figures: Position of points, angles, regions, etc. can be assumed to be in the order shown; and angle measures can be assumed to be positive.

Lines shown as straight can be assumed to be straight.

Figures can be assumed to lie in a plane unless otherwise indicated.

Figures that accompany questions are intended to provide information useful in answering the questions. However, unless a note states that a figure is drawn to scale, you should solve these problems NOT by estimating sizes by sight or by measurement, but by using your knowledge of mathematics (see Example 2 below).

Directions: Each of the questions 1–15 consists of two quantities, one in Column A and one in Column B. You are to compare the two quantities and choose

A if the quantity in Column A is greater;
B if the quantity in Column B is greater;
C if the two quantities are equal;
D if the relationship cannot be determined from the information given.

Note: Since there are only four choices, NEVER MARK (E).

Common Information: In a question, information concerning one or both of the quantities to be compared is centered above the two columns. A symbol that appears in both columns represents the same thing in Column A as it does in Column B.

	Column A	**Column B**	**Sample Answers**
Example 1:	2×6	$2 + 6$	Ⓐ Ⓑ Ⓒ Ⓓ Ⓔ

Examples 2–4 refer to $\triangle PQR$.

	Column A	**Column B**	**Sample Answers**
Example 2:	PN	NQ	Ⓐ Ⓑ Ⓒ Ⓓ Ⓔ (since equal measures cannot be assumed, even though PN and NQ appear equal)
Example 3:	x	y	Ⓐ Ⓑ Ⓒ Ⓓ Ⓔ (since N is between P and Q)

FIGURE 13-9

GRE analytical ability sample items.

Directions: Each question or group of questions is based on a passage or set of conditions. In answering some of the questions, it may be useful to draw a rough diagram. For each question, select the best answer choice given.

Questions 1–3
(1) There are five people standing on a flight of six steps, with no more than one person to a step.
(2) R is two steps lower than J.
(3) L is one step lower than M.
(4) J is as far above R as L is below.
(5) P is one step above R.

1. The order of the people from top to bottom is

   (A) PRJLM   (B) JPRML   (C) LMJPR   (D) MPRJL   (E) MJRPL

2. Where is the empty step?

   (A) It could only be the top step.
   (B) It is between P and J.
   (C) It is between R and J.
   (D) It could be either the top or the bottom step.
   (E) It could be anywhere on the flight of steps.

3. Which condition by itself repeats all the information given by one of the other statements?

   (A) (2)   (B) (3)   (C) (4)   (D) (5)   (E) None of the above

chances for going to graduate school and on my future career?" One answer is that many schools have developed their own norms and psychometric documentation and can use the GRE, either independently or with other sources of data, to predict success in their programs. Furthermore, many graduate selection committees use the GRE broadly, as in requiring a minimum cutoff score to apply. Because more qualified students apply for graduate school than exist available resources to train them and job markets to absorb them, the difficult job of selection must have some base.

Finally, by looking at a GRE score in conjunction with GPA, graduate success can be predicted with greater accuracy than without the GRE (Morrison & Morrison, 1995).

Graduate schools also frequently complain that grades no longer predict scholastic ability well, because of *grade inflation*—the phenomenon of rising average college grades despite declines in average SAT scores. Thus, many people claim that a *B* today is equivalent to a *C* 15 or 20 years ago, and that an *A* today is equivalent to a *B* then. This grade inflation has led to a corresponding restriction in the range of grades. Thus, the median grade point average for applicants to clinical psychological Ph.D. programs can exceed 3.5. Another

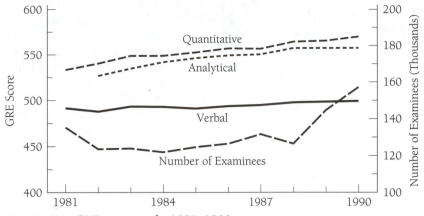

FIGURE 13-10   *GRE score trends, 1981–1990.*

(From "Performance at the Top: From Elementary Through Graduate School," p. 33. Copyright © 1991 by Educational Testing Service. Reprinted by permission of Educational Testing Service, the copyright holder.)

reason for reliance on GRE scores is that the Freedom of Information Act grants students the right to examine their files, including letters of recommendation. Schools argue that professors and others cannot be candid knowing the student may someday read the letter. Thus, as the validity of grades and letters of recommendation becomes more questionable, greater reliance on test scores results. Fair or not, this is the reality. However, students with relatively poor GRE scores need not feel devastated and can take heart in the knowledge that their score does not necessarily predict performance in graduate school.

Nevertheless, the definite trend of GRE scores is upward. As Figure 13-10 illustrates, quantitative scores were up 36 points between 1981 and 1990, from a mean of 534 to a mean of 570. During this same period, analytical scores increased from a mean of 527 to a mean of 557, up 30 points. The verbal mean rose a modest 8 points, from 491 to 499. These increases are particularly impressive because they occurred during a time of a substantial increase in the numbers of students taking the GRE, from 135,339 in 1981 to 157,023 in 1990.

One trend in graduate selection in psychology concerns nontraditional factors such as research experience and publications. Saccuzzo and Schulte (1978), for example, surveyed APA-approved and APA-nonapproved clinical and nonclinical psychology programs. They found that the most important consideration beyond grades and GRE scores was research experience and professional publications. Although apparently rare, research publications can do more to enhance a new application or previously rejected application for graduate study than can retaking the GRE, taking additional courses to improve grades, or even obtaining a master's degree. The message is clear. Students who believe themselves to be more capable than their undergraduate grades and GRE scores indicate simply must demonstrate their ability through research endeavors.

Another issue one must consider is whether or not to study for the GRE. In addition to study books and guides, many courses are offered to those who hope to increase their chances of success (see Anastasi, 1981). Though recognized universities offer some of these courses there are no restrictions on who can offer them or for how much. Students can pay more than $850 for such courses. Unfortunately, no published data support the value of such courses or study guides. Certainly, one should attempt to prepare as much as possible for this important exam; however, many of those who offer study programs have not yet bothered to document their value. Well-established programs such as the Stanley Kaplan and Princeton Review at least help structure one's preparation and provide practice in the actual items. Such programs probably help students most who are poor test takers or fall toward the low end of the scale. The higher one's scores without coaching, the more difficult it is to raise one's score with coaching.

Miller Analogies Test

A second major graduate school entrance test is the Miller Analogies Test (MAT). Like the GRE, the MAT is designed to measure scholastic aptitudes for graduate studies. However, unlike the GRE, the MAT is a strictly verbal test. A 50-minute test, it requires the student to discern logical relationships for 100 varied analogy problems, including the most difficult items found on any test (see Figure 13-11). Knowledge of specific content and a wide vocabulary are extremely useful in this endeavor. However, the most important factors appear to be the ability to see relationships and a knowledge of the various ways analogies can be formed (by sound, number, similarities, differences, and so forth). Used in a variety of specializations and fields, the MAT offers special norms for various fields.

Odd-even reliability data for the MAT are adequate, with coefficients in the high .80s reported in the manual. Unfortunately, as with the GRE, the MAT lacks predictive validity support. Despite a substantial correlation with the GRE (coefficients run in the low .80s), validity coefficients reported in the manual for grades vary considerably from sample to sample and are only modest (median in the high .30s). Generally, the psychometric adequacy of the MAT is reasonable when compared with ability tests in general, but GRE scores and grade point average remain its primary correlates. Furthermore, the MAT does not predict research ability, creativity, and other factors important to graduate school and professional performance. However, as an aid in discriminating among graduate school applications and adults at the highest level of verbal ability, the MAT is an excellent device.

The Law School Admissions Test

The Law School Admissions Test (LSAT) provides a good example of tests for professional degree programs. LSAT problems require almost no specific

FIGURE 13-11

MAT sample items.

Look at the first sample analogy below. **Pain** is the right answer because **pain** is related to PLEASURE as DARK is related to LIGHT. On the **Answer Sheet** mark **c** for the first sample to show that choice **c. pain** is the right answer. The diagram at the right shows you how to mark on your **Answer Sheet.**

SAMPLES

How to Mark on Answer Sheet

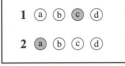

1. LIGHT : DARK :: PLEASURE : (*a.* picnic, *b.* day, *c.* pain, *d.* night)
2. LEAVE : DEPART :: (*a.* stay, *b.* go, *c.* home, *d.* come) : REMAIN
3. STAPLE : (*a.* clamp, *b.* paper, *c.* glue, *d.* food) :: NAIL : WOOD
4. (*a.* 4, *b.* 5, *c.* 7, *d.* 6) : 12 :: 12 : 24

Choose the proper word in the **parentheses** in Sample 2 and mark the corresponding letter in the proper place on **your Answer Sheet**. Do the same thing in the third and fourth samples.

knowledge. Students of any major can take it without facing bias. As with the MAT, some of the problems on the LSAT are among the most difficult one can encounter on a standardization test. The LSAT is taken under extreme time pressure. Some of the sections almost no one is expected to finish.

The LSAT contains three types of problems: Reading Comprehension, Logical Reasoning, and Analytical Reasoning. Reading Comprehension problems are similar to those found on the GRE. The student is given four 450-word passages followed by about seven questions per passage. The content of the passages may be drawn from just about any subject—history, the humanities, the women's movement, African-American literature, and science. Each passage is purposefully chosen to be complicated and densely packed with information. The questions that follow may be long and complicated. Students may be asked what was not covered as well as to draw inferences about what was covered. All of this must be done in 35 minutes.

About half the problems on the LSAT are logical reasoning problems. These provide a test stimulus as short as four lines or as long as half a page and ask for some type of logical deduction. An example of a logical reasoning question, as provided by law services (*LSAT/LSDAS Registration and Information Handbook,* 1994–1995, p. 42. Copyright 1994 Law School Admission Council. Reprinted by permission). is as follows:

> "Electrons orbit around the nucleus of an atom the way the earth orbits around the sun. It is well known that gravity is a major force that determines the orbit of the earth. We may therefore, expect that gravity is the main force that determines the orbit of an electron."
>
> The argument attempts to prove its case by:
>
> **(A)** applying well-known general laws to a specific case
>
> **(B)** appealing to well-known specific cases to prove a general law about them
>
> **(C)** testing the conclusion by a definite experiment
>
> **(D)** appealing to an apparently similar case
>
> **(E)** stating its conclusions without giving any kind of reason to think that it might be true

According to Law Services, this question is a "middle difficulty" item. Approximately 60% of test takers answered it correctly. Approximately 25% incorrectly chose *A* (*LSAT/LSDAS Registration and Information Book,* 1994–1995). A student has about 35 minutes to complete 25 problems such as this. (For an example of an analytical reasoning problem, see Chapter 1.)

Applying for law school is a little less mystical than applying to graduate school. Unlike graduate schools, the weight given to the LSAT score is openly published for each school approved by the American Bar Association. Although many law schools consider special factors such as overcoming hardship, entrance into most approved schools is based almost solely on a weighted sum of GPA and LSAT scores.

The publishers of the LSAT make available every single previously administered test since the format changed in 1991. And, with little variation from year to year, one can know what to expect by examining old tests. For each administration, scores are adjusted according to test difficulty; one can then compare scores from one test to the next. Law Services also provides booklets that analyze questions from past tests and explain various test-taking strategies.

Application to law school is also more structured (and humane) than to psychology Ph.D. programs. One's transcripts are sent to a central location and all GPAs calculated according to a clearly prescribed set of rules. Test scores go to the same location. To apply to a school, one simply has to inform the school, which will request your official GPA and test scores directly from Law Services. Thus, one need not send transcripts all over the country or worry about whether something is lost in the mail. Law Services provides periodic updates to applicants informing them of what has been received and what is missing. Graduate programs in psychology could learn much from such an organized system.

The LSAT is psychometrically sound, with reliability coefficients in the .90s. It predicts first-year GPA in law school. Its content validity is exceptional in that the skills tested on the LSAT resemble the ones needed for success in the first year of law school.

Nonverbal Group Ability Tests

As we have noted, nonverbal tests are needed for evaluating certain individuals. Like their individual test counterparts, nonverbal group tests may be performance tests, which require the subject to do something (draw, solve maze problems), or they may be paper-and-pencil tests, which provide printed nonverbal relationship items and instruct the subject to select the best of two or more multiple-choice responses. Some nonverbal group tests can be administered without the use of language.

Raven Progressive Matrices

The Raven Progressive Matrices (RPM) test is one of the best known and most popular nonverbal group tests. Only the SAT, Wechsler, and Binet tests are referenced more in *The Mental Measurements Yearbook*. One may administer the RPM to groups or individuals, from 5-year-olds to elderly adults. Instructions are simple and, if necessary, the RPM can be administered without the use of language. The RPM consists exclusively of one of the most common types of stimuli in nonverbal tests of any kind—matrices (see Figures 13-12 and 13-13). The 60 matrices of the standard RPM are graded in difficulty. Each contains a logical pattern or design with a missing part. The subject must select the appropriate design from up to eight choices. The test can be used with or without a time limit.

Research supports the RPM as a measure of general intelligence, or Spearman's g factor (S. M. Paul, 1985). In fact, the Raven may be the best single measure of g available, as shown by a multidimensional scaling by Marshalek, Lohman, and Snow (1983). (See Figure 13-14.)

Figure 13-12 is the only illustration of an RPM problem that the test publisher allows to be reproduced. Recently, N. E. Johnson et al. (1993) developed a parallel form for the RPM. Initial studies with the parallel form have revealed

FIGURE 13-12

Sample Progressive Matrices items.

(Reprinted by permission of J. C. Raven, Ltd.)

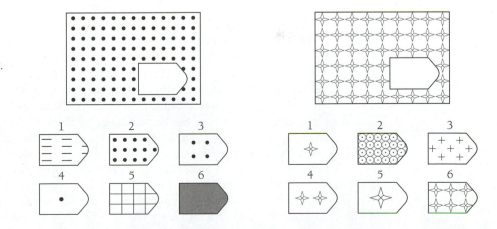

FIGURE 13-13
An advanced problem from the alternate Raven by N. E. Johnson et al., 1993.

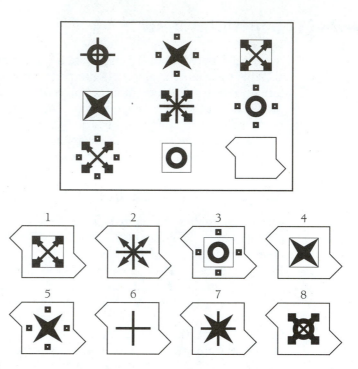

an alternate form reliability coefficient of .90 with comparable internal reliability coefficients between the two versions of the test (.94). Figure 13-13 illustrates one of the more difficult items from the parallel form.

A product of England, the RPM was originally designed to assess military recruits independently of educational factors. For years, the lack of adequate U.S. norms for the RPM and weaknesses in the manual received criticism. In spite of these limitations, the RPM and PM-like tests flourished. One can see the versatility of matrices in their wide application for such groups as young children, the culturally deprived, and the language-handicapped (Saccuzzo, Johnson, & Guertin, 1994). Analysis of available reliability studies shows a rather respectable range of coefficients, from the high .70s to low .90s (see Bortner, 1965). Early studies also revealed a fairly high correlation between the RPM and the Stanford-Binet ($r = .60$) (Keir, 1949), Wechsler performance IQ ($r = .70$), and Wechsler verbal IQ ($r = .58$) (J. C. Hall, 1957).

More recently, the manual for the Raven has been updated along with the publication of an impressive set of norms (Raven, 1986, 1990). With these new norms, one can compare the performance of children from major cities around the world. Thus, a major criticism of the Raven has finally been corrected and in a rather marvelous way.

The Raven appears to minimize the effects of language and culture. For example, whereas Hispanics and African Americans typically score about 15 points lower on the Wechsler and Binet scales than Caucasians (see Chapters 10 and 11), there is only about a seven- or eight-point difference with the

FIGURE 13-14
*Marshalek,
Lohman, and
Snow's radix
analysis of the
Raven.*
(Courtesy of Richard
Snow.)

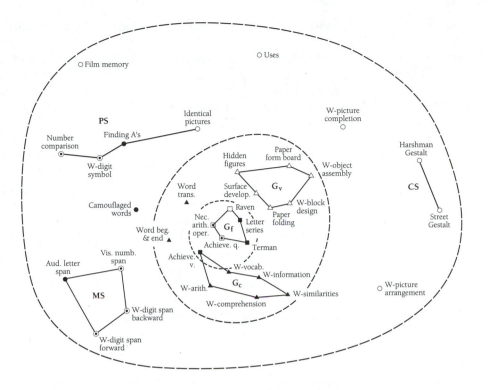

Raven. Thus, the Raven tends to cut in half the selection bias that occurs with the Binet or Wechsler. Consequently, it has great utility for use in selecting disadvantaged African-American and Hispanic children for giftedness (Saccuzzo & Johnson, 1995). Moreover, unlike the Kaufman, which also has a reduced African-American–Caucasian and Hispanic–Caucasian discrepancy (see Chapter 12), the Raven is actually a better measure of general intelligence than the Wechsler scales. With its new worldwide norms and updated test manual, the Raven holds promise as one of the major players in the testing field in the 21st century.

Goodenough-Harris Drawing Test

A remarkable nonverbal intelligence test that can be either group or individually administered is the Goodenough-Harris Drawing Test (G-HDT). The G-HDT is one of the simplest, quickest, easiest to administer, and least expensive of all ability tests. A pencil and white unlined paper are the only needed materials. The subject is instructed to draw a picture of a whole man and to do the best job possible. The G-HDT was standardized by determining those characteristics of human figure drawings that differentiated subjects in various age groups. More than 70 scoreable items were discerned. Subjects get credit for each item included in their drawings. As a rule, each detail is given one point. For example, if only a head is included with no facial features, then the subject receives only one point. Points are added for additional details, such as facial features and clothing.

The G-HDT was originally standardized in 1926 and restandardized in 1963 (D. B. Harris, 1963). Scoring of the G-HDT follows the principle of age differentiation—older children tend to get more points because of the greater accuracy and detail of their drawings. Thus, one can determine mental ages by comparing scores with those of the normative sample. Raw scores can be converted to standard scores with a mean of 100 and a standard deviation of 15. Split-half, test-retest, and interscorer reliability coefficients are good, with ranges in the high .60s to low .90s for both old and revised forms (J. A. Dunn, 1972). Scores begin leveling off at about age 14 or 15 (Anastasi, 1972b), so the use of the G-HDT is restricted primarily to children, working best with younger children (L. H. Scott, 1981). Correlations with the Stanford-Binet (Form L-M) have ranged from .36 to .74 (J. A. Dunn, 1972).

Because of their ease of administration and short administration time, the G-HDT and other human-figure drawing tests are used extensively in test batteries (Lubin, Wallis, and Paine, 1971). Relatively recent representative norms and good validity documentation allow the examiner to obtain a quick rough estimate of a child's intelligence. However, the G-HDT is most appropriately used in conjunction with other sources of information in a battery of tests; results based on G-HDT data alone can be quite misleading.

IPAT Culture Fair Intelligence Test

All cultures tend to reinforce certain skills and activities at the expense of others. One purpose of nonverbal and performance tests is to remove factors related to cultural influences so that one can measure pure intelligence—independent of learning, culture, and the like. Experience and empirical research have shown that such a test has yet to be developed (see Olmedo, 1981). Indeed, many doubt whether such an accomplishment lies within the realm of possibility (Tannenbaum, 1968), although the Raven probably comes as close to this goal as any test.

The IPAT Culture Fair Intelligence Test was designed to eliminate language influences in an ability test and to provide an estimate of intelligence relatively free of cultural influence. Although this test succeeds no more in this regard than any other such attempt, the popularity of the Culture Fair Intelligence Test reflects the strong desire among users for a test that reduces cultural factors as much as possible.

Constructed in the 1940s under the direction of R. B. Cattell, the Culture Fair Intelligence Test is a paper-and-pencil procedure that covers three levels (ages 4–8 and mentally defective adults, ages 8–12 and randomly selected adults, and high-school age and superior adults). Two parallel forms are available.

Standardization varies according to age level. Kuder-Richardson reliabilities are only in the .70s, with substantially lower test-retest coefficients. The test has been correlated with a wide variety of other tests with mixed results. Correlations with the Wechsler and Binet tests are quite good, with a range of .56 to .85 (Tannenbaum, 1968). Also, normative data from Western European countries, the United States, and Australia are comparable. Thus, if one wishes to estimate intelligence in a Western-European or Australian individual, the Culture Fair Intelligence Test is probably the instrument of choice. However, the norms are becoming outdated and more work is needed if the Culture Fair Test is to compete with the Raven.

Group Tests for Specific Purposes

An almost uncountable number of group tests serve an endless variety of purposes. In addition to group tests used to assess intelligence, academic aptitude, and factors relevant to personnel and occupation selection, tests for specific populations abound. The Black Intelligence Test of Cultural Homogeneity (BITCH), for example, is designed to be a culture-fair intelligence test for blacks (see Chapter 20). The Barranquilla Rapid Survey Intelligence Test (BRSI) purports to measure intelligence in Spanish-speaking people. Inasmuch as intelligence tests for specific groups are new and poorly documented, we mention them here only to make you aware of the richness and variety of available tests.

Tests for Use in Industry: Wonderlic Personnel Test

Business and industry make extensive use of tests, especially as an aid in making decisions concerning employment, placement, and promotion. One such test widely used is the Wonderlic Personnel Test (WPT). Based on a popular instrument, the Otis Self-Administering Tests of Mental Ability, the WPT is a quick (12-minute) test of mental ability in adults. Normative data are available on more than 50,000 adults 20 to 65 years old. Five forms, whose intercorrelations range from .82 to .94, are available. Odd-even reliability coefficients are also excellent, with a range of .88 to .94 reported in the manual. The main drawback of the WPT is its validity documentation, although available studies tend to support it (Dodrill & Warner, 1988; Rosenstein & Glickman, 1994). Moreover, the WPT is a quick, stable, paper-and-pencil intelligence test with extensive norms. Widely used for employee-related decisions in industry, it has its greatest value when local validity data are available. In the absence of local data, test scores must be interpreted with some caution. Figure 13-15 shows a sample question from the Wonderlic.

Tests for Assessing Occupational Aptitude

The number and variety of group ability tests for measuring aptitude for various occupations are staggering. The General Aptitude Test Battery (GATB), for

FIGURE 13-15
Sample questions from the Wonderlic.

Sample Questions

Look at the row of numbers below. What number should come next?

8   4   2   1   1/2   1/4   ?

Assume the first 2 statements are true. Is the final one: (1) true, (2) false, (3) not certain?
The boy plays baseball. All baseball players wear hats. The boy wears a hat.

One of the numbered figures in the following drawing is most different from the others. What is the number in that figure?

A train travels 20 feet in 1/5 second. At this same speed, how many feet will it travel in three seconds?

How many of the six pairs of items listed below are exact duplicates?

3421	1243
21212	21212
558956	558956
10120210	10120210
612986896	612986896
356471201	356571201

The hours of daylight and darkness in SEPTEMBER are nearest equal to the hours of daylight and darkness in
(1) June   (2) March   (3) May   (4) November

example, is a reading ability test that purportedly measures aptitude for a variety of occupations.

The U.S. Employment Service developed the GATB for use in making employment decisions in government agencies. It attempts to measure a wide range of aptitudes, from general intelligence (g) through manual dexterity. The GATB also produces scores for motor coordination, form perception (awareness of relevant details and ability to compare and discriminate various shapes), and clerical perception (for example, the ability to proofread). Scores are also available for verbal, numerical, and spatial aptitudes.

The GATB was originally standardized in 1952 on a sample of 4000 people believed to represent the working population of the United States in 1940.

Stratified according to gender, education, occupation, and geographic location, the sample ranged in age from 18 to 54. The mean education level of the sample of 11.0 years reveals that the GATB is most appropriate for those who have not graduated from college. Moreover, with rapidly changing times and the advent of high technology, the GATB may be out of date (see, for example, Avolio & Waldman, 1990; Vandevijver & Harsveld, 1994).

The GATB has engendered considerable controversy because it used within-group norming prior to the passage of the Civil Rights Act of 1991. In within-group norming, individuals are compared with others within a specific subgroup. For example, women may be compared with other women; African Americans only with other African Americans. Such norming practices were justified on the basis of fairness. If men consistently outperform women on a particular test, then, given an equal number of men and women applying for a job, more men will be selected. However, the Civil Rights Act of 1991 outlawed within-group norming, arguing that such norming was reverse discrimination (see D. C. Brown, 1994). Today, any kind of score adjustments through within-group norming in employment practices are strictly forbidden by law. (For more on these issues, see Chapters 20 and 21.)

To measure potential ability (aptitude) for specific vocations, one can choose from a number of fine tests. The Differential Aptitude Test (DAT) is especially useful in assessing clerical competence, such as speed, accuracy, and grammar. The Bennett Mechanical Comprehension Test and the Revised Minnesota Paper Form Board Tests are two popular measures of mechanical ability. The Accounting Orientation Test has shown some promise in measuring accounting skills. To assess business skills and readiness for graduate study in business, one can use the Admission Test for Graduate Study in Business. Special ability tests also exist for advanced study in dentistry (for example, the Dental Admission Testing Program) and medicine (for example, the Medical College Admission Test).

Armed Services Vocational Aptitude Battery

Designed for the Department of Defense, the Armed Services Vocational Aptitude Battery (ASVAB) is administered to more than 1.3 million students each year. A multiple aptitude battery, the ASVAB was designed for students in grades 11 and 12 and in postsecondary schools. The test yields scores used in both educational and military settings. In the latter, ASVAB results can help identify students who potentially qualify for entry into the military and can recommend assignment to various military occupational training programs.

The ASVAB consists of ten subtests: general science, arithmetic reasoning, word knowledge, paragraph comprehension, numeral operations, coding speed, auto and shop information, mathematics knowledge, mechanical comprehension, and electronics information. These subtests are grouped into various composites, including three academic composites—academic ability, verbal, and math; four occupational composites—mechanical and crafts, business and clerical, electronics and electrical, and health and social; and an overall composite reflecting general ability.

The psychometric characteristics of the ASVAB are excellent (Ree & Carretta, 1994, 1995). The most recent form of the test was normed on a nationally representative group of nearly 12,000 men and women between the ages of 16 and 23 who took the ASVAB-8a between July and October 1980.

African Americans, Hispanics, and economically disadvantaged whites were oversampled and then weighted to represent the national population distribution for all groups. Reliability coefficients for composite scores based on the Kuder-Richardson formula (KR_{20}) are excellent, ranging from .84 to .92 for women and .88 to .95 for men. The test manual and supporting documents strongly support the ASVAB as a valid predictor of performance during training for a variety of military and civilian occupations.

Recently, the military has been involved in presenting the ASVAB via microcomputer rather than in the traditional paper-and-pencil format. Through this new computerized format, subjects can be tested adaptively, meaning that the questions given each person can be based on his or her unique ability. Briefly, adaptive testing of ability involves presenting an item of a known level of difficulty and then presenting either a more difficult or a less difficult item, depending on whether the subject is correct. The procedure cuts testing time almost in half and is far less fatiguing than the complete test. Preliminary results have supported computerized adaptive testing in U.S. Army recruiting (W. A. Sands & Gade, 1983). By the 21st century, this format may become a normal part of the military testing procedure.

Summary

Group ability tests are available for just about any purpose. There appears to be no end to the construction of this type of test. Relative ease in scoring and administration gives group ability tests a major advantage over individual tests. In many cases, the results from group tests are as stable and valid as those from individual tests. However, low scores, wide discrepancies between two group-test results, or wide discrepancies between a group test result and some other indicator such as grades should be a reason for exercising caution in interpreting results. When in doubt, users of group ability tests should refer the problem to a competent professional who can administer an individual ability test.

The public school system makes the most extensive use of group ability tests. Indeed, many sound tests exist for all levels, from kindergarten through 12th grade. College and graduate school entrance tests also account for a large proportion of the group ability tests used in the United States.

In addition to being used in the educational system, a considerable number of group ability tests play an important role in personnel decisions. Some ability tests have been developed for personnel selection in business and industry. Other group ability tests can help vocational counselors assess ability for certain occupations. Still other group ability tests measure aptitude for advanced or professional training. In viewing group ability tests, one gets the impression that there is almost no limit to the scope and applicability of psychological tests.

CHAPTER 14

Tests for Choosing Careers

LEARNING OBJECTIVES

When you have completed this chapter, you should be able to:

□ Describe the use of the criterion-keying method in the development of the SVIB

□ List some of the criticisms of the SVIB

□ Describe how the SCII and the CISS improved on the SVIB

□ Describe how the KOIS differs from the SVIB, the SCII, and the CISS

□ Outline some of the controversial issues in interest measurement

□ Compare the approaches to career placement taken by Osipow, Super, and Roe

□ State why one should study the characteristics of work environments

□ Discuss several ways work environment can affect behavior

□ List several methods of job analysis

□ Describe the template-matching method of assessment

At age 35, Harry found himself faced with a dilemma. He had studied hard for many years to become a dentist, but what he had suspected for many years was becoming obvious: He really did not like dentistry. Although Harry had chosen this occupation, he had not considered dentistry in detail before making a commitment to the field.

Harry could trace his interest in becoming a dentist to an experience he had during his childhood. As a young boy, he liked to play golf. While on the course one day, Harry met a dentist who explained that the practice of dentistry was lucrative but still allowed practitioners enough time to play golf and engage in other activities. Harry was a good student, and the encounter with the golfer-dentist made him think that dentistry would afford him the ideal lifestyle. Harry liked his science classes when he entered college, and he continued to be an outstanding student. After four years at a state university, he was accepted by a good dental school.

In dental school, Harry began to question his career choice. Two things were apparent by the end of his third year. First, he did not really enjoy doing dental work. He found himself uneasy when his patients fussed in the chair, and he disliked subjecting people to the discomfort associated with some dental procedures. Second, Harry discovered that he did not share many interests with other people in the field of dentistry.

After completing dental school, Harry did a brief tour of duty in the Air Force as a dentist. When he left the service, he decided he wanted to get away from dentistry for a while and enrolled in art school. However, despite his dislike for dentistry, he returned to the practice because of the large personal and financial investment he had already made in the profession. Dentistry paid well, and retraining in a field of more interest to him would be difficult and costly. During the ten years following dental school, Harry quit and reentered his dental practice on three separate occasions. Throughout the entire experience, he remained unhappy with his choice of profession.

Although Harry is not the dentist's original name, this story is true, and it recounts the lives of many people in many careers who feel they have made the wrong career choice. Some of the misery that talented people like Harry experience could be avoided with proper career counseling and guidance. In this chapter, we examine the contribution of psychological tests to the selection of and preparation for a career.

The term *career* denotes adventure to many people. As a noun it means swift course, and as a verb, it means to go swiftly or wildly. The Latin root is *carrus,* "chariot." Thus, the term for today's rat race has its roots in the exciting Roman races (Super & Hall, 1978). Careers can indeed be exciting and the essence of life if they are properly selected. They can also lead to misery if not carefully chosen. Psychological tests help one select the right career. The first step in the identification of an appropriate career path is the evaluation of interests.

Measuring Interests

If you want to enter an appropriate career, you must identify your interests. Some people need little help finding work that interests them; others can benefit from the guidance given by a psychological test. In the more than 75 years since the introduction of interest inventories, millions of people have received feedback about their own interests to help them make wise career choices.

The first interest inventory, introduced in 1921, and was called the Carnegie Interest Inventory. When *The Mental Measurements Yearbook* was first published in 1939, it discussed 15 different interest measures (Datta, 1975). The two most widely used interest tests were introduced relatively early: the Strong Vocational Interest Blank in 1927 and the Kuder Preference Survey in 1939. Today there are more than 80 interest inventories in use; however, the Strong (which has now evolved into the Campbell Interest and Skill Survey) remains the most widely used test in research and practice.

The Strong Vocational Interest Blank

Shortly after World War I, E. K. Strong, Jr., and some of his colleagues began to examine the activities that members of different professions liked and disliked. They came to realize that people in different professional groups had different patterns of interests. To some extent, one might expect this, because people tend to choose lines of work that interest them. One might expect carpenters to like woodworking, and painting might interest an artist more than a salesperson. However, Strong and his colleagues also found that people in the same line of work had similar hobbies, liked the same types of entertainment, and read the same sort of books and magazines.

With this research as a base, Strong set out to develop a test that would match the interests of a subject to the interests and values of a criterion group of people who were happy in the careers they had chosen. This procedure is called *criterion keying,* or the *criterion-group approach* (see Chapter 15). The test created with this method was called the Strong Vocational Interest Blank (SVIB).

In the early studies, groups of individuals from many professions and occupations responded to approximately 400 items dealing with likes and dislikes related to these occupations and to leisure activities. The Strong procedure then determined whether the interests of new subjects resembled those of the criterion groups.

In the revised 1966 version of the SVIB, the 399 items were related to 54 occupations for men. A separate form presented 32 different occupations for women. Items in the SVIB were weighted according to how frequently an interest occurred in a particular occupational group as opposed to how frequently it occurred in the general population. Raw scores were converted to standard scores, with a mean of 50 and a standard deviation of 10. Each criterion group used in the construction of the SVIB contained about 300 persons, which made for a good normative sample. Numerous reliability studies produced impressive results, with odd-even and short-term test-retest figures generally running between the low .80s and low .90s. Long-term (20-year) test-retest coefficients ran in the respectable .60s. Validity data indicated that the SVIB predicted job satisfaction well (for example, Strong & Campbell, 1966).

One of the most interesting findings to emerge from the hundreds of published studies using the SVIB is that patterns of interest remain relatively stable over time. Strong made a practice of asking a group of Stanford University students who took the test in the 1930s to take the test again as they grew older. These studies showed that interests remain relatively stable for as long as 22 years. Of course, most people did modify their interests slightly over this period, and a few people made complete turnabouts; nevertheless, the great majority remained consistent.

Studies with the SVIB also showed that interest patterns are fairly well established by age 17. For example, Stanford premed students who eventually became physicians scored high on the physician scale of the SVIB. When recontacted throughout life, they tended to remain high on that scale (Tyler & Walsh, 1979). Other studies showed some instability of interests during adolescence, with the patterns becoming stable by one's senior year of high school (Hansen & Campbell, 1985).

Despite the widespread acceptance and use of the SVIB, disenchantment with the test began to mount in the late 1960s and early 1970s. Critics cited a sex bias in the scales because different tests were used for men and women. Others complained about the lack of theory associated with the test.

The Strong-Campbell Interest Inventory

In 1974, Campbell published a new version of the SVIB, which he called the Strong-Campbell Interest Inventory (SCII). The SCII was Campbell's (1974) response to the shortcomings of the SVIB. Items from both the men's and women's forms of the SVIB were merged into a single form that included scales devoid of sex bias. For example, the scales for waiter and waitress were merged, and items that referred to gender (for example, salesman) were appropriately modified.

The SVIB had been attacked because it lacked a theoretical orientation. In developing the SVIB, Strong had focused on the match between the interests of a subject and those of people who enjoyed working in various fields. However, he shied away from providing a theoretical explanation for why certain types of individuals liked some fields and disliked others. In the SCII, Campbell incorporated J. L. Holland's (1975) theory of vocational choice. After many years of study, Holland postulated that interests express personality and that people can be classified into one or more of six categories according to their interests. These categories are listed in Table 14-1. One detailed study using all 437 occupation titles from the Bureau of the Census demonstrated that Holland's system can better describe work activities, general training

TABLE 14-1

Holland's Six Personality Factors

Factor	Interest Pattern
Realistic	Enjoys technical material and outdoor activities
Investigative	Is interested in science and the process of investigation
Artistic	Enjoys self-expression and being dramatic
Social	Is interested in helping others and in activities involving other people
Enterprising	Is interested in power and political strength
Conventional	Likes to be well organized and has clerical interests

Adapted from J. L. Holland (1985b).

requirements, and occupational rewards than can a variety of competing vocational classification systems (Gottfredson, 1980). Holland's work came to the attention of Campbell because the six personality factors in Holland's theory were quite similar to the patterns of interest that emerged from many years of research with the SVIB. In addition, the factors postulated by Holland could be used for either men or women. Thus, Holland's theory and his six personality factors became incorporated into the SCII (Tyler & Walsh, 1979).

The SCII in its current form is divided into seven parts, summarized in Table 14-2. The test, which still retains the core of the SVIB, now has 325 items, to which a person responds "like," "dislike," or "indifferent."

Various agencies provide automated scoring services for the SCII, and most of them summarize several scores for each profile. The first score is a summary of general themes based on Holland's six personality types (see Table 14-1). For example, the profile might provide information about the general types of activities the person enjoys, the kinds of people the person might work well with, and the most suitable general occupational environment.

TABLE 14-2

Summary of the Seven Parts of the Strong-Campbell Interest Inventory

Section	Name	Number of Items	Examples of Items
1	Occupations	131	Actor/actress, criminal lawyer, freelance writer, office clerk, X-ray technician
2	School subjects	36	Algebra, art, economics, literature, zoology
3	Activities	51	Cooking, taping a sprained ankle, watching an open-heart operation
4	Amusements	39	Fishing, boxing, listening to religious music, skiing, attending lectures
5	Types of people	24	Military officers, ballet dancers, very old people
6	Preference between two activities	30	Being an airline pilot or being an airline ticket agent, taking a chance or playing it safe, reading a book or watching TV
7	Your characteristics	14	Wins friends easily, can prepare successful advertisements, has patience when teaching others

Adapted from Hansen & Campbell (1985).

The second score summary given in a report is for the administrative indices. Of less personal importance to the test taker, these are needed to ensure that errors were not made in the administration, scoring, or processing of the test.

The third set of scores provides a summary of a person's basic interests. For example, they suggest whether a person scored high, low, or about average in preference for science, mechanical activities, and athletics. This information is reported in standardized **T scores** (see Chapter 2). Remember that T scores have a mean of 50 and a standard deviation of 10. Thus, a T score of 60 would be one standard deviation above the mean or in approximately the 84th percentile.

The final set of summary scores given in the SCII profile is for the occupational scales. These scales occupy most of the space on the SCII profile. The profile shows the person's score for each of 124 occupations, which are broken into six general occupational themes. The scoring for the occupational scales differs from that for the general theme and basic interest scales because the occupational scale compares the test taker's score with the scores of people working in the various professions. The general theme and basic interest scales compare the test taker's score with those of people in general. If you took the SCII, for each scale you would be assigned a score indicating the degree of similarity—very dissimilar, dissimilar, average, similar, or very similar—between your interests and the interests of people happy in their chosen occupations. Many of the occupations are divided so that different criterion groups are provided for men and women. For example, if you scored in the "very similar" category for the occupation social worker (for female), this finding would suggest that your interests were close to those of women who had been employed as social workers and had enjoyed the profession.

Evidence suggests that the interests measured by these tests are stable. For example, we tested a 39-year-old woman college professor named Jean A. on the SCII. The test was given twice, separated by 11 years. At the first testing, Jean was a 28-year-old psychology graduate student who had not started her professional career. Table 14-3 compares her SCII profiles at ages 28 and 39. During this 11-year interval, Jean completed her Ph.D., held three different jobs, and had two children. As the table shows, her interests remained remarkably stable.

The last version of the SCII was released in spring 1985. Although the testing materials (that is, test booklets and answer sheets) did not change, the SCII profile was expanded to include 207 occupational scales, 144 of which have been developed since 1977. In the 1985 revision, a national sample represents every occupational criterion group. In addition, special precautions were taken to rule out potential difficulties in interpretation. For example, one criticism of the SCII has been that members of the criterion groups were older than those who would be just entering the work force. In the revised SCII, younger and older members of each criterion group were compared to determine whether the interests and values of the recent entrants to the work force

Theme	Age 28	Age 39
Investigative	58	58
Artistic	51	51
Social	45	46
Enterprising	42	37
Conventional	37	44
Realistic	36	36
Similarity Scores	**Age 28**	**Age 39**
High Similarity		
Physician	58	53
Optometrist	52	47
Psychologist	50	47
College professor	49	50
Low Similarity		
Librarian	32	27
Beautician	28	31
Flight attendant	27	31
Army officer	27	25

differed from those of workers who had been on the job for many years (Hansen & Campbell, 1985).

The Campbell Interest and Skill Survey

The Strong scales have had an interesting and turbulent recent history. David Campbell began working on the Strong Vocational Interest Blank in 1960 when he was a graduate student at the University of Minnesota. When Strong died in 1963, Campbell, then an assistant professor at the University of Minnesota, became the primary representative of the SVIB. Later versions were published under the authorship of Strong and Campbell. The first version of the Strong-Campbell Interest Inventory was published in 1974. Because Strong had been a professor at Stanford University, Stanford and the University of Minnesota became engaged in a legal dispute over ownership. In an out of court settlement in 1988, Stanford and Campbell "got divorced." Stanford received the rights to publish the Strong Interest Inventory while Campbell received the rights to most of the cumulative work. In 1992 Campbell published the Campbell Interest and Skill Survey (CISS) (Campbell, Hyne, & Nilsen, 1992).

The CISS asks respondents to assess their degree of interest in 200 academic and occupational topics. Further, it assesses the degree of skill in 120 specific occupations. The system produces an 11-page profile and a 2-page report summary (see Focused Example 14-1; Campbell, 1995). The CISS ultimately yields a variety of different types of scales. These are summarized in Table 14-4.

Focused Example 14.1

CAMPBELL INTEREST AND SKILL SURVEY INDIVIDUAL PROFILE

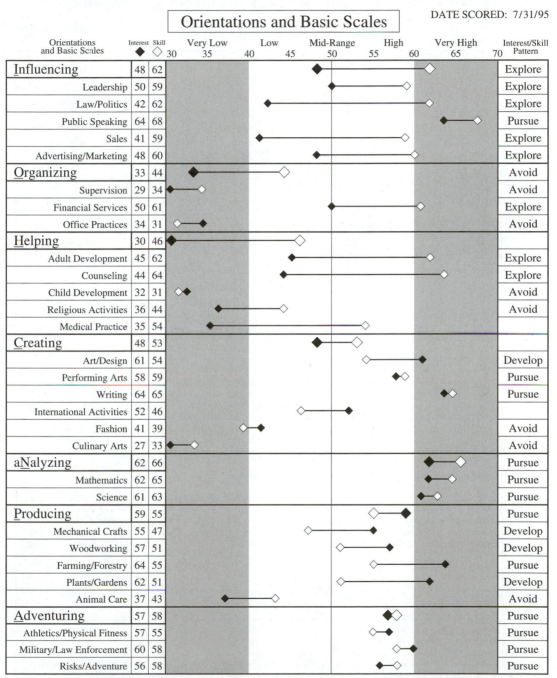

Orientations and Basic Scales

DATE SCORED: 7/31/95

Orientations and Basic Scales	Interest ◆	Skill ◇	Interest/Skill Pattern
Influencing	48	62	Explore
Leadership	50	59	Explore
Law/Politics	42	62	Explore
Public Speaking	64	68	Pursue
Sales	41	59	Explore
Advertising/Marketing	48	60	Explore
Organizing	33	44	Avoid
Supervision	29	34	Avoid
Financial Services	50	61	Explore
Office Practices	34	31	Avoid
Helping	30	46	
Adult Development	45	62	Explore
Counseling	44	64	Explore
Child Development	32	31	Avoid
Religious Activities	36	44	Avoid
Medical Practice	35	54	
Creating	48	53	
Art/Design	61	54	Develop
Performing Arts	58	59	Pursue
Writing	64	65	Pursue
International Activities	52	46	
Fashion	41	39	Avoid
Culinary Arts	27	33	Avoid
aNalyzing	62	66	Pursue
Mathematics	62	65	Pursue
Science	61	63	Pursue
Producing	59	55	Pursue
Mechanical Crafts	55	47	Develop
Woodworking	57	51	Develop
Farming/Forestry	64	55	Pursue
Plants/Gardens	62	51	Develop
Animal Care	37	43	Avoid
Adventuring	57	58	Pursue
Athletics/Physical Fitness	57	55	Pursue
Military/Law Enforcement	60	58	Pursue
Risks/Adventure	56	58	Pursue

Scale ranges: Very Low 30–35, Low 40–45, Mid-Range 50–55, High 55–60, Very High 65–70

From *The Campbell Interest and Skills Survey.* Paper presented at the annual meeting of the American Psychological Association, New York, August 1995. Reprinted by permission of David P. Campbell.

Continued

CAMPBELL INTEREST AND SKILL SURVEY INDIVIDUAL PROFILE

Influencing Orientation

DATE SCORED: 7/31/95

Orientation Scale

	Standard Scores	Very Low 30 35	Low 40 45	Mid-Range 50 55	High 60 65	Very High 70	Interest/Skill Pattern
Influencing	I 48 / S 62		◆		◇		Explore

Basic Interest and Skill Scales

	Standard Scores	Very Low 30 35	Low 40 45	Mid-Range 50 55	High 60 65	Very High 70	Interest/Skill Pattern
Leadership	I 50 / S 59		◆	◇			Explore
Law/ Politics	I 42 / S 62	◆		◇			Explore
Public Speaking	I 64 / S 68			◆ ◇			Pursue
Sales	I 41 / S 59	◆	◇				Explore
Advertising/ Marketing	I 48 / S 60		◆	◇			Explore

Occupational Scales

	Orientation Code	Standard Scores	Very Low 25 30 35	Low 40 45	Mid-Range 50 55	High 60 65	Very High 70 75	Interest/Skill Pattern
Attorney	I	I 48 / S 65		◆		━━━ ◇		Explore
Financial Planner	IO	I 50 / S 66			◆	━━ ◇		Explore
Hotel Manager	IO	I 26 / S 52	◆		◇ ▭	━━━		
Manufacturer's Representative	IO	I 54 / S 60			◆	◇		Explore
Marketing Director	IO	I 48 / S 71		◆		━━ ◇		Explore
Realtor	IO	I 36 / S 69	◆			━━ ◇		Explore
CEO/President	IOA	I 54 / S 64			◆	━━ ◇		Explore
Human Resources Director	IOH	I 53 / S 69			◆	━━ ◇		Explore
School Superintendent	IOH	I 26 / S 62	◆		━━━━	◇		Explore
Advertising Account Executive	IC	I 46 / S 63		◆		◇		Explore
Media Executive	IC	I 42 / S 69		◆	━━━	◇		Explore
Public Relations Director	IC	I 49 / S 63			◆	◇		Explore
Corporate Trainer	ICH	I 66 / S 73		━━		◆ ◇		Pursue

The Influencing Orientation focuses on influencing others through leadership, politics, public speaking, sales, and marketing. Influencers like to make things happen. They are often visible because they tend to take charge of activities that interest them. They typically work in organizations where they are responsible for directing activities, setting policies, and motivating people. Influencers are generally confident of their ability to persuade others and they usually enjoy the give-and-take of debating and negotiating. Typically high-scoring individuals include company presidents, corporate managers, school superintendents, sales representatives, and attorneys.

Your Influencing interest score is mid-range but your skill score is very high. People who have this pattern of scores typically report moderate interest but very substantial confidence in leading, negotiating, marketing, selling, and public speaking.

Explore how your Influencing skills could be transferred to more appealing areas.

Your scores on the Influencing Basic Scales, which provide more detail about your interests and skills in this area, are reported above on the left-hand side of the page. Your scores on the Influencing Occupational Scales, which show how your pattern of interests and skills compares with those of people employed in Influencing occupations, are reported above on the right-hand side of the page. Each occupation has a one-, two-, or three-letter code that indicates its highest Orientation score(s). The more similar the Orientation code is to your highest Orientation scores (which are reported on page 2), the more likely it is that you will find satisfaction working in that occupation.

---

* Standard Scores: I (◆) = Interests; S (◇) = Skills
** Interest/Skill Pattern: Pursue = High Interests, High Skills; Develop = High Interest, Lower Skills; Explore = High Skills, Lower Interests; Avoid = Low Interest, Low Skills
*** Orientation Code: I = Influencing; O = Organizing; H = Helping; C = Creating; N = aNalyzing; P = Producing; A = Adventuring
▭▭▭ Range of middle 50% of people in the occupation: Solid Bar = Interests; Hollow Bar = Skills

CAMPBELL INTEREST AND SKILL SURVEY INDIVIDUAL PROFILE

DATE SCORED: 7/31/95

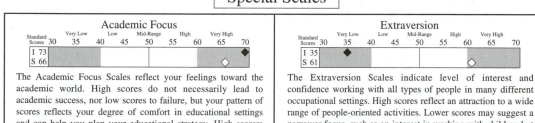

Academic Focus

Standard Scores	30	Very Low 35	40	Low 45	Mid-Range 50	55	High 60	Very High 65	70
I 73									◆
S 66								◇	

The Academic Focus Scales reflect your feelings toward the academic world. High scores do not necessarily lead to academic success, nor low scores to failure, but your pattern of scores reflects your degree of comfort in educational settings and can help you plan your educational strategy. High scorers are attracted to intellectual ideas, academic pursuits, and scientific research. Typical high-scoring individuals include university professors, research scientists, technical writers, and other scholars. People who score low usually see themselves as more action-oriented and practical. Business people, especially those in sales and marketing, tend to score low on the Academic Focus Scales.

Your Academic Focus interest and skill scores are both very high. People who have scores as high as yours typically report very strong interest and very substantial confidence in academic activities, such as studying, conducting research, and writing scientific papers. Your scores suggest that earning an advanced degree would be a rewarding experience for you.

Extraversion

Standard Scores	30	Very Low 35	40	Low 45	Mid-Range 50	55	High 60	Very High 65	70
I 35		◆							
S 61							◇		

The Extraversion Scales indicate level of interest and confidence working with all types of people in many different occupational settings. High scores reflect an attraction to a wide range of people-oriented activities. Lower scores may suggest a narrower focus, such as an interest in working with children but not adults, or confidence in counseling others but not selling. Low scores may indicate a preference for less contact with people on the job.

Occupational Extraverts (such as guidance counselors, hotel managers, corporate trainers, and realtors) are energized by frequent social contact and enjoy working closely with others. People who score low on the Extraversion Scales may prefer more independent work assignments and the opportunity for private time and space. Low-scoring individuals include scientists, skilled craftsworkers, and veterinarians.

Your Extraversion interest score is very low but your skill score is very high. People who have this pattern of scores typically report almost no interest but very substantial confidence in work situations requiring a great deal of personal contact with others. You may want to explore the factors leading to your lower interest in people-oriented activities or perhaps discover new outlets for your Extraversion skills.

Procedural Checks

The Procedural Checks are designed to detect possible problems in the administration, completion, or processing of answer sheets. See the CISS manual for details.

All Procedural Checks are VALID

Interest Items

Response Percentage Check - **Valid**							Inconsistency Check - **Valid**	
Topic	STRONGLY LIKE	Like	slightly like	slightly dislike	Dislike	STRONGLY DISLIKE	# Inconsistent Pairs	0
Occupations	13	26	14	9	15	22		
School Subjects	12	33	23	9	12	12		
Varied Activities	7	21	11	8	17	36	Omitted Items Check - **Valid**	
Overall Percentage	11	26	15	9	15	25	# Omitted Items	0

Skill Items

Response Percentage Check - **Valid**							Inconsistency Check - **Valid**	
	EXPERT	Good	above average	below average	Poor	NONE	# Inconsistent Pairs	0
Varied Activities	16	19	31	11	16	8		
							Omitted Items Check - **Valid**	
							# Omitted Items	0

TABLE 14.4

Summary of the Components of the Campbell Interest and Skill Survey

Orientation Scales

Seven scales describe the test taker's occupational orientation: influencing, organizing, helping, creating, analyzing, producing, and adventuring.

Basic Scales

The basic scales provide an overview for categories of occupations. Examples of basic scales include law/politics, counseling, and mathematics.

Occupational Scales

Sixty occupational scales describe matches with particular occupations, including attorney, engineer, guidance counselor, and math teacher.

Source: Campbell, (1995).

In addition to these specific scales, the CISS offers an academic focus scale that helps test takers understand how comfortable or successful they may be in an academic setting, and an extroversion scale that helps guide them to occupations with the appropriate amount and intensity of interpersonal relations. For each of these scales, an interest level and a skill score are offered.

To a large extent, the CISS is a continuation of the research on the SVIB and the SCII. The CISS is now shorter and more efficient than the older SCII. The scales are standardized with means of 50 and standard deviations of 10. As with the earlier versions, the CISS uses the theoretical structure of John Holland. The manual provides extensive evidence for validity and reliability (Campbell, 1995).

The Kuder Occupational Interest Survey

Although the SCII is probably the most widely used interest inventory today, many other interest inventories compete for large shares of the market. The Kuder Occupational Interest Survey (KOIS) ranks second in popularity. It is one of several interest scales that grew out of the original Kuder Preference Survey published in 1939. Throughout the years, the Kuder has always offered a unique alternative to the SVIB-SCII-CISS.

The KOIS presents the test taker with 100 triads (sets of three) of alternative activities. For each triad, the test taker selects the most preferred and the least preferred alternatives. Scoring of the KOIS scales gives the same information yielded by the earlier Kuder Preference Surveys—data on 10 general occupational interests (for example, outdoor interests versus social service interests). However, in its current form (Kuder, 1979), the KOIS examines the similarity between a test taker's interests and those of people employed in different occupations in a manner very like that of the SCII and CISS. Further, the KOIS has developed separate norms for men and women. The KOIS also has a separate set of scales for college majors. Thus, in addition to suggesting which occupational group might work best with a test taker's interests, the KOIS may also help students choose a major.

To emphasize nontraditional occupations for men and women, a series of new scales have been added to the KOIS. Examples of these new scales are architect (female norms), journalist (female norms), and film/television producer/director (male norms) (Zytowski, 1985).

Although each test taker is evaluated with regard to the norms for many occupational and college major groups, the KOIS provides a summary of an individual's highest scores by signaling them with an asterisk. Table 14-5 shows one of these summaries. The scores are rank-ordered in the table. Those toward the top reflect the vocations in which this test taker showed the highest interest. The higher the score, the greater the similarity between the test taker and people actually engaged in that line of work or enrolled in that college major. A score higher than .45 is typically obtained by about 80% of the people in the actual vocation or college major. Most students will have some scores above this level and may want to pay particular attention to them. For example, the scores in Table 14-5 suggest that the woman has interests that resemble those of women working in professional jobs and in computer programming.

TABLE 14-5

Summary Report for Kuder Occupational Interest Survey

	Report of Scores		Kuder Occupational Interest Survey				Form DD	
Name	**Student One**		**Female**			**99991** **Date**	**01/20/81**	
Occupational Scales	**Norms**		**Occupational Scales**	**Norms**		**College Major**	**Norms**	
	M	**F**	**(Continued)**	**M**	**F**	**Scales**	**M**	**F**
>COMPUTR PROGRAMR		.60*	MATHEMATICIAN	.48*		ENG,HEAT/AIR CON	.43	
>DENTIST		.57*	PSYCH,COUNSELING	.48*		METEOROLOGIST	.43	
SOC WORKR,SCHOOL		.57*	DIETITIAN, ADMIN		.47	>SOC NORKER,GROUP		.42
>ARCHITECT		.56*	CHEMIST	.47*		AUTO SALESPERSON	.42	
>PHYSICIAN		.56*	>LAWYER	.47*		>COUNSELOR, HI SCH	.42	
>FILM/TV PROD/DIR		.55*	>JOURNALIST		.46	ENGINEER, ELEC	.42	
>PHYS THERAPIST		.54*	>SCIENCE TCHR, HS		.46	ENG.MINING/METAL	.42	
ENGINEER		.53	>SOCIAL CASEWORKR		.46	TRAVEL AGENT	.42	
>ACCT.CERT PUBLIC		.52	>INTERIOR DECORAT	.46*		>VETERINARIAN	.42	
>COMPUTR PROGRAMR	.52*		OSTEOPATH	.46*		>XRAY TECHNICIAN	.42	
>FILM/TV PROD/DIR	.52*		PHARMACIST	.46*		STENOGRAPHER		.41
PSYCHIATRIST	.52*		>SCIENCE TCHR, HS	.46*		ENGINEER, CIVIL	.41	
>PSYCH, CLINICAL	.52*		>SOCIAL CASEWORKR	.46*		RADIO STATON MGR	.41	
STATISTICIAN	.52*		>INTERIOR DECORAT		.45	DENTAL ASSISTANT		.40
>AUDIOL/SP PATHOL		.51	>LAWYER		.45	ENGINEER, INDUS	.40	
PSYCHOLOGIST		.51	NUTRITIONIST		.45	>FLORIST	.40	
>PSYCH, CLINICAL		.51	>BANKER		.44	>LIBRARIAN	.40	
>AUDIOL/SP PATHOL	.51*		DIETITIAN, SCHOOL		.44	PLANT NURSRY WKR	.40	
OPTOMETRIST	.51*		HOME EC TCHR COL		.44	>FLORIST		.39
>ARCHITECT	.50*		>INSURANCE AGENT		.44	BUYER	.39	
PEDIATRICIAN	.50*		SOC WORKER,MEDIC		.44	CLOTHIER, RETAIL	.39	
PHOTOGRAPHER	.50*		>XRAY TECHNICIAN		.44	>JOURNALIST	.39	
>PHYS THERAPIST	.50*		>ACCT, CERT PUBLIC	.44		>MATH TCHR,HI SCH	.39	
PODIATRIST	.50*		>BOOKSTOR MANAGER	.44		PERSONNEL MANAGR	.39	
PSYCH,INDUSTRIAL	.50*		ENGINEER, MECH	.44		TV REPAIRER	.39	
ELEM SCHL TCHR	.49*		PHARMACEUT SALES	.44		COUNCELOR,HI SCH		.38
>NURSE	.49*		>PHYSICIAN	.44		SECRETARY		.38
PSYCHOLOGY PROF	.49*		>SOC WORKER,GROUP	.44		FORESTER	.38	
>SOC WORKER,PSYCH	.49*		>BOOKSTORE MANAGER		.43	>LIBRARIAN		.37
OCCUPA THERAPIST		.48	DEAN OF WOMEN		.43	>MATH TCHR,HI SCH		.37
>SOC WORKER,PSYCH		.48	>NURSE		.43	RELIGIOUS ED DIR		.37
>DENTIST	.48*					MINISTER	.37	

Continued

TABLE 14-5

Continued

Occupational Scales	Norms M	Norms F	Occupational Scales (Continued)	Norms M	Norms F	College Major Scales	Norms M	Norms F
REAL ESTATE AGT	.37		>BIOLOGICAL SCI		.64*	NURSING		.51
SCHOOL SUPT	.37		>PSYCHOLOGY		.64*	>ENGLISH	.49	
BEAUTICIAN		.36	HEALTH PROFES		.59*	>HISTORY	.49	
PRIMARY SCH TCHR		.35	>MATHEMATICS		.59*	LAWGRAD SCHOOL	.49	
PRINTER	.35					MILITARY CADET	.49	
HOME DEMONST AGT		.34	>ART AND ART EDUC	.58		>POLITICAL SCI	.48	
>VETERINARIAN		.34	>BIOLOGICAL SCI	.58*		ENGINEERING, CHEM	.47	
>INSURANCE AGENT	.34		>FOREIGN LANGUAGE		.57	ENGINEERING,ELEC	.47	
YMCA SECRETARY	.34		>FOREIGN LANGUAGE	.57*				
>BANKER	.33		>MUSIC & MUSIC ED	.57*		>PHYSICAL EDUC	.47	
>BOOKKEEPER	.33		>PSYCHOLOGY	.57*		BUS ED COMMERC		.46
BANK CLERK		.32	DRAMA		.56	ECONOMICS	.46	
>BOOKKEEPER		.31	>HISTORY		.56	ENGINEERING,MECH	.46	
BLDG CONTRACTOR	.31					ENGINEERING,CIVIL	.44	
COUNTY AGRI AGT	.31		>POLITICAL SCI		.56	BUS ACCT AND FIN	.43	
PLUMBING CONTRAC	.31		PREMED/PHAR/DENT	.56*		BUS & MARKETING	.43	
POSTAL CLERK	.31		>SOCIOLOGY	.56*		BUS MANAGEMENT	.43	
DEPT STORE SALES		.30	>ART AND ART EDUC		.55			
OFFICE CLERK		.30	PHYSICAL SCIENCE	.55*		FORESTRY	.43	
SUPERVSR,INDUSTR	.30		>ENGLISH		.54	ANIMAL HUSBANDRY	.42	
ELECTRICIAN	.29		SOCIAL SCI, GENL		.54	AGRICULTURE	.39	
WELDER	.29		HOME ECON EDUC		.54	TCHG CATH SISTER		.38
BRICKLAYER	.28							
PAINTER, HOUSE	.28		MUSIC & MUSIC ED		.54		V 52	
POLICE OFFICER	.28		>PHYSICAL EDUC		.54			
AUTO MECHANIC	.27		AIR FORCE CADET	.54*		M .42		S .49
FARMER	.27		ARCHITECTURE	.53*				
MACHINIST	.25		>MATHEMATICS	.53*		MBI .30		F .42
PLUMBER	.24		>SOCIOLOGY		.52			
CARPENTER	.22		>ELEMENTARY EDUC	.52*		W .45		D .53
			>ELEMENTARY EDUC		.51			
						WBI .34		MO .40

Scores are reported to you in rank order, on all scales. They show to what extent the choices you marked were like those typical of satisfied people in the occupations and college majors listed. Your top scores are followed by an asterisk (*). (For additional information and for an alphabetical list of scales, see the other side of this report.) > INDICATES TWIN SCALES, WITH SCORES IN M AND F COLUMNS.

From "Report of Scores" in Kuder Occupational Interest Survey, Form DD. © 1979, 1970, 1968, 1965 Science Research Associates, Inc. Reprinted by permission of CTB Macmillan/McGraw-Hill.

Studies show that the psychometric properties of the KOIS are very good. Short-term reliabilities tend to be high (between .80 and .95), and increasing evidence indicates that scores remain stable for as long as 19 years (Zytowski, 1976). One study on the predictive validity of the KOIS showed that half of one group of adults who had taken an early version of the KOIS while they were high-school students were working in fields that the high-school KOIS suggested they enter. Predictive validity for the college major scales was even better. There was closer correspondence between interests and the occupation a person was working in for those who had completed college. A college degree provides more freedom than a high school diploma does in finding personally desirable work (Zytowski, 1976).

Other studies on the KOIS reveal that high-school students reported greater confidence in their knowledge of themselves when they received KOIS results than when they did not. But knowing the results of the KOIS did not make the high-school students more confident or more satisfied with their career plans, except when the students expressed a special interest in learning about the test results (Zytowski, 1977). Even though the KOIS has been less thoroughly studied than the SVIB-SCII, a growing amount of evidence indicates that it may be quite useful for guidance decisions for high-school and college students. New refinements published in 1985 reflect continuing development of this measure (Zytowski, 1992).

The Jackson Vocational Interest Survey

The Jackson Vocational Interest Survey (JVIS), revised in 1995, is used for career education and counseling of high-school and college students. It can also be used to plan careers for adults, including those who want to make mid-life career changes. The JVIS consists of 289 statements describing job-related activities. It takes about 45 minutes to complete, and the scoring yields 34 basic interest scales. The test construction carefully avoided sex bias. The scale employs forced-choice formats in which the respondent must indicate a preference between two equally popular interests.

Studies suggest that the reliability for 10 general occupational themes is about .89 and that the test-retest stability of the 44 basic interest scales ranges from .84 to .88. Validity studies suggest that the JVIS predicts university and academic major more accurately than most other interest inventories. Available in both hand-scored and machine-scored forms, the JVIS offers computer software to administer and score the measure (Jackson & Livesley, 1995).

The Minnesota Vocational Interest Inventory

Some criticize the SCII, CISS, and the KOIS because they emphasize professions that require college and professional training. Although an increasing number of Americans eventually obtain a college degree, most workers still do not graduate from college. The Minnesota Vocational Interest Inventory (MVII) is designed for men who are not oriented toward college and emphasizes skilled and semiskilled trades (Clark, 1961; Clark & Campbell, 1965). Modeled after the SVIB scales, the MVII has nine basic interest areas, including mechanical interests, electronics, and food service, as well as 21 specific occupational scales, including those for plumber, carpenter, and truck driver. The MVII has been used extensively by the military and by guidance programs for individuals not going to college.

The Career Assessment Inventory

A more modern interest inventory for nonprofessionally oriented adults than the MVII is the Career Assessment Inventory (CAI). Developed by

Charles B. Johansson, the CAI is written at the sixth-grade reading level and is designed for the 80% of Americans who have fewer than four years of postsecondary education. The CAI provides information similar to that yielded by the SCII and CISS. Each test taker is evaluated on Holland's six occupational theme scales: realistic, investigative, artistic, social, enterprising, and conventional. The second portion of the CAI report describes basic interests. Each test taker is evaluated in 22 specific areas, including carpentry, business, and food service. The third section of the report is a series of occupational scales. Scores for the 89 occupational scales on the CAI were obtained by using a criterion-keying method. The interests of the test takers are matched to the interests of truck drivers, secretaries, waitresses, and so forth.

Validity and reliability studies reported in the test manual suggest that the CAI has desirable psychometric properties. Scores tend to be quite stable, and people who find employment in occupations for which they have expressed strong interest tend to remain at their jobs and find more satisfaction with work than do those with low scores for those occupations. The test developer also took special pains to make the CAI culturally fair and eliminate sex bias. In many ways, the CAI has become the workingperson's CISS (Johansson, 1976; Johansson & Johansson, 1978).

The Self-Directed Search

Most interest inventories require professional or computer-automated scoring. In addition, they typically require interpretation by a trained counselor. J. L. Holland developed the Self-Directed Search (SDS) to be a self-administered, self-scored, and self-interpreted vocational interest inventory. The SDS attempts to simulate the counseling process by allowing the respondent to list occupational aspirations, indicate occupational preferences in six areas, and rate abilities and skills in these areas. Then the test taker can score his or her own inventory and calculate six summary scores, which he or she can use to obtain codes that reflect the highest areas of interest. The SDS is linked to an occupational finder. In the 1994 edition of the system, the individual can locate over 1300 occupations and match his or her own interest codes to corresponding occupational choices.

The SDS includes 228 items. Six scales with 11 items each describe activities. Another 66 items assess competencies, with six scales of 11 items each. Occupations are evaluated in six scales of 14 items each. Self-estimates are obtained in two sets of six ratings. Studies have demonstrated that respondents accurately score their own tests. Validity studies reflect a moderate, but not high, association between SDS categories and stated vocational aspirations (J. L. Holland, 1985b).

Another approach similar to the self-directed search is to allow subjects to interact with a computer-assisted guidance system. One study analyzed "dialogue" used in interactions with the computer. The analysis suggests that most people do not do comprehensive searches. They seek information on only some alternatives. The larger the number of choices, the smaller the number explored. This is not unexpected, since most people need to simplify information and gather it very selectively (Gati & Tikotzki, 1989).

Despite the common and enthusiastic use of interest inventories, several problems have repeatedly surfaced, including faking, sex bias, and mismatches between abilities and interests.

Eliminating Sex Bias in Interest Measurement

Not all members of society have found the use and development of interest inventories acceptable. In particular, advocates of women's rights justifiably pointed out that the early interest inventories contributed to the discrimination against women (Birk, 1974; Campbell, 1995; Diamond, 1979; Peoples, 1975; Tittle, 1983). The Association for Evaluation in Guidance appointed the Commission on Sex Bias in Measurement, which concluded that interest inventories contributed to the policy of guiding young men and women into sex-typed careers. The interest inventories were much more likely to direct women into their traditional work roles, such as nursing, clerical service, and elementary-school teaching. The SVIB, the major interest inventory at the time of the commission report, had separate forms for men and for women. Careers on the women's form, it was noted, tended to be lower in status and to command lower salaries (Harmon et al., 1973).

In response to these criticisms, the SCII began using the same forms for both men and women. However, in the 1977 SCII manual, Campbell (1977) noted that Strong (who was no longer alive) may have felt that using the same norming tables for both men and women would have harmed the validity of the test. A unisex interest inventory, according to Strong, ignores the social and statistical reality that men and women have different interests. In other words, knowing the sex of the test taker tells us a lot about his or her interests. Nevertheless, the SCII made major efforts to reduce sex bias, and newer measures, such as the CISS (Campbell, 1995) have gone even further.

We must emphasize that most measures have reduced but not eliminated sex bias. Although the basic interest and general theme portions of the SCII and CISS compare a respondent's responses with those from a combined male/female reference group, the occupational scales are normed separately for men and women. Furthermore, the interpretive comments that are provided by most scoring services are geared toward the test taker's gender (Minton & Schneider, 1980). We expect that using the same or different norms for men and women will continue to engender controversy and debate. The current versions of both the CISS and the KOIS reflect the growing concern about sex bias (Campbell, 1995; Hansen & Campbell, 1987).

Aptitudes and Interests

Extensive research on interest inventories reinforces an important but often overlooked point: Interest inventories measure interests; they do not measure the chances that people will succeed in the jobs they find interesting.

The norm groups for the Strong inventories consist of people successful enough in various fields to remain working in them for defined periods. However, degree of success is not defined. If you obtain a high score for a particular occupation, you have interests similar to those of people in that field. Self-rated satisfaction with chosen careers does appear to be higher for people whose interests match those of others working in the field. But repeated studies have emphasized that the chances of succeeding in that job depend on aptitudes and abilities.

Measuring Personal Characteristics for Job Placement

Interests are just one of the many factors to be considered in career planning and placement. Career choices also depend on matches between people and jobs. Employers want to find the right person for the job, and job hunters continually seek that one position that perfectly suits their personal skills and interests. Thus, psychologists and vocational guidance specialists look at job placement from many different perspectives. Some focus on the person and his or her characteristics, others attend the work environment, while still others concentrate on unique combinations of people and situations. To begin, let's look at some of the theories and measurement methods that focus on the person.

Trait Factor Approach: Osipow's Vocational Dimensions

Samuel Osipow has been a leading figure in the field of counseling psychology for many years. Like Holland's method of trait assessment, Osipow's (1983) approach to career guidance is to give extensive tests covering personality, abilities, interests, and personal values to learn as much about a person's traits as possible. This approach involves the administration of an extensive battery of tests, including many we have already covered (Purdue pegboard, see Fleishman & Quaintance, 1984; Seashore Measure of Musical Talents, see Lezak, 1983; SCII; KOIS). The results of this large battery of tests were factor analyzed (see Chapter 3) to find common factors or traits that characterize different occupational groups. People requiring guidance take the battery of tests to learn about their traits. Then the counselor matches their traits to those that characterize the different occupations.

Used extensively in research and practice, Osipow's approach has undoubtedly helped many people find their occupational niches. However, the approach has also come under fire for overemphasizing the person and paying too little attention to the work environment. Furthermore, some critics suggest that Osipow's system focuses too much on a single point in time and does not attend sufficiently to the process of reaching a career decision (Tyler & Walsh, 1979).

The Career Maturity Inventory: Super's Development Theory

Many theories of career choice draw on stage theories from life-span developmental psychology, or the study of personal development throughout the life cycle (Osipow, 1987). Super (1953) proposed that individuals go through five developmental stages that are relevant to their career choices and aspirations. Table 14-6 summarizes these stages. Super believes that people enter careers in order to express themselves. Activities in the world of work are expressions of the worker's self-concept. The developmental stages define the vocational behavior that is expected of an individual during given portions of the life cycle. The correspondence between vocational behavior and the expected behavior for that age period is called *vocational maturity*.

Several tests measure vocational maturity. The best known and most widely used of these is the Vocational Maturity Inventory (VMI), which later became the Career Maturity Inventory (CMI) (Crites, 1973). This test provides scores for vocational maturity, attitude, self-knowledge or vocational competence, choosing a job, problem solving, occupational information, and looking ahead. Most of the psychometric data on the CMI are impressive. In particular, the vocational competence portion is well constructed, and data obtained with it seem to demonstrate the expected properties. For example, high-school students show an expected year-to-year increase in scores on the vocational competence scale. One would expect this result as the students become more vocationally mature (Crites, 1974). Unfortunately, some problems with the CMI still remain; for example, scores suggest that 12th-graders are less vocationally mature than 11th-graders, which is inconsistent with the notion that students should become more vocationally mature with age (Crites, 1973).

The California Occupational Preference Survey: Roe's Career-Choice Theory

In her theory, Roe claims that career choice results from the type of relationship a person has had with his or her family during childhood. After extensive research on the personalities of scientists who had entered different fields of study, Roe concluded that some people are interested primarily in other people, whereas other people are not. Children reared in a warm and accepting

TABLE 14-6

Stages in Super's Developmental Vocational Maturity Model

Stage	Age Range
Crystallization	14–18
Specification	18–21
Implementation	21–24
Stabilization	25–35
Consolidation	35 and up

environment, according to Roe, become people-oriented adults, whereas those exposed to a cold and aloof environment at home become more interested in things than people (Roe & Klos, 1969; Roe & Siegelman, 1964).

Roe's theory identifies person or nonperson orientation as the main factor in career choice. Those who are people oriented seek careers in which they will have contact with others, in such fields as service, the arts, or entertainment. Individuals who are not person oriented may prefer occupations that minimize interpersonal relationships, such as those in science or technology or those involving outdoor activities. In an elaboration of the theory, Roe and Klos (1969) classified occupational roles according to two independent continua. The first had orientation to purposeful communication at one extreme and orientation to resource utilization at the other. The second had orientation to interpersonal relations at one extreme and orientation to natural phenomena at the other. Table 14-7 summarizes the vocations that fall within these two continua. Placement in a particular job within a field depends on an individual's ability and training.

To measure the characteristics described in Roe's theory, Knapp and associates developed the California Occupational Preference Survey (COPS). This test requires respondents to indicate on a four-point scale the degree to which they like or dislike 168 different occupational activities. The COPS gives scores in six fields: aesthetic, business, linguistic, scientific, service, and technical. Scores are also given for professional versus skilled orientation as well as for outdoor versus clerical orientation. (The COPS has been expanded to become the California Preference System Inventory, which includes nine occupational clusters.) Reliabilities for the COPS have been reported to be in the .90s. Normative data have been reported for 512 high-school boys and 589 high-school girls.

Are There Stable Personality Traits?

Imagine that you have the responsibility for hiring employees for a large business, and you want to do everything you can to convince your supervisors that you have done a good job. You want to make decisions about the personalities

TABLE 14-7

Examples of Career Fields for Individuals Rated on Roe's Continua

	High on Orientation to Purposeful Communication	High on Orientation to Resource Utilization
High on Orientation to Interpersonal Relations	Arts and entertainment; uses tastes	Business contacts; uses persuasive techniques
High on Orientation to Natural Phenomena	Science; uses "laws"	Technology; uses mechanics

Adapted from Roe & Klos (1969).

of the people you interview, and you need to communicate this information to the people who will supervise the employees. For example, you might ask whether they have the traits of kindness, honesty, trustworthiness, reliability, and dedication. People often believe knowledge of such personality traits provides them with a convenient way of organizing information about others, for describing how they have behaved in the past and for predicting how they will act in the future (Bradbury & Fincham, 1990; Higgins & Bargh, 1987; E. E. Jones & Nisbett, 1971; Kelly, 1967).

Much of the study of personality has been devoted to creating categories of traits, developing methods for measuring them, and finding out how groups of traits cluster. Indeed, the very concept of personality assumes that the characteristics of a person are stable over time. If Richard is hard working, we expect him to work hard in many different situations. Although we commonly use trait names in this way to describe other people, the evidence that personality characteristics are stable is a little shaky. For example, Mischel (1984) has shown that personality traits are simply not good predictors of how people will behave in particular situations. In a classic, well-argued attack on trait theorists, Mischel (1968) demonstrated that knowing how someone scores on measures of psychological traits sometimes gives little better than chance insight into how the person will act in a given situation. Thus, trait theorists were forced to rethink their assumptions.

Another problem for traditional trait theories arises from research on *attribution theory*. Originally, attribution theory considered only how people make judgments about others; however, research in this area now covers all aspects of how people attempt to understand the causes of events in their lives.

First presented by Heider (1944, 1958), the ideas behind attribution theory became popular in the late 1960s. Attribution theorists suggest that events in a person's environment can be caused by one of three sources: persons, entities (things or some aspect of the environment), and times (situations) (Kelly, 1967). To determine which of these (or which combination) has caused an event, an observer uses three criteria: distinctiveness, consensus, and consistency. For example, if one wants to explain why John is unhappy with his job today, one needs to ask whether it has to do with something that happened on the job this particular day (distinctiveness), whether others in the same situation also dislike the job (consensus), or whether John is unhappy on all workdays (consistency).

Attribution theory is thus less concerned with predicting behavior situations than with studying how individuals make judgments about the causes of behavior. Some researchers have suggested that selecting an explanation for behavior depends on the role played by the person offering the judgment. The person making the judgment acts like a scientist in using all data to come to the best conclusion (Weiner, 1991). When we observe others and make judgments about them, we tend to use dispositional, or trait, explanations; however, we do not use trait explanations for our own behavior (Forsterling, 1988). When we are the actors in a situation, we see our own behavior in terms of the situation. In other words, we describe others in terms of traits, but we explain our own behavior in terms of situations. Why is there a difference between the attributions of actors and observers? E. E. Jones and Nisbett (1971) suggest that we know more about ourselves than about others. By searching our memory, we can remember behaving in many different situations. However, when we make judgments about others, we do not have as much information about how situations caused them to act differently. Yet we may be able to identify with others when they tell us that situations have influenced their behavior. For example, juries may be forgiving of a criminal defendant who claims to have been influenced by a situation and makes a confession (Weiner et al., 1991).

To summarize, Mischel and the attribution theorists feel that psychologists have devoted too much attention to personality traits and not enough attention to situations. Thus, they recommend attention to the effect of situations on behavior.

Measuring Characteristics of the Work Setting

To study the influence of situations, one needs methods to describe and measure them. This section describes these methods.

The Social-Ecology Approach

Ecology is the branch of biology that studies the relationship between living organisms and their environments. Organisms must adapt to the physical environment to survive. Similarly, environments can impact the social lives of their inhabitants. Thus, psychologists have recently come to recognize the importance of studying people in their natural environments and of analyzing the effects of physical environments on social behavior (Wicker, 1979). As Stokols (1978, p. 253) states, "At a time when environmentalists and economists are proclaiming that 'small is beautiful,' the research literature on human behavior in relation to its environmental settings continues to expand at a staggering rate." This field of study is called *environmental psychology*. A similar area, *ecological psychology,* focuses on events that occur in a behavioral setting. We refer to these topics of study together as **social ecology** (Stokols, 1992). One of the most important areas in social ecology is the study of behavioral settings.

Each day, you participate in a variety of behavioral settings. For example, your psychological testing class is one such setting, which might include a lecturer who comes to deliver a prepared talk to a group of students. Let's say the lecturer arrives two or three minutes late, entering a room in which students are enjoying conversation with one another. The room then grows quiet and, as the presentation begins, students focus their attention on the speaker. Physical arrangements in the room facilitate this social interaction. For example, the chairs face the front of the room, where a chalkboard hangs. Barker has made the study of behavioral settings his life's work. For many years, he and his colleagues described the publicly available behavioral settings in two small towns: Oskaloosa, Kansas, and Leyburn, England. Each of these towns included many behavioral settings such as card games, court sessions, and special businesses. Barker's work involved documenting each setting by describing how long interactions lasted, who participated, the genders of the people in the setting, and so on (Barker, 1979; Barker & Schoggen, 1973; Schoggen, 1979; Wicker, 1979).

The study of behavioral settings reveals a great deal about the social rules of the environment. For example, in both Oskaloosa and Leyburn, women spent less time in public behavioral settings than men. The studies also confirmed what many feminists have been saying all along—that women are limited to certain settings. For example, women in both towns were observed most often in such settings as churches and schools. They were more often found in settings that favored social talking than in business and government settings.

Behavioral settings are truly self-regulating ecologies. When a component of the system is missing, the activities in the program are changed to correct the imbalance. For example, if there are no chairs in your psychological testing class, students will probably go out looking for them in order to bring the situation into balance. If someone in the class makes too much noise, social forces will attempt to eliminate the disruption (Wicker, 1979). Thus, to avoid social condemnation, one must act according to the rules for that behavioral setting. A catcall during psychology class might bring you strange and rejecting looks. Yet, in a rock concert, it is perfectly appropriate. Social adjustment requires that one know and follow the rules of many social behavioral settings.

The study of behavioral settings also involves examining the relationship between work satisfaction and the requirements of the job. Wicker and Kirmeyer (1976) used this approach in a study of coping behavior among rangers in Yosemite National Park. During the summer, as the workload for the rangers increases, the rangers feel more challenged and needed on the job and also use more strategies to cope with their jobs. By the end of the summer, when the work load peaks, the challenge of heavy crowds is no longer associated with job satisfaction. Instead, the rangers are less able to cope and they feel physically and emotionally drained. To understand the relationship between work setting and satisfaction, one must consider many aspects of the ecology, including the workload, coping strategies, and the duration of work overload. One must also make a precise description of the work environment.

There are many applications of the social ecology approach in clinical and health psychology. For example, characteristics of the work environment can influence health-damaging behaviors such as smoking and lack of exercise. Restructuring the environment may modify these dangerous behaviors (Johansson et al., 1991). Considerable work has gone into characterizing family environments and the interaction between spouses. The social environment may affect cigarette smoking, diet, and other health behaviors (S. Cohen & Lichtenstein, 1990; Ewart, 1991).

Classifying Environments

How do different environments affect your behavior? Are you able to work better when the sun is out? Do you get more tired and irritable on hot days? Most of social psychology is based on the premise that situations influence behavior. Some of the early work in the field of environmental psychology involved building classification systems for various situations (Holahan, 1986). You might think of this as similar to the work done by many early personality psychologists who built elaborate systems to classify personality types (for example, aggressive, confident). The environmental psychologists built elaborate systems to classify the characteristics of environments that had been shown to affect individual or group behavior.

Table 14-8 shows a classification system created by Moos (1973). It includes six characteristics of environments and gives some examples. Many studies demonstrate that the characteristics of the people in one's environment affect one's behavior. The likelihood that a high-school girl will begin to smoke, for example, can be greatly influenced by the number of other girls who already smoke or who approve of smoking (Pierce et al., 1992). Over the years, Moos and his colleagues have developed many different measures to evaluate the characteristics of environments. A summary of these scales is shown in Table 14-9.

Moos's work on measuring the characteristics of environments demonstrates how personal characteristics of the work environment affect job choice and worker satisfaction. For example, workers are more satisfied with work environments that promote quality interactions between workers and supervisors than they are with environments that keep these relationships more distant. The quality of the relationship between workers and supervisors also

TABLE 14-8

Six Characteristics of Environments

Characteristics	Examples
Ecological dimensions	Architectural design, geographic location, weather conditions
Behavioral settings	Office, home, store
Organizational structure	Percentage of women in the student body, number of people per household, average age of group
Characteristics of inhabitants	Proportion of students who date, drink, or vote
Psychosocial and organizational climate	Work pressure, encouragement of participation, orientation toward helping with personal problems
Functional or reinforcing properties	Is aggression reinforced on the football field; is it reinforced at home?

Adapted from Moos (1973).

TABLE 14-9

Summary of Scales Used to Evaluate Different Environments

Type of Environment	Scale	Reference
Treatment	Ward Atmosphere Scale	Moos (1987d)
	Community-oriented Programs Environment Scale	Moos (1987a)
Institutional	Correctional Institutions Environment Scale	Moos (1987b)
Educational	University Residence Environment Scale	Moos (1987c)
	Classroom Environment Scale	Moos and Truckett (1986)
Community	Work Environment Scale	Moos (1986b)
	Group Environment Scale	Moos (1986a)
	Family Environment Scale	Moos and Moos (1986)

enhances productivity (Moos, 1986c). Some evidence also indicates that workers in supportive work environments will less likely develop disabilities caused by stress on the job than will workers in nonsupportive environments (Holahan & Moos, 1986). A pleasant work environment is also good for business. Bank customers who perceive employees as friendly and supportive tend to stay at their bank more than customers who dislike the bank's social environment (Moos, 1986b).

Lemke and Moos (1986) have expanded the work on characterization of the environment to create a multiphasic environmental assessment procedure (MEAP). One use of this approach is to describe sheltered-care settings, including skilled nursing homes and other housing situations for older adults. This complex approach includes evaluating the settings according to physical and architectural features, policy and program information, resident and staff information, physical attractiveness and other characteristics, and a general environment scale. Each of these features has many subscales. For example, policy and program information includes how selective the home is in admitting new patients, how clearly its policies are specified, how much control residents have over policies, and so on. The resident and staff information includes the ratio of staff members to residents, the resident activity level, and the functional abilities of the residents. Figure 14-1 describes the physical and architectural resources of two nursing homes: Pacific Place and Bella Vista. As the figure shows, the homes are very similar on some variables such as community accessibility and safety features. However, Bella Vista receives a much better score for social recreational activities, whereas Pacific Place receives a better score for orientational aids. Using this sort of information, one can quantitatively measure the characteristics of a work or home environment (Moos & Lemke, 1984).

FIGURE 14-1
*Physical and
architectural
resources profile
for two nursing
homes.*
(From Moos and
Lemke, 1984, p. 22).

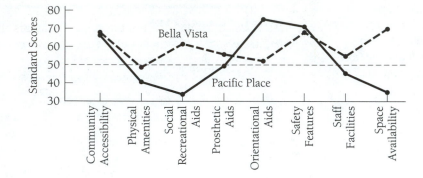

In sum, behavioral settings and social environments are coming to be recognized as important factors in job and personal satisfaction. The study of work environments is a relatively new area that we expect to blossom in the coming decade.

Job Analysis

In addition to classifying work environments, the industrial psychologist must describe and measure characteristics of the job. Employers often want to detail the activities of their workplace to determine what type of personnel is needed or why some employees are unhappy working in the setting. Zedeck and Blood (1974) summarize five basic methods for doing so: checklists, critical incidents, observations, interviews, and questionnaires.

Checklists are used by job analysts to describe the activities and working conditions usually associated with a job title. An example of a checklist for a research assistant in behavioral research is shown in Table 14-10. The first column of the checklist shows the activities associated with the job title, while the other columns list the frequency of occurrence of these activities. The job analyst must simply record how frequently each activity occurs for people in this job classification.

TABLE 14-10

*Job Checklist for
Research
Assistant**

Activity	Frequency of Occurrence Per Hour	Per Day	Per Week	Per Month	Per Year
Photocopying		1			
Typing			2		
Attending meetings				1	
Meeting with subjects			3		
Ordering supplies				1	
Writing reports					1

* The assistant would be expected to photocopy materials once per day, type twice per week, meet with subjects three times per week, and so on.

Some criticize checklists for providing neither an integrated picture of the job situation nor information about specific behaviors. In contrast to Moos's environment scales, checklists do not well predict whether someone will like a particular job environment.

Critical incidents are observable behaviors that differentiate successful from unsuccessful employees. The critical-incident method was developed by J. C. Flanagan (1954). By acquiring specific descriptions of the behaviors of successful employees and their unsuccessful counterparts, one can learn something about the differences between the two groups. For example, a critical incident that might describe a successful employee is "always arrives at meetings on time." A critical incident describing an unsuccessful employee might be "leaves work area disorganized."

Observation is another method for learning about the nature of the job. As we discussed in Chapter 8, information gathered through observational methods can sometimes be biased because people change their behavior when they know they are being watched. To avoid this problem, the participant-observation method is sometimes used. A participant-observer is someone who participates in the job and functions as though he or she were one of the workers.

Interviews can also be used to find out about the job. However, some workers may give an interviewer information that differs from what they would give another employee because they are uncomfortable or fear that what they say will be held against them. Another problem is that an interviewer unfamiliar with the job may not ask the right questions. Some methods that can help one get more information out of an interview were discussed in Chapter 9.

Questionnaires are commonly used to find out about job situations, but we do not recommend using them without special precautions. Many employers favor questionnaires because they are inexpensive. However, the employer may never know whether the respondent understood the questions. Further, the type of information gained is limited to the specific questions. A more serious problem concerns the selective return rate in questionnaire studies. Those employees who feel very favorable or very unfavorable toward the company are the most likely to complete the questionnaire and return it.

The task of constructing methods of job analysis is extremely difficult (Hakel, 1986). Fleishman and Quaintance (1984) reviewed the methodological issues in developing taxonomies for job analysis and found that characterization of jobs is often done poorly. Job analysis faces many of the same challenges as creating alternative tests and performance instruments.

Measuring the Person-Situation Interaction

In this chapter, we have presented two different perspectives First, we reviewed research and methods from counseling psychology that emphasized the importance of persons' characteristics or traits in their career satisfaction. Then we discussed the characteristics of work situations and how they may affect people.

To a growing number of psychologists, whether traits or situations are more important in determining behavior is a "pseudo-question" (Anastasi, 1986; Endler, 1973; McFall & McDonell, 1986; I. G. Sarason, Sarason, & Pierce, 1990). It is meaningless to ask whether trait or situation is more important in explaining behavior because behavior is clearly a joint function of the characteristics of both person and situation. A compromise between trait and situational approaches to personality assessment, this position acknowledges the importance of personality characteristics as well as the role of situations (Endler, 1973; Endler & Hunt, 1968; Endler & Magnusson, 1976; Magnusson & Endler, 1977). The interactionists support their position by reporting the proportion of variance in behavior explained by person, by situation, and by the interaction between person and situation. You might think of this as a pie divided to represent all the different influences on human behavior (see Figure 14-2). The slices represent the proportion of the variation attributable to personality traits, by situational influences, the interaction between the two, and unknown causes. Unique combinations of traits and situations cause this interaction. For example, an interaction might describe how Harry reacts to being a dentist. This cause is different from the characteristics of Harry (in all situations) or the effects of performing the role of a dentist. Careful studies that apply a statistical method known as *analysis of variance* have separated the proportion of variance attributable to each of these factors. As shown in Figure 14-2, the interaction accounts for a larger portion of the variance in behavior than does either the person or the situation (Endler et al., 1991).

As you can see, the interaction position explains only some of the people some of the time (Bem & Allen, 1974). As Figure 14-2 shows, the largest slice of the pie represents *error variance,* the proportion of the total not explained by the three sources of influence. After reviewing many studies on the influences of person and situation, I. G. Sarason, Smith, and Diener (1975) concluded that none of the three sources account for an impressive share of the variation when compared with the amount of variation left unexplained. Although the interaction is a better predictor than either trait or situation, it is only slightly better. Thus, the need persisted for measurement methods that one could use to predict more of the people more of the time.

Bem and Funder (1978) introduced the *Template-Matching Technique,* a system that takes advantage of people's ability to predict their own behavior in particular situations. The system attempts to match personality to a specific template of behavior. For example, consider how to answer the question "Should Tom become an insurance salesperson?" Assuming you know nothing about Tom, perhaps the best way to guide him would be to describe how several hypothetical people might react to working in this job. You might say that shy people may have difficulty approaching new customers or that people with families may not like insurance sales because of the irregular work hours. Tom could then predict his own reaction to the job by matching his characteristics with the set of templates you have provided for him.

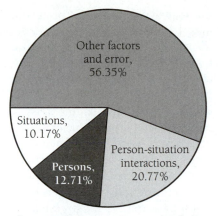

FIGURE 14-2 *Factors influencing behavior. A pie is divided according to the proportion of variation in behavior accounted for by trait, situation, and the interaction between trait and situation. The interaction is greater than either of the other two sources of influence. However, unexplained or error variance is much greater than any other factor.*

(Adapted from data in Bowers, 1973.)

Along the same lines, Bem and Funder (1978, p. 486) proposed that "situations be characterized as sets of template-behavior pairs, each template being a personality description of an idealized type of person expected to behave in a specified way in that setting." The probability that a particular person will behave in a particular way in a situation is a function of the match between his or her characteristics and a template. For example, if Tom's personality characteristics matched the template for those who hated being insurance salespersons, he might be best advised to avoid that career.

Because the template-matching idea arose from research in personality and social psychology, it is not often discussed in other areas of psychology. However, the person-situation interaction resembles what educational psychologists call *the aptitude-treatment interaction* (Snow, 1991). Furthermore, the template-matching idea resembles a popular theory of career choice that J. L. Holland (1985a) proposes. Holland suggests that there are six clusters of personality and interest traits; these are the same clusters represented as the six general themes on the SCII (see Table 14-1). Holland contends that six vocational environments correspond to these traits and that people will be happiest if they can match their traits to the characteristics of the work environment (Holland, 1975; Holland & Gottfredson, 1976). For example, an investigative individual will be most content if he or she can work in an investigative field such as science. The idea of matching traits to situations is intuitively appealing. The concept of "different strokes for different folks" seems like a good way to structure one's search for the right job, the right apartment, or the right psychotherapist. However, there are some problems. First, there are an enormous number of combinations of persons and situations. For example, predicting how 10 personality types will perform in 20 different work environments produces $10 \times 20 = 200$ unique combinations. Most real-life decisions require many more factors. One of the most important problems with the interaction concept is illustrated by research on psychotherapy. Studies have shown that psychotherapeutic effectiveness often falls short of expectations. When challenged by these results, therapists argue that weak results should be expected because therapies must be tailored to the specific personalities of clients. Some people will do well in behavior therapy, whereas others will have better success with a more cognitive approach. However, research has typically failed to correlate personalities with treatments. When these interactions are found, other studies tend not to replicate them (B. Smith & Sechrest, 1991). As a result, researchers must go back to the theoretical drawing board for new insights into the selection of treatment.

One finding supported by research is that people often predict their own behavior better than experts. However, some people tend to be overly positive in their self-evaluations. This self-enhancement can be evaluated by comparing self-ratings with those provided by friends and professionals (Funder, 1993: Funder & West, 1993). Longitudinal studies show that self-enhancers tend to have poor social skills and poor psychological adjustment. Positive mental health may be associated with accurate self appraisal (Colvin et al, 1995).

In general, career satisfaction depends on an appropriate match between person and job. The developing technology for finding job-person matches holds great promise for the field of career counseling and guidance testing.

Summary

In the beginning of this chapter we presented the real-life case of Harry, a dentist who felt he had made the wrong career choice. Harry's problem might have been avoided through proper interest testing and career counseling. Several methods for assessing vocational interests are available. The best known of these was the SVIB, an empirically keyed test that matches the interests of male and female test takers with those of people satisfied with their career choices. Although one of the most widely used tests in the history of psychology, the SVIB has been harshly criticized for its sexist and atheoretical orientation. Newer versions, such as the SCII and the CISS, respond to these criticisms by including male and female keys in the same form and by embracing Holland's theory of occupational themes.

The KOIS is the next most frequently used interest test. In contrast to earlier versions, the present KOIS provides occupational scores similar to those given by the SVIB. A unique feature of the KOIS is that it provides scores for college majors. Other occupational interest measures are also available, including the MVII and the CAI, both designed for use with non-college-oriented individuals.

Several prominent counseling psychologists have proposed that career placement be guided by personality traits. Osipow used multivariate statistics to identify clusters of interests and abilities that characterized people in different occupations. Super and Crites favored a developmental perspective, suggesting that career satisfaction is related to vocational maturity. Roe believed that different approaches to child-rearing produced some individuals who were people oriented and others who were thing oriented. People-oriented individuals find their way into people-oriented careers, and individuals not oriented toward people gain more satisfaction from work that involves less contact with people.

In 1968, Mischel demonstrated that personality measures may not always accurately predict behavior in particular situations. At about the same time, many attribution theorists began demonstrating that people explain the behavior of others by using personality traits; however, when asked about their own behavior, they tend to attribute cause to the situation. These ideas gave rise to the development of measures to assess the characteristics of social environments and work settings.

Out of these developments grew the interactional perspective, which emphasized that all behavior is the product of both personal characteristics and the situation in which the behavior occurs. The interactional perspective gave rise to new assessment techniques such as the Template-Matching Technique, which attempts to predict behavior by finding the optimal match between characteristics of people and aspects of the situation.

CHAPTER 15

Structured Personality Tests

LEARNING OBJECTIVES

When you have completed this chapter, you should be able to:

☐ Identify the major characteristics of a structured personality test

☐ Identify the underlying assumption of the first structured personality test (the Woodworth Personal Data Sheet)

☐ Identify the assumptions of early structured personality tests based on the logical-content strategy

☐ Briefly discuss the strategy used in construction of the MMPI and MMPI-2

☐ Describe the K and F scales on the MMPI and MMPI-2

☐ Identify strengths and weaknesses of the MMPI and MMPI-2

☐ Explain how one uses factor analysis to build structured personality tests

☐ Briefly describe the Millon Clinical Multiaxial Inventory-II (MCMI-II)

☐ Explain the approach to test construction used in the NEO Personality Inventory

☐ Briefly describe the EPPS and explain the meaning of an ipsative score

*I*n his junior year in college, Mike went to the university counseling center for help in finding a direction in life. To aid him in his quest, a psychologist suggested that he respond to a long list of items known as the California Psychological Inventory (CPI). The CPI is a structured personality test that provides a list of statements and asks the subject to respond "True" or "False" to each. It is widely used as a tool in career assessment (Gough, 1995). The statements went something like these: "I like to read mystery stories." "I am usually alert to my environment." "I would rather follow others than be the leader." "I like to solve difficult problems." "My father is a good man." It took Mike about an hour to respond to the 462 items.

A week later, he returned for an interpretation of his test scores. The psychologist told Mike that the test indicated he was highly effective in dealing with other people; his response pattern resembled that produced by individuals who make effective leaders. The CPI also indicated that Mike could control his desires and impulses and express them effectively and appropriately.

How did the psychologist decide that Mike's responses to certain items reflected specific traits and characteristics (such as leadership ability and control of impulses)? Did the interpretations really reflect Mike's characteristics? How stable are the results? Can one expect the CPI to indicate after 10 years that Mike still has leadership qualities? We explore these and other questions in this chapter.

People have developed tests in part to help solve the problems that face modern societies. Tests of mental ability were created to distinguish those with subnormal mental abilities from those with normal abilities in order to enhance the education of both groups. However, there is far more to being human than having normal or subnormal mental capabilities. It is not enough to know that a person is high or low in such factors as speed of calculation, memory, range of knowledge, and abstract thinking. To make full use of information about a person's mental abilities, one must also know how that person uses these abilities. All the mental abilities in the world remain inert in a totally withdrawn individual who sits in the corner of a room all day. But even modest mental abilities can go far in a high-energy individual who relates well to others and is organized, persistent, determined, and motivated. These nonintellective aspects of human behavior, typically distinguished from mental abilities, are called *personality characteristics*.

One can define *personality* as the relatively stable and distinctive patterns of behavior that characterize an individual and his or her reactions to the environment. Structured personality tests attempt to evaluate personality traits, personality types, personality states, and other aspects of personality, such as self-concept. *Personality traits* refer to relatively enduring dispositions—tendencies to act, think, or feel in a certain manner in any given circumstance—that distinguish one person from another. *Personality types* refer to general descriptions of people, such as the avoiding types, whom Adler (1933/1964) described as individuals of low social interest and low activity who cope by avoiding situations. *Personality states* refer to emotional reactions that vary from one situation to another. Finally, *self-concept* refers to a person's self-definition or, according to C. R. Rogers (1959a), an organized and relatively consistent set of assumptions that a person has about himself or herself. In this chapter, we focus on personality traits, with some discussion of personality types and self-concept. In Chapter 18, we shall examine personality states and compare and contrast them with personality traits.

Prior to the development of the first Binet scale, A. Binet had hypothesized that a person's pattern of intellectual functioning might reveal information about personality factors (Binet & Henri, 1895, 1896). Subsequent investigators agreed with Binet's hypothesis (Hart & Spearman, 1912; Terman, 1916; E. L. Thorndike, 1921; Webb, 1951), and the hypothesis continues to find support (Eysenck, 1967; G. H. Frank, 1970, 1976; Wechsler, 1943, 1958, 1981). However, specific tests of human personality were not developed until World War I created a need to distinguish people on the basis of emotional functioning. Thus, the impetus for the development of measures of functioning above and beyond mental abilities came from a need to separate groups on the basis of emotional well-being.

As with tests of mental ability, early developers of personality tests traveled in uncharted territory. Imagine yourself faced with the task of measuring some aspect of human behavior. How would you begin? You could observe and record a person's behavior. This approach, however, would not have helped early investigators, because they had to identify emotionally unstable military recruits. The volume of applicants for military service in the United States during World War I was so great that it became impossible to use the one available method of the time, the psychiatric interview. Psychologists needed a measure of emotional functioning so they could evaluate large numbers of people and screen out those unfit for military service. To meet this need, psychologists used **self-report questionnaires,** which provide a list of statements and require subjects to respond in some way to each, such as marking "True" or "False" to indicate whether the statement applies to them.

The general procedure in which the subject is asked to respond to a written statement is known as the *structured,* or objective, method of personality assessment, as distinguished from the projective method (see Chapter 16). As their name implies, structured measures of personality are characterized by structure and lack of ambiguity. A clear and definite stimulus is provided, and the requirements of the subject are evident and specific. An example of a structured personality test item is "Respond 'yes' or 'no' to the statement 'I am happy.' " In contrast, a projective test item may provide a picture on an inkblot and ask, "What might this be?" In a projective personality test, the stimulus is ambiguous and the subject has few guidelines about what type of response is required.

Strategies of Structured Personality Test Construction

Many approaches to test construction have been tried during the evolution of structured personality tests.

Overview of the Strategies

Like measures of mental ability, personality measures evolved through a number of phases. New features appeared as problems with the old approaches became evident. In the realm of structured personality testing, a number of approaches or strategies have been tried. Psychologists disagree on how these strategies should be classified, what they should be called, and even how many distinctly different strategies exist (Ben-Porath & Butcher, 1991; Gynther & Gynther, 1976). At the broadest level, the strategies are empirical or nonempirical (deductive). One can divide each of these strategies into two substrategies. Empirical strategies may use either the method of criterion groups or the method of factor analysis. Deductive strategies may be of either the logical-content variety or the theoretical variety. We shall discuss these four strategies in the approximate order in which they came to prominence. In addition, we shall discuss procedures that combine two or more strategies. Figure 15-1 provides an overview of the strategies.

Deductive strategies use reason and deductive logic to determine the meaning of a test response; empirical strategies use statistical or experimental methods or both. For the deductive strategies, the logical-content method has designers select items on the basis of simple face validity; in the theoretical approach, test construction is guided by a particular psychological theory. For the empirical strategies, the criterion-group approach has designers choose items to distinguish a group of individuals with certain characteristics, known as the criterion group, from a control group; the factor analytic approach uses the statistical technique of factor analysis to determine the meaning of test items.

Deductive Strategies

The two deductive strategies are the logical-content and theoretical approaches.

Logical-content strategy. The logical-content strategy, as its name implies, uses reason and deductive logic in the development of personality measures. This strategy has also been referred to as the content approach (Maloney & Ward,

FIGURE 15-1
Overview of strategies for structured personality test construction.

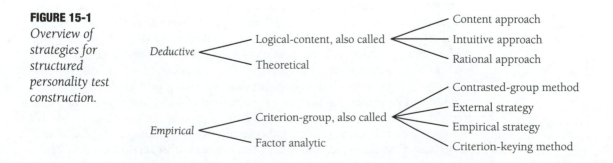

1976), the intuitive approach (Goldberg, 1974), and the rational approach (J. S. Wiggins, 1973). In the most general use of this strategy, the test designer tries to logically deduce the type of content that should measure the characteristic to be assessed. For example, if one wants to measure eating behavior, it makes sense to include statements such as "I frequently eat between meals." Statements that have no direct logical relevance to eating behavior, such as "I enjoy solving complex puzzles," would not be included in tests that use the logical-content strategy. The principal distinguishing characteristic of this strategy is that it assumes that the test item describes the subject's personality and behavior. If a person marks "True" for the statement "I am outgoing," then testers assume that he or she is outgoing. Initial efforts to measure personality used the logical-content approach as the primary strategy.

Theoretical strategy. As its name implies, the theoretical strategy begins with a theory concerning the nature of the particular characteristic to be measured. As in the logical-content approach, an attempt is then made to deduce items. In the theoretical approach, however, items must be consistent with the theory. If the theory hypothesizes that personality can be broken down into six major areas, then developers strive to create items that tap each of these six areas. In addition, theoretical strategies demand that every item in a scale be related to the characteristic being measured. Thus, the theoretical approach attempts to create a homogeneous scale and, toward this end, may use statistical procedures such as item analysis.

Empirical Strategies

Empirical strategies rely on data collection and statistical analyses to determine the meaning of a test response or the nature of personality. These strategies retain the self-report features of the deductive strategies in that subjects are asked to respond to items that describe their own views, opinions, and feelings. However, empirical strategies attempt to use experimental research to determine empirically the meaning of a test response, the major dimensions of personality, or both.

Criterion-group strategy. The criterion-group strategy is sometimes known as the contrasted-group method (Goldberg, 1972b), the external strategy (Goldberg, 1974), or even the empirical strategy (Maloney & Ward, 1976). It begins with a criterion group, or a collection of individuals who share a characteristic, such as aggressiveness or schizophrenia. Test constructors select and administer a group of items to all the people in this criterion group as well as to a control group that represents the general population. They then attempt to locate items that distinguish the criterion and control groups. This procedures always involves both the use of an external criterion—a group known to possess certain characteristics—and contrasting the criterion and control groups. Thus, the terms *contrasted-group* and *external-criterion strategy* are frequently used interchangeably with the term *criterion-group strategy.*

Suppose that a group of aggressive individuals mark "True" to items such as "I am not aggressive," "I like to attend concerts," and "I would rather read than write" significantly more often than individuals in a control group. These items could then be included on an aggression scale. When new subjects endorse a large proportion of items on the aggression scale, one may hypothesize that they are aggressive because they endorsed the same items that distinguished aggressive individuals from control individuals. The content of the items is of little consequence. What matters is that aggressive individuals marked "True" to these items, thereby discriminating the aggressive individuals from the control group. As J. S. Wiggins (1973, p. 394) noted, depressed individuals respond "False" significantly more than controls to the statement "I sometimes tease animals." There is no logical or rational reason for this response. The actual content or face validity of an item in the criterion-group strategy is of little importance. Instead, the approach attempts to determine which items discriminate the criterion and control groups.

Once distinguishing items have been determined for one sample of subjects representing the criterion group, the next step is to cross-validate the scale by checking how well it distinguishes an independent criterion sample—individuals also known to possess the characteristics to be measured—from a control group. If the scale significantly distinguishes the two groups, then it is said to have been *cross-validated.* Once a scale has been developed, data from the normal controls can be used to obtain standard scores. One can then determine how far above or below the mean of the normal group each new subject scores in standardized units. Thus, a subject's score on each scale can be converted to percentiles (see Chapter 2).

After a scale has been constructed and cross-validated, the third step in the criterion approach is to conduct additional research to ascertain empirically what it means when subjects endorse a large number of items on a particular scale (for example, Cripe, Maxwell, & Hill, 1995; Sinnett, Holen, & Albott, 1995). An independent group of people who score two standard deviations above the mean on an aggression scale, for example, may be studied intensely to determine how they describe themselves, how others describe them, the characteristics of their family backgrounds, and so on.

Factor analytic strategy. The factor analytic strategy uses factor analysis to derive empirically the basic dimensions of personality. As you will recall from Chapter 3, factor analysis boils down or reduces data to a small number of descriptive units or dimensions. A test, for example, may have two scales that correlate highly, such as hostility and aggression. This correlation means that the two overlap in what they measure; that is, they share common variance. Both, for example, may be related to paranoid personality, a problem characterized in part by aggression and hostility. The same test may also have two other scales, suspicion and defensiveness, variables also associated with the paranoid personality. These two scales may correlate not only with each other but also with the hostility and aggression scales. Thus, all four scales may share common variance. If one can show that a substantial proportion of the variability in all four scales is related to some common factor, then a factor analyst could argue that the test actually has only one scale, which is related to the paranoid personality.

Factor analysts begin with an empirical database consisting of the inter-correlation of a large number of items or tests. They then factor analyze these intercorrelations, typically to find the minimum number of vectors of common variance that account for as much of the variability in the data as possible. They then attempt to label these factors by ascertaining what the items related to a particular factor have in common.

Criteria Used in Selecting Tests for Discussion

There are far too many structured personality tests to adequately discuss them all in a book devoted exclusively to the subject, let alone in a single chapter. (We prefer the term *tests* for general purposes, although for specific procedures other terms like *inventories, techniques, scales,* and *assessment procedures* are often preferred.) However, all available structured personality tests can be classified according to whether they use one or some combination of the four strategies just discussed: logical-content, theoretical, criterion-group, and factor analytic. We selected the tests included in the discussion that follows because (1) they illustrate each of the major strategies; (2) they are widely used, as indicated by surveys of psychological test usage in the United States (Lubin, Larson, & Matarazzo, 1984; Lubin, Wallis, & Paine, 1971; Polyson, Peterson, & Marshall, 1986); (3) they interest the research community, as determined by publication in major journals; and (4) they show historical value, as determined by the introduction of new concepts in structured personality testing.

The Logical-Content Strategy

We begin our discussion with the first personality test ever developed—the Woodworth Personal Data Sheet. We then present two examples of early logical-content tests. The Mooney Problem Checklist is a relatively recent example of the logical-content approach.

Woodworth Personal Data Sheet

The first personality inventory ever, the Woodworth Personal Data Sheet, was developed during World War I and published in its final form after the war

(Woodworth, 1920). Its purpose was to identify military recruits likely to break down in combat. The final form of the Woodworth contained 116 questions to which the individual responded "Yes" or "No." The items were selected from lists of known symptoms of emotional disorders and from the questions asked by psychiatrists in their screening interviews. In effect, the scale was a paper-and-pencil psychiatric interview. The Woodworth consisted of questions similar to these: "Do you drink a fifth of whiskey a day?" "Do you wet the bed at night?" "Do you frequently daydream?" "Do you usually feel in good health?" "Do you usually sleep soundly at night?" The Woodworth yielded a single score, providing a global measure of functioning. Only those recruits who reported many symptoms received an interview. In this way, the military could concentrate its efforts on the most likely candidates for rejection.

Although its items were selected through the logical-content approach, the Woodworth had two additional features. First, items endorsed by 25% or more of a normal sample in the scored direction were excluded from the test. This technique tended to reduce the number of false positives—that is, subjects identified by the test as risks who would most likely be cleared in an actual interview. Second, only those symptoms that occurred twice as often in a previously diagnosed neurotic group as in normals were included in the first version of the test.

The success of the Woodworth in solving the problem of mass screening stimulated the development of a host of structured tests (inventories) aimed at measuring personality characteristics. These tests borrowed items from each other, particularly the Woodworth, and used a variety of methods for clustering and scoring items. However, all were alike in that they assumed that test items could be taken at face value; that is, they assumed the face validity of a test response. If someone marked "No" to "I wet the bed," for example, it was assumed that they did not wet the bed.

Early Multidimensional Logical-Content Scales

Two of the best-known early tests developed with the logical-content strategy were the Bell Adjustment Inventory and the Bernreuter Personality Inventory. The Bell attempted to evaluate the subject's adjustment in a variety of areas such as home life, social life, and emotional functioning. The Bernreuter could be used for subjects as young as 13 years old and included items related to six personality traits such as introversion, confidence, and sociability. Each was first published in the 1930s and, in contrast to the Woodworth, produced more than one score. These multidimensional procedures laid a foundation for the many modern tests that yield multiple scores rather than a single overall index.

Mooney Problem Checklist

Few modern tests rely extensively on the logical-content method of test construction. Perhaps the most recent important example is the Mooney Problem

Checklist, published in 1950. The Mooney contains a list of problems that recurred in clinical case history data and in the written statements of problems submitted by approximately 4000 high-school students. It resembles the Woodworth in that subjects who check an excessive number of items are considered to have difficulties. The main interpretive procedure is to assume the face validity of a test response. Thus, if a subject checks an item related to finances, testers assume that the person is having financial difficulties.

Criticisms of the Logical-Content Approach

Psychologists involved in the development of the Woodworth and the plethora of subsequent tests satisfied an important need. These tests proved extremely useful as screening devices and methods of obtaining information about a person without an extensive interview. Before long, however, the weaknesses of the logical-content strategy became evident.

In assuming that one can interpret test items at face value, the logical-content strategy also assumes that the subject takes a normal approach to the test, complies with the instructions, reads each item, and answers as honestly as possible. Even if this were all so, subjects might not be able to evaluate their own behavior objectively in the area covered by the test item (for example, "I never drink too much alcohol"). And even if subjects can provide accurate self-evaluation, they still may not interpret the test item in the same way as the test constructor or test user, which is also an implicit assumption of the logical-content strategy. For example, what does "wet the bed" really mean?

A. Ellis (1946) argued that none of these assumptions is necessarily true and that assuming they are is certain to produce errors. Indeed, structured personality tests based on the logic of face validity were so sharply criticized that the entire structured approach to personality was all but discarded (Landis, 1936; Landis, Zubin, & Katz, 1935; O. W. McNemar & Landis, 1935). It was finally rescued by the introduction of a new conceptualization in personality testing, the empirical criterion-group strategy (Dahlstrom, 1969a).

The Criterion-Group Strategy

Just when the development of an adequate structured personality test seemed nothing more than a pipe dream, the Minnesota Multiphasic Personality Inventory (MMPI) introduced a number of innovations in the construction of structured personality tests. The main idea—assume nothing about the meaning of a subject's response to a test item—though not entirely new, was the only possible way of meeting objections to face validity. Since critics had beaten to death the logical-content approach because of its many assumptions, developers of the MMPI argued that the meaning of a test response could be determined only through empirical research. In this section, we discuss the MMPI as well as its most recent offspring, the MMPI-2.

Minnesota Multiphasic Personality Inventory

The Minnesota Multiphasic Personality Inventory (MMPI and MMPI-2) is a true-false self-report questionnaire. Statements are typically of the self-reference type, such as "I like good food" and "I never have trouble falling asleep." Subjects marked "True" or "False" for each statement as it applies to themselves. The heart of the test consists of its validity scales, clinical scales, and content scales. The validity scales provide information concerning the person's approach to testing, such as whether an attempt was made to fake bad by endorsing more items of pathological content than any person's actual problems could justify or whether an attempt was made to fake good by avoiding pathological items. The clinical scales were designed to identify psychological disorders such as depression and schizophrenia. Today, clinicians use formulas, the pattern of scores, codebooks that provide extensive research summaries on the meaning of test scores, and clinical judgment to assess the meaning of the clinical scales. Content scales consist of groups of items empirically related to a specific content area. For example, the anger scale contains references to irritability, hotheadedness, and other symptoms of anger or control problems. Subjects obtain a raw score on each scale based on the number of items they have marked in the scored direction. Raw scores are then converted to *T* scores, with a mean of 50 and a standard deviation of 10. (See Figure 15-2.)

Purpose. Like the Woodworth, the purpose of the MMPI and MMPI-2 is to assist in distinguishing normal from abnormal groups. Specifically, the test was designed to aid in the diagnosis or assessment of the major psychiatric or psychological disorders. For the most part it is still used for this purpose. The MMPI requires at least a sixth-grade reading ability; the MMPI-2 an eighth-grade reading ability. Administrators must take great care to make sure the individual can read at the appropriate level and has an IQ within normal limits (see Focused Example 15-1).

Original development of the scales. Beginning with a pool of 1000 items selected from a wide variety of sources, including case histories, psychological reports, textbooks, and existing tests, the original authors of the test, S. R. Hathaway, a psychologist, and J. C. McKinley, a physician, selected 504 items judged to be relatively independent of one another. The scales were then determined empirically by presenting the items to criterion and control groups.

The criterion groups used to develop the original MMPI consisted of psychiatric inpatients at the University of Minnesota Hospital. These psychiatric patients were divided into eight groups, according to their psychiatric diagnoses. Though the original pool of patients had 800 people, this number was substantially reduced in order to find homogeneous groupings, with sufficient agreement on diagnoses. The final eight criterion groups each consisted of about 50 patients: hypochondriacs—individuals preoccupied with the body and fears of illness; depressed patients; hysterics—primarily individuals who

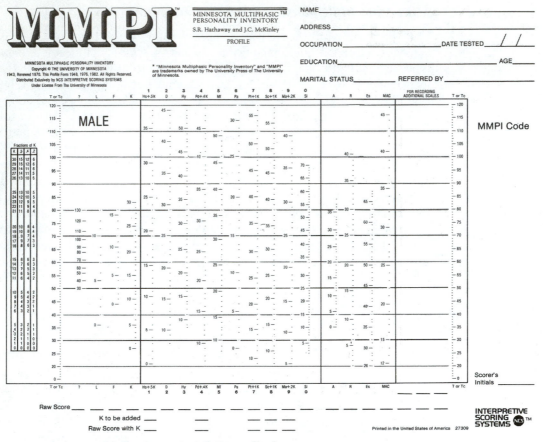

FIGURE 15-2 *An MMPI profile sheet.*
(Reproduced by permission of University of Minnesota Press.)

showed a physical problem with no physical cause, such as physical pain without cause; psychopathic deviates—delinquent, criminal, or antisocial individuals; paranoids—individuals who showed symptoms including poor reality testing (for example, delusions in which they falsely believed that people were plotting against them); psychasthenics—individuals with a neurotic disorder characterized by excessive doubts and unreasonable fears; schizophrenics—individuals with a psychotic disorder involving dramatic symptoms such as hallucinations, and thinking problems such as illogical reasoning; and hypomanics—individuals with a disorder characterized by hyperactivity and irritability. (See Table 15-1.)

Those in the criterion groups were then compared with about 700 controls consisting primarily of relatives and visitors of the patients, excluding mental patients, in the University of Minnesota Hospital. The use of this control group was perhaps the original MMPI's greatest source of criticism. Clearly, there is little basis for calling the relatives of patients in a large city university hospital representative of the general population, although the control group was augmented by other subjects such as a group of recent high-school graduates. The MMPI-2, as you will see, has a large and relatively good representative control sample.

Despite its weakness, the original control group did provide a reference sample. After an item analysis was conducted, items that separated the criterion from the control group were included on one or more of the eight scales. To cross-validate the scales, independent samples of the criterion and control groups were administered the items. To qualify as cross-validated, a scale had to distinguish the criterion group from the control group at the .05 level of significance (i.e., the probability of obtaining differences by chance is less than 5 out of 100).

Focused Example 15.1

READING THE MMPI

In one interesting case that we had the opportunity to observe, a 16-year-old girl was detained by the juvenile court. Her mother had reported her to the police, stating she could not be controlled. A few hours before the girl's preliminary hearing, the judge requested psychological testing to aid in the assessment process. A psychology intern was the only professional staff member available. Though inexperienced with the MMPI, he tried to carry out the judge's orders by administering the test. The intern warned the girl of the validity scales, stating that he could tell if she tried to fake. When presented with the test booklet, the girl groaned and stated, "This test is too hard." The intern assured her not to worry, that there were no right or wrong answers. "Oh, I hope I pass," the girl said. "I'm not good at tests."

She finished moments before the time of her court hearing, after taking more than 3 hours rather than the usual 1–2 hours required to complete the MMPI. The intern immediately scored it and found that she had marked nearly half of the 64 items in the scored direction on the F scale, one of the validity scales containing highly pathological content. Since the average for the general population on this scale is 4 items in the scored direction, with an average of 8 items in the scored direction for adolescents, the girl's endorsement of 30 items clearly indicated she had not taken a normal approach to testing and suggested to the intern that she had faked by deliberately endorsing pathological items to appear disordered.

In court the judge asked the intern what the results showed. "I can't tell," said the intern, "because she tried to fake." "Did you fake?" asked the judge. "No sir," said the girl, "I swear I didn't." The judge told her to go back and take the test again.

Irate, the intern again warned the girl not to fake. "Oh, I hope I pass," she moaned. "Just answer truthfully and you'll pass," said the intern. She completed the test, and the intern immediately scored it. The results were almost identical to those for the previous testing. The intern rushed into the testing room and scolded the girl for faking again. "I knew I'd flunk that test," she said. "It was too hard for me." Finally, it dawned on the intern to ask whether she could read the test. A reading test revealed that she could read at only the fourth-grade level. Most of the items were therefore incomprehensible to her. The embarrassed intern was forced to go back into court and explain what had happened. No doubt he never again administered the MMPI without checking the subject's reading level.

TABLE 15-1

Original Criterion Groups for the MMPI

Hypochondriacs	Patients suffering from overconcern of bodily symptoms; express conflicts through bodily (somatic) symptoms
Depressives	Patients with depressed mood, loss of appetite, loss of interest, suicidal thoughts, and other depressive symptoms
Hysterics	Immature individuals who overdramatize their plight and may exhibit physical symptoms for which no physical cause exists
Psychopathic deviates	Individuals who are antisocial and rebellious, exploit others without remorse or anxiety
Paranoids	Individuals who show extreme suspicions, hypersensitivity, and delusions
Psychasthenics	Individuals plagued by excessive self-doubts, obsessive thoughts, anxiety, and low energy
Schizophrenics	Disorganized, highly disturbed individuals out of contact with reality and having difficulties with communication, interpersonal relations, sensory abnormalities (e.g., hallucinations), or motor abnormalities (e.g., catatonia)
Hypomanics	Individuals in a high-energy, agitated state with poor impulse control, inability to sleep, and poor judgment

In addition to the eight scales just described, two content scales were added: the masculinity-femininity (MF) scale, which contained items differentially endorsed by men and women, and the social-introversion (Si) scale, which was developed by Drake (1946) to identify extroverted individuals. These two scales plus the eight scales already described constitute the original ten clinical scales of the MMPI.

Because the logical-content approach had been criticized for its many assumptions, Hathaway and McKinley developed validity scales to measure test-taking attitude and to assess whether the subject took a normal, honest approach to the test (see Table 15-2). The L, or lie, scale was rationally designed to detect individuals who attempted to present themselves in an overly favorable way.

The K scale served the same purpose but was empirically constructed. In deriving the K scale, Hathaway and McKinley compared the MMPI scores of

TABLE 15-2

Original Validity Scales of the MMPI

Lie scale (L)	Fifteen rationally derived items included in both the MMPI and MMPI-2 designed to evaluate a naive attempt to present oneself in a favorable light. The items reflect personal weaknesses such as "I never lose control of myself when I drive." Most people are willing to admit to these weaknesses. People who score high on this scale are unwilling to acknowledge minor flaws.
Infrequency scale (F)	Of the original 64 items from the MMPI developed to detect deviant response patterns, 60 were retained for the MMPI-2. These are items that are scored infrequently (less than 10%) by the normal population. The F scale contains items like "I am aware of a special presence that others cannot perceive." High scores on the F scale invalidate the profile.
K scale	30 items included on both the MMPI and MMPI-2 that detect attempts to deny problems and present oneself in a favorable light. People who score high on this scale are attempting to project an image of self-control and personal effectiveness. Very high scores on this scale invalidate the profile.

nondisturbed individuals showing normal patterns with the MMPI scores of disturbed individuals who produced normal MMPI patterns, in that they showed no scales that deviated significantly from the mean. The K scale thus attempts to locate those items that distinguished normal from abnormal groups when both groups produced a normal test pattern. It was assumed that pathological groups would produce normal patterns because of defensiveness, a tendency to hide or deny psychological problems, and that this defensiveness could be determined by comparing these individuals to nondisturbed normals.

The F scale, designed to detect individuals who attempted to fake bad, consists of those items endorsed by less than 10% of the control group. Of the 64 items on the F scale, most of which contain pathological content such as "Odd odors come to me at times," the average number of items endorsed in the scored direction is four. Clearly, anyone who marks a lot of these items is taking an unusual approach to the test. Thus, high F scores bring the validity of the whole profile into question.

Finally, although it is referred to as a validity scale, the "cannot say" scale consists simply of the items to which the subject failed to respond either "True" or "False." If as few as 10% of the items are omitted, the entire profile becomes invalid.

Initial interpretations. For all the scales, the control group provided the reference for which standard scores were determined. McCall's *T*, with a mean of 50 and a standard deviation of 10, was used to compute standard scores. Subjects with *T* scores of 50 were thus at the mean of the control sample for any given scale; *T* scores of 70, two standard deviations above the mean, were considered significantly elevated for the MMPI. With the new norms for the MMPI-2, *T* scores of 65 are now considered significant.

The original approach taken to interpret the MMPI was simple and straightforward. Because the scales significantly discriminated the criterion from control groups and withstood the test of cross-validation, most users assumed that individuals with characteristics similar to those of a criterion group would have significant elevation on the appropriate scale. Schizophrenics, for example, would show significant elevation on the schizophrenia scale, hysterics would show elevation on the hysteria scale, and so on. Unfortunately, this turned out to be a false assumption. Experience with the MMPI rapidly revealed that only a relatively small number of disturbed subjects showed elevation on only a single scale. More often, elevation was found in two, three, four, or even all the scales. Thus, a problem had arisen: What did the test mean when someone showed elevation on the hysteria, psychopathic deviate, schizophrenia, and hypomania scales? There is no such thing as a hysterical psychopathic hypomanic schizophrenic!

To deal with multiple-scale elevations, clinicians made use of pattern (configural) analysis, which the test authors had originally suggested (Hathaway & McKinley, 1943). This change led to an avalanche of studies and proposals for identifying clinical groups on the basis of patterns of MMPI scores (Henrichs, 1964; Meehl & Dahlstrom, 1960; Taulbee & Sisson, 1957). However, early investigations (Garfield & Sineps, 1959; Loy, 1959) as well as more recent studies (Fowler & Coyle, 1969; Meikle & Gerritse, 1970) revealed the futility of this approach. Either the rules were so complex that only an extremely small portion of the profiles met the criteria, like the Gilberstadt and Duker (1965) rules, or the rules led to diagnoses that were no more accurate than those made by untrained nonprofessionals (Meehl, 1954, 1956, 1957; Meehl & Rosen, 1955). Led by Meehl, clinicians began to look at the highest two scales.

Meehl's extension of the empirical approach. Pointing to the possible advantages of analyzing the two highest scales, or *two-point code,* Meehl (1951) emphasized the importance of conducting research on individuals who showed specific two-point codes and other configural patterns. This way, developers could empirically determine the meaning of MMPI elevations. Thus, the validity of the MMPI was extended by finding homogeneous profile patterns and determining the characteristics of individuals who show these patterns. In other words, new criterion groups were established, consisting of individuals grouped on the basis of similarities in their MMPI profiles. In this approach, the characteristics of a criterion group, consisting of subjects who showed elevation on two scales (for example, the psychopathic deviate and hypomania scales), could be empirically determined. The difference in approach meant that MMPI configural patterns, rather than psychiatric diagnosis, became the criterion for the selection of homogeneous criterion groups.

Because the original idea of the contrasted-group method was extended by the use of criterion groups, we use the term *criterion-group strategy* rather than *contrasted-group strategy* to describe the MMPI and related tests. The most recent approach does not attempt to distinguish the criterion group from a control group. Instead, the characteristics of the criterion groups are evaluated through empirical means such as peer ratings, physician ratings, and demographic characteristics. The upshot has been numerous studies describing the characteristics of individuals who show specific MMPI patterns.

Along with an empirical approach, Meehl and others (Hathaway, 1947; G. S. Welsh, 1948) began to advocate a change in the names of the scales. Since elevation on the schizophrenia scale did not necessarily mean the person was schizophrenic, the use of such a name was awkward as well as confusing. They therefore suggested that the scales be identified by number rather than name. Table 15-3 lists the scales by their number. Only clinical scales received numbers; validity scales retained their original names.

At this point, MMPI patterns could have a numerical code. For each of the two most commonly used coding systems (Hathaway, 1947; G. S. Welsh, 1948), the clinical scales are listed in rank order from highest *T* score to lowest. A symbol indicates the level of elevation. In Welsh's (1948) system, for example, *T* scores of 90 (four standard deviations above the mean) and greater

TABLE 15-3
Original MMPI Scales

Symbol Currently in Use	Old Name	Number of Items in Scale*	Common Interpretation of Elevation
Validity Scales			
L	Lie scale	15	Naive attempt to fake good
K	K scale	30	Defensiveness
F	F scale	64	Attempt to fake bad
Clinical Scales			
1	Hypochondriasis	33	Physical complaints
2	Depression	60	Depression
3	Hysteria	60	Immaturity
4	Psychopathic deviate	50	Authority conflict
5	Masculinity-femininity	60	Masculine or feminine interests
6	Paranoia	40	Suspicion, hostility
7	Psychasthenia	48	Anxiety
8	Schizophrenia	78	Alienation, withdrawal
9	Hypomania	46	Elated mood, high energy
0	Social Introversion	70	Introversion, shyness

*Because of item overlap, the total number of items here is 654.

Note: The validity scales (L, K, and F) determine the individual's approach to testing (normal or honest, fake bad or fake good). Of the ten clinical scales, two were developed rationally (5 and 0). The remaining eight scales were developed through the criterion-group method. Numerous interpretive hypotheses can be associated with each MMPI scale; however, the meaning of any MMPI scale depends on the characteristics of the subject (age, race, sex, socioeconomic status, education, IQ, and so forth).

are designated by ★; *T* scores between 80 and 89 are designated by ″; *T* scores between 70 and 79, by ′; *T* scores between 60 and 69, by –; and so on for each ten-point interval down to # placed to the right of *T* scores below 29. For example, the code 13★ 2″ 7′ 456890– means that Scales 1 and 3 have *T* scores above 90, Scale 2 above 80, Scale 7 above 70, and the remaining scales between 60 and 69. This pattern is referred to as a one-three two-point pattern or, more simply, a 13 code, based on the two highest scales.

The restandardization: MMPI-2. Beginning in 1982, a major effort was made to update and restandardize the MMPI. The result was the MMPI-2 (J. N. Butcher, Graham, Dahlstrom, et al., 1989). The purpose of the revision was to update and expand the norms; revise items that were out of date, awkward, sexist, or problematic; and broaden the item pool to extend the range of constructs that one could evaluate. At the same time, developers strove to retain all the features of the original MMPI, including the original validity and clinical scales. Finally, they wanted to develop a separate form for adolescents. Each of these goals was accomplished in masterful fashion. (See Figure 15-3.)

All 550 of the original items were retained. Of these, 82 were modified and 154 added. Research presented in the manual (Ben-Porath & Butcher, 1989) has indicated that the item rewording did not alter the psychometric properties of the items.

Profile for Basic Scales

Minnesota Multiphasic Personality Inventory-2
Copyright © by THE REGENTS OF THE UNIVERSITY OF MINNESOTA
1942, 1943 (renewed 1970), 1989. This Profile Form 1989.
All rights reserved. Distributed exclusively by NATIONAL COMPUTER SYSTEMS, INC.
under license from The University of Minnesota.

"MMPI-2" and "Minnesota Multiphasic Personality Inventory-2" are trademarks owned by
The University of Minnesota. Printed in the United States of America.

FIGURE 15-3 *An MMPI-2 profile sheet.*
(*Reproduced by permission of University of Minnesota Press.*)

In developing new norms, the MMPI project committee, which consisted of James Butcher of the University of Minnesota, Grant Dahlstrom of the University of North Carolina, Jack Graham of Kent State University, and Auke Tellegen of the University of Minnesota, selected 2900 subjects from seven geographic areas of the United States: California, Minnesota, North Carolina, Ohio, Pennsylvania, Virginia, and Washington. Of these, 300 were eliminated because of incomplete or invalid profiles, resulting in a final sample of 2600 men and women. Potential subjects for the restandardization were initially identified by telephone and then contacted by letter. Testing centers were set up in major cities to make personal contact and arrange for the testing. The goal was to obtain a sample that reflected the demographics of the 1980 census. However, because participation was completely voluntary, the final sample was more educated and had greater economic means than the general population.

A major feature of the MMPI-2 is the inclusion of additional validity scales. On the original MMPI, all the F items are in the first 370 items and appear on the front of the answer sheet. The MMPI-2 expanded the F scale to the back of the scoring sheet as well. The FB (Back F) score provides a check on validity and cooperation throughout the test and permits a confirmation of F scores obtained in the first half of the test. Two additional validity scales, the Variable Response Inconsistency Scale (VRIN) and the True Response Inconsistency Scale (TRIN), are included to evaluate response styles. VRIN attempts to evaluate random responding. The scale consists of matched pairs of items that have similar content. Each time the pairs are marked in opposite directions, a point is scored on the scale. The TRIN attempts to measure acquiescence—the tendency to agree or mark "True" regardless of content. This scale consists of matched pairs of items with opposite content. For example to receive a point on the TRIN Scale, the person might mark "True" to both "I feel good" and "I feel bad."

The additional 154 items of the MMPI-2 permit the evaluation of a number of content areas (J. N. Butcher, Graham, Williams, et al., 1990). The MMPI-2 contains 15 content scales including HEA (health concerns) and TPA, which evaluates for the hard-driving, irritable, impatient Type A personality. (For more on the Type A personality, see Chapter 18.) Other MMPI-2 content scales include FAM (family problems), which evaluates family disorders and possible child abuse, and WRK (work interference), which examines behaviors or attitudes likely to interfere with work performance.

Psychometric properties. The psychometric properties of the MMPI and MMPI-2 are comparable; the newer version maintains strong continuity with the original. For example, the factor structures of the new and original versions are very similar. Median split-half reliability coefficients for both the original MMPI and the MMPI-2 run in the .70s, with some coefficients as high as .96 but others much lower. Median test-retest coefficients range from the low .50s to the low .90s (median .80s). Although these coefficients are not as solid as those for the major ability tests, such as the Binet and Wechsler, they are as high as or better than those reported in comparable tests. Moreover, when one looks at the basic higher-order factor structure, the MMPI and MMPI-2 are extremely reliable, with coefficients running in the high .90s.

Although the reliability of the MMPI is generally adequate, developers have not yet dealt with some notable problems. For example, because of the way scales were originally constructed, many items are on more than one scale, with some items on as many as six. Scale 8, which has more items than any other scale (78 items), contains only 16 unique items (Dahlstrom, Welsh, & Dahlstrom, 1972, p. 232). This problem of item overlap was not confronted in the MMPI-2 revision because the goal was to retain all the original scales.

Perhaps as a result of item overlap, intercorrelations among the clinical scales are extremely high. For example, Scales 7 and 8 correlate between .64 and .87, depending on the sample studied (J. N. Butcher, Graham, Dahlstrom, et al., 1989; Dahlstrom & Welsh, 1960). This high intercorrelation among the scales has led to a number of factor analytic studies (Block, 1965; Dahlstrom & Welsh, 1960; Dahlstrom, Welsh, & Dahlstrom, 1972, 1975; G. S. Welsh, 1956), which consistently show that two factors account for most of the variance in the original MMPI scales. These factors have been variously labeled throughout the literature (for instance, as negative or positive affectivity). Because of the high intercorrelations among the scales and the results of factor analytic studies, the validity of pattern analysis is questionable.

Another problem with the MMPI and MMPI-2 is the imbalance in the way items are keyed. Many individuals approach structured tests with a **response style,** or bias, which is a tendency to mark an item in a certain way regardless of content. One of these tendencies is **acquiescence,** the tendency to agree with or to endorse an item as true. Given the possibility of response tendencies, one would expect an equal number of items keyed true and keyed false. Not so; all the items on the L scale and 29 of the 30 items on the K scale are keyed false. Scales 7, 8, and 9 are keyed on a 3:1 true-false ratio. The VRIN and TRIN scales of the MMPI-2 allow the examiner to evaluate response tendencies and represent a clear positive step toward overcoming this imbalance.

Major works devoted to the MMPI and MMPI-2 strongly emphasize the importance of taking into account the subjects' demographic characteristics when interpreting profiles (J. N. Butcher, 1990; J. N. Butcher, Graham, Williams et al., 1990; Dahlstrom & Welsh, 1960; Dahlstrom, Welsh, & Dahlstrom, 1972; Graham, 1990; Hathaway & McKinley, 1967). This advice is indeed warranted in that most of the studies have shown that age (J. N. Butcher, Aidwin et al., 1992), gender (J. N. Butcher, Graham, Dahlstrom et al., 1989; J. T. Webb, 1970), race (J. N. Butcher, 1990; Gynther, 1972; M. E. Strauss, Gynther, & Wallhermfechtel, 1974), place of residence (Erdberg, 1969), and other demographic factors such as intelligence, education, and socioeconomic status (J. N. Butcher, 1990; J. N. Butcher, Graham, Williams et al., 1990; Gynther & Shimkunas, 1965; Thumin, 1969) are all related to the MMPI and MMPI-2 scales. This overwhelming evidence supporting the covariation between demographic factors and the meaning of MMPI and MMPI-2 scores clearly shows that two exact profile patterns can have quite different meanings, depending on the demographic characteristics of each subject. Despite these differences in interpretation, some evidence suggests that the MMPI-2 predicts equally well for at least whites and African Americans (Timbrook & Graham, 1994).

The major source of validity for the MMPI and MMPI-2 comes from the multitude of research studies that describe the characteristics of particular profile patterns. Volume II of the revised MMPI handbook (Dahlstrom, Welsh, & Dahlstrom, 1975) cites approximately 6000 studies, with the number of new studies increasing every year. In conjunction with this older base, literature devoted to the MMPI-2 has mushroomed, with the number of studies published or in press already in the thousands. In fact, our survey of the relevant literature between 1993 and 1995 revealed more citations for the MMPI-2 than for any other personality test. This body of research provides ample evidence for the construct validity of the MMPI-2.

A number of studies, for example, have related MMPI response patterns to alcoholism (McMahon et al., 1991). For example, evidence indicates that the MMPI and MMPI-2 might help detect individuals who might later become alcoholics (Hoffman, Loper, & Kammeier, 1974; Kammeier, Hoffman, & Loper, 1973; Malinchoc et al., 1994). The items of the original MMPI were administered to a group of men while they were still in college. The response patterns of those individuals who later became alcoholics were compared with those of a control group who did not become alcoholics. Results showed that the subjects who eventually became alcoholics had significantly higher scores on one validity scale (F) and two clinical scales (4 and 9). Thus, these scales may be related to characteristics that contribute to alcoholism in men. Interestingly, the response pattern of those in the alcoholic group was the same as their retest pattern after they had become alcoholics.

Indeed, the range of problems for which the MMPI and MMPI-2 have been shown to be of value spans everything from eating disorders (Shisslak, Pazda, & Crago, 1990; Strassberg, Ross, & Todt, 1995), posttraumatic stress syndrome (Lyons & Scotti, 1994; Munley et al., 1995), prediction of surgical outcome in chronic low-back-pain patients (J. A. Turner, Herron, & Weiner, 1986), and prediction of delinquent behavior (Lindgren et al., 1986) to prediction of neurologic disorders (Cripe, Maxwell, & Hill, 1995). Of course, not all MMPI studies report positive results (Levenson et al., 1986), but the vast majority attest to its utility and versatility (Harkness, McNulty, & Ben-Porath, 1995; Iverson, Franzen, & Hammond, 1995).

Current status. The restandardization of the MMPI has eliminated the most serious drawback of the original version: the inadequate control group. With its already widespread use and acceptance, the future of the MMPI appears extremely bright. And with the addition of new items, we are sure to see many new applications. In addition, the newer items can be added to the original scales when appropriate to increase their reliability as well as their predictive validity. It is unlikely that the MMPI and MMPI-2 will soon be replaced as the premiere structured personality tests.

California Psychological Inventory

The California Psychological Inventory (CPI) (Gough, 1957, 1969, 1987) is second only to the MMPI in popularity as a structured personality test constructed primarily by the criterion-group strategy. For 11 of the 20 CPI scales in the 1987 revision, criterion groups (for example, men versus women; homosexual men versus heterosexual men) were contrasted to produce measures of personality categorized as (1) introversion-extroversion, (2) conventional versus unconventional in following norms, and (3) self-realization and sense of integration.

In contrast to the MMPI (and MMPI-2), the CPI attempts to evaluate personality in normally adjusted individuals. The test contains 18 scales, each of which is grouped into one of four classes. Class I scales measure poise, self-assurance, and interpersonal effectiveness. Individuals who score high on these scales tend to be active, resourceful, competitive, outgoing, spontaneous, and self-confident. They are also at ease in interpersonal situations. Individuals who score high on Class II scales, which evaluate socialization, maturity, and responsibility, tend to be conscientious, honest, dependable, calm, practical, cooperative, and alert to ethical and moral issues. Class III scales measure achievement potential and intellectual efficiency. High scores in this class tend to indicate organized, efficient, sincere, mature, forceful, capable, and well-informed people. Class IV scales examine interest modes. High scorers tend to respond well to the inner needs of others and adapt well socially.

More than a third of the 462 items are almost identical to items in the MMPI, and many others resemble them (Megargee, 1972). However, the test does more than share items with the MMPI. Like the MMPI, the CPI shows considerable intercorrelation among its scales. Factor analytic studies have shown that only two factors in the CPI, associated with internal controls (Class II scales) and interpersonal effectiveness (Class I scales), account for a large part of the variance (Megargee, 1972). Also like the MMPI, true-false scale keying is often extremely unbalanced. Furthermore, reliability coefficients are similar to those reported for the MMPI. Short-term test-retest coefficients range from .49 to .90, depending on the sample; long-term coefficients range from .38 to .77 (Megargee, 1972). The method used to establish some criterion groups for the CPI has been questioned. For example, for some of the scales, subjects were placed in criterion groups on the basis of ratings by friends. Nevertheless, one must consider the psychometric properties of the CPI adequate by today's standards, because they are comparable to those of most widely used personality tests.

The CPI is commonly used in research settings to examine everything from the personality of nursing students (Houldin & Forbes, 1990) to career choices (Gough, 1995). The advantage of the CPI is that it can be used with normal subjects. The MMPI (and MMPI-2) generally does not apply to normal subjects, and the meaning of nonelevated profiles is not well established. Therefore, if one intends to assess normal individuals for interpersonal effectiveness and internal controls, the CPI is a good candidate for the measure. Furthermore, as with the MMPI, a considerable body of literature has focused on the CPI. Each new piece of literature extends the utility of the test and adds to its construct validity. Therefore, the future of the CPI as a measure of normal personalities has good potential despite its limitations.

The Factor Analytic Strategy

Structured personality tests, as they exist today, share one common set of assumptions. These assumptions, simply stated, are that humans possess characteristics or traits that are stable, vary from individual to individual, and can be measured. Nowhere are these assumptions better illustrated than in the factor analytic strategy of test construction.

As you will recall, factor analysis is a statistical procedure for reducing the redundancy in a set of intercorrelated scores. For example, one major technique of factor analysis, the principal-components methods (Hotelling, 1933), finds the minimum number of common factors that can account for an interrelated set of scores. As noted in the previous section, two factors can account for most of the variance in both the CPI and the MMPI, which suggests that these tests are actually measuring only two unique components and that all scales are related to these two components.

The advantages of factor analysis are quite evident. However, before computers, even simple factor analyses required several weeks or even months of tedious arithmetic operations on a hand calculator. Therefore, the development of the factor analytic strategy awaited computer technology. One individual, R. B. Cattell, has distinguished himself in using the factor analytic strategy of structured personality assessment; this section focuses on his work.

Guilford's Pioneer Efforts

One usual strategy in validating a new test is to correlate the scores on the new test with the scores on other tests that purport to measure the same entity. J. P. Guilford's approach was related to this procedure. However, instead of individually comparing one test to a series of other tests, Guilford and his associates determined the interrelationship (intercorrelation) of a wide variety of tests and then factor analyzed the results in an effort to find the main underlying dimensions common to all personality tests. If the results from existing personality tests could be reduced to a few factors, then items that correlated highly with these factors could be used in a new test, which would therefore capture the major dimensions of personality.

The result of the initial attempt to apply this strategy was a series of inventories, which Guilford and his associates published in the 1940s (the STDCR, Guilford, 1940; the GAMIN, Guilford & Martin, 1943; the Temperament Survey, Guilford & Zimmerman, 1949). These procedures were ultimately collapsed into a single scale—the Guilford-Zimmerman Temperament Survey (Guilford & Zimmerman, 1956).

The Guilford-Zimmerman Temperament Survey reduces personality to 10 dimensions, each of which is measured by 30 different items (Guilford, 1959). The 10 dimensions are general activity, restraint, ascendance (leadership), sociability, emotional stability, objectivity, friendliness, thoughtfulness, personal relations, and masculinity. The test presents a list of statements, most of which are self-statements as in the MMPI. The subject must indicate "Yes" or "No" for each statement. As in the MMPI, three validity, or verification, keys are included to detect falsification and to evaluate the validity of the profile. Standard scores were obtained from college group reference samples, and split-half reliabilities are good, ranging from .75 to .85. However, this first major factor analytic structured personality test failed to catch on, perhaps because it was overshadowed by the MMPI and because of its arbitrary, subjective way of naming factors. Now, the Guilford-Zimmerman Temperament Survey primarily serves only historical interest.

Cattell's Contribution

Rather than attempt to uncover the major dimensions of personality by intercorrelating personality tests, R. B. Cattell began with all the adjectives applicable to human beings so he could empirically determine and measure the essence of personality. Beginning with a monumental catalog of all the adjectives (trait names) in an unabridged dictionary that apply to humans, Allport and Odbert (1936) reduced their list to 4504 "real" traits. Adding to the list traits found in the psychological and psychiatric literature, Cattell then reduced the list to 171 items that he believed accounted for the meaning of all items on the original list. College students rated their friends on these 171 terms, and the results were intercorrelated and factor analyzed. The 171 terms were reduced to 36 dimensions, called *surface traits* (Cattell, 1957). Subsequent investigation by factor analysis finally produced 16 distinct factors that accounted for all the variables. Thus, Cattell had reduced personality to 16 basic dimensions, which he called *source traits*. Table 15-4 lists these source traits.

The product of Cattell's marathon task was the Sixteen Personality Factor Questionnaire, better known as the 16PF (Cattell, 1949), which was subsequently revised based on continued factor analysis (Cattell, Eber, & Tatsuoka, 1970). Consistent with the factor analytic strategy, items that correlated highly with each of the 16 major factors, or source traits, were included, and those with relatively low correlations were excluded.

Developers took great care in standardizing the 16PF. Separate norms were provided for men alone, women alone, and men and women combined for each of three U.S. groups: adults, college students, and high-school seniors. Thus, nine sets of norms are available. To deal further with the covariation of structured personality test data and demographic variables that plagues the MMPI, the 16PF provides age corrections for scales that change significantly with age. Six forms of the test are available: two parallel forms for each of three levels of vocabulary proficiency, ranging from newspaper-literate adults through the educationally disadvantaged. For the latter, a tape-recorded (oral) form is also available. Norms for the various forms are based on more than 15,000 subjects representative of geographic area, population density, age, family income, and race according to figures provided by the U.S. census.

Unlike the MMPI and CPI, the 16PF contains no item overlap, and keying is balanced among the various alternative responses. Short-term test-retest correlation coefficients for the 16 source traits are impressive, with a range of .65 to .93 and a median coefficient of .83. Long-term test-retest coefficients, however, which range from .21 to .64, are not so impressive, and most such

TABLE 15-4

The Primary Source Traits Covered by the 16PF Test

Factor	Low Sten Score Description (1–3)	High Sten Score Description (8–10)
A	*Cool,* **reserved, impersonal, detached, formal, aloof** Sizothymia*	*Warm,* **outgoing, kindly, easygoing, participating, likes people** Affectothymia
B	*Concrete-thinking,* **less intelligent** Lower scholastic mental capacity	*Abstract-thinking,* **more intelligent, bright** Higher scholastic mental capacity
C	*Affected by feelings,* **emotionally less stable, easily annoyed** Lower ego strength	*Emotionally stable,* **mature, faces reality, calm** Higher ego strength
E	*Submissive,* **humble, mild, easily led, accommodating** Submissiveness	*Dominant,* **assertive, aggressive, stubborn, competitive, bossy** Dominance
F	*Sober,* **restrained, prudent, taciturn, serious** Desurgency	*Enthusiastic,* **spontaneous, heedless, expressive, cheerful** Surgency
G	*Expedient,* **disregards rules, self-indulgent** Weaker superego strength	*Conscientious,* **conforming, moralistic, staid, rule-bound** Stronger superego strength
H	*Shy,* **threat-sensitive, timid, hesitant, intimidated** Threctia	*Bold,* **venturesome, uninhibited, can take stress** Parmia
I	*Tough-minded,* **self-reliant, no-nonsense, rough, realistic** Harria	*Tender-minded,* **sensitive, overprotected, intuitive, refined** Premsia
L	*Trusting,* **accepting conditions, easy to get on with** Alaxia	*Suspicious,* **hard to fool, distrustful, skeptical** Protension
M	*Practical,* **concerned with "down-to-earth" issues, steady** Praxernia	*Imaginative,* **absent-minded, absorbed in thought, impractical** Autia
N	*Forthright,* **unpretentious, open, genuine, artless** Artlessness	*Shrewd,* **polished, socially aware, diplomatic, calculating** Shrewdness
O	*Self-assured,* **secure, feels free of guilt, untroubled, self-satisfied** Untroubled adequacy	*Apprehensive,* **self-blaming, guilt-prone, insecure, worrying** Guilt proneness
Q$_1$	*Conservative,* **respecting traditional ideas** Conservatism of temperament	*Experimenting,* **liberal, critical, open to change** Radicalism
Q$_2$	*Group-oriented,* **a "joiner" and sound follower, listens to others** Group adherence	*Self-sufficient,* **resourceful, prefers own decisions** Self-sufficiency
Q$_3$	*Undisciplined self-conflict,* **lax, careless of social rules** Low integration	*Following self-image,* **socially precise, compulsive** High self-concept control
Q$_4$	*Relaxed,* **tranquil, composed, has low drive, unfrustrated** Low ergic tension	*Tense,* **frustrated, overwrought, has high drive** High ergic tension

*Titles in roman type are the technical names for the factors and are explained more fully in the *Handbook.*
From the *Administrator's Manual for the Sixteen Personality Factor Questionnaire,* copyright © 1972, 1979, 1986 by the Institute for Personality and Ability Testing, Inc. Reproduced by permission.

coefficients reported in the literature are lower than those reported for the MMPI and MMPI-2 (Schuerger, Tait, & Tavernelli, 1982). Also a bit disappointing are the correlations between the various forms, which range from a low of .16 to a high of .79, with median coefficients in the .50s and .60s, depending on which forms are correlated. Moreover, despite the method used for deriving the factors, the 16 source traits of the 16PF do intercorrelate, with some correlations as high as .75 (Cattell, Eber, & Tatsuoka, 1970). To deal with this overlap, the 16 factors themselves were factor analyzed, resulting in four second-order factors, for which one can obtain scores. Analysis of the psychometric properties of the 16PF thus reflects the efforts Cattell and his colleagues have made in attempting to provide a psychometrically sound instrument.

Other important features of the test are its provision of a parallel inventory for ages 12 to 18, the Jr. Sr. High School Personality Questionnaire, and still another parallel extension for use with ages 8 to 12, the Children's Personality Questionnaire. Cross-cultural studies have been conducted in Western Europe, Eastern Europe, the Middle East, Australia, and Canada (Gynther & Gynther, 1976). Furthermore, various research investigations have supported the validity of Cattell's personality test (Cattell, Eber, & Tatsuoka, 1970). To extend the test to the assessment of clinical populations, items related to psychological disorders have been factor analyzed (Cattell & Bolton, 1969; Delhees & Cattell, 1971a), resulting in 12 new factors in addition to the 16 needed to measure normal personalities. These new factors were then used to construct a clinical instrument, the Clinical Analysis Questionnaire (CAQ) (Delhees & Cattell, 1971b).

Despite the care that has gone into the 16PF, its research base and use pale when compared with those of the MMPI. The fact is, neither clinicians nor researchers have found the 16PF to be as useful as the MMPI. Moreover, the claims of the 16 PF to have identified the basic source traits of the personality are simply not true. Factor analysis is one of many ways of constructing tests. Factor analysis will identify only those traits about which questions are asked; it has no more claim to uniqueness than any other method. Even so, the 16PF remains an exemplary illustration of the factor analytic approach to structured personality testing.

Problems with the Factor Analytic Strategy

One major criticism of factor analytic approaches centers on the subjective nature of naming factors. To understand this problem, one must understand that each score on any given set of tests or variables can be broken down into three components: common variance, unique variance, and error variance. *Common variance* is the amount of variance a particular variable holds in common with other variables. It results from the overlap of what two or more variables are measuring. Highly specific, *unique variance* refers to factors uniquely measured by the variable. In other words, it refers to some construct measured only by the variable in question. *Error variance* is variance attributable to error. Factor analytic procedures generally identify sources of common variance at the expense of unique variance. Thus, important factors may be overlooked when the data are categorized solely on the basis of blind groupings by computers. Furthermore, all the computer can do is identify the groupings. The factor analyst must determine which factors these groupings measure, but no definite criteria or rules exist for naming factors. If five items such as daring, outgoing, determined, excitable, and fearless load high on a factor, what should one call this factor? In factor analysis, one name for this factor has about as much validity as any other.

The Theoretical Strategy

To avoid the potential disagreement and biases that stem from factor analytic approaches, structured personality tests guided in their construction by theory have been proposed. In this approach, items are selected to measure the variables or constructs specified by a major theory of personality. After the items have been selected and grouped into scales, a construct validity approach is taken. Presumably, predictions are made concerning the nature of the scale, and if the predictions hold up, the scale is supported.

Edwards Personal Preference Schedule

One of the best-known examples of a structured personality test developed using the theoretical strategy is the Edwards Personal Preference Schedule (EPPS) (A. L. Edwards, 1954, 1959). Again, we use the term *test* in the general sense. According to Edwards, the EPPS is not a test in the strict sense of the word because there are no right or wrong answers. At one time, the EPPS was used widely in counseling centers (Lubin, Wallis, & Paine, 1971). It has also been widely researched (Gynther & Gynther, 1976). Today, the test is not used extensively. However, in addition to illustrating the theoretical strategy, the EPPS elucidates some interesting concepts in personality test construction, such as the concept of ipsative scores, which we shall discuss later.

The theoretical basis for the EPPS is the need system proposed by Murray (1938), probably the most influential theory in personality test construction to date. The human needs proposed by Murray include the need to accomplish (achievement), the need to conform (deference), and the need for attention (exhibition). In developing the EPPS, Edwards selected 15 needs from Murray's list and constructed items with content validity for each (see Table 15-5).

Having selected items based on theory, Edwards could avoid the blind, subjective, and atheoretical approaches of other strategies. However, he still faced the perpetual problems of response styles and biases, which the MMPI had dealt with by including special scales to detect faking or unusual test-tak-

TABLE 15-5

List and Description of Murray's Psychogenic Needs

Need	Description
Abasement	To submit passively to external force. To accept injury, blame, criticism, punishment. To surrender. To become resigned to fate. To admit inferiority, error, wrong-doing, or defeat. To confess and atone. To blame, belittle, or mutilate the self. To seek and enjoy pain, punishment, illness, and misfortune.
Achievement	To accomplish something difficult. To master, manipulate, or organize physical objects, human beings, or ideas. To do this as rapidly and as independently as possible. To overcome obstacles and attain a high standard. To excel one's self. To rival and surpass others. To increase self-regard by the successful exercise of talent.
Affiliation	To form friendships and associations. To greet, join, and live with others. To cooperate and converse sociably with others. To love. To join groups.
Aggression	To overcome opposition forcefully. To fight. To revenge an injury. To attack, injure, or kill another. To oppose forcefully or punish another.
Autonomy	To get free, shake off restraint, break out of confinement. To resist coercion and restriction. To avoid or quit activities prescribed by domineering authorities. To be independent and free to act according to impulse. To be unattached, unconditioned, irresponsible. To defy convention.
Blamavoidance	To avoid blame, ostracism, or punishment by inhibiting asocial or unconventional impulses. To be well-behaved and obey the law.
Counteraction	Proudly to refuse admission of defeat by restriving and retaliating. To select the hardest tasks. To defend one's honor in action.
Defendance	To defend oneself against blame or belittlement. To justify one's actions. To offer extenuations, explanations, and excuses. To resist "probing."
Deference	To admire and support a superior other. To praise, honor, or eulogize. To yield eagerly to the influence of an allied other. To emulate an exemplar. To conform to custom.
Dominance	To influence or control others. To persuade, prohibit, dictate. To lead and direct. To restrain. To organize the behavior of a group.
Exhibition	To make an impression. To be seen and heard. To excite, amaze, fascinate, entertain, shock, intrigue, amuse, or entice others.
Harmavoidance	To avoid pain, physical injury, illness, and death. To escape from a dangerous situation. To take precautionary measures.
Infavoidance	To avoid humiliation. To quit embarrassing situations or to avoid conditions that may lead to belittlement; the scorn, derision, or indifference of others. To refrain from action because of the fear of failure.
Nurturance	To nourish, aid, or protect a helpless other. To express sympathy. To "mother" a child.
Order	To put things in order. To achieve cleanliness, arrangement, organization, balance, neatness, tidiness, and precision.
Play	To relax, amuse oneself, seek diversion and entertainment. To "have fun," to play games. To laugh, joke, and be merry. To avoid serious tension.
Rejection	To snub, ignore, or exclude another. To remain aloof and indifferent. To be discriminating.
Sentience	To seek and enjoy sensuous impressions.
Sex	To form and further an erotic relationship. To have sexual intercourse.
Succorance	To seek aid, protection, or sympathy. To cry for help. To plead for mercy. To adhere to an affectionate, nurturant parent. To be dependent.
Understanding	To analyze experience, to abstract, to discriminate among concepts, to define relations, to synthesize ideas.

ing approaches. Edwards was especially concerned with faking and social desirability, the tendency to say good things about yourself or to mark items that you believe will be approved by the examiner, regardless of accuracy.

To deal with these sources of bias, Edwards attempted to rate each of his items on social desirability. He then formed pairs of items roughly comparable in social desirability and required subjects to select the item in the pair that was more characteristic of their likes or feelings. Subjects cannot simply provide the socially desirable or expected response, because both items in the pair are presumably equal on social desirability. There is also not much point in faking—that is, selecting the less characteristic item. In addition, no problem of balancing scored items arises, as the true-false imbalance of the MMPI has.

As a further check on the validity of EPPS results, Edwards included a consistency scale with 15 pairs of statements repeated in identical form. In other words, of the 210 pairs of statements, only 195 are unique. The 15 that occur twice are presented more or less randomly throughout the test. With this format, the number of times a subject makes the identical choice can be converted to a percentile based on normative data. The approach provided the precursor to the VRIN and TRIN scales of the MMPI-2. The EPPS also permits an analysis of within-subject consistency, which consists of the correlation of odd and even scores in the 15 scales.

Norms for the EPPS were based on more than 1500 college men and women and approximately 9000 adults from the general population selected from urban and rural areas in 48 states. Separate normative data are available for each of these two groups and high-school students as well. For a given raw score on each of the 15 scales, a percentile can be obtained immediately from the profile sheet.

To better understand the EPPS, you should bear in mind that in constructing it, Edwards listed items for each of the scales and then paired them with items from the other 14 scales. When subjects make a choice, they select between one of two needs. In other words, in each choice, a subject selects one need at the expense of another. With this procedure, one can express the selection of items on one scale relative to the selection of items on another, thereby producing an **ipsative score.** Ipsative scores present results in relative terms rather than as absolute totals. Thus, two individuals with identical relative, or ipsative, scores may differ markedly in the absolute strength of a particular need. Ipsative scores compare the individual against himself or herself and produce data that reflect the relative strength of each need for that person; each person thus provides his or her own frame of reference (see Mullins, Weeks, & Wilbourn, 1978).

Although the manual presents only short-term (one-week) test-retest reliability figures, the coefficients, which range from .74 to .88, are quite respectable for personality test data. Though not so impressive, split-half reliabilities, which range from .60 to .87 as reported in the manual, are generally satisfactory. Furthermore, intercorrelations among the scales are lower than for either the MMPI or 16PF, ranging between −.34 and .46.

The EPPS has a number of interesting features. Its forced-choice method, which requires subjects to select one of two items rather than to respond "True" or "False" ("Yes" or "No") to a single item, is an interesting solution to the problem of faking and other sources of bias. Because each subject provides his or her own frame of reference, one can determine the relative strength of needs as well as the internal consistency of each individual subject. Item content follows established theoretical lines. The 15 identical pairs aid in the evaluation of the validity of the profile. Norms are based on large samples and are available for adults from the general population as well as for high-school and college students. Ipsative scores based on these norms can be converted to percentiles. Reliability data generally are adequate for the short term, and the 15 scales of the EPPS have lower intercorrelations than do the scales of the major tests developed by using factor analytic and criterion-group strategies. Last, but not least, the test is among the most researched of the personality inventories and is used widely in applied settings.

Despite its impressive features and extensive use and the widespread interest it has engendered, the EPPS has not been well received by reviewers, such as Radcliffe (1965), Stricker (1965), and Heilbrun (1972). Studies have shown that, like other structured personality tests, the EPPS can be faked in spite of its forced-choice procedure (Dicken, 1959). Other data raise questions concerning the test's ability to adequately control social-desirability effects (Feldman & Corah, 1960; N. Wiggins, 1966). The appropriateness of converting ipsative scores, which are relative, to normative percentiles is also questionable. Gynther and Gynther (1976) believe that the main problem with the EPPS is the rather meager data supporting its validity. Although many studies have attempted to discriminate a variety of groups (for example, smokers versus nonsmokers) with the EPPS, the EPPS has a "paucity" of nontest correlates (Gynther & Gynther, 1976), with little being done to correct the problem.

Since the first attempts at test construction, tests have followed a trend of gradual improvement following criticism and the identification of problems. The EPPS seems to have originated in this spirit, but efforts are not being made to improve it. Many more validity studies are needed (Stricker, 1965), and new norms are long overdue (D. Cooper, 1990).

Personality Research Form and Jackson Personality Inventory

Other attempts to use the theoretical strategy in constructing a structured personality test are the Personality Research Form (PRF) (D. N. Jackson, 1967) and the Jackson Personality Inventory (JPI) (D. N. Jackson, 1976a, 1976b.) Like the EPPS, the PRF and JPI were based on Murray's (1938) theory of needs. However, unlike Edwards, the constructors of these tests developed specific definitions of each need. In this way, items for each scale could be as independent as possible, an important consideration in creating homogeneous scales. To further increase the homogeneity of scales, more than 100 items were tentatively written for each scale and administered to over 1000 college students. Biserial correlational analysis then located the items that correlated highest with the proposed scale while showing relatively low correlations with other scales, particularly social desirability. In other words, strict definitional standards and statistical procedures were used in conjunction with the theoretical approach. This use of a combination of procedures is the latest trend in personality test construction.

To aid in the assessment of validity, a scale analogous to the F scale of the MMPI was constructed. Like the F scale, the PRF and JPI infrequency scales consist of items with low endorsement rates in a standard sample. Thus, high rates of endorsement on this scale throw doubt on the validity of the results. A social-desirability scale similar to the K scale of the MMPI is also included in the PFR. Two sets of parallel forms (four forms in all) as well as a form based on the best items from other forms were developed for the PFR. The JPI has one form consisting of 320 true-false items and 16 scales for use with high-school students through college students and adults. The PFR, as its name implies, is primarily for research purposes. The JPI is for use on normal individuals to assess various aspects of personality including interpersonal, cognitive, and value orientations. See Figure 15-4 for a profile sheet from the Jackson Personality Inventory.

Items for the PFR and JPI are balanced in true-false keying. Unlike the scales of the MMPI, the PRF and JPI scales have no item overlap. Furthermore, the scales are relatively independent, with most intercorrelation coefficients at ±.30 (Gynther & Gynther, 1976). (See Table 15-6.)

The internal consistency coefficients reported in the test manuals are extremely good, with a range of .80 to .94. Factor analytic studies have supported the validity of the tests (D. N. Jackson, 1970). Furthermore, many studies have supported the construct validity of the tests (Mungas, Trontel, & Weingardner, 1981; Murray-Jobsis, 1991; Trott & Morf, 1972.

Clearly, the PRF and JPI possess sound psychometric properties, which perhaps accounts for the preponderance of favorable reviews (Anastasi, 1972a; E. C. Kelly, 1972; J. G. Wiggins, 1973). In any case, by combining theory with rigorous statistical procedures, these tests appear to have established a new trend in the construction of structured personality tests. As with other structured personality tests, however, the PRF has yet to challenge the MMPI and MMPI-2 in terms of use (both clinical and research) and status.

Temperament: The Myers-Briggs Type Indicator

The Myers-Briggs Type Indicator, developed by I. B. Myers and K. C. Briggs, is a theoretically constructed test based on Carl Jung's theory of psychology types (I. B. Myers, 1976, 1977; I. B. Myers & Briggs, 1943/1962). Jung had theorized that there are four main ways in which we experience or come to know the world: *sensing,* knowing through our sensory systems of sight, hearing,

Jackson Personality Inventory

PROFILE SHEET: MALE

Name _____ Age _____ Form Administered _____

Date Tested _____ Other Information _____

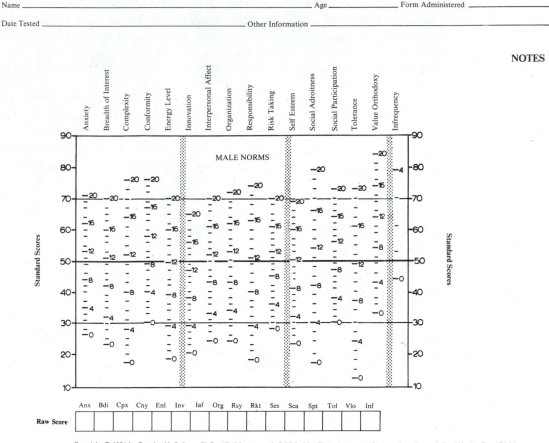

FIGURE 15-4 *Jackson Personality Inventory profile sheet.*

(Reprinted with permission of Sigma Assessment Systems, Inc., P.O. Box 610984, Port Huron, MI 48061-0984, copyright 1976.)

touch, and so on; *intuition,* guessing what underlies sensory inputs; *feeling,* focusing on the emotional aspect of experience; and *thinking,* reasoning or thinking abstractly. Jung argued that though we must strive for balance in the four modes, each person tended to emphasize one over the others. In addition, Jung believed that one could distinguish all individuals in terms of introversion versus extroversion. The purpose of the Myers-Briggs test is to determine where people fall on the introversion-extroversion dimension and on which of the four modes they rely.

In line with Jung's theory, the underlying assumption of the Myers-Briggs Type Indicator is that people have specific preferences in the way they con-

TABLE 15-6
Trait Descriptions for the Jackson Personality Inventory

Scale	Trait
Anxiety	Tendency to worry over minor matters
Breadth of interest	Curiosity; inquisitiveness
Complexity	Preference for abstract versus concrete thought
Conformity	Compliance; cooperativeness
Energy level	Energy; enthusiasm
Innovation	Originality; imagination
Interpersonal affect	Ability to identify with others
Organization	Planfulness; systematic versus disorganized
Responsibility	Responsibility; dependability
Risk taking	Reckless and bold versus cautious and hesitant
Self-esteem	Self-assured versus self-conscious
Social adroitness	Skill in persuading others
Social participation	Sociable and gregarious versus withdrawn loner
Tolerance	Broad-minded and open versus intolerant and uncompromising
Value orthodoxy	Moralistic and conventional versus modern and liberal
Infrequency	Validity of profile

strue their experiences. These preferences, moreover, are believed to underlie our interests, needs, values, and motivation.

The most recent norms for the Myers-Briggs test are based on more than 2000 boys and girls in grades 4 through 12 spanning three public and four private schools (I. B. Myers, 1976). Reliability for the test is adequate, with split-half figures ranging in the .70s and .80s. The Myers-Briggs test appears to hold special promise in predicting vocational preference when used in conjunction with interest and ability tests (Lowman, 1991).

Self-Concept

A number of personality tests have evolved from a theoretical strategy to evaluate self-concept—the set of assumptions a person has about himself or herself. Presumably, what you believe to be true about yourself will strongly affect your behavior. If you believe you are honest, then you will tend to act in conformity with this belief. If you believe you are effective with others, you will more likely assume a leadership role than if you believe you are ineffective. The extent to which you use your leadership skills or other abilities is influenced by your self-concept.

Many tests have been developed to evaluate self-concept. The Tennessee Self-Concept Scale is a formal paper-and-pencil test designed to measure self-concept data. Several adjective checklists are also available in which a list of adjectives is presented and subjects are asked to indicate which apply to them. Gough's Adjective Checklist, for instance, contains 350 adjectives in alphabetical order (Gough, 1960; Gough & Heilbrun, 1980). The Piers-Harris Children's Self-Concept Scale contains 80 self-statements (e.g., "I like my looks") and requires a "Yes" or "No" response.

A novel approach to the assessment of self-concept is based on Carl Rogers's theory of the self. According to Rogers, the self is organized to remain consistent. New experiences consistent with a person's self-concept are easily integrated; experiences inconsistent with the self-concept tend to be denied or distorted. For example, if you view yourself as honest and moral and find yourself looking at another student's exam during the pressure of a difficult test, you might try to distort the experience by thinking your classmate purposefully flashed her paper in front of your eyes.

To evaluate self-concept, Rogers uses a Q-Sort technique, in which a person receives a set of cards with appropriate self-statements such as "I am a good person." The individual then sorts the cards in piles from least to most personally descriptive. The person is asked to make two sorts of the cards. The first describes who the person really is (real self). The second describes what the person believes he or she should be (ideal self). Rogers's theory predicts that large discrepancies between the real and ideal selves reflect poor adjustment and low self-esteem (Rogers, 1961b).

Combination Strategies

Clearly, the modern trend is to use a mix of strategies. Indeed, almost all of the tests we have examined use factor analytic methods regardless of their strategy of scale development. In this final section, we briefly discuss two newer tests that rely on a combination of strategies in scale development: the Millon Clinical Multiaxial Inventory and the NEO Personality Inventory.

The Millon Clinical Multiaxial Inventory

The Millon Clinical Multiaxial Inventory (MCMI) is a structured inventory designed to evaluate personality disorders. There are two versions, both of which continue to instigate research and debate (Grossman & Craig, 1995; Wetzler, 1990). The manual for the MCMI was published in 1983 (Millon, 1983). Following some controversy concerning whether the MCMI provided a good measure of personality disorders as defined by the *Diagnostic and Statistical Manual of Mental Disorders,* third edition (DSM-III) (APA, 1980), Millon (1985) wrote that the MCMI was never intended to be such a measure. A few years later, the MCMI-II was published (Millon, 1987). In this revision, developers had added two new scales to the original 20 and attempted to accommodate the personality disorders of the revised version of the DSM-III, the DSM-III-R. In the MCMI-II, Millon also replaced 45 of the original items and introduced a weighting scheme, whereby he gave certain items greater weight based on earlier validity studies.

The purpose of the MCMI-II is to help the clinician make a diagnosis on Axis II of the DSM-III-R. These disorders are pervasive, stable, and deeply ingrained patterns of behaving that influence the individual's thinking, feeling, and acting in a wide range of situations. Controversy continues over how much the MCMI-II really improves on the original MCMI. However, the test is in widespread use (L. C. Ward, 1995; Weeks et al., 1995) and follows Millon's highly influential theory of personality disorders (Craig & Olson, 1995).

According to Millon's theory (1969), personality disorders are rooted in how an individual deals with dependency needs. Because detached individuals give up on having their dependency needs met, they avoid or are indifferent to others. Dependent individuals either passively submit to others or actively try to obtain reassurance and support by dramatic displays. Ambivalents cannot decide whether they want to rely on themselves or others, so their moods and behaviors often fluctuate. Independents trust no one, relying on themselves to satisfy dependency needs.

The MCMI-II, like the MCMI, has a reliability similar to that of other personality tests. A wide variety of validity studies supports it. Primarily used for clinical populations, it is not intended for normal subjects.

Development of the items and scales followed Millon's personality theory (see Millon, 1969). The final item pool and scale composition were refined through a variety of internal consistency methods and external criterion checks. In using a variety of approaches, the MCMI-II represents the latest trend in personality test construction.

The NEO Personality Inventory

One of the newest major personality inventories is the NEO Personality Inventory (Costa & McCrae, 1985, 1995; Costa, McCrae, & Kay, 1995), which used both factor analysis and theory in item development and scale construction. Quite ambitious, the NEO attempts to provide a multipurpose inventory for predicting interests, health and illness behavior, psychological well-being, and characteristic coping styles. Of the personality tests, the NEO has been among the most heavily researched in the 1990s (e.g., Caprara, Barbaranelli, & Comrey, 1995).

Based on their review of extensive factor analytic studies and personality theory, the authors of the NEO identified three broad domains: neuroticism (N), extroversion (E), and openness (O). Each domain has six specific facets. Neuroticism (N) is defined primarily by anxiety and depression. In fact, the six facets of this domain are anxiety, hostility, depression, self-consciousness, impulsiveness, and vulnerability (describing people who don't feel safe). Extroversion (E) refers to the degree of sociability or withdrawal a person tends to exhibit. The six facets of extraversion are warmth, gregariousness, assertiveness, activity, excitement seeking, and positive emotions. Finally, openness refers to the breadth of experience to which a person is amenable. Its six dimensions are fantasy, esthetics, feelings (openness to feelings of self and others), actions (willingness to try new activities), ideas (intellectual curiosity), and values. Figure 15-5 is a profile from the NEO Personality Inventory.

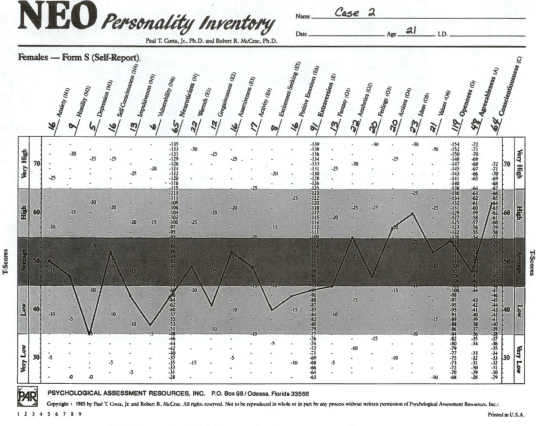

FIGURE 15-5 *NEO Personality Inventory profile.*

(Reprinted by permission of Psychological Assessment Resources, Inc.)

Guided by personality theory and factor analytic findings, the authors of the NEO took a rational approach in constructing items. For each of the 18 facets, 14 items were written. Seven were positively worded and seven negatively worded to create a balance. Subjects respond on a five-point Likert scale format ranging from "strongly disagree" to "strongly agree." Initial items were then refined using a variety of statistical procedures.

Data presented in the manual support the NEO Personality Inventory. Factor analytic studies support the grouping of three major areas and associated facets. Reliabilities for the three domains are in the high .80s to low .90s for both internal consistency and test-retest reliability. As true of all major personality tests, reliabilities of the individual facets are lower. Preliminary predictive and concurrent validity studies have been encouraging, with coefficients ranging into the .80s.

The NEO has, in particular, supported what is perhaps becoming one of the most accepted notions in personality and personality assessment—the big five dimensions of personality. Recall that through factor analysis, researchers have repeatedly attempted to find the minimum number of independent personality dimensions to describe the human personality. Research with the NEO has supported the notion of the following five dimensions (after J. G. Wiggins, 1994):

1. *Surgency* is the degree to which a person is sociable, leaderlike, and assertive, as opposed to withdrawn, quiet, and reserved.
2. *Emotional Stability* is the degree to which a person is calm and self-confident, as opposed to anxious and insecure.
3. *Conscientiousness* is the degree to which a person is persevering, responsible, and organized, as opposed to lazy, irresponsible, and impulsive.
4. *Agreeableness* is the degree to which a person is warm and cooperative as opposed to unpleasant and disagreeable.
5. *Intellectance* is the degree to which a person is imaginative and curious as opposed to concrete minded and narrow in thinking.

The NEO Personality Inventory reflects modern trends in personality test construction by its reliance on theory, logic, and liberal use of factor analysis and statistical approaches in test construction. It appears to be exceptionally promising for a wide range of characteristics.

Summary

Structured personality tests are self-report procedures that provide statements to which the subject must either respond "True" or "False" ("Yes" or "No") or choose the most characteristic of two or more alternatives. These tests are highly structured and provide a definite, unambiguous stimulus for the subject. Scoring is straightforward and usually involves summing the number of items marked in a scored direction.

The original pressure to develop personality tests came from the demands created by World War I for a screening instrument to identify emotionally unstable recruits who might break down under the pressures of combat. The first structured personality instrument, the Woodworth Personal Data Sheet, was based on a logical-content strategy in which items were interpreted in terms of face validity.

Not long after their appearance, tests based on the logical-content strategy fell into disrepute. The problem with these tests was the numerous assumptions underlying them, such as the subject complies with the instructions and provides an honest response; the subject understands the items and is an accurate observer capable of evaluating his or her own behavior and responding in a nondefensive manner; and the subject, test constructor, and test interpreter all define the questions in the same way. A review by A. Ellis (1946) seriously questioned all these assumptions.

The first major advance in structured personality assessment came with the MMPI, which used a strategy involving criterion groups. In this criterion-group strategy, groups who had known characteristics were contrasted with a control population. Items that distinguished the criterion group were included in a scale that was then cross-validated on an independent sample of criterion and control subjects. The MMPI revitalized structured personality tests. Rather than making assumptions about the meaning of a subject's response to a test item, it attempted to empirically discern the response's meaning. In the criterion-group strategy, the content of the item is irrelevant. If a subject marks "True" to the statement "I hear loud voices when I'm alone," testers do not assume that he or she really does hear loud voices when alone.

In addition to its advantages over logical-content tests in avoiding assumptions, the MMPI featured validity scales. The two most important MMPI validity scales are the K scale, which measures social desirability, and the F scale, which consists of 64 infrequently endorsed items to pick out subjects who take an unusual or unconventional approach to testing. Theoretically, excessively high scores on the validity scales can identify biased results, thus avoiding the problems of faking and social desirability inherent in the logical-content approach.

Despite its extensive use, researchers' widespread interest in it, and its recent restandardization (the MMPI-2), the MMPI does have problems, including item overlap among the scales, an imbalance in true-false keying, high intercorrelation among the scales, and lack of generalizability across demographic variables.

The factor analytic strategy of test construction has been used in an effort to overcome some of the problems inherent in the criterion strategy. Factor analytic strategies attempt to find areas of common variance in order to locate the minimum number of variables or factors that account for a set of intercorrelated data. R. B. Cattell has been the most important representative of this approach.

Using the factor analytic approach to find the common variance of all trait-descriptive terms in the dictionary, Cattell reduced an original pool of more than 4000 items to 16 and created the 16PF. Great care was taken to provide adequate norms. Nine separate normative samples based on demographic variables, plus an age-correction scale, are available. Also available are three sets of parallel forms that accommodate different levels of subjects' vocabulary proficiency.

The EPPS has found its primary use in counseling centers. It employs a forced-choice strategy that requires subjects to choose the more applicable of two statements. *Ipsative scores,* which use the subject as his or her own frame of reference, express results in terms of the relative strength of a need.

A number of tests have been developed with the theoretical strategy. Among these are the Myers-Briggs Type Indicator, which measures temperament, and the Q-sort technique, which measures self-concept.

The modern trend is to use a combination of strategies in scale construction. This approach is used in the Millon Clinical Multiaxial Inventory and the NEO Personality Inventory.

CHAPTER 16

Projective Personality Tests

LEARNING OBJECTIVES

When you have completed this chapter, you should be able to:

- Define the projective hypothesis
- Identify five individuals who played a dominant role in the development of the Rorschach
- Describe the Rorschach stimuli
- Briefly describe Rorschach administration and scoring
- List the pros and cons of the Rorschach
- Describe the Holtzman
- Describe the TAT stimuli
- Briefly describe TAT administration
- Identify the factors that should be considered in evaluating the TAT
- List some of the major similarities and differences between the Rorschach and the TAT

few years ago the wife of an army sergeant sued him for divorce after 14 years of marriage. The wife claimed that her husband was "mentally unstable and deranged." She accused him of beating her, often for no apparent reason. The sergeant went to a psychologist to "prove" his sanity. In addition to an interview, an ability test (the WAIS-III), and an objective personality test (the MMPI-2), the psychologist administered the Rorschach inkblot test. The Rorschach is one of the best known and most widely used of the projective personality tests. According to the psychologist's evaluation, the Rorschach indicated that the sergeant was free of unusual or bizarre thought processes. The psychologist concluded that, based on the Rorschach and other test results, the sergeant was mentally stable, contrary to his wife's claims.

When the matter went to court, the psychologist was called to the witness stand. The cross-examination by the wife's attorney proceeded as follows:

> Attorney: Based on the Rorschach and other tests, you concluded that this man is mentally stable.
>
> Psychologist: I did.
>
> Attorney: What is the Rorschach?
>
> Psychologists: The Rorschach is a projective psychological test that contains ten cards with inkblots on them. Five of the inkblots are black and gray; two are black, gray, and red; and the remaining three are composed of a variety of pastel colors of various shades.
>
> Attorney: How do you administer a Rorschach?
>
> Psychologist: The subject—that is, the person taking the test—is shown each of the cards, one at a time. The subject is required to state what the inkblot might be.
>
> Attorney: You mean to say that you can tell whether a person is sane or insane by the way he or she interprets ten black, gray, and variously colored inkblots?
>
> Psychologist: That is correct.
>
> Attorney: Your honor, this is ridiculous. For 14 years, a man beats his wife for no apparent reason, but the psychologist says he's normal because he passed an inkblot test!

You should keep in mind that this example does not represent the uses of the Rorschach. This test, as you will see, plays an important role in clinical assessment. The example is meant to illustrate why feelings about the Rorschach run so high.

Projective personality tests, such as the Rorschach, are among the most controversial and misunderstood psychological tests (Aronow, Reznikoff, & Moreland, 1995; Blatt, 1990). The Rorschach has been vigorously attacked on a variety of scientific and statistical grounds (Eysenck, 1959; Jensen, 1965; Knutson, 1972). Yet, in Lubin, Wallis, and Paine's (1971) survey of psychological test usage in the United States, the Rorschach was reported to be used in 91% of the 251 clinical settings surveyed. And things have not changed much since then (Lubin, Larsen, & Matarazzo, 1984). The Rorschach is used extensively in clinical settings and widely taught in doctoral training programs for clinical psychologists (Meloy & Singer, 1991; Piotrowski, 1984; Piotrowski, Sherry, & Keller, 1985; Ritzler & Alter, 1986). Moreover, our survey of the testing literature revealed that between 1993 and 1995 the Rorschach was, by far, the most referenced projective personality test and continued to rank second only to the MMPI/MMPI-2 in the number of research citations.

Why are there such widespread use and acceptance of projective tests such as the Rorschach in spite of severe attacks from prominent researchers and psychometricians? To answer this question, we need to take a look at the rationale for and the nature of projective tests.

The Projective Hypothesis

The primary rationale underlying projective tests is the **projective hypothesis.** Numerous definitions have been advanced for the projective hypothesis, with credit for the most complete analysis usually given to L. K. Frank (1939). Simply stated, the projective hypothesis proposes that when people attempt to understand an ambiguous or vague stimulus, their interpretation of that stimulus reflects their needs, feelings, experiences, prior conditioning, thought processes, and so forth. When a frightened little boy looks into a dark room and sees a huge shadow that he interprets as a monster, he is projecting his fear onto the shadow. The shadow itself is neutral—neither good nor bad, fearsome nor pretty. What the child really sees is a reflection of the inner workings of his mind.

The concept of projection is not new. Exner (1976) notes, for example, that Leonardo da Vinci used ambiguous figures to evaluate young art students. The artist presented potential students with an ambiguous figure and presumably evaluated their imaginations according to the quality of the artistic form the students created from it. The concept of projection is also reflected in Shakespeare's "Nothing is either good or bad, but thinking makes it so."

Although what the subject finally sees in a stimulus is assumed to be a reflection of personal qualities or characteristics, some responses may be more revealing than others. If, for example, you say that a round figure is a ball, you provide a relatively straightforward interpretation of the stimulus. The stimulus itself has little ambiguity; it is round and shaped like a ball. In viewing this stimulus, a high percentage of people probably see, though not necessarily report, a ball. Even this simple response, however, can reveal a lot about you. Your response indicates that you accurately perceive simple objects in the external environment and are willing to provide a conventional response. Suppose, however, you said that this same stimulus looked like a square peg in a round hole. Assuming the stimulus is actually round and contains no lines or shapes resembling a square peg, your perception of the stimulus does not conform to its actual property (roundness). Thus, your perceptions in general may not be accurate. Your response may also indicate that you are unwilling to provide the obvious, conventional response. Or it may indicate that you feel out of place, like a square peg in a round hole.

In understanding projective tests, you should realize from the start that one should never draw absolute, definite conclusions from any single response to an ambiguous stimulus. The examiner may only hypothesize what a test response means. Even the same response to the same stimulus may have several possible meanings, depending on the characteristics of the people who make the response. Many factors can influence a response to a stimulus on a projective test. A response, for example, may reflect a recent experience or an early experience of which one is unaware. It may reflect something one has witnessed (a bloody murder) or something one imagines (flunking out of college) rather than something one has actually experienced. It may reflect day-to-day problems, such as an argument with a boyfriend or girlfriend. With all these possible factors influencing a response, no wonder that the validity of projective tests is difficult to document. The interpretation of projective tests requires highly trained, experienced practitioners. Even an expert, however, can easily draw the wrong conclusions; further, even the most experienced experts often disagree among themselves (Exner, 1995; Nezworski & Wood, 1995). As in the example at the beginning of the chapter, the experts claim that they can use projective tests to draw valid conclusions. Researchers, however, remain unconvinced.

The Rorschach Inkblot Test

As an example of a psychological test based on the projective hypothesis, the Rorschach has few peers. Indeed, no general discussion of psychological tests is complete without reference to the Rorschach.

Historical Antecedents

Like most concepts, the notion of using inkblots to study human functioning did not simply appear out of thin air. More than 25 years before the birth of Herman Rorschach, the originator of the test that bears his name, Kerner (1857) noted that individuals frequently report idiosyncratic or unique personal meanings when viewing inkblot stimuli. The wide variety of possible responses to inkblots makes them valuable in studying individuals. Indeed, Binet proposed the idea of using inkblots to assess personality functioning (Binet & Henri, 1896) when Rorschach was only 10 years old. Several investigators then supported Binet's position concerning the potential value of inkblots for investigating human personality (G. Dearborn, 1897; Kirkpatrick, 1900). Their support led to the publication of the first set of standardized inkblots, by Whipple (1910). Rorschach receives credit for finding an original and important use for inkblots: identifying psychological disorders. His investigation of inkblots began in 1911 and culminated in 1921 with the publication of his famous book *Psychodiagnostik.* A year later, he suddenly and unexpectedly died of a serious illness at age 37.

Like many unconventional ideas, Rorschach's work was initially viewed with suspicion and even disdain. Not even the sole psychiatric journal of Switzerland, Rorschach's homeland, reviewed *Psychodiagnostik* (Allison, Blatt, & Zimet, 1968). In fact, only a few foreign reviews of the book appeared, and these tended to be critical. When David Levy first brought Rorschach's test to the United States from Europe, he found a cold, unenthusiastic response. American psychologists judged the test to be scientifically unsound, and psychiatrists found little use for it. Nevertheless, the use of the test gradually increased, and eventually it became quite popular.

Five individuals have played dominant roles in the use and investigation of the Rorschach. One of these, Samuel J. Beck, was a student of Levy's. Beck was especially interested in studying certain patterns or, as he called them, "configurational tendencies" in Rorschach responses (S. J. Beck, 1933). Beck, who died in 1980, eventually wrote several books on the Rorschach and influenced generations of Rorschach practitioners (S. J. Beck, 1944, 1945, 1952). Like Beck, Marguerite Hertz stimulated considerable research on the Rorschach during the years when the test first established its foothold in the United States (Hertz, 1937, 1938). Bruno Klopfer, who emigrated to the United States from Germany, published several key Rorschach books and articles and played an important role in the early development of the test (Klopfer & Davidson, 1944; Klopfer & Kelley, 1942). Zygmunt Piotrowski (1947, 1964) and David Rapaport (Rapaport, Gill, & Schafer 1945–1946) came somewhat later than Beck, Hertz, and Klopfer, but like them continue to exert an influence. As Exner (1976, p. 75) notes, the development of the Rorschach can be attributed primarily to the efforts of these five individuals. Like most scholars, however, the five often disagreed. Their disagreements are the source of many of the current problems with the Rorschach. Each expert developed a unique system of administration, scoring, and interpretation (Blais et al., 1995). They all found disciples willing to accept their biases and use their systems.

Stimuli, Administration, and Interpretation

Rorschach constructed each stimulus card by dropping ink onto a piece of paper and folding it. The result was a unique, bilaterally symmetrical form on a white background. After experimenting with thousands of such blots, Rorschach selected ten. Five were black and gray, two contained black, gray, and red, and three contained pastel colors of various shades. An example of a Rorschach card is shown in Figure 16-1.

The Rorschach is an individual test. In the administration procedure, each of the 10 cards is presented to the subject with minimum structure. After some preliminary remarks concerning the purpose of testing, the examiner hands the first card to the subject and asks something like, "What might this be?" No

FIGURE 16-1

A Rorschach-type image is created by dropping ink onto a piece of paper and folding it. This is a reproduction of an actual card from the Rorschach.

restriction is placed on the type of response permitted, and no clues are given concerning what is expected. If the subject asks for guidance or clarification, the examiner gives little information. If, for example, the subject asks, "Do I use the whole thing or just part of it?" the examiner replies, "As you like" or "Whatever you choose." Anxious subjects or individuals who are made uncomfortable by unstructured situations frequently ask questions, attempting to find out as much as possible before committing themselves. The examiner, however, must not give any cues that might reveal the nature of the expected response. Furthermore, in view of the finding that the examiner may inadvertently reveal information or reinforce certain types of responses through facial expressions and other forms of nonverbal communication (E. Lord, 1950), Exner (1993) advocated an administration procedure in which the examiner sits next to the subject rather than face to face, as in Rapaport's system (Blais et al., 1995).

Notice that the examiner is nonspecific and largely vague. This lack of clear structure or direction with regard to demands and expectations is a primary feature of all projective tests. The idea is to provide as much ambiguity as possible so that the subject's response reflects only the subject. If the examiner inadvertently provides too many guidelines, then the response may simply reflect the subject's tendency to perform as expected or to provide a socially desirable response, as discussed in Chapter 15. Therefore, an improper administration that provides too much structure invalidates the results. Interpretations from such administrations are dubious.

Each card is administered twice. During the free-association phase of the test, the examiner presents the cards one at a time and asks, "What might this be?" If the subject gives only one response to the first card, the examiner may say, "Some people see more than one thing here." The examiner usually makes this remark only once. If the subject rejects the card—that is, states that he or she sees nothing—the examiner may reply, "Most people do see something here. Just take your time." The examiner records every word and even every sound made by the subject verbatim. In addition, the examiner records how long it takes a subject to respond to a card (reaction time) and the position of the card when the response is made (upside down, sideways).

In the second phase of the Rorschach administration, the inquiry, the examiner scores the subject's responses. Responses are scored according to at least five dimensions, including location (where the perception was seen), determinant (what determined the response), form quality (to what extent the response matched the stimulus properties of the inkblot), content (what the perception was), and frequency of occurrence (to what extent the response was popular or original; popular responses occur once in every three protocols on the average). A complete discussion of these special scoring categories is beyond the scope of this text. For more information on scoring and interpretation, see Exner's (1993) Rorschach textbook and Exner and Weiner (1981).

In scoring for location, the examiner must determine where the subject's perception is located on the inkblot. To facilitate determining this location, a small picture of each card, known as the location chart, is provided. If necessary, on rare occasions, an examiner may give a subject a pencil and ask the subject to outline the perception on the location chart. In scoring for location, the examiner notes whether the subject used the whole blot (W), a common detail (D), or an unusual detail (Dd). Location may be scored for other factors as well, such as the *confabulatory response* (DW). In this response, the subject overgeneralizes from a part to the whole. We will discuss this response in detail later on.

A summary of a subject's location choices can be extremely valuable. The examiner may, for example, determine the number and percentage of W, D, and Dd responses. This type of information, in which scoring categories are summarized as a frequency or percentage, is known as the *quantitative,* structural, or statistical aspect of the Rorschach as opposed to the *qualitative* aspects, which pertain to the content and sequence of responses. Normal subjects typically produce a balance of W, D, and Dd responses. When a subject's pattern deviates from the typical balance, the examiner begins to suspect problems. However, no one has been able to demonstrate that a particular deviation is linked to a specific problem (e.g., see Acklin, 1995; Bartell & Solanto, 1995; G. Frank, 1995). A substantial deviation from what is typical or average may suggest a number of possibilities. The protocol may be invalid. Or the subject may be original or unconventional and thus fail to respond according to the typical pattern. Or the subject may have a perceptual problem associated with certain types of brain damage or severe emotional problems. The relative proportion of W, D, and Dd location choices varies with maturational development. Ames, Metraux, and Walker (1971), for example, note that W responses occur most frequently in the 3- to 4-year-old group. As the child grows older, the frequency of W responses gradually decreases until young adulthood. Thus, adult protocols with a preponderance of W responses may suggest immaturity or low mental age.

Like other quantitative aspects of the Rorschach, location patterns and frequencies have been studied in many experimental investigations. These investigations provide information concerning the meaning of various response patterns and thus contribute to the construct validity of the Rorschach. Unfortunately, many of the results of the studies conflict with the opinions of experts. Furthermore, many studies that support the validity of the Rorschach have not been successfully replicated. The ability to form W responses, for example, has been linked to intelligence. Presumably, the W response requires an ability to organize the entire inkblot into a single, meaningful percept, and this organization process requires intelligence. However, because W responses are related to intelligence only for specific cards, there is a low correlation (about .40) between the number of W responses and IQ (Abrams, 1955; Holzberg & Belmont, 1952; Lotsoff, 1953; McCandless, 1949; Wishner, 1948).

Having ascertained the location of a response, the examiner must determine what it was about the inkblot that led the subject to see that particular percept. This factor is known as the *determinant*. One or more of at least four properties of an inkblot may determine or lead to a response: its form or shape, its perceived movement, its color, and its shading. If the subject uses only the form of the blot to determine a response, then the response is scored F and is called a pure form response. Responses are scored for form when the subject justifies or elaborates a response by statements such as "It looks like one," "It is shaped like one," or "Here are the head, legs, feet, ears, and wings." In all these examples, the response is determined exclusively on the basis of shape. In addition to form, a perception may be based on movement, color, shading, or some combination of these factors. These other determinants can be further subdivided. Movement may be human (M), such as two people hugging; animal (FM), such as two elephants playing; or inanimate (m), such as sparks flying.

Focused Example 16.1

EXPERT INTERPRETATION OF THE RORSCHACH

Rorschach experts resolutely maintain that, if properly used, the Rorschach can be an invaluable tool. Scientists remain unconvinced. In our judgment, the key issue revolves around test use. As we have stated, Rorschach interpretations should be viewed only as tentative hypotheses. Those hypotheses that can be confirmed by other sources of data can be seen as having more validity than those that cannot be confirmed. When the Rorschach is rigidly or blindly interpreted, the scientists' disdain becomes justified. When the Rorschach is interpreted cautiously and in conjunction with other sources of data, however, a highly trained expert may astound even the most critical scientist.

One of us had a predoctoral internship at a Veterans Administration hospital in which Marguerite Hertz, one of the five original Rorschach experts, was a consultant. Every second Thursday of the month, Hertz would interpret an actual Rorschach protocol presented by interns or staff members. Her interpretations were so detailed and exact that we, as scientists inexperienced with the Rorschach, doubted the validity of her interpretations. When other interns or the staff psychologists agreed with everything Hertz said, we became even more skeptical. We thought they were just awed by Hertz's reputation and were afraid to challenge this spirited woman.

When our turn came to present a Rorschach, we used the protocol of a patient we had been see-

As with location, the presence (or absence) of each determinant as well as the relative proportion of the various determinants can be related to a number of hypotheses and empirical findings (Exner, 1986; Perry et al., 1995). Consider the movement response. Most Rorschach experts agree that whether and how a subject uses movement can be revealing. The meaning of movement, however, is unclear because of disagreements among experts and contradictory or unclear experimental findings. Many experts believe the movement response is related to motor activity and impulses. Numerous movement responses, for example, may suggest high motor activity or strong impulses. The ratio of M (human movement) to FM (animal movement) responses has been linked by some experts to a person's control and expression of internal impulses. In addition, like many other quantitative aspects of the Rorschach, the movement category varies with development. Ames, Metraux, and Walker (1971), for example, found more FM than M responses from children than from adults. Thus, a high proportion of FM responses in an adult may indicate immaturity or a primitive capacity to deal with impulses. As you think about these inferences, keep in mind that they are no more than hypotheses. An examiner who blindly accepts one interpretation of a particular quantitative aspect can be making a big mistake. Certainly one who blindly accepts a particular interpretation of a Rorschach pattern is ignoring the available literature. Focused Example 16-1 illustrates the value of using highly trained experts to interpret Rorschach patterns.

---

ing in psychotherapy for several months. We knew this patient very well. We fully expected Hertz to make errors in her interpretation. We were determined to point these out to the group, thus exposing the group's error in accepting Hertz's previous interpretations. We were shocked, however, when Hertz was able to describe this patient after reading only the first four or five responses and examining the quantitative summary of the various scoring categories and ratios. Within 25 minutes, Hertz told us not only what we already knew but also things we hadn't seen but were obviously true once pointed out. This experience was most unsettling. Having started with a strong bias against the Rorschach, we could not dismiss what Hertz had done without concluding that there must be some value in it.

Later, we found that Hertz's secret was her experience. She had given or studied so many Rorschachs that she had an intuitive feeling for the meaning of a particular pattern. After having seen the Rorschach patterns of dozens, if not hundreds, of disturbed individuals, she could easily identify a problem. Indeed, her knowledge and experience were so broad that she could even distinguish specific types of disturbances based on the Rorschach.

We still feel the scientific status of the Rorschach leaves much to be desired. However, our experiences with the Rorschach, which include direct observation of interpretations from prominent experts, have led us to reconsider its value. If experts can make accurate interpretations, then it may be premature to reject the Rorschach without more experimental investigations. However, until the experts can specify the exact processes underlying correct interpretations from the Rorschach, the criticism from scientists will continue, as Hertz herself (1986), who has repeatedly called for innovation and rigorous research, has acknowledged.

Making sure the determinant can be identified is the most difficult aspect of Rorschach administration. Because of the difficulties of conducting an adequate inquiry and the present lack of standardized administration procedures, examiners vary widely in the conduct of their inquiries (Blais et al., 1995). It has been known for years that examiner differences influence the subject's response (Gibby, Miller, & Walker, 1953). As a result of this problem, much of the Rorschach literature is confounded by differences in administration and scoring alone. This is one reason why reliable experimental investigations of the Rorschach are rare (Lewandowski & Saccuzzo, 1976).

Scoring content, however, is a relatively simple matter. Most authorities list content categories such as human (H), animal (A), and nature (N). An inquiry is generally not necessary to determine content.

Similarly, most experts generally agree on the so-called populars, those responses frequently given for each card. Furthermore, Exner's (1993) comprehensive system, which includes as populars only those responses that occur once in three protocols on the average, provides a standardized method for scoring populars.

Scoring form quality, the extent to which the percept matches the stimulus properties of the inkblot, is difficult. Some experts argue that if the examiner can also see the percept, then the response has adequate form quality. If the examiner cannot see it, then the response has poor form quality and is scored F−. Obviously, such a subjective system is grossly inadequate, because scoring for form quality may then depend on the intelligence, imagination, skill, and even psychological state of the examiner. Exner's (1993) comprehensive system, which uses the usual frequency of the occurrence of various responses in evaluating form quality, is more objective and thus more scientifically acceptable than the method based on the examiner's ability to see the percept.

Table 16-1 summarizes our discussion of Rorschach scoring. Though the discussion has been incomplete, perhaps you now have an idea of how a projective test can be scored to yield quantitative data. These quantitative data, in turn, are important because they permit the accumulation of norms for particular groups. If subjects deviate from the typical or expected performance, then the examiner must determine the reason underlying the deviation. This process often leads to valuable information about the individual (Acklin, 1995; J. E. Smith et al., 1991).

Rorschach scoring is obviously difficult and complex. The purpose of the preceding discussion is to familiarize you with some of its many possibilities. Use of the Rorschach requires advanced graduate training. You should not attempt to score or use a Rorschach without formal and didactic graduate instruction and supervised experience. Without this detailed training, you might make serious errors because the procedure is so complex.

In addition to the quantitative aspects, Rorschach protocols may be evaluated for qualitative features, including the specific content (Moreland, Reznikoff, & Aronow, 1995) as well as the sequence of responses. One important aspect of a qualitative interpretation is an evaluation of content reported frequently by emotionally disturbed, mentally retarded, or brain-damaged indi-

TABLE 16-1

Summary of Rorschach Scoring

I. Location

Definition: Where on the blot was the percept seen (located)?

Types: *
1. Whole (W). The whole inkblot was used.
2. Common detail (D). A common or well-defined part of the inkblot was used.
3. Unusual detail (Dd). An unusual or poorly defined part of the inkblot was used.

II. Determinant

Definition: What feature of the inkblot determined the response?

Types: *
1. Form (F). The shape or outline of the blot determined the response ("because the inkblot looked like one").
2. Movement (M, FM, m). Movement was seen ("two animals walking up a hill").
3. Color (C). Color played a role in determining the response ("a brown bear," "pink clouds").
4. Shading (T). Texture or shading features played a role in determining the response ("a furry bear because of the shading").

III. Form Quality

Definition: To what extent did the percept match the stimulus properties of the inkblot?

Types: *
1. F+ or +. Percept matched stimulus properties of the inkblot in an exceptionally good way.
2. F. Percept matched stimulus properties of the inkblot.
3. F− or −. Percept matched the stimulus properties of the inkblot poorly.

IV. Content

Definition: What was the percept?

Types: *
1. Human (H).
2. Animal (A).
3. Nature (N).

V. Popular-original

Definition: How frequently is the percept seen in normative samples? (Popular responses are seen in about one of every three protocols.)

*This list is incomplete and does not cover the entire range of possibilities. The information given is designed to illustrate quantitative scoring of a projective test.

viduals but infrequently by the normal population. Such responses can be used to discriminate normal from disordered conditions (Moreland, Reznikoff, & Aronow, 1995). Confabulatory (DW) responses also illustrate the value of qualitative interpretations. In the DW response, the subject overgeneralizes from a part to a whole: "It looked like my mother because of the eyes. My mother has large piercing eyes just like these." Here the subject sees a detail—"large piercing eyes"—and overgeneralizes so that the entire inkblot looks like his or her mother. Although one such response has no clear or specific meaning, when a subject makes a number of confabulatory responses, a disordered state becomes increasingly likely. Given infrequently by the normal population, these responses are given often by brain-damaged, mentally retarded, or emotionally disturbed individuals. Naturally, the examiner must evaluate interviews, the case history, the presenting problem, and results from other tests before accepting the validity of a qualitative analysis of a Rorschach protocol. A problem arises when the examiner or a researcher tries to use a single Rorschach feature to predict or define a specific disordered state (see Focused Example 16-2).

Focused Example 16.2

THE DANGER OF BASING RORSCHACH INTERPRETATIONS ON INSUFFICIENT EVIDENCE

We had the opportunity to become involved in a forensic case in which an individual claimed that the negligence of a large company in sealing pipes together caused a gas leak that resulted in brain damage. This individual consulted an attorney, who sent him to a psychologist. The psychologist administered a Rorschach test. Based on her findings, the psychologist concluded that the person was brain damaged and thus had a legitimate case. The company called us and asked whether the Rorschach could be used to diagnose or identify brain damage. We replied that certain Rorschach patterns may be consistent with brain damage but that you can't prove a person is brain damaged simply on the basis of Rorschach results.

Lawyers for the company brought in the psychologist's report and a copy of the Rorschach protocol. The person suspected of brain damage provided only 6 responses, far fewer than the 22 to 32 responses typically found for the ten Rorschach cards. The protocol was as follows:

	Free Association	*Inquiry*	*Scoring*
Card 1	A bat.	Here are the wings; there is the head.	W F A P

Discussion

The W indicates the whole inkblot was used in the percept. The F indicates that only the form or shape (not color, movement, or shading) determined the response. The A stands for animal content. The P indicates this response is a popular (that is, one that is commonly given).

Card 2	I don't know.	No, I still don't.	Rejection

Discussion

When the subject fails to provide a response, this is known as a rejection. Some examiners present the card again in the inquiry and ask, "Now do you see anything?" A rejection could indicate a number of things. The typical or classical interpretation of a rejection is guardedness or defensiveness.

Card 3	I don't know. (Q) No, I don't see anything.	I said I don't know.	Rejection

Discussion

The (Q) indicates the examiner questioned the subject further, thus attempting to elicit a response. Notice the defensive quality in the subject's response during the inquiry.

Card 4	A gorilla.	All of it; big feet, head, body.	W F A
Card 5	A moth.	Whole thing; wings, feelers, head.	W F A P
Card 6	I don't know.	No, nothing.	Rejection
Card 7	A bird without a head.	Wings, but no head. (Q) All of it.	W F−A

Discussion

The F− indicates a poor correspondence between the response, bird, and the stimulus properties of the inkblot. Bird is an unusual response to this inkblot.

	Free Association	*Inquiry*	*Scoring*
Card 8	Animals, maybe rats trying to steal something.	Just two animals on the sides.	D F A P

Discussion

The two animals were formed from two common details (D). It was scored P because this response is a popular (that is, frequently occurring).

Card 9	I don't know.	No, it doesn't look like anything to me.	Rejection
Card 10	Nothing, wait, looks like a bug here.	Just a bug, legs, pinchers, head.	D F Insect

The psychologist who conducted this Rorschach administration stretched the interpretation, in our judgment, when she claimed this person was brain damaged. The argument presented was that a small number of responses, a preponderance of W responses, a lack of determinants other than form, and misperception (the poor form quality response to card 7) were all consistent with brain damage. Because the protocol contained qualities commonly found in the protocols of brain-damaged individuals, the psychologist argued that she had found evidence for brain damage.

We looked at this Rorschach protocol and concluded that its information alone could in no way be considered sufficient evidence for brain damage. First, a small number of responses in itself cannot be attributed to any single factor. A small number of responses can be found in retarded, depressed, and extremely defensive individuals as well as in those who are brain damaged. Second, the small number of responses led to an imbalance in the proportion of W to D responses. Data on the typical ratio of W to D responses are based on protocols with 20 to 30 responses. With only six responses, all bets are off. No one can say anything about the balance with so few responses. And, in any case, there is no clear evidence that brain-damaged people give a preponderance of W responses. Third, the one F− response proves nothing. A single F− response does not necessarily indicate anything in particular, let alone brain damage or disturbed perceptions. On the contrary, the subject gave three popular responses, indicating he was capable of accurate perceptions. How else could he see things that are so commonly seen by others? Fourth, the lack of determinants other than form can have several possible interpretations. The significance of the exclusive use of form in this protocol is dubious, however, in view of the small number of responses. A protocol with 30 responses, all determined exclusively by form, would have quite a different meaning. Notice how the total number of responses can influence or alter the meaning of Rorschach data. The Rorschach places no limit on the number of possible responses.

We suggested that other tests be used to evaluate brain damage in this individual. Taking a conservative approach, we did not deny that this person was brain damaged. We simply stated that the Rorschach in no way documented the presence of brain damage. The person in question, however, dropped his suit after our analysis was communicated to his attorney and psychologist.

Psychometric Properties

Evaluating the Rorschach on classical psychometric properties (standardization, norms, reliability, validity) has proven exceptionally difficult. Indeed, this attempt to document or refute the adequacy of the Rorschach has produced one of the greatest divisions of opinion within psychology. Time and again, psychologists have evaluated the available empirical data and concluded that the Rorschach is inadequate when judged by scientific standards. Yet, despite these negative evaluations, the Rorschach has flourished in clinical settings (Lubin, Larsen, & Matarazzo, 1984; Lubin, Wallis, & Paine, 1971).

In evaluating the Rorschach, you should keep in mind that there is no universally accepted method of administration. Some examiners provide lengthy introductions and explanations; others provide almost none. Most of the experts state that the length, content, and flavor of administrative instructions should depend on the subject. Yet, empirical evidence indicates that the method of providing instructions and the content of the instructions influence a subject's response to the Rorschach (Blais et al., 1995). Given the lack of standardized instructions, which has no scientifically legitimate excuse, comparisons of the protocols of two different examiners are tenuous at best. Suppose, for example, one hypothesizes that the total number of responses to a Rorschach is related to the level of defensiveness. Even with an adequate criterion measure of defensiveness, if examiner instructions influence the number of responses, one examiner might obtain an average of 32 responses, whereas a second might obtain 22, independent of defensiveness. If protocols from both examiners are averaged in a group, any direct relationship between number of responses and defensiveness can easily be masked or distorted. Until a universally accepted method of Rorschach administration is used, researchers must standardize the Rorschach administration procedures themselves or risk confounding their results.

In addition to nonuniform administration, Rorschach scoring procedures are not standardized. One system scores for human movement whenever a human is seen, whereas another has elaborate and stringent rules for scoring human movement. The former system obviously finds much more human movement than does the latter, even when the same test protocols are evaluated. Without standardized scoring, determining the frequency, consistency, and meaning of a particular Rorschach response is extremely difficult. One result of unstandardized Rorschach administration and scoring procedures is that reliability investigations have produced varied and inconsistent results and, even when reliability is shown, validity is questionable. Moreover, scoring as well as interpretation procedures do not enjoy criterion-related validity and are not linked to any theory, which limits the evaluation of construct validity. Researchers must also share in the responsibility for the contradictory and inconclusive findings that permeate the Rorschach literature. Many research investigations of tests such as the Rorschach have failed to control important variables such as race, sex, age, socioeconomic status, and intelligence. If race, for example, influences test results as research indicates (see Lewandowski & Saccuzzo, 1976; Saccuzzo & Johnson, 1995), then studies that fail to control for race may lead to false conclusions. Other problems attributable to the research rather than to psychometric properties include lack of relevant training experience in those who score the protocols, poor statistical models, and poor validating criteria (Blatt, 1975; G. Frank, 1995; Meloy & Singer, 1991).

Whether the problem is lack of standardization, poorly controlled experiments, or both, there is little agreement regarding the scientific status of the Rorschach (Exner, 1995; Nezworski & Wood, 1995). As Buros (1970) noted, "This vast amount of writing and research has produced astonishingly little, if any, agreement among psychologists regarding the specific validities of the Rorschach" (p. xxvi). In brief, the meaning of the thousands of published Rorschach studies is still debatable. For every supportive study, there appears to be a negative or damaging one. (See Table 16-2.)

Traditional belief, especially among opponents of the Rorschach, is that the Rorschach is unreliable. Indeed, when one views individual studies in isolation, especially those published before 1985, the results appear confusing. For every study reporting internal consistency coefficients in the .80s and .90s, one can find another with coefficients of .10 or even .01. Two recent developments, however, show a much brighter picture: the use of meta-analysis to analyze Rorschach reliability and validity and new approaches to the evaluation of the Rorschach's internal consistency.

Meta-analysis is a statistical procedure in which the results of numerous studies are averaged in a single, overall investigation. In a meta-analysis of Rorschach reliability and validity, Parker (1983) found an overall internal reliability coefficient of .83 based on 530 statistics from 39 papers published between 1971 and 1980 in the *Journal of Personality Assessment*, the main outlet for research on projective techniques. Moreover, when one uses the Kuder-Richardson formula (which examines all possible ways of splitting the test in two) to calculate internal consistency coefficients rather than the more traditionally used odd-even procedure, Rorschach reliability coefficients are markedly increased. In one study, E. E. Wagner and co-workers (1986) compared the split-half coefficients using the odd-even and the Kuder-Richardson

TABLE 16-2

Summary of Arguments for and Against the Rorschach

Against	In Favor
1. Lacks a universally accepted standard of administration, scoring, and interpretation.	1. Lack of standardized procedures is a historical accident that can be corrected.
2. Evaluations of data are subjective.	2. Test interpretation is an art, not a science; all test interpretation involves a subjective component.
3. Results are unstable over time.	3. A new look at the data reveals that the Rorschach is much more stable than is widely believed.
4. Is unscientific.	4. Has a large empirical base.
5. Is inadequate by all traditional standards.	5. Available evidence is biased and poorly controlled and has therefore failed to provide a fair evaluation.

techniques for 12 scoring categories. With the odd-even technique, coefficients ranged between −.075 and +.785, which reflects the general findings in the literature through the mid-1980s. However, with the Kuder-Richardson, commonly used for evaluating the major ability tests, the coefficients ranged from .55 to .88, with a mean of .77. Thus, results from both meta-analysis and application of Kuder-Richardson techniques reveal a higher level of Rorschach reliability than has generally been attributed to the test.

Clearly, the final word on the Rorschach has yet to be spoken. Far more research is needed, but unless practitioners can agree on a standard method of administration and scoring, the researchers' hands will be tied. Fortunately for the Rorschach, the first steps toward an adequate evaluation have already been taken. In a heroic effort, Exner (1993) distilled the best elements of the various Rorschach systems and proposed a comprehensive system that provides standard administration procedures developed and refined by empirical analysis. Likewise, scoring has been designed to increase interscorer reliability. Normative frequency tables based on empirical investigations are available to aid in evaluating quantitative factors.

Despite these efforts, criticism remains intense. Wood, Nezworski, and Stejskal (1996), for example, have pointed to what these authors believe are significant problems with Exner's comprehensive system. They contend that the interrater reliability of most scoring indices in the system has never been adequately demonstrated. Further, they maintain that the validity of such indices is questionable. Finally, they note that much of the data cited in support of the system remains unpublished and thus unavailable for examination by the scientific community.

Although additional work is still needed, Exner and his colleagues have improved the psychometric qualities of the Rorschach. Interpretive suggestions are based on experimental investigations rather than on theoretical dogma or personal bias (Exner, 1996). In any event, both opponents and proponents still have a long way to go before the psychological community achieves consensus on this most controversial test (Hertz, 1986; C. Piotrowski, 1984). As the Rorschach expert, and recipient of the Society for Personality Assessment Distinguished Contributor Award, Sidney J. Blatt (1990) stated it is best to view the Rorschach "as an experimental procedure that systematically presents an individual with ambiguity and allows us to observe and study how the individual constructs meaning from relative ambiguity" (p. 401).

In line with Blatt's suggestion is some excellent work by Aronow, Reznikoff, and Moreland (1995). These authors prefer an emphasis on the Rorschach as a semi-structured interview (see Chapter 9). The inkblots are used as standard stimuli to elicit information about the unique qualities of the individual. In their projective technique approach, they emphasize interpretation of content rather than scoring indices. The focus is on "what the subject sees" rather than on "how the subject perceives" (Aronow, Reznikoff, & Moreland, 1995, p. 214). These authors' approach represents a promising alternative for clinically-oriented practitioners.

An Alternative Inkblot Test: The Holtzman

Among the prime problems of the Rorschach, from a psychometric viewpoint, are its variable number of responses from one subject to another, lack of standard procedures, and lack of an alternative form. The Holtzman Inkblot Test was created (Holtzman et al., 1961) to meet these difficulties while maintaining the advantages of the inkblot methodology. In this test, the subject is permitted to give only one response per card. Administration and scoring procedures are standardized and carefully described. An alternative form is available that correlates well with the original test stimuli. Interscorer as well as split-half reliabilities are comparable to those found for objective personality tests (Gamble, 1972).

Both forms, A and B, of the Holtzman contain 45 cards. Each response may be scored on 22 dimensions. Many of these dimensions resemble those found in the Rorschach and include location, determinant, and content. Responses may also be scored for such factors as anxiety and hostility. For each scoring category or variable, norms are presented for several samples ranging from 5-year-olds through adults. Given the psychometric advantages of the Holtzman, it is interesting that the test hasn't even begun to challenge the Rorschach's popularity.

Gamble (1972) reviewed the literature on the Holtzman and concluded that there were insufficient data to compare the Holtzman to the Rorschach adequately. The main difficulty with the Holtzman appears to be its validity (Gamble, 1972; Zubin, 1972). The few available validity studies are hardly impressive. As Zubin (1972) notes, those studies that show a positive relationship between the Holtzman and various criterion measures are based on qualitative rather than quantitative features. Thus, the available supportive evidence is highly subjective, depending on examiner skill rather than formal interpretive standards. In short, one cannot currently consider the Holtzman any more useful than the Rorschach, despite the former's superior psychometric features. Nevertheless, because the Holtzman is a relatively young test, it is still too early to judge its clinical utility compared with the Rorschach (Leichsenring, 1990, 1991).

The Thematic Apperception Test

The Thematic Apperception Test (TAT) was introduced in 1935 by Christina Morgan and Henry Murray of Harvard University. It is comparable to the Rorschach in many ways, including its importance and psychometric problems. As with the Rorschach, use of the TAT grew rapidly after its introduction, though its psychometric adequacy was (and still is) vigorously debated (Alvarado, 1994; Keiser & Prather, 1990). Unlike the Rorschach, the TAT has been relatively well received by the scientific community. Also, the TAT is based on Murray's (1938) theory of needs (see Chapter 15), whereas the Rorschach is basically atheoretical. The TAT and the Rorschach differ in other respects as well. The TAT authors were conservative in their evaluation of the TAT and scientific in their outlook. The TAT was not oversold as was the Rorschach, and no extravagant claims were made. Unlike the Rorschach, the TAT was not billed as a diagnostic instrument—that is, a test of disordered emotional states. Instead, the TAT was presented as an instrument for evaluating human personality characteristics. (See Table 16-3.)

This test also differs from the Rorschach because the TAT's nonclinical uses are just as important as its clinical ones. Indeed, the TAT is one of the most important techniques used in personality research (for example, J. W. Atkinson, 1981; Cramer & Blatt, 1990; McClelland et al., 1953; J. H. Turner, 1970). As stated, the TAT is based on Murray's (1938) theory, which distinguishes 28 human needs, including the needs for sex, affiliation, and dominance. Many of these needs have been extensively researched through use of the TAT. Murray's need for achievement—"the desire or tendency to do things as rapidly and/or as well as possible" (1938, p. 164)—alone has generated countless studies involving the TAT. A review of the relevant literature by Birney (1968) cites well over 100 studies on this one need, most of them by McClelland (1951a, 1951b, 1958, for example). The TAT measure of the achievement need has been related to factors such as parental perceptions, parental expectations, and parental attitudes toward offspring. Need achievement is also related to the standards you as a student set for yourself (for example, academic standards). The higher your need for achievement, the more likely you are to study and ultimately achieve a high economic and social position in society. Studies such as those on the achievement motive have increased the construct validity as well as the scientific respectability of the TAT.

Stimuli, Administration, and Interpretation

The TAT is more structured and less ambiguous than the Rorschach. TAT stimuli consist of pictures that depict a variety of scenes. There are 30 pictures and one blank card. Specific cards are designed for male subjects, others for female. Some of the cards are appropriate for older people, others for young

TABLE 16-3

A Comparison of the Rorschach and TAT

Rorschach	TAT
Rejected by scientific community	Well received by scientific community
Atheoretical	Based on Murray's (1938) theory of needs
Oversold by extravagant claims	Conservative claims
Purported diagnostic instrument	Not purported as diagnostic
Primarily clinical use	Clinical and nonclinical uses

ones. A few of the cards are appropriate for all subjects, such as Card 1. This card shows a boy, neatly dressed and groomed, sitting at a table on which lies a violin. In his description of Card 1, Murray stated that the boy is "contemplating" the violin. According to experts such as Bellak (1986), Card 1 of the TAT tends to reveal a person's relationship toward parental figures.

Other TAT cards tend to elicit other kinds of information. Card 4 is a picture of a woman "clutching the shoulders of a man whose face and body are averted as if he were trying to pull away from her" (Bellak, 1975, p. 51). This card elicits information concerning male-female relationships. Bellak (1975, 1986) and others (Rapaport, Gill, & Schafer, 1945–1946) provide a description of the TAT cards along with the information each card tends to elicit. This knowledge is essential in TAT interpretation. Figure 16-2 shows Card 12F, which sometimes elicits conflicting emotions about the self. Other feelings may also be elicited.

Standardization of administration and especially scoring procedures of the TAT are about as poor as, if not worse than, those of the Rorschach. Most examiners typically state something like, "I am going to show you some pictures. I want you to tell me a story about each picture. Tell me what led up to

FIGURE 16-2 *Card 12F from the Thematic Apperception Test. This card often gives the subject a chance to express attitudes toward a mother or daughter figure. Sometimes attitudes toward marriage and aging also emerge.*

(Reprinted by permission of the publishers from Henry A. Murray, Thematic Apperception Test, Cambridge, MA: Harvard University Press, Copyright © 1943 by the President and Fellows of Harvard College, © 1971 by Henry A. Murray.)

the story, what is happening, what the characters are thinking and feeling, and what the outcome will be." In the original design of the test, 20 cards were to be administered to each subject, 10 cards in each of two separate one-hour sessions. In actual practice, however, only 10 or 12 cards are typically used (Bellak, 1975, p. 47). As with the Rorschach and almost all other individually administered tests, the examiner records the subject's responses verbatim. The examiner also records the reaction time—the time interval between the initial presentation of a card and the subject's first response. By recording reaction time, the examiner can determine whether the subject has difficulty with a particular card. Because each card is designed to elicit its own themes, needs, and conflicts, an abnormally long reaction time may indicate a specific problem. If, for example, the reaction time substantially increases for all cards involving heterosexual relationships, then the examiner may hypothesize that the subject is experiencing difficulty in this area.

There are by far more interpretive and scoring systems for the TAT than for the Rorschach. In his comprehensive review of the TAT literature, Murstein (1963, p. 23) states, "There would seem to be as many thematic scoring systems as there were hairs in the beard of Rasputin." Murstein summarizes most of the major methods of interpretation for the TAT, grouping them into quantitative and nonquantitative methods. Unlike the quantitative aspects of the Rorschach, which most examiners consider extremely important, the quantitative methods of TAT interpretation are unpopular (Alvarado, 1995; Westen, 1991). Most TAT examiners find the available scoring systems to be overly elaborate, complex, and time consuming. They therefore tend to use only nonquantitative methods of interpretation.

Almost all methods of TAT interpretation take into account the hero, needs, press, themes, and outcomes. The hero is the character in each picture with whom the subject seems to identify. In most cases, the story revolves around one easily recognizable character. If a number of characters seem to be important, the character most like the storyteller is selected as the hero. Of particular importance are the motives and needs of the hero. Most systems, including Murray's original, consider the intensity, duration, and frequency of each need to indicate the importance and relevance of that need. In TAT interpretation, *press* refers to the environmental forces that interfere with or facilitate satisfaction of the various needs. Again, factors such as frequency, intensity, and duration are used to judge the relative importance of these factors. The frequency of various themes (for example, depression) and outcomes (for example, failures) also indicates their importance.

To understand the potential value of the TAT in evaluating personality characteristics, you should realize that different individuals offer quite different responses to the same card. For example, given Card 1, in which a boy is contemplating a violin, one subject may say, "This boy's mother has just reminded him to practice the violin. The boy hates the violin and is wondering what he can do to make his practice session less boring. As he daydreams, his mother scolds him, so he picks up the violin and plays, resenting every minute." Another subject may respond, "The boy has just come home from school and is getting ready to practice the violin. He hopes to become a great violin player someday but realizes he's just an average, ordinary person. He picks up the violin and plays, dreaming about success." A third story may go as follows: "It's violin practice again and the boy is fed up. Do this, do that; his parents are always trying to live his life. This time he fixes them. He picks up the violin, smashes it, and goes out to play baseball."

Think about these three different stories. Because the stimulus was the same in each case, differences in the stories must in some way reflect differences in the storytellers. The primary issue is exactly what is revealed in these stories. Many years ago, Lindzey (1952) analyzed a number of assumptions underlying the TAT. Table 16-4 lists these major assumptions. Although there were problems with many of the studies cited by Lindzey, positive evidence was found to support these assumptions, the validity of which holds to this day (J. L. Johnson, 1994; Keiser & Prather, 1990). By understanding these assumptions, you can get an idea of the complexity of TAT interpretation.

Although Lindzey's analysis was conducted some time ago, many TAT practitioners are guided by the assumptions listed in Table 16-4. The primary assumption—in completing an incomplete or unstructured situation, the individual may reveal his or her own strivings, dispositions, and conflicts—provides a rationale and support for projective tests in general. Most of the other assumptions, however, pertain specifically to the TAT. As these assumptions indicate, although a story reflects the storyteller, a multitude of factors may influence the story. There-

---

TABLE 16-4

Lindzey's Assumptions for TAT Interpretation

Primary assumption

In completing an incomplete or unstructured situation, the individual may reveal his or her own characteristics (strivings, dispositions, conflicts).

Other assumptions

1. The storyteller ordinarily identifies with one person in the drama. The characteristics (wishes, strivings, conflicts) of this imaginary person may reflect those of the storyteller.

2. The storyteller's characteristics may be represented indirectly or symbolically.

3. All stories are not of equal importance.

4. Themes directly related to stimulus material are less likely to be significant than those unrelated to stimulus material.

5. Recurrent themes (those that show up in three or four different stories) are particularly likely to mirror the characteristics of the storyteller.

6. The stories may reflect momentary characteristics of the storyteller (those aroused by temporary environmental factors) as well as enduring characteristics

7. Stories may reflect events from the past that the storyteller has only observed or witnessed. However, the selection of these stories suggest that the events may still reflect the storyteller's own characteristics.

8. The stories may also reflect group membership or sociocultural factors.

9. Dispositions and conflicts inferred from the storyteller's creations may be unconscious and thus may not always be reflected directly in overt behavior or consciousness.

Adapted from Lindzey (1952).

fore, all TAT experts agree that a complete interview and a case history must accompany any attempt to interpret the TAT. No matter how careful and thorough such an interview, however, final conclusions and interpretations are still based on many factors, including the skill and experience of the examiner.

Psychometric Properties

Many experts consider the TAT to be psychometrically unsound. Given the TAT's unstandardized procedures for administration, scoring, and interpretation, one can easily understand why psychometric evaluations have produced inconsistent, unclear, and conflicting findings. Division of opinion is so wide that, whereas one expert finds impressive evidence of intrinsic validity (Harrison, 1965), others have found TAT validity to be almost nil (Varble, 1971). Subjectivity affects not only the interpretation of the TAT, but also analysis of the TAT literature. In other words, as with the Rorschach, two experts can look at the same research data and draw different or even opposite conclusions. It should be no surprise, then, that for almost every positive empirical finding there is a negative counterpart.

An analysis of existing results does reveal that the study of specific variables, such as the achievement need, produces respectably high reliability figures. (Exner, 1976; Murstein, 1963). Test-retest reliabilities appear to fluctuate, however, and to diminish as the interval between the two testing sessions increases. The median test-retest correlation across studies is only about .30 (Kraiger, Hakel, & Cornelius, 1984; Winter & Stewart, 1977). However, J. W. Atkinson (1981) has argued that the validity of the TAT does not depend on test-retest reliability. Split-half reliabilities have been consistently poor. Many TAT proponents, though, do not consider the split-half method appropriate, because each card is designed to produce its own theme and content. What is needed is a study with Kuder-Richardson reliabilities, as has recently been done with the Rorschach.

Validity studies have produced even murkier findings. Most experts agree that the TAT has content validity for evaluating human personality; however, criterion validity has been difficult to document. In an early but often cited study, Harrison (1940) found that his own inferences based on TAT stories correlated at .78 with hospital records for specific variables. And he reported that he was 75% correct in diagnosing patients into major categories, such as psychotic versus neurotic, using TAT data. Little and Shneidman (1959) found, however, that when 12 specialists for each of four tests (TAT, Make-a-Picture Story, Rorschach, MMPI) were asked to match the judgments of a group of criterion judges who had conducted extensive interviews with each of the subjects, not only was there little agreement between the test judges and the criterion judges, but the TAT fared poorest, having both the lowest reliability and the poorest predictive validity of the four tests. Newer studies also report discouraging reliability coefficients (Singh, 1986).

As we review the psychometric properties of the TAT, we find that, like the Rorschach, the TAT has a number of significant problems. In spite of these problems, however, the TAT continues to find widespread application in clinical as well as research settings. As with the Rorschach, the most pressing need appears to be establishing standardized administration and scoring procedures. Until such standardization is achieved, the TAT will continue to fare poorly according to traditional psychometric standards.

Alternative Apperception Procedures

An alternative thematic apperception test (Ritzler, Sharkey, & Chudy, 1980; Sharkey & Ritzler, 1985) has been constructed with pictures from the *Family of Man* photo-essay collection (Museum of Modern Art, 1955). According to these authors, the new procedure can be scored quantitatively. It provides a balance of positive and negative stories and a variety of action and energy levels for the main character. In comparison, the TAT elicits predominantly negative and low-energy stories (Ritzler, Sharkey, & Chudy, 1980). Preliminary results with this new procedure, known as the Southern Mississippi TAT (or SM-TAT), have been encouraging. These results indicate that the SM-TAT preserves many of the advantages of the TAT while providing a more rigorous and modern methodology. Naturally, more research is needed, but the authors of this new attempt to modernize the TAT are to be applauded.

The versatility and usefulness of the TAT approach are illustrated not only by attempts such as that of Ritzler, Sharkey, and Chudy (1980) to update the test but also by the availability of special forms of the TAT for children and others for the elderly. The Children's Apperception Test (CAT) was created to meet the special needs of children aged 3 through 10 (Bellak, 1975). The CAT stimuli contain animal rather than human figures as in the TAT.

A special children's apperception test has been developed specifically for Hispanic children (Malgady, Constantino, & Rogler, 1984). The Tell Me A Story Test (TEMAS) is a TAT technique consisting of 23 chromatic pictures depicting minority and nonminority characters in urban and familial settings (Constantino et al., 1992). Initial research has shown the promise of the TEMAS, but more work is needed (Constantino et al., 1991).

The Gerontological Apperception Test uses stimuli in which one or more elderly individuals are involved in a scene with a theme relevant to the concerns of the elderly, such as loneliness and family conflicts (Wolk & Wolk, 1971). The Senior Apperception Technique is an alternative to the Gerontological Apperception Test and is parallel in content (Bellak, 1975; Bellak & Bellak, 1973). All hold promise as clinical tools (Mark, 1993).

Nonpictorial Projective Procedures

Projective tests need not involve the use of a pictorial stimulus. Words or phrases sometimes provide the stimulus, as in the Word Association Test and incomplete sentence tasks. Or a subject can be asked to create or draw something, as in the Draw-A-Man Test. In our final section, we briefly describe each of these procedures.

Word Association Test

Imagine yourself comfortably seated in a psychologist's examining office. Your task is simple, or at least it seems so. The psychologist says a word and you say the first word that comes to mind. The test begins. The first word is *hat.* You reply *coat,* the most common response of college students according to Rapaport, Gill, and Schafer (1968). The test goes on as follows:

Lamp

Love

Father

Paper

Masturbation

Chair

Breast

Car

Penis

Suicide

Do some of these words arouse any feelings in you? Words like *love, mother, breast,* and *masturbation* do in many people. The purpose of word association tests is to infer possible disturbances and areas of conflict from an individual's response to words.

The use of word association tests dates back to Galton (1879) and was first used on a clinical basis by Jung (1910) and G. H. Kent and Rosanoff (1910). The first to attempt to standardize word association procedures, Kent and Rosanoff developed a list of 100 standard words and presented them to a sample of 1000 normal adults who were partially stratified by geographic location, education, occupation, age, and intelligence. An objective scoring system was developed and the Kent-Rosanoff word association test enjoyed moderate popularity in the 1920s and 1930s.

Rapaport, Gill, and Schafer (1968) subsequently developed a 60-item word association test. The range of words covered familial, household, oral, anal, aggressive, and phobic content. Responses were quantified by collecting norms on college students and schizophrenics, although interpretations were clearly psychoanalytic in nature.

Interest in word association techniques dropped considerably after Rapaport, Gill, and Schafer (1968) concluded that the procedures did not live up to their clinical promise. Although the techniques are still in use (deGroot, 1988; Pons, 1989), they play only a limited role in clinical and counseling settings.

Sentence Completion Tasks

Another family of projective techniques involving words are incomplete sentence tasks. These tasks provide a stem that the subject is asked to complete; for example,

1. I am_____
2. I enjoy_____
3. What annoys me_____
4. It pains me to _____
5. Men_____
6. Dancing_____
7. Sports _____

As with all projective techniques, the individual's response is believed to reflect that person's needs, conflicts, values, and thought processes. In clinical use these tasks also give a person the opportunity to provide information that may have been too embarrassing to present in a face-to-face verbal interview. Clinicians look for recurring themes of conflict and pathological content.

A number of incomplete sentence tasks with scoring procedures are available. Among the most widely used of these is the Rotter Incomplete Sentence Blank (Rotter & Rafferty, 1950). The Rotter provides 40 stems, each of which is scored on a seven-point system. In general, short sentences with some humor and positive content get the highest scores—for example, "Men <u>have their advantages and disadvantages.</u>" Long complex sentences with negative or depressed content receive the lowest scores—for example, "Men <u>who I can't stand and would like to sometimes kill and do away with really know how to make a person feel crazy all the time.</u>"

Sentence completion procedures are used widely in clinical as well as research settings. A relatively recent addition to this family is the Incomplete Sentences Task of Lanyon and Lanyon (1980). Sentences are scored on a three-point scale (0, 1, 2), and norms are available as a function of age and gender. The initial reviews of Lanyon and Lanyon's incomplete sentence task have been positive and encouraging (Cundick, 1985; Dush, 1985).

Figure Drawing Tests

Another set of projective tests uses expressive techniques, in which the subject is asked to create something, usually a drawing. In the Draw-A-Person Test (Machover, 1949), the subject, most often a child, is asked to draw the picture of a person. Later the child is asked to tell a story about the person. A similar technique is the House-Tree-Person Test (Buck, 1948), in which the subject draws the picture of a house, tree, and person and then makes up a story about it. In the Kinetic Family Drawing Test (R. C. Burns & Kaufman, 1970, 1972), the subject draws a picture of his or her family.

Projective drawing tests are scored on a number of dimensions, including absolute size, relative size, omissions, and disproportions. For example, in drawing her family, a young child may omit herself. One might then assume that the child feels alienated from the family. In drawing a house-tree-person, the child might draw himself in the house looking out, perhaps reflecting a feeling of being isolated or trapped.

If there is a tendency to overinterpret projective test data without sufficient empirical foundation, then projective drawing tests are among the worst offenders. Although experienced clinicians can gain insights into an individual through a skillful and cautious interpretation, there is a tendency to go too far in what one can infer. For instance, in the Draw-A-Person Test, a clinician is advised to interpret a large head as indicating an overconcern with matters of intellectual functioning—or even brain damage, according to one system (Machover, 1949). Although figure drawing tests have a place in a test battery, great caution is called for in their use until rigorous research can document the valid inferences one can make from them.

Summary

According to the *projective hypothesis,* interpretations of an ambiguous or vague stimulus reflect the subject's own needs, feelings, experiences, prior conditioning, thought processes, and so forth.

The Rorschach is the preeminent projective test. Five individuals played a dominant role in its development: S. J. Beck, Hertz, Klopfer, Z. Piotrowski, and Rapaport. Rorschach stimuli consist of ten black, gray, red, and various pastel inkblots. These stimuli were formed by dropping ink onto a piece of paper and folding the paper.

Rorschach administration involves two phases. During the free-association phase, the examiner presents each card with a minimum of structure. During the second phase—the inquiry—the examiner presents each card again to obtain sufficient information for scoring purposes. The five major Rorschach scoring categories are location (where), determinant (why), content (what), frequency of occurrence (popular-original), and form quality (correspondence of percept to stimulus properties of the inkblot).

The Rorschach is highly controversial. On the negative side, it has been attacked for its lack of standardized methods for administration, scoring, and interpretation. It has also been criticized because interpretations are subjective and results are unstable over time. With the exception of recent reliability studies, scientific evidence has generally weighed against it. On the positive side, efforts are being made to establish standardized procedures. In the hands of an expert, the Rorschach can reveal a wealth of information about a single individual. Unfavorable scientific evidence is disputable.

The Holtzman is a recently developed alternative to the Rorschach. Though it overcomes much of the scientific criticism of the Rorschach, the value and importance of this relatively new procedure have not yet been determined.

Another projective test, the TAT, enjoys wide research as well as clinical use. The TAT stimuli consist of 30 pictures, depicting a variety of scenes, and one blank card. Card 1, for example, shows a scene in which a boy, neatly dressed and groomed, sits at a table on which is a violin. The boy is looking at the violin. Specific cards are suited for adults, children, men, and women. In administering the TAT, the examiner asks subjects to make up a story; he or she looks for the events that led up to the scene, what the characters are thinking and feeling, and the outcome.

Like the Rorschach, the TAT has strong supporters but has also been attacked on a variety of scientific grounds. Though not psychometrically sound by traditional standards, the TAT is in widespread use. Like the Rorschach, it can provide a wealth of information about an individual.

Some of the similarities between the TAT and Rorschach are as follows: They are both individual projective tests for measuring human functioning and personality characteristics. Both are poorly standardized for administration, scoring, and interpretation. Reliability coefficients for both tests vary widely. Both are highly criticized, yet both are used extensively and adopted enthusiastically by practitioners. Both provide a rich source of information about a single individual. And both are supported by a wide body of empirical findings.

Some of the differences between the TAT and Rorschach are as follows: The Rorschach stimuli are inkblots; the TAT stimuli depict scenes. Thus, TAT stimuli are more meaningful than Rorschach stimuli. The TAT is based on Murray's (1938) theory of needs; the Rorschach is atheoretical. Formal scoring and quantitative features, important in the Rorschach, are of little significance in the TAT. The TAT finds extensive use in research as well as in clinical settings; the Rorschach is primarily a clinical tool. TAT interpretation is guided by a variety of assumptions, listed and explored by Lindzey (1952). Rorschach interpretation still depends on the opinion of experts and on research surveys such as those described in Exner's (1974) Rorschach textbook.

A number of nonpictorial projective tests are available, including word association tests and incomplete sentence tests. Expressive techniques require a person to make something, such as draw a picture of a person or of one's family.

CHAPTER 17

Alternatives to Traditional Psychological Tests

LEARNING OBJECTIVES

When you have completed this chapter, you should be able to:

☐ Identify the differences between behavior and traditional assessment procedures

☐ Identify the difference between the beliefs underlying traditional tests and the beliefs underlying behavioral tests

☐ Briefly describe behavioral assessment based on operant conditioning

☐ Identify the main difference between behavioral self-report techniques and traditional self-report techniques

☐ List four types of behavioral self-report techniques

☐ Briefly describe the functional, or behavior-analytic, approach to behavioral assessment

☐ Explain how cognitive-behavioral assessment differs from others types of behavioral assessment

☐ List four types of cognitive-behavioral assessment

☐ Describe a cognitive functional analysis

☐ Briefly describe psychophysical assessment

☐ Describe two major ways in which computers play a role in testing

A high-school teacher once contacted us regarding her 7-year-old son. At the age of 4, the boy had suffered from an illness in which he could not eat solid food for 25 days because it made him gag. If he managed to swallow, he became extremely nauseous. Ever since he had recovered from the illness, he was reluctant to eat all but a few select foods. His usual menu was cold cereal for breakfast, a peanut butter sandwich for lunch, and plain spaghetti for dinner. He refused to eat meat or vegetables of any kind. His parents tried everything, but nothing worked. The mother was concerned that the boy was not developing properly. She had taken him to a pediatrician who told her that unless something could be done to get the boy to eat, he would have to be hospitalized. The physician suggested psychiatric intervention and gave the boy one month to improve.

After explaining this problem, the mother asked us whether we could administer a test that might explain why the child wasn't eating. A school psychologist had suggested to her that psychological tests might help facilitate the treatment process. If we could understand why the boy wasn't eating, perhaps this information would help us treat him. During our interview, we discovered that the boy had been in psychiatric treatment when he was 5. The treatment had lasted about one year with little improvement. Partly because of this previous failure and partly because of her desperation, the mother insisted we do some testing. As we thought about the various tests we might use, we could see little value in using any of the traditional tests for this presenting problem.

We did administer the Wechsler Intelligence Scale for Children—III (WISC-III) and found that the boy had above-average intelligence (full-scale IQ = 115). In achievement, as measured by the Wide Range Achievement Test, the boy was functioning about half a grade level above his present grade placement in both reading and arithmetic. Thus, intellectual and achievement factors could not account for the problem; the ability tests yielded little information in this case. Though more revealing than the ability tests, personality tests unfortunately were not very useful. After administering the Children's Apperception Test (see Chapter 16), our interpretation confirmed our suspicion that the boy's eating problem originated with the trauma he had suffered when he could not eat solid foods. In simple terms, the boy had a fear of eating.

Knowing why the boy wasn't eating certainly wasn't much help. One of the weaknesses of the traditional tests we had used in this case is that they provide little information concerning possible treatment approaches. When we explained the situation to the mother, she pleaded, "Isn't there any other type of test you can give him? Isn't there a test that might also indicate what type of treatment would be most effective?" Thanks to advances within scientific psychology, we could answer "Yes."

We told the mother that an alternative approach to testing had been developed by psychologists in the specialty based on learning principles known as behavior modification, or behavior therapy. Collectively, these nontraditional testing techniques are known as *behavioral assessment*. "Please try these alternative procedures," she said. "I don't care if they are nontraditional," she continued. "If they might help, by all means use them."

Would you be willing to try a nontraditional testing procedure? If so, you are not alone. In the hands of highly trained experts, traditional psychological tests may be extremely valuable, but they still fall short on several grounds. The traditional tests that we have discussed thus far offer little information concerning treatment approaches. As a rule, these traditional procedures also provide little information about how a person might behave in a particular situation. Even if these traditional procedures do explain the reason behind a particular symptom, this information is often of little value to the overall treatment process. Thus, in addition to limitations in reliability, validity, norms, and the like, traditional psychological tests have been criticized on other grounds. The result has been an explosion of alternative approaches.

The Status of Traditional Psychological Tests and an Overview of the Alternatives

In 1953, L. Shaffer conducted a survey asking clinical psychological practitioners to rank order their primary responsibilities. The practitioners ranked psychological testing first among all their duties. Only 14 years later, Holt wrote, "Diagnostic testing today is in a funk" (1967, p. 44). A number of authors have explored the reasons for this dramatic decline in the role and status of psychological testing (Lewandowski & Saccuzzo, 1976; Saccuzzo, 1976). In addition to the unreliability and poorly documented validity of many traditional procedures, many psychologists have rejected traditional tests because of these tests' lack of grounding in the psychological sciences, poor relationship to treatment, and poor validity (Ziskin, 1995).

The psychologists' aversion to traditional testing procedures was paralleled by attacks from the public. As noted by Rapaport, Gill, and Schafer (1968), books written for the general public strongly attacked psychological tests during the interval between L. Shaffer's (1953) survey and Holt's (1967) assessment of the status of testing. In summarizing the general spirit of these attacks, Rapaport, Gill, and Schafer provided this statement: "Although their instruments are unscientific and invalid, psychologists are reading our minds, invading our privacy, imposing a yoke of conformity on employees, and stifling originality in school children, driven by morbid sexual curiosity and the cynical pursuit of money" (1968, p. 32). These accusations led to an inquiry by the Senate Subcommittee on Constitutional Rights and the House Subcommittee on Invasion of Privacy (Dahlstrom, 1969b). Although neither of these subcommittees succeeded in documenting deliberate and widespread misuse of tests (Brayfield, 1965), public attacks against testing continued. For example, a call arose for a moratorium on all tests until improved procedures were developed (APA, 1974). Hardly a year goes by without some major challenge to psychological tests (National Commission on Testing and Public Policy, 1990).

In response to these criticisms, psychologists began to develop testing techniques based on the psychological sciences, on principles and concepts developed in psychological laboratories. Grounded in psychological findings and theories, these tests, though relatively new, provide genuine alternatives to traditional testing procedures.

The alternatives fall into four main categories (see Table 17-1). The first, and by far the largest, category is generally referred to as *behavioral assessment,* which can be broken down into the subcategories of procedures based on operant conditioning, self-report techniques, and Kanfer and Saslow's behavior-analytic (or functional) approach. The second category consists of cognitive techniques; the third, psychophysiological techniques. The fourth category consists of assessment procedures involving the use of computers. We discuss each of these procedures in the sections that follow.

Behavioral Assessment Procedures

Traditional testing procedures are based on a medical model. According to this model, the overt manifestations of a disordered psychological condition (for example, overeating or undereating) are only symptoms—surface expressions of an underlying cause. Disordered behavior is believed to be caused by some underlying characteristic such as an early traumatic experience. In the example at the beginning of this chapter, the boy's avoidance of food was, in a sense, caused by the trauma of an illness in which solid food made him nauseous. Treatment in the medical model is based on the idea that unless the cause of a symptom is removed, a new symptom may develop. Thus, one major function of traditional psychological tests is to ascertain the possible underlying causes of disordered behaviors.

In behavioral assessment, by contrast, the behaviors, cognitions, or physiological responses that define a disordered condition are considered the real problem. If the person eats too much, then the problem is simply overeating and not some possible underlying cause. The overeating may, in fact, have been caused by some early experience, just as in the 7-year-old boy. However, in behavioral assessment, the eating behavior becomes the direct target of treatment. Therefore, the testing procedure evaluates eating behavior.

TABLE 17-1

Categories of Alternatives to Traditional Testing Procedures

Behavioral assessment
Operant conditioning techniques
Self-report techniques
Kanfer and Saslow's behavior-analytic technique
Cognitive techniques
Psychophysiological techniques
Psychophysical and signal detection procedures

You shouldn't assume that behavioral assessment denies, ignores, or negates the causes of psychological disorders. On the contrary, certain techniques of behavior assessment include an evaluation of the factors that precede, coexist with, and follow (maintain) disordered behavior (Haynes, 1990, 1992). These may be environmental factors (such as working conditions, home situation), thought processes (such as internal dialogue), or both. Thus, behavioral assessment often includes an evaluation of the internal and external factors that lead to and maintain disordered behavior as well as an evaluation of the behavior itself (Bellack & Hersen, 1988).

Behavioral assessment is more direct than traditional psychological tests. All the major reviewers of the distinction between traditional and behavioral assessment agree that behavioral assessment is characterized by fewer inferential assumptions and remains closer to observables (Goldfried, 1976; Haynes, 1992; Mischel, 1968). Through behavioral assessment, one might find that just prior to eating, the 7-year-old boy in our example says to himself, "I don't want to eat; it will make me sick." Subsequently, the boy refuses to eat. As he leaves the dinner table, his mother might say, "That's OK, honey, you don't have to eat." The boy's statement, "I don't want to eat," precedes the disordered behavior. His avoidance of food is the core of the disorder. His mother's comment, plus the boy's relief that he doesn't have to eat, reinforces or maintains the disorder. In behavioral assessment, psychologists analyze preceding and subsequent factors and focus on behavioral change. The treatment process thus involves an attempt to alter the disordered behavior (for example, increasing the frequency of eating behavior). Treatment may also involve modifying the internal dialogue before and after the boy eats and modifying the mother's behavior so that she no longer reinforces avoidance of food and instead reinforces eating.

In traditional procedures, the boy's failure to eat would be viewed as only a symptom. Testing would be aimed at determining the cause of this symptom (the early trauma of the illness he had when he was 4), and treatment would be directed at the cause rather than at the behavior itself. Presumably, by giving the boy insight into the causes of his behavior, a psychologist could get the boy to understand why he wasn't eating. When he achieved this understanding, he would no longer need to avoid eating. Table 17-2 compares traditional and behavioral assessment.

It is beyond the scope of this text to debate the pros and cons of the behavioral and medical models. Our goal is to help you understand the differences between the two. Suffice it to say that behavioral testing procedures have added a whole new dimension to the field of psychological testing.

TABLE 17-2

Traditional versus Behavioral Assessment

	Traditional Assessment	Behavioral Assessment
Target	Underlying cause	Disordered behavior
Symptoms	Superficial	Focus on treatment
Assessment	Indirect; not related to treatment	Direct; related to treatment
Theory	Medical model	Behavioral model
Goal	Determine cause of symptoms	Analyze disordered behavior

Procedures Based on Operant Conditioning

In operant conditioning, psychologists observe the behaviors of an individual. After the individual has made a response, they can do something to the individual to alter the probability of the recurrence of the response. They may present something positive or remove something negative following the response, to increase the rate of recurrence, or else they may present something aversive or remove something positive preceding the response, to reduce the rate of recurrence. In behavioral assessment based on operant conditioning, one must first identify the critical response or responses involved in the disorder. One can then evaluate these critical responses for frequency, intensity, or duration. This evaluation establishes the baseline (usual rate of occurrence) for the particular behavior. According to an early system developed by Kanfer and Saslow (1969), if the behaviors occur too frequently, they are called behavioral *excesses*. If they occur too infrequently, they are called behavioral *deficits*. Obviously, with a behavioral excess, treatment centers on reducing the frequency, intensity, or duration of the behavior in question. With a behavioral deficit, treatment focuses on increasing the frequency, intensity, or duration of the behavior. Table 17-3 outlines the steps in behavioral assessment based on operant conditioning.

After attempting to increase or decrease the behavior (treatment intervention), psychologists observe the effect of the intervention on the behavior in question relative to the baseline. If the goal was to decrease the behavior, then there should be a decrease relative to the baseline. If the critical behavior remains at or above baseline levels, then the intervention has failed.

In the example at the beginning of this chapter, we decided to use behavioral assessment based on operant conditioning. The critical behavior was obvious: frequency of eating. Furthermore, the critical behavior was a deficit; that is, the boy wasn't eating enough. To evaluate the critical behavior (Step 3), we asked the boy's mother to record the amount and kind of food that the boy ate each day. Using standard calorie references, we converted the amount of food the boy ate into calories. The baseline looked something like the graph in Figure 17-1. The boy was eating an average of about 800 calories a day, with a range of 600 to 1000 calories on any given day. This number of calories is too few to prevent a small, gradual weight loss.

TABLE 17-3

Steps in a Behavioral Assessment

Step 1:	Identify critical behaviors.
Step 2:	Determine whether critical behaviors are excesses or deficits.
Step 3:	Evaluate critical behaviors for frequency, duration, or intensity (that is, obtain a baseline).
Step 4:	If excesses, attempt to decrease frequency, duration, or intensity of behaviors; if deficits, attempt to increase behaviors.

FIGURE 17-1

Baseline of eating.

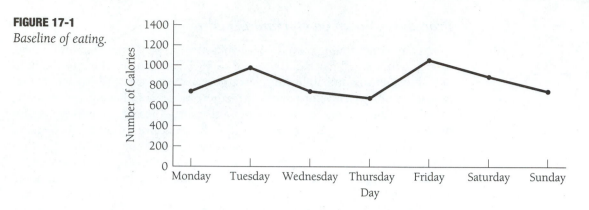

Because the behavior was a deficit, we tried to increase the boy's frequency of eating. For our intervention, we used a reward system based on points. The boy would receive points for everything he ate. The more he ate, the more points he could get. Following each meal, his mother recorded the number of points that he received as well as the cumulative total. She posted this record on a bulletin board in the boy's room so he could observe his own progress. She also posted a chart that we had worked out with her and the boy. The chart listed toys and other rewards that he could trade for points. For example, he could exchange 10 points for a package of baseball cards any time he wanted. He could also save his points for bigger prizes. For 350 points he could get a miniature pinball machine he had been wanting, and so on. In the treatment procedure, his mother recorded exactly what he ate each day just as she did during the pretreatment assessment in which the baseline was obtained. This record was then converted into calories, and each week we made a graph of his day-to-day calorie intake.

The intervention proved highly effective. Within one week, the boy had earned about 200 points and was well on the way to securing a pinball machine. The graph for this first week of treatment is shown in Figure 17-2. As the graph indicates, the boy doubled his average intake of calories to about 1600 (range 1400 to 1800). Thus, his intake of calories was far above baseline following the intervention. Assessment continued throughout the treatment and also provided feedback concerning the effects of the treatment. In the second week, the boy's consumption of calories fell below the dramatic increases of the first week, but it never fell below baseline levels. In six weeks, the boy gained about 8 pounds. He had earned just about every toy he had ever wanted. At this point his mother became concerned that he might gain too much weight or that she might go broke paying for rewards. After consultation with us, she terminated the point system. Following termination, there was a substantial drop in his eating behavior for three or four days, but then it increased to about a normal level for his age.

Apparently, the boy's parents had developed a different attitude about his eating behavior. So had the boy. Everybody concerned now knew the boy

FIGURE 17-2
Eating behavior during the first week of intervention.

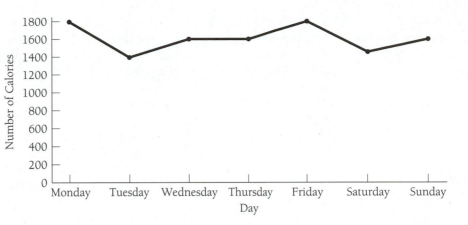

could eat without negative consequences. The parents refused to permit the boy to get away without eating, and the boy no longer had an excuse not to eat. Although the therapy never attempted to get at an original or hypothetical underlying cause of the behavior, the boy was in every sense cured. He wasn't hospitalized, and his eating behavior was adequate six months following treatment. His mother complained that he was still a finicky eater, but his weight fell within normal limits.

One can use the operant approach to solve a variety of problems, including smoking cessation, increasing studying time, and losing weight. In each case, one first calculates a baseline. Then one implements an intervention. Finally, one observes the effects of this intervention on the baseline. If you feel you don't study enough, for instance, you can try the approach yourself. To assess your study behavior, record the number of minutes you study each day for one week. This is your baseline. Then decide on a reward you can give yourself. Every day record how long you study. Give yourself the reward whenever you study longer than 75% of the average time for your baseline. See whether this procedure doesn't increase the time you spend studying.

Self-Report Techniques

In our example, the frequency of the 7-year-old boy's disordered eating behavior was recorded by his mother because the assessment process required that someone observe the boy. Not all problems, however, can be so easily and readily observed. Furthermore, when a patient or relative of the subject does the observing and recording, the practitioner must depend on the skill, accuracy, and honesty of the well-meaning but untrained relative. Thus, in the ideal situation, the practitioner or a trained assistant observes the individual to be assessed. The practitioner directly observes and records specific problem behaviors in a variety of situations and notes the factors that precede and maintain these behaviors. Like any observer, the practitioner must make himself or herself as inconspicuous (unobtrusive) as possible so as not to interfere with or influence the subject. Unfortunately, following a subject around to record behaviors is difficult, time consuming, and often unrealistic. In most cases, furthermore, the observer can hardly avoid influencing the subject. Indeed, the mere presence of an observer may alter the behavior of an individual (Polansky et al., 1949).

One attempt to deal with the problems inherent in observation is the self-report technique (Klieger & McCoy, 1994; Maisto, McKay, & Connors, 1990). The typical self-report is a list of statements about particular situations. The subject's task may be either to respond "True" or "False" to each statement or to circle a number (1 to 5, for example) to indicate the importance or relevance of the statement. Table 17-4 gives examples of the types of statements used. Self-report techniques assume that the person's responses reflect individual differences and measure some other observable phenomenon (Tasto, 1977). If, for example, one person circles 5 for fear of snakes and another person circles 1, one would assume that direct observation of these two individuals in the presence of snakes would reveal different, measurable responses. The person who circled 5 might scream and run. The person who circled 1 might simply ignore the snakes. Thus, psychologists assume that a person's response is related to an observable behavior. In place of direct observation, the practitioner accepts the face validity of the subject's responses.

That behavior assessment has concentrated on phenomena such as fear illustrates the major distinction between behavioral and traditional self-report procedures. The former focus on situations that lead to particular response patterns. The latter center on relatively enduring internal characteristics of the individual (personality traits) that lead to particular response patterns. In the behavior approach, one sees situations as the primary determinant of behavior. In the traditional approach, one sees characteristics that the person brings to a situation (for example, traits) as the primary determinant of behavior. Thus, in the behavioral approach, a person is not simply fearful and therefore fearful no matter what the situation; a person is fearful only in certain circumstances or situations because these circumstances elicit fear in that person. For more on traits versus states, see Chapters 15, 18, and 22.

The Fear Survey Schedule. The Fear Survey Schedule (FSS) is the oldest and most researched of the behavioral self-report procedures. In clinical and experimental use since the 1950s, it continues to be used for a variety of purposes (Klingberg, 1994). Since the FSS was introduced into the literature by Akutagawa (1956) as a 50-item test, it has undergone a variety of changes, and various versions have from 50 to 122 items (Lawlis, 1971), with ratings of fear on either five- or seven-point scales. It has been adapted for use with children (King et al., 1994) and adolescents (Gullone & King, 1992) as well as adults (Klieger & Franklin, 1993). It has been used worldwide (Abdelkhalek, 1994), and cross-cultural studies are available (Milgrom et al., 1994).

Items are typically related to situations that involve fear and avoidance behaviors, such as fear of open places, fear of snakes, fear of dead animals.

TABLE 17-4

Examples of a Behavioral Self-Report

Circle 1 if the item elicits no fear
     2 if the item elicits some fear
     3 if the item elicits a little fear
     4 if the item elicits a lot of fear
     5 if the item elicits extreme fear

Worms	1	2	3	4	5
Bats	1	2	3	4	5
Psychological tests	1	2	3	4	5
Dogs	1	2	3	4	5
Snakes	1	2	3	4	5
Highways	1	2	3	4	5
Men	1	2	3	4	5

Circle true or false as the item applies to you.

I like to talk when in a group.	True	False
I relate easily to persons of the opposite sex.	True	False
I like to walk in dark places.	True	False
I like to give speeches to large groups.	True	False
I feel most comfortable with strangers.	True	False
I feel most comfortable with family.	True	False
I feel most comfortable with friends.	True	False
I like to be the leader in a group.	True	False
I would rather follow than lead in a group.	True	False

Subjects rate each item according to the degree to which they experience that particular fear. Developers have derived items on the FSS from both clinical observation of actual cases (Wolpe & Lang, 1964) and experimental investigations in laboratory settings (Geer, 1965). The FSS attempts to identify those situations that elicit fear and thus avoidance. Once one has identified these situations, one can aim treatment at helping the person deal with these situations, thus reducing fear.

Social avoidance and depression. Since the introduction of the FSS, behavioral practitioners have developed numerous other self-report techniques to measure a variety of problems. D. Watson and Friend (1969) attempted to measure anxiety in society situations with their 28-item true/false Social Avoidance

Distress (SAD) scale and 30-item Fear of Negative Evaluation (FNE) scale. Lubin (1965) published a Depression Adjective Check List (DACL) to assist in the behavioral treatment of depression. In Lubin's depression scale, subjects indicate whether each of 32 adjectives "applies to me" or "does not apply to me." Eight forms are available. A recent tendency has been to combine two or more measures into a single, more effective one (see Blanchard et al., 1986).

Assertiveness. Many individuals have difficulty speaking up for themselves. Often, when they finally do speak up, they are aggressive. Suppose someone cuts in front of you in a long line to see a popular movie. Assertiveness experts might suggest that you calmly and firmly inform this person of the location of the end of the line. If you encounter resistance, you calmly explain that everyone has been waiting in line and that the only polite and appropriate thing for the intruder to do is to go to the end of the line. Many people, however, have difficulty acting appropriately in this type of situation. They may stew inside or go to the other extreme and display aggression, such as striking the intruder or throwing a temper tantrum.

A number of clinical practitioners have constructed measures of assertiveness. Table 17-5 illustrates the type of item found in a behavioral assessment self-report questionnaire for assertiveness, such as the Assertive Behavior Survey Schedule (ABSS). If you were taking the ABSS, you would indicate the responses you would make in specific situations in which assertiveness is indicated. You would also be asked to speculate on the consequences of assertiveness for you. Thus, the ABSS can help determine whether you can be assertive if necessary, situations in which you might have difficulty being assertive, and your personal attitude toward assertiveness.

The availability of many other assertiveness questionnaires illustrates the importance of this topic in behavioral assessment. Another approach, developed by Rathus (1973), the Rathus Assertiveness Schedule (RAS) consists of 30 items that subjects rate on a six-point scale, depending on the extent to which the item applies to them. McFall and Lillesand (1971) developed yet another assertiveness procedure, the 35-item Conflict Resolution Inventory (CRI). The CRI describes a series of unreasonable requests and asks whether the subject would refuse each request. For example, a fellow classmate who missed the last lecture asks you to recopy your notes, neatly of course, and bring them to his house that night so he can study for the exam scheduled for the next day. Would you comply? What would you say to this person? How would you feel about your response?

Self-report battery. Cautela and Upper (1976) have proposed the use of a self-report battery that incorporates many of the commonly used self-report techniques, such as a variety of behavioral self-rating checklists and the FSS. The battery contains three types of scales. Primary scales request general information, such as historical data, and assess general needs. Secondary scales yield information about the need for specific techniques such as relaxation or

TABLE 17-5

*Sample Questions
from a Behavioral
Assertiveness
Questionnaire*

I. Suppose you were in the following situations. How would you respond? Indicate by circling number 1, 2, or 3.

  A. You have ordered filet mignon for you and your date at an expensive restaurant. You wanted yours cooked rare. The waiter brings it well done. What would you do?

    1. Tell the waiter to bring you another, cooked the way you wanted it.

    2. Complain to the waiter, but eat what he had brought for you anyway.

    3. Say nothing.

  B. You are at a bank. You've been waiting in line for nearly 10 minutes. Finally, you reach the head of the line. A man with a large briefcase comes from the outside and steps right in front of you. What would you do?

    1. Tell him to go to the end of the line.

    2. Tell him there is a long line, but let him go in front of you anyway.

    3. Say nothing.

II. In those situations in which you say nothing, what are you afraid of? (Check the best answer.)

  A. Being yelled at ( )

  B. Being beat up ( )

  C. Being embarrassed ( )

  D. Being rejected ( )

  E. Violating a personal or religious belief ( )

  F. Expending excessive energy ( )

Adapted from Cautela & Upper (1976, pp. 97–98).

assertiveness training. Requiring a highly specific response, tertiary scales yield information about specific problems such as alcohol and drug abuse, overeating, and inappropriate sexual behavior (Cameron & Evers, 1990).

Evaluation of self-report procedures. Obviously, any practitioner with a problem to assess can simply devise and publish a self-report device. Indeed, there appears to be no shortage of such practitioners. Unfortunately, little psychometric data, if any, are ever presented to aid in an evaluation of these devices. The little information presented is usually based on poorly controlled correlational studies with highly variable results (Maisto, McKay, & Connors, 1990).

In their use of self-report techniques, some psychologists reinvent the wheel. For example, Cautela and Upper (1976) do not hesitate to admit that the prototypes of current self-report techniques are tests such as the Woodworth Personal Data Sheet, discussed in Chapter 15. Early paper-and-pencil structured personality tests, finally abandoned in the 1930s, are indeed difficult to distinguish from many modern self-report procedures. Both implicitly assume that a test response can be interpreted on the basis of face validity. Thus, all the problems of interpretation in terms of face validity (subject capacity and willingness to be truthful, response bias, poor reliability, poor validity, lack of norms) usually apply to current behavioral self-report techniques. Unfortunately, only one of the currently available self-report techniques, the FSS, has been subjected to anything close to an adequate psychometric analysis.

Practitioners appear to have a long way to go before they can offer behavioral self-report procedures as established clinical tools. However, when used in conjunction with other sources of data, such as psychophysiological recordings and direct observation, self-report data can provide useful information in clinical as well as research settings. Indeed, the modern trend is to use self-report data in conjunction with more direct observations and physiological recordings (Haynes, 1991, 1992; Matias & Turner, 1986).

Kanfer and Saslow's Functional Approach

In our discussion of behavioral assessment procedures based on operant conditioning, we mentioned Kanfer and Saslow's (1969) original concepts of behavioral deficits and excesses. Now we shall discuss this approach in detail, because it goes beyond the principles of operant conditioning. Indeed, Kanfer and Saslow are among the most important pioneers in the field of behavioral assessment.

Kanfer and Saslow's (1969) method of behavioral assessment provides an alternative to the traditional diagnostic labeling of the medical model (neurotic, psychotic, and so forth). These authors propose what they call a *functional (behavior-analytic) approach* to assessment. Rather than labeling people schizophrenic or neurotic, the psychologist would focus on behavioral excesses and deficits. As previously indicated, a *behavioral excess* is any behavior or class of behaviors described as problematic by an individual because of excesses in its frequency, intensity, duration, or because of its inappropriateness. The functional approach adheres to the assumptions of the learning approach (to the study of disordered behavior). The functional approach assumes that normal and disordered behavior both develop according to the same laws and differ only in extremes. Taking a shower, for example, is a normal behavior. What about taking two showers a day? Clearly, the laws that govern the acquisition of the behaviors involved in taking one shower are the same as those for taking two showers. What about eight showers a day? Consider three hour-long showers a day, or a two-hour-long shower taken within minutes after company arrives for an unexpected visit. Behavior is abnormal only because of excessive frequency, intensity, duration, or inappropriateness. Similarly, most of us blow off steam by yelling every now and then. However, if you yell intensely every 30 seconds for half an hour at a time, especially when you go to the public library, then your yelling behavior is clearly extreme and maladaptive.

Behavioral deficits are classes of behaviors described as problematic because they fail to occur with sufficient frequency, with adequate intensity, in appropriate form, or under socially expected conditions (Kanfer & Saslow, 1969). For example, one may view lack of assertiveness as a behavioral deficit.

Again, the behavior, or lack of it, is not by itself a disorder. If, for example, a gang of high-school dropouts drive their motorcycles into the parking spot you were prepared to pull into, then it may not be too wise to say, "That's my spot; there's another around the block." Finding another parking spot yourself is probably far more adaptive behavior.

Besides isolating behavioral excesses and deficits, a functional analysis involves other procedures, including clarifying the problem and making suggestions for treatment. In the traditional approaches, knowing a person has a particular disorder or conflict does little to suggest treatment strategies. However, when behavioral excesses are identified, one can make efforts to reduce the behaviors' intensity, frequency, and so forth. When behavioral deficits are identified, one can make efforts to provide new behaviors or increase the frequency of existing behaviors.

Cognitive Assessment Procedures

Whereas behavioral assessments based on operant conditioning, self-reports, and Kanfer and Saslow's functional analysis are relatively established, cognitive-behavioral assessment is a relatively new and exciting development. The more established techniques of behavioral assessment, in general, concentrate on overt behavior and the situations that lead to particular behavioral patterns. Cognitive-behavioral assessment, however, evaluates the thinking patterns and other processes that presumably lead to behavior, including beliefs, expectations, and self-statements. As with other areas of behavioral assessment, treatment interventions and the testing processes are linked.

The Dysfunctional Attitude Scale

A major pillar of cognitive behavioral assessment is A. T. Beck's (1967, 1976) Cognitive Model of Psychopathology. The model is based on *schemas,* which are cognitive frameworks or organizing principles of thought. For example, in your first impression of an individual, you create a schema of that person. In your subsequent interactions with that person, you add to or subtract from that original schema. Moreover, the original schema influences your subsequent perceptions. For instance, if you originally pegged the person as a nerd, then you will likely label subsequent behavior accordingly. According to Beck, schemas serve to organize prior experience, guide the interpretations of new experiences, and shape expectancies and predictions. Beck's theory holds that dysfunctional schemas predispose an individual to develop psychopathology (A. T. Beck et al., 1991).

To evaluate negative schemas, Beck and colleagues have developed the Dysfunctional Attitude Scale (DAS) (A. N. Weissman, 1979; A. N. Weissman & Beck, 1978). The DAS has two parallel forms (Power et al., 1994). The DAS identifies beliefs that might interact with a stressor to produce psychopathology. For instance, one may believe that one cannot find happiness without being loved by another or that turning to someone else for advice or help is an admission of weakness. The subject is provided with a list of statements such as "Others can care for me even if they know all my weaknesses" and is asked to respond on a seven-point Likert scale ranging from "totally agree" to "totally disagree." The validity of the scale is supported by a variety of factor analytic data (A. T. Beck et al., 1991; Cane et al., 1986).

Irrational Beliefs Test

According to the social-learning viewpoint, human behavior is often determined by beliefs and expectations rather than reality. If, for example, your instructor announces that there will be an exam in the third week of classes, you will do most of your studying for it the day or two before it if you are like most students. Suppose, however, you miss the class just before the announced exam. And suppose that a "friend" of yours plays a trick on you. He telephones and tells you the exam has been canceled. If you believe him and therefore expect that there will be no exam, will you study as hard as you would have before (if at all)? It's unlikely. The exam will still be given (reality), but your behavior has changed because you believe the exam has been canceled. In view of the influence of beliefs and expectations, a number of behavioral tests have been developed to measure them. R. A. Jones (1968), for example, developed a 100-item Irrational Beliefs Test (IBT) to measure irrational beliefs (for example, the belief that you must always succeed to be worthwhile).

The IBT has found widespread use, in clinical as well as research settings, and has received considerable attention (Deffenbacher et al., 1986; T. E. Ellis, 1985; Lohr & Bonge, 1982). The IBT requires subjects to indicate their level of agreement or disagreement with each of the 100 items on a five-point scale (for example, "I frequently worry about things over which I have no control"). Half of the items indicate the presence of a particular irrational belief, the other half, its absence.

The reliability of the IBT appears to be similar to that of structured personality tests, with test-retest coefficients for short intervals (two weeks or less) ranging from .48 to .90 for individual scales and .88 for the full scale. The validity documentation of the IBT is weak and questionable (T. W. Smith & Zurawski, 1983), although the IBT does appear to be related to both anxiety and depression (Cook & Peterson, 1986; Deffenbacher et al., 1986).

Cognitive Functional Analysis

What people say to themselves also influences behavior. If you tell yourself that you can't learn statistics, then you will likely avoid statistics. Furthermore, when confronted with a difficult statistics problem, you are likely to give up easily. If you tell yourself you like statistics, however, you probably look forward to studying statistics. When you confront a difficult statistics problem, you will probably take your time and systematically figure out the answer. Self-statements have been shown to influence behaviors as diverse as assertiveness (Schwartz & Gottman, 1976) and coping behavior in cardiac patients (Kendall et al., 1979). Interestingly, positive and negative self-statements do not function in the same way. Apparently, negative self-statements do far more harm than positive self-statements do good. Thus, treatment generally involves identifying and then eliminating negative self-statements rather than increasing positive self-statements. Try to become aware of your own self-statements for a moment. What do you say to yourself as you go about your daily activities? Odds are, if you make a lot of negative self-statements, you are hindering your personal efficiency and ability to cope.

One of the most important examples of the cognitive-behavioral assessment approach is *cognitive functional analysis* (Meichenbaum, 1976). The premise underlying a cognitive functional analysis is that what a person says to himself or herself plays a critical role in behavior. The cognitive functional analyst is thus interested in internal dialogue such as self-appraisals and expectations. Again, what do you say to yourself about yourself as you go about your daily activities? Do you constantly criticize or belittle yourself? Or do you always reassure yourself of your capabilities? Research clearly indicates these self-statements influence your behavior and even your feelings (Meichenbaum, 1976).

Meichenbaum's cognitive functional analysis is an extension of previously discussed behavioral assessment procedures. Like behavioral assessment, cognitive functional analysis is concerned with ascertaining the environmental factors that precede behavior (environmental antecedents) as well as those that maintain behavior (environmental consequences). In addition, however, a cognitive functional analysis attempts to ascertain the internal or cognitive antecedents and consequences for the behavioral sequence (the internal dialogue). What does the person say to himself or herself before, during, and following the behavior? What is said before the behavior may influence what is done. What is said during the behavior may influence the way the behavior manifests itself. What is said following the behavior may influence its probability of recurrence (Meichenbaum & Turk, 1976).

If thoughts influence behavior, then modifying one's thoughts can lead to modifications in behavior. That is, to the extent that thoughts play a role in eliciting or maintaining a behavioral sequence, modification of the thoughts underlying the sequence should lead to behavioral changes. If, for example, the thought "I must have a cigarette" is consistently associated with the behavioral sequence involved in smoking, then changing that thought to "My lungs are clean, I feel healthy, and I have no desire to smoke" could help to modify the person's pattern of smoking behavior.

TABLE 17-6
*Summary of
Cognitive-
Behavioral
Procedures*

Scale or Technique	Author	Goal
Dysfunctional Attitude Scale (DAS)	Beck and colleagues	Evaluates negative schemas
Thought Sampling Questionnaire (TSQ)	Klinger	Samples thoughts randomly
Irrational Beliefs Test (IBT)	Jones	Measures irrational beliefs
Cognitive functional analysis	Meichenbaum	Analyzes internal dialogue

Paralleling Meichenbaum's technique of cognitive functional analysis are procedures and devices that allow a person to test himself or herself, or *self-monitoring devices*. Because behavioral practitioners value the role and responsibility of the individual in the therapeutic process, they have developed a wide variety of these devices. In the simplest case, an individual must record the frequency of a particular behavior—that is, to monitor it so that he or she becomes aware of the behavior. To monitor your smoking behavior, simply count the number of cigarettes you smoke each day. To monitor your weight, weigh yourself each morning and record the number of pounds.

Some self-monitoring procedures are quite sophisticated (Mahoney, 1974). For example, a mechanical counter, marketed to the general public, attached to the jaw can count the number of bites a person takes when eating. The idea is to take fewer bites each day, even if it's only one fewer than the day before. Presumably, this procedure will ultimately result in a lower intake of food and eventually weight loss. Similarly, timing devices and procedures allow one to assess how long one engages in an activity. In one method, the subject plugs in a clock every time he or she studies, thus recording total study time. The goal is to increase this length of time, either by increasing the length of individual study sessions or by increasing the total study time within a specific period. These self-monitoring assessment tools are limited only by the imagination of the practitioner. Azrin and Powell (1968) developed an electronic device that counts the number of times a cigarette case is opened. Treatment is aimed at opening the case fewer times each day. Naturally, one can easily cheat with these devices, but to think of this possibility is to miss the point of these procedures. These devices help people help themselves by increasing awareness through feedback. You test yourself. If you cheat, you cheat yourself. (See Table 17-6.)

Psychophysiological Assessment Procedures

Seen as a variant of behavioral assessment by some and as an independent category by others, psychophysiological methods of assessment utilize such indicators as heart rate, blood pressure, galvanic skin response (GSR), and skin temperature to assess psychological problems (Iacono, 1991; Morales, 1994). In essence, psychophysiological assessment procedures attempt to quantify physiological responses (Roscoe, 1994). This quantification is then translated into psychological factors (Steptoe & Johnston, 1991). Thus, physiological data are used to draw inferences concerning the psychological state of the individual (Fredrikson, 1991). As Haynes (1991) states, "A fundamental tenet of [psychophysiological assessment] is that social, behavioral, cognitive, and emotional phenomena are often a function of, and are often reflected in, physiological processes" (p. 307).

Physiological Variables with Treatment Implications

The feasibility of psychophysiological assessment received support in an early study conducted by Ax (1953). Ax demonstrated that the fear response was related to specific physiological changes such as increases in blood pressure and skin conductance levels. He found that he could distinguish fear and anger based on physiological data. Ax's early work, which has subsequently been supported (see Ekman, Levenson, & Friesen, 1983; Turpin, 1991), had interesting implications. For instance, it suggested the possibility of assessing abnormally chronic and intense anger or fear through strictly physiological methods. This type of assessment would be a quantum leap from traditional procedures, which depend on voluntary responses from subjects. In addition, as with other methods of behavioral assessment, psychophysiological assessment has direct implications for treatment (Haynes, 1992).

The polygraph and related devices that measure blood pressure, heart rate, and GSR have been the primary tools of the psychophysiological assessment specialist. However, imaginative researchers continue to augment this hardware. For example, psychophysiologists have been particularly interested in measuring adult sexual responses (Janssen et al., 1994; Morales, 1994).

Measures of sexual arousal make use of the fact that it is directly related to the flow of blood into the penis in men and into the vagina in women (Masters & Johnson, 1966). Using this knowledge, researchers have developed measures of human sexual arousal. For example, penile erection can be measured by the penile transducer, a device that encircles the penis (Baxter, Barbaree, & Marshall, 1986; Zuckerman, 1971). As erection occurs, an electrical signal is generated, and this signal can then be recorded. The procedure can be used to determine the type of stimuli (pictures, fantasies, men, women, and so forth) that lead to arousal in men as well as the strength of the male sexual response. The penile transducer and related devices are much more objective than traditional tools.

Evaluation of Physiological Techniques

Support for psychophysiological assessment has come from investigations that have revealed a systematic covariation between measurable physiological processes and cognitive processes (Iacono, 1991; Jennings, 1986). For example, Ahern and Beatty (1979) found that more-intelligent subjects show smaller task-evoked pupillary dilations than less-intelligent subjects (as evaluated by their scores on the

SAT). These results reveal physiological differences in individuals with differing mental abilities. In other studies, Beatty and colleagues (for example, Geiselman, Woodward, & Beatty, 1982) used measures of heart-rate variability and skin conductance to evaluate processing intensity, the amount of effort or energy devoted to a cognitive task. Presumably, brighter individuals expend less of their total available processing resources in solving a different problem, either because they have greater resources or because they make more efficient use of them.

Psychophysiological hardware seems to hold considerable promise for raising the scientific respectability of psychological testing. Problems still remain, however, and considerably more research and development are needed. One of the most serious problems in psychophysiological assessment concerns artifacts. For instance, movement by a subject may result in the recording of a physiological response that did not occur. In many cases, furthermore, direct measurement is difficult if not impossible. To measure brain-wave patterns, for example, one places electrodes on the head, whereas the electrical current measured actually comes from the brain. Thus, the skull distorts the electrical impulse measured by the recording device. There are other problems as well, including the long-known effect of initial values (Wilder, 1950), by which the strength of a response is influenced by the absolute prestimulus strength. Which is the stronger response: an increase in heart rate from 60 to 85 beats per minute or an increase from 110 to 125 beats per minute? Obviously, one must take initial values into account in evaluating the strength, intensity, and significance of a physiological response. Another problem, which you have seen throughout this book, is that demographic factors such as age, gender, and ethnicity influence psychophysiological responses (N. B. Anderson & McNeilly, 1991). Thus, one must always consider cultural, ethnic, economic, gender, and other variables in making any kind of assessment. In spite of these problems, psychophysiological procedures appear to hold great promise for the future of psychological testing.

Computers and Psychological Testing

A major development has been the application and use of computers in testing (Farrell, 1989, 1992a). In this regard, one can use computers two basic ways: (1) to create new tasks and perhaps measure abilities that traditional procedures cannot tap and (2) to administer, score, and even interpret traditional tests. In this last section on alternatives to traditional procedures, we briefly discuss each of these recent applications of computers to the testing field.

Psychophysical and Signal Detection Procedures

An early impetus for using computers to generate tasks that one cannot present through traditional methods came from the application of psychophysical and signal detection procedures. In these procedures, a signal is presented and the subject is required to report whether he or she saw it. Many variations in presenting a signal are possible. The examiner can vary the strength of the signal, use more than one signal and require the subject to guess which one has been presented, or follow the signal with noise or another signal to determine the effects of one signal on another.

Saccuzzo and colleagues (Saccuzzo, 1977, 1981; Saccuzzo & Braff, 1981, 1986; Saccuzzo et al., 1979; Saccuzzo & Miller, 1977; Saccuzzo & Schubert, 1981) suggest that one can use psychophysical methods to evaluated psychological disorders and perhaps detect them in their early stages. In a series of studies, beginning with Saccuzzo, Hirt, and Spencer (1974), Saccuzzo has provided considerable evidence that schizophrenia may be related to the speed with which information is transferred throughout the nervous system (Saccuzzo, 1993). If schizophrenia does in fact develop because of slow processing by the individual, then it would seem sensible to use a direct measure of processing speed to assess schizophrenia rather than indirect procedures such as the Rorschach.

Indeed, one can assess information-processing speed by flashing two stimuli in brief succession on a microcomputer screen or a tachistoscope. If a stimulus, such as the letter *T,* is presented and then terminated, the information is first registered by the nervous system. After the information is registered, it theoretically enters a brief perceptual memory system, which Neisser (1967) calls *iconic storage.* The person does not become consciously aware of the stimulus until it is transferred to the higher brain centers, where it is compared with previous learning. The rate of this transfer of information is the speed of information processing (Saccuzzo, Hirt, & Spencer, 1974).

If a stimulus is presented and terminated, then followed by a second, noninformational stimulus such as a random pattern, the second and first stimuli may integrate in the visual system. Only this unidentifiable composite will then be transferred to the higher brain centers. Obviously, if this occurs, the individual is not able to identify the originally presented *T.* However, if the *T* is transferred to the higher centers before the noninformational stimulus is presented, the person can identify the letter. By finding the minimum interval between presentation of the letter and presentation of the noninformational stimulus at which the noninformational stimulus no longer interferes with processing of the letter, one can estimate how long it took the letter to reach the higher centers (Saccuzzo & Miller, 1977). Thus, the speed of information processing can be determined by finding this minimum interval. (See Figure 17-3.)

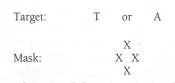

FIGURE 17-3 *Target and mask in signal detection. In signal detection experiments, the target and mask are presented to the same visual area in close temporal succession. The minimum interval between presentation of the target and presentation of the mask at which the mask no longer interferes with processing of the target is used to evaluate the information-processing speed.*

Saccuzzo and colleagues have shown that schizophrenic people can be distinguished from normal people and others (for example, neurotic people) on the basis of information-processing speed (see Saccuzzo and Johnson, 1995). Normal people require a much shorter interval to avoid the effects of the noninformational stimulus. For example, Saccuzzo, Hirt, and Spencer (1974) showed that normal people and hospitalized nonschizophrenic people reached maximum performance with only a 150-millisecond interval between presentation of the letter and presentation of a second, noninformational stimulus. The schizophrenic people, however, required an interval of 300 milliseconds to reach maximum performance. This finding suggests that schizophrenics process information more slowly than normal people do and can be distinguished from normal people by the length of the interval between the two stimuli required for maximum performance. This approach, as yet in its infancy, offers a variety of advantages over other procedures: Scoring can be simplified, administration can be easily standardized, and the effects of the examiner can be minimized.

Psychophysical and signal detection procedures have also been applied to ability testing (Jensen, 1982; Nettelbeck, 1982). Reaction time and backward masking tasks (in which a briefly presented informational target stimulus is followed by a noninformational noise stimulus, known as a mask) are used to measure the speed, capacity, or efficiency of information processing (Saccuzzo, Larson, & Rimland, 1986). The general idea is that variations among individuals who differ in psychometric intelligence reflect different information-processing capabilities (E. Hunt, 1980; Jensen, 1986).

Support for a relationship between information-processing capabilities and individual differences in intelligence has come from studies in which the individual must make a rapid response to two or more choices (Jensen, 1979; Jensen & Munro, 1979; Lunneborg, 1978; G. A. Smith & Stanley, 1983). When one uses parameters such as median reaction time, slope of reaction time as a function of the number of choices, and intraindividual standard deviations of reaction-time performance, large differences emerge between groups with mental retardation and those with normal IQs as well as between groups of vocational college students and university students (Jensen, 1980, 1982). However, results differ across samples (Lunneborg, 1978). Although the correlations vary widely, with estimates ranging from the high .60s to the low .20s, the correlations are almost always in the expected direction (Jensen, 1982).

The visual paradigm for studying the relationship between information processing and intelligence, in which the subject must respond to a visual stimulus, parallels the backward masking approach used by Saccuzzo and colleagues to study schizophrenia. The subject is required to discriminate between two briefly exposed target stimuli, such as identifying which of two lines presented to the right and left of central fixation is longer (see Figure 17-4). The targets are then followed by a spatially overlapping, noninformational mask (for example, two uniform lines that completely superimpose the lines of the target stimulus). Extensive literature indicates that the mask limits the time the informational impulse is available for processing in the nervous system (Felsten &

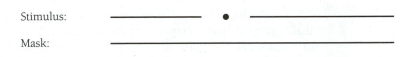

FIGURE 17-4 *Stimuli used in signal detection studies of intelligence. The stimulus and mask are presented in close temporal succession. The subject must estimate which line is longer.*

Wasserman, 1980). Speed of processing, or inspection time (Vickers, Nettelbeck, & Willson, 1972), can be evaluated by systematically varying the exposure duration of the target and estimating the minimum duration needed for accuracy (Brand, 1981; Lally & Nettelbeck, 1977; Nettelbeck & Lally, 1976) or by keeping the stimulus duration constant and varying the interval between target and mask (Saccuzzo et al., 1979; Saccuzzo & Marcus, 1983).

Numerous studies have reported a statistically significant (nonchance) difference between mentally retarded and nonretarded (average IQ) individuals in their speed of visual information processing as evaluated in a backward masking paradigm (Saccuzzo et al., 1979; Saccuzzo & Michael, 1984). Such differences occur in spite of wide variations in the nature of the stimuli, method of stimulus presentation, and technique used to estimate visual processing speed (Saccuzzo & Michael, 1984). In addition, there are clear-cut developmental differences, with a direct relationship between chronological and/or mental age and performance (Black, 1974; Liss & Haith, 1970; Saccuzzo et al., 1979). Gifted children have a greater speed of processing than nongifted children (Saccuzzo, Johnson, & Guertin, 1994). Finally, the evidence supports a significant relationship between degrees of normal intelligence and visual information processing. As in reaction-time studies, however, correlations vary widely, and the magnitude of the relationship remains highly controversial (Mackintosh, 1981; Nettelbeck, 1982).

Developers have adapted the reaction time and backward masking tasks for presentation by personal computers such as the Macintosh and IBM PC (see Brand, 1981; Saccuzzo & Larson, 1987; Saccuzzo, Larson, & Rimland, 1986). With standard software, independent investigators can readily verify results from psychophysical and signal detection procedures. Thus far, the findings seem to indicate a clear but modest relationship between information-processing capabilities and intelligence (Saccuzzo, Johnson, & Guertin, 1994). In their present state of development, however, such procedures cannot replace traditional tests. If they eventually prove to be a valid substitute, however, the objectivity of assessment may be markedly enhanced.

The Computerization of Traditional Tests

Another major application of computers is the computerization of traditional tests. A number of studies have shown that presentation of traditional test content by computer does not appreciably reduce reliability or validity (Greaud & Green, 1986; Lee, Moreno, & Sympson, 1986).

As Fowler (1985) has noted, computers began to be applied to psychological testing almost as soon as they were available. However, the increase in application of computer technology to traditional testing has been all but geometric during the 1990s. Currently, there are numerous programs for administering, scoring, and even interpreting a host of personality tests, including the MMPI and Rorschach (see Butcher, Keller, & Bacon, 1985; Fowler, 1985).

Of course, developments in computerized testing have not avoided controversy and problems (Hofer & Green, 1985). Although computers may be able to score and even administer traditional tests without reducing reliability or validity, interpretations based on a computer program must be approached with great caution (Moreland, 1985). If the clinicians who use such reports are not adequately trained to recognize errors and be cognizant of the limitations of computerized test interpretations, consumers of psychological testing services can suffer great harm. Again, cautious optimism and far more empirical research are called for. (For more on computers in testing, see Chapter 22.)

The Computerization of Behavioral Assessment

Farrell (1992b) has identified seven major applications of computers to behavioral assessment: (1) collecting self-report data, (2) coding observational data, (3) directly recording behavior, (4) training, (5) organizing and synthesizing behavioral assessment data, (6) analyzing behavioral assessment data, and (7) supporting decision making. As Farrell notes, the computerization of behavioral self-report tests, such as those discussed earlier in the chapter, would be a relatively simple endeavor. Once computerized, such questionnaires could be easily administered and immediately scored by the computer, thus saving valuable professional time.

According to Farrell (1991), a number of factors continue to impede the widespread use of computers in behavioral assessment. Perhaps first among these is lack of acceptance by practitioners. Many simply have no experience with computers and so avoid them, although attitudes seem to be becoming more favorable (Farrell, 1989). Another obstacle to the use of computers in behavioral assessment involves evaluation of software (Farrell, 1992b). Apparently, vendors are reluctant to make their products available for review; consequently, potential users do not have sufficient information to evaluate the quality of the software. Despite such obstacles, it seems inevitable that the future will see a greater use of computers in all areas of assessment.

Summary

Behavioral procedures differ from traditional tests in that they are more direct, have fewer inferential assumptions, and remain closer to observables. Traditional tests are based on the medical model, which views the overt manifestations of psychological disorders merely as symptoms of some underlying cause. This underlying cause is the target of the traditional procedures. Behavioral tests are based on the belief that the overt manifestations of psychological disorders are more than mere symptoms. Although possibly caused by some other factor, behaviors themselves are the targets of behavioral tests.

In behavioral assessment based on operant conditioning, one must first identify the critical response or responses involved in a disorder. These critical responses are then evaluated for frequency, intensity, or duration. The resulting data provide the baseline for the particular behaviors. Once a baseline is obtained, an intervention is introduced. The effect of this intervention on the baseline is then observed.

Self-report techniques of behavioral assessment focus on situations that lead to particular response patterns, whereas traditional procedures focus on determining the internal characteristics of the individual that lead to particular response patterns. Furthermore, the behavioral procedures purport to be more related to observable phenomena than traditional procedures are.

Kanfer and Saslow (1969) developed the functional, or behavior-analytic, approach to behavioral assessment. Rather than labeling people as schizophrenic or neurotic, this approach focuses on behavioral deficits and behavioral excesses. A behavioral excess is any behavior described as problematic because of excesses in its frequency, intensity, duration, or because of its inappropriateness; a behavioral deficit is the opposite (occurs too infrequently, etc.).

Behavioral assessment based on operant conditioning, self-reports, and functional analyses concentrates on overt behaviors and the situations that lead to particular behavioral patterns. Cognitive-behavioral assessment, by contrast, evaluates thinking patterns and thinking processes that lead to certain behavior, including beliefs and expectations. Kendall and Korgeski (1979) discuss several approaches to cognitive-behavioral assessment, including thought sampling, assessing imagery, assessing beliefs, and assessing self-statements.

One of the most important examples of the cognitive-behavioral assessment approach is Meichenbaum's (1976) technique, cognitive functional analysis. The premise underlying cognitive functional analysis is that what a person says to himself or herself plays a critical role in determining behavior. A cognitive functional analysis ascertains the environmental factors that precede behavior as well as those that maintain it. In addition, a cognitive functional analysis attempts to ascertain the internal or cognitive antecedents and consequences of a behavioral sequence.

An important recent development is the application of computers to testing. Computers can be used to present new traditional tasks. In the psychophysical and signal detection approaches, computers present tasks that cannot be given by traditional means. For example, the subject is required to make a visual discrimination or to respond rapidly to a stimulus in an effort to measure information-processing capabilities.

CHAPTER 18

Measures of Anxiety and Stress

LEARNING OBJECTIVES

When you have completed this chapter, you should be able to:

- List the three major types of situations that cause stress

- Define anxiety and describe how it is usually expressed

- Describe the difference between state anxiety and trait anxiety

- Describe the type of anxiety the Taylor Manifest Anxiety Scale was designed to measure

- Name the first test designed to measure test anxiety

- Discuss some of the theoretical orientations that underlie the different test-anxiety measures

- Describe treatments that can be used to reduce test anxiety

- Describe the strengths and weaknesses of two different approaches for the assessment of life stress

- Discuss why it is important to measure coping

- Discuss the relationship between measures of coping, of life stress, and of social support

*I*t is the day of your final exam. You have studied hard and you have every reason to expect an A. As you enter the classroom, you have a stiff feeling in the back of your neck. Your hands sweat as you get out your pencil. Finally, the long, complicated instructions are over, the materials are distributed, and it is time to work. Yet, despite all your preparation, the test does not go the way you had hoped. Instead of concentrating on the task of test taking, you worry about not doing well, or you think about running out of time. When it is all over, you feel cheated. You knew the material well, but your grade on the exam does not reflect your knowledge.

If this story describes a situation you have experienced, you have company. Although there are no good figures, this experience typifies that of thousands of students and other test takers each year. Test anxiety is a common problem among college students and a major factor in diminishing the validity of tests.

Test anxiety is also an important and active area in psychological research. Many theories about the relationship of anxiety to performance have led to the development of a variety of specific test-anxiety scales and measures (Endler, Kantorn & Parker, 1994; Flett & Blankstein, 1994; I. G. Sarason & Sarason, 1990; Williams, 1994). In this chapter, we review the general concepts of anxiety and stress, and then we review in some detail the theory and measurement of the same.

Stress and Anxiety

Stress is a response to situations that involve demands, constraints, or opportunities (I. G. Sarason & Sarason, 1980). During our lifetimes, all of us will experience some psychological stress. The extent to which it bothers us at various times in our lives, however, differs for each of us. For some people, stress is a debilitating problem that interferes with virtually every aspect of their lives. For others, stress causes problems in particular situations. For still others, stress helps them accomplish important goals. The study of psychological stress has gained an increasingly central position within the psychological and biomedical sciences. It has become clear that psychological stress can interfere with performance on mental and academic tests (I. G. Sarason, Sarason & Pierce, 1990), and it is increasingly apparent that stress is a major factor in disease. Some medical investigators now believe that stress is involved in 50% to 80% of all illnesses.

Psychological stress has three components: frustration, conflict, and pressure. Frustration occurs when the attainment of a goal is blocked. Though frustration takes different forms, the principle remains the same. If, after being a premed student for four years, you are rejected by all major medical schools, frustration will likely result. Or if you want to get into a concert and are refused entrance, you may become frustrated. In each case, something or someone has blocked the attainment of a goal. Conflict is a type of stress that occurs when one must make a choice between two or more important goals. For example, you must decide between going to law school and going to graduate school in psychology. The final type of stress is pressure to speed up activities. External pressure occurs when your professor assigns a lot of extra reading right before the midterm exam; internal pressure occurs when no such reading is assigned but you take it on yourself because it fits your style and aspirations (J. C. Coleman, 1973).

Exposure to stressful situations can cause an observable reaction known as **anxiety**, an unpleasant emotional state marked by worry, apprehension, and tension. When you are anxious, your autonomic nervous system becomes activated: Your heart beats fast, your pulse rate goes up, your hands tend to sweat. The amount of anxiety you experience depends, in part, on the intensity of the stress-producing stimulus as you perceive it. It results from your evaluation of a situation (Spielberger & Sydeman, 1994): How potentially harmful is the situation for you? How threatening? How dangerous?

General Measures of Anxiety

The State-Trait Anxiety Inventory

Actually, there are two types of anxiety. The preceding paragraph described state anxiety, an emotional reaction that varies from one situation to another. Trait anxiety is a personality characteristic reflecting the noticeable differences among the frequencies and intensities of people's emotional reactions to stress—a characteristic of the person, not of the situation confronted. Interest in these two types of anxiety led Charles D. Spielberger to develop the state-trait anxiety theory, which in turn led to the development of the State-Trait Anxiety Inventory (STAI). The STAI provides two separate scores: one for state anxiety (A-State) and another for trait anxiety (A-Trait). The STAI A-Trait scale consists of 20 items. On a four-point scale, subjects indicate how they generally feel about each item. A similar set of items is used to evaluate the A-State.

Good evidence exists for the validity and the reliability of the STAI. Test-retest reliabilities range from .73 to .86 for the trait scale. The state scale, which is supposed to be inconsistent over time, indeed has low test-retest reliability (.16 to .54). As noted in Chapter 5, validity defines the range of inferences that one can make on the basis of a score or measure. Validity studies have shown that the STAI can be used to make several important and useful generalizations. For example, concurrent validity studies have shown that the STAI trait scale correlates well with other measures of trait anxiety. Spielberger and Sydeman (1994) report a variety of studies in which the STAI trait scale was correlated with the Taylor Manifest Anxiety Scale, to be discussed. It was also associated with another trait-anxiety scale known as the IPAT Anxiety Scale (Cattell & Scheier, 1961) for the same groups of college students and psychiatric patients. The correlations with the Taylor and the IPAT ranged from .75 to .85, which are quite impressive and suggest that these three scales measure much of the same psychological dimension. Other scales that attempt to measure trait anxiety do not do so well. One example is the Affect Adjective Checklist developed by Zuckerman (1960), which correlated only moderately with other tests designed to measure trait anxiety. In this case, the concurrent validity correlations ranged from .41 to .57 (Spielberger, Gorsuch, & Lushene, 1970). Overall, the STAI seems to measure the same thing as other scales that purport to assess trait anxiety.

To give a test a positive recommendation, we must go beyond the observation that it correlates well with other tests that supposedly measure the same thing. At least two other conditions must be met. First, we must show that the test measures something that the other tests do not, offering discriminant evidence for construct validity (see Chapter 5). If a new test does just what the old tests could already do, there is no need to further develop the new test. Second, the test must be shown to have meaning beyond what is known through its relationships to other tests. Just because a test correlates with other tests does not mean that it is valid for the inferences one wants to make; the other tests may themselves be meaningless.

One good example of a validity study for the STAI (Spielberger et al., 1975) took advantage of the natural anxiety associated with the anticipation of surgery. Patients scheduled to undergo surgery took the STAI before and after the medical procedure. Patients who had undergone major surgery showed less state anxiety after they had been told they were recovering well than they had before the operation. This finding demonstrates that state anxiety fluctuates with the situation—just as the test constructors say it will. Trait anxiety was not affected by the situation; it remained the same before and after surgery. People high in trait anxiety simply continued to respond in an anxious way, even in situations that evoked little or no anxiety among people low in trait anxiety. Each component of the STAI thus appears to measure what it is supposed to measure, and the two components clearly assess different aspects of anxiety.

Over the course of several decades, studies have continually supported the value of the STAI. Recent factor analysis studies have continued to show the two-factor structure. For example, a study involving 205 patients with panic disorder confirmed that state and trait anxiety are two different dimensions, even among people with fairly serious emotional problems (Oei, Evans, & Crook, 1990).

Other multidimensional measures. Although the STAI continues to be the most widely used multidimensional measure, several others are now available. For example, Endler et al. (1991) produced the Endler Multidimensional Anxiety Scales (EMAS). The four factors of the EMAS are based on a factor analysis of responses by more than 2000 subjects. The first scale, social evaluation trait anxiety, measures an individual's predisposition to react to situations perceived as evaluative. Physical danger, the second subscale, measures the fear of being physically damaged or hurt. The third subscale, ambiguous anxiety, describes ambiguous, new, or uncertain situations. The final subscale, daily routines, is related to anxiety associated with routines in daily life (Endler et al., 1991; Endler & Parker, 1994).

Other recent developments emphasize a larger number of dimensions. For example, Koksal and Power (1990) have developed a Four Systems Anxiety Questionnaire (FSAQ), which presents recent research that identifies four separate components of anxiety. The first component is somatic, which is reflected in physiological signs such as increased heart rate or sweating. The next component is cognitive. This component of anxiety often includes two aspects: awareness of one's own irrationality and negative self-statements. The third dimension represents feelings about anxiety or the affective-emotional component. The FSAQ separates the feeling components, like the cognitive, into different dimensions. The final component is behavioral, which describes alterations in behaviors as a function of anxiety.

The FSAQ was administered to 218 first-year university students. In addition, a group of 54 anxiety patients from a psychology clinic and 14 agoraphobic (afraid to go outside) patients were evaluated. The analysis demonstrated that a behavioral treatment improved the behavioral dimension for agoraphobic patients. Treatment also affected feelings but did not affect the cognitive component. University students and anxiety patients differed on all four dimensions. Measures such as the FSAQ help one redefine the construct of anxiety. In particular, separating feeling from cognitive components may help clinical psychologists identify the appropriate treatments for people who suffer from anxiety.

The Taylor Manifest Anxiety Scale

The Taylor Manifest Anxiety Scale grew out of a different tradition within psychology. Originally, J. A. Taylor (1951) was interested in the conditioning of the eyelid response. In eyelid-conditioning experiments, puffs of air are administered to the eyelids to cause a blinking response. Over a series of trials, subjects learn to anticipate the puff, and the blink comes to precede rather than follow the air puff. Taylor noticed that some individuals learned to anticipate the air puff more rapidly than others. *Manifest anxiety* refers to the effect of anxiety on the performance of a learned task.

According to Spence's learning theory, which Taylor followed (Taylor, 1953), the performance of a response is partially a function of motivation. In Taylor's case, the motivation was anxiety. To measure it, she began by selecting items from the MMPI (see Chapter 15) that described anxiety states. A partial list of these items and the answers that indicate high anxiety are presented in Table 18-1. Taylor reasoned that her list of items about these rather private events tapped an inferred drive state (J. A. Taylor, 1953). When she divided subjects into groups high and low on manifest anxiety, she found that the rate

TABLE 18-1

*Ten Items from
the Taylor
Manifest Anxiety
Scale*

I have very few headaches. (False)
I cannot keep my mind on one thing. (True)
I frequently notice my hand shakes when I try to do something. (True)
I practically never blush. (False)
I have nightmares every few nights. (True)
I sweat very easily even on cool days. (True)
I have a great deal of stomach trouble. (True)
I am usually calm and not easily upset. (False)
I am happy most of the time. (False)
I have been afraid of things or people that I know could not hurt me. (True)

From J. A. Taylor (1953, p. 286). Copyright 1953 by the American Psychological Association. Reprinted by permission.

of anticipatory eye blinking was greater for the high-anxiety subjects than for the low-anxiety subjects. This experiment demonstrates both the validity of the scale for learning experiments and the plausibility of Taylor's hypothesis about eyelid conditioning and anxiety (J. A. Taylor, 1951).

In recent years, the Taylor scale has declined in value because anxiety research has often required measures that are more specific. Anxiety is no longer regarded as a global trait; rather, there has been a growing tendency to consider specific types of anxiety and to use specific measures. One type of anxiety that has attracted an enormous amount of research attention is test anxiety.

Measures of Test Anxiety

Few topics in contemporary psychology are as well studied as test anxiety. This anxiety affects large numbers of students at many educational levels. Most readers of this book have experienced this; some may even have suffered a debilitating form of test anxiety that interfered with performance on an exam.

We discuss research on test anxiety in more detail than research on other topics for three reasons. This topic is relevant to many college students, test-anxiety research relates to many major psychological theories, and test anxiety is a factor that may interfere with performance on all sorts of tests, including psychological ones.

For more than 40 years, much theoretical research within psychology has been centered on test anxiety. A lot of this research was stimulated by a theory of test anxiety proposed by Mandler and Sarason (1952), who described test anxiety as a drive, or motivational state, that could become manifest in two different types of responding—task relevant and task irrelevant. Task-relevant responses are directed toward accomplishing the task at hand. They direct the energy associated with the test situation toward the goal of achieving a good grade. These responses may actually reduce anxiety. Students with test anxiety suffer the most from task-irrelevant responses. In a test-taking situation, these students begin to respond in a way that interferes with their performance. Usually, they begin thinking in self-oriented ways; they entertain thoughts such as "I am going to fail." Because they focus on these thoughts at the expense of attention to the items on the test, they often do a poor job.

Although Mandler and Sarason were from the same theoretical persuasion as Taylor, they concluded that the Taylor Manifest Anxiety Scale was too general a measure of test anxiety. They decided instead to develop a specific measure of test anxiety, the Test Anxiety Questionnaire. Over the years, people have discovered some inadequacies with this questionnaire and have transformed it into other measures such as the Test Anxiety Scale (I. G. Sarason, 1958), the Liebert-Morris Emotionality and Worry Scales (Liebert & Morris, 1967), and the Test Anxiety Inventory (Spielberger, Anton, & Bedell, 1976). Others have used different sources of items to construct tests such as the Achievement Anxiety Test (Alpert & Haber, 1960) and the Suinn Test Anxiety Behavior Scale (Suinn, 1969b). In the following sections, we review some of these test-anxiety measures.

The Test Anxiety Questionnaire

The grandparent of all test-anxiety measures, the Test Anxiety Questionnaire (TAQ) was the outgrowth of the Mandler and Sarason (1952) test-anxiety theory. The theory distinguishes between two different drives, or motivational states, that operate in test-taking situations. One is the learned task drive, which is the motivation to emit responses relevant to the task at hand. The other is the learned anxiety drive, which has two components, which you will recall: task-relevant responses and task-irrelevant responses. Mandler and Sarason developed a 37-item questionnaire (the TAQ) that assesses a person's predisposition to think or act in a way that interferes with the completion of a task. In other words, they attempted to build a measure to assess task-irrelevant responses. Some of the items from the TAQ are presented in Table 18-2. You might check the items to see whether they describe the way you feel during testing situations. Responses to the TAQ items are obtained on a 15-centimeter graphic scale. On the scale, the endpoints and the midpoint are identified. For example, a student is asked whether he or she avoids intelligence tests more or less than other students avoid them. The endpoints of the scale are "More often than other students" and "Less often than other students." The midpoint is simply labeled "Midpoint."

The reliability of the TAQ is very good. Early studies using a group of 100 Yale students demonstrated that the split-half reliability was .99, and a coefficient of .82 was obtained in a test-retest study over a six-week period. Some validity evidence showed that students who were high in test anxiety actually did more poorly on intellectual tasks than did students low in test anxiety (Mandler & Sarason, 1952).

TABLE 18-2

Some of the Questions Used in the Test Anxiety Questionnaire

---

4. If you know that you are going to take a group intelligence test, how do you feel beforehand?

I . . . . .I I

Feel very confident   Midpoint   Feel very unconfident

9. While taking a group intelligence test, to what extent do you perspire?

I . . . . .I I

Perspire not at all   Midpoint   Perspire a lot

17. Before taking an individual intelligence test, to what extent are you (or would you be) aware of an "uneasy feeling"?

I . . . . .I I

Am not aware of it at all   Midpoint   Am very much aware of it

24. In comparison to other students, how often do you (would you) think of ways of avoiding an individual intelligence test?

I . . . . .I I

More often than other students   Midpoint   Less often than other students

26. When you are taking a course examination, to what extent do you feel that your emotional reactions interfere with or lower your performance?

I . . . . .I I

Do not interfere with it at all   Midpoint   Interfere a great deal

---

From Mandler & Sarason (1952). Copyright 1952 by the American Psychological Association. Reprinted by permission.

The Test Anxiety Scale

One of the early criticisms of the TAQ was that it dealt with state anxiety rather than trait anxiety. The first revision of the TAQ began to consider individual or personality differences in test anxiety. In 1958, Irwin Sarason, the brother of Seymour Sarason (the original codeveloper of test-anxiety theory), rewrote the TAQ items in a true/false format to create the 21-item Test Anxiety Scale (TAS). I. Sarason agreed with the earlier theory that test anxiety produced interfering responses during test-taking situations, but he also recognized personality differences between people high and those low in test anxiety. He believed that less test-anxious people respond to test-taking situations by increasing their effort and attention toward the problem they are working on. Highly test-anxious persons react to the threatening situation by making self-oriented and personalized responses, often criticizing themselves rather than working on the test problems.

As you can see, the focus on the test-anxiety problem shifts from the situation in the TAQ to the person in the TAS. Although the two measures are quite similar and are indeed highly correlated, one measure assesses anxiety associated with situations, whereas the other determines which persons are highly test anxious.

Since the introduction of the TAS, Sarason has accumulated convincing evidence of a meaningful distinction between more and less test-anxious individuals. For example, they respond differently to instructions. In some experiments, the experimenter intentionally gives instructions that produce stress—for example, by telling the students that they must finish in a limited time or by telling them that the test they are taking correlates well with measures of intelligence. For subjects who score low on the TAS, these instructions may actually help. Usually, less test-anxious students score better under stress-producing conditions. The opposite seems to be true for the more test-anxious group. These individuals tend to do better when the instructions are neutral or reassuring rather than stress producing (G. L. Paul & Eriksen, 1964; I. G. Sarason, 1958, 1959, 1961, 1975). These studies are valuable for at least two reasons. First, they show that the TAS does make meaningful distinctions among people. Second, they suggest that differences in school performance may be associated with personality characteristics other than intelligence.

Furthermore, the research gives specific hints about the nature of test anxiety. Only the more test anxious say negative things to themselves instead of thinking about the problems on the test. This interference with thought is most severe for test-anxious people while they are working on difficult tasks (I. G. Sarason & Palola, 1960).

Some studies demonstrate that students who score high and low on the TAS also use information in different ways. Those with low scores on the TAS tend to increase their efforts when they are told they have not done well. In other words, if they do not do well, they may try to do better. Given the same feedback, test-anxious people plunge into themselves instead of plunging themselves into the task (Mandler & Sarason, 1952; Marlett & Watson, 1968; I. G. Sarason, 1975).

The differences between more and less test-anxious individuals also appear in the way they respond to neutral feedback. After receiving neutral feedback, students who score high on the TAS tend to respond as though they had just been given bad news, and they do not have much faith in their future success. Those who score low on the TAS tend to be optimistic about their future performance after they have been given neutral feedback (Meunier & Rule, 1967).

Some studies have even shown that when test-anxious individuals are placed in situations in which they will be evaluated (like describing themselves orally for half an hour), they attend most to negative references to themselves. They probably do not expect others to evaluate them well, and they actively search their environment for information to prove to themselves that this is true. For example, if someone leaves the room during a test, a test-anxious subject may interpret the behavior as an indication that he or she is not working fast enough (I. G. Sarason, 1975).

Among the most extensive in the test-anxiety literature, TAS confirms the validity of the TAS as a personality measure. The research shows that poor performance on tests may result from a combination of two factors: being a test-anxious person and being in a situation that arouses anxiety. When they come to an anxiety-arousing testing situation, highly test-anxious individuals may not be able to focus on the task at hand, performing well on the test. Instead, they may have to contend with many interfering thoughts such as "My mind's a blank" or "I feel really stupid." Those of you who have had this experience know how distressing it can be. When you should be concentrating on calculating the statistics problem or picking the correct multiple-choice alternative, you begin instead to think that you are running out of time or that you are going to fail.

You may also experience some physiological changes: Your heart rate may speed up, your mouth may get dry, you may begin to sweat, you may get an upset stomach or a stiff neck. Recognizing these physical side effects of test taking, some researchers have proposed that these emotional responses be measured separately.

Other Measures of Test Anxiety

A number of other measures of test anxiety are commonly used in research and practice. Liebert and Morris (1967) suggested that test anxiety has two components: emotionality and worry. Emotionality, the physical response to test-taking situations, is associated with conditions such as accelerated heart rate and muscle stiffness. Worry is the mental preoccupation with failing and with the personal consequences of doing poorly. The Liebert-Morris scales tap these components separately.

Spielberger, Anton, and Bedell (1976) also created a test-anxiety scale that has both emotionality and worry factors. Spielberger's 20-item Test Anxiety Inventory conceptualizes test anxiety in terms of state and trait. According to Spielberger, worry is a trait that is more consistent over the course of time. Each person worries about tests to a characteristic degree. Emotionality is the manner in which arousal is expressed in particular situations. Thus, this theory proposes that the emotional component is a state, or situational, aspect. Systematic studies have confirmed that emotionality and worry are independent dimensions of test anxiety. Furthermore, these two dimensions have been observed in both male and female subjects. The latter score significantly higher than the former on the emotionality components but not on the worry components (Everson, Millsap, & Rodriguez, 1991; Zeidner, 1990).

Another approach to the measurement of test anxiety was proposed by Alpert and Haber (1960). Their Achievement Anxiety Test (AAT) is a 19-item scale that gives scores for two different components of anxiety: facilitating and debilitating. Debilitating anxiety resembles the anxiety that all the other scales attempt to measure. The debilitating anxiety scale measures the extent to which anxiety interferes with performance on tests. The novel component of the AAT is facilitating anxiety, a state that can motivate performance. This type of anxiety gets one worried enough to study hard. If one is not anxious at all, one may not be motivated enough to gear up for the exam. Thus, facilitating anxiety is helpful, and debilitating anxiety harmful.

Treatments for Test Anxiety

Throughout this chapter, we have stressed how debilitating test anxiety can be for many college students. If you have problems with test anxiety, you may gain some comfort from knowing that clinical psychologists have sharpened their skills for dealing with it. The most successful approaches have centered on some form of behavior modification. The most popular treatments are systematic desensitization (Wolpe, 1969) and cognitive behavior modification. In the former, a student systematically learns to relax and then experiences the thought of successively more threatening situations. Cognitive behavior modification combines systematic desensitization with training in which a student learns to say positive things to himself or herself (R. M. Kaplan, McCordick & Twitchell, 1979; Wessel & Mersch, 1994). For example, the student may learn to relax muscles in order to combat emotional responses during a test and then may also learn to make self-statements such as "I am not going to let this get to me" or "Just relax; I'm in control; concentrate on the exam."

The success of these approaches depends to some extent on the measures used to evaluate them. For example, systematic desensitization is quite effective when it is evaluated by changes in the TAQ, the TAS, or the AAT. However, systematic desensitization and most other therapies are less effective if the measure used is an increase in grade point average. When combined with training in study skills, however, systematic desensitization appears to be effective even when the measure is grade point average (G. J. Allen, 1972; Anton, 1976; S. H. Smith, 1977; Spielberger, Anton, & Bedell, 1976).

Thus, test-anxious college students may need help not only reducing their test anxiety but also improving their study skills. Additional benefits appear when a self-talk component is added. Thus, clinical psychologists now feel they have begun to develop the technology to help college students cope with the debilitating effects of test anxiety. Furthermore, these new approaches appear to effect improvements in classroom performance in addition to positive changes in scores on anxiety inventories (Flett & Blankstein, 1994; Wessel & Mersch, 1994). Other methods have also been shown to be valuable. For example, both relaxation exercises and regular physical activity may reduce test anxiety among college students (Topp, 1989). Focused Example 18-1 describes a different approach to treating test anxiety.

Measures of Life Stress

The research on the relationship between stress and illness requires measures of stressful life events. Table 18-3 shows an early measure called the Survey of Recent Events (SRE), which lists events that may have occurred in a person's life. This instrument is commonly used in psychiatric research (Holmes & Rahe, 1967; Rahe, 1972). The designers of the SRE assumed that specific life events have a cumulative impact on well-being. In Table 18-3, each of the events is associated with a life change unit (LCU) value; LCUs are social values that need to be measured. It is thought that all the events listed in the table represent life changes, one cannot count each as having the same effect. Getting a traffic ticket cannot be considered as disrupting as getting a divorce.

To determine the weight of each event, the investigators had people of different social backgrounds rate the degree of turmoil, upheaval, and social readjustment each of the events causes. These people compared each event with getting married, which was arbitrarily assigned the score of 50. For example, people were asked to give a number to the readjustment required by the death of a spouse (if the amount of readjustment necessitated by marriage is 50). Remarkably, little disagreement about these values arose among raters

---

Focused Example 18.1

TEST ANXIETY AND THE FUNNY TEST

Perhaps the most unusual treatment for test anxiety was reported by R. E. Smith and colleagues (1971). These psychologists knew that some students in their classes had difficulties with test anxiety. They also knew of several theories that suggest that a good laugh may help alleviate anger and anxiety. Smith and his colleagues used the TAS to determine which of their students were low and which were high in test anxiety. Then half the students in each group were given a funny version of their midterm. The other half were given a serious version. For comparison, some items on each version of the test were identical.

In the funny version, one-third of the items were intended to be humorous. For example, one of the items about abnormal behavior read,

Claiming to be a slot machine, Julius has been standing against a wall in a Las Vegas casino for six years making bell-like sounds and occasionally complaining that he is being tilted. Which other member of Julius's family is most likely to exhibit bizarre behavior? Alternatives: (a) his mother; (b) his sister; (c) his identical twin; (d) it is impossible to make a probability statement.

The results demonstrated that the humorous items did help relieve some of the test anxiety. On the serious version of the test, the highly anxious students did not do as well as those who did not experience much test anxiety. However, on the test with some funny items, the differences between high and low test-anxious students disappeared.

TABLE 18-3
*Values of Life
Change Events**

	LCU Values
Family	
Death of spouse	100
Divorce	73
Marital separation	65
Death of close family member	63
Marriage	50
Marital reconciliation	45
Major change in health of family	44
Pregnancy	40
Addition of new family member	39
Major change in arguments with spouse	35
Son or daughter leaving home	29
In-law troubles	29
Spouse starting or ending work	26
Major change in family get-togethers	15
Personal	
Detention in jail	63
Major personal injury or illness	53
Sexual difficulties	39
Death of a close friend	37
Outstanding personal achievement	28
Start or end of formal schooling	26
Major change in living conditions	25
Major revision of personal habits	24
Changing to a new school	20
Change in residence	20
Major change in recreation	19
Major change in church activities	19
Major change in sleeping habits	16
Major change in eating habits	15
Vacation	13
Christmas	12
Minor violations of the law	11
Work	
Being fired from work	47
Retirement from work	45
Major business adjustment	39
Changing to different line of work	36
Major change in work responsibilities	29
Trouble with boss	23
Major change in working conditions	20

TABLE 18-3
Continued

Financial

Major change in financial state	38
Mortgage or loan over $10,000	31
Mortgage foreclosure	30
Mortgage or loan less than $10,000	17

*Scoring directions: Mark the changes that may have happened in your life within the last six months. Add up the life change unit (LCU) values associated with each of the events you have checked, People who experience the most life changes also experience the most illness (see text).
From Rahe (1972).

who differ in age, gender, marital status, education, social class, race, and creed. In addition, there was substantial agreement among people from different cultures. Swedes, Danes, Japanese, and North Americans appeared to regard the impact of life changes in similar ways.

Once the scoring system had been developed, one could create life stress scores and compare these scores with the amounts of illness contracted (Komaroff, Masuda, & Holmes, 1968). A variety of studies demonstrated that there is a small but significant correlation between the life change score for the last six months and the probability of developing an illness. In one study conducted with U.S. Navy personnel, life stress scores were obtained for entire crews before their vessels were sent out to sea. After six months, the sailors and their health records were examined. It was observed that sailors who were in the top 10% in life change scores were twice as likely to become ill as sailors in the bottom 10%. Life crises may have weakened the immune system and made the sailors easier targets for disease.

The relationship between stress and illness continues to be documented in a wide variety of studies (Zales, 1985), including studies on heart disease (Rosenman & Chesney, 1985) and cancer (Biondi & Pancheri, 1985). Recent research is beginning to illuminate the relationship between stress and illness. For example, Irwin and co-workers (1987) have demonstrated how two aspects of the immune system (natural killer-cell activity and t-cell subpopulations) are affected by bereavement. Women who recently lost a husband had more severe depressive symptoms and lower ratios of helper to suppressor t-cells. Newer evidence has suggested that these same biochemical changes can be induced by a brief (12-minute) stressful mental arithmetic exam (Naliboff et al., 1991). These biochemical events are associated with impaired immunity.

Debate continues about the effect of life stress on illness (R. M. Kaplan, 1990). However, at least some evidence suggests that serious health outcomes are related to the inability to cope with stress. For example, Eysenck (1990) has shown that inability to cope with stress, which often results in feelings of hopelessness, helplessness, and desperation, may predict death from serious disease such as cancer. Certainly, this is an area that will continue to attract research attention.

The Survey of Recent Events has been criticized by G. W. Brown, Bhrolchain, and Harris (1975) because the weighting system and interview format are arbitrary and do not apply to all groups of people. G. W. Brown and Harris (1978) proposed an alternative method that requires personal interviews to determine when life events occurred and how much ongoing difficulty these events pose in people's lives. Some have argued that Brown's interview method is most appropriate for studies of the elderly (Wilkinson, James, & Davies, 1985). Wilkinson and colleagues (1986) have shown that the test-retest reliability for the Brown scale is indeed adequate for elderly populations. Another approach based on a similar criticism of the SRE is the Life Experiences Survey.

Life Experiences Survey

The SRE was based on the assumption that specific life events have a cumulative impact on well-being, that the degree of impact is the same for any individual, and that a mean societal evaluation of the desirability or undesirability of an event is appropriate for any individual. For example, the desirability of pregnancy would be determined by the mean scale value that a community assigned to this event, and the mean value would be applied to any woman who became pregnant within some defined time interval. I. G. Sarason, Johnson, and Siegel (1978) note that this is not a palatable assumption. A positive pregnancy test may be received as good news by some women and as a disaster by others. Life change measures, they argue, must allow for individual differences in reactions to stress.

A similar assumption in the life stress literature is that positive and negative life events both contribute to probabilities of poor future functioning. This assumption, evident in theories of stress, has been so widely accepted that few investigators have attempted to separate positive and negative life events.

I. G. Sarason and Sarason (1985a) showed the importance of these points by presenting data from a new Life Experiences Survey (LES). The measure includes 47 events that may be appropriate for any subjects and an additional section with 10 items specifically designed for students. The subject must indicate which events have occurred within a specific time period and record the perceived impact of the event on a scale ranging from -3 for extremely negative to $+3$ for extremely positive. Separating those events with negative weights from those with positive ones yields separate scores for negative and positive events.

Validity data suggest that the LES negative score correlates with depression, external locus of control, state and trait anxiety, and low grade point average. These variables were not correlated with positive life events. In addition, the LES showed good discriminant validity. To evaluate discriminant validity, estimates of SRE life change units and LES scores were obtained for the same group of subjects; the SRE tended not to correlate as highly as the LES with a variety of different measures. The LES performed better than the SRE because it allowed individuals to express the extent to which different events bothered them as individuals. For example, with the SRE, any person who had been fired from a job would get the same score. The LES allows the respondent to specify how stressful the event was.

A variety of other measures have been created to record perceived stress. For example, S. Cohen, Karnarack, and Mermelstein (1983) developed a measure that focuses on the perceived stressfulness of various events. Respondents are asked how often they felt upset because something had happened to them, how often they felt stressed or nervous, how often they felt they could not cope with what was happening, how often they felt angered by things that were happening beyond their control, how often they found themselves thinking about things they had to accomplish, and how often they felt difficulties were piling so high that they could not overcome them.

Some research also shows that more than just major life events cause problems. Daily irritations accumulate. Kanner and colleagues (1981) have begun to measure the minor "hassles" in daily life. In addition, they record the small pleasures that may make life more bearable. Some research has demonstrated that daily hassles are better predictors of poor health than are major life events (DeLongis et al., 1982). Thus, the minor irritations may be the most difficult to cope with. Conversely, small uplifts may improve the ability to cope. Although research on daily hassles has attracted a lot of attention, no one has yet established a strong association between hassles and health. For example, among students, daily stress does not predict variations in mental health measures (J. G. Johnson & Bernstein, 1991). In the next section, we examine measures of coping with stress.

Measures of Coping

Measuring the stressfulness of one's environment may not provide an adequate understanding of the relationship between stress and poor health. Different people confronted with the same stressful situation may respond quite differently. Feifel, Strack, and Nagy (1987) compared the coping styles of two different patient groups. Some of the patients had life-threatening illnesses such as cancer or heart attacks. The comparison group had non-life-threatening illnesses such as skin problems or arthritis. The coping styles of the two groups differed. In particular, those with life-threatening illnesses used confrontation more frequently. Interestingly, neither group used acceptance and resignation often. Several measures have been developed to assess the ways people cope with stress (Dupue & Monroe, 1986; Folkman & Lazarus, 1980). One of these measures, the Ways of Coping Scale (Lazarus, 1995; Lazarus & Folkman, 1984), is a 68-item checklist. Individuals choose from a list those thoughts and actions that they use to deal with stressful situations. The scale includes seven subscales for problem solving, growth, wishful thinking, advice seeking, minimizing threat, seeking support, and self-blame. Studies using this scale have suggested that the seven subscales can be divided into problem-focused and emotion-focused strategies for dealing with stressful situations. Problem-focused strategies involve cognitive and behavioral attempts to change the course of the stress. In other words, these are active methods of coping. Emotion-focused strategies do not attempt to alter the stressor but instead focus on ways of dealing with the emotional responses to stress (F. Cohen & Lazarus, 1994). The Ways of Coping questionnaire is one of the most widely used measures in health psychology. However, some have offered criticism. For example, using factor analysis, some studies have failed to replicate the basic factor structure (D. Parker, Endler, & Bagby, 1993).

A related measure is the Coping Inventory (Horowitz & Wilner, 1980), a 33-item measure derived from clinical interview data. Of three categories of items, the first describes activities and attitudes people use to avoid stress. The second involves items that characterize strategies for working through stressful events. The third category considers socialization responses, or how each strategy would help the respondent cope with a specific stressful event. These measures and related tests, such as the Coping Resources Inventory (Hammer & Marting, 1985), have been very useful in research on both adults and adolescents. For example, one study demonstrated that coping resources predict lower rates of both psychological and physical symptoms independent of stressful life events. In other words, having good coping capabilities is important whether or not you are under stress (Zeidner & Hammer, 1990).

Ecological Momentary Assessment

Most psychological tests are designed to evaluate traits, which are constant over the course of time. Even measures of state anxiety are presumed to be reliable. However, levels of stress vary over the course of time. Stress, as measured today, may tell one very little about stress experienced next week. If one asks today about experiences last week, the measurements may be inaccurate because memory fades over time. Recall affects virtually all autobiographical information.

New technical developments have made it possible to obtain information on an ongoing basis. One can obtain information repeatedly and average the results to get an overall impression of stress. Or, one can assess information with reference to a particular event. For example, one might determine if levels of perceived stress coincide with particular stressors. Ecological Momentary Assessment (EMA) uses computers to collect information on a continuing basis. The equipment might measure blood pressure or hormonal state at specific points in time. Further, a subject might be prompted to record information about mood, symptoms, or fatigue.

One of the advantages of EMA is that the information is collected in the subject's natural environment. Most information in clinical studies is collected in clinics, offices, or laboratories—not necessarily the situations in which people ordinarily experience life events. The EMA method usually involves a substantial number of repeated observations and shows variability within the subject over time (Stone & Shiffman, 1994).

One study of the co-use of alcohol and tobacco provides an example of EMA. Traditional studies of alcohol consumption might actually miss much of the information about drinking, because the assessment is typically done during the day, but alcohol consumption often occurs in the evening. EMA allows the continuous assessment of these behaviors in the subject's own environment. In one study, 57 subjects were given minicomputers that randomly prompted them to record their behaviors. The study showed that drinking was likely to occur between 8:00 P.M. and midnight. Smoking was more than twice as likely when subjects had been drinking as when they had not. In other words, smoking and drinking were linked (Shiffman et al., 1995). Other studies have used daily assessments to evaluate life stress. In one study, 74 patients with arthritis rated stress, mood, and pain for 75 days. The results showed that the experience of major recent life stresses affected the association between daily stress and pain. Those who had experienced major stresses were more likely to experience pain the day after a stressful event than other days. The results suggest that life stress may amplify the relationship between life events and pain (Affleck et al., 1994). We expect technical developments, such as EMA, to improve significantly the assessment of variable behaviors and emotions (Stone 1995; Stone, Kennedy-Moore, & Neale, 1995).

Measures of Social Support

In recent years, health psychologists have devoted considerable effort to the study of social support. Social resources and support apparently serve as significant buffers for stressful life events and moderators of psychological and physical well-being (Sarason & Sarason, 1994; R. J. Turner, 1981). Family, friends, and other social contacts may aid in reducing emotional distress and problems resulting from injuries or other disabilities. Several lines of research suggest that those confronted with serious life events may cope better if they have friends or family to help them absorb shock.

Although definitions vary, most measures of social support include both tangible (financial assistance and physical aid) and intangible (encouragement and guidance) support. Social support has been shown to help mediate stressful life events, speed recovery from illness, and increase the likelihood that a person will follow the advice of his or her doctor. However, there are many inconsistent findings in the literature, and it is difficult to resolve discrepancies because measures of social support vary widely from study to study. When Heitzmann and Kaplan (1988) reviewed 26 measures for evaluating social support, they looked for documented validity and reliability coefficients greater than .80. Correlations between various social support and criterion measures were simulated in order to demonstrate the consequences of choosing a measure with low reliability (see also R. M. Kaplan, 1994a).

According to the review, few social support measures offered adequate documentation of reliability. In addition, documentation of validity was available for only some measures. Evidence for discriminant validity was almost never presented. Perhaps the best example of a social support measure has been presented by I. G. Sarason and co-workers (1983). This measure, known as the Social Support Questionnaire (SSQ), includes 27 items, each with two parts. For each item the respondent must (1) list the people whom he or she can count on for support in given circumstances and (2) indicate the overall level of satisfaction with these supports. The SSQ yields two scores: the number (N) score for each item is the number of supports the person lists. The satisfaction (S) score ranges from 1 for very dissatisfied to 6 for very satisfied for each of these items. The number of people someone can count on is averaged from the 27 items to get a mean N score, and the satisfaction ratings are also averaged to get a mean S score.

Sarason and colleagues (1983) conducted a series of studies to determine the reliability and validity of their measure. Based on a normative sample of 602 undergraduate college students, coefficient alpha for satisfaction (S) was .94 and for number (N) was .97. Test-retest correlations over a four-week period were .90 for N and .83 for S. These results indicate that the SSQ is a very stable instrument with high internal consistency. Validity data were based on a number of comparisons between the SSQ and other measurement techniques. A sample of 277 undergraduate students were given the SSQ, the Multiple Affect Adjective Check List (MAACL), and the Lack of Protection scale (LP). There were significant negative correlations between the SSQ-N and SSQ-S and measures of emotional discomfort as tapped by the MACCL. Similarily, items on the LP that deal with recollections of separation anxiety in childhood also correlated negatively with the SSQ.

As the interest in social support grows, so does the number of measures. Most of the newer measures attempt to identify multiple factors of social support (R. M. Kaplan, 1994). For example, a Multidimensional Scale of Perceived Social Support (MSPSS) has been introduced to separate support obtained from family, friends, and significant others (Zimet et al., 1990). The psychometric properties of some of the new measures are better than those of earlier ones. However, this field continues to require rigorous research investigation.

Comment on theory. This chapter has emphasized the measurement of stress and anxiety. The complex theory that links stress to illness and to performance lies beyond a book on psychological testing, yet measurement is central to the evaluation of these theoretical models. For example, the same levels of stress may cause mental health symptoms for some people but not for others. This may be because stress activates a mental disorder (Monroe & Simons, 1991) or because some people have better social relationships to help them buffer the stress. Evaluating these theories is difficult. For instance, mental health symptoms may bias the report of life stress. New theories about the role of stress in the development of physical and mental problems may stimulate a better understanding of its role in depression or other forms of psychopathology (Monroe & Simons, 1991). Ultimately, research and theory development should stimulate better measures and clinical interventions.

Summary

Test anxiety is a fact of life for many students. In this chapter, we reviewed some of the existing research on the theory and measurement of test anxiety. Research on test anxiety grew from general theories of learning. Early studies by J. Taylor identified anxiety as a motivational state that one could measure with a short scale. Using the scale, she could relate anxiety to a general theory that had previously depended primarily on evidence from animal studies. Later developments divided anxiety into state and trait components.

Eventually, specific test-anxiety theories were proposed, and test anxiety became an area of study in itself. As test-anxiety theory developed, many scales were devised to measure test-anxiety problems. Different theories emphasized that test anxiety is a general motivational state, is a personality trait, or is related both to situations and to the characteristics of the test taker. In other words, there are many different theories of test anxiety and many different ways of measuring it. Recent developments in psychotherapy hold great promise for the successful treatment of test anxiety.

In recent years, considerable interest has developed in the measurement of life stress. The Survey of Recent Events (SRE) is a list of occurrences that could cause disruption in an individual's life. The events are weighted by the perceived amount of readjustment required to cope with them. Studies have linked scores on these measures with the onset of illness. However, a variety of critiques have demonstrated the SRE's weaknesses. An alternate approach, the Life Experiences Survey (LES), allows individuals to weight the amount of readjustment required by particular events in their own lives. The LES may be a superior measure of life stress. Future research will illuminate the relationship among life stress, perceived disruption, and health outcomes. The measurement of health outcomes will be described in more detail in Chapter 19.

In addition to measures of test anxiety and life stress, a variety of measures quantify adaptation to stressful situations. These include measures of coping and measures of social support. Not all individuals faced with the same stresses have the same reactions. Measures of social support and coping help explain why some people can better adapt to stressful situations than others.

Testing in Health-Care Settings

LEARNING OBJECTIVES

When you have completed this chapter, you should be able to

☐ Describe at least two important health-care situations in which psychological tests are used

☐ Define *clinical neuropsychology*

☐ Discuss the use of neuropsychological instruments in both childhood and adulthood

☐ Describe the Halstead-Reitan test battery

☐ Describe the Luria-Nebraska test battery

☐ Discuss the advantages of the California Verbal Learning Test

☐ Differentiate psychometric and decision theory approaches to quality of life measurement

☐ Describe the Sickness Impact Profile

☐ Discuss the advantages and disadvantages of measures such as the Index of Activities of Daily Living, the Karnofsky Performance Status, and the McMaster Health Index Questionnaire

☐ Discuss the concept of a quality-adjusted life-year

oday more than 5% of all psychologists are directly employed by hospitals, medical centers, and clinics, and projections indicate that this figure will increase. One of the main functions of psychologists in these settings is to use and interpret measurement instruments. Although we cannot discuss the wide variety of measures used in medical settings, we focus on two areas that have experienced rapid development in the last few years: neuropsychological assessment and quality of life assessment.

Neuropsychological Assessment

Clinical Neuropsychology

Linda was an intelligent, extremely cooperative 7-year-old when she was hit by a car. Unconscious for only a short time, she appeared to show a rapid physical recovery from the accident. However, by the time one year had passed, her parents had become very concerned about behavioral changes they had observed after the accident. She had become introverted, did not interact well with others, and seemed anxious, prone to temper tantrums, frustrated, and unable to take criticism. The doctor who had originally examined Linda referred her to a neurologist, who could not find anything abnormal in her CAT scans and EEG tests. Unable to determine the source of her difficulties, the neurologist referred Linda to a specialized psychologist trained in neuropsychological assessment. The psychologist discovered that Linda's visual functioning and her ability to talk were superior; however, she had difficulties in hearing and in the ability to write down phonemes she had heard. Furthermore, tests showed that she had done very well on things she had learned before the accident but that she had lost the ability to discriminate among the sounds of letters closely related to one another. This in turn caused a great deal of strain and created her belief that she was stupid and unable to keep up with other children. The test that helped identify Linda's specific problem is called the Luria-Nebraska Neuropsychological Battery. After discovering that Linda's problem was very specific, her teachers designed a special education program to adapt learning materials to a visual approach and to avoid auditory presentations. Her parents could also adapt to their child's problem once they realized its nature. Given this support and the reduced pressure, Linda's introversion, sensitivity to criticism, and frustration decreased. Over time, as her injuries healed, she returned to normal (Golden, 1981).

Linda's case shows the importance of a rapidly expanding new field known as **clinical neuropsychology.** This field is a scientific discipline that focuses on psychological impairments of the central nervous system and their remediation. One formal definition of *neuropsychology* is the application of methods from experimental and clinical psychology to the analysis of cognitive and behavioral problems caused by injury, disease, or abnormal development of the brain (Levin et al., 1989). The activities of neuropsychologists include identification, description, multivariate quantification, and treatment of diseases of the brain and spinal cord. Clinical neuropsychology is a multi-disciplinary endeavor, overlapping neurology, psychiatry, and psychometric testing in the following ways: Neuropsychology and neurology both focus on sensations and perceptions and on motor movements. Neuropsychology and psychiatry both study mood and adaptations to psychosocial situations. Finally, neuropsychology and psychometrics both use psychological tests. Neuropsychology differs from these other clinical disciplines because it is finely specialized, focusing on attention, memory, learning, language and communication, spatial integration, and cognitive flexibility. In summary, neuropsychology is a field of study that actively attempts to relate brain dysfunction and damage to observable and measurable behavioral problems (Crockett, Clark, & Kalonoff, 1981; Grant & Adams, 1986).

Clinical neuropsychology has developed rapidly over the last few decades. In 1970, neuropsychology was viewed as a new field characterized by rapid growth (Parsons, 1970). During the 1970s and early 1980s, research in neuropsychology exploded, and a practice specialty rapidly developed. Currently, neuropsychology has formally joined the ranks of other neurosciences. Using powerful measurement techniques, neuropsychologists have developed many procedures for identifying the relationship between brain problems and behavior problems (Butters, Delis, & Lucas, 1995). The activities of neuropsychologists are extremely varied and require some complex technology. An exploration of this important new discipline in any depth would require a review of neuroanatomy and other topics in neuroscience, which we cannot discuss here. Instead, we describe some current activities of active neuropsychological research and practice. The interested reader should consult Baddeley, Wilson, and Watts (1995), Grant and Adams (1995), Hooper and March (1995), Lezak (1995), and Mapou & Spector (1986).

Neuropsychologists are very specialized. Some focus on the study of brain dysfunction in children (Fletcher et al., 1995; Hooper & March, 1995), whereas others work with adults (Heaton & Pendleton, 1981) or older adults (Kaszniak & Christenson, 1994; K. Welsh et al., 1991). Most of the work in neuropsychology is directed at the assessment of brain dysfunction, but some neuropsychologists are actively developing interventions for those who suffer brain injuries or related problems (Dikmen & Machamer, 1995). Neuropsychologists also study the impact of mental illness (McKenna, Clare, & Baddeley, 1995) as well as alcohol abuse (Grant, 1987) or serious diseases such as AIDS (Grant & Heaton, 1990) on cognitive processes. Neuropsychologists differ in the methods they apply. Some prefer to use batteries of psychological tests, whereas others prefer specific tasks derived from experimental psychology (Delis et al., 1994; Satz & Fletcher, 1981).

Neuropsychological assessment has been used to evaluate specific problems in memory. Clearly, memory is a heterogeneous phenomena, and there are probably different memory systems. Perhaps the most important distinction is between short-term memory and long-term memory. Short-term memory occurs when one recollects or produces material immediately after it has been presented. The capacity for short-term memory is probably limited; without repetition one can hold information only a few minutes. Conversely, long-term memory may be stored for a long time (more than a few days), and the capacity for long-term memory is very large.

Examiners use a variety of clinical techniques to measure memory dysfunction, including the Wechsler Memory Scale—Revised (WMS-R), the Memory Assessment Scales (MAS), the RANDT Memory Test (RMT), and the Luria-Nebraska battery (Butters, Delis, & Lucas, 1995). Short-term memory is best assessed using verbal tests. These include the immediate recall span, the digit span, and several word tests (Butters, Delis, & Lucas, 1995). The techniques used to assess short-term memory include tests that evaluate memory for specific stories or memory for lists of unrelated words.

Significant progress has been made in linking performance on neuropsychological tests to specific clinical problems. For example, dementia associated with Alzheimer's disease is associated with an anterograde amnesia for semantic or episodic types of information. Adults affected by Alzheimer's disease have difficulty learning new information or retaining it over time. However, their long-term memory may be less affected. These types of dementias can be differentiated from other memory problems. For example, alcoholic dementia, caused by long-term chronic alcoholism, is characterized by further dysfunction in visuospatial skills in comparison with verbal abilities. Patients with subcortical dementias, such as Huntington's disease, may demonstrate a different pattern of performance on neuropsychological tests. For example, patients with Huntington's disease perform much better on recognition than do patients with Alzheimer's disease. Patients with Huntington's disease may have retrograde amnesia with equally deficient recall of events from all decades. In contrast, patients with Alzheimer's disease have more severe difficulties with recall for recent events (Butters, Delis, & Lucas, 1995).

Developmental Neuropsychology

The study of childhood brain dysfunction is extremely important. Neuropsychological problems appear in speech and reading disorders known as *learning disabilities*, which account for problems in significant numbers of young children. **Dyslexia** is a specific reading disorder characterized by reading backward (Rutter, 1978). Unfortunately, it is difficult to estimate the exact number of children affected by dyslexia, because different studies apply different definitions. Nevertheless, federal law now requires that children with specific disabilities receive individualized instruction programs and special attention. Thus, the identification of a disability such as dyslexia means that considerable attention will be devoted to the child at enormous public expense. In other words, learning disabilities represent major public health problems. Therefore, considerable effort has been devoted to defining subcategories of learning disabilities, developing procedures to identify them, and instituting methods for helping children overcome these problems (Leong & Joshi, 1995; Pennington & Welsh, 1995; Shaywitz, Fletcher, & Shaywitz, 1995).

Other clinical neuropsychologists have been busy identifying the **cognitive** consequences of early brain lesions. For example, studies have shown that high-risk infants show poor performance on tests of verbal ability, coordination, visual-spatial ability, and the like by the time they are 3½ years old (Francis-Williams, 1974). Other studies focus on recovery from accidents and trauma. For example, a few years after children have been in accidents involving head injuries, neurological tests often show no remaining problems. Nevertheless, neuropsychological tests of intellectual abilities often show that these functions remain somewhat impaired (Butters, Delis, & Lucas, 1995). In summary, developmental neuropsychologists actively work toward understanding brain-behavior relationships in children. They have created extensive diagnostic procedures for identifying different learning disabilities, including articulation disorders, speech disorders, and dyslexia. Furthermore, they have attempted to link specific medical problems such as birth complications and prematurity to later intellectual function. Finally, they have attempted to identify the cognitive consequences of early brain disease and injury.

Developmental neuropsychology is a difficult field because it requires several levels of assessment. Figure 19-1 shows a seven-step model used by neuropsychologists in the development of rehabilitation plans. The first step requires the application of formal tests to determine the nature of the problem. The second step calls for an assessment of the environment. For example, demands of the school environment and other academic expectations must be taken into consideration. The third and fourth steps require the formulation of treatment plans, which involve a prediction of the short- and long-term consequences of the brain problem and the chances that intervention will make a difference. The fifth level of assessment concerns the availability of resources. For example, is there a family member who can assist in treatment? Are there facilities and therapists in the community? The sixth step calls for the development of a realistic treatment plan that considers the information gained in Steps 1–5. Even if the neuropsychologist does not deliver the treatment, he or she may remain involved in the seventh step, evaluating progress made in the course of clinical care. When treatment is not achieving its objectives, modifications may be suggested (Fletcher et al., 1995).

As suggested by Figure 19-1, the neuropsychologist has many complex and important tasks that require the administration and interpretation of assessment devices.

Adult Neuropsychology

There are many different approaches to identifying the consequences of brain injury in adults. Perhaps the two best known approaches involve administra-

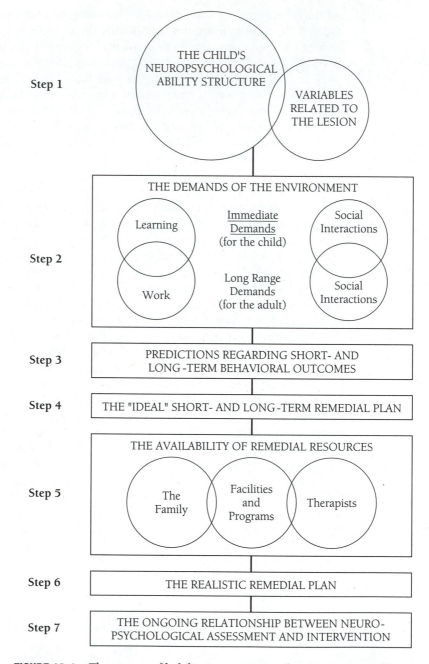

FIGURE 19-1   *The process of habilitation requires at least seven steps: (1) assessment of the child, (2) assessment of the environment, (3) predictions about short- and long-term outcomes, (4) development of an ideal plan, (5) assessment of resources, (6) development of a realistic intervention plan, and (7) ongoing assessment.*
(From Fletcher et al. (1995, p. 585). Reprinted by permission of Guilford Publications.)

tion of the Halstead-Reitan and Luria-Nebraska test batteries. We discuss each of these psychological test batteries briefly.

Halstead-Reitan neuropsychological battery. In 1935, Ward Halstead opened a laboratory to study the impact of impairments of brain function on a wide range of human abilities. Some of Halstead's observations were formal, while others involved observations in work and social settings. The formal observations were obtained through modifications of existing psychological tests. Over time, Halstead realized that determining inadequacy in brain function required a wide range of tests that measured characteristics and abilities beyond those targeted by existing psychological tests. In 1944, Halstead was joined in his neuropsychological laboratory by his first graduate student, Ralph M. Reitan. Halstead and Reitan worked together until 1950, when Reitan received his Ph.D. Reitan contributed by adding several tests to the assessment procedures. The full battery includes many psychological tests and sometimes requires 8 to 12 hours to administer. In addition, patients assessed by the Halstead-Reitan procedures often receive the full Minnesota Multiphasic Personality Inventory (MMPI) to evaluate their emotional state in response to a medical situation.

The full Halstead-Reitan Neuropsychological Battery is available in different versions for children and adults. See Table 19-1 for a summary of the components in the adult battery.

A large number of studies validate the Halstead and Reitan procedures (Reitan, 1986). Most of the studies show that performance on specific subtasks of the Halstead-Reitan battery is associated with dysfunction in one of the two hemispheres of the brain. For example, tactile, visual, and auditory problems on one side of the body reflect damage in the opposite hemisphere of the brain. Difficulty on the right side of the body indicates a problem in the left side of the brain (Wheeler & Reitan, 1962). Later studies by Reitan (1968) demonstrated that the battery can locate tumors or lesions in the right or left hemisphere of the brain and in the front or back portion of the brain in a significant number of cases. By studying performance in a systematic way, neuropsychologists have been able to provide important information about the location and the impact of brain problems (Reitan & Wolfson, 1995; Wolfson & Reitan, 1995).

Luria-Nebraska neuropsychological battery. A different approach to neuropsychological assessment is found in the work of Luria, who has been recognized for many years as an expert on the functions of the human brain (Luria, 1966, 1973). Luria's theory and methods differ from those applied by Halstead, Reitan, and others. The most important concepts in Luria's theory are that the brain is a functional system and that many areas within the system coordinate to produce observable behavior. Other researchers attempted to find specific areas within the brain that correspond to particular behaviors. Luria differed because he did not acknowledge any single area in the brain as solely responsi-

TABLE 19-1   *Components of the Halstead-Reitan Neuropsychology Battery for Adults*

Test	Description
Halstead category test	This test is a learning experiment for current learning skills, mental efficiency, and abstract concept formation.
Tactual test (time, memory, localization)	The patient must put variously shaped blocks into holes of the same shape. The test assesses several abilities, including motor speed and tactual and kinesthetic psychomotor performance, as well as memory.
Rhythm test	Thirty pairs of rhythm beats are presented, and the patient is to identify which pairs are the same and which are different. The task measures auditory perception, concentration, and attention.
Speech-sounds perception test	Sixty nonsense words are presented on a tape recorder. After hearing each word, the patient must choose the word from among four alternatives presented visually. The test measures auditory-verbal perception, auditory-visual coordination, and some aspects of language and concentration.
Finger oscillation test	The patient taps the index finger as rapidly as possible, alternating hands on consecutive trials. The test is used to analyze motor speed and right-left hand preference.
Related Procedures	The following tests are often given in conjunction with the Halstead-Reitan battery.
Trail-making test	This test requires patients to connect numbers and letters as rapidly as possible. The test measures speed, visual scanning, and ability to process information in sequence.
Strength-of-grip test	A mechanical device (the hand dynamometer) is used to measure the strength of grip in each hand.
Sensory-perceptual examination	In a variety of sensory modalities, such as touch, hearing, and vision, the patient receives information on one side of the body and then on the other side. The test is used to determine whether stimuli presented on one side of the body are perceived when presented alone and also to determine whether competition with other stimulation reduces the perception of the stimulus.

From Saccuzzo & Kaplan (1984, pp. 226–227).

ble for any particular behavior. Instead, Luria used the brain as a functional system, with a limited number of brain areas involved in each behavior. Each area in the functional system might be considered a necessary link in a chain. If any link is injured, the total system will break down.

Luria also introduced the concept of *pluripotentiality*—that is, any one center in the brain can be involved in several different functional systems (Golden, 1981). For example, one center in the brain may be involved in both visual and tactile senses. Luria also felt that multiple systems might be responsible for the same behavior. Thus, if a child's injury affects one system, another system may take over.

In practice, Luria applied his theory clinically to make intuitive judgments about deficits in functional systems. Because he did not use a standardized procedure, the amount of time he spent testing individuals varied greatly. In addition, it was difficult for others to repeat the exact steps Luria had used to reach conclusions about particular patients. Reitan (1976b) criticized him on the grounds that Luria's opinion was the only known evidence for the validity of the tests.

Although Luria's procedures were widely regarded as important, they did not meet the psychometric standards of many American psychologists. To face

TABLE 19-2   *Subsections of Luria-Nebraska Neuropsychological Battery*

Item	Description
Motor functions	Examines basic and complex motor skills. Some items ask patients to perform fine tasks with the right and left hand and with the eyes open or closed. Other items involve mouth, tongue, and speech movements.
Rhythm	Evaluates rhythm and pitch skills. Patients must reproduce melodic sounds such as those from the song "Home on the Range." They are also to identify soft and loud sounds and musical patterns.
Tactile	Evaluates a variety of kinesthetic (movement) and tactile (touch) abilities. Patients are blindfolded and asked to identify where they have been touched. Then they must identify a variety of shapes and letters written on the back of the patients' hands. In addition, patients must identify common objects such as quarters, keys, paper clips, and so on.
Visual	Investigates visual and spatial skills. Patients are asked to identify objects through pictures and through progressively more difficult items. They are asked to put pieces together or identify objects in overlapping sketches.
Receptive speech	Tests ability to understand the spoken language. Items range from simple phonemes to comprehension of complex sentences.
Expressive speech	Estimates ability to express speech orally. The word sounds range from "see" to "Massachusetts" to "episcopal."
Writing	Identifies basic writing skills including simple spelling, copying letters and words, and writing names.
Reading	Similar to writing section. It tests whether patients can identify individual letters and read symbols, words, sentences, and stories.
Arithmetic skills	Tests a variety of simple numeric and algebraic abilities.
Memory	Assesses verbal and nonverbal memory skills. Items range from very simple recall to complex memorization tasks.
Intellectual processes	Evaluates intellectual level using items similar to those on traditional intelligence tests.

From Saccuzzo & Kaplan (1984, p. 230).

these criticisms, Golden (1981) developed a standardized version of Luria's procedures. Because Golden worked at the University of Nebraska, the test has become known as the Luria-Nebraska Neuropsychological Battery. The battery includes 269 items that can be administered in about 2½ hours. The items are divided into 11 subsections; these subsections are listed in Table 19-2. A similar test for children has also been developed (Plaisted et al., 1983).

The inventory is scored by finding a standardized performance level for each of the 11 subtests. In addition, three more scores are reported. First, a pathognomonic scale consists of 32 items found in previous studies to be highly sensitive to brain dysfunction. The other two scores indicate whether dysfunction is in the right or the left hemisphere of the brain. They are taken from the sections of the battery that independently test the function of the right or left side of the body. A variety of studies (summarized by Golden, 1981) have demonstrated that the Luria-Nebraska battery can make fine dis-

FIGURE 19-2

Profile of a patient tested with the Luria-Nebraska Battery.

(From Golden (1981). Copyright © 1981 by John Wiley & Sons, Inc. Reprinted by permission of John Wiley & Sons, Inc.)

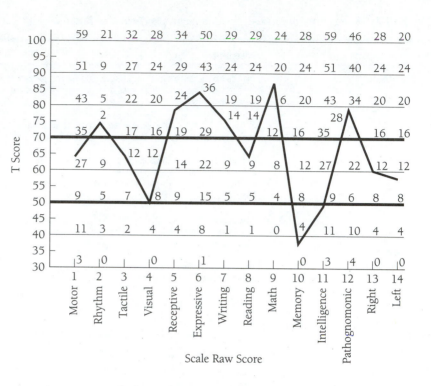

tinctions in neuropsychologic functions. Many of these studies used the battery to estimate the area of the brain damaged by a tumor or lesion. In many of these studies, confirmation of localization is made by surgery, angiogram, or CAT scan. In one study, the Luria-Nebraska battery localized problems in 22 of 24 right-hemisphere and 29 of 36 left-hemisphere cases (Golden, 1981). Some evaluations of the Luria-Nebraska battery are very encouraging, whereas others fail to show that these tests give significantly more information than IQ tests (Carr, Sweet, & Rossini, 1986). Statistical methods for interpreting results are continually improving (Reynolds, 1982; Moses, Pritchard, & Faustman, 1994; J. S. Webster & Dostrow, 1982); nevertheless, the approach still has some serious critics (Spiers, 1982).

An example of a profile from a patient tested with the Luria-Nebraska Battery is shown in Figure 19-2. The two dark horizontal lines in the figure represent the normal ranges for performance on the various subtests. Scores above the top dark line indicate significant problem areas. As the figure shows, the patient demonstrates significant impairment in both expressive and receptive language, as well as problems in arithmetic and writing. There were no problems on the visual memory scales. Neuropsychologists have learned that memory problems are associated with damage in the temporal lobe of the brain. Thus, the good performance on memory rules out a temporal lobe problem. Receptive and expressive language abilities seem to be localized more in the left than the right side of the brain. The difficulties seen in this profile in the language areas thus imply a problem in the brain's left side. Comparing the profile with information acquired in other studies, the neuropsychologists estimated that there was damage in the left side of the brain in the parietal-occipital area (toward the back of the left side). A neurological report confirmed that a stroke had damaged this very area.

Using information from neuropsychological test batteries, clinical neuropsychologists can evaluate damage and suggest programs for rehabilitation. Despite important improvements in the Luria-Nebraska battery, several methodological questions still remain. After a detailed review of the test and the standardization procedures, Lezak (1983) concluded that one must exercise caution in the use of the measure. She argued that "examiners must be cautious about the conclusions they draw when using this battery." Some neuropsychologists prefer to use specific experimental tasks in addition to test batteries.

California Verbal Learning Test

Most psychological tests evaluate performance by summing the number of correct responses. For many years, psychologists have known that people can get a wrong response for different reasons. More than half a century has passed since Werner (1937) objected to the use of global scores based only on the number of right or wrong items. Instead, Werner favored tests that assess how problems are solved in addition to the overall level of achievement.

Modern cognitive psychology has identified many levels of human information processing (Squire & Butters, 1984). Contemporary cognitive psychology suggests that many factors determine performance on any given task. It is not enough to know that there is an impairment in cognitive functioning. Instead, one needs to know which aspects of the human information-processing system are defective and which aspects are functioning well. This information is essential in designing rehabilitation strategies for patients who have selective problems.

The California Verbal Learning Test (CVLT) is a new approach to clinical neuropsychology that builds on research in psychological testing, cognitive psychology, and computer science (Delis et al., 1987). The test determines how errors are made in learning tasks. In other words, the intent is to identify different strategies, processes, and errors associated with specific deficits. The test attempts to link memory deficits with impaired performance on specific tasks for people who have known neurological problems. The CVLT assesses a variety of different variables, including levels of recall and recognition, semantic and serial strategies, serial position effects, learning rates across trials, consistency of item recall across trials, degree of vulnerability to proactive and retroactive interference, retention of information over short and long delays, and learning errors in recall and recognition.

In one component of the CVLT, the subject is asked to imagine that he or she is going to go shopping. Then the subject receives a list of items to buy.

The examiner lists 16 items verbally at a pace of about one word per second. The respondent is asked to repeat the list. This process is repeated through a series of five trials.

Performance on these tasks is analyzed in many ways. For example, learning across trials gives the test taker considerable information. Those who are very anxious may perform poorly on the first trial but improve as the task is repeated (Lezak, 1983). However, adults with limited learning capacity may do relatively well on early trials but reach a plateau where repeated trials do not reflect improved performance. Adults with limited learning capacity may also have inconsistent recall across trials. This can happen when they abandon one strategy and adopt another. Studies have demonstrated that inconsistent recall across trials characterizes patients with amnesia caused by frontal lobe pathology.

The CVLT also includes other features derived from experimental cognitive psychology. For example, after five trials of exposure to the 16-word lists, a second interference list of 16 words is given. Subjects are tested immediately and after a 20-minute delay for free recall, cued recall, and recognition of the first list.

Another unique feature of the CVLT is that one can administer it either in a paper-and-pencil form or with a microcomputer. Versions for both the IBM PC and the Macintosh are available. The computer does not replace test administrators, but instead works to assist them. In the computer-assisted form of the test, the examiner can enter responses directly into the computer using a single key or a light pen to touch the words on a monitor screen. This greatly facilitates and speeds up the scoring process.

Several studies have evaluated the CVLT's validity. For example, the test correlates with other measures such as the Wechsler memory scale (Delis et al., 1987). In addition, factor analysis studies of the CVLT suggest independent factors for learning strategy, acquisition rate, serial position, discriminability, and learning performance. These constructs correspond to empirical findings from modern cognitive psychology. The diversity of deficits identified by the CVLT could not be identified using more traditional psychometric tests (Delis et al., 1987).

The CVLT has been used to compare patients with Alzheimer's disease, Korsakoff syndrome, and Huntington's disease. As you may know, Alzheimer's disease is a serious neurological disorder that causes loss of short-term memory. Korsakoff's syndrome is an organic brain disorder, often associated with long-term alcohol use, that also results in the loss of short-term memory. Finally, Huntington's disease is an inherited disorder emerging in adulthood and associated with memory loss. Although all three organic brain problems are associated with memory loss, the nature of the deficit may be different. For example, patients with Alzheimer's and Huntington's may score about the same on measures of recall and memory tests but may differ in measures of forgetting. Studies of brain pathology show that these two diseases affect dif-

FIGURE 19-3

Long-delay recall on CVLT in three patient groups.

(*Adapted from Delis et al., 1991.*)

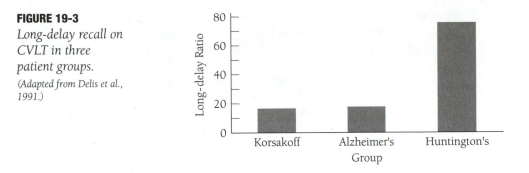

ferent parts of the brain. An advantage of the CVLT is that it allows a more precise evaluation of the nature of the problems than other tests.

When representative groups of patients from these three diagnostic groups are compared on the CVLT, those with Alzheimer's disease and with Korsakoff's syndrome appear very similar, with comparable scores for recall, learning and forgetting, semantic clustering, and several other cognitive factors. However, each of these groups performed at a lower level than patients with Huntington's disease on measures of retention, intrusion errors, and recognition. Figure 19-3 shows an example of this finding. The figure compares CVLT scores for long-delay savings for the three patient groups. Long-delay savings require that subjects learn a list of words. Then, after a long delay, they are given a free recall test. The results are reported as a ratio of all responses given to correct for the fact that different subjects give different numbers of responses. The figure shows that Huntington's patients have significantly higher recall than those in the other two groups, a finding consistent with the neuroanatomy of the illnesses. Huntington's disease is a subcortical dementia, while Alzheimer's disease is associated with cortical lesions. The CVLT may be helpful in identifying the location of the organic problem; however, the results may be less useful in differentiating Korsakoff's syndrome from Alzheimer's disease (Delis et al., 1991).

In 1994, Delis and colleagues released a children's version of the CVLT, the CVLT-C. Appropriate for children age 5–16, this individually administered test can be used to evaluate mild to severe learning disabilities, Attention Deficit Disorder (ADD), mental retardation, and other neurological disorders. In addition, the CVLT-C provides information for the diagnosis of psychiatric disorders. Like the adult version, the CVLT-C assesses both recall and recognition of words. In a typical testing session, the child may receive a list of 15 words on Monday and an interference list of 15 words on Tuesday. After the interference list, the child is tested on the Monday list. After a 20-minute delay, a nonverbal test is administered, followed by tests of long-delay free recall and long-delay cued recall, then a test designed to assess recognition of the words administered the day before. These procedures produce several different scores including total recall, learning strategy, serial position effect, learning rate, consistency of item recall, proactive and retroactive interference, retention over long and short delays, and several others.

The test was standardized on a large national sample. Internal consistency and alpha reliabilities for the test are generally high (usually above .80 for all age levels). Validity studies consistently show that the test is moderately correlated (between .32 and .40) with the WISC-R vocabulary subtest. In contrast to other tests, however, the CVLT-C provides substantially more diagnostic information (Delis, et al., 1994).

In summary, clinical neuropsychology is an emerging and important area in psychological testing. It is linked closely to basic research in neuroscience and in cognitive psychology. We expect clinical neuropsychology to continue its rapid development over the next few decades.

Quality of Life Assessment

Studies on the preference for different states of being sometimes exclude ratings of health because people rate their health the most important thing they can obtain in life. Despite the almost universal feeling that health is important, the definition of health status has remained ambiguous. Among the many definitions of health, we find two common themes. First, everyone agrees that premature mortality is undesirable, so one aspect of health is the avoidance of death. The health status of nations is often evaluated in terms of mortality rates or infant mortality rates. (Infant mortality is the number of children who die before one year of age per thousand live births.)

Second, quality of life is also very important. Disease and disability are of concern because they affect either life expectancy or life quality. For example, cancer and heart disease are the two major causes of premature death in the United States. In addition, disease or disability can make life less desirable. A person with heart disease may face restrictions on daily living activities and may be unable to work or participate in social activities. Even relatively minor diseases and disabilities affect quality of life. A cold, for example, may interfere with your ability to concentrate or attend school. The cold, however, impinges on your life for only a limited time. A serious disease may affect the quality of your life for a long time.

Within the last few years, medical scientists have come to realize the importance of quality of life measurement. Many major diseases, including arthritis, heart disease, and diabetes, are evaluated in terms of the degree to which they affect life quality and life expectancy. One can also evaluate treatments for these conditions by the amount of improvement they produce in quality of life. The Food and Drug Administration now considers quality of life data in their evaluations of new products. In the remainder of this chapter, we review several approaches to quality of life measurement.

What Is Health-Related Quality of Life?

Numerous quality of life measurement systems have evolved during the last 20 years and represent various traditions in measurement. Recent articles have presented at least two different conceptual approaches. One grows out of the tradition of health status measurement. In the late 1960s and early 1970s, the National Center for Health Services Research funded several major projects to develop general measures of health status. All the projects were guided by the World Health Organization's (WHO) definition of health status, which states that "health is a complete state of physical, mental, and social well-being and not merely absence of disease" (WHO, 1948). The projects resulted in a variety of assessment tools, including the Sickness Impact Profile (Bergner et al., 1981), the Quality of Well-Being Scale (R. M. Kaplan & Anderson, 1990), the McMaster Health Index Questionnaire (Chambers, 1996), the SF-36 (Ware et al., 1995), and the Nottingham Health Profile (McEwen, 1992). Many of the measures examined the effect of disease or disability on performance of social role, ability to interact in the community, and physical functioning. Some of the systems have separate components for the measurement of social and mental health.

Other authors refer to quality of life as independent of health status. For instance, Follick and co-workers (1988) suggest that quality of life represents a broader outcome than traditional measures of symptoms and mortality. Croog and colleagues (1986) used a wide variety of outcome measures, collectively referring to these as quality of life. The measures included the patients' subjective evaluation of well-being, physical symptoms, sexual function, work performance and satisfaction, emotional status, cognitive function, social participation, and life satisfaction. Other investigators, including McEwen and McKenna (1996), have regarded quality of life as subjective appraisals of life satisfaction. In summary, a variety of dimensions have all been described as quality of life. Though people disagree on which dimensions researchers should assess, a consideration of recurrent themes in the methodologic literature can help one evaluate existing instruments.

There are two major approaches to quality of life assessment: psychometric and decision theory. The psychometric approach attempts to provide separate measures for the many different dimensions of quality of life. Perhaps the best known example of the psychometric tradition is the Sickness Impact Profile (SIP). The SIP is a 136-item measure that yields 12 different scores displayed in a format similar to an MMPI profile.

The decision theory approach attempts to weight the different dimensions of health in order to provide a single expression of health status. Supporters of this approach argue that psychometric methods fail to consider that different health problems are not of equal concern. One hundred runny noses are not the same as 100 missing legs (Bush, 1984). In an experimental trial using the psychometric approach, one will often find that some aspects of quality of life improve while others get worse. For example, a medication might reduce high blood pressure but also produce headaches and impotence. Many argue that the quality of life notion is the subjective evaluation of observable or objective health states. The decision theory approach attempts to provide an overall measure of quality of life that integrates subjective function states, preferences for these states, morbidity, and mortality.

Common Methods for the Measurement of Quality of Life

A variety of methods have been proposed to measure quality of life, but we cannot review and critique them all here. Instead, we present some of the most widely used methods. Readers interested in more detailed reviews should consult Shumaker and Berzon (1995) or S. Walker and Rosser (1993).

Some of the most commonly used assessment methods are the Sickness Impact Profile (SIP), the Index of Activities of Daily Living scales, the Karnofsky Performance Status, the McMaster Health Index Questionnaire, the SF-36, the Quality of Well-Being Scale, and the Nottingham Health Profile.

Sickness Impact Profile. One of the best known and widely used quality of life measures, the Sickness Impact Profile (SIP) is a general measure applicable to any disease or disability group (Bergner et al, 1981). Furthermore, the SIP has been successfully used with a variety of different cultural subgroups.

The SIP includes 136 items, divided into 12 categories, that describe the effect of sickness on behavioral function. Each of the 12 categories is clustered into three groups: independent categories, physical, and psychosocial. Independent categories include sleep and rest, eating, work, home management, and recreation and pastimes. Physical categories include ambulation, mobility, and body care and movement. The psychosocial categories are social interaction, alertness behavior, emotional behavior, and communication. Table 19-3 shows the categories for the SIP and gives sample items.

Each SIP item has been evaluated by an independent group of judges on a 15-point scale of dysfunction. The judges' ratings determine the weighting of each item in the SIP scoring. The respondent does not consider the judges' weightings in deciding to endorse an item. The overall SIP percent score is obtained by separating the items endorsed by the respondent, summing their scale values, and dividing by the sum of all values for all items on the SIP. Then this proportion is multiplied by 100 to compute a total percent impaired score. Similarly, scores are obtained for each category. Percent scores for each category can be plotted on a graphic display that looks similar to an MMPI profile. A variety of studies attest to the reliability and validity of the SIP for various patient groups and clinical applications (see Bergner et al., 1981). An example of an application of the SIP in cardiovascular disease is shown in Figure 19-4, which compares 50 patients who have angina (chest pain) with 50 healthy volunteers. Angina patients have more impairment in all categories.

With less impact on body care, mobility, and eating, angina most seriously affects work and recreation (Vandenburg & Vogler, 1985).

TABLE 19-3   *Sickness Impact Profile Categories and Selected Items*

Dimension	Category	Items Describing Behavior Related to:	Selected Items
Independent categories	SR	Sleep and rest	I sit during much of the day.
			I sleep or nap during the day.
	E	Eating	I am eating no food at all; nutrition is taken through tubes or intravenous fluids.
			I am eating special or different food.
	W	Work	I am not working at all.
			I often act irritable toward my work associates.
	HM	Home management	I am not doing any of the maintenance or repair work around the house that I usually do.
			I am not doing heavy work around the house.
	RP	Recreation and pastimes	I am going out for entertainment less.
			I am not doing any of my usual physical recreation or activities.
Physical	A	Ambulation	I walk shorter distances or stop to rest often.
			I do not walk at all.
	M	Mobility	I stay within one room.
			I stay away from home only for brief periods of time.
	BCM	Body care and movement	I do not bathe myself at all but am bathed by someone else.
			I am very clumsy in body movements.
Psychosocial	SI	Social interaction	I am doing fewer social activities with groups of people.
			I isolate myself as much as I can from the rest of the family.
	AB	Alertness behavior	I have difficulty reasoning and solving problems, for example, making plans, making decisions, learning new things.
			I sometimes behave as if I were confused or disoriented in place or time, for example, where I am, who is around, directions, what day it is.
	EB	Emotional behavior	I laugh or cry suddenly.
			I act irritable and impatient with myself, for example, talk badly about myself, swear at myself, blame myself for things that happen.
	C	Communication	I am having trouble writing or typing.
			I do not speak clearly when I am under stress.

From Bergner et al. (1981). Reprinted by permission.

FIGURE 19-4
Differences between angina patients and healthy adults for various SIP categories.

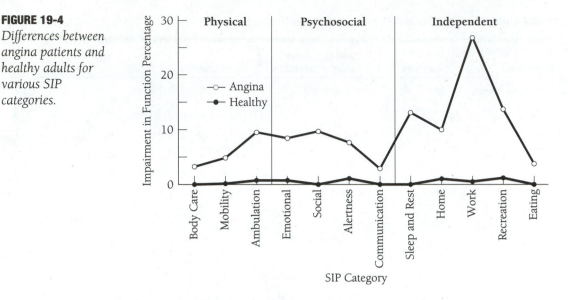

Index of Activities of Daily Living. Perhaps the oldest general quality of life measure is the Index of Activities of Daily Living (ADL), contributed by Katz and associates (1963). Katz argued very early that the main impact of disease and disability was on function and ability to perform the roles of everyday life.

Most commonly used in studies of the elderly, the system includes six subscales for bathing, dressing, toileting, transfer, continence, and feeding. These categories are listed in Table 19-4. For each category, a judgment is made as to whether the person is independent or dependent. For the category of bathing, people are judged to be independent if they need assistance only in bathing a single part of the body or can bathe themselves. They are judged to be dependent if they need assistance in bathing more than one part of the body. Once a judgment of dependence or independence is obtained for each of the six categories, an overall grade is assigned. To receive the top grade, or grade A, the person must be independent in all six categories. Grade B is assigned to those who are independent in only five functions. The bottom grade, G, is assigned to people dependent in all six functions. Several reliability and validity studies for the ADL have been reported (Katz et al., 1970). Despite its many important applications in studies of aging, the ADL has been criticized because it does not make distinctions toward the well end of the quality of life continuum. Stewart and co-workers (1978) have suggested that nearly 80% of the noninstitutionalized population have no gross functional limitations and would obtain the top score in the ADL system. However, other population surveys have demonstrated that more than 80% of the population experiences one or more symptoms during any one week (R. M. Kaplan, Bush, & Berry, 1976). Most of these symptoms cause minor irritation but do not cause the type of dysfunction detected using ADL measures. For example, chest pain, shortness of breath, and dizziness would not be recorded by the ADL

TABLE 19-4 *Definitions and Grades for the Katz Index of Activities of Daily Living*

Index of Independence in Activities of Daily Living

The Index of Independence in is based on an evaluation of the functional independence or dependence of patients in bathing, dressing, going to the toilet, transferring, continence, and feeding. Specific definitions of functional independence and dependence appear below the index.

A   Independent in feeding, continence, transferring, going to toilet, and bathing

B   Independent in all but one of these functions

C   Independent in all but bathing and one additional function

D   Independent in all but bathing, dressing, and one additional function

E   Independent in all but bathing, dressing, going to toilet, and one additional function

F   Independent in all but bathing, dressing, going to toilet, transferring, and one additional function

G   Dependent in all six functions

Other   Dependent in at least two functions, but not classifiable as C, D, E, or F

Independence means without supervision, direction, or active personal assistance, except as specifically noted below. This is based on actual status and not on ability. A patient who refuses to perform a function is considered as not performing the function, even though he is deemed able.

Bathing (sponge, shower, or tub)

Independent: assistance only in bathing a single part (as back or disabled extremity) or bathes self completely
Dependent: assistance in bathing more than one part of body; assistance in getting in or out of tub or does not bathe self

Dressing

Independent: gets clothes from closets and drawers;
puts on clothes, outer garments, braces; manages fasteners; act of tying shoes is excluded
Dependent: does not dress self or remains partly undressed

Going to toilet

Independent: gets to toilet; gets on and off toilet,
arranges clothes, cleans organs of excretion (may manage own bedpan used at night only and may or may not be using mechanical supports)
Dependent: uses bedpan or commode or receives assistance in getting to and using toilet

Transfer

Independent: moves in and out of bed independently and moves in and out of chair independently (may or may not be using mechanical supports)
Dependent: assistance in moving in or out of bed and/or does not perform one or more transfers

Continence

Independent: urination and defecation entirely self-controlled
Dependent: partial or total incontinence in urination or defecation; partial or total control by enemas, catheters, or regulated use of urinals and/or bedpans

Feeding

Independent: gets food from plate or its equivalent into mouth (precutting of meat and preparation of food, as buttering bread, are excluded from evaluation)
Dependent: assistance in act of feeding (see above); does not eat at all or parental feeding

From Katz et al. (1963). Copyright 1963, American Medical Association.

scales in cases where they did not disrupt major role activities. Given the wide array of behaviors and symptoms relevant to life quality, the ADL has some significant limitations. One needs other measures in order to discriminate among impaired individuals who land toward the healthy end of the functioning continuum.

Karnofsky Performance Status. Often in quality of life assessment, general measures are tailored for use with a specific disease category. For example, a measure may be designed to assess the effect of arthritis on quality of life. In cancer research, however, a different trend seems to have occurred. One general quality of life measure, known as the Karnofsky Performance Status (KPS), has found widespread use in cancer research, but it has not been used for populations other than cancer patients. The term *quality of life* first appeared as a heading in the Index Medicus in 1977. Grieco and Long (1984) reviewed the 45 studies listed in the *Index Medicus* that used quality of life measures. Among those cited, the Karnofsky Performance Status was used in about 18% of the studies. However, because of the diversity of outcome measures used in the studies, the KPS was actually used more often than any other technique. Even so, all studies that used the KPS involved cancer patients.

The KPS is a simple rating form that requires a physician, an observer, or even the patient to assign a percentage score. The scores range from 0 for dead to 100 for normal with no complaints and no evidence of disease. Each 10-point interval is labeled with a description. For example, 90% is associated with "ability to carry out normal activity, with minor signs or symptoms of disease," while 50% is labeled "requires considerable assistance and frequent medical care."

The KPS is easy to use and attempts to relate disease or disability to daily functioning. However, it has several deficiencies. First, because it has never been published, guidelines for its use are not available. Use of the KPS requires subjective judgments, and there are not adequate data to suggest that these judgments can be made reliably. For example, Hutchinson, Boyd, and Feinstein (1979) found interrater agreement to be only .29 to .34. Yates, Chalmer, and McKegney (1980) reported more positive results, with a correlation of .69 between nurses' and social workers' ratings of cancer patients. Even this higher estimate, however, is less than acceptable for research or clinical practice. Despite its poor reliability, the KPS does correlate with survival in lung cancer (Hyde et al., 1973; K. E. Stanley, 1980).

To improve the KPS's psychometric profile, Grieco and Long (1984) tried to make the assessment more objective by using behaviorally oriented procedures. The revised procedure includes three components: (1) a structured interview, (2) a review of the medical chart, and (3) a supplemental interview with people closely associated with the patient. Using trained observers, Grieco and Long boosted the interrater reliability to .96 and demonstrated the validity of the KPS by showing its correlation with other established quality of life scales and its ability to discriminate among different patient groups.

In summary, the KPS is an interesting approach that has found widespread use in cancer research. It offers the advantages of brevity and ease of administration. In a carefully controlled study, adequate reliability was obtained. However, the scores on the KPS are somewhat arbitrary, and how the KPS deals with the transition between health states over time is not clear. Also, the KPS depends most of the time on a clinical judgment of functional status. E. Nelson and co-workers (1983) have demonstrated serious discrepancies between the functional status reported by patients and that reported by their doctors. Physicians tend to miss much of the dysfunction and may systematically underestimate the impact of illness on the quality of life. The work of Grieco and Long is very important and may lead to substantial improvements in the KPS.

The McMaster Health Index Questionnaire. A similar approach developed by Chambers and colleagues (Chambers, 1996) is the McMaster Health Index Questionnaire (MHIQ), named after the sponsoring university. In developing their questionnaire, a group of specialists in internal medicine, family medicine, psychiatry, epidemiology, statistics, and social science reviewed existing health status questionnaires. They tried to develop an instrument that conforms with the World Health Organization's definition of health as "not merely the absence of disease or infirmity" (WHO, 1948). Similar to the SIP, the MHIQ has separate scales. For example, some of the physical health items were taken from the Index of Activities of Daily Living Scale (Katz et al., 1970). The emotional function items were adapted or taken verbatim from a variety of sources, including the Social Readjustment Rating Scale (Holmes & Rahe, 1967), resulting in an initial questionnaire of 172 items.

After validation testing, the pool of items was reduced to 59. The criteria for selection of the final items included association with observed functional changes before and after patients entered the hospital and correlation with ratings by family physicians. Later studies validated the MHIQ against a variety of other quality of life measures such as the Lee Index of Functional Capacity, the Spitzer Quality of Life Index, and the Bradburn Psychological Well-Being Scale. The MHIQ is a self-administered questionnaire, and validity studies have demonstrated that these self-reports correlate significantly with ratings by external observers. One study showed that the physical function portion of the index changes in response to therapies designed to affect physical function. The physical function portion of the MHIQ has adequate but not impressive reliability. In one study of patients in a physiotherapy clinic, the MHIQ was administered twice within a one-week period. The physiotherapists reported that functional status should not change over a short interval in this patient population. Using test-retest assessment, the interclass correlation coefficients were .53, .70, and .48 for the physical, emotional, and social function portions of the MHIQ, respectively. Another study evaluated the internal consistency of the MHIQ as assessed by KR_{20} coefficients. For the physical, emotional, and social function indices, the coefficients were .76, .67, and .51, respectively. Although these levels of reliability may be acceptable for group comparisons in large clinical trials, they are less than optimal. Low reliability, causing attenuation in correlations between variables, may reduce the chances of detecting important relationships. Unfortunately, many predictors of quality of life are also measured with substantial error. For instance, some measures of social support have reliabilities of around .50.

An example may help clarify the consequences of low reliability. Suppose that the reliability of a social support measure was .50 and you wish to show its association with the physical health portion of the MHIQ, which also has a reliability of approximately .50. Furthermore, suppose that the true correlation between these two constructs is .50. Because of attenuation from measurement error, the observed correlation would be .25. For a sample size of 50, this would not be statistically significant. In other words, many problems in health psychology require the detection of moderate relationships with moderate sample sizes. For instruments with reliabilities near .50, there will be attenuation in correlations, so that the detection of important relationships may be missed.

SF-36. Another commonly used measure is the Medical Outcome Study Short Form-36 (SF-36). The SF-36 grew out of work by the RAND Corporation and the Medical Outcomes Study (MOS) (Stewart & Ware, 1992). Originally, it was based on the measurement strategy from the RAND Health Insurance Study. The MOS attempted to develop a very short, 20-item instrument known as the Short Form-20 or SF-20. However, the SF-20 did not have appropriate reliability for some dimensions. The SF-36 includes eight health concepts: physical functioning, role-physical, bodily pain, general health perceptions, vitality, social functioning, role-emotional, and mental health. The SF-36 can be either administered by a trained interviewer or self-administered. It has many advantages. For example, it is brief, and there is substantial evidence for its reliability and validity. The SF-36 can be machine scored and has been evaluated in large population studies. The reliability and validity of the SF-36 are well documented (Haley, McHorney, & Ware, 1994; McHorney & Ware, 1995; Ware, 1996).

Despite its many advantages, the SF-36 also presents some disadvantages. For example, it does not have age-specific questions and one cannot clearly determine whether it is equally appropriate at each level of the age continuum. The items for older retired individuals are the same as those for children (Stewart & Ware, 1992). Nevertheless, the SF-36 has become the most commonly used behavioral measure in contemporary medicine.

Nottingham Health Profile. Another major approach, the Nottingham Health Profile (NHP), has particularly influenced the European community. The NHP has two parts. The first includes 38 items divided into six categories: sleep, physical mobility, energy, pain, emotional reactions, and social isolation. Items within each of these sections are rated in terms of relative importance. Items are rescaled in order to allow them to vary between 0 and 100 within each section.

The second part of the NHP includes seven statements related to the areas of life most affected by health: employment, household activities, social life, home life, sex life, hobbies and interests, and holidays. The respondent indicates whether or not a health condition has affected his or her life in these areas. Used in a substantial number of studies, the NHP has considerable evidence for its reliability and validity.

The NHP is consumer based and arises from definitions of health offered by individuals in the community. Furthermore, this scale uses language easily interpreted by people in the community and conforms to minimum reading requirements. Substantial testing has been performed on the NHP. However, the NHP does not provide relative-importance weightings across dimensions. As a result, it is difficult to compare the dimensions directly with one another (McEwen, 1992).

Decision theory approaches. Within the last few years, interest has grown in using quality of life data to help evaluate the cost/utility or cost-effectiveness of health-care programs. Cost studies have gained in popularity because health-care costs have grown so rapidly in recent years. Not all health-care interventions equally return benefit for the expended dollar. Objective cost studies might guide policymakers toward an optimal and equitable distribution of scarce resources. Cost-effectiveness analysis typically quantifies the benefits of a health-care intervention in terms of years of life, or quality-adjusted life-years (QALYs). Cost/utility is a special use of cost-effectiveness that weights observable health states by preferences or utility judgments of quality (R. M. Kaplan, Anderson, & Ganiats, 1993). In cost/utility analysis, the benefits of medical care, behavioral interventions, or preventive programs are expressed in terms of well-years (R. M. Kaplan, 1994).

If a man dies of heart disease at age 50 and we expected him to live to age 75, we might conclude that the disease precipitated 25 lost life-years. If 100 men died at age 50 (and also had a life expectancy of 75 years), we might conclude that 2500 (100 men × 25 years) life-years had been lost. Yet death is not the only relevant outcome of heart disease. Many adults suffer myocardial infarctions that leave them somewhat disabled for a long time. Though still alive, they suffer diminished quality of life. Quality-adjusted life-years take into consideration such consequences. For example, a disease that reduces quality of life by one-half will take away .5 QALY over the course of each year. If the disease affects two people, it will take away one year (2 × .5) over each year. A medical treatment that improves quality of life by .2 for each of five individuals will result in the equivalent of 1 QALY if the benefit persists for one year. This system has the advantage of considering both benefits and side effects of programs in terms of the common QALY units.

The need to integrate mortality and quality of life information is clearly apparent in studies of heart disease. Consider hypertension. People with high blood pressure may live shorter lives if untreated, longer if treated. Thus, one benefit of treatment is to add years to life. However, for most patients, high blood pressure does not produce symptoms for many years. Conversely, the treatment for high blood pressure may cause negative side effects. If one evaluates a treatment only in terms of changes in life expectancy, the benefits of the program will be overestimated because one has not taken side effects into consideration. On the other hand, considering only current quality of life will underestimate the treatment benefits, because information on mortality (death) is excluded. In fact, considering only current function might make the treatment look harmful because the side effects of the treatment might be worse than the symptoms of hypertension. A comprehensive measurement system takes into consideration side effects and benefits and provides an overall estimate of the benefit of treatment (Russell, 1986).

Of the several different approaches for obtaining quality-adjusted life-years, most are similar (R. M. Kaplan, 1990). The approach that we prefer involves several steps. First, patients are classified according to objective levels of functioning. These levels are represented by the scales of mobility, physical activity, and social activity. Next, once observable behavioral levels of functioning have been classified, each individual is placed on the 0 to 1.0 scale of wellness, which describes where a person lies on the continuum between optimum function and death.

Most traditional measures used in medicine and public health consider only whether a person is dead or alive. In other words, all living people get the same score. Yet we know that there are different levels of wellness, and a need to score these levels exists. To accomplish this, the observable health states are weighted by quality ratings for the desirability of these conditions. Human value studies have been conducted to place the observable states onto a preference continuum, with an anchor of 0 for death and 1.0 for completely well (R. M. Kaplan, Bush, & Berry, 1976). Studies have shown that the weights are highly stable over a one-year period and that they are consistent across diverse groups of raters (R. M. Kaplan, 1993). Finally, one must consider the duration of stay in various health states. Having a cough or a headache for one day is not the same as having the problem for one year. A health measure must take these durations into consideration. Using this information, one can describe health-related quality of life in terms similar to years of life. For example, one year in a state assigned the weight of .5 is equivalent to .5 of a quality-adjusted life-year.

This system has been used to evaluate many different health-care programs. For example, it was used to demonstrate that a new medication for patients with arthritis produced an average of .023 QALY per year, whereas a new medication for AIDS produced nearly .46 of these units per year. However, the benefit of the arthritis medication may last as long as 20 years, ultimately producing .023 × 20 years = .46 year. The AIDS treatment produced a benefit for only one year, so its total effect was .46 × 1 year = .46 year. In other words, the general system allows the full potential benefits of these two very different treatments to be compared (R. M. Kaplan et al., 1995).

Summary

In this chapter, we considered two broad areas relevant to testing in medical settings. First, we reviewed clinical neuropsychology. This remarkable new area of investigation has generated new research and clinical opportunities for psychologists. Neuropsychology involves the application of tests to evaluate the status of the central nervous system. Some of the more common approaches are the Halstead-Reitan and the Luria-Nebraska batteries. Each of these approaches is based on different principles of cognitive psychology. A newer approach, the California Verbal Learning Test, attempts to evaluate brain function by considering not only errors but also how people make errors.

Another major area for the application of tests in medical settings involves health status and quality of life assessment. Health-care practitioners try to help people live longer and to live higher quality lives than they might without health care. The quantification of life quality, however, is difficult. Two approaches to this type of assessment use psychometric methods and decision theory methods. Psychometric methods include the Sickness Impact Profile, the Index of Activities of Daily Living, the MOS Short Form-36, the McMaster Health Index Questionnaire, and the Karnofsky Performance Status. Decision theory approaches include methods for estimating the value of the equivalent of a life-year. We expect the fields of psychological measurement and medical measurement to continue to merge over the next few decades.

Issues

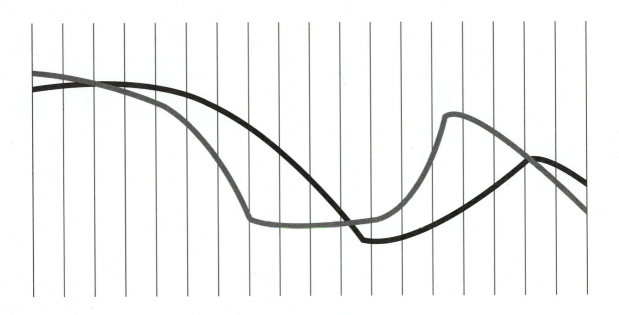

CHAPTER 20

Test Bias

LEARNING OBJECTIVES

When you have completed this chapter, you should be able to

☐ Discuss some of the current controversies surrounding the use of intelligence tests

☐ Give some of the arguments for and against the belief that the content of standardized tests is biased in favor of white, middle-class children

☐ Explain how criterion validity studies, which review the slopes and intercepts of regression lines, are used in the study of test bias

☐ Discuss some of the problems with popular tests such as the Chitling Test and the BITCH

☐ List the components of the SOMPA and some of its advantages and disadvantages

☐ Describe how different social, political, and ethical viewpoints are represented by different definitions of test fairness

☐ Discuss some of the opportunities for developing improved predictors for minority-group members

☐ Describe some of the problems with the criteria commonly used to evaluate standardized tests

☐ Describe how one can use differences in test scores to justify efforts to change the social environment

☐ Using the information from this chapter and from other sources, write an essay for or against the use of standardized tests for minority children

S ince the early 1970s, serious, emotional debates have flourished about the meaning of tests for the placement and classification of individuals. This chapter reviews test bias, which lies at the heart of the controversy. This issue is so controversial that it has inspired some court evaluations of the meaning of tests for minority group members.

Although test bias is unmistakably an important issue, it is not the first controversy about mental testing. Controversy has surrounded mental testing since test reports began in 1905, and psychologists and others have debated the issues since the 1920s (Cronbach, 1975b; Haney, 1981).

Why Is Test Bias Controversial?

That all persons are created equal is the cornerstone of political and social thought in U. S. society. Yet all individuals are not treated equally. The history of social action is replete with attempts to remedy this situation. Among the many practices that counteract the idea that all people are the same, psychological tests are designed to measure differences among people, often in terms of desirable personal characteristics such as intelligence and aptitude. Test scores that demonstrate differences among people may suggest to some that people are not created with the same basic abilities.

The most difficult problem is that certain ethnic groups, on the average, obtain lower scores on some psychological tests. The most controversial case concerns intelligence tests. On the average, African Americans score 15 points lower than white Americans on standardized IQ tests. (See Chapter 11 for the meaning of IQ scores.) This difference equates to about one standard deviation. Nobody disagrees that the two distributions overlap greatly and that some African Americans score as high as the highest whites. Similarly, some whites score as low as the lowest African Americans. Yet only about 15% to 20% of the African-American population score above the average white score, and only about 15% to 20% of the white population score below the average African-American score. Figure 20-1 shows the overlap between these two populations.

This is not a debatable issue. If you were to administer the Stanford-Binet or the Wechsler scale (see Chapter 11) to large random samples of African Americans and white Americans, you would most likely get the same results. The dispute has not been over whether these differences exist but over why they do. Many have argued that the differences are due to environmental factors (Kamin, 1974; Rosenthal & Jacobson, 1968; Turkheimer, 1991; Zuckerman, 1990), while others have suggested that the differences are biological (Eysenck; 1991, Jensen, 1969, 1972; Munsinger, 1975; Rushton, 1991). We shall not discuss the environmental versus the biological debate, however, because this is a technical issue independent of the problems with tests.

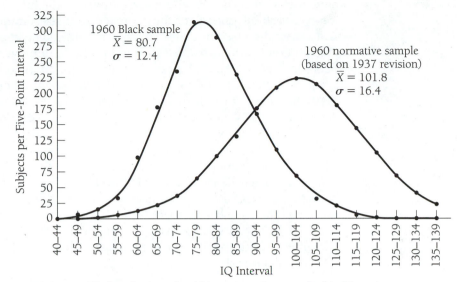

FIGURE 20-1   *IQ distributions for African Americans and white Americans. Although the distributions overlap, the means differ. Only about 15% to 20% of the African-American population scored above the white mean. The IQs were measured using the Stanford-Binet scale.*

(From Kennedy, Van de Riet, & White, 1963. Reprinted by permission.)

Test Fairness and the Law

The U.S. government has attempted to establish clear standards for the use of psychological tests. Regulation of tests comes in many forms, including executive orders, laws, and court actions. The most important legal development was the passage of the 1964 Civil Rights Act. Title VII of this act created the Equal Employment Opportunity Commission (EEOC). In 1970, **EEOC guidelines** were published for employee selection procedures. In 1978, the EEOC released a new document entitled *Uniform Guidelines on Employee Selection Procedures*. These are the major guidelines for the use of psychological tests in education and in industry.

Regarding allowable uses of psychological test scores, the 1978 guidelines are stricter, more condensed, and less ambiguous than the 1970 guidelines. The original act clearly prohibited discrimination in employment on the basis of race, color, religion, gender, or national origin. However, the 1978 guidelines made clear that the government will view any screening procedure, including the use of psychological tests, as having an **adverse impact** if it systematically rejects substantially higher proportions of minority than nonminority applicants. When any selection procedure does so, the employer must demonstrate that the procedure has validity for the inferences the employer wants to make. These criteria for the validity of a selection procedure are similar to those discussed in Chapter 5. However, the guidelines detail the acceptable criteria for the use of a test; we shall therefore review these criteria in detail in Chapter 21. The guidelines have been adopted by several federal agencies, including the Civil Service Commission, the Department of Justice, the Department of Labor, and the Department of the Treasury. The Office of Federal Contract Compliance has the direct power to cancel government contracts held by employers who do not comply with these guidelines. The guidelines became the focus of several political controversies in 1991. For example, when Clarence Thomas was nominated for a position on the U.S. Supreme Court, he was challenged because of his enforcement of the guidelines while he was the head of the EEOC. The President, George Bush, also opposed some aspects of the guidelines. In fact, he had planned to relax these standards in the 1991 Civil Rights Bill; however, last-minute political pressure successfully encouraged Bush to leave the guidelines unchanged. The guidelines have remained in place since then.

The Traditional Defense of Testing

In this chapter, we focus on a central issue: Are standardized tests as valid for African Americans and other minority groups as they are for whites? All the types of validity we discussed in Chapter 5 come into play when the issue of test bias is considered (Cole, 1981). Some psychologists argue that the tests are differentially valid for African Americans and whites. Because **differential validity** is so controversial and emotional, it has forced psychologists to think carefully about many issues in test validation. Differences among ethnic groups on test performance do not necessarily indicate test bias. The question is whether the test has different meanings for different groups. In psychometrics, validity defines the meaning of a test.

Content Validity

In 1968, *Newsweek* magazine published an article on cultural fairness in testing. The article listed several items from the general information portion of the Stanford-Binet scale that people with disadvantaged backgrounds might find problematic. Test constructors and users were accused of being biased because some children have never had the opportunity to learn about some of the items, and other items may be answered differently (but still correctly) by members of ethnic groups.

Many researchers have also argued that scores on intelligence tests are affected by language skills inculcated as part of a white, middle-class upbringing but foreign to inner-city children (Castenell & Castenell, 1988; Kagan,

Moss, & Siegel, 1963; Lesser, Fifer, & Clark, 1965; Mercer, 1971; Pettigrew, 1964; Waldman, Weinberg, & Scarr, 1994). Children unfamiliar with the language have no chance of doing well on standardized IQ tests. For example, an American child does not usually know what a shilling is, but a British child probably does. Similarly, the American child would not know where one puts the petrol; a British child would. Some psychologists argue that asking an inner-city child about opera is just as unfair as asking an American child about petrol. In both cases, the term is not familiar to the child (Hardy et al., 1976).

Flaugher (1978) considered the accusations about bias in psychological tests and concluded that many perceived problems are based on misunderstandings. Many people feel that a fair test asks questions they can answer. By contrast, a biased test does not ask about things a test taker knows. Flaugher argued that the purpose of aptitude and achievement tests is to measure performance on items sampled from a wide range of information. Not particularly concerned about individual items, test developers focus on test performance, making judgments about it based on correlations between the tests and external criteria. Many test critics, though, focus attention on specific items. For example, Owen (1985) reported that several intelligent and well-educated people had difficulty with specific items on the SAT and LSAT examinations. He also asserted that some items on standardized tests are familiar only to those with a middle-class background. Test developers are indifferent to the opportunities people have to learn the information on the tests. Again, the meaning they eventually assign to the tests comes from correlations of test scores with other variables.

However, some research evidence suggests that the linguistic bias in standardized tests does not cause the observed differences (Scheuneman, 1987). Quay (1971) administered the Stanford-Binet test to 100 children in an inner-city Head Start program. Half of the children took a version of the test that used African-American dialect, while the others took the standard version. The results demonstrated that the advantage produced by having the test in African-American dialect translates into less than a one-point increase in test scores. This finding is consistent with other research findings demonstrating that African-American children can comprehend standard English about as well as they can comprehend African-American dialect (Clarizio, 1979a; Copple & Succi, 1974). This finding does not hold for white children, who seem to comprehend only the standard dialect.

Systematic studies have failed to demonstrate that biased items in well-known standardized tests account for the differences in scores among ethnic groups (Flaugher, 1978). In one approach, developers ask experts to judge the unfairness of particular items. Without these unfair items, the test should be less biased. Unexpectedly, the many attempts to purify tests using this approach have not yielded positive results. In one study, 16% of the items in an elementary reading test were eliminated after experts reviewed them and labeled them as potentially biased toward the majority group. However, when the "purged" version of the test was used, the differences between the majority and the minority school populations were no smaller than they had been originally (Bianchini, 1976).

Another approach to the same problem is to find those classes of items most likely to be missed by members of a particular minority group. If a test is biased against that group, significant differences between minority and nonminority groups should appear in certain categories of items. These studies are particularly important; if they identify certain types of items that discriminate among groups, these types of items can be avoided on future tests. Again, the results have not been encouraging; studies have not clearly identified such categories of items (Wild et al., 1989). The studies show that groups differ for certain items but not whether these are real or chance differences. When groups are compared for large numbers of items, some differences will occur by chance.

Differential item functioning (DIF) analysis. Another approach to the analysis of test bias has been developed by the Educational Testing Service (ETS, 1991). The ETS creates and administers a variety of aptitude tests, including the Graduate Record Examination (GRE), the Scholastic Aptitude Test (SAT), and the Law School Admissions Test (LSAT). In each of these programs, the performance of white test takers differs significantly from the performances of other racial/ethnic groups on verbal and analysis measures. On quantitative measures, Asian Americans tend to have the highest scores. On the Graduate Records Examination, men and women score equivalently on verbal and analytic measures. Men, however, obtain higher scores on the quantitative measures.

Differential item functioning (DIF) analysis attempts to identify items that are specifically biased against an ethnic/racial or gender group (Holland & Wainer, 1993; Kok, 1992). The analysis first equates groups on the basis of overall score. For example, it would find subgroups of test takers who obtain equivalent scores. These might be groups of men and women who obtain scores of about 500 on the verbal portion of the GRE. Using these groups, it evaluates differences in performance between men and women on particular items. Items that differ significantly between the groups are thrown out and the entire test is rescored.

Similarly, items that show differences among racial and ethnic groups can be eliminated and the test rescored. In one study, 27 items from the SAT were eliminated because ethnic groups consistently answered them differently. Then the test was rescored for everyone. Although it seems this procedure should have eliminated the differences between the two groups, it actually had only slight effects because the items that differentiated the groups tended to be the easiest items in the set. When these items were eliminated, the test was harder for everyone (Flaugher & Schrader, 1978).

There is at least some evidence that test items depicting people do not accurately portray the distribution of genders and races in the population.

Zores and Williams (1980) reviewed the WAIS, WISC-R, Stanford-Binet, and Slosson Intelligence test items for race and gender characterization and found that white male characterization occurred with disproportionate frequency. Nevertheless, no one has yet established that the frequency of different groups appearing in items affects the outcome of tests. Studies have failed to demonstrate serious bias in item content. Most critics argue that the verbal content of test items is most objectionable because it is unfamiliar to minority groups. However, Scheuneman (1981) reviewed the problem and concluded that verbal material reflects the life experiences of African-Americans more closely than nonverbal material. Studies that manipulate gender bias by creating neutral, male, and female items demonstrate little effect on the performance differences between male and female test takers (McCarty, Noble, & Huntley, 1989).

Other statistical models have been used to evaluate item fairness. In these studies, which use a variety of populations and methods of analysis, little evidence has been produced of bias in test items (Gotkin & Reynolds, 1981). However, different models may identify different items in the same test as biased. In one comparison, Ironson and Sebkovial (1979) applied four different methods to analyze item bias in the National Longitudinal Study test battery. Three differential statistical methods identified many of the same items as biased in evaluating 1691 African-American high school seniors in contrast to 1794 white 12th-graders. However, there was little agreement among these item evaluations and the bias items selected by a method proposed by D. R. Green and Draper (1972).

How do biased test items affect the differential validity of a test? In one theoretical example, 25% of the items on a test were presumed to be so biased that minority test takers would be expected to perform at chance level. Despite random performance, there would be only slight and perhaps undetectable differences in validity coefficients for minority and majority group members (Drasgow, 1982). However, this result may be artificial and depend on an unusual use of the phrase *test bias* (Dobko & Kehoe, 1983). Using a relatively general definition of test bias and biased items, they suggested that failure to find differences in validity coefficients is consistent with the belief that the tests are equally valid for members of different ethnic and racial groups.

In spite of the many studies about item bias, its role remains poorly understood. For example, students who have taken many tests may be better able to answer questions irrelevant to the knowledge base being assessed. Since such test-wise students tend to get these items correct, item analysis may incorrectly identify the irrelevant items as useful. These problems magnify the differences between high-achieving and low-achieving students (B. N. Masters, 1988).

In summary, studies have not supported the popular belief that items have different meanings for different groups; however, people must continue to scrutinize the content of tests. On some occasions, careful reviews of tests have turned up questionable items. Many tests are carelessly constructed, and every effort should be taken to purge items that have the potential for being biased.

FIGURE 20-2

A sample regression plot. The slope of the line shows the relationship between a test and a criterion. The steeper the slope of the line, the better the prediction of the criterion score.

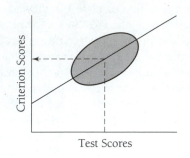

Criterion Validity

Each night on the evening news, the weatherperson forecasts the conditions for the next day. If these forecasts have a history of being accurate, we come to depend on them. In evaluating the weather report, we make a subjective assessment of validity. Similarly, one evaluates tests by asking whether they forecast future performance accurately. Standardized tests such as the SAT have been found to satisfactorily predict performance during the first year of college. These tests clearly do not give one all the information needed for perfect prediction; yet they do give enough information to make one pay attention to them.

College administrators who use the test scores face difficult problems. On the average, minority applicants have lower test scores than nonminority applicants. At the same time, most universities and colleges are attempting to increase their minority enrollments. Because minority applicants are considered as a separate category, one should ask whether the tests have differential predictive power for the two groups of applicants.

As we mentioned in Chapter 5, one assesses the criterion validity of a test by the coefficient of correlation between the test and some criterion. The higher the correlation, the more confident one feels about making predictions. If college grades are the criterion (the variable one is trying to forecast), the validity of a test such as the SAT is represented by the correlation between the SAT score and first-year college grades. If students who score well on the SAT do well in college and students who score poorly on it get lower grades, then the test might be considered valid for helping one decide which college students to admit.

In Chapter 3, we reviewed the interpretation of regression plots as they relate to the validity of psychological tests. Showing plots like the one in Figure 20-2, we explained how to obtain a predicted criterion score from a test score. First, you find the test score on the horizontal axis of the graph and draw a line directly upward until it hits the regression line. Then you draw a line directly left until it comes to the vertical axis. This gives the predicted criterion score. The only difference between Figure 20-2 and Figure 3-9 is that we have added an ellipse around the regression line. Called an **isodensity**

FIGURE 20-3

A single regression slope can predict performance equally well for two groups. However, the means of the groups differ.

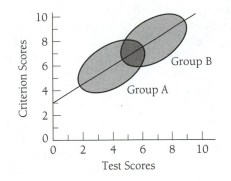

curve, this ellipse is used to encircle a specified portion of the cases that constitute a particular group.

Figure 20-3 shows a regression line that represents two groups equally well. Group A appears to be performing less well than Group B on both the test (predictor) and the criterion scores. You can demonstrate this for yourself by selecting some points from the test scores for Group A and finding the expected scores on the criterion. By repeating this exercise for a few points in Group B, you will find that Group A is expected to do poorly on the criterion because it did more poorly on the test. However, for both Group A and Group B, the relationship between the test score and performance on the criterion is the same. Thus, Figure 20-3 shows there is little evidence for test bias.

Figure 20-4 represents a different situation—a separate regression line for each group. Because their slopes are the same, the lines are parallel. However, the *intercepts*, or the points where the regression lines cross the vertical axis, differ. If you pick a particular test score, you get one expected criterion score if you use regression line A and another if you use B. For a test score of 8, the expected criterion score from regression line A is 6, whereas the expected criterion score from regression line B is 10. The broken line in Figure 20-4 is based on a combination of regression lines A and B. Now try finding the predicted score for a test score of 8 from this combined (broken) regression line.

FIGURE 20-4

Regression lines with equal slopes but different intercepts.

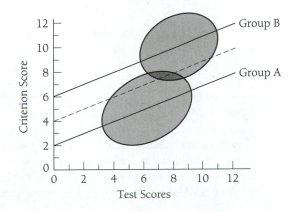

You should get 8. Thus, the combined regression line actually overpredicts performance on the criterion for Group A and underpredicts it for Group B. According to this example, the use of a single regression line produces discrimination in favor of Group A and against Group B.

This situation seems to fit the use of the SAT (Cleary, 1968; Jensen, 1984; Kallingal, 1971; Pfeifer & Sedlacek, 1971; Reynolds, 1986; Schneider & Briel, 1990; Temp, 1971). Each of these studies showed that the relationship between college performance and SAT scores was best described by two separate regression equations. Using a combined regression equation, a common practice, overpredicts how well minority students will do in college and underpredicts the performance of majority group students. In other words, it appears that the SAT used with a single regression line yields biased predictions in favor of minority groups and against majority groups.

The equal slopes of the lines in Figure 20-4 suggest equal predictive validity. Most standardized intelligence, aptitude, and achievement tests in fact do confirm the relationships shown in the figure (Reschly & Sabers, 1979; Reynolds, 1980; Reynolds & Nigl, 1981). Thus, there is little evidence that tests such as the SAT predict college performance differently for different groups or that IQ tests have different correlations with achievement tests for African-American, white, or Hispanic children. This finding has been reported for the SAT (Temp, 1971), preschool tests (Reynolds, 1980), and IQ tests such as the WISC-R (Reschly & Sabers, 1979). Whether separate or combined regression lines are used depends on different definitions of bias. (We shall return to this issue later in the chapter. As you will see, the interpretation of tests for assessing different groups can be strongly influenced by personal and moral convictions.) The situation shown in Figure 20-4 is independent of differences in mean scores, which are equal to the differences between the two regression lines.

Some studies have shown that these problems are not specific to American culture. Psychometric aptitude tests are currently used by all Israeli universities. A wide variety of cultural and ethnic groups makes up Israeli society. As in the United States, there is interest in determining whether or not aptitude tests include biases against specific ethnic or cultural groups. In a study of 1538 Israeli college candidates of varying ethnic backgrounds, the predictive validity of the test was the same across groups in spite of mean differences among the groups (Zeidner, 1987).

A third situation outlined by Cleary and co-workers (1975) is shown in Figure 20-5. In this figure, the two regression lines, are not parallel; the coefficient of one group differs from that of the other. In the situation presented in Figure 20-4, each group was best represented by its own regression line. Using a common regression line causes error in predicting the scores for each group. However, the situation depicted in Figure 20-4 is not hopeless, and indeed some psychologists feel that this situation is useful because it may help increase the accuracy of predictions (Cleary, 1968). In Figure 20-5, however, the test is differentially valid for the two groups, meaning that the test has an

FIGURE 20-5

Regression lines with different slopes suggest that a test has different meanings for different groups. This is the most clear-cut example of test bias.

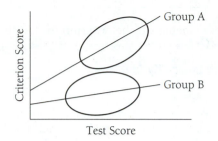

entirely different meaning for each group. Although empirical studies have rarely turned up such a case, there are some known examples of differential slopes (Mercer, 1979). An example of differential validity might be a test designed to predict performance in a mechanical training program. This test might predict performance much better for men than for women. Women might tend to score poorly on the test because women have traditionally had less previous experience with mechanical concepts than men. However, when taking the course, many women would easily acquire this information and perform well. Thus, the test would provide relatively little information about how these women would perform in the program, but it would tend to predict how men would perform. Furthermore, poor test performance by a man would indicate that he might never learn mechanical concepts, given that most men would have been previously exposed to this information. An extensive discussion of differential validity is presented by Bartlett and O'Leary (1969). Focused Example 20-1 illustrates the application of both content and criterion validity.

Other Approaches to Testing Minority-Group Members

To many American psychologists, the defense of psychological tests has not been totally satisfactory. Although some consider the defense of the tests strong enough, others emphasize that developers must try to find selection procedures that will end all discriminatory practices and protect the interests of minority-group members. Those who do not think that the tests are fair suggest one of two alternatives: Outlaw the use of psychological tests for minority students (R. L. Williams, 1974) or develop psychological assessment strategies that suit minority children. Advocates of the first alternative have launched a legal battle to restrict the use of tests. (This battle is discussed in detail in Chapter 21.) In this section, we review various approaches to the second alternative. In particular, we look at three different assessment approaches: the Chitling Test, the Black Intelligence Test of Cultural Homogeneity, and the System of Multicultural Pluralistic Assessment. Though each approach differs, they are all based on one common assumption: Minority children have not had the opportunity to learn how to answer items on tests that reflect traditional, white, middle-class values.

Focused Example 20-1

Scoring the WISC-R for Inner-City Children

The WISC-R requires that a test administrator follow a rigid protocol in allowing credit for certain types of responses. Over the years, many people have questioned whether these scoring procedures should be so stringent. In particular, they have suggested that some children may be giving an appropriate response for the subculture they are familiar with, but that response may not be given credit. The Johns Hopkins Child Development Study favors this conclusion (Hardy et al., 1976).

As part of the Johns Hopkins study, 200 children from the inner city of Baltimore received selected questions from the WISC-R. For this study, however, the standard WISC-R scoring instructions were abandoned, and an attempt was made to understand the reasoning behind the children's answers. For example, this WISC-R question was given: "What would you do if you were sent to buy a loaf of bread, and the grocer said he did not have anymore?" The WISC-R scoring instructions state that the correct answer is "Go to another store." Among the 200 children in the study, 61 gave an incorrect response. However, when the examiners probed the children about their responses, they discovered that many of the children had given replies that were reasonable considering their circumstances. For instance, the rigid WISC-R scoring procedures do not allow credit for the response "Go home." Yet many of the inner-city children explained that there were no other stores near their homes and they were not allowed to go away from home without permission. Others reported that they used family credit to shop and would need to go home to get money if they had to go to another store. In each of these cases, the researchers suggested that the children had given correct and reasonable responses to the question (Hardy et al., 1976).

Other psychologists, however, emphasize the need for strict scoring procedures if intelligence tests are to be reliable. Standardization implies that all children take the test with the same set of rules. Beyond this objection, Sattler (1979b) carefully reviewed the study and found a variety of methodological problems. In particular, there was no control group of children not from the inner city. Thus, one cannot determine whether children in general would have benefited from a more liberal interpretation of the criteria for a correct answer. Abundant evidence suggests that permitting a tester to exercise judgment about the reasonableness of a response results in higher scores for children from many different walks of life. Under most circumstances, this procedure does not result in greater validity for the test (Sattler, 1988).

Another of Sattler's objections is that the study may have had serious rater bias. Quite likely, the psychologists who tested the inner-city children knew that the study was on test bias, and their interpretations of a reasonable response were thus influenced by a subjective predisposition.

Ultimately, a test is evaluated by its criterion validity. How well does it do its job in predicting performance on some criterion of interest? Some have argued that any scoring procedure is valid if it enhances the relationship between a test and a criterion (Barrett & Depinet, 1991). In the Johns Hopkins study, no information was offered about the benefits of a liberal scoring system for the criterion validity of the test (Hardy et al., 1976). Thus, different scoring procedures may make the scores of inner-city children higher, but whether the revised procedures would make the tests more meaningful remains to be seen (Sattler, 1979b). Most studies on criterion validity suggest that IQ tests are not differentially meaningful for different groups of children (Barrett & Depinet, 1991; Hall, Huppertz, & Levi, 1977; Hartigan & Wigdor, 1989; Hartlage & Steele, 1977; Henderson et al., 1973; Lamp & Traxler, 1973; Lunemann, 1974; Palmer, 1970; Valencia & Lopez, 1992).

Ignorance Versus Stupidity

In a California trial about the use of testing in public schools, *Larry P. v. Wilson Riles*, the judge made an abrasive but insightful comment. Both sides in the case agreed that minority children perform more poorly than white children on standardized tests. The main issue debated was the meaning of the scores. One side argued that the scores reflect the underlying trait of intelligence. In other words, the tests allegedly measure how smart a child is. Witnesses for the other side suggested that the tests measure only whether the child has learned the appropriate responses needed to perform well on the test. This position claims that the tests do not measure how smart the child is but only whether the child has been exposed to the information on the test. After hearing the testimony for the different points of view, the judge commented that the issue was really one of ignorance versus stupidity. Although this comment appears insensitive and racist, it deserves reflection. There are two potential explanations for why some children do more poorly on standardized tests than other children. One explanation is that they are less intelligent, or the "stupidity" explanation. The other is that some children do more poorly because they are ignorant. In other words, they are ignorant of the right responses for a particular test. If ignorance is the explanation, then differences in IQ scores are of less concern because they can be changed. The stupidity explanation is more damning because it implies that the lower test scores obtained by African-American students are a product of some deficit that cannot easily be changed.

Ignorance implies that differences can easily be abolished. Just as some minority children have not learned how to answer items that might predict success in white, middle-class culture, so many white, middle-class children have not learned how to succeed in the world of an inner-city child. This proposition is illustrated by the Chitling Test.

The Chitling Test

Many years ago, animal psychologists talked about higher and lower animals. The higher animals were considered to be intelligent because they could do some of the same things humans can do, and the lower animals were considered to be unintelligent because they could not perform like humans. However, in 1969 a famous article by Hodos and Campbell changed the thinking of many students of animal behavior. Hodos and Campbell argued that all animals are equally intelligent for the environments in which they live. We cannot compare the intelligence of a rat with that of a cat because a rat is adapted to a rat's environment and a cat to a cat's environment.

The same insight seems not to have permeated the world of human affairs. Because of poverty and discrimination, minority and nonminority children grow up in different environments. To succeed in each requires different skills and knowledge. A psychological test may consider survival in only one of these environments, usually the white, middle-class one. Thus, using one of these tests for impoverished children is analogous to testing a cat on a task designed to determine how well a rat is adapted to a rat's environment.

The Chitling Test was developed to demonstrate that there is a body of information about which the white middle class is ignorant. Named the Dove Counterbalance General Intelligence Test, it has become known as just the Chitling Test (Dove, 1968). A major aim in developing the Chitling Test was to show that African Americans and whites are just not talking the same language.

Some of the items from the Chitling Test are listed in Table 20-1. Try to answer the questions and tally up your scores. Many of you may not do too well because you have not been exposed to African-American, mid-1960s culture. People who have grown up in a ghetto in this era should clearly outperform you. On this test, a white, middle-class student would probably score as culturally deprived.

However, we must caution you about the meaning of the test. At present, no more than face validity has been established. No body of evidence demonstrates that the test successfully predicts performance on any important criterion. If we want to predict which students will do well in college, the Chitling Test will not help us. In fact, standardized tests predict performance for both minority and nonminority students, but the Chitling Test predicts performance for neither group. It may well be that the Chitling Test will turn out to be a valid test for inferring how streetwise someone is. Yet we must await

TABLE 20-1   *Selected Items from the Dove Counterbalance General Intelligence Test (the Chitling Test)* *

---

1.   A "handkerchief head" is: (a) a cool cat, (b) a porter, (c) an Uncle Tom, (d) a hoddi, (e) a preacher.

2.   Which word is most out of place here? (a) splib, (b) blood, (c) gray, (d) spook, (e) African-American.

3.   A "gas head" is a person who has a: (a) fast-moving car, (b) stable of "lace," (c) "process," (d) habit of stealing cars, (e) long jail record for arson.

4.   "Bo Diddley" is a: (a) game for children, (b) down-home cheap wine, (c) down-home singer, (d) new dance, (e) Moejoe call.

5.   If a pimp is uptight with a woman who gets state aid, what does he mean when he talks about "Mother's Day"? (a) second Sunday in May, (b) third Sunday in June, (c) first of every month, (d) none of these, (e) first and fifteenth of every month.

6.   If a man is called a "blood," then he is a: (a) fighter, (b) Mexican-American, (c) Negro, (d) hungry hemophile, (e) Redman or Indian.

7.   What are the "Dixie Hummingbirds"? (a) part of the KKK, (b) a swamp disease, (c) a modern gospel group, (d) a Mississippi Negro paramilitary group, (e) deacons.

8.   T'Bone Walker got famous for playing what? (a) trombone, (b) piano, (c) "T-flute," (d) guitar, (e) "hambone."

From Dove (1968).

validity evidence before we can make any generalizations. Dove described his efforts to develop an intelligence test as "half serious." But we have seen that the test does identify an area of content in which the races differ and African Americans outperform whites.

The Black Intelligence Test of Cultural Homogeneity

Some psychologists regard most achievement and intelligence tests as instruments of racism. Most racist actions are felt to be illogical and emotional. However, the use of intelligence tests is seen as a subtle and thus more dangerous racist move because the tests are supported by scientific validity studies (Garcia, 1981). R. L. Williams (1974) has labeled this phenomenon *scientific racism.* He views IQ and standardized achievement tests as "nothing but updated versions of the old signs down South that read 'For Whites Only' " (1974, p. 34).

Of particular interest to Williams and his colleagues is the assessment of the ability to survive in the African-American community. Indeed, they feel that assessment of survival potential with a survival quotient (SQ) is more important than assessment of IQ, which indicates only the likelihood of succeeding in the white community. As a beginning, Williams developed the Black Intelligence Test of Cultural Homogeneity (BITCH), which asks respondents to define 100 vocabulary words relevant to African-American culture. The words came from the *Afro-American Slang Dictionary* and from Williams's personal experience interacting with African Americans. African-American people obtain higher scores than their white counterparts on the BITCH. When Williams administered the BITCH to 100 16- to 18-year-olds from each group, the average score for African-American subjects was 87.07 (out of 100). The mean score for the whites was significantly lower (51.07). Williams argues that traditional IQ and achievement tests are nothing more than culture-specific tests that assess how much white children know about white culture. The BITCH is also a culture-specific test, but one on which African-American subjects outperform whites.

Although the BITCH does tell one a lot about the cultural loading in intelligence and achievement tests, it has received mixed reviews. The reliability data reported by Williams show that the BITCH is quite reliable for African-American test takers (standard error less than 3 points on the 100-point scale) and acceptably reliable for white test takers (standard error about 6). (Conventional tests have similar reliabilities for both groups; see Oakland & Feigenbaum, 1979.) However, little convincing validity data on the BITCH are available. Although the test manual does report some studies, the samples are small and do not represent any clearly defined population (Cronbach, 1978). The difficulty is that one cannot determine whether the BITCH predicts how well a person will survive on the streets or how well he or she will do in school, in life, or in anything else. To support the conclusion that the BITCH is an intelligence test, one must have some evidence. Though the test does assess word association, it gives no information on reasoning abilities.

More studies are needed to determine whether the BITCH does what it is supposed to do. One of the rationales for the test is that it will identify children who have been unfairly assigned to classes for the educable mentally retarded (EMR) on the basis of IQ scores. In one study, P. A. Long and Anthony (1974) attempted to determine how many African-American EMR children would be reclassified if they were retested with the BITCH. Among a small and limited sample of 30 African-American EMR high-school students from Gainesville, Florida, all the students who performed poorly on the WISC also performed below the first percentile on the BITCH. Using the BITCH served to reclassify none of the students. However, this was just one small and nonrepresentative study. In its present state, the BITCH can be a valuable tool for measuring white familiarity with the African-American community. When white teachers or administrators are sent to schools that have predominantly African-American enrollments, the BITCH can help determine how much they know about the culture. Furthermore, the BITCH can help assess the extent to which an African American is in touch with his or her own community. As Cronbach (1978) has noted, people with good abstract reasoning skills may function poorly if they are unfamiliar with the community in which they live. Similarly, people with poor reasoning skills may get along just fine in a familiar community.

The System of Multicultural Pluralistic Assessment

No assessment technique covered in this book challenges traditional beliefs about testing as much as the System of Multicultural Pluralistic Assessment (SOMPA) (Mercer, 1979). This system has been adopted by several states. Before we discuss the SOMPA, we shall review Mercer's beliefs about the social and political implications of testing.

Mercer asserted that people's beliefs about what is fair and what knowledge exists are related to the social structure. She agreed with Mannheim (1936) that members of the politically dominant group provide the interpretation of events within a society and that they do so from their own perspective. The traditional psychometric literature on IQ tests provides a scientific rationale for the dominant group to keep minority group members in their place by demonstrating that such members do not have the language and knowledge skills to perform well in a white cultural setting. The feedback given to the minority groups is not that they are ignorant about the rules for success in another culture (just as the dominant group would be in a minority culture) but that they are stupid and unlikely to succeed. Mercer emphasized that one must take into consideration that people work from different bases of knowledge.

We cannot give a complete description of the SOMPA here. The system is complex, and many technical issues have been raised about its validity and its applicability (F. G. Brown, 1979a, 1979b; Clarizio, 1979a, 1979b; Goodman, 1977, 1979; Mercer, 1979; Oakland, 1979; Oakland & Parmelee, 1985; R. L. Taylor, Sternberg, & Partenio, 1986).

One important philosophical assumption underlies the development of the SOMPA—that all cultural groups have the same average potential. Any differences among cultural groups are assumed to be caused by differences in access to cultural experiences. Those who do not perform well on the tests are not well informed about the criteria for success usually set forth by the dominant group. Within groups that have had the same cultural experiences, however, not all individuals are expected to be the same, and assessment of these differences is a better measure of ability than is assessment of differences among cultural groups.

Mercer (1972) has been concerned about the consequences of labeling a child as mentally retarded. She has convincingly argued that many children are incorrectly identified as retarded and that they suffer severely as a result. In particular, she was distressed that classes for EMR students have disproportionate numbers of minority children. Mercer maintained that some minority students score low on the traditional tests because they are ignorant about the ways of the dominant culture, and they are not in any way mentally retarded. Because misclassification may also stem from medical problems, a fair system of evaluation must include medical assessment. It must also include the assessment of children relative to other children who have had similar life experiences. The basic point of divergence between the SOMPA and earlier approaches to assessment is that the SOMPA attempts to integrate three different approaches to assessment: medical, social, and pluralistic.

One of the most consistent findings in the field of public health is that members of low-income groups have more health problems than those who are economically better off. The *medical* component of the SOMPA system asks, "Is the child an intact organism?" (Mercer, 1979, p. 92). The rationale for this portion is that medical problems can interfere with a child's performance on mental measures and in school.

The *social-system* component attempts to determine whether a child is functioning at a level that would be expected by social norms. For example, does the child do what is expected by family members, peer groups, and the community? Mercer felt that test users and developers typically adopt only a social-system orientation. For example, if a test predicts who will do well in school, it forecasts behavior expected by the dominant social system. Mercer has emphasized that the social-system approach is narrow because only the dominant group in society defines the criteria for success (Reschly, 1981).

The *pluralistic* component of the SOMPA recognizes that different subcultures are associated with different life experiences. Only within these subgroups do individuals have common experiences. Thus, tests should assess individuals against others in the same subculture. One must recognize the distinction between the criteria for defining deviance in the pluralistic model and those in the social-system model. The latter uses the norms of society as the criteria, whereas the former uses the norms within a particular group.

The SOMPA attempts to assess children relative to each of these models. The medical portion of the SOMPA includes physical measures such as tests of vision, hearing, and motor functioning. The social-system portion resembles most assessment procedures in that the entire WISC-R is given and evaluated according to the regular criteria. Finally, the pluralistic portion evaluates WISC-R scores against those for groups that have similar social and cultural backgrounds. In other words, the WISC-R scores are adjusted for socioeconomic background. These adjusted scores are known as **estimated learning potentials (ELPs)**. An example of a SOMPA profile is shown in Figure 20-6.

The main dispute between Mercer and her many critics has centered on the validity of the SOMPA. Mercer (1979) pointed out that validity applies not to tests themselves but to inferences made on the basis of test scores. She insisted that one cannot validate ELPs in the same way as other test scores. (Validating a test by predicting who will do well in school is appropriate only for the social-system model.) The appropriate validity criterion for ELPs should be the percentage of variance in WISC-R scores that is accounted for by sociocultural variables. Even so, many SOMPA critics (F. G. Brown, 1979a; Clarizio, 1979b; Goodman, 1979; Oakland, 1979) felt that one should always validate a test by demonstrating that it predicts performance. The correlation between ELPs and school achievement is around .40, whereas the correlation between the WISC-R and school achievement is around .60 (Oakland, 1979). Thus, ELPs are a poorer predictor than WISC-R scores of school success. Mercer refuted these critics by arguing that the test is not designed to identify which children will do well in school but to determine which children are mentally retarded. One can do this only by comparing children with others who have had the same life experiences.

Accepting Mercer's argument may produce a quota system for EMR classes. Using ELPs should make the proportions of ethnic groups in EMR classes more representative than they now are. Because several states have adopted the SOMPA, researchers may soon be able to determine the ultimate effect of the system. It will certainly identify far fewer minority children as EMR students, which may please some taxpayers, because the costs of educating EMR students are higher than average. Yet, researchers still do not know whether children no longer considered EMR students will benefit. Mercer's (1972) work has suggested that a big part of the battle is just getting more children labeled as normal. Her critics have retaliated by claiming that the effects of labeling are weak and inconsequential. They argue that no matter what these children are called, they will need some special help in school. The critics may have won the argument. Over the years since its introduction, the use of the SOMPA has decreased significantly.

Suggestions for Solutions

Centering on problems associated with ethnic differences in test scores, we have presented many different arguments from various perspectives. In the following pages, we offer some solutions; however, we must warn you that these

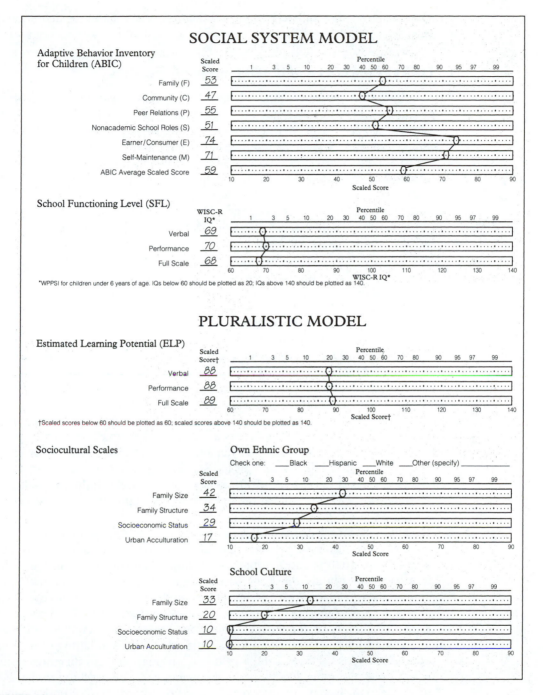

FIGURE 20-6

Sample SOMPA profile.

(*From the* System of Multicultural Pluralistic Assessment. *Copyright © 1978 by The Psychological Corporation. Reproduced by permission. All rights reserved.*)

solutions depend on different social and political beliefs about the definition of bias.

Ethical Concerns and the Definition of Test Bias

It is difficult to define *test bias;* different authors present various views (Barrett & Depinet, 1991; Cole, 1981; Darlington, 1978; Flaugher, 1978; Hunter & Schmidt, 1976). These definitions represent commitments to ethical viewpoints about the way one should treat certain groups. Hunter and Schmidt (1976) identify three ethical positions that set the tone for much of the debate: unqualified individualism, the use of quotas, and qualified individualism. These positions focus on the use of tests to select people either for jobs or for training programs (including college).

Supporters of *unqualified individualism* would use tests to select the most qualified individuals they could find. In this case, users of tests would remain indifferent to the race or gender of applicants. The goal would be to predict those who would perform best on the job or in school. According to this viewpoint, a test is fair if it finds the best candidates for the job or for admission to school. If race or gender was a valid predictor of performance over and above the information in the test, the unqualified individualist would see nothing wrong with considering this information in the selection process.

In a quite different ethical approach to selection, one uses *quotas,* which explicitly recognize race and gender differences. If the population of a state is 20% African American, then supporters of a quota system might argue that 20% of the new medical students in the state-supported medical school should also be African American. Selection procedures are regarded as biased if the actual percentage of applicants admitted differs from the percentage in the population; each group should demonstrate a fair share of the representation (Gordon & Terrell, 1981). This fair-share process gives less emphasis than testing does on how well people in the different groups will do once selected (Darlington, 1971; Gottfredson, 1994; Hunter & Schmidt, 1976; Sackett & Wilk, 1994; R. L. Thorndike, 1971).

The final moral position considered by Hunter and Schmidt might be viewed as a compromise between unqualified individualism and a quota system. Like unqualified individualism, *qualified individualism* embraces the notion that one should select the best qualified people. But unqualified individualists also take information about race, gender, and religion into consideration if it helps to predict performance on the criterion; not to do so results in underprediction of performance for one group and overprediction for another. Qualified individualists, however, recognize that although failing to include group characteristics (race, gender, and religion) may lead to differential accuracy in prediction, this differential prediction may counteract known effects of discrimination. It may, for example, lead to underprediction of performance for the majority group and overprediction for the minority group. The qualified individualist may choose not to include information about personal characteristics in selection because ignoring this information may serve the interests of minority-group members. Many people have argued that increased minority hiring will result in lower average job performance, because some applicants with lower test scores will be hired. However, systematic study of this issue has not always supported these arguments. For example, increased minority hiring in some industries has resulted in only a small loss in job performance. There may be circumstances in which average job performance drops with the overselection of low-scoring job applicants, but the data from these studies typically are complex (Silva & Jacobs, 1993).

One can relate each of these ethical positions to a particular statistical definition of test bias. Table 20-2 shows several different models of test bias, based on different definitions of fairness. All these models are based on regression lines, as we discussed. The models in Table 20-2 also apply to tests used for selection purposes, such as job placement and college or for advanced-degree programs.

The regression model described in this table (see also Cleary, 1968) represents the unqualified individualism position. The result of this approach is that a large number of majority group members may be selected. This approach maintains that an employer or a school should be absolutely color and gender blind. The reason for considering ethnicity or gender is to improve the prediction of future performance. This approach has been favored by business because it ensures the highest employee productivity.

At the other extreme is the quota system. To achieve fair-share representation, separate selection procedures are developed. One procedure, for example, is used to select the best available African-American applicants, and another to select the best available non-African-American applicants. If a community has 42% African-American residents, the first procedure would be used to select 42% of the employees, the other procedure to select the other 58%.

The quota system, though, may lead to greater rates of failure among some groups. Suppose that a test devised to select telephone operators did indeed predict who would succeed on the job, but it selected 70% women and 30% men. The quota system would encourage the use of separate cutoff scores so that the proportion of men selected would approach 50%. But because the women scored higher on the average, they would perform better on the job, resulting in a higher rate of failure among the men. Thus, although quota systems often increase the selection of underrepresented groups, they also make it likely that the underrepresented groups will experience failure.

Table 20-2 shows two other models (Cole, 1973; Darlington, 1971; R. L. Thorndike, 1971), which represent compromises between the quota and the unqualified individualism points of view. Each of these cases reflects an attempt to select the most qualified people, yet there is some adjustment for minority-group members. When people from two different groups have the same test score, these procedures give a slight edge to those from the lower group and put those from the higher group at a slight disadvantage.

TABLE 20-2 *Different Models of Test Fairness*

Model	Reference	Use of Regression	Rationale	Effect on Minority Selection	Effect on Average Criterion Performance
Regression	Cleary (1968)	Separate regression lines are used for different groups. Those with the highest predicted criterion scores are selected.	This is fair because those with the highest estimated level of success are selected.	Few minority group members selected	Good peformance on criteria
Constant ratio	Thorndike (1971)	Points equal to about half the average difference between the groups are added to the test scores of the group with the lower score. Then a single regression line is used, and those with the highest predicted scores are selected.	This is fair because it best reflects the potential of the lower scoring group.	Some increase in the number of minority group members selected	Somewhat lower
Cole/ Darlington	Cole (1973), Darlington (1971, 1978)	Separate regression equations are used for each group, and points are added to the scores of those from the lower group to ensure that those with the same criterion score have the same predictor score.	This is fair because it selects more potentially successful people from the lower group.	Larger increase in the number of minority group members selected	Lower
Quota	Dunnette and Borman (1979)	The proportion of people to be selected from each group is predetermined. Separate regression equations are used to select those from each group who are expected to perform highest on the criterion.	This is fair because members of different subgroups are selected based on their proportions in the community.	Best representation of minority groups	About the same as for the Cole/ Darlington model

Based on Dunnette & Borman (1979).

Although these approaches have been attacked for being based on faulty logic (Hunter & Schmidt, 1976, 1978), plausible defenses have been offered. These procedures increase the number of people selected from underrepresented groups. However, these procedures also reduce the average performance score on the criterion. We cannot tell you which of these approaches is right and which wrong. That decision depends on your own values and judgment about what is fair. (See Focused Example 20-2.)

Focused Example 20-2

Quotas in the Civil Rights Act of 1991

The difference between unqualified individualism and quota systems became a central issue in the 1991 Civil Rights Bill. The bill never mentioned the word *quota;* however, the structure of the bill emphasized selection systems that would support affirmative action and increase the percentage of minority-group members in federal jobs. President George Bush initially refused to support the bill and accused the Democratic Congress of pushing discriminatory quotas. Bush favored an unqualified individualism position and emphasized that many prominent minority-group members had achieved success without special programs. During the 1980s, President Ronald Reagan had appointed a director of the Equal Employment Opportunity Commission (EEOC) who had, in effect, also supported unqualified individualism over quota systems. During that era, the EEOC failed to act on a substantial number of adverse selection cases. In the fall of 1991, newspapers reported that President Bush would add language to the bill that would halt the use of quota selection systems. However, last-minute lobbying by civil rights groups persuaded the president to leave undisturbed the federal policies encouraging affirmative action. (For more details, see Chapter 21.)

Despite these problems and controversies, surveys show that psychologists and educational specialists generally have positive attitudes about intelligence and aptitude tests. In one survey, 1020 experts agreed that there were some sociocultural biases in the tests (Snyderman & Rothman, 1987). However, these experts also generally agreed that the tests were valid for predictive purposes. Their main concerns centered on the interpretation and application of test results by elementary and secondary schools.

Perhaps the most controversial defense of testing was presented in a 1994 book entitled *The Bell Curve.* The book is reviewed in Focused Example 20-3.

Improving the Use of Selection Devices

We have contended that the observed differences between minority and non-minority groups on standardized tests are a problem. Sometimes a problem stimulates us to think differently; in the words of the famous entrepreneur, Henry Kaiser, "A problem is an opportunity in work clothes." Differences in test scores may also reflect patterns of problem solving that characterize different subcultures. Knowing how groups differ in their approaches to problem solving can be helpful for two reasons. First, it can teach one important things about the relationship between socialization and problem-solving approaches. This information can guide the development of pluralistic education programs (Castaneda & Ramirez, 1974). Second, knowing more about the ways different groups approach problems can lead to the development of improved predictors of success for minority groups (R. D. Goldman, 1973; Sternberg, 1991).

Focused Example 20-3

The Bell Curve

In 1994 Richard Herrnstein, a noted Harvard psychologist, and Charles Murray, a professional writer, published a controversial book entitled *The Bell Curve: Intelligence and Class Structure in American Life*. The controversial book drew immediate reaction from the mass media and serious scholars alike. In contrast to the many testing professionals who question the value of intelligence tests, Herrnstein and Murray argued that, indeed, intelligence tests are the primary correlates of success in American life. Consistent with Spearman, they argued that the *g* factor is essential to a variety of different skills and abilities.

The Bell Curve used data from the National Longitudinal Study of Youth, started in 1979. The study has involved a representative sample of 12,686 youths, between the ages of 14–21 in 1979, who have been restudied each year. The book used data collected through 1990. For the analysis, testers used the Armed Services Vocational Battery (ASVB). Various analyses showed that IQ scores are related to a wide variety of indices of success in life ranging from completion of a college degree through the attainment of substantial income. Some researchers argued that IQ tests predict who will fill the important leadership roles in society. According to the book, those with low IQ are more likely to become involved in crime and delinquency, to end up on welfare, and to have illegitimate children.

Herrnstein and Murray are unusually optimistic about the relationship between job performance and IQ. From their data, they suggest that the correlation between IQ and job performance rating is .53, with the correlation between education and job performance at .22, between college grades and performance at .11. They even argue that the Supreme Court case of *Griggs* vs. *Duke Power Company* (see Chapter 21), which restricted the use of IQ testing for job selection, has cost American companies billions of dollars because it prevented the most qualified individuals from being selected for various jobs. They attribute most social problems, ranging from school dropouts to unemployment to work-related injury and crime, to low intelligence. Further, they suggest that the differences in economic attainment for various ethnic groups probably reflect differences in IQ. They conclude by arguing that the United States must face up to differences in intelligence. Further, they suggest that we must recognize that not all people are created equal and that traditional approaches to these problems will simply not work.

Upon publication, *The Bell Curve* was robustly attacked for a variety of reasons. First, many complained of its arrogant writing style. For example, Herrnstein and Murray described themselves as classicists who favor the traditional view of *g* intelligence. They discussed alternative views of intelligence proposed by "revisionists" and "radicals." They then wrote off these theories as approaches that scholars do not take seriously, even though scholars consider alternative approaches very seriously. Critics of the book's statistical methods focus on the simplified analyses. For example, many of the correlations between IQ and outcome depend highly on those in the lowest decimal of intelligence. Indeed, it may be that those with very low IQ (under 80) may have difficulty in various aspects of their lives. However, removing the bottom decile from the analyses would significantly reduce the relationship between IQ and several of the outcome variables.

Others have attacked *The Bell Curve* for not using measures of intelligence but measures of developed ability as captured by the ASVB. It has been argued that people from higher social classes would be expected to do better on the ASVB because the test better reflects their culture (Leman, 1995).

Along these lines, R. D. Goldman (1973) has proposed the differential process theory, which maintains that for many tasks, different strategies may lead to an effective solution. According to this theory, strategies—ways people go about solving problems (Frederiksen, 1969; Sternberg, 1985)—mediate abilities and performance.

For example, African-American college students (on average) tend to score higher on the verbal subtest of the SAT than they do on the quantitative subtest. White students (on average) score about the same on both subtests. As the result of their socialization, African-American students possibly structure the task of getting through school differently; they develop their verbal skills rather than their quantitative abilities. This result may also reflect differences in the opportunity to learn proper quantitative skills. In any case, African-American students tend to choose college majors that emphasize their verbal abilities. It may thus be appropriate to build specific tests that predict how well these students will do in the majors they choose. These tests could deemphasize quantitative skills if shown to be unrelated to success for these particular majors. In other words, the test would be validated for the specific majors chosen by African-American students.

In a related argument, H. Gardner (1993; H. Gardner et al., 1994) suggests seven distinct types of intelligence: linguistic, musical, logical-mathematical, spatial, bodily-kinesthetic, and two different forms of personal intelligence. Gardner sees no reason to call logical thinking "intelligence" and musical ability a "talent." Instead, he believes that these abilities are equal. Groups that perform best on tests of general intelligence do not necessarily excel in all of Gardner's talent domains.

Developing Different Criteria

Criterion validity is the correlation between the test and the criterion. But what are the criteria used to validate the tests for assessing the potential of children? Most of these tests are simply valid predictors of how well children will do on other standardized tests. In other words, most standardized tests are evaluated against other standardized tests. However, the criterion simply may be the test dressed in different clothes. For example, one may evaluate an intelligence test to determine how well it predicts performance on a standardized achievement test. This test measures achievement, not native ability. Differences in scores on this test between minority and nonminority groups are therefore due to the opportunity to learn rather than the ability to learn. This is recognized by the Educational Testing Service, which requests special care in interpreting SAT and GRE scores for students who have had "an educational and cultural experience somewhat different from that of the traditional majority" (*GRE Guide*, 1991, p. 14).

If one does not accept standardized tests as a validity criterion for other tests, how can one determine the meaning of the tests? A considerable debate concerns whether classroom grades should serve as this criterion. Supporters of the use of classroom grades claim that these grades are the only independent measure of how well the child is doing. It is no surprise, they maintain, that a correlation exists between IQ tests and scores on standardized achievement tests because both measure similar content. However, they argue that because they do not predict classroom grades for minority children, IQ tests are not valid for such youngsters. The support for this position comes from studies like one by R. D. Goldman and Hartig (1976). This study found scores on the WISC to be unrelated to teacher ratings of classroom performance for minority children. For the nonminority children, it found a significant relationship between IQ and teacher ratings. If the criterion becomes classroom grades rather than another standardized test, the IQ test appears valid for nonminority but not for minority children.

Supporters of the use of the tests give three reasons one should not use grades as the criterion. First, teacher-assigned grades are unstandardized and open to subjective bias (Sattler, 1979a). For example, teachers sometimes reward effort more than ability (Weiner, 1994). Second, few available studies have used grades as the criterion. Third, the most frequently cited study (Goldman & Hartig, 1976) is open to other explanations. In this study, the teachers rated the classroom performance of nearly all the minority children as poor. These low ratings resulted in little variance on the criterion measure. As you learned in Chapter 3, any variable for which there is no variability cannot correlate well with other variables.

The problem with criterion measures becomes even more apparent in relation to measures used with adults. For example, the Medical College Admission Test (MCAT) predicts success in medical school. Yet, as Focused Example 20-4 demonstrates, it does not predict who will be a successful doctor. Similarly, the Law School Admission Test (LSAT) predicts performance in law school, yet there is little evidence that it predicts who will be a good attorney. The professional school admission tests may thus be eliminating people who are potentially better doctors and lawyers than those who are admitted. Imagine, for example, that an Anglo and a Hispanic doctor, trained equally well in the science of medical care, both practice in a public hospital in a Hispanic neighborhood. The Hispanic doctor will more likely be effective because he or she understands the culture and the language of the patients and thus can better understand specific complaints and symptoms. The Anglo doctor may do a poorer job at diagnosing the problems. The MCAT would have done its job poorly by focusing on the short-term criterion of medical school grades. More work is needed to develop measures that are good predictors of the long-range goal of clinical success (Altmaier et al., 1992).

Changing the Social Environment

It is not hard to determine that majority and minority children grow up in different social environments. You can learn this by reading any sociology textbook or by getting in your car and driving to the inner city. Given this

Focused Example 20-4

Evaluating the Medical College Admission Test

The ultimate goal in medical practice is the successful diagnosis and treatment of patients. Thus, the selection of medical students should proceed with this objective in mind. However, the MCAT is designed to predict only how well students will do in medical school. Studies do show that the MCAT adequately predicts medical school grades. But how meaningful are such grades?

Much debate has centered on the importance of medical school grades. For example, one study that considered measures of physician success in practice found that grades were unassociated with measures of real-life performance (Loughmiller et al., 1970). In another study of 217 physicians practicing in Utah, 76 measures of doctor performance were taken. Among more than 1000 correlations between grades and performance on these measures, 97% were nearly 0. On the basis of these results, the criteria for admission to medical school were seriously questioned (C. W. Taylor et al., 1965). Although tests may predict medical school grades, it is unclear whether grades or the tests offer much information about who will be a successful doctor.

After students graduate from medical school, they must enter medical residency programs to obtain training in their specialty areas. To select the best residents, specialty training programs have typically used test scores and personal interviews. These interviews and tests determine where a physician will get training and which physicians will gain entry into the most prestigious programs. Studies have suggested that programs increasingly rely on academic test performance as selection criteria. In addition, most residency programs require inter-

views. During the interview process, prospective specialists are evaluated on their personality characteristics, professional maturity, enthusiasm and energy, and interpersonal rapport. Detailed studies have evaluated the relationship between these cognitive (test performance) and noncognitive (interview) predictors of success in the residency program. The studies have produced consistent results: Traditional tests and interviews are terrible predictors of success as a physician (Altmaier et al., 1990, 1992; P. S. Wood et al., 1990).

Why are these predictors inadequate? One explanation is that the practice of medicine is very complicated. Physicians need more than knowledge one can test. The tests often evaluate the physicians' understanding of the basic biological constructs but may not tap into their motivation, ability to interact with people, or judgment. Although interviews are designed to capture some of these characteristics, personal interviews are notoriously poor at identifying the appropriate information (see Chapter 9). To target some of these abilities, newer approaches use techniques of job analysis and analysis of specific skills appropriate to the practice of medicine. Studies have identified specific behavioral skills related to lack of confidence, conscientiousness, interpersonal skills, curiosity, and a variety of other behaviors. Each of these was linked to specific behavioral incidents that could be self-reported. The early analysis has suggested that these techniques successfully predict performance in the residency programs as evaluated by senior physicians and patients (P. S. Wood et al., 1990). In the future, we expect more use of behavioral-based measures for the selection of medical residents.

disparity in environment, it is not surprising that tests favor the majority. Many critics of tests, though, seem to hold the tests responsible for inequality of opportunity (Flaugher, 1978). Another view claims test scores accurately reflect the effects of social and economic inequality (B. F. Green, 1978).

To understand these arguments, one must consider the purpose of testing. In educational settings, tests such as the SAT and the GRE or even IQ tests are usually considered to be tests of aptitude: They measure some inborn trait unlikely to change with environment. But most experts now agree that tests measure not just inborn potential but also the effects of cumulative experience. With proper nurturing, a subject can change his or her score. Verbal and numerical abilities are acquired through experience. Thus, low test scores should not be viewed as insurmountable problems; they can improve.

Much of what we have said in this chapter is consistent with the view that tests do point out differences between minority and nonminority students. Furthermore, systematic attempts to show that the tests have created this problem have not been convincing. Many minority students do well on the tests, which accurately predict that these students will do well on the criterion. An African-American student and a white student who both achieve a score of 1100 on the SAT are predicted to do equally well in college, and studies show that indeed they do perform at about the same level.

Blaming the tests for observed differences between groups may be a convenient way to avoid a much larger problem. No one has suggested that the tuberculin test is unfair because it demonstrates that poor people have the disease more often than wealthy people. Public health officials have correctly concluded that some people live in environments that predispose them to the disease. Getting rid of scales that identify underweight children will not cure malnutrition (Flaugher, 1978). Although measuring intelligence may not be the same as testing for tuberculosis or measuring weight, the analogy may be worth considering.

If unequal access to adequate education and to stimulating experiences results in differences in test scores, it would be more useful to change the social environment than to continuously bicker about the tests. The tests may merely be the bearers of bad news. By documenting the problem's severity, the tests may be telling us that overcoming this problem will be expensive, will be difficult, and may take many years. Blaming the tests for a problem that they did not cause seems to be shortsighted and nonproductive (Elliot, 1988).

Summary

In this chapter, we examined two sides of the issue of test bias. Table 20-3 offers a summary of some of the arguments for and against the use of tests. As the table shows, there are strong differences of opinion about the value of intelligence and aptitude tests for minority group members. As a result of the challenge to traditional tests, new approaches such as the Chitling Test, the BITCH, and the SOMPA have been developed. Among these, the SOMPA is clearly the most sophisticated. All these approaches are based on the assumption that social groups do not differ in their average potential. These approaches have been challenged because they do not have the same sort of validity evidence as traditional tests.

Part of the debate about test bias results from different moral views about what is fair. Some have argued that a testing and selection program is fair if it

TABLE 20-3 *For and Against the Use of Tests*

Against	For
The Stanford-Binet was standardized on only 1000 children and 400 adults. None of these people were African-American (Guthrie, 1976).	Although not standardized on minority group members, tests appear to have the same validity for minority students as they do for majority students. Therefore, neglecting to include minorities in the original validation studies was not relevant (Barrett & Depinet, 1991; Herrnstein & Murray, 1994).
The use of intelligence tests can have a damaging social impact. For example, the IQ scores of ethnic groups were used to limit immigration of certain groups into the United States during the early years of the 20th century (Kamin, 1974).	Examination of the Congressional Record covering the debates about the 1924 Immigration Act failed to uncover discussion of intelligence test data or claims that the mean IQ of Americans would decline if the immigration of certain groups was allowed (DuBois, 1972).
If a teacher just thinks some children have higher IQs, the actual test scores of those children will improve (Rosenthal & Jacobson, 1968).	Studies documenting the effects of self-fulfilling prophecies and teacher expectations overinterpreted their original data, contained some results that are statistically impossible, and cannot be depended on (Elashoff & Snow, 1971; Snow, 1969; R. L. Thorndike, 1968).
Minority children can only be damaged by the continued use of psychological tests.	Psychological tests can be used to identify the most capable members of each group. Without the tests, people will be selected on the basis of personal judgment, which might be more racist than the tests (Ones, Chockalingham, & Schmidt, 1995).
The validity of IQ tests was documented using other standardized tests as the criterion rather than measures of classroom performance (Mercer, 1988).	The objective tests are better validity criteria than classroom performance, which is more subjective. Teachers may grade on the basis of effort rather than ability (Sattler, 1979a).
Most test administrators are white; the scores of African-American children would improve if they were tested by African-American examiners (Forrester & Klaus, 1964; Pasamanick & Knobloch, 1955).	Some studies do indeed show that the race of the examiner is an important factor. However, most studies do not. Among 28 different studies on the effects of the examiner's race, 24 fail to show that the race of the examiner significantly affects scores (Sattler, 1979a).

selects the best-suited people, regardless of their social group. This approach, however, may lead to overrepresentation of one group. Another moral position supports procedures that select members from different racial and ethnic groups according to their proportions in the general population. A third moral position is a compromise between the other two.

Although test bias will surely remain an area of considerable controversy, some positive potential solutions have come to light. For example, one might evaluate tests against outcome criteria relevant to minority groups.

A current controversy rages on about the nature of differences in test performance. One group believes the differences are genetic or biological in origin (Hernstein, 1982; Rushton, 1991; Vandenburg & Vogler, 1985), while another believes the differences result from the influence of social environment (Kamin, 1974; Olmedo, 1981; Zuckerman, 1990). Some people believe there

is evidence for both genetic and environmental explanations (Turkheimer, 1991). The social-environment explanation (Gould, 1981) seems to be the most popular. If people accept this view, differences in test performance might suggest that people need to escalate their efforts to wipe out inequality. If one endorses the genetic position, one acknowledges that little can be done to equalize performance among different groups.

CHAPTER 21

Testing and the Law

LEARNING OBJECTIVES

When you have completed this chapter, you should be able to

☐ Describe the basis on which the federal government can regulate the use of psychological tests

☐ Describe the EEOC guidelines and their importance

☐ Describe how the New York Truth in Testing Law affects the use of psychological tests

☐ Discuss the impact of PL 94-142

☐ Discuss the importance of *Hobson* v. *Hansen*

☐ Describe the issue in *Diana* v. *State Board of Education* and how it differs from the major issue in *Larry P.* v. *Wilson Riles*

☐ Compare and contrast the decisions in *Larry P.* v. *Wilson Riles* and *Parents in Action* on *Special Education* v. *Hannon*

☐ Discuss the importance of *Regents of the University of California* v. *Bakke*

☐ Describe how the courts are involved in the use of personnel tests

☐ Discuss the events that led to the Civil Rights Act of 1991

In 1969, the California Department of Education began requiring the use of standardized IQ tests to diagnose retardation. Students who scored below 85 on the WISC or the Stanford-Binet were sent to special classes for the educable mentally retarded (EMR). Larry P. was one of approximately 6000 African-American children assigned to EMR classes on the basis of the tests. However, a few years later, Larry P. and five of his African-American schoolmates were retested by African-American psychologists, who reported higher IQ scores. On the basis of these new, higher test scores, Larry and the others were placed back in the regular school track.

Larry P.'s battle was not as simple as being retested to gain an appropriate placement. Instead, a class-action lawsuit was filed on behalf of the six African-American children (representing the class of all similar students). This case challenged the right of the state to use IQ tests for classroom placement, arguing that the tests discriminated by race and therefore violated both the California Constitution and the 14th Amendment to the U.S. Constitution, which guarantees equal protection under the law.

It took until 1977 for the case to be heard in the U.S. District Court. After hearing and reviewing more than 11,000 pages of testimony by psychologists and interested parties, judge Robert Peckham released a 131-page opinion in October 1979 forbidding the placement of African-American children in EMR classes on the basis of standardized test scores. The same judge reversed his own decision in a 1992 opinion. Thus, the ultimate decision about the use of psychological tests was made not by trained psychologists, professional educators, or interested citizens, but by the courts.

The same year the decision in Larry P.'s case was released, the state of New York passed a Truth in Testing Law, and a similar bill was introduced in the U.S. House of Representatives. In addition, a Florida judge ruled that African-American students who did not receive all their education in integrated schools could not be denied a high-school credential on the basis of a minimum competence test. By the end of the 1970s, the use of psychological tests had become a major legal issue. The focus broadened to employment testing in the 1980s and early 1990s. These courtroom and legislative battles over the appropriate use of psychological tests set the stage for the many current conflicts over testing.

In this chapter, we present major legal issues concerning the use of psychological tests. We begin by covering some of the basic laws that regulate the use of tests, and then we report on how the courts have interpreted some of these laws. Focused Example 21-1 discusses the meaning of the word *law*.

Laws Governing the Use of Tests

Federal Authorities

Many people believe that the federal government has unlimited authority to regulate almost any activity. Actually, the circumstances under which the fed-

Focused Example 21-1

What Is a Law?

 As common as it is to refer to laws, many people are confused about what exactly constitutes the law. Most people think of law only as *statutes*, or the rules written by legislative bodies at any level of government. Before proposed statutes become law, they are called *bills* or *propositions*.

In addition to statutes, *constitutions* have the force of law. In the United States, there is a federal Constitution, and each state has its own constitution. In lawsuits (or litigation), lawyers frequently argue that a policy violates a constitutional rule or principle. The U.S. Constitution is considered the supreme law of the land because any federal, state, or local law is invalid if judged to conflict with it. State or local laws inconsistent with a state constitution can also be declared invalid.

Statutes and constitutions are typically worded in general terms. Often, they give authority to a specific agency to write *regulations*. For all intents and purposes, these regulations are also laws. For example, the Civil Rights Act of 1964 (a statute) created the Equal Employment Opportunity Commission (EEOC), which wrote guidelines for fair employment practices; these guidelines are regulations. Although not created by any elected officials, they are laws that one must follow.

The final form of law is *judicial opinion*. Statutes, constitutions, and regulations must be applied to the specific facts. Thus, courts of law are frequently called on to interpret the law in view of a given situation. In doing so, the courts offer opinions that consider specific cases against the background of statutes, constitutions, and regulations. Once a court offers an opinion on a specific case, the opinion becomes law (Wing, 1976). For example, in the case of *Larry P.* v. *Wilson Riles*, a judge rendered the opinion that IQ tests could not be used to place African-American children in EMR classes. This opinion is the law in California. The opinion was reversed in 1992.

eral government can regulate are limited. Until fairly recently, the most commonly used authority for regulation was interstate commerce.

Interstate commerce. The Constitution gives most of the ruling power to the states. Each state has its own constitution, which defines the general relationship between the state and its citizens. The states must make policies for the other administrative units, such as cities and counties, that exist within them. The U.S. Constitution does not directly recognize cities, counties, or school districts. The only restriction on the states' authority to pass laws is that no state can pass or enforce a law that is inconsistent with the Constitution.

Because each state has only that authority necessary to attend to its own affairs, the federal government regulates interstate commerce, or business activity involving two or more states. For example, a test developed by a New Jersey company and shipped (to Kansas) to be administered for profit clearly involves interstate commerce. Some legal authorities now believe that interstate commerce involves almost all activities. Thus, the federal government can regulate many activities under this umbrella.

The regulation of interstate commerce is clear and direct. Federal agencies such as the Federal Trade Commission create policies to regulate specific products and activities. Congress also devotes much of its energy to creating laws that regulate specific business activities. These extensive and well-documented policies represent direct regulation. The other form of government regulation—the power to control spending—is indirect.

Control of spending. The U.S. government is a big spender—so big, in fact, that virtually all major American business institutions depend to some extent on federal revenues. This spending gives the federal government considerable leverage. It can withhold money whenever federal authorities consider it just to do so. In effect, the government has the right to say, "Do it our way or we will not pay."

This policy is straightforward when the government is a customer. For example, when the federal government is paying for the development of a test, it has the right to withhold payment unless the work is done according to government standards. However, this power is frequently exercised indirectly. For example, the government can say in effect "Conform to our employment guidelines or we will not pay you to develop a test."

Most school districts are happy to receive federal funds to implement certain programs; however, they may not be enthusiastic about implementing governmental policies. For example, a district may have a school lunch program for underprivileged children, which it enthusiastically supports. What happens if the government asks the district to build ramps for handicapped children? If the district does not follow through, there is no criminal penalty for deciding not to build the ramps; however, the government has the authority to withhold the funds for the lunch program until the district agrees to the ramps.

Virtually all public and most major private institutions can be regulated in this way because of their dependence on federal contracts and grants. Institutions in the private sector that do not depend as heavily on federal funds can be regulated through interstate commerce. Government regulation is thus difficult to escape.

Guidelines of the Equal Employment Opportunity Commission. The government exercises its power to regulate testing in large part through interpretations of the 14th Amendment to the Constitution. This amendment guarantees all citizens due process and equal protection under the law. However, specifying the conditions under which due process and equal protection are afforded has taken a long time. Gradually, the way in which these principles are implemented has been carefully refined. The clearest statement from the federal government has concerned employee testing and personnel procedures.

During the presidency of Lyndon Johnson, Congress enacted the Civil Rights Act of 1964, one of this century's most important pieces of legislation. Title VII of the act and its subsequent amendments created an Equal Employment Opportunity Commission (EEOC). In 1970, the EEOC released a set of guidelines that defined fair employee-selection procedures. In 1978, the guidelines were revised and simplified, published as the *Uniform Guidelines on Employee Selection Procedures*, and jointly adopted by the EEOC, the Civil Service Commission, and the Departments of Justice, Labor, and the Treasury. These guidelines thus affect most public employment and institutions that receive government funds (Novick, 1981).

The guidelines clearly state that an employer cannot discriminate on the basis of race, color, gender, national origin, or religion. Selection procedures that might have adverse impact receive particular attention. *Adverse impact* is interpreted according to one of the most controversial components of the guidelines, the **four-fifths rule:**

> A selection rate of any race, sex, or ethnic group which is less than four-fifths (4/5) (or 80%) of the rate for the group with the highest rate will generally be regarded by the federal enforcement agencies as evidence of adverse impact, while a greater than four-fifths rate will generally not be regarded by federal enforcement agencies as evidence of adverse impact.

Thus, a selection procedure may be suspected of having adverse impact if it gives any homogeneous group of employees four-fifths or more of the jobs. For example, if an employer hires 90% of the white male applicants and only 20% of the African-American male applicants, the selection procedure violates the four-fifths rule. The employer then has to demonstrate that extenuating circumstances make the standard unreasonable. One of the most interesting problems with the four-fifths rule has been that efforts to recruit minorities can reduce the percentage from each group hired. By actively recruiting members of many minority groups an employer can hire a smaller percentage of each group and still maintain the four-fifths rule. Thus, this rule designed to protect minorities may actually discourage the aggressive recruiting of these groups. The EEOC acknowledges these problems and has developed exceptions for particular circumstances. The authorization of these exceptions for specific individual cases is left up to the EEOC and, in many cases, has been left to the courts (McCormick & Ilgen, 1980).

The guidelines include many careful definitions of terms such as *validity*. Whenever using a psychological test or other selection device results in adverse impact (or overselection in one group), the employer must present extensive evidence for the validity of the selection procedure. Much of the text of the EEOC guidelines is devoted to a discussion of the minimum requirements for the validity of a selection procedure. In essence, the guidelines parallel the discussion presented in Chapter 5. Technical Box 21-1 gives the EEOC requirements for criterion validity.

If prospective employees feel they have been treated unfairly, they can file complaints with the commission. The EEOC regional and district offices handle about 70,000 complaints each year. The EEOC also gathers information. Any organization with more than 100 employees must complete a form each year that describes the number of women and members of four different minority groups employed in nine different job categories within the organiza-

(Text continues on p. 573.)

TECHNICAL BOX 21-1

EEOC Guidelines for Criterion Validity

Technical standards for criterion-related validity studies—(1) *Technical feasibility.* Users choosing to validate a selection procedure by a criterion-related validity strategy should determine whether it is technically feasible (as defined in section 16) to conduct such a study in the particular employment context. The determination of the number of persons necessary to permit the conduct of a meaningful criterion-related study should be made by the user on the basis of all relevant information concerning the selection procedure, the potential sample, and the employment situation. Where appropriate, jobs with substantially the same major work behaviors may be grouped together for validity studies, in order to obtain an adequate sample. These guidelines do not require a user to hire or promote persons for the purpose of making it possible to conduct a criterion-related study.

(2) *Analysis of the job.* There should be a review of job information to determine measures of work behavior(s) or performance that are relevant to the job or group of jobs in question. These measures or criteria are relevant to the extent that they represent critical or important job duties, work behaviors, or work outcomes as developed from the review of job information. The possibility of bias should be considered both in selection of the criterion measures and their application. In view of the possibility of bias in subjective evaluations, supervisory rating techniques and instructions to raters should be carefully developed. All criterion measures and the methods for gathering data need to be examined for freedom from factors which would unfairly alter scores of members of any group. The relevance of criteria and their freedom from bias are of particular concern when there are significant differences in measures of job performance for different groups.

(3) *Criterion measures.* Proper safeguards should be taken to ensure that scores on selection procedures do not enter into any judgments of employee adequacy that are to be used as criterion measures. Whatever criteria are used should represent important or critical work behavior(s) or work outcomes. Certain criteria may be used without a full job analysis if the user can show the importance of the criteria to the particular employment context. These criteria include but are not limited to production rate, error rate, tardiness, absenteeism, and length of service. A standardized rating of overall work performance may be used where a study of the job shows that it is an appropriate criterion. Where performance in training is used as a criterion, success in training should be properly measured and the relevance of the training should be shown either through a comparison of the content of the training program with the critical or important work behavior(s) of the job(s) or through a demonstration of the relationship between measures of performance in training and measures of job performance. Measures of relative success in training include but are not limited to instructor evaluations, performance samples, or tests. Criterion measures consisting of paper-and-pencil tests will be closely reviewed for job relevance.

(4) *Representativeness of the sample.* Whether the study is predictive or concurrent, the sample subjects should insofar as feasible be representative of the candidates normally available in the relevant labor market for the job or group of jobs in question, and should insofar as feasible include the races, sexes, and ethnic groups normally available in the relevant job market. In determining the representativeness of the

sample in a concurrent validity study, the user should take into account the extent to which the specific knowledges or skills which are the primary focus of the test are those which employees learn on the job.

Where samples are combined or compared, attention should be given to see that such samples are comparable in terms of the actual job they perform, the length of time on the job where time on the job is likely to affect performance, and other relevant factors likely to affect validity differences; or that these factors are included in the design of the study and their effects identified.

(5) *Statistical relationships.* The degree of relationship between selection procedure scores and criterion measures should be examined and computed, using professionally acceptable statistical procedures. Generally, a selection procedure is considered related to the criterion, for the purposes of these guidelines, when the relationship between performance on the procedure and performance on the criterion measure is statistically significant at the .05 level of significance, which means that it is sufficiently high as to have a probability of no more than one (1) in twenty (20) to have occurred by chance. Absence of a statistically significant relationship between a selection procedure and job performance should not necessarily discourage other investigations of the validity of that selection procedure.

(6) *Operational use of selection procedures.* Users should evaluate each selection procedure to assure that it is appropriate for operational use, including establishment of cutoff scores or rank ordering. Generally, if other factors remain the same, the greater the magnitude of the relationship (e.g., correlation coefficient) between performance on a selection procedure and one or more criteria of performance on the job and the greater the importance and number of aspects of job performance covered by the criteria, the more likely it is that the procedure will be appropriate for use. Reliance upon a selection procedure which is significantly related to a criterion measure but which is based upon a study involving a large number of subjects and has a low correlation coefficient will be subject to close review if it has a large adverse impact. Sole reliance upon a single selection instrument which is related to only one of many job duties or aspects of job performance will also be subject to close review. The appropriateness of a selection procedure is best evaluated in each particular situation and there are no minimum correlation coefficients applicable to all employment situations. In determining whether a selection procedure is appropriate for operational use, the following considerations should also be taken into account: the degree of adverse impact of the procedure, the availability of other selection procedures of greater or substantially equal validity.

(7) *Overstatement of validity findings.* Users should avoid reliance upon techniques which tend to overestimate validity findings as a result of capitalization on chance unless an appropriate safeguard is taken. Reliance upon a few selection procedures or criteria of successful job performance when many selection procedures or criteria of performance have been studied, or the use of optimal statistical weights for selection procedures computed in one sample, are techniques which tend to inflate validity estimates as a result of chance. Use of a large sample is one safeguard; cross validation is another.

(8) *Fairness.* This section generally calls for studies of unfairness where technically feasible. The concept of fairness or unfairness of selection procedures is a developing concept. In addition, fairness studies generally require substantial numbers of employees in the job or group of jobs being studied. For these reasons, the federal enforcement agencies recognize that the obligation to conduct studies of fairness

Continued

Continued

imposed by the guidelines generally will be upon users or groups of users with a large number of persons in a job class, or test developers; and that small users utilizing their own selection procedures will generally not be obligated to conduct such studies because it will be technically infeasible for them to do so.

(a) *Unfairness defined.* When members of one race, sex, or ethnic group characteristically obtain lower scores on a selection procedure than members of another group and the differences in scores are not reflected in differences in a measure of job performance, use of the selection procedure may unfairly deny opportunities to members of the group that obtains the lower scores.

(b) *Investigation of fairness.* Where a selection procedure results in an adverse impact on a race, sex, or ethnic group identified in accordance with the classifications set forth in section 4 above and that group is a significant factor in the relevant lab or market, the user generally should investigate the possible existence of unfairness for that group if it is technically feasible to do so. The greater the severity of the adverse impact on a group, the greater the need to investigate the possible existence of unfairness. Where the weight of evidence from other studies shows that the selection procedure predicts fairly for the group in question and for the same or similar jobs, such evidence may be relied on in connection with the selection procedure at issue.

(c) *General considerations in fairness investigations.* Users conducting a study of fairness should review the A.P.A. Standards regarding investigation of possible bias in testing. An investigation of fairness of a selection procedure depends on both evidence of validity and the manner in which the selection procedure is to be used in a particular employment context. Fairness of a selection procedure cannot necessarily be specified in advance without investigating these factors. Investigation of fairness of a selection procedure in samples where the range of scores on selection procedures or criterion measures is severely restricted for any subgroup sample (as compared to other subgroup samples) may produce misleading evidence of unfairness. That factor should accordingly be taken into account in conducting such studies and before reliance is placed on the results.

(d) *When unfairness is shown.* If unfairness is demonstrated through a showing that members of a particular group perform better or poorer on the job than their scores on the selection procedure would indicate through comparison with how members of other groups perform, the user may either revise or replace the selection instrument in accordance with these guidelines, or may continue to use the selection instrument operationally with appropriate revisions in its use to ensure compatibility between the probability of successful job performance and the probability of being selected.

(e) *Technical feasibility of fairness studies.* In addition to the general conditions needed for technical feasibility for the conduct of a criterion-related study, an investigation of fairness requires the following.

(i) An adequate sample of persons in each group available for the study to achieve findings of statistical significance. Guidelines do not require a user to hire or promote persons on the basis of group classifications for the purpose of making it possible to conduct a study of fairness, but the user has the obligation otherwise to comply with these guidelines.

(ii) The samples for each group should be comparable in terms of the actual job they perform, length of time on the job where time on the job is likely to affect performance, and other relevant factors likely to affect validity differences; or such factors should be included in the design of the study and their effects identified.

(f) *Continued use of selection procedures when fairness studies not feasible.* If a study of fairness should otherwise be performed, but is not technically feasible, a selection procedure may be used which has otherwise met the validity standards of these guidelines, unless the technical infeasibility resulted from discriminatory employment practices which are demonstrated by facts other than past failure to conform with requirements for validation of selection procedures. However, when it becomes technically feasible for the user to perform a study of fairness and such a study is otherwise called for, the user should conduct the study of fairness.

From "EEOC Guidelines," Equal Employment Opportunity Commission, 1978.

tion. The specific minority groups are African American, Hispanic (Cuban, Spanish, Puerto Rican, or Mexican), Asian, and American Indian. After collecting these forms from 260,000 organizations, the EEOC can estimate broad patterns of discrimination. The EEOC is involved in hundreds of lawsuits concerning discrimination each year.

Although the validity requirements apply specifically to psychological tests, they also apply to other selection devices such as employment forms and interviews. See Focused Example 21-2 for an example. In addition, they apply to other job requirements, including educational and work-experience requirements. In summary, the EEOC guidelines provide clear, unambiguous regulations for the use of any assessment device in the selection of employees.

As you might expect, many employers were furious about the EEOC guidelines. They saw them as additional government interference with their conduct of business and as a means of inhibiting them from hiring the best person for a job. Although one can easily sympathize with their concern about excessive bureaucratic red tape, historical evidence supports the implementation of the guidelines. The basic rationale for the EEOC guidelines was provided by the equal protection clause in the 14th Amendment to the Constitution. Though ratified in the post–Civil War era, the equal protection clause did not strongly affect public policy for nearly 100 years—until the court battles over school desegregation and the activities of the civil rights movement led to the passage of the 1964 Civil Rights Act. Even then, many employers did not follow fair employment practices. The specific EEOC guidelines were therefore necessary to enforce the law. Before these specific guidelines, more than 100 years had passed without employers recognizing the legal requirements of equal protection.

In 1980, the EEOC added specific guidelines on sexual harassment in the workplace. Sexual harassment was defined as unsolicited sexual advances, requests for sexual favors, or any other implicit or explicit conduct that might be interpreted as a condition of an individual's employment. The EEOC ruled that a company is always liable for sexual harassment by supervisors even when company officials are unaware of the problem, but the Supreme Court overturned this policy in a 1986 decision. Nevertheless, the Supreme Court affirmed that sexual harassment is sexual discrimination and underscored the need for employers to eliminate any form of sexual harassment (Wermiel &

Focused Example 21-2

Content Validity and Sexual Harassment During a Paramedic Exam

 The EEOC guidelines make it clear that questions asked on employment tests and during employment interviews must relate to performance on the job. However, not all agencies are in full compliance with this regulation, particularly with regard to job interviews. This noncompliance irritated Sandra Buchanan when she appeared before the Los Angeles City Fire Department to interview for a paramedic job. During the interview, she was asked as much about her sex life as she was about her four years of paramedic training and experience. For example, she was asked: "Have you ever had semi-public sex?" "Have you had sex on the beach?" "Have you had sex in a parked car?" "Have you ever exposed yourself indecently?" "Have you molested any children?" "Do you have any homosexual contacts?"

Buchanan was so disturbed by these questions that she filed a complaint with the Civil Service Commission. In the ensuing investigation, the fire department was asked to show how the questions about sex related to the paramedic job.

Its response was that the questions create stress and therefore give the department a chance to observe how a person handles himself or herself in stressful situations. The department also argued that it needed to delve deeply into the backgrounds of applicants because paramedics are entrusted with important responsibilities. One member of the fire department argued that the question on indecent exposure was necessary because "they have a dormitory situation that is quite different from other jobs; the nature of this job makes some of the questions job related that would not be related in other jobs."

The commission decided that the department had to review the questions and eliminate those that were not job related, then reinterview Buchanan. It appeared that the commission agreed with Buchanan's attorney, who argued, "It is time that the city of Los Angeles stop asking 'How's your sex life?' and get back to the business of finding the most qualified person for the job of Los Angeles paramedic" (*Los Angeles Times*, June 29, 1979).

Trost, 1986). When traveling abroad, some Americans are surprised by evidence of sexual discrimination and the sexist standards apparent in job-selection procedures. Consider the advertisement in Focused Example 21-3.

In November 1991, the 1991 Civil Rights Bill became law. The bill essentially reaffirmed the EEOC guidelines. However, it was a reaction to a trend that had eroded the impact of these guidelines during the 1980s and early 1990s. We shall return to a discussion of the 1991 Civil Rights Bill later in the chapter.

Specific Laws

Other regulatory schemes attempt to control the use of tests. Two examples are the New York Truth in Testing Law of 1979 and the Education for All Handicapped Children Act of 1975.

Focused Example 21-3

Sexism in Other Countries

 The fairness in employment policies that characterizes American and European countries is not observed throughout the world. Consider this advertisement placed in a 1985 Hong Kong newspaper:

> OBEDIENT YOUNG SECRETARY
>
> Very obedient young woman required by American Director of position as Secretary/Personal Assistant. Must be attractive and eager to submit to authority, have good typing and filing skills, and be free to travel. Knowledge of Mandarin an advantage. Most important, she should enjoy following orders without question and cheerfully accept directions. Send handwritten resume on unlined paper and recent photo to G.P.O. Box 6132, Hong Kong.

From Cascio (1987, p. 29).

Truth in testing laws. One of the most controversial measures in the testing field, the New York Truth in Testing Law sprang from an extensive investigation of the Educational Testing Service (ETS) by the New York Public Interest Research Group (NYPIRG). Though it affects other testing companies, the New York law was written specifically for ETS.

In 1948, ETS was created by the College Entrance Examination Board, the American Council on Education, and the Carnegie Foundation. Its original and best-known mission was to create and administer aptitude tests such as the SAT. ETS is responsible for more than 300 testing programs, including the Graduate Management Admission Test (GMAT), the Graduate Record Examination (GRE), the Multi-State Bar Exam, and the Law School Admission Test (LSAT). The assets and income of the company are substantial.

Though apparently upset by the wealth and success of ETS, NYPIRG objected even more to the power ETS wielded. Even now, each year several million persons take tests designed and administered by ETS, and the results of these tests profoundly affect their lives (Brill, 1973, Kiersh, 1979; Levy, 1979). Many educational programs take the scores seriously. Students who score poorly on the LSAT, for example, may be denied entrance to law school; this rejection may eventually affect many important aspects of their lives. Higher scores might have resulted in a higher income, occupational status, and self-esteem for them.

In its investigation, NYPIRG became dissatisfied with the available information on test validity, the calculation of test scores, and the financial accounting of ETS. The Truth in Testing Law addresses these objections by requiring testing companies to (1) disclose all studies on the validity of a test, (2) provide a complete disclosure to students about what scores mean and how they were calculated, and (3) on request by a student, provide a copy of the test questions, the correct answers, and the student's answers.

The first two portions are essentially noncontroversial. The test developers argue that they already disclose all pertinent information on validity and release many public documents highlighting the strengths and weaknesses of their tests. We have written to ETS many times and have never been refused any report. Furthermore, ETS strongly encourages institutions that use its tests to perform local validity studies. Any of these studies can be published in scholarly journals (found in most college libraries) with no interference from ETS. However, NYPIRG provided some evidence that ETS and other testing companies have files of secret data that they do not make public because these data may reflect poorly on the product. The second aspect of the law was included because ETS sometimes reports index scores to schools without telling students how the index was calculated and the exact index value being reported.

The controversial third portion of the law may turn out to decrease the value of testing programs seriously. Requiring that the test questions be returned to students means that the same questions cannot be used in future versions of the test. Several problems have resulted from this policy. First, it decreases the validity of the test. With the items constantly changing, the test essentially becomes a new test each time the items change. As a result, it is impossible to accumulate a record of construct validity.

Second, it is difficult to equate scores across years. For example, a graduate school must often consider students who took the GRE in different years. Because the test itself differs each year, comparing the scores of students who took the test at different times is difficult. Although the bill eventually adopted in New York did allow testing companies to keep some of the items secret for equating purposes, this practice falls short of a satisfactory solution. Equating can be accomplished, but only at the risk of increasing the chances of error.

Third, the most serious problem associated with the disclosure of test items was that it increased the costs to ETS and other testing companies. ETS passes these inflated costs on to the consumer.

ETS does make booklets available to the public that present information on the scoring system, validity, reliability, and standard error of measurement for each of their tests. Each of you, after completing this testing course, will have little difficulty interpreting the manuals, but, as you know, it has taken you a long term of hard study to get to this point. People with no background in testing, though, probably will not comprehend all this information. The authors of the bills fail to recognize that the proper use of tests and test results requires technical training in advanced courses such as psychological testing. After all, we do not expect people to be able to practice medicine without medical school training. Surveys suggest that testing experts agree that primary and secondary schools misuse test scores. Those who do not understand the limitations of tests may rely too much on test scores (Snyderman & Rothman, 1987).

Consider the ultimate impact of the truth in testing legislation. One side argues that the laws have made for a fairer and more honest testing industry.

The other argues that students now have to pay a higher price for a poorer product. As a result of these laws, other tests are given on only a limited number of occasions and test items are not reused. With the distribution of test items, tests are not as thoroughly validated prior to their use as they were 15 years ago. This may cause greater error in selecting students. In addition, continuing the development of the tests has increased expense. Ultimately, students may need to pay more to take a lower quality test. In response to these concerns, ETS argues that the validity of its tests has not declined. In fact, it suggests that the concurrent validity of the tests is still significant (ETS, 1991).

The American Psychological Association has issued a statement expressing a conservative attitude toward truth in testing laws. This statement is summarized in Table 21-1.

The Education for All Handicapped Children Act of 1975. In 1975, Congress passed a law that is having a major impact on the use of psychological tests. PL 94-142 (the 142nd Public Law passed by the 94th Congress) guarantees a publicly financed education to all handicapped children. The law details its main requirement—that an individual education plan be developed for each handicapped child. The additional requirement that the educational characteristics of each handicapped child be assessed necessitates the use of tests. In particular, children may be identified for placement in programs funded through PL 94-142 by the use of psychological tests. For example, tests may

TABLE 21-1

Summary of the American Psychological Association's Statement on Testing Legislation

1. We recommend a "wait and see" period prior to enacting further legislation. The legislation enacted in New York and California has created a situation that can be viewed as a naturally occurring field experiment. A few years of studying this "experiment" are warranted before other legislation is passed or rejected.

2. We strongly support provisions encouraging the dissemination of information about test content, test purpose, validity, reliability, and interpretation of test scores. Test takers should have access to their individual results and interpretative information, especially where such test results are used for educational or employment decisions.

3. We oppose total disclosure of items from low-volume tests or tests where item domains are finite (for instance, measuring specific content areas).

4. We oppose disclosure of tests where interpretation is dependent upon a long history of research (for example, extensive norming); disclosure would result in loss of valid interpretation. This is particularly true of interest and personality measures.

5. In disclosure cases involving large-volume tests testing a broad domain, we recommend at a minimum that only items used to determine test performance be disclosed. Pretesting and equating items should be protected from disclosure.

6. Where disclosure is deemed desirable, we encourage examination of alternative methods of conveying this information to test takers, such as partial disclosure (disclosure of one test after several administrations) or making sample tests available for perusal at a secure location.

7. We urge that any personnel selection or licensing procedure in use should be subject to the same scrutiny as tests, provided that sample size is sufficient for meaningful statistical analyses.

From American Psychological Association Statement on Test Item Disclosure Legislation (August 1983).

be used to identify children for EMR classes, which receive funding under the law.

The law clearly specifies that the tests must be reliable, valid, and nondiscriminatory with regard to the non-English-speaking, the poor, members of minority groups, and the bilingual. A debate has erupted about which tests meet these criteria. Mercer, the creator of the SOMPA (see Chapter 20), argues that her test meets the requirements of the law, whereas the WISC and Stanford-Binet scales do not. In fact, she suggests that the SOMPA system is the only test that conforms to the law (Mercer, 1979). Her critics interpret the law as requiring traditional tests such as the Stanford-Binet and WISC scales and assert that the SOMPA cannot be used under the law (Clarizio, 1979a; Sattler, 1979a).

Some Major Lawsuits

Legislation is not the only way to change policy; other options exist for those with particular conflicts. One option used with increasing frequency is litigation, or the lawsuit. One usually considers this as a last resort for resolving personal conflicts. For example, if you feel you have been wronged, but you cannot persuade those who have offended you through other legal means, you may file a lawsuit. In doing so, you trust the court to make a fair judgment about your case.

There have already been many lawsuits concerning the use of psychological tests, and we expect the number to increase in the years to come. We shall now discuss some of the most important of these. Keep in mind that each of these complex cases involved considerably more evidence than we can cite here.

Early Desegregation Cases

The 14th Amendment requires that all citizens be granted equal protection under the law. At the end of the 19th century, some people argued that segregated schools did not offer such protection. In the famous 1896 case of *Plessy* v. *Ferguson*,[1] the Supreme Court ruled that schools could remain segregated but that the quality of the schools must be equal. This was the much-acclaimed separate-but-equal ruling.

Perhaps the most influential ruling in the history of American public school education came in the case of *Brown* v. *Board of Education*[2] in 1954. In this case, the Supreme Court overturned the *Plessy* v. *Ferguson* decision by ruling that the schools must provide nonsegregated facilities for African-American and white students. In this opinion, the court raised several issues that would eventually affect the use of psychological tests.

---

[1]163 U.S. 537 (1896).
[2]347 U.S. 483 (1954), 349 U.S. 294 (1955).

The most important pronouncement of *Brown* was that segregation denied equal protection. In coming to its decision, the court made extensive use of testimony by psychologists that suggested African-American children could be made to feel inferior if the school system kept the two races separate.

The story of the *Brown* case is well known, but what is less often discussed is the ugly history that followed. Many school districts did not want to desegregate, and the battle over busing and other mechanisms for desegregation continues today in many areas. Many of the current arguments against desegregation are based on fear of children leaving their own neighborhoods or the stress on children who must endure long bus rides. The early resistance to the *Brown* decision was more clearly linked to the racist belief in African-American inferiority.

Stell v. Savannah-Chatham County Board of Education[3]

The most significant reactionary court case occurred when legal action was taken to desegregate the school system of Savannah, Georgia, on behalf of a group of African-American children. The conflict began when the attorneys for two white children intervened. They argued that they were not opposed to desegregating on the basis of race but that African-American children did not have the ability to be in the same classrooms as whites. Testimony from psychologists indicated that the median IQ score for African-American children was 81, whereas that for white children was 101. Because there was such a large difference in this trait (assumed to be genetic), the attorneys argued that it could be to the mutual disadvantage of both groups to teach them in the same schools. Doing so might create even greater feelings of inferiority among African-American children and might create frustration that would eventually result in antisocial behavior.

The court essentially agreed with this testimony and ruled that the district should not desegregate. The judge's opinion reflected his view of the best interest of all the children. Later, this decision was reversed. In doing so, the court used the precedent set forth by *Brown* as the reason for requiring the Savannah district to desegregate. It is important to note that the validity of the test scores—the primary evidence—was never discussed (Bersoff, 1979, 1981).

Hobson v. Hansen[4]

Stell was just one of many cases that attempted to resist the order set forth in the *Brown* desegregation case. Like *Stell*, many of these cases introduced test scores as evidence that African-American children were genetically incapable of learning or being educated in the same classrooms as white children. The

---

[3]210 F. Supp. 667, 668 (S.D. Ga. 1963), rev'd 333 F.2d 55 (5th Cir. 1964), cert. denied, 379 U.S. 933 (1964).
[4]269 F. Supp. 401 (D.D.C. 1967).

courts routinely accepted this evidence. Given the current controversy over the use of psychological tests, it is remarkable that several years passed before the validity of the test scores became an issue.

The first major case to examine the validity of psychological tests was *Hobson* v. *Hansen*. The *Hobson* case is relevant to many current lawsuits. Unlike the early desegregation cases, it did not deal with sending African-American and white children to different schools. Instead, it concerned the placement of children once they arrived at a school. Although the courts had consistently required schools to desegregate, they tended to take a hands-off approach with regard to the placement of students in tracks once they arrived at school.

The *Hobson* case contested the use of group standardized ability tests to place students in different learning tracks. Julius W. Hobson was the father of two African-American children placed in a basic track by the District of Columbia School District. Carl F. Hansen was its superintendent. Within the district, children were placed in honors, regular, general, and basic tracks on the basis of group ability tests. The honors track was designed to prepare children for college, while the basic track focused on skills and preparation for blue-collar jobs. Placement in the basic track made it essentially impossible to prepare for a high-income, high-prestige profession.

In *Hobson,* racial groups were not equally represented among those assigned to the basic track. In effect, the tracking system segregated groups by placing African-American children in the basic track and white children in the other tracks. Psychological tests were the primary mechanism used to justify this separation.

The *Hobson* case was decided in 1967. Just two years before the decision, the Supreme Court had ruled that a group is not denied equal protection by "mere classification" (Bersoff, 1979). Nevertheless, Judge Skelly Wright ruled against the use of the tracking system when based on group ability tests. After extensive expert testimony on the validity of the tests for minority children, the judge concluded that the tests discriminated against them. An interesting aspect of the opinion was that it claimed that grouping would be permissible if based on innate ability. The judge asserted that ability test scores were influenced by cultural experiences, and that the dominant cultural group had an unfair advantage on the tests and thereby gained admission to the tracks that provided the best preparation for high-income, high-prestige jobs.

Diana v. State Board of Education[5]

The decision in *Hobson v. Hansen* opened the door for a thorough examination of the use of standardized tests for the placement of students in EMR tracks. The case of *Diana* has particular implications for the use of standardized tests for bilingual children. Diana was one of nine Mexican-American elementary-

---

[5]C.A. No. C-70 37 RFP (N.D. Cal., filed Feb. 3, 1970).

school children placed in EMR classes on the basis of scores on the WISC or Stanford-Binet test. Representing bilingual children, these nine students brought a class-action suit against the California State Board of Education, contending that the use of standardized IQ tests for placement in EMR classes denied equal protection because the tests were standardized only for whites and had been administered by a non-Spanish-speaking psychometrist. Although only 18% of the children in Diana's school district had Spanish surnames, this group made up nearly one-third of the enrollment in EMR classes.

When tested in English, Diana had achieved an IQ score of only 30. However, when retested in Spanish and English, her IQ bounced to 79, high enough to keep her out of EMR classes. Seven of the other eight plaintiffs also achieved high enough scores on the retest to be taken out of the EMR classes.

When faced with this evidence, the California State Board of Education decided not to take the case to court. Instead, they adopted special provisions for the testing of Mexican-American and Chinese-American children. These provisions included the following: (1) The children would be tested in their primary language. (2) Questions based on certain vocabulary and information that the children could not be expected to know would be eliminated. (3) The Mexican-American and Chinese-American children already assigned to EMR classes would be reevaluated with tests that used their primary language and nonverbal items. (4) New tests would be developed by the state that reflected Mexican-American culture and that were normed for Mexican-American children (Bersoff, 1979). Later studies confirmed that bilingual children do score higher when tested in their primary language (Bergan & Parra, 1979).

The combination of the judgment in *Hobson* and the change in policy brought about by *Diana* forced many to question seriously the use of IQ tests for the assignment of children to EMR classes. However, these decisions were quite specific to the circumstances in the particular cases. *Hobson* dealt with group tests but not individual ones, even though individual tests are used more often than group tests to make final decisions for EMR placement. The ruling in *Diana* was limited to strictly bilingual children. These two cases thus did not apply to African-American children placed in EMR classes on the basis of individual IQ tests. This specific area was left for the most important court battle of them all—*Larry P. v. Wilson Riles.*

Larry P. v. Wilson Riles[6]

In October 1979, Judge Robert Peckham of the Federal District Court for the Northern District of California handed down an opinion that declared that "the use of IQ tests which had a disproportionate effect on Black children

---

[6]343 F. Supp. 1306 (N.D. Cal. 1972), affd 502 F.2d 963 (9th Cir. 1979).

violated the Rehabilitation Act, the Education for All Handicapped Children Act, Title VI, and the 14th Amendment when used to place children in EMR classes." Attorneys for Larry P., one of six African-American elementary-school students assigned to EMR classes on the basis of IQ test results, had argued that the use of standardized IQ tests to place African-American children in EMR classes violated both the California constitution and the equal protection clause of the 14th Amendment (Opton, 1979), as well as the laws mentioned.

The court first ruled in the case of *Larry P.* in 1972. It found that the school district had incorrectly labeled Larry as EMR and violated his right to equal educational opportunity. As a result, a preliminary injunction was issued to prohibit that particular school district from using IQ tests for EMR placement decisions. Later, the California Department of Education called for a temporary moratorium on IQ testing until another court opinion on the validity of the tests could be obtained (Opton, 1977). To this end, the *Larry P.* case came before the same court that had issued the preliminary injunction.

During the trial, both sides geared up for a particularly intense battle. Wilson Riles was the African-American superintendent of public instruction in California; he had instituted many significant reforms that benefited minority children. Thus, it was particularly awkward to have a nationally recognized spokesperson for progressive programs named as the defendant for an allegedly racist scheme.

In defense of the use of tests, Riles and the state called many nationally recognized experts on IQ tests, including Lloyd Humphreys, Jerome Sattler, Robert Thorndike, Nadine Lambert, and Robert Gordon. These witnesses presented extensive evidence that IQ tests, particularly the Stanford-Binet and the WISC (used to test Larry and the others), were not biased against African Americans. Although the tests had not originally been normed for African-American populations, studies had demonstrated that they were equally valid for African-American and white children. (Many of the arguments that support the use of tests for all races are summarized in Chapter 20.) Yet, if the tests were not biased, then why did Larry and the others receive higher scores when they were retested by African-American psychologists? The defense argued that the African-American psychologists did not follow standard testing procedures and that IQ test scores are not changed when standardized procedures are followed.

Statements from special education teachers were also presented. The teachers argued that the children involved in the case could not cope with the standard curriculum and that they required the special tutoring available in the EMR classes. The children had not been learning in regular classes, and the schools investigated classes in which there was doubt about the placement. For all these children, the assignment to EMR classes was deemed appropriate (Sattler, 1979a).

The Larry P. side of the case also had its share of distinguished experts, including George Albee, Leon Kamin, and Jane Mercer. The arguments for

Larry varied widely. His lawyers argued that all humans are born with equal capacity and that any test that assigns disproportionate numbers of children from one race to an EMR category is racist and discriminatory. The witnesses testified that dominant social groups had historically used devices such as IQ tests to discriminate against less powerful social groups and that the school district had intentionally discriminated against African-American children by using unvalidated IQ tests. Specifically, the tests were used to keep African Americans in dead-end classes for the mentally retarded, in which they would not get the training they needed to move up in the social strata. Furthermore, the plaintiffs suggested that labeling someone as EMR has devastating social consequences. Children labeled as EMR lose confidence and self-esteem (Mercer, 1973); eventually, the label becomes a self-fulfilling prophecy (Rosenthal & Jacobson, 1968). In other words, labeling a child as mentally retarded may cause the child to behave as though he or she really is mentally retarded.

Clearly persuaded by the plaintiffs, the judge declared that the tests "are racially and culturally biased, have a discriminatory impact on African-American children, and have not been validated for the purpose of (consigning) African-American children into educationally dead-end, isolated, and stigmatizing classes." Furthermore, the judge stated that the Department of Education had "desired to perpetuate the segregation of minorities in inferior, dead-end, and stigmatizing classes for the retarded."

The effect of the ruling was a permanent discontinuance of IQ testing to place African-American children in EMR classes. The decision immediately affected all African-American California schoolchildren who had been labeled as EMR. More than 6000 of these children had to be reassessed in some other manner.

There are strong differences of opinion about the meaning of the *Larry P.* decision. Harold Dent, one of the African-American psychologists who had retested Larry P. and the other children, hailed the decision as a victory for African-American children:

> For more than 60 years, psychologists had used tests primarily to justify the majority's desire to "track" minorities into inferior education and dead-end jobs. The message of *Larry P.* was that psychologists must involve themselves in the task mandated in the last sentence of the court's opinion: "This will clear the way for more constructive educational reform." (Quoted in Opton, 1979.)

Others did not share the belief that the *Larry P.* decision was a social victory. Nadine Lambert, an expert witness for the state, felt it was a terrible decision: "I think the people who will be most hurt by it are the African-American children" (quoted in Opton, 1979). Banning the use of IQ tests opens the door to completely subjective judgments, perhaps even more racist than the test results. Opponents of the *Larry P.* decision cite many instances in which gifted African-American children were assumed to be average by their teachers but were recognized as highly intelligent because of IQ test scores.

The *Larry P.* decision has been frequently cited in subsequent cases, some of which are actually remote from the issues in *Larry P.* For example, in the case of *Ana Maria R.* v. *California Department of Education*,[7] parental rights were terminated on the grounds that the mother was mentally retarded. However, the mother was Spanish-speaking, and *Larry P.* was cited as precedent that tests used for classification of mental retardation discriminate against African Americans and Hispanics. In contrast to the case of *Ana Maria R.*, the factual situation in an Illinois case strongly resembled that of *Larry P*, as you will see in the following section.

Parents in Action on Special Education v. *Hannon*[8]

Just as the case of *Larry P.* was making headlines in California, a similar case came to trial in Illinois. The case was a class-action lawsuit filed on behalf of two African-American children who had been placed in special classes for the educable mentally handicapped (EMH) on the basis of IQ test scores. Attorneys for the two student plaintiffs argued that the children were inappropriately placed in EMH classes because of racial bias in the IQ tests. They suggested that the use of IQ tests for African-American children violates the equal protection clause of the Constitution and many federal statutes.

In their presentation to the court, the plaintiffs relied heavily on the *Larry P.* decision, which held that the WISC, the WISC-R, and the Stanford-Binet IQ tests are biased and inappropriate for the testing of minority children. However, Judge John Grady came to exactly the opposite conclusion that Judge Robert Peckham had in the *Larry P.* case. Judge Grady found evidence for racial bias in the three major IQ tests to be unconvincing. In his opinion, he noted that the objectionable items comprised only a fraction of the entire test. For example, witnesses for the plaintiffs never mentioned whole subtests on the WISC and WISC-R, such as arithmetic, digit span, block design, mazes, coding, and object assembly. The judge noted that these subtests were not biased in favor of either African-American or white children because most youngsters of both groups would never have confronted problems of this type before. The items for which there were legitimate objections were too few to affect test scores.

Thus, less than one year after the historic *Larry P.* case, another court concluded, "Evidence of racial bias in standardized IQ tests is not sufficient to render their use as part of classification procedures to place African-American children in 'educable mentally handicapped' classes violative of statutes prohibiting discrimination in federal funded programs." Focused Example 21-4 presents conflicting statements from the two judges in these cases.

---

[7]96 U.S. 2040(c) (1976).
[8]USDC NIII; J. Grady pub. 7/7/80.

Focused Example 21-4

Different Opinions from Different Judges

 People often think that two judges looking at the same evidence will come to the same conclusion. However, many times judges differ sharply in this regard. When confronted with different opinions from Judges Peckham (*Larry P.* v. *Wilson Riles*) and Grady (*Parents in Action on Special Education* v. *Hannon*), Sattler (1980) juxtaposed quotes from the two judges on selected issues in the cases. Below are some of the statements demonstrating how differently the judges viewed the issues.

Judge Robert Peckham	Judge John Grady

What are the functions of special classes for the educable mentally retarded or educable mentally handicapped?

"EMR classes are designed to separate out children who are incapable of learning in the regular classes. . . . Further, the curriculum was not and is not designed to help students learn the skills necessary to return to the regular instructional program. . . . Finally, consistent with the first two aspects of EMR classes, the classes are conceived of as 'dead-end classes.' Children are placed there, generally at about eight to ten years of age, because they are thought to be incapable of learning the skills inculcated by the regular curriculum. They are provided with instruction that deemphasizes academic skills in favor of adjustment, and naturally they will tend to fall farther and farther behind the children in the regular classes."

"The EMH curriculum is designed for the child who cannot benefit from the regular curriculum. It is designed for children who learn slowly, who have short attention spans, slow reaction time, and difficulty retaining material in both the short term and the long term. The curriculum also recognizes the difficulty an EMH child has in seeing similarities and differences, in learning by implication, in generalizing and in thinking abstractly. The curriculum thus involves much repetition and concrete teaching. Subjects are taught for short periods of time, in recognition of the children's short attention spans."

How much emphasis is given to the IQ in placing children in mentally retarded or educable mentally handicapped classes?

"The available data suggest very strongly that, even if in some districts the IQ scores were not always determinative, they were pervasive in the placement process. . . . Retardation is defined in terms of the IQ tests, and a low score in effect establishes a *prima facie* case of retardation."

"The IQ score is not the sole determinant of whether a child is placed in an EMH class. First, the score itself is evaluated by the psychologist who administers the test. The child's responses are recorded verbatim, and the significance of his numerical score is a matter involving judgment and interpretation. . . . The examiner who knows the milieu of the child can correct for cultural bias by asking the questions in a sensitive and intelligent way. . . . Finally, the IQ test and the psychologist's evaluation of the child in the light of that test are only one component of several which form the basis for an EMH referral."

Continued

Was the issue of test validity important in the trial?

"If defendants could somehow have demonstrated that the intelligence tests had been 'validated' for the purpose of EMR placement of Black children, those tests could have been utilized despite their disproportionate impact. . . . However, defendants did not make these showings."

"We do not address the broader questions of whether these IQ tests are generally valid as measures of intelligence, whether individual items are appropriate for that purpose, or whether the tests could be improved. Those questions are not involved in this case."

To what extent do socioeconomic factors account for the findings that Black children score lower than White children on intelligence tests?

"It is clear that socioeconomic status by itself cannot explain fully the undisputed disparities in IQ test scores and in EMR placements. . . . The insufficiency of the above explanation leads us to question the cultural bias of IQ tests. The first important inferential evidence is that the tests were never designed to eliminate cultural biases against Black children, it was assumed in effect that Black children were less 'intelligent' than Whites."

"It is uncontradicted that most of the children in the EMH classes do in fact come from the poverty pockets of the city. This tends to suggest that what is involved is not simply race but something associated with poverty. It is also significant that many Black children who take the tests score at levels high enough to preclude EMH placement. Plaintiffs have not explained why the alleged cultural bias of the tests did not result in EMH-level scores for these children. Plaintiffs' theory of cultural bias simply ignores the fact that some Black children perform better than most Whites. Nationally, 15 to 20 percent of the Blacks who take the tests score above the White mean of 100."

To what extent does Black children's use of nonstandard English affect their performance on intelligence tests?

"At the outset, it is undeniable that to the extent Black children speak other than standard English, they will be handicapped in at least the verbal component of the tests. . . . Dr. [Asa] Hilliard and other witnesses pointed out that Black children are more likely to be exposed to nonstandard English, and that exposure will be reflected in IQ scores."

"The evidence does not establish how the use of nonstandard English would interfere with performance on the Wechsler and Stanford-Binet tests. . . . Dr. [Robert J.] Williams testified that a Black child might say, 'John go to town' instead of 'John is going to town,' or 'John book' instead of 'John's book.' . . . What is unclear is how the use of such nonstandard English would handicap a child either in understanding the test items or in responding to them. . . . Moreover, responding to a test item in nonstandard English should not affect a child's score on the item, since the examiners are specifically instructed by the test manuals to disregard the form of the answer so long as the substance is correct. . . . But there are no vocabulary items on the IQ tests, so far as I can tell, which are peculiar to White culture."

To what extent do differences between Black culture and White culture affect Black children's performance on intelligence tests?

"To the extent that a 'Black culture'—admittedly a vague term—exists and translates the phenomenon of intelligence into skills and knowledge untested by the standardized intelligence tests, those tests cannot measure the capabilities of Black children. . . . On the basis of their different cultural background, which results particularly in lower scores on IQ tests, Black children are subjected to discrimination analogous to that borne by many San Francisco Chinese, who, because of their cultural background, could not communicate effectively in English. Certainly many Chinese Americans would succeed in those schools even without remedial English. Nevertheless, the failure to provide English-language teaching foreclosed substantial numbers of students from any meaningful educational opportunity. This same result occurs from the use of IQ tests and a biased placement process."

"Dr. Williams did not explain how he relates the other characteristics of Black culture to performance on the tests. It is not clear, for instance, how the extended family as opposed to the nuclear family would pertain to performance on the tests. Like Dr. [Leon] Kamin's description of the racist attitudes of Goddard, Yerkes and Terman, Dr. Williams's description of African-American culture has not been connected to the specific issue in this case. . . . Dr. Kamin's argument that the Black child does not obtain the same 'information,' and Dr. [George] Albee's argument that the Black child does not share in the dominant White culture, seem inapplicable to most items on all three of the tests in question. As already noted, many of the categories of test items have no precise counterpart in the experience of any children, of whatever race. Others have almost precise counterparts in the everyday experience of American children of all races. Any number of test items could be cited to illustrate this point."

Generally, to what extent are intelligence tests racially biased?

"The answer, as should be clear from the earlier discussion of the history and biases of IQ tests, is that validation has been assumed, not established, for Blacks. The tests were developed and standardized in the United States on White, essentially middle-class groups."

"All but a few of the items on their face appear racially neutral. . . . I conclude that the possibility of the few biased items on these tests causing an EMH placement that would not otherwise occur is practically nonexistent."

Does the use of intelligence tests violate some provisions of Public Law 94-142 (Education for All Handicapped)?

"Defendants have failed to take the steps necessary to assure the tests' validity. They have committed a serious error that Title VII regulations warn against in the employment situation: 'Under no circumstances will the general reputation of a test, its author, or its publisher, or casual reports of test utility be accepted in lieu of evidence of validity.' Whether or not the tests in fact do what they are supposed to do, the law is that defendants must come forward and show that they have been validated for each minority group with which they are used. This minimal burden has not been met for diagnosing the kind of mental retardation justifying EMR placement."

"The requirement that 'materials and procedures' used for assessment be nondiscriminatory, and that no single procedure be the sole criterion for assessment, seems to me to contemplate that the process as a whole be nondiscriminatory. It does not require that any single procedure, standing alone, be affirmatively shown to be free of bias. The very requirement of multiple procedures implies recognition that one procedure, standing alone, could well result in bias and that a system of cross-checking is necessary."

From Sattler (1980).

Crawford et al. v. Honig et al.[9]

In 1986, the court modified the *Larry P.* court order to expand the intelligence testing ban to all African-American children. The California Department of Education and the public interest lawyers who represented Larry P. gained an order from judge Peckham to ban the use of standardized intelligence tests for African-American children for assignment to special education programs. However, African-American children could take intelligence tests to be considered for the state-supported gifted and talented education program (GATE).

After the 1986 strengthening of the *Larry P.* decision, several new problems arose. One of them is represented by the case of *Crawford v. Honig*. Some children do have special needs and may benefit from special education programs. Indeed, such programs were developed to identify learning problems and to provide special assistance. Under the 1986 modification of the *Larry P.* decision, one can evaluate white, Hispanic, Asian-American, and Native-American students with intelligence tests for placement in special education. However, these tests cannot be used for African-American children. In fact, these tests cannot be given to African-American children even if the families request them. Crawford's mother was African-American but her father was not. Recognizing that the child was struggling in school, the mother requested testing.

Citing *Larry P.*, the school denied the request because the child had been identified as African American. However, the mother was told that if she changed the child's racial identification to match the father's, testing would be permitted. The lawsuit that followed claimed that California Superintendent of Public Education Bill Honig and the California Board of Education violated Crawford's civil rights by denying a public service on the basis of race. The arguments in court suggested that a race-conscious testing policy promoted inequities and indignities. Eventually, the case was heard by Judge Peckham, the same judge who had issued the *Larry P.* ruling and the 1986 modification strengthening the original judgment. Crawford's case was vigorously opposed by the California Department of Education. However, since this 1991 case was not a class-action suit, it was uncertain whether or not the ruling would apply to all children. The plaintiffs petitioned the court to extend the judgment to all similar African-American children (Bredemeier, 1991). In September 1992, Judge Peckham issued an order reversing the earlier ban on IQ tests for African-American students.

---

[9]C.A. No. C-89-0014-RFP.

Marchall v. Georgia

One of the first major decisions that opposed the *Larry P.* judgment was *Marchall* v. *Georgia*. This class-action suit was filed in 1981 on behalf of a group of African-American students. Allegedly, students had received unfair treatment by being disproportionately placed in classes for the educable mentally retarded (EMR) and underrepresented in classes for learning disabilities (LD). The defendants in the case were 13 school districts, most in the state of Georgia. The key witness for the plaintiff was Robert Calfee, an educational psychologist from Stanford University. Calfee noted that racial differences accounted for differential performance in school more than socioeconomic status did. Through a series of complex analyses, Calfee concluded that the school experience itself was actually creating differences between groups. Thus, the practice of assigning students to groups was damaging. As a remedy, Calfee suggested that students be assigned to classrooms on a random basis.

The defense argued that, indeed, placement into certain classrooms did provide benefits for students. The court ultimately ruled that the grouping of students was to their benefit. Thus, they allowed the use of tests to separate students because these procedures ultimately resulted in better outcomes. The critical result of the decision was that the focus shifted to emphasize the ultimate benefit to students. An important issue in the case was the focus on curriculum-based assessment rather than IQ testing. Perhaps the most important difference between the *Marchall* decision and previous court cases was the judge's belief that test information could be used to structure interventions that would help the children (*Marchall et al.* v. *Georgia*, 1984, 1985; Reschly, Kicklighter, & McKee, 1988; Reschly & Ward, 1991).

Debra P. v. Turlington[10]

Some people feel that a test is biased if it contains questions that particular test takers cannot answer. One 1979 lawsuit in Florida involved ten African-American students, including Debra P., who had failed in their first attempt to pass Florida's minimum competence test, the State Student Assessment Test. In Hillsborough County, where the suit was filed, about 19% of the students in the public school system were African American; however, African-American students constituted 64% of those who failed the test.

More than 30 states have adopted minimum competence tests similar to the one used in Florida, and 19 states require the exam for graduation. If they meet other requirements, students who do not pass the exam receive a certificate of completion, which acknowledges that they attended high school but does not carry the same status as a high-school diploma. Examples of items from a minimum competence test are shown in Table 21-2.

---

[10] 474 F. Supp. 244 (M.D. Fla. 1979).

TABLE 21-2

Examples of Items from a Minimum Competence Test

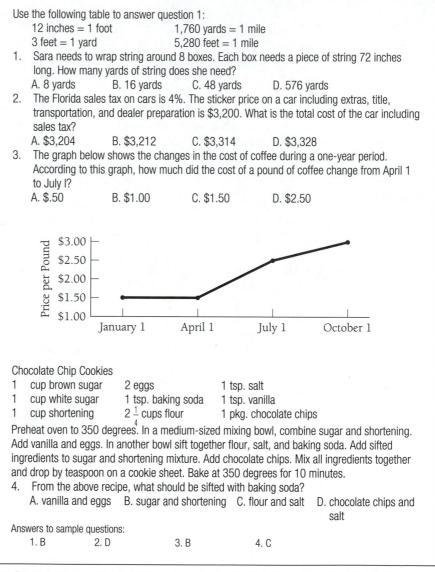

Use the following table to answer question 1:

| 12 inches = 1 foot | 1,760 yards = 1 mile |
| 3 feet = 1 yard | 5,280 feet = 1 mile |

1. Sara needs to wrap string around 8 boxes. Each box needs a piece of string 72 inches long. How many yards of string does she need?

    A. 8 yards   B. 16 yards   C. 48 yards   D. 576 yards

2. The Florida sales tax on cars is 4%. The sticker price on a car including extras, title, transportation, and dealer preparation is $3,200. What is the total cost of the car including sales tax?

    A. $3,204   B. $3,212   C. $3,314   D. $3,328

3. The graph below shows the changes in the cost of coffee during a one-year period. According to this graph, how much did the cost of a pound of coffee change from April 1 to July I?

    A. $.50   B. $1.00   C. $1.50   D. $2.50

Chocolate Chip Cookies

1	cup brown sugar	2 eggs	1 tsp. salt
1	cup white sugar	1 tsp. baking soda	1 tsp. vanilla
1	cup shortening	2 $\frac{1}{4}$ cups flour	1 pkg. chocolate chips

Preheat oven to 350 degrees. In a medium-sized mixing bowl, combine sugar and shortening. Add vanilla and eggs. In another bowl sift together flour, salt, and baking soda. Add sifted ingredients to sugar and shortening mixture. Add chocolate chips. Mix all ingredients together and drop by teaspoon on a cookie sheet. Bake at 350 degrees for 10 minutes.

4. From the above recipe, what should be sifted with baking soda?

    A. vanilla and eggs   B. sugar and shortening   C. flour and salt   D. chocolate chips and salt

Answers to sample questions:

| 1. B | 2. D | 3. B | 4. C |

From *State Student Assesment Test. Part II: Answers to your Questions.* Reprinted with permission of the State of Florida, Department of Education.

The Florida suit charged that the test should not be used for those minority students taught primarily in segregated schools. Thus, the dispute was over whether the same test should be used for students with unequal opportunities to learn in school. Attorneys for the students argued that their clients had attended inferior schools and had suffered continued discrimination; thus, they should not be held to the standards for majority students, who had received better opportunities.

Ralph D. Turlington was the commissioner of education and one of the defendants in the case. He argued that basic minimum standards must be applied to certify that students have enough information to survive in situations that require high-school level sophistication. These standards, he argued, must be absolute. Either students know the basic information or they do not. According to the commissioner, "To demand that a 12th-grade student with a 3rd-grade reading level be given a diploma is silly."

The Florida case illustrates the kind of lawsuit we might expect in the future. It pits two sides with reasonable arguments against each other. One side argues that minority children have worked hard in school under great disadvantage and cannot be expected to have learned the things majority children know. In recognition of their work, they deserve a diploma. The other side argues that there should be an absolute standard for basic information (Seligmann et al., 1979).

The court essentially sided with the commissioner. The judge did not challenge the validity of the test. However, he did suspend the use of the test for four years, after which all the students who had any part of their education in segregated schools would have graduated. Then, according to the opinion, the test could be used.

In a 1981 article, Lerner argued that minimum competence exams, such as the SSAT II used in the state of Florida, benefit both students and society. As an attorney, she found little legal justification for court involvement. However, the court reopened the *Debra P.* case that same year. This new consideration came after those students who had begun their education under a segregated system had graduated, and thus differences in performance could not be attributed to segregation. In the new evaluation, the U.S. District Court of Appeals considered the validity of the test. It stated that the test would violate the equal protection clause if "the test by dividing students into two categories, passers and failers, did so without a rational relation to the purpose for which it was designed, then the Court would be compelled to find the test unconstitutional." [11]However, in this case, the court concluded that the test did have adequate construct validity and that it could be used to evaluate functional literacy. In the same opinion, the court stressed that the test must reflect what is taught in school and that continual surveillance of test fairness is warranted.

---

[11]474 F. Supp. 260.

Regents of the University of California v. Bakke[12]

Alan Bakke was an engineer in his 30s who decided to apply to medical school at the University of California, Davis, in the early 1970s. Although Bakke had a high grade point average and good MCAT scores, he was denied admission. Bakke decided to investigate the matter. He discovered that his test scores were higher than those of minority students who had gained admission to the medical school under a special affirmative action program. Bakke eventually sued the university on the grounds that he had been discriminated against because he was not a minority group member. The suit ended in the Supreme Court.

Of the many arguments presented in the *Bakke* case, a major one concerned the use of test scores. Under the affirmative action program, the cutoff value for MCAT scores was higher for nonminority than for minority students. The defense argued that the tests were not meaningful (valid) for minority students. However, evidence was also presented that the tests were equally meaningful for both groups.

The Supreme Court ruling did not specifically address the use of tests, but ruled that the university had to admit Bakke and that it had denied him due process in the original consideration of the case. It also implied that the use of different cutoff scores was not appropriate. However, the court did acknowledge that race could be taken into consideration in selection decisions. The EEOC interpreted this acknowledgement as a green light for affirmative action programs based on numerical quotas (Norton, 1978). However, the *Bakke* case signified a change in attitude about affirmative action programs.

As President, Ronald Reagan openly opposed selection goals and affirmative action and made a political issue out of "racial quotas." In the 1980s, Reagan appointed several people to key positions who agreed with his beliefs. For example, his assistant attorney general for civil rights, Bradford Reynolds, became an advocate for unqualified individualism (see Chapter 20). He argued for "color blind" equal opportunity in which skin color is not considered in selection decisions. According to Reynolds, selecting African Americans with lower test scores to remediate past discrimination would be "borrowing the tools of the racist." He emphasized that government must "never support the use of quotas or any other numerical formulas" (Bareak & Lauter, 1991, p. A18). Many Reagan appointees held similar beliefs. Even the Reagan-appointed director of the EEOC stressed the importance of individual qualifications over racial identification. Thus, by the late 1980s and early 1990s, the mood toward affirmative action had changed. This mood change has most clearly affected personnel cases.

---

[12]438 U.S. 265, 17 Fair Empl. Prac. Cas. (BNA) 1000 (1978).

Golden Rule Insurance Company et al. v. Washburn et al.

In 1976, the Golden Rule Insurance Company of Lawrenceville, Illinois, sued the Educational Testing Service (ETS) and the Illinois Department of Insurance over "cultural bias" in the Illinois Insurance Licensing Examination, created by the ETS for the state of Illinois. A 1978 study showed that 77% of white applicants passed the exam, while only 52% of African Americans passed. The case was settled out of court. ETS made no admission of guilt but did agree to change the test, mainly in the way items are selected for the test. An expert committee of insurance officials and testing experts now oversee the selection of the items, now selected on the criterion that the proportions of correct answers for white and African-American test takers differ by no more than .15.

When the *Golden Rule* case was settled in 1984, civil rights experts predicted that there would be a major revision in the way insurance tests were administered in 22 other states. About 200,000 applicants for insurance licenses take these tests every year ("Insurance License Exams . . . ," 1984, p. 5). In 1985, a related case (*Allen v. Alabama State Board of Education*[13]) followed similar lines of reasoning. However, in this case, a much more stringent rule was used. The Alabama State Board of Education agreed to use items for which the African-American/white proportion of correct answers differed by no more than .05. The *Golden Rule* case is important because it sets a new precedent within the testing industry. Although ETS admitted no guilt, it clearly agreed to revise its method of operation. (See Focused Example 21-5.)

Adarand Constructors, Inc. v. Pena, Secretary of Transportation et al.[14]

In 1995, the U.S. Supreme Court weakened the legal basis for affirmative action. The case which involved Adarand Constructors, Inc., which was competing for a subcontract from the federal government. Prior to 1995, most federal contracts had included a compensation clause giving the primary contractor a financial incentive to hire as subcontractors small businesses controlled by socially and economically disadvantaged individuals. This particular case involved a contract from the U.S. Department of Transportation. After submitting the low bid to complete construction work, Adarand Constructors, Inc. was denied the job in favor of a small business controlled by minority group members. The Supreme Court, by a vote of 5–4, suggested that giving business to firms owned by minority group members violated the equal protection component of the 14th Amendment. This policy, the court argued, denied Adarand and other contractors their due process. The decision had immediate impact. Hundreds of millions of dollars in federal grants were awarded under special

---

[13]612 Fed Supp 1046 (1985).
[14]115 U.S. 2097 (1995).

Focused Example 21-5

The Twists and Turns of University Affirmative Action Policies

 Federal regulation of college admissions policies has taken many interesting twists and turns. Initially, affirmative action policies were designed to guarantee that institutions of higher learning would be ethnically diverse. Indeed, most disciplinary actions have been taken because universities had not successfully attracted an ethnically diverse student body. However, some institutions have been very successful. For example, Boalt Hall, the School of Law at the University of California, Berkeley, has made aggressive efforts to attract an ethnically diverse student body. In the class of 1996 (made up of students admitted in 1992), 39% of the students were from minority groups.

In September 1992, Boalt Hall's admissions policies came under scrutiny. The U.S. Department of Education's Office of Civil Rights argued that the university had engaged in policies inconsistent with Title VI of the 1964 Civil Rights Act in that the law school had allowed discrimination on the basis of race, color, or national origin. Because Boalt Hall set aside a portion of their entering class positions for minority students and used separate decision processes for minority and nonminority students, it was argued that discrimination was taking place against Asians and to some extent Caucasians.

When faced with the complaint, the university agreed to alter their admissions policies. They were required to report by 1994 the number of applicants in each racial and ethnic category and to list how many of these applicants were admitted. By the time the 1994 report was completed, the university faced several similar lawsuits. In 1995 the Regents of the University decided to end their affirmative action programs.

From Merl & Trombley, (1992).

preference programs. The ultimate impact of the decision on affirmative action programs will be determined by future policies and decisions.

University of California Board of Regents Decision

In addition to the *Adarand* case, other policy decisions have weakened affirmative action. For example, in the summer of 1995 the Regents of the University of California voted to end affirmative action programs within the university. In particular, the regents passed a resolution suggesting that race, per se, could not be considered a factor in the university hiring or admissions policies. The impact of these decisions has yet to be assessed.

Personnel Cases

Though most of the cases we have discussed involved educational tests, several other important lawsuits have dealt with testing in employment settings. Through a series of Supreme Court decisions, specific restrictions have been placed on the use of tests for the selection of employees. The most important of these cases are *Griggs* v. *Duke Power Company*,[15] *Albemarle Paper Company* v. *Moody*,[16] and *Washington* v. *Davis*.[17] Effectively, these decisions have forced employers to define the measure of job performance as well as how it relates to test scores. However, none of the decisions denies that tests are valuable tools in the personnel field and that the use of tests can continue.

In Chapter 5, we mentioned *Griggs* v. *Duke Power Company*. The case involved 14 African-American employees of the Duke Steam Plant in North Carolina who were concerned about their lack of opportunity. In the steam plant, few employees, either African-American or white, had graduated from high school. In 1966, the most an African-American employee could earn was $1.65 per hour, while whites started at $1.81. Furthermore, white men generally rose through the ranks of the company and became managers or supervisors, with comfortable offices and bathrooms down the hall. Though assigned to clean the toilets in those bathrooms, African-American men were not allowed to use them. Instead, the company built a "colored" bathroom and placed it across the railroad tracks behind the coal pile. The leader of the African-American employees, Willie Boyd, had learned about the EEOC and become acquainted with a civil rights leader who persuaded Boyd and his co-workers to file a complaint. When they presented their complaint to the company, they were told that education and training were necessary for advancement. Yet, few African-American or white employees had much educational background. In fact, only 15 white employees had finished high school. The company reacted by creating a test and telling the African-American employees that they needed to pass it in order to gain advancement. The test included 50 items such as this:

> In printing an article of 24,000 words, a printer decides to use two sizes of type. With the larger type, a printed page contains 900 words. With the smaller type, a page contains 1200 words. The article is allotted 21 full pages in the magazine. How many pages must be in small type?

None of the African-American employees passed this difficult test. Neither did any of the white employees. The validity of the test became the central issue in the lawsuit that followed. Specifically, evidence was required on the relationship between the test and the job duties. Although Boyd led the group, the lawsuit was filed under the name of Willie Griggs, the youngest of the group with the least seniority and the least to lose. After five years, the case worked its way to the U.S. Supreme Court, which ruled that employment tests must be valid and reliable. The *Griggs* case set the tone for the next two decades of civil rights action in the United States (Bareak & Louter, 1991).

---

[15]401 U.S. 424(a) (1971).
[16]442 U.S. 405 (1975).
[17]96 U.S. 2040(c) (1976).

In the 1988 Supreme Court case, *Watson v. Fort Worth Bank and Trust*[18], it was argued that any procedure that appears to discriminate because of the ratio of minorities selected violates the law. The case involved Clara Watson, an African American employee of the Fort Worth Bank and Trust. After being passed over for promotion to a supervisory position, Watson filed suit. She argued that African-Americans made up 13% of the bank's work force and 10% of Forth Worth's population. However, the bank had only one African-American supervisor. Thus, there was a misrepresentation in selection for higher jobs. The lower courts had rejected Watson's petition, arguing that statistical evidence for bias applied only to objective selection devices, such as psychological tests, and that subjective judgments could be defended when there was evidence of "business necessity." The Supreme Court disagreed, suggesting that employers could protect themselves from discrimination suits by adding just one subjective item to objective tests. The court affirmed that statistical selection ratios are sufficient evidence of adverse impact.

Sometimes trends in one direction spur reactions in another. The *Watson* case was among the first important civil rights cases that had been decided by a conservative group of Supreme Court justices. Unhappy with the trend set in earlier decisions, the Reagan administration emphasized the "color blind" selection of employees. The next major case that came to the court was *Wards Cove Packing Company v. Antonio.*[19] The case concerned salmon canneries in Alaska. Most of the workers were nonskilled Filipinos and Eskimos who sliced up the fish during fishing season. Because these jobs were unsteady and dirty, they were the worst in the company. The employees claimed that the company was biased against them and kept them out of the better-paying skilled jobs such as machinery repair. The nine Supreme Court justices decided not to hear the case, returning it to the lower courts. This decision reversed a central theme of the *Griggs* decision. In refusing to hear the case, the court noted that the burden of proof should be shifted from the employer to the employee. In other words, instead of requiring the employer to show that a psychological test is valid and reliable, the burden fell to the employee to demonstrate that it did not have these properties. This may seem like a minor point, but in practice it could have had an enormous impact. Employers know how to interpret their own tests, financial records, and selection procedures. Requiring the plaintiff to discredit these procedures gives him or her an almost impossible task. Even the most skilled lawyers felt that the long fight for equal employment opportunity had been lost (Bareak & Louter, 1991).

The *Wards Cove Packing Company v. Antonio* decision upset the Democratic-controlled 1991 Congress. Both the House and the Senate introduced new legislation. For example, the Senate enacted Senate Bill 45 of the 102nd Congress and stated specifically that the Supreme Court decision had weakened

---

[18]Los Angeles Times, June 30, 1988, Part 1, pp. 1, 16.
[19]490, U.S. 642 (1989).

the scope and effectiveness of federal civil rights protection. In response to court actions, they felt that new and stronger legislation was required. The purposes of the 1991 Civil Rights Act are listed here:

1. Provide appropriate redress for intentional discrimination and unlawful harassment in the workplace.
2. Overrule proof burdens and the meaning of business necessity in *Wards Cove Packing Company* v. *Antonio* and codify the proof burdens and the meaning of business necessity used in *Griggs* v. *Duke Power Company*.
3. Confirm the basic aspects of the 1964 Civil Rights Act.
4. Provide a clear response to the Supreme Court decision.

The bill placed the burden of proof back on the employer.

One provision of the 1991 Civil Rights Act deals specifically with test scores. Section 9—"Prohibition Against Discriminatory Use of Test Scores"—states,

> It shall be an unlawful employment practice for a respondent in connection with the selection or referral of applicants or candidates for employment or promotion to adjust the scores of, use different cutoff scores, or otherwise alter the results of employment related tests on the basis of race, color, religion, sex, or natural origin.

This part of the bill appears to outlaw the use of differential cutoff scores by race, gender, or ethnic background; thus, it may cause a shift away from the use of quotas.

The early 1990s saw the beginning of a new type of lawsuit. Affirmative action programs did not necessarily benefit all minority groups. For example, Asian students have historically done very well on college admissions tests such as the SAT. Some people have argued that affirmative action programs systematically discriminate against both minority and majority students. In 1991, a California congressman requested an investigation of the University of California in San Diego (UCSD). The university admits about 60% of its first-year class according to grade point average and SAT scores. Admission to the university is extremely competitive. Those who are admitted often have a nearly perfect grade point average and high SAT scores. However, 40% of the spots are reserved for students admitted under special considerations, including special achievements in fields such as music, athletics, or student government. In addition, the supplemental criteria can include race and ethnicity. Students admitted under these criteria are often from traditionally underrepresented groups such as Latinos and African Americans. The USCD case was initiated by a Filipino student denied admission under both standard and supplemental criteria. However, if all students had been admitted under the standard criteria, this student would probably have been admitted, because both his grade point average and SAT scores were high. The congressman argued that Asian Americans had been systematically denied admission

Focused Example 21-6

Different Views of Affirmative Action

African Americans and whites differ in their views of affirmative action. For example, a 1991 poll conducted by the *Los Angeles Times* suggested that nearly two-thirds of whites felt that affirmative action was either adequate or had gone too far. One-third thought that it had not gone far enough. Among African-American respondents, 60% felt that it had not gone far enough.

On average, African Americans have less desirable jobs, income, and housing than whites. Sixty-five percent of African-American respondents said that discrimination was the cause of this problem, while only 33% of whites came to the same conclusion. These data, shown in the accompanying bar graphs, suggest important attitudinal differences between African Americans and whites that we must address to resolve these problems.

effectively increased the number of African American and other underrepresented groups in various jobs. The increase in African Americans in professional jobs over the last few decades is undeniable. However, some believe that the trend was established prior to affirmative action programs. For example, there was a sharp increase in the percentage of African Americans in professional and technical jobs prior to the 1964 Civil Rights Act. Since then the slope of the trend in technical and professional jobs has been less steep and appears unaffected by the *Griggs* decision and the EEOC guidelines (see line graph) (Herrnstein & Murray, 1994). However, one cannot assume that the *Griggs* decision and the Civil Rights Act did not affect the hiring of African Americans. It is possible that the number of African Americans in professional jobs would have reverted back to the 1960s level had these programs not helped.

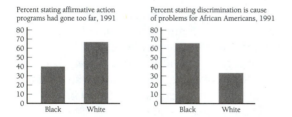

In addition to differences of opinion about whether affirmative action is fair, opinion differs about how effective these programs have been. Most observers believe that the programs have

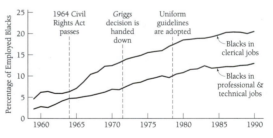

Sources: Bureau of Labor Statistics 1983, 1989; U.S. Department of Labor 1991. Figures prior to 1973, reported for "blacks and others," are adjusted pro-rata to the black-only population.

because of their race. They did not receive extra consideration under the supplemental criteria because they were not underrepresented in the first 60% of students selected. On the other hand, their test scores and grade point averages were higher than other minority-group members who were selected under the special admissions policies.

Focused Example 21-7

Coaching and the Bias in Aptitude Tests

 One criticism of standardized achieve-ment tests is that coaching may improve performance. So widespread is this belief that SAT, LSAT, and GRE preparatory schools have become a big business. If coaching does improve performance on these tests, then they are not really aptitude tests but achieve-ment tests. Those who believe that coaching works have accused the ETS of bias and fraud because its tests do not measure pure aptitude.

One major problem with studies on coaching is that few of them include a proper control group. Thus, when students improve after coaching classes, it is not clear whether this was due to the coaching, their commitment to improve perfor-mance (as evidenced by enrollment in the course), or some other personality characteristic associated with taking a coaching course. The few studies with proper control groups show a small but significant gain in performance as a function of obtaining coaching, but is the small gain worth the effort?

Systematic reviews of the coaching literature suggest that the more time spent in preparation for the test, the greater the increase in score. However, the relationship is nonlinear. Small increases in preparation time result in some improvement in test performance, but as preparation time increases, lesser returns in performance are realized. Accord-ing to Messick and Jungeblut (1981, p. 191), who completed the review, "the student contact time required to achieve average score increases much greater than 20 to 30 points (on a 200- to 800-point scale) for both the SAT-V and the SAT-M rapidly approaches that of full-time schooling."

Despite these studies, ETS critics still maintain that coaching is useful. Owen (1985), for example, suggested that coaching schools can improve scores by teaching skills in multiple-choice test taking. He cited one test preparation course that has achieved success by teaching students to analyze answer choices. In some cases, students can im-prove their scores without even studying alternative choices and without referring to the questions. Rebuffing the ETS claim that coaching makes little difference, Owen pointed out that ETS itself sells (at a hand-some price) its own version of coaching booklets.

Similar complaints were filed at other University of California campuses. The university's defense was that it does not discriminate on the basis of race. Selection criteria are not ironclad. In other words, the university reserves the right to have some flexibility in its decision to select students. Ethnic diversity, they argue, is an appropriate goal for a public university. (See Focused Exam-ples 21-6 and 21-7). In 1995, the Regents of the University of California voted to give up all affirmative action programs.

The courts have also been asked to decide on issues of test administration. For example, because of a low test score, an employee of the Detroit Edison Company was not promoted. In his defense, his union suggested that the low score might have been an error and requested a copy of the test to check the scoring. Detroit Edison did not want to release the test because it feared that the union would distribute the items to other employees. By a vote of five to four, the Supreme Court ruled on the side of Detroit Edison (*Detroit Edison Co.*

v. *N.L.R.B.*[20]). It is interesting that in a major decision such as this, a single vote can make a difference in policy (Cronbach, 1980).

A 1982 Supreme Court decision (*Connecticut* v. *Teal*[21]) considered the issue of discrimination against an individual when there has been no adverse impact. In this case, a written test unrelated to any specific job was used as an initial screening device. This screening device significantly reduced the number of African Americans in the application pool. However, at the next step in the screening process, African Americans who had passed the test had a better chance of being hired than whites. In short, the total number of African Americans hired did not reflect an adverse impact.

On review of the situation, the U.S. Supreme Court ruled that Title VII protects individuals, not just the groups to which they belong. Thus, it ruled that African-American applicants had been discriminated against by the use of a test that did not have validity for the particular job. The court suggested that these individuals were not compensated just because other members of their minority group received favorable treatment if they could pass the initial test. In other words, one cannot defensibly argue that a particular result justifies discrimination against individuals. In more recent decisions, the court has upheld hiring goals that favor formerly underrepresented groups as interim relief for past discrimination while new and more valid selection procedures are being established (*United States* v. *City of Buffalo*, 1985). In one summary article, Hogan and Quigley (1986) reviewed all the cases involving physical standards used in employment decisions.[22] Physical tests, including height, weight, and physical strength, must be subjected to the same validity criteria as psychological tests. Reviewers expect many future lawsuits to arise concerning these issues.

A major issue that has plagued job discrimination cases is the evidence that one can use to prove bias. Proof of discrimination has often been difficult. In blue-collar jobs, employers have defended their hiring practices on the basis of the validity of aptitude tests. Challenges were typically based on the test criterion validity and the ratio of minority applicants that the test selected. In contrast, decisions about the selection and advancement of people in white-collar jobs have been based on subjective impressions of job performance and interviews. This promotes a double standard. White-collar employees have promoted the use of tests, even though tests are not used for blue-collar evaluations.

Cases Relevant to the Americans with Disabilities Act

One of the major challenges in test administration was created by the passage of the Americans with Disabilities Act (ADA) in 1991. The major focus of the

---

[20]99 S. Ct. 1123 (1979).
[21]102 S. Ct. 2525 (1982).
[22]37 U.S. 628 (W.D.N.Y. 1985).

ADA is the removal of physical barriers in work places that make it difficult for people with disabilities to gain employment and education. However, according to some interpretations of the act, people with learning or other disabilities may request accommodations including substantially more time, rest breaks, or testing over multiple days.

The ADA, in effect, made private entities responsible for the same requirements public agencies had addressed under Section 504 of the 1973 Rehabilitation Act. Section 504 creates a specific conflict with regard to testing:

> A recipient (of federal funds) shall make reasonable accommodations to the known physical or mental limitations of an otherwise qualified handicapped applicant or employee unless the recipient can demonstrate that the accommodation would impose an undue hardship on the operation of its program.

This passage has been interpreted to mean that those with disabilities should be afforded extra time or other accommodations in the completion of psychological or achievement tests. This policy contrasts with the APA Standards for Educational and Psychological Tests, which states,

> In typical applications, test administrators should follow carefully the standardized procedures for administration and scoring specified by the test publisher. Specifications regarding instructions to test takers, time limits, a form of item presentation or response, and test materials or equipment should be strictly observed. Exceptions should be made only on the basis of carefully considered professional judgment, primarily in clinical applications (P-83). (Geisinger, 1994)

The Americans with Disabilities Act has provoked a variety of lawsuits. One of the earliest cases, *Brock Brookhart* v. *Illinois State Board of Education* (1983) concerned minimum competency tests. Because they failed a minimum competency test, several disabled students were denied high-school diplomas. They filed a lawsuit arguing that they had completed individualized educational programs and, therefore, qualified for a diploma. The test, they argued, denied them due process. In particular, the disabled students, including those with learning disabilities, may have had difficulty completing the test within the required time. In their decision, the federal court suggested that schools must provide accommodations for disabled students. However, the court argued that the test administrator did not have to modify the test substantially. Further, the court noted that the test need not be modified to assure a passing grade for a person unable to learn because of a disability. On the other hand, the court left unanswered many decisions about the degree of accommodation required of test administrators.

Following the *Brookhart* case, there have been several other challenges. For example, in one case, the Hawaii Department of Education refused to allow a reader to assist a learning disabled boy in a statewide graduation test. Because the student did not have impaired vision, the court decided that the use of a reader for the reading portions of the test would be inappropriate; that is, the decision by the Hawaii Department of Education was not discriminatory. However, the court also concluded that readers could be provided for aspects of the test that did not measure reading competency. Further, the ruling suggested that denying a reader for these portions of the test did constitute unlawful discrimination against those with disabilities (Phillips, 1994).

A Critical Look at Lawsuits

As surely as the sun rises, court battles over the use of psychological tests will continue to develop. The problems that psychologists cannot resolve themselves will eventually be turned over to someone else for a binding opinion. This move, though, may not be in the best interest of the field of psychology or of the people whom the profession serves.

As Lerner (1979) notes, inconsistencies in court decisions are commonplace. Even worse, judges who make important decisions about the use of tests often have little background in psychology or testing. On completing this course, you should be better able to evaluate most of the evidence than some judges who ultimately make the decisions in courtrooms. Often, judges obtain their entire education about testing during the course of a trial.

In the near future, society must grapple with many difficult issues. For example, many current social problems seem related to the differential distribution of resources among the races in the United States. Changing the income distribution seems to be one of the only ways to effect social change. To accomplish this redistribution, society must get minority children in appropriate educational tracks, into professional schools, and into high-income positions. The courts have ruled that psychological tests are blocking this progress.

Psychologists themselves are not of one mind regarding the use of psychological tests. Though some researchers do not agree with the predominant court opinion, the courts have the power, and their judgment is the law.

Summary

With increasing frequency, tests are coming under legal regulation. One of the major sets of regulations has been provided by the EEOC. This commission, created by the Civil Rights Act of 1964, has issued strict guidelines for the use of tests. The guidelines clearly spell out the minimum criteria for validity and reliability of psychological measures. The role of the EEOC became the focus of considerable debate in the 1980s, and the power of the commission was questioned by two court decisions at the end of that decade. However, the 1991 Civil Rights Bill reaffirmed commitment to affirmative action programs.

Tests have also come to be regulated by statute. The states of California and New York were among the first to pass truth in testing laws that place many requirements on commercial testing companies. These laws have required testing companies to disclose actual test items to test takers. In the past, test items were protected by copyright. Items on tests affected by these laws must now be rewritten frequently, and this procedure may damage the reliability and the validity of the tests. In 1975, Congress passed PL 94-142, which outlined standards for the assessment of potential among handicapped children. This law continues to affect the use of tests in the educational system.

Many lawsuits have also affected the use of tests. In *Stell v. Savannah-Chatham County Board of Education*, the court ruled that differences between African Americans and whites in IQ scores could not justify segregation. In *Hobson v. Hansen*, group tests were found to be inappropriate for the assignment of African-American children to EMR classes. The concern over IQ tests was extended in *Diana v. State Board of Education*. This case, settled out of court, established that IQ tests could not be used with bilingual children, and it stimulated the development of new methods of assessment for these children. The impact of each of these decisions was magnified in *Larry P. v. Wilson Riles*, in which tests were banned as a means of assigning African-American children to EMR classes. In 1980, a court apparently reversed this decision in the case of *Parents in Action on Special Education v. Hannon*. In *Debra P. v. Turlington*, a court ruled that a minimum competence test could be used only when the students had received their entire education in integrated schools. The courts have created new challenges in the *Adarand* case, which eliminated affirmative action.

The regulation of testing through statute (laws passed by legislators), regulation (rules created by agencies), and litigation (lawsuits) has only recently become common. The passage of the Americans with Disabilities Act is one example of a set of laws likely to affect the testing industry. One can expect more interactions between testing and the law.

CHAPTER 22

The Future of Psychological Testing

LEARNING OBJECTIVES

When you have completed this chapter, you should be able to

- Explain why the question of whether people possess stable traits is an issue in the testing field

- Explain the issue of actuarial versus clinical prediction

- Identify human rights as they pertain to testing

- Explain the problem of labeling

- Explain the issue of divided loyalties

- Identify some important responsibilities of test users and constructors

- Identify four important current trends in the testing field

- Describe the future prospects of testing

*I*n a special issue of *Psychological Assessment,* specialists in psychological test-ing received a glimpse of the field's future (Haynes, 1995). This future involves the assimilation of new concepts such as chaos theory, nonlinear dynamical models, and mathematical models recently applied to fields such as economics, ecology, biology, and physics (Haynes, Blaine, & Meyer, 1995; Heiby, 1995a, 1995b). Indeed, the future of testing will depend on the appli-cation of ultramodern theoretical notions and technologies. Of all these tech-nologies, the high-speed computer clearly presents the key to this future. To discuss the future of testing, we must not only look ahead, but also remain cognizant of the many interacting, and sometimes conflicting, issues that presently shape the field.

No one can predict the future with certainty. However, by examining cur-rent trends in conjunction with the forces shaping the testing field, we can deepen our understanding of testing and venture a few educated guesses about its future. Keep in mind that the forces influencing this future do not operate in isolation but rather interact with one another in highly complicated ways, even though we treat each separately here.

Pressures Shaping the Field of Testing

The pressures currently shaping the testing field include professional issues, moral issues, ethical issues, and social issues.

Professional Issues

Three major professional issues play an especially important role in the cur-rent status and the future of psychological testing: theoretical concerns, the adequacy of tests, and actuarial versus clinical prediction.

Theoretical concerns. One of the most important considerations underlying tests is the dependability (reliability) of test results. Reliability places an upper limit on validity. According to the *Standards for Educational and Psychological Testing* of the American Education Research Association, the American Psycho-logical Association, and the National Council on Measurement in Education (AERA et al., 1985; see also APA, 1974), a test that is totally unreliable (unsta-ble) has no meaning. There may be exceptions to this rule (J. W. Atkinson, 1981), but current practice generally demands that tests possess some form of stability. As a corollary, whatever is being measured must itself have stability. When one says that a test has reliability, one implies that test results are attrib-utable to a systematic source of variance, which is stable itself. In other words, the test is presumed to measure a stable entity. There are various types of relia-bility, depending on the different purposes of the tests. Each test must possess the type of reliability appropriate to the test's uses (AERA et al., 1985; APA, 1974).

Most existing tests measure a presumably stable entity—either the individual as he or she presently functions or some temporally stable characteristic of the individual. In measuring current functioning, one may say something like, "The person is emotionally unstable" or "The person is out of contact with reality," or else one may provide a diagnostic label such as "schizophrenic" or "neurotic." In describing current functioning, psychologists imply that the person functions this way in a fairly stable, though perhaps short-term, manner, independent of the situation or environment. In other words, they assume that they can describe the person in absolute terms, as if in a vacuum, independent of external factors. Similarly, and even more strikingly, when psychologists purport to measure a temporally stable characteristic of an individual, they assume that they are measuring an enduring quality that will manifest itself over time regardless of immediate or long-term external (situational, environmental, and so forth) factors. Again, they assume that what they are measuring exists in absolute terms.

Whether measuring current functioning or a temporally stable characteristic, one always assumes that the systematic source of variance measured by the test is due entirely to the person as opposed to some other factor. When one tries to measure a stable characteristic of an individual and finds less than perfect temporal reliability, one assumes that the imperfections proceed from test-related inadequacies, such as measurement error, or from minor fluctuating subject variables, such as fatigue. Presumably, then, the characteristic or variable being measured is stable, it exists, and only the test instrument limits one's ability to measure it. Therefore, the more accurate a test, the more stable the results should be.

In simple terms, testers assume that people possess stable characteristics (for example, intelligence) and stable response tendencies (for example, traits) that hold up across situations and exist independent of the environment. However, many empirical investigations (Cacioppo, Berntson, & Anderson, 1991; Rowe, 1987) show that even the best tests have yet to achieve such temporal stability. That is, testers cannot readily attribute differences over time solely to measurement error or fluctuating subject variables. Hence, this primary assumption underlying tests is not entirely correct. Moreover, the social environment affects behavior, as illustrated in a model by Cacioppo, Berntson, and Anderson (1991) that shows the relationship between the psychological and the physiological domain. (See Figure 22-1.)

The trait question applies to psychology as a whole and to personality psychology in particular. Early formulations of human personality tended to view personality as comprising stable and lasting traits (behavioral dispositions). Freud and many of his followers, for example, believed that early experiences, memories, traumas, and anxieties often resulted in behavioral dispositions that persisted throughout life. Views such as Freud's, however, were challenged by those who saw human personality as changing rather than fixed and stationary as well as by those who saw that situations and external factors influence behavior.

Psychophysiological Response Space

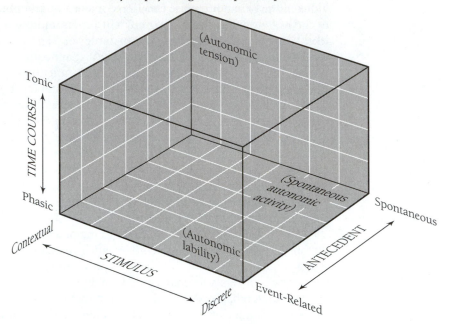

FIGURE 22-1 *Dimensions of psychophysiological response space. One dimension represents the antecedent of the physiological event (event-related/spontaneous), a second dimension represents the nature of the stimulus (discrete/contextual), and a third represents the time course of the physiological event (tonic/phasic). Each of the pairs of terms in this figure represents endpoints on a continuum rather than narrowly and absolutely defined categories of activity.*
(From Cacioppo, Berntson, and Andrews, 1991. Copyright 1991 by the American Psychological Association. Reprinted by permission.)

Most tests discussed in this text are based on the assumption that one can measure human characteristics independently of the context in which these characteristics occur, a theory not only disputable but also without significant support (Bandura, 1986; Mischel, 1968). Psychological tests can be no better than the science of psychology that underlies them. As the science clarifies basic theoretical issues, testing conforms to the available knowledge. In the meantime, perhaps the single most important theoretical assumption of tests—that human characteristics are stable and can be measured independently of the environment—is debatable.

Human behavior may be the result of long-term stable behavioral tendencies (traits); the external or internal environments that precede, coexist with, and follow behavior; or some other factor such as the interaction between traits and environments (Mischel, 1968; Rowe, 1987). Either tests have a long way to go before they will be able to measure the precise determinants of human behavior, or else current conceptualizations and underlying assumptions of tests are not precise enough to make accurate predictions.

After reviewing the psychometric qualities and the limits of mental ability and personality tests, we have concluded that, although people exhibit a core of stability, they continually change. One explanation for the relatively poor long-term reliability of personality tests is that as the individual adjusts to the environment, he or she changes. Most definitions of intelligence include the ability to adapt or change according to circumstances.

A theory consistent with the available data would postulate that all normal people possess the ability to adapt to changing circumstances. This ability is itself a combination of factors that can and do change. We refer to these combined factors as the individual's *index of adjustment,* which we believe is correlated with scores on major ability tests in use today. An individual with a high index of adjustment can adapt more readily and perhaps find more effective solutions to environmental pressures than can those with a low index. However, reacting to the environment may change not only behavioral tendencies but also the index of adjustment. Repeated failures or consistent success, for example, may increase rigidity, which in turn can lower the index of adjustment. However, an extremely demanding environment, such as one that forces the individual to call on latent reserves, may increase the index. In this theory, ability and personality are always changing and can be measured only within the context in which they occur.

The point here is that all psychological tests are based on implicit theories of human functioning. Unfortunately, the validity of these theories and their underlying assumptions is far from proven. Furthermore, there is no consensus concerning either a definition of human intelligence or the essence of human personality, normal or abnormal. A revolution in psychological theory, therefore, could revolutionize psychological tests. In any case, today's tests are no better than the theories and assumptions that underlie them.

The adequacy of tests. A second professional issue in testing concerns the adequacy of existing tests. This entire book has been aimed at providing you with the knowledge you need to evaluate tests. To this end, the book is filled with statements about standardization, norms, scoring, interpretation, test design, reliability, and validity. Thus far, however, we have evaluated tests relative to traditionally accepted psychometric standards rather than against absolute external criteria. Many psychologists and others have questioned whether even the best existing tests possess sufficiently sound psychometric qualities to warrant their use (Ziskin, 1995).

As we have noted, the real issue in testing is how tests are used. In support of this position, the APA (1974) argued that decisions will be made whether or not tests are used in the process. However, one could argue that no test at all is better than a test that often leads to an incorrect conclusion. No doubt, situations exist in which all concerned would be better off without test results than they would be with them.

We do not think all tests should be eliminated until better ones are developed, but we do believe that one should view the adequacy of tests from all possible perspectives. Some tests, such as certain ability tests, are generally adequate in reliability. However, just about any test could benefit from greater validity documentation. Clearly, the quality or adequacy of existing tests viewed in absolute rather than relative terms is a factor that one must consider when evaluating current and future trends in testing.

Actuarial versus clinical prediction. A third issue concerns the accuracy of predictions made by test users. Throughout this book we have argued that tests provide a standard setting in which one can observe behavior. Also, practitioners can use this situation in conjunction with experience and local norms to gain accuracy in their observations and decisions. Certainly, users of psychological tests must feel this way or they simply would not waste their time with tests. However, test users rarely, if ever, receive feedback on the accuracy of their predictions and decisions based on tests. Do tests, then, truly enhance assessment, or are practitioners fooling themselves, repeating their errors and teaching their errors to students?

One can examine this question from all sides. The early work of Meehl (Meehl, 1954; Meehl & Rosen, 1955) and Little and Shneidman (1959) drew attention to the limits of test data even in the hands of trained practitioners. In subsequent analyses, Sawyer (1966) and Sines (1970) reviewed a number of studies that compared an actuarial approach, in which test results were interpreted by using a set of rules, with a clinical approach, in which trained professionals interpreted test results. These reviews indicated that the set of rules was more accurate than the trained professional practitioners, even when the practitioners knew the rules. This research confirmed Meehl's (1954) earlier finding that trained practitioners could not surpass predictions based on statistical formulas. Most recently, Ziskin (1995) has argued that simple tables of actuarial data, such as number of prior arrests and severity of crime, predict recidivism better than any test or any clinical judgment. Do we really need trained clinicians and sophisticated tests to make decisions? Other studies and analyses indicate that the trained practitioner is a better predictor than actuarial formulas, especially when using data from a variety of sources including a test battery, interview, and case history (for example, Goldberg, 1970; Holt, 1970; N. Wiggins & Kohen, 1971). In either case, we again find professional disagreement at the most basic levels.

The issue of actuarial versus clinical prediction has recently reemerged with the proliferation of computerized test interpretations, briefly discussed in Chapter 17. Can a computer accurately interpret a psychological test? The many problems inherent in such interpretations have kept the computer's potential far from realized (Saccuzzo, 1994). As Hartman (1986b) noted, a number of potential abuses accompany the use of computer software to interpret psychological tests, including trivialization of assessment, use of software inappropriate to the client, inadequate contribution of the clinician to the assessment process, and whether the computer's interpretations can be as good (or better) than those of the clinician. (See Figure 22-2).

Moral Issues

Professional issues alone will not determine the future of testing. The field is also being shaped by moral issues—human rights, labeling, and invasion of privacy.

Human rights. Several different kinds of human rights are relevant to psychological testing. Among these is the right not to be tested (APA, 1974). Individuals who do not want to subject themselves to testing should not, and ethically cannot, be forced to do so. The APA (1974) also states that test takers have the right to know test scores and interpretations as well as the bases of any decisions that affect their lives. The position on the right to know reflects a change in policy stemming from current realities. In the past, guarding the security of tests was of paramount importance. Now, one must still take all precautions to protect test security but not at the expense of an individual's right to know the basis of detrimental or adverse decisions. Other human rights, some of which are only now being widely accepted, are the right to know who will have access to test data and the right to confidentiality of test results.

Test interpreters have a moral as well as an ethical obligation to protect human rights. Potential test takers have the responsibility of knowing and demanding their rights. The increasing awareness among test users and the public of human rights is an important influence on the testing field.

Labeling. In standard medical practice, a person's disease or disorder is first identified (diagnosed). Once diagnosed, the disease can be labeled and standard medical intervention procedures implemented. It is no embarrassment to be diagnosed as having gall bladder or kidney disease. However, labeling people with certain medical diseases, such as AIDS, and psychiatric disorders can be extremely damaging (D. Smith, 1981). The public has little understanding of the label *schizophrenia,* for example. Therefore, someone with this label could be stigmatized, perhaps for life. Labels may also affect one's access to help. Chronic schizophrenia, for example, has no cure. Labeling someone a chronic schizophrenic may be a self-fulfilling prophecy. Because the disorder is incurable, nothing can be done. Because nothing can be done, why should one bother to help? Because no help is given, the person is a chronic case.

FIGURE 22-2
Schematic summary of professional issues.

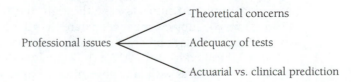

Professional issues — Theoretical concerns / Adequacy of tests / Actuarial vs. clinical prediction

Still another problem with labels, which people unfortunately often justify with psychological tests, is theoretical. As Szasz (1961) originally noted, a medical label such as schizophrenia implies that a person is ill or diseased. Because no one can be blamed for becoming ill, a medical or psychiatric label implies that the person is not responsible for the condition. However, it may very well be that those labeled as psychiatrically disturbed must take responsibility for their lives in order to get better.

When we take responsibility for our lives, we believe that we can exercise some degree of control over our fates (after all, what is intelligence?) rather than simply being the victims of uncontrollable external forces. Individuals who feel a sense of control or responsibility for themselves should be able to tolerate more stress, frustration, and pain than those who feel like passive victims. Certainly, a person who feels responsible or in control has more incentive to alter negative conditions than one who does not.

Labels that imply a person is not responsible may increase the risk that the person so labeled will feel passive. Thus, the labeling process may not only stigmatize the person but also lower tolerance for stress and make treatment more difficult. In view of the potentially negative effects of labels, the APA (1974) states that a person has the right not to be labeled and suggests that the person be described instead.

Invasion of privacy. Another moral issue centers on invasion of privacy. As we stated earlier, people have a right to privacy. When people respond to psychological tests, they have little idea what is being revealed, but they often feel that their privacy has been invaded in a way not justified by the test's benefits. Public concern over this issue once became so strong that tests were investigated by the Senate Subcommittee on Constitutional Rights and the House Subcommittee on Invasion of Privacy. Neither found evidence of deliberate and widespread misuse of tests (see Brayfield, 1965).

There are two sides to the issue. Dahlstrom (1969b) argued that the issue of invasion of privacy is based on serious misunderstandings. He states that because tests have been oversold, the public doesn't realize their limitations. Psychological tests are so limited they can't invade one's privacy. Another issue, according to Dahlstrom (1969b), is the ambiguity of the notion of invasion of privacy. It isn't necessarily wrong, evil, or detrimental to find out about a person. The person's privacy is invaded when such information is used inappropriately. Psychologists, though, are morally, ethically, and often legally bound to maintain confidentiality and do not have to reveal any more information about a person than is necessary to accomplish the purpose for which testing was initiated. Furthermore, psychologists must inform subjects of the limits of confidentiality, and subjects have the right not to be tested. As Dahlstrom (1969b) noted, subjects must cooperate in order to be tested. On the whole, those tested by today's procedures must be willing participants.

The ethical code of the APA (1992) includes confidentiality. Guaranteed by law in most states with laws governing the practice of psychology, this principle means that personal information obtained by the psychologist from any source is communicated only with the person's consent. Exceptions include circumstances in which withholding information causes danger to the person or society, as well as cases that require subpoenaed records. Therefore, people have the right to know the limits of confidentiality and to know that test data can be subpoenaed and used as evidence in court or in employment decisions (Ones, Viswesvaran, & Schmidt, 1995). (See Figure 22-3).

Ethical Issues

Ethical issues are closely related to professional and moral issues and indeed often cannot be easily separated from them. Two extremely important ethical issues are divided loyalties and the responsibilities of test users and test constructors.

Divided loyalties. D. N. Jackson and Messick (1967, Chap. 69) argue that no one has formulated a coherent set of ethical principles that govern all legitimate uses of testing. They believe the core of the problem lies in divided loyalties—the often conflicting commitments of the psychologist who uses tests. Despite the more than 30 years that have elapsed since D. N. Jackson and Messick (1967) first articulated the problem of divided loyalties, this problem remains a central dilemma to all psychologists who use tests in clinics, schools, business, industry, government, and the military.

One ethical principle is that the psychologist must protect the welfare and privacy of the client or consumer of tests. A conflict arises, however, when the individual's welfare is at odds with that of the institution that employs the psychologist. For example, a psychologist working for an industrial firm to identify individuals who might break down under stress has a responsibility to the institution to identify such individuals as well as a responsibility to protect the rights and welfare of clients seeking employment with the firm. Thus, the psychologist's loyalty is divided. Similarly, the psychologist must maintain test security but also not violate the client's right to know the basis for an adverse decision. However, if the basis for an adverse decision is explained to one client, this information may leak out, and others with the same problem might then outsmart the test. Again, the test user is trapped between two opposing forces and principles.

The conflict is presently being resolved as follows. Ethically, psychologists must inform all concerned where their loyalty lies. They must tell clients or subjects in advance how tests are to be used and describe the limits of confi-

FIGURE 22-3
Schematic summary of moral issues.

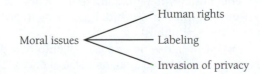

dentiality. To the institution, they provide only the minimum information needed, such as "This subject has a low probability of breaking down under stress, and the probability that this conclusion is accurate is 68/100." Unnecessary or irrelevant personal information remains confidential.

In addition, the person's right to know the basis of an adverse decision may override issues of test security. Either the results are explained to the client or they are given to a representative of the client who is qualified to explain them (AERA et al., 1985). A law in the state of New York prohibits the distributors of standardized tests used in selection procedures (for example the SAT, the GRE, and the MCAT) from keeping the items secret. The implication of the law is that the person has the right to see the items missed. In other words, the dilemma of test security versus client welfare has been decided by the courts, with the decision clearly favoring the client.

Responsibilities of test users and test constructors. A second ethical issue in testing concerns the responsibilities of test users. Because even the best test can be misused, the testing profession has become increasingly stringent and precise in outlining the ethics of responsible test use. According to the APA (1974), almost any test can be useful in the right circumstances, but even the best test, when used inappropriately, can hurt the subject. To reduce potential damage, the APA (1974) makes users of tests responsible for knowing the reason for using the test, the consequences, and the procedures necessary to maximize the test's effectiveness and to minimize unfairness. Test users must thus possess sufficient knowledge to understand the principles underlying the construction and supporting research of any test they administer. They must also know the psychometric qualities of the test being used as well as the literature relevant to the test. In addition, they are to ensure that interpretations based on the test are justified and that the test is properly used. In our judgment, a test user cannot claim ignorance ("I didn't realize normative data were not representative"). The test user is responsible for finding out all pertinent information before using any test.

It is the test developer's responsibility to provide this information. Current standards for test use state that test constructors must provide a test manual with sufficient data to permit appropriate use of the test, including adequate validity and reliability data, clearly specified scoring and administration standards, and a clear description of the normative sample (AERA et al., 1985; APA, 1974). It is not unusual for a researcher to receive requests from test designers to investigate a newly developed test. These designers hope that others will conduct the necessary research to provide adequate psychometric documentation. The standards also state that the test manual should warn against possible misinterpretation and identify necessary qualifications for responsible test use. Despite these guidelines, tests that do not meet specified standards continue to be published.

A test user has no excuse for employing an inadequately documented instrument that has damaging consequences. The test user must know enough to tell the difference between a test that meets present standards and one that does not. D. N. Jackson and Messick (1967, Chap. 69) wisely suggest that the test user ask two questions whenever a test is proposed for a particular use. First, "Is the test any good as a measure of the characteristics it purports to measure?" The answer lies in the psychometric qualities of the test, such as reliability and validity documentation. Second, "Should the test be used for this purpose?" The answer to this question rests on the ethical and social values of the test user, who must think about the test's effect on the person and his or her human rights. Thus, though test constructors bear some responsibility for a poorly designed test or an inadequate manual, the ethical use of tests ultimately rests with the test user.

Social Issues

In addition to professional, moral, and ethical issues, a number of social issues play an important role in the testing field. We discuss three of these social issues: dehumanization, the usefulness of tests, and access to psychological testing sources.

Dehumanization. One social issue in the testing field concerns the dehumanizing tendencies that lurk in the testing process. For example, as noted in Chapter 17, some corporations provide computerized analyses of the MMPI-2 and other test results. Such technology tends to minimize individual freedom and uniqueness. With high-speed computers and centralized data banks, the risk that machines will someday make important decisions about our lives is always increasing. Thus, society must weigh the risks against the benefits of the growing application of modern technology to the testing field. People must make this evaluation now, before an undesirable but unalterable situation develops. If psychologists or the public allow test results to be stored and analyzed by computers, it may become extremely difficult to reverse this trend. U.S. society is founded on principles of individual rights and freedom. Anything that might threaten these principles—such as computerized test interpretations—must be evaluated. One should make decisions concerning such issues with an awareness of potential risks as well as benefits. Only when the benefits far outweigh the risks and the risks are minimized can the decision be socially acceptable.

Usefulness of tests. Tests need not be perfect in all ways. Society often finds uses for initially crude tools that become precise with research and development. One can discriminate the useful and the true or correct. For example, when Western society believed the sun revolved around the earth, the available formulas and principles were useful in that they led to some accurate predictions, even though the underlying theories were incorrect. This may also be the situation with testing as it is currently practiced. The assumptions underlying tests may be fundamentally incorrect and the resulting test instruments far from perfect. However, the tests may still be useful as long as they provide information that leads to better predictions and understanding than can otherwise be obtained. The point is that a test may be useful to society even if all the principles that underlie tests are totally incorrect.

Thus, the crucial social issue in testing is not whether tests are perfect but whether they are useful to society. Obviously, the answer to this question to date has been a strong but disputed "Yes" (see Camara & Schneider, 1994; Ones, Chockalingam, & Schmidt, 1995). However, as new knowledge is gained, society must continually weigh the risks of tests against the benefits. The risks, of course, include the possible misuse of tests, which in turn may adversely affect the life of an individual or may discriminate systematically against a specific cultural group (see Henry, Bryson, & Henry, 1990). The benefits include the potential for increased precision and fairness in the decision-making process. Obviously, the resolution of this recurring issue will profoundly affect the field of testing.

Society has used modern tests on a wide scale. First the military, then the schools and psychiatric facilities, and finally business and industry have found important uses for psychological tests. Indeed, there appears to be no end to the proliferation of tests, despite criticisms and heated debates. If the pervasiveness of tests indicates society's opinion of their usefulness, then certainly society has found them useful. As long as tests continue to serve a function, they most likely will be used.

Access to psychological testing services. Who will have access to psychological testing services? Being tested can be expensive. A practitioner in a large metropolitan area often commands a fee of $2000 or more to administer a full battery of individual tests, score and interpret the findings, and produce a written report. Fees for neurological testing can be two to three times higher. Moreover, the cost of test materials continues to skyrocket. A WAIS-R kit cost $98 in 1983. In 1997, the new WAIS-III cost more than $450, with further price increases in the works. Such high prices for materials increase the cost of psychological assessments. As with many other commodities, this price tag places testing beyond the reach of many. Yet, if a person's well-being depends on information from a psychological test battery, how will the decision be made about who will have access to testing and who will not?

As it stands now, the expensive test batteries for neurological and psychiatric assessment are available to those who can afford them and to those who have enough insurance. In California, developmentally disabled persons (for example, the mentally retarded) or those with suspected developmental disabilities have access to psychological testing services at regional centers throughout the state. Unless California laws are changed, anyone suspected of having a handicap that originated during the developmental years can request (or have someone request on his or her behalf) an evaluation, which may include a medical examination and psychological testing. The service is free, and if a team of specialists finds the person developmentally disabled, additional services are available.

Anyone with a developmental disability in California may be eligible to receive Medi-Cal, which provides free medical care, including the services of a psychologist. The individual may also be eligible for federal assistance such as Medicare and SSI, which provide cash benefits. Thus, current California and federal laws and policies help ensure that certain disabled persons will have access to psychological testing services. However, such guarantees are not available in all states, and only certain disabled persons are covered.

Some in our society have offered national health insurance as a way to provide adequate medical care to everyone. As of this writing, no program of national health insurance has been implemented, but talk about it continues. One of the controversies in proposals for national health insurance concerns the extent of mental health coverage and whether psychological services will be included. Presumably, if psychological testing services are included in a national health insurance program, then anyone who needs such services will have access to them. If not, then the availability of testing services may be substantially limited. In a sense, society will be judging the value of tests in deciding whether or not to include them in a national health insurance program. Because resources are limited, testing services may preclude some other needed service, or vice versa. (See Figure 22-4).

Current Trends

Professional, moral, ethical, social, and even legal issues have interacted to produce today's trends in testing. These trends can be placed into four main categories: the proliferation of new tests; higher standards, improved technology, and increased objectivity; greater public awareness and influence; and computer applications.

Proliferation of New Tests

New tests keep coming out all the time, with no end in sight. If we count revised and updated tests, we find hundreds of new tests being published each year. The impetus for developing these new tests comes from professional disagreement over the best strategies for measuring human characteristics, over the nature of these characteristics, and over theories about the causes of human behavior. [For example, see the discussion of the Kaufman Assessment

FIGURE 22-4
Schematic summary of social issues.

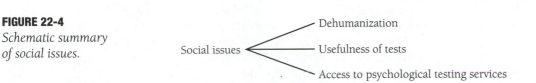

Battery for Children (K-ABC) in Chapter 12.] The impetus also stems from public and professional pressure to use only fair, accurate, and unbiased instruments. Finally, if tests are used, then the authors and publishers of tests stand to profit financially. As long as one can make a profit publishing tests, new tests will be developed and marketed.

An examination of major reference books on tests indicates that the majority of new tests are based on the same principles and underlying theories as the more established tests. Indeed, most newly developed tests are justified on the grounds that they are either psychometrically superior to the existing tests or more specific and thus more appropriate for particular problems. However, as you saw in Chapter 17, some of the newer tests, especially the most recent ones, are based on models, theories, and concepts that fundamentally differ from those underlying traditional, established tests. These nontraditional tests stem from modern concepts and theories from learning, social, physiological, and experimental psychology. Most of these newer tests are rooted in empirically derived data (Iacono, 1991).

The proliferation of nontraditional tests is related to two other trends in testing. First, the development of these nontraditional tests reflects the increasing application and role of the science of psychology in testing (Haynes, 1991, 1995). Even critics of testing must admit that a responsiveness to criticism and an honest and persistent effort to improve the quality of tests have characterized testing. The application of insights and empirical findings from psychological laboratories currently reflects this responsiveness.

Second, efforts are being made to integrate tests with other aspects of applied psychology. Many psychologists, especially the behaviorally oriented (Haynes, 1992), have long regretted the poor relationship among clinical assessment, traditional tests, and subsequent treatment interventions. They would most prefer test results that not only have a direct relationship to treatment but also can be used to assess the effectiveness of treatment. Because psychologists continually try to devise such procedures, their products add to the list of the many new tests published each year.

Higher Standards, Improved Technology, and Increasing Objectivity

Various pressures and issues have led to another current trend. The minimum acceptable standards for tests are becoming higher and more stringent. Before the APA (1974) clearly and specifically defined their responsibilities, test constructors had neither a uniform nor a widely accepted set of guidelines. As a result, the quality of newly published tests varied greatly. With published standards, test constructors no longer have to work in the dark. One can already see that an increasing percentage of new tests provide the information necessary for test users to make a fully informed choice in test selection, thus maximizing the chance of proper test use.

Higher standards of test construction have encouraged better and more appropriate use of tests. The APA (1974) and the AREA et al. (1985) standards have helped considerably by reemphasizing the critical importance of proper test use and by articulating the responsibilities of test users. More recently, a working group of the Joint Committee on Testing Practices sponsored by the American Association for Counseling and Development, the American Educational Research Association, the American Psychological Association, the American Speech-Language-Hearing Association, and the National Council on Measurement in Education has published a thorough document delineating the qualifications of test users (Eyde, Moreland, & Robertson, 1988). This comprehensive guide clearly specifies the competencies needed to use various types of tests and will provide a beacon for some time to come. Moreover, as we indicated earlier, the ethics of testing have been modified to encourage the proper use of tests and to avoid misuse. Now that test users have a published set of standards, there is no excuse for misusing a test. Naturally, misuse and even abuse will never be entirely eliminated; however, the trend toward better and more appropriate use of existing tests is most desirable.

Related to higher standards, improved technology is currently being applied in the testing field. Those in the testing field now enjoy the benefits of the remarkable technology that has developed during the previous few decades (Farrell, 1991, 1992; Haynes, 1992; Lowman, 1991; Matarazzo, 1990). Primarily because of advances in computer technology, statistical procedures such as factor analysis and item analysis can be performed with great ease. This technology thus contributes to the current trend toward better tests.

Also related to high standards is the trend toward increasing objectivity in test interpretation. Although we generally spoke in favor of projective tests such as the Rorschach, many practitioners have been displeased with the often subjective nature of the interpretation of such tests. As a result, many have shown a tendency to rely heavily on objective data such as that provided by the MMPI-2. One can readily see this trend toward increased objectivity in testing in how the relative proportion of references devoted to the Rorschach and the MMPI in *The Mental Measurements Yearbook* and other sources has changed (for example, Archer et al., 1991; C. Piotrowski, Sherry, & Keller, 1985; Polyson, Peterson, & Marshall, 1986).

The continuing research interest in testing also reflects the trend toward objectivity in the field. In view of the tens of thousands, if not hundreds of thousands, of published studies directly or indirectly related to psychological tests, a casual observer might conclude that little remains to be done. This conclusion is far from correct. Despite the thousands of published articles devoted to the MMPI and MMPI-2, for example, hundreds more creative and scientifically rigorous articles are published each year on these tests, not to mention the hundreds of other tests listed in *The Mental Measurements Yearbook* and other resource books. As long as tests are anything but perfect, and in this regard they are a long way off, psychological researchers will no doubt keep conducting investigations to facilitate the objective use of tests.

Greater Public Awareness and Influence

Greater public awareness of the nature and use of psychological tests has led to increasing external influence on the practice of testing, as well as other trends in the field. At one time, the public knew little about psychological tests; psychologists played an almost exclusive role in governing how tests were used. With the greater assertiveness on the part of the public during the 1980s and 1990s, the days when psychologists alone called the shots are gone forever (Saccuzzo, 1994). In our opinion, this is a desirable trend that has affected the field positively.

Public awareness has led to the current trend toward an increased demand for psychological services, including testing services. This demand is balanced by the tendency toward restrictive legislative and judicial regulations and policies such as the judicial decision restricting the use of standard intelligence tests in diagnosing mental retardation. These restrictions originate in real and imagined public fears. In short, the public seems to be ambivalent about psychological testing, simultaneously desiring the benefits yet fearing the power they attribute to tests.

Perhaps the greatest benefit of increased public awareness of tests has been the extra focus on safeguarding human rights. As more individuals share the responsibility of encouraging the proper use of tests by becoming informed of their rights and insisting on receiving them, the probability of misuse and abuse of tests will be reduced. The commitment of the field of psychology to high standards in ethics, morals, and human rights can be easily seen in the published ethical guidelines, position papers, and debates that have evolved during the relatively short period beginning in 1947 with the development of formal standards for training in clinical psychology (Shakow et al., 1947). Practitioners of psychology as well as their instructors and supervisors show a deep concern for social values and the dignity of the individual human being. However, the pressure of public interest in psychological tests has led psychological practitioners to even greater awareness of safeguarding the rights and dignity of the individual.

Interrelated with all of these issues is the trend toward greater protection for the public. Nearly every state has laws that govern the use of psychological tests. Limiting testing to reduce the chance that unqualified persons will use psychological tests, sensitivity among practitioners to the rights of the individual, relevant court decisions, and a clearly articulated set of ethical guidelines and published standards for proper test use give the public significant protection against the inherent risks of testing.

The Computerization of Tests

Throughout this book we have discussed how computers are being applied to testing on a rapid and widespread basis. The computerization of tests is a major trend, and computers, as you saw in Chapter 17, are being used in a number of different ways.

In adaptive computerized testing, different sets of test questions are administered, via computer, to different individuals depending on each individual's status on the trait being measured (Weiss, 1983, 1985). In ability testing, for example, the computer adapts the level of item difficulty depending on the subject's response. If the subject's answer is incorrect, an easier item is given; if correct, a more difficult item appears next. Such an approach individualizes a test and reduces total testing time. Research currently in progress may some day lead to the conversion of the Armed Services Vocational Aptitude Battery, given to millions, to an adaptive computerized format (see Chapter 13). In addition, by the year 2000 most students will probably be taking tests such as the SAT, GRE, and LSAT through adaptive computer programs.

Computers are also being used to administer, score, and even interpret psychological tests. In addition, computers are being used to generate tasks that cannot be presented by traditional methods (see Chapter 17). Through computer technology, one might be able to tap a whole new range of abilities heretofore beyond the scope of traditional tests (Saccuzzo, Johnson, & Guertin, 1994). Objective personality tests such as the MMPI-2 can be processed by a computer that generates a typed report. Each year, developers create more programs that score tests and produce written reports (Prince & Guastello, 1990). The use of the computer extends to all types of tests, including behavioral assessment (Farrell, 1991, 1992).

Future Trends

Having analyzed the major relevant issues and forces in testing and identified current trends, we are now ready to venture a few guesses about what the future holds for the field. Certainly, we are reasonably safe in stating that the trends identified above will continue and become established as realities of the field. However, our predictions for the future are educated guesses based on limited knowledge.

Future Prospects for Testing Are Promising

Our studies lead us to conclude that testing has a promising future. We base our optimism on the integral role testing has played in the development and recognition of psychology. The field gained its first real status from its role in the development of screening tests for the military in World War I. Later, psychologists' creativity and skill in the testing field during World War II no doubt numbered among the factors that ultimately led to government funding through the Veterans Administration to encourage the development of professional psychology. Indeed, this federal funding, first earmarked for psychology in 1945, played an important role in the birth of clinical psychology and formal training standards.

The central role played by testing in the development and recognition of psychology, however, does not alone ensure an important future role for testing. Despite division within psychology concerning the role and value of testing, psychological testing remains one of the few unique functions of the professional psychologist. When one sees psychological testing as encompassing not only traditional but also new and innovative uses—as in behavioral assessment, psychophysiology, evaluation research, organizational assessment, community assessment, and investigations into the nature of human functioning—one can understand just how important tests are to psychologists.

Thus, with their traditional and fundamental tie with tests, psychologists remain the undisputed leaders in the field. We do not believe that attacks on and dissatisfaction with traditional psychological tests will suddenly compel psychologists to abandon tests. Instead, we predict that psychologists will continue to take the lead in this field to produce better and better tests, and that such a direction will benefit psychologists, the field, and society.

In addition, tests are used in most institutions—schools, colleges, hospitals, industry, business, the government, and so forth—and new applications and creative uses continue to emerge in response to them. Tests will not suddenly disappear with nothing to replace them. If anything, current tests will continue to be used until they are replaced by still better tests, which of course may be based on totally new ideas. Though current tests may gradually fade from the scene, we believe psychological testing will not simply survive but instead flourish and thrive through the rest of this and the next century.

The Proliferation of New and Improved Tests Will Continue

In conjunction with our prediction of a promising future for psychological testing, we feel safe claiming that the future will see the development of many more tests. In Chapters 10, 11, and 12, we presented our belief that currently available intelligence tests are far from perfect and that we have a long way to go before the ultimate in such tests is seen. Consistent with this belief, we believe the dominant role of the Stanford-Binet and Wechsler tests is far from secure. These two major intelligence scales are probably about as technically adequate as they will ever be. They can, of course, be improved through minor revisions to update test stimuli and to provide larger and even more representative normative samples with special norms for particular groups and through additional research to extend and support validity documentation. However, despite the changes in the modern Binet and the WAIS-III, the fundamental characteristics and underlying concepts resemble those of the original scales.

During the next few decades, we shall be surprised if these two major intelligence scales are not challenged at least once or twice by similar tests with superior standardization and normative data. However, if history indicates what is to be, a true challenge can come only from a test based on original concepts and a more comprehensive theoretical rationale than that of the present scales. The Kaufman Assessment Battery for Children may be one such contender in its age range (see Chapter 12). We believe that the development of such a test is only a question of time (see, for example, Sternberg, 1981). Just how soon such a test appears will, of course, depend primarily on need. Should a compelling need for such an instrument arise, then we shall see it sooner rather than later.

In structured personality testing, the MMPI-2 appears destined to be the premier test of the 21st century. This favorable prediction for the MMPI-2 is a turnabout from the 1982 prediction made in the first edition of this book. We had not anticipated the innovative approach of Butcher and colleagues. Their restandardization, as we noted in Chapter 15, also deals with the main problem of the original MMPI: its inadequate normative sample. Thus, future prospects for the MMPI-2 are indeed bright.

Regarding *projective personality testing,* we believe that the Rorschach will achieve a new level of acceptance and respectability as the 21st century dawns. Used on a wide scale in clinical settings, the Rorschach has few competitors. Computer programs that generate reports are available for projective tests (Exner, 1980, 1986). The Holtzman Inkblot Test takes care of just about every psychometric criticism of the Rorschach, yet it still has not found widespread clinical use. Our view of the Rorschach is that it is fundamentally sound and will ultimately be vindicated because of the work of psychologists such as Exner and Weiner. Most likely, though, the Rorschach will never achieve the prominence it enjoyed during its heyday. In fact, relative to other personality tests, the Rorschach may show even further declines. However, only when the mysteries of schizophrenia are better understood and new ways to measure the pathology of schizophrenia are perfected will the Rorschach be seriously threatened.

The future of the TAT is more difficult to predict. Affixed to some of the main arteries of psychological theory, the TAT has an incredibly extensive research base and is a prominent clinical tool. Unfortunately, the TAT stimuli are out of date. In a projective test, outdated stimuli are not a devastating weakness because projective stimuli are by nature ambiguous. Nevertheless, because the TAT stimuli have been revised (Ritzler, Sharkey, & Chudy, 1980) the TAT may enjoy increased respectability as data are acquired on the latest version.

Revolutionary Changes: "Perestroika" in School Testing

Recently, we attended a meeting on testing in Washington, D.C. Speaker after speaker, including the U.S. Secretary of Education, predicted changes in testing in schools. Whereas some speakers emphasized national standardized tests, others rejected the idea. According to one speaker, there would soon be a "perestroika" in the field of testing in the schools. Performance tests would replace standardized multiple-choice tests by the year 2000.

Panic is indeed raging in Washington, D.C., because of the poor performance of American school children compared with children from other industrialized nations including Japan, Korea, Canada, and the European Community. At the heart of this panic is how we evaluate school performance and measure progress.

A report of the National Commission on Testing and Public Policy (1990) made the following points:

1. "America must revamp the way it develops and utilizes human talent, and to do that, educational and employment testing must be restructured" (p. ix).
2. "Current testing, predominantly multiple choice in format, is overrelied upon, lacks adequate public accountability, sometimes leads to unfairness in the allocation of opportunities, and far too often undermines vital social policies" (p. ix).
3. "To help promote greater development of the talents of all our people, alternative forms of assessment must be developed and more critically judged and used, so that testing and assessment open gates of opportunity rather than close them off" (p. x).

The "new" assessment currently being called for by the National Education Association and others is performance testing. As you have seen, such testing requires a subject to do something rather than to provide a verbal response or fill in a blank. In performance testing in the schools, students would write essays, provide written responses to specified problems, or solve open-ended math problems (see Table 22-1).

Multifaceted, performance testing includes such procedures as observing a foreign-language student having a conversation in the foreign language; requiring science students to conduct a real experiment; asking students to work together as a group and observing the interaction; and giving problems that have no answer or more than one correct answer and observing a stu-

TABLE 22-1

Performance Testing

Purchasing an Automobile

You are considering two used cars: a 1988 Ford Taurus priced at $3800 and a 1988 Honda Accord priced at $4100. How would you go about determining which is the best decision for you? Your task is to design and carry out a study to answer this question.

Grade level:	12th
Curriculum topics:	Computational skills: ability to work with money, ability to make relative judgments and comparisons, ability to analyze and write conclusions in a clear narrative form
Suggested length of time:	1–2 weeks
In class:	2 periods
Out of class:	4 periods

Based on the Connecticut Common Core of Learning Performance Assessment Project sponsored by the National Science Foundation.

dent's approach. A related idea is the portfolio, a collection of samples of the student's work.

We presently see two contrary positions, each purporting to solve the problems in the U.S. school system: national standardized testing versus performance testing and portfolios. This battle is not new. As you saw back in Chapter 1, performance tests were replaced by standardized achievement tests in the 1930s because they were seen as more objective. Now, more than 65 years later, certain educators are calling for a return to the older method. Whichever force ultimately wins out, we are sure to see substantial change in how tests are used in the schools as the new century begins.

Controversy, Disagreement, and Change Will Continue

We feel quite safe in predicting continued controversy and disagreement in the testing field, which will no doubt produce further change. Disagreement and controversy are second nature to psychologists; it doesn't matter whether the topic is testing or animal learning. Because of disagreement, however, new data are sought, found, and ultimately produce some clarification of old controversies along with brand-new contradictions and battle lines (Jensen, 1988). This is the way of psychology. Therefore, it's not likely that psychologists will ever agree that any one test is perfect. As a consequence, change will be a constant characteristic of the field. We continue to be optimistic because we see the change as ultimately resulting in more empirical data, better theories, continuing innovations and advances, and higher standards.

The Integration of Cognitive Science and Computer Science Will Lead to Several Innovations in Testing

As you saw in Chapter 17, concepts from basic psychological sciences have worked their way into the field: learning theory in the 1960s and 1970s, psychophysiological and psychophysical concepts in the 1980s. Today, the integration of concepts from experimental cognitive psychology, computer science, and psychometrics are rapidly shaping the field.

Multimedia computerized tests form the most recent cutting edge in the new generation of assessment instruments. The test taker sits in front of a computer that presents realistically animated situations with full color and sound. The program is both interactive and adaptive. The computer screen freezes and asks the test taker to provide a response. If the response is good, a more difficult item is presented. For example, in research programs presently being developed at companies such as IBM, the computer may show a scene involving sexual harassment. The screen freezes just after an employee has made an inappropriate joke. The test taker, who is applying for a manager's job, is given four choices to deal with the situation. If an effective choice is made, the computer moves on to an even more difficult situation, such as a threat from the offensive employee.

The computer offers test developers unlimited scope in developing new technologies. As we noted at the outset, the computer holds one of the major keys to the future of psychological testing.

Summary

Anything is possible, especially in a field as controversial as testing. Psychology is now better equipped in technique, methodology, empirical data, and experience than ever before, and the members of this new and expanding field, as a group, are relatively young. Therefore, it does not seem unrealistic or overly optimistic to expect that the next 50 years will see advances equal to those of the last 50. On the other hand, psychology has come so far in the last 50 years that a comparable advance in the next 50 years could easily produce results unimaginable today. What happens to testing in the future will depend on the goals and objectives chosen by those in the field and by their persistence and creativity in accomplishing their goals.

Appendix 1

Areas of a Standard Normal Distribution

PART I

Percentiles Associated with Various Z Scores

Z	% Rank	Z	% Rank
−3.0	.13	0	50.00
−2.9	.19	.1	53.98
−2.8	.26	.2	57.93
−2.7	.35	.3	61.79
−2.6	.47	.4	66.54
−2.5	.62	.5	69.15
−2.4	.82	.6	72.57
−2.3	1.07	.7	75.80
−2.2	1.39	.8	78.81
−2.1	1.79	.9	81.59
−2.0	2.28	1.0	84.13
−1.9	2.87	1.1	86.43
−1.8	3.59	1.2	88.49
−1.7	4.46	1.3	90.32
−1.6	5.48	1.4	91.92
−1.5	6.68	1.5	93.32
−1.4	8.08	1.6	94.52
−1.3	9.68	1.7	95.54
−1.2	11.51	1.8	96.41
−1.1	13.57	1.9	97.13
−1.0	15.87	2.0	97.72
− .9	18.41	2.1	98.21
− .8	21.19	2.2	98.61
− .7	24.20	2.3	98.93
− .6	27.43	2.4	99.18
− .5	30.58	2.5	99.38
− .4	34.46	2.6	99.53
− .3	38.21	2.7	99.65
− .2	42.07	2.8	99.74
− .1	46.02	2.9	99.81
0	50.00	3.0	99.87

PART II

Areas Between Mean and Various Z Scores

Z	.00	.01	.02	.03	.04	.05	.06	.07	.08	.09
.0	.0000	.0040	.0080	.0120	.0160	.0199	.0239	.0279	.0319	.0359
.1	.0398	.0438	.0478	.0517	.0557	.0596	.0636	.0675	.0714	.0753
.2	.0793	.0832	.0871	.0910	.0948	.0987	.1026	.1064	.1103	.1141
.3	.1179	.1217	.1255	.1293	.1331	.1368	.1406	.1443	.1480	.1517
.4	.1554	.1591	.1628	.1664	.1700	.1736	.1772	.1808	.1844	.1879
.5	.1915	.1950	.1985	.2019	.2054	.2088	.2123	.2157	.2190	.2224
.6	.2257	.2291	.2324	.2357	.2389	.2422	.2454	.2486	.2517	.2549
.7	.2580	.2611	.2642	.2673	.2704	.2734	.2764	.2794	.2823	.2852
.8	.2881	.2910	.2939	.2967	.2995	.3023	.3051	.3078	.3106	.3133
.9	.3195	.3186	.3212	.3238	.3264	.3289	.3315	.3340	.3365	.3389
1.0	.3413	.3438	.3461	.3485	.3508	.3531	.3554	.3577	.3599	.3621
1.1	.3643	.3665	.3686	.3708	.3729	.3749	.3770	.3790	.3810	.3830
1.2	.3849	.3869	.3888	.3907	.3925	.3944	.3962	.3980	.3997	.4015
1.3	.4032	.4049	.4066	.4082	.4099	.4115	.4131	.4147	.4162	.4177
1.4	.4192	.4207	.4222	.4236	.4251	.4265	.4279	.4292	.4306	.4319
1.5	.4332	.4345	.4357	.4370	.4382	.4394	.4406	.4418	.4429	.4441
1.6	.4452	.4463	.4474	.4484	.4495	.4505	.4515	.4525	.4535	.4545
1.7	.4554	.4564	.4573	.4582	.4591	.4599	.4608	.4616	.4625	.4633
1.8	.4641	.4649	.4656	.4664	.4671	.4678	.4686	.4693	.4699	.4706
1.9	.4713	.4719	.4726	.4732	.4738	.4744	.4750	.4756	.4761	.4767
2.0	.4772	.4778	.4783	.4788	.4793	.4798	.4803	.4808	.4812	.4817
2.1	.4821	.4826	.4830	.4834	.4838	.4842	.4846	.4850	.4854	.4857
2.2	.4861	.4864	.4868	.4871	.4875	.4878	.4881	.4884	.4887	.4890
2.3	.4893	.4896	.4898	.4901	.4904	.4906	.4909	.4911	.4913	.4916
2.4	.4918	.4920	.4922	.4925	.4927	.4929	.4931	.4932	.4934	.4936
2.5	.4938	.4940	.4941	.4943	.4945	.4946	.4948	.4949	.4951	.4952
2.6	.4953	.4955	.4956	.4957	.4959	.4960	.4961	.4962	.4963	.4964
2.7	.4965	.4966	.4967	.4968	.4969	.4970	.4971	.4972	.4973	.4974
2.8	.4974	.4975	.4976	.4977	.4977	.4978	.4979	.4979	.4980	.4981
2.9	.4981	.4982	.4982	.4983	.4984	.4984	.4985	.4985	.4986	.4986
3.0	.4987	.4987	.4987	.4988	.4988	.4989	.4989	.4989	.4900	.4990.

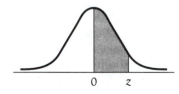

Standard score values are listed in the column headed "Z." To find the proportion of the total area occurring between the mean and any given Z score, locate the entry indicated by the Z score. For example, a Z score of $+1.85$ is located by reading across to the column for .05 from the value of 1.8 in the "Z" column. The value in the table is .4678. Since the total area above the mean is equal to .5000, this means that only .0322 of the area is beyond the Z score of $+1.85$.

Publishers of Major Tests

Listed are the names and addresses of the publishers of major tests mentioned in this book.

Bayley School of Infant Development
Psychological Corporation
555 Academic Court
San Antonio, TX 78204

Bender Visual Motor Gestalt Test
American Orthopsychiatric Association, Inc.
330 7th Avenue
New York City, NY 10001

Bennett Mechanical Comprehension Test
Psychological Corporation
555 Academic Court
San Antonio, TX 78204

Benton Visual Retention Test
Psychological Corporation
555 Academic Court
San Antonio, TX 78204

Beta Examination—Revised
Psychological Corporation
555 Academic Court
San Antonio, TX 78204

California Psychological Inventory
Consulting Psychologists Press, Inc.
3803 East Bayshore
Palo Alto, CA 94303

Cattell Infant Intelligence Scale
Psychological Corporation
555 Academic Court
San Antonio, TX 78204

Children's Apperception Test
CPS, Inc.
P.O. Box 83
Larchmont, NY 10538

Children's Personality Questionnaire
Institute for Personality and Ability Testing
P.O. Box 1188
Champaign, IL 61824

Clinical Analysis Questionnaire (research edition)
Institute for Personality and Ability Testing
P.O. Box 1188
Champaign, IL 61824

Cognitive Abilities Test
Riverside Publishing
8240 Bryn Mawr
Chicago, IL 60631

Columbia Mental Maturity Scale
Psychological Corporation
555 Academic Court
San Antonio, TX 78204

Cooperative School and College Ability Test—Series II
Out of print—no longer available

Culture Fair Intelligence Test
Institute for Personality and Ability Testing
P.O. Box 1188
Champaign, IL 61824

Dental Admission Testing Program
Division of Educational Measurements
Council of Dental Education
American Dental Association
211 East Chicago Avenue, Ste. 1846
Chicago, IL 60611

Differential Aptitude Test
Psychological Corporation
555 Academic Court
San Antonio, TX 78204

Edwards Personal Preference Schedule
Psychological Corporation
555 Academic Court
San Antonio, TX 78204

Fear Survey Schedule
Educational and Industrial Testing Service
P.O. Box 7234
San Diego, CA 92167

Goodenough-Harris Drawing Test
Psychological Corporation
555 Academic Court
San Antonio, TX 78204

Graduate Record Examination Aptitude Test
Educational Testing Service
Princeton, NJ 08540

Guilford-Zimmerman Temperament Survey
Consulting Psychological Press, Inc.
3803 East Bayshore
Palo Alto, CA 94303

Henmon-Nelson Test of Mental Ability (1973 revision)
Riverside Publishing
8420 Bryn Mawr
Chicago, IL 60631

Holtzman Inkblot Test
Psychological Corporation
555 Academic Court
San Antonio, TX 78204

Illinois Test of Psycholinguistic Abilities
Out of print—no longer available

Junior Senior High School Ability Questionnaire
Institute for Personality and Ability Testing
P.O. Box 1188
Champaign, IL 61824

Kuder Occupational Interest Survey
CTB McGraw Hill
20 Ryan Ranch Road
Monterey, CA 93960

Kuhlmann-Anderson Test (seventh edition)
Personnel Press
191 Spring Street
Lexington, MA 02173

Law School Admission Test
Law Services
661 Penn Street
Newtown, PA 18940

Leiter International Performance Scale
C. H. Stoeling Company
620 Wheat Lane
Wooddale, IL 60191

McCarthy Scales of Children's Abilities
Psychological Corporation
555 Academic Court
San Antonio, TX 78204

Memory-for-Designs Test
Psychological Tests Specialists
Box 1441
Missoula, Montana 59801

Miller Analogies Test
Psychological Corporation
555 Academic Court
San Antonio, TX 78204

Minnesota Multiphasic Personality Questionnaire
University of Minnesota
Minneapolis, MN 55455

Mooney Problem Checklist
Psychological Corporation
555 Academic Court
San Antonio, TX 78204

Otis Lennon Test of School Ability
Psychological Corporation
555 Academic Court
San Antonio, TX 78204

Peabody Picture Vocabulary Test
American Guidance Services
P.O. Box 99
Circle Pines, MN 55014

Pictorial Test of Intelligence
Out of print—no longer available

Porteus Maze Test
Psychological Corporation
555 Academic Court
San Antonio, TX 78204

Quick Neurological Screening Test
Psychological Corporation
555 Academic Court
San Antonio, TX 78204

Raven Standard Progressive Matrices
Psychological Corporation
555 Academic Court
San Antonio, TX 78204

Minnesota Paper Form Board Test—Revised
Psychological Corporation
555 Academic Court
San Antonio, TX 78204

Rorschach Inkblot Test
Psychological Corporation
555 Academic Court
San Antonio, TX 78204

Scholastic Achievement Test
Educational Testing Service
Princeton, NJ 08540

Senior Apperception Technique
CPS, Inc.
P.O. Box 83
Larchmont, NY

Sixteen Personality Factor Questionnaire
Institute for Personality and Ability Testing
P.O. Box 1188
Champaign, IL 61824

Stanford Binet Intelligence Scale
Riverside Publishing
8420 Bryn Mawr Avenue
Chicago, IL 60631

State-Trait Anxiety Inventory
Consulting Psychologists Press, Inc.
3803 East Bayshore
Palo Alto, CA 94303

Strong Interest Inventory
Consulting Psychologists Press, Inc.
3803 East Bayshore
Palo Alto, CA 94303

System of Multicultural Pluralistic
Psychological Corporation
555 Academic Court
San Antonio, TX 78204

Thematic Apperception Test
Harvard University Press
79 Garden Street
Cambridge, MA 02138

Torrance Tests of Creative Thinking
Personnel Press
191 Spring Street
Lexington, MA 02173

Wechsler Adult Intelligence Scale
Psychological Corporation
555 Academic Court
San Antonio, TX 78204

Wechsler Intelligence Scale for Children—Revised
Psychological Corporation
555 Academic Court
San Antonio, TX 78204

Wechsler Preschool and Primary Scale of
   Intelligence
Psychological Corporation
555 Academic Court
San Antonio, TX 78204

Wide Range Achievement Test III
Psychological Corporation
555 Academic Court
San Antonio, TX 78204

Wonderlic Personnel Test
Psychological Corporation
555 Academic Court
San Antonio, TX 78204

Critical Values of r for α = .05 and α = .01 (*Two-Tailed Test*)

df*	α = .05	α = .01	df*	α = .05	α = .01
1	.99692	.999877	17	.456	.575
2	.9500	.99000	18	.444	.561
3	.878	.9587	19	.433	.549
4	.811	.9172	20	.423	.537
5	.754	.875	25	.381	.487
6	.707	.834	30	.349	.449
7	.666	.798	35	.325	.418
8	.632	.765	40	.304	.393
9	.602	.735	45	.288	.372
10	.576	.708	50	.273	.354
11	.553	.684	60	.250	.325
12	.532	.661	70	.232	.302
13	.514	.641	80	.217	.283
14	.497	.623	90	.205	.267
15	.482	.606	100	.195	.254
16	.468	.590			

*df are equal to N − 2, where N is the number of paired observations.

Reprinted with permission from Table IX-1. Percentage Points. Distribution of the Correlation Coefficient. When $p = 0$, *CRC Handbook of Tables for Probability and Statistics* (2nd ed.). Copyright 1968, CRC Press, Inc., Boca Raton, Florida.

Critical Values of *t**

For any given *df*, the table shows the values of *t* corresponding to various levels of probability. Obtained *t* is significant at a given level if it is equal to or greater than the value shown in the table.

---

*Appendix 4 is taken from Table III of R. A. Fisher and R. Yates, 1967, *Statistical Tables for Biological, Agricultural and Medical Research* (6th ed.), New York: Hafner. With permission of the authors and publishers.

	Level of Significance for One-Tailed Test					
	.10	.05	.025	.01	.005	.0005
	Level of Significance for Two-Tailed Test					
df	.20	.10	.05	.02	.01	.001
1	3.078	6.314	12.706	31.821	63.657	636.619
2	1.886	2.920	4.303	6.965	9.925	31.598
3	1.638	2.353	3.182	4.541	5.841	12.941
4	1.533	2.132	2.776	3.747	4.604	8.610
5	1.476	2.015	2.571	3.365	4.032	6.859
6	1.440	1.943	2.447	3.143	3.707	5.959
7	1.415	1.895	2.365	2.998	3.499	5.405
8	1.397	1.860	2.306	2.896	3.355	5.041
9	1.383	1.833	2.262	2.821	3.250	4.781
10	1.372	1.812	2.228	2.764	3.169	4.587
11	1.363	1.796	2.201	2.718	3.106	4.437
12	1.356	1.782	2.179	2.681	3.055	4.318
13	1.350	1.771	2.160	2.650	3.012	4.221
14	1.345	1.761	2.145	2.624	2.977	4.140
15	1.341	1.753	2.131	2.602	2.947	4.073
16	1.337	1.746	2.120	2.583	2.921	4.015
17	1.333	1.740	2.110	2.567	2.898	3.965
18	1.330	1.734	2.101	2.552	2.878	3.922
19	1.328	1.729	2.093	2.539	2.861	3.883
20	1.325	1.725	2.086	2.528	2.845	3.850
21	1.323	1.721	2.080	2.518	2.831	3.819
22	1.321	1.717	2.074	2.508	2.819	3.792
23	1.319	1.714	2.069	2.500	2.807	3.767
24	1.318	1.711	2.064	2.492	2.797	3.745
25	1.316	1.708	2.060	2.485	2.787	3.725
26	1.315	1.706	2.056	2.479	2.779	3.707
27	1.314	1.703	2.052	2.473	2.771	3.690
28	1.313	1.701	2.048	2.467	2.763	3.674
29	1.311	1.699	2.045	2.462	2.756	3.659
30	1.310	1.697	2.042	2.457	2.750	3.646
40	1.303	1.684	2.021	2.423	2.704	3.551
60	1.296	1.671	2.000	2.390	2.660	3.460
120	1.289	1.658	1.980	2.358	2.617	3.373
∞	1.282	1.645	1.960	2.326	2.576	3.291

Code of Fair Testing Practices in Education

*Prepared by the Joint Committee
on Testing Practices*

The Code of Fair Testing Practices in Education states the major obligations to test takers or professionals who develop or use educational tests. The Code is meant to apply broadly to the use of tests in education (admissions, educational assessment, educational diagnosis, and student placement). The Code is not designed to cover employment testing, licensure or certification testing, or other types of testing. Although the Code has relevance to many types of educational tests, it is directed primarily at professionally developed tests such as those sold by commercial test publishers or used in formally administered testing programs. The Code is not intended to cover tests made by individual teachers for use in their own classrooms.

The Code addresses the roles of test developers and test users separately. Test users are people who select tests, commission test development services, or make decisions on the basis of test scores. Test developers are people who actually construct tests as well as those who set policies for particular testing programs. The roles may, of course, overlap as when a state education agency commissions test development services, sets policies that control the test development process, and makes decisions on the basis of the test scores.

The Code has been developed by the Joint Committee on Testing Practices, a cooperative effort of several professional organizations, that has as its aim the advancement, in the public interest, of the quality of testing practices. The Joint Committee was initiated by the American Educational Research Association, the American Psychological Association, and the National Council on Measurement in Education. In addition to these three groups, the American Association for Counseling and Development/Association for Measurement and Evaluation in Counseling and Development and the American Speech-Language-Hearing Association are now also sponsors of the Joint Committee.

This is not copyrighted material. Reproduction and dissemination are encouraged. Please cite this document as follows:
Code of Fair Testing Practices in Education. (1988) Washington, D.C. Joint Committee on Testing Practices. (Mailing Address: Joint Committee on Testing Practices, American Psychological Association, 1200 17th Street, NW, Washington, D.C. 20036.)

The Code presents standards for educational test developers and users in four areas:

A. Developing/Selecting Tests
B. Interpreting Scores
C. Striving for Fairness
D. Informing Test Takers

Organizations, institutions, and individual professionals who endorse the Code commit themselves to safeguarding the rights of test takers by following the principles listed. The Code is intended to be consistent with the relevant parts of the *Standards for Educational and Psychological Testing* (AERA, APA, NCME, 1985). However, the Code differs from the Standards in both audience and purpose. The Code is meant to be understood by the general public, it is limited to educational tests, and the primary focus is on those issues that affect the proper use of tests. The Code is not meant to add new principles over and above those in the Standards or to change the meaning of the Standards. The goal is rather to represent the spirit of a selected portion of the Standards in a way that is meaningful to test takers and/or their parents or guardians. It is the hope of the Joint Committee that the Code will also be judged to be consistent with existing codes of conduct and standards of other professional groups who use educational tests.

Developing/Selecting Appropriate Tests*

Test developers should provide the information that test users need to select appropriate tests.

Test users should select tests that meet the purpose for which they are to be used and that are appropriate for the intended test-taking populations.

Test Developers Should:

1. Define what each test measures and what the test should be used for. Describe the population(s) for which the test is appropriate.

2. Accurately represent the characteristics, usefulness, and limitations of tests for their intended purposes.

3. Explain relevant measurement concepts as necessary for clarity at the level of detail that is appropriate for the intended audience(s).

Test Users Should:

1. First define the purpose for testing and the population to be tested. Then, select a test for that purpose and that population based on a thorough review of the available information.

2. Investigate potentially useful sources of information, in addition to test scores, to corroborate the information provided by tests.

3. Read the materials provided by test developers and avoid using tests for which unclear or incomplete information is provided.

---

*Many of the statements in the Code refer to the selection of existing tests. However, in customized testing programs test developers are engaged to construct new tests. In those situations, the test development process should be designed to help ensure that the completed tests will be in compliance with the Code.

4. Describe the process of test development. Explain how the content and skills to be tested were selected.

5. Provide evidence that the tests meets its intended purpose(s).

6. Provide either representative samples or complete copies of test questions, directions, answer sheets, manuals, and score reports to qualified users.

7. Indicate the nature of the evidence obtained concerning the appropriateness of each test for groups of different racial, ethnic, or linguistic backgrounds who are likely to be tested.

8. Identify and publish any specialized skills needed to administer each test and to interpret scores correctly.

4. Become familiar with how and when the test was developed and tried out.

5. Read independent evaluations of a test and of possible alternative measures. Look for evidence required to support the claims of test developers.

6. Examine specimen sets, disclosed tests or samples of questions, directions, answer sheets, manuals, and score reports before selecting a test.

7. Ascertain whether the test content and norms group(s) or comparison group(s) are appropriate for the intended test takers.

8. Select and use only those tests for which the skills needed to administer the test and interpret scores correctly are available.

Interpreting Scores

Test developers should help users interpret scores correctly.

Test users should interpret scores correctly.

Test Developers Should:

9. Provide timely and easily understood score reports that describe test performance clearly and accurately. Also explain the meaning and limitations of reported scores.

10. Describe the population(s) represented by any norms or comparison group(s), the dates the data were gathered, and the process used to select the samples of test takers.

11. Warn users to avoid specific, reasonably anticipated misuses of test scores.

12. Provide information that will help users follow reasonable procedures for setting passing scores when it is appropriate to use such scores with the test.

Test Users Should:

9. Obtain information about the scale used for reporting scores, the characteristics of any norms or comparison group(s), and the limitations of the scores.

10. Interpret scores taking into account any major differences between the norms or comparison groups and the actual test takers. Also take into account any differences in test administration practices or familiarity with the specific questions in the test.

11. Avoid using tests for purposes not specifically recommended by the test developer unless evidence is obtained to support the intended use.

12. Explain how any passing scores were set and gather evidence to support the appropriateness of the scores.

13. Provide information that will help users gather evidence to show that the test is meeting its intended purpose(s).

13. Obtain evidence to help show that the test is meeting its intended purpose(s).

Striving for Fairness

Test developers should strive to make tests that are as fair as possible for test takers of different races, gender, ethnic backgrounds, or handicapping conditions.

Test users should select tests that have been developed in ways that attempt to make them as fair as possible for test takers of different races, gender, ethnic backgrounds, or handicapping conditions.

Test Developers Should:

14. Review and revise test questions and related materials to avoid potentially insensitive content or language.

15. Investigate the performance of test takers of different races, gender, and ethnic backgrounds when samples of sufficient size are available. Enact procedures that help to ensure that differences in performance are related primarily to the skills under assessment rather than to irrelevant factors.

16. When feasible, make appropriately modified forms of tests or administration procedures available for test takers with handicapping conditions. Warn test users of potential problems in using standard norms with modified tests or administration procedures that result in noncomparable scores.

Test Users Should:

14. Evaluate the procedures used by test developers to avoid potentially insensitive content or language.

15. Review the performance of test takers of different races, gender, and ethnic backgrounds when samples of sufficient size are available. Evaluate the extent to which performance differences may have been caused by inappropriate characteristics of the test.

16. When necessary and feasible, use appropriately modified forms of tests or administration procedures for test takers with handicapping conditions. Interpret standard norms with care in the light of the modifications that were made.

Informing Test Takers

Under some circumstances, test developers have direct communication with test takers. Under other circumstances, test users communicate directly with test takers. Whichever group communicates directly with test takers should provide the information described below.

Under some circumstances, test developers have direct control of tests and test scores. Under other circumstances, test users have such control. Whichever group has direct control of tests and test scores should take the steps described below.

Test Developers or Test Users Should:

17. When a test is optional, provide test takers or their parents/guardians with information to help them judge whether the test should be taken, or if an available alternative to the test should be used.

Test Developers or Test Users Should:

19. Provide test takers or their parents/guardians with information about rights test takers may have to obtain copies of tests and completed answer sheets, retake tests, have tests rescored, or cancel scores.

18. Provide test takers the information they need to be familiar with the coverage of the test, the types of question formats, the directions, and appropriate test-taking strategies. Strive to make such information equally available to all test takers.

20. Tell test takers or their parents/guardians how long scores will be kept on file and indicate to whom and under what circumstances test scores will or will not be released.

21. Describe the procedures that test takers or their parents/guardians may use to register complaints and have problems resolved.

Note: The membership of the Working Group that developed the Code of Fair Testing Practices in Education and of the Joint Committee on Testing Practices that guided the Working Group was as follows:

Theodore P. Bartell
John R. Bergan
Esther E. Diamond
Richard P. Duran
Lorraine D. Eyde
Raymond D. Fowler
John J. Fremer
　(Co-chair, JCTP and Chair, Code Working Group)

Edmund W. Gordon
Jo-Ida C. Hansen
James B. Lingwall
George F. Madaus
　(Co-chair, JCTP)
Kevin L. Moreland
Jo-Ellen V. Perez
Robert J. Solomon
John T. Stewart

Carol Kehr Tittle
　(Co-chair, JCTP)
Nicholas A. Vacc
Michael J. Zieky
Debra Boltas and Wayne Camara of the American Psychological Association served as staff liaisons.

Glossary

Achievement Previous learning.

Acquiescence The tendency to agree or to endorse a test item as true.

Adverse impact The effect of any test used for selection purposes if it systematically rejects substantially higher proportions of minority than majority job applicants.

Age differentiation Discrimination based on the fact that older children have greater capabilities than younger children.

Age scale A test in which items are grouped according to age level. (The Binet scale, for example, grouped into one age level items that two-thirds to three-quarters of a representative group of children at a specific age could successfully pass.)

Anxiety An unpleasant emotional state marked by worry, apprehension, and tension.

Aptitude Potential for learning a specific skill (for example, musical aptitude).

Assessment A procedure used to evaluate an individual so that one can describe the person in terms of current functioning and also so that one can predict future functioning. Tests are used in the assessment process.

Basal age In the Stanford-Binet scale, the highest year level at which the subject successfully passes all tests.

Base rate In decision analysis, the proportion of people expected to succeed on a criterion if they are chosen at random.

Biserial correlation An index used to express the relationship between a continuous variable and an artificially dichotomous variable.

Category format A rating-scale format that often uses the categories 1 to 10.

Ceiling In the Stanford-Binet scale, the year level at which all tests are failed.

Class interval The unit for the horizontal axis in a frequency distribution.

Closed-ended question In interviewing, a question that can be answered specifically (for example, "Yes" or "No"). Such questions generally require the interviewee to recall something.

Coefficient alpha A generalized method for estimating reliability. Alpha is similar to the KR_{20} formula, except that it allows items to take on values other than 0 and 1.

Coefficient of alienation In correlation and regression analysis, the index of nonassociation between two variables.

Coefficient of determination The correlation coefficient squared; gives an estimate of the percentage of variation in Y that is known as a function of knowing X (and vice versa).

Concurrent validity A form of criterion validity in which the test and the criterion are administered at the same point in time.

Confrontation A statement that points out a discrepancy or inconsistency.

Construct validity A process used to established the meaning of a test through a series of studies. To evaluate construct validity, a researcher simultaneously defines some construct and develops the instrumentation to measure it. In the studies, observed correlations between the test and other measures come to define the meaning of the test. See also *convergent evidence* and *discriminant evidence*.

Content validity The extent to which the content of a test represents the conceptual domain it is designed to cover.

Convergent evidence Evidence obtained to demonstrate that a test measures the same attribute as other measures do that purport to measure the same thing. A form of construct validity.

Correction for attenuation Correction of the reduction, caused by low reliability, in the estimated correlation between a test and another measure. The correction for attenuation formula is used to estimate what the correlation would have been if the variables had been perfectly reliable.

Correlation coefficient A mathematical index used to describe the direction and the magnitude of a relationship between two variables. The correlation coefficient ranges between -1.0 and 1.0.

Criterion-referenced test A test that describes the specific types of skills, tasks, or knowledge of an individual relative to a well-defined mastery criterion. The content of criterion-referenced tests is limited to certain well-defined objectives.

Criterion validity The extent to which a test score corresponds to an accurate measure of interest. The measure of interest is called the criterion.

Cross validation The process of evaluating a test or

a regression equation for a sample other than the one used for the original studies.

Descriptive statistics   Methods used to provide a concise description of a collection of quantitative information.

Deciles   Points that divide the frequency distribution into equal tenths.

Developmental quotient   In the Gesell Developmental Schedules, a test score that is obtained by assessing the presence or absence of behaviors associated with maturation.

Diagnostic interview   An interview designed to elicit information concerning emotional functioning, including feelings, thoughts, and attitudes.

Dichotomous format   A test item format in which there are two alternatives for each item.

Differential validity   The extent to which a test has different meanings for different groups of people. For example, a test may be a valid predictor of college success for white but not for black students.

Discriminability   In item analysis, how well an item performs in relation to some criterion. For example, items may be compared according to how well they separate groups who score high and low on the test. The index of discrimination would then be the correlation between performance on an item and performance on the whole test.

Discriminant analysis   A multivariate data analysis method for finding the linear combination of variables that best describes the classification of groups into discrete categories.

Discriminant evidence   Evidence obtained to demonstrate that a test measures something different from what other available tests measure. A form of construct validity.

Distractor   An alternative on a multiple-choice exam that is not correct or for which no credit is given.

Drift   The tendency for observers in behavioral studies to stray from the definitions they learned during training and to develop their own idiosyncratic definitions of behaviors.

Dyslexia   A specific reading disorder characterized by reading backwardness.

EEOC guidelines   A set of procedures created by the Equal Employment Opportunity Commission (EEOC) to ensure fairness in employment practices. The EEOC guidelines discuss the minimum requirements for the validity and reliability of psychological tests used for employee selection.

Empathy response   In interviewing, a statement that communicates understanding (also called an *understanding response*).

Employment interview   An interview designed to elicit information pertaining to a person's qualifications and capabilities for particular employment duties.

Estimated learning potentials (ELPs)   In the SOMPA system, WISC-R scores adjusted for the socioeconomic background of the children. ELPs take the place of IQ scores.

Evaluative statement   A statement in interviewing that judges or evaluates.

Expectancy effect   The tendency for results to be influenced by what an experimenter or a test administrator expects to find (also known as the Rosenthal effect, after the psychologist who has studied this problem intensively).

Face validity   The extent to which items on a test appear to be meaningful and relevant. Actually not a form of validity because face validity is not a basis for inference.

Factor analysis   A set of multivariate data analysis methods for reducing large matrixes of correlations to fewer variables. The variables are linear combinations of the variables that were in the original correlation matrix.

False negative   In test-decision theory, a case in which the test suggests a negative classification, yet the correct classification is positive.

False positive   In test decision analysis, a case in which the test suggests a positive classification, yet the correct classification is negative.

Four-fifths rule   A rule used by federal agencies in deciding whether there is equal employment opportunity. Any procedure that results in a selection rate for any race, gender, or ethnic group that is less than four-fifths (80%) of the selection rate for the group with the highest rate is regarded as having an adverse impact.

Frequency distribution   The systematic arrangement of scores on a measure to reflect how frequently each value on the measure occurred.

General cognitive index   In the McCarthy Scales of Children's Abilities, a standard score with a mean of 100 and standard deviation of 16.

Group test   A test that a single test administrator can give to more than one person at a time.

Hit rate   In test decision analysis, the proportion of cases in which a test accurately predicts success or failure.

Hostile statement A statement in interviewing that reflects anger.

Human ability Behaviors that reflect either what a person has learned or the person's capacity to emit a specific behavior; includes *achievement, aptitude,* and *intelligence.*

Individual test A test that can be given to only one person at a time.

Inference A logical deduction (from evidence) about something one cannot observe directly.

Inferential statistics Methods used to make inferences from a small group of observations, called a sample. These inferences are then applied to a larger group of individuals, known as a population. Typically, the researcher wants to make statements about the larger group but cannot make all the necessary observations.

Intelligence General potential, independent of prior learning.

Intelligence quotient A unit for expressing the results of intelligence tests. The intelligence quotient is based on the ratio of the individual's mental age (*MA*) (as determined by the test) to actual or chronological age (*CA*): $IQ = MA/CA \times 100$.

Intercept On a two-dimensional graph, the point on the *y* axis where *x* equals 0. In regression, this is the point at which the regression line intersects the *y* axis.

Interquartile range The interval of scores bounded by the 25th and the 75th percentiles.

Interval scale A scale that one can use to rank order objects and on which the units reflect equivalent magnitudes of the property being measured.

Interview A method of gathering information by talk, discussion, or direct questions.

Ipsative scores Test results presented in relative rather than absolute terms. Ipsative scores compare the individual against himself or herself. Each person thus provides his or her own frame of reference.

Isodensity curve An ellipse on a scatterplot (or two-dimensional scatter diagram) that encircles a specified proportion of the cases constituting particular groups.

Item analysis A set of methods used to evaluate test items. The most common techniques involve assessment of item difficulty and item discriminability.

Item characteristic curve A graph prepared as part of the process of item analysis. One graph is prepared for each test item and shows the total test score on the *x* axis and the proportion of test takers passing the item on the *y* axis.

Item difficulty A form of item analysis used to assess how difficult items are. The most common index of difficulty is the percentage of test takers who respond with the correct choice.

Item discriminability See *discriminability.*

Kuder-Richardson 20 A formula for estimating the internal consistency of a test. The KR_{20} method is equivalent to the average split-half correlation obtained from all possible splits of the items. For the KR_{20} formula to be applied, all items must be scored either 0 or 1.

Likert format A format for attitude scale items in which subjects indicate their degree of agreement to statements using these categories: strongly disagree, disagree, neither disagree nor agree, agree, strongly agree.

McCall's *T* A standardized score system with a mean of 50 and a standard deviation of 10. McCall's *T* can be obtained from a simple linear transformation of *Z* scores ($T = 10Z + 50$).

Mean The arithmetic average of a set of scores on a variable.

Measurement error The component of an observed test score that is neither the true score nor the quality you wish to measure.

Median The point on a frequency distribution marking the 50th percentile.

Mental age A unit for expressing the results of intelligence tests. This unit is based on comparing the individual's performance on the test with the average performance of individuals in a specific chronological age group.

Multiple regression A multivariate data analysis method that considers the relationship between a continuous outcome variable and the linear combination of two or more predictor variables.

Multivariate analysis A set of methods for data analysis that considers the relationships between combinations of three or more variables.

Nominal scale A system of arbitrarily assigning numbers to objects. Mathematical manipulation of numbers from a nominal scale is not justified. For example, numbers on the backs of football players' uniforms are a nominal scale.

Normative sample A comparison group consisting of individuals who have been administered a test under standard conditions—that is, with the instructions, format, and general procedures outlined in the test manual for administering the test (also called a *standardization sample*).

Norm-referenced test   A test that evaluates each individual relative to a normative group.

Norms   A summary of the performance of a group of individuals on which a test was standardized. The norms usually include the mean and the standard deviation for the reference group and information on how to translate a raw score into a percentile rank.

Open-ended question   In interviewing, a question that usually cannot be answered specifically. Such questions require the interviewee to produce something spontaneously.

Ordinal scale   A scale that one can use to rank order objects or individuals.

Parallel forms reliability   The method of reliability assessment used to evaluate the error associated with the use of a particular set of items. Equivalent forms of a test are developed by generating two forms using the same rules. The correlation between the two forms is the estimate of parallel forms reliability.

Pearson product moment correlation   An index of correlation between two continuous variables.

Percentile band   The range of percentiles that are likely to represent a subject's true score. It is created by forming an interval one standard error of measurement above and below the obtained score and converting the resulting values to percentiles.

Percentile rank   The proportion of scores that fall below a particular score.

Performance scale   A test that consists of tasks that require a subject to do something rather than to answer questions.

Personality test   A test that measures overt and covert dispositions of the individual (the tendency that the individual will show a particular behavior or response in any given situation). Personality tests measure typical human behavior.

Point scale   A test in which points (0, 1, or 2, for example) are assigned to each item. In a point scale, all items with a particular content can be grouped together.

Polytomous format   A format for objective tests in which three or more alternative responses are given for each item. This format is popular for multiple-choice exams. Also called *polychotomous format.*

Predictive validity   The extent to which a test forecasts scores on the criterion at some future time.

Probing statement   A statement in interviewing that demands more information than the interviewee has been willing to provide of his or her own accord.

Projective hypothesis   The proposal that when a person attempts to understand an ambiguous or vague stimulus, his or her interpretation reflects needs, feelings, experiences, prior conditioning, thought processes, and so forth.

Projective personality test   A test in which the stimulus or the required response or both are ambiguous. The general idea behind projective tests is that a person's interpretation of an ambiguous stimulus reflects his or her unique characteristics.

Prophecy formula   A formula developed by Spearman and Brown that one can use to correct for the loss of reliability that occurs when the split-half method is used and each half of the test is one half as long as the whole test. The method can also be used to estimate how much the test length must be increased to bring the test to a desired level of reliability.

Psychological test   A device for measuring characteristics of human beings that pertain to overt (observable) and covert (intraindividual) behavior. A psychological test measures past, present, or future human behavior.

Psychological testing   The use of psychological tests. Psychological testing refers to all the possible uses, applications, and underlying concepts of psychological tests.

Quartiles   Points that divide the frequency distribution into equal fourths.

Randomly parallel tests   Tests created by successive random sampling of items from a domain or universe of items.

Ratio scale   An interval scale with an absolute zero, or point at which there is none of the property being measured.

Reactivity   The phenomenon that causes the reliability of a scale in behavior studies to be higher when an observer knows that his or her work is being monitored.

Reassuring statement In interviewing, a statement intended to comfort or support.

Receptive vocabulary In the Peabody Picture Vocabulary Test, a nonverbal estimate of verbal intelligence; in general, the ability to understand language.

Regression line The best-fitting straight line through a set of points in a scatter diagram.

Reliability The extent to which a score or measure is free of measurement error. Theoretically, reliability is the ratio of true score variance to observed score variance. This ratio can be estimated using a variety of correlational methods, including *coefficient alpha, Kuder-Richardson 20, test-retest,* and *parallel forms.*

Representative sample A sample (group) composed of individuals with characteristics similar to those for whom the test is to be used.

Residual The difference between predicted and observed values from a regression equation.

Response style The tendency to mark a test item in a certain way irrespective of content.

Rosenthal effect See *expectancy effect.*

Scaled score On the Wechsler tests, a standard score with a mean of 10 and a standard deviation of 3.

Scatter diagram A picture of the relationship between two variables. For each individual, a pair of observations is obtained, and the values are plotted in a two-dimensional space created by variables X and Y.

Selection ratio In test decision analysis, the proportion of selected applicants to unselected ones.

Self-report questionnaire A questionnaire that provides a list of statements about an individual and requires him or her to respond in some way to each, such as "True" or "False."

Shrinkage Many times a regression equation is created for one group and used to predict the performance of another group of subjects. This procedure tends to overestimate the magnitude of the relationship for the second group. The amount of decrease in the strength of the relationship from the original sample to the sample with which the equation is used is known as *shrinkage.*

Social ecology A relatively new field of study that deals with the relationship between environments and behavior, the description of behavioral settings, and other related topics.

Social facilitation Tendency of people to behave like the models around them.

Spearman's rho A method for finding the correlation between two sets of ranks.

Split-half reliability A method for evaluating reliability in which a test is split into halves. The correlation between the halves of the test, corrected for the shortened length of the halves, is used as an estimate of reliability.

Standard administration The procedures outlined in the test manual for administering a test.

Standard deviation The square root of the average squared deviation around the mean (or the variance). It is used as a measure of variability in a distribution of scores.

Standard error of estimate An index of the accuracy of a regression equation. It is equivalent to the standard deviation of the residuals from a regression analysis. Prediction is most accurate when the standard error of estimate is small.

Standard error of measurement An index of the amount of error in a test or measure. The standard error of measurement is a standard deviation of a set of observations for the same test.

Standardization sample A comparison group consisting of individuals who have been administered a test under standard conditions—that is, with the instructions, format, and general procedures outlined in the test manual for administering the test (also called a *normative sample*).

Standardized interview An interview conducted under standard conditions that are well defined in a manual or procedure book.

Stanine system A system for assigning the numbers 1 through 9 to a test score. The system was developed by the U.S. Air Force. The standardized stanine distribution has a mean of 5 and a standard deviation of approximately 2.

State anxiety An emotional reaction to a situation. State anxiety varies from one situation to the next.

Stress A response to situations that pose demands, place constraints, or give opportunities.

Structured personality test A test that provides a statement, usually of the self-report variety ("I like rock and roll music"), and requires the subject to choose between two or more alternative responses ("True" or "False," for example). Sometimes called an objective personality test.

Subtest scatter On the Wechsler tests, the degree of subtest variability.

T **score**   On the MMPI, a standard score with a mean of 50 and a standard deviation of 10. (See also *McCall's T.*)

Taylor-Russell tables   A series of tables one can use to evaluate the validity of a test in relation to the amount of information it contributes beyond what would be known by chance.

Test   A measurement device that quantifies behavior.

Test administration   The act of giving a test.

Test administrator   Person giving a test.

Test anxiety   Anxiety that occurs in test-taking situations.

Test battery   A collection of tests the scores of which are used together in appraising an individual.

Test-retest reliability   A method for estimating how much measurement error is caused by time sampling, or administering the test at two different points in time. Test-retest reliability is usually estimated from the correlation between performances on two different administrations of the test.

Third variable   A variable that may account for the observed relationship between two other variables.

Tracking   The tendency to stay at about the same level of growth or performance relative to other peers who are the same age.

Trait   An enduring or persistent characteristic of an individual that is independent of situations.

Trait anxiety   A personality characteristic reflecting the differences among people in the intensity of their reaction to stressful situations.

True score   The score that would be obtained on a test or measure if there were no measurement error. In practice, the true score can be estimated but not directly observed.

Understanding response   In interviewing, a statement that communicates understanding (also called an *empathy response*).

Unstructured interview   An interview conducted without any specific or particular questions or sequences of questions.

Validity   The extent to which a test measures the quality it purports to measure. Types of validity include *content validity, criterion validity,* and *construct validity.*

Variance   The average squared deviation around the mean; the standard deviation squared.

References

Abdelkhalek, A. M. (1994). Normative results on the Arabic Fear Survey Schedule 3. *Journal of Behavior Therapy and Experimental Psychiatry, 25*(1), 61–67.

Abrams, E. W. (1955). Predictions of intelligence from certain Rorschach factors. *Journal of Clinical Psychology, 11*, 81–94.

Abramson, L. Y., Alloy, L. B., & Metalsky, G. I. (1995). Hopelessness depression: Explanatory style. In G. M. Buchanan & E. P. Seligman (Eds.), *Explanatory style*. (pp. 113– 134). Hillsdale, NJ: Lawrence Erlbaum Associates.

Abramson, L. Y., Metalsky, G. I., & Alloy, L. B. (1989). Helplessness depression: A theory based system of depression. *Psychological Review, 96*, 358–372.

Abramson, T. (1969). The influence of examiner race on first-grade and kindergarten subjects' Peabody Picture Vocabulary Test scores. *Journal of Educational Measurement, 6*, 241–246.

Ackerman, P. T., Dykman, R. A., & Gardner, M. Y. (1990). ADD students with and without dyslexia differ in sensitivity to rhyme and alliteration. *Journal of Learning Disabilities, 23*, 279–283.

Acklin, M. W. (1995). Rorschach assesment of the borderline child. *Journal of Clinical Psychology, 51*(2), 294–302.

Adler, A. (1964). *Social interest: A challenge to mankind.* New York: Capricorn. (Original work published 1933.)

Affleck, G., Tennen, H., Urrows S., & Higgins, P. (1994). Person and contextual features of daily stress reactivity: Individual differences in relations of undesirable daily events with mood disturbance and chronic pain intensity. *Journal of Personality and Social Psychology, 66*(2) 329–340.

Ahern S., & Beatty, J. (1979). Pupillary responses vary during information-processing with scholastic aptitude test score. *Science, 205*, 1289–1292.

Aiken, L. R. (1987). *Assessment of intellectual functioning.* Newton, MA: Allyn and Bacon.

Akutagawa, D. A. (1956). *A study in construct validity of the psychoanalytic concept of latent anxiety and a test of projection distance hypothesis.* Unpublished doctoral dissertation, University of Pittsburgh, PA.

Alarcon, R. D., Libb, J. W., & Boll, T. J. (1994). Neuropsychological testing in obsessive-compulsive disorder: A clinical review. *Journal of Neuropsychiatry and Clinical Neurosciences, 6*, 217–228.

Albert, M. S. (1981). Geriatric neuropsychology. *Journal of Consulting and Clinical Psychology, 49*, 835–850.

Alexander, G. E., Prohovnik, I., Stern, Y., & Mayeux, R. (1994). WAIS-R subtest profile and cortical perfusion in Alzheimer's disease. *Brain and Cognition, 24*(1), 24–43.

Allen, F. (1994). The diagnostic interview for genetic studies. *Archives of General Psychiatry, 51*(11), 863–864.

Allen, G. J. (1972). The behavioral treatment of text anxiety: Recent research and future trends. *Behavior Therapy, 3*, 253–262.

Allen, J. G., & Smith, W. H. (1993). Diagnosing dissociative disorders. *Bulletin of the Menninger Clinic, 57*(3), 328–343.

Allen, J. J., Iacono, W. G., & Danielson, K. (1992). The development and validation of an event-related potential memory assessment procedure: A methodology for prediction in the face of individual differences. *Psychophysiology, 29*, 504–522.

Allen, M. J., & Yen, W. M. (1979). *Introduction to measurement theory.* Pacific Grove, CA: Brooks/Cole.

Allison, J., Blatt, S. J., & Zimet, C. N. (1968). *The interpretation of psychological tests.* New York: Harper & Row.

Allport, G. W., & Odbert, H. S. (1936). Trait-names, a psycholexical study. *Psychological Monographs, 47*(1)

Alpert, R., & Haber, R. N. (1960). Anxiety in academic achievement situations. *Journal of Abnormal and Social Psychology, 61*, 207–215.

Als, H. (1984). Newborn behavioral assessment. In W. J. Burns & J. V. Lavigne (Eds.), *Progress in pediatric psychology.* New York: Grune & Stratton.

Als, H., Tronick, E., Adamson, L., & Brazelton, T. B. (1976). The behavior of the full-term yet underweight newborn infant. *Developmental Medicine and Child Neurology, 18*, 599–602.

Als, H., Tronick, E., Lester, B. M., & Brazelton, T. B. (1979). Specific neonatal measures: The Brazelton neonatal behavioral assessment scale. In J. Osofsky (Ed.), *Handbook of infant development.* New York: Wiley.

Altmaier, E. M., McGuinnes, S. G., Wood, P., Ross, R. R., Bartley, J., & Smith, W. L. (1990). Defining successful performance among pediatric residents. *Pediatrics, 85*, 139–143.

Altmaier, E. M., Smith, W. L., O'Halloran, C. M., & Franken, E. A., Jr. (1992). The predictive utility of behavior-based interviewing compared with traditional interviewing in the selection of radiology residents. *Investigative Radiology, 27*(5), 385–389.

Alvarado, N. (1994). Empirical validity of the Thematic Apperception Test. *Journal of Personality Assessment, 63*(1), 59–79.

647

American Education Research Association, American Psychological Association, & National Council on Measurement in Education. (1985). *Standards for educational and psychological testing.* Washington, DC: American Psychological Association.

American Psychiatric Association. (1980). *Diagnostic and statistical manual of mental disorders* (3rd ed.). Washington, DC: American Psychiatric Association.

American Psychiatric Association. (1995). *Diagnostic and statistical manual of mental disorders* (4th ed.) (DSM-IV: Primary care version). Washington, DC: American Psychiatric Association.

American Psychological Association (APA) (1954). *Psychology and its relations with other professions.* Washington, D.C.: American Psychological Association.

American Psychological Association (APA) (1974). *Standards for educational and psychological tests.* Washington, D.C.: American Psychological Association.

American Psychological Association (APA). (1981). Ethical principles of psychologists. *American Psychologist, 36,* 633–638.

Ames, L. B. (1967). Predictive value of infant behavior examination. In J. Hellmuth (Ed.), *Exceptional infant. The normal infant* (Vol. 1). Seattle: Straub & Hellmuth.

Ames, L. B., Metraux, R. W., & Walker, R. N. (1971). *Adolescent Rorschach responses.* New York: Brunner/Mazel.

Ammons, R. B., & Ammons, C. H. (1962). The quick test (QT): Provisional manual. *Psychological Reports, 11,* 111–161.

Anastasi, A. (1972a). Personality research form. In O. K. Buros (Ed.), *The seventh mental measurements yearbook* (Vol. 1). Highland Park, NJ: Gryphon Press.

Anastasi, A. (1972b). Review of the Goodenough-Harris Drawing Test. In O. K. Buros (Ed.), *The seventh mental measurements yearbook* (Vol. 1). Highland Park, NJ: Gryphon Press.

Anastasi, A. (1976). *Psychological testing* (4th ed.). New York: Macmillan.

Anastasi, A. (1981). Coaching, test sophistication, and developed abilities. *American Psychologist, 36,* 1086–1093.

Anastasi, A. (1984). The K-ABC in historical and contemporary perspective. *Journal of Special Education, 78*(3), 357–366.

Anastasi, A. (1986). Evolving concepts of test validation. *Annual Review of Psychology, 37,* 1–15.

Anastasi, A. (1993). A century of psychological testing: Origins, problems, and progress. In T. K. Fagan & G. R. VandenBos (Eds.), *Exploring applied psychology: Origins and critical analyses* (pp. 13–36). *American Psychological Association.* Washington, D.C.

Anastasi, A. (1995). Psychology evolving: Linkages, hierarchies, and dimensions. F. Kessel, (Ed.) *Psychology, science, and human affairs: Essays in honor of William Bevan.* (pp. 245–260). Boulder, CO: Westview Press.

Anastopoulos, A. D., Spisto, M. A., & Maher, M. C. (1994). The WISC-III freedom from distractibility factor: Its utility in identifying children with attention deficit hyperactivity disorder. *Psychological Assessment, 6*(4), 368–371.

Anderson, N. B., & McNeilly, M. (1991). Age, gender, and ethnicity as variables in psychophysiological assessment: Sociodemographics in context. *Psychological Assessment: A Journal of Consulting and Clinical Psychology, 3,* 376–384.

Anderson, N. H. (1991). Contributions to information integration theory. Hillsdale, NJ: Erlbaum.

Angoff, W. H. (1993). Perspectives on differential item functioning methodology. W. Holland & Wainer, (Eds.), *Differential item functioning,* (pp. 3–23). Hillsdale, NJ: Lawrence Erlbaum Associates.

Ansorge, C. J. (1985). Review of the Cognitive Abilities Test, Form 3. In J. V. Mitchell (Ed.), *The ninth mental measurements yearbook* (Vol. 1). Highland Park, NJ: Gryphon Press.

Anton, W. D. (1976). An evaluation of outcome variables in the systematic desensitization of test anxiety. *Behaviour Research and Therapy, 14,* 217–224.

Archer, R. P., Maruish, M., Imhof, E. A., & Piotrowski, C. (1991). Psychological test usage with adolescent clients: 1990 survey. *Professional Psychology: Research & Practice, 22,* 247–252.

Arkes, H. R. (1991). Costs and benefits from judgment errors: Implications for debiasing. *Psychological Bulletin, 110,* 486–489.

Aronow, E., Reznikoff, M., & Moreland, K. L. (1995). The Rorschach: Projective technique or psychometric test. *Journal of Personality Assessment, 64*(3), 213–228.

Aronow, E., Reznikoff, M., & Rauchway, A. (1979). Some old and new directions in Rorschach testing. *Journal of Personality Assessment, 43,* 227–234.

Arthur, G. (1930). *Arthur point scale of performance tests.* Chicago: Stoelting.

Arthur, W., & Day, D. V. (1994). Development of a short form for the Raven Advanced Progressive Matrices Test. *Educational and Psychological Measurement, 54*(2), 394–403.

Arvey, R. D., & Campion, J. E. (1982). The employment interview: A summary and review of recent research. *Personnel Psychology, 35,* 281–322.

Asher, J. J., & Sciarrino, J. A. (1974). Realistic work sample tests: A review. *Personnel Psychology, 27,* 519–533.

Atkinson, J. W. (1981). Studying personality in the context of an advanced motivational psychology. *American Psychologist, 36,* 117–128.

Atkinson, L. (1990a). Intellectual and adaptive functioning: Some tables for interpreting the Vineland in combination with intelligence tests. *Journal of Mental Retardation, 95,* 198–203.

Atkinson, L. (1990b). Reliability and validity of ratio developmental quotients from the Cattell Infant Intelligence Scale. *American Journal of Mental Retardation, 95,* 215–219.

Avolio, B. J., & Waidman, D. A. (1990). An examination of age and cognitive test performance across job complexity and occupational types. *Journal of Applied Psychology, 75,* 43–50.

Ax, A. F. (1953). The physiological differentiation between fear and anger in humans. *Psychosomatic Medicine, 15,* 433–442.

Azrin, N. H., Holz, W., Ulrich, R., & Goldiamond, I. (1961). The control of the content of conversation through reinforcement. *Journal of the Experimental Analysis of Behavior, 4,* 25–30.

Azrin, N. H., & Powell, J. (1968). Behavioral engineering: The reduction of smoking behavior by a conditioning apparatus and procedure. *Journal of Applied Behavior Analysis, 1,* 193–200.

Baddeley, A. D., Wilson, B. A., & Watts, F. N. (1995). *Handbook of memory disorders.* Chichester, England: Wiley.

Baehr, M. (1987). A review of employee evaluation procedures and a description of "high potential" executives and professionals. *Journal of Business and Psychology, 1,* 172–202.

Baglan T. (1981). Effects of interpersonal attraction and type of behavior on attributions. *Psychological Reports, 48,* 299–304.

Baird, L. L. (1972). Review of the Torrance Tests of Creative Thinking. In O. K. Buros (Ed.), *The seventh mental measurements yearbook* (vol. 1). Highland Park, NJ: Gryphon Press.

Baker, E. L., O'Neil, H. F., & Linn, R. L. (1994). Policy and validity prospects for performance-based assessment [Special issue: Reformers speak]. *Journal for the Education of the Gifted, 17,* 331–353.

Ball, J. D., Archer, R. P., & Imhof, E. A. (1994). Time requirements of psychological testing: A survey of practitioners. *Journal of Personality Assessment, 63,* 239–249.

Balzer, W. K., Rohrbaugh, J., & Murphy, K. R. (1983). Reliability of actual and predicted judgments across time. *Organizational Behavior and Human Performance, 32,* 109–123.

Bandura, A. (1977). Self-efficacy: Toward a unifying theory of behavioral change. *Psychological Review, 84,* 191–215.

Bandura, A. (1986). *Social foundations of thought and action: A social cognitive theory.* Englewood Cliffs, NJ: Prentice-Hall.

Bandura, A. (1992). Exercise of personal agency through the self-efficacy mechanism. In R. Schwarzer (Ed.), *Self-efficacy: Thought control of action* (pp. 3–38). Washington, DC: Hemisphere.

Bandura, A. (1994). Regulative function of perceived self-efficacy. M. G. Rumsey, C. B. Walker, & J. H. Harris (Eds.) *Personnel selection and classification,* (pp. 261–271). Hillsdale, NJ: Lawrence Erlbaum Associates.

Banerji, M. (1992a). Factor structure of the Gessell-School

Readiness Screening Test. *Journal of Psychoeducational Assessment, 10*(4), 342–354.

Banerji, M. (1992b). An integrated study of the predictive properties of the Gessell School Readiness Screening Test. *Journal of Psychoeducational Assessment, 10*(3), 240–256.

Barber, T. X., & Silver, M. J. (1968). Fact, fiction, and the experimenter bias effect. *Psychological Bulletin Monograph Supplement, 70,* 1–29.

Bareak, B., & Lauter, D. (1991, November 5). 1991 rights bill a return to earlier path of bias redress. *Los Angeles Times,* pp. A1, A18.

Barker, R. G. (1979). Settings of a professional lifetime. *Journal of Personality and Social Psychology, 37,* 2137–2157.

Barker, R. G., & Schoggen, P. (1973). *Qualities of community life.* San Francisco: Jossey-Bass.

Barnes, J. H., Banahan, B. F., & Fish, K. E. (1995). The response effect of question order in computer-administered questioning in the social sciences. *Social Science Computer Review, 13,* 47–63.

Baron, R. A. (1986). Self-presentation in job interviews: When there can be "too much" of a good thing. *Journal of Applied Social Psychology, 16,* 16–28.

Barrett, G. V., & Depinct, R. L. (1991). A reconsideration of testing for confidence rather than for intelligence. *American Psychologist, 46,* 1012–1024.

Bartell, S. S., & Solanto, M. V. (1995). Usefulness of the Rorschach Inkblot Test in assessment of attention deficit hyperactivity disorder. *Perceptual and Motor Skills, 80*(2), 531–541.

Bartlett, C. J., & O'Leary, B. S. (1969). A differential prediction model to moderate the effects of heterogeneous groups in personnel selection and classification. *Personnel Psychology, 22,* 117.

Baxter, D. J., Barbaree, H. E., & Marshall, W. L. (1986). Sexual responses to consenting and forced sex in a large sample of rapists and nonrapists. *Behaviour Research and Therapy, 24,* 513–520.

Bayles, K. A. (1990). Language and Parkinson disease. *Alzheimer Disease and Associated Disorders, 4,* 171–180.

Bayley, N. (1949). Consistency and variability in the growth of intelligence from birth to 18 years. *Journal of Genetic Psychology, 75,* 165–196.

Bayley, N. (1969). *Manual: Bayley Scales of Infant Development.* New York: Psychological Corporation.

Beal, J. A. (1991). Methodological issues in conducting research on parent-infant attachment. *Journal of Pediatric Nursing, 6,* 11–15.

Beck, A. T. (1967). *Depression: Clinical, experimental, and theoretical aspects.* New York: Harper & Row.

Beck, A. T. (1976). *Cognitive therapy and the emotional disorders.* New York: International Universities Press.

Beck, A. T., Brown, G., Steer, R. A., & Weissman, A. N. (1991). Factor analysis of the Dysfunctional Attitude Scale in a clinical population. *Psychological Assessment: A Journal of Consulting and Clinical Psychology, 3,* 478–583.

Beck, S. J. (1933). Configurational tendencies in Rorschach responses. *American Journal of Psychology, 45,* 433–443.

Beck, S. J. (1944). *Rorschach's test: Vol. 3. Basic processes.* New York: Grune & Stratton.

Beck, S. J. (1945). *Rorschach's test: Vol. 2. A variety of personality pictures.* New York: Grune & Stratton.

Beck, S. J. (1952). *Rorschach's test. Vol. 3. Advances in interpretation.* New York: Grune & Stratton.

Bell, T. K. (1990). Rapid sequential processing in dyslexic and ordinary readers. *Perceptual and Motor Skills, 71,* 1155–1159.

Bellack, A. S., & Hersen, M. (1988). *Behavioral assessment: A practical handbook* (3rd ed.). New York: Pergamon Press.

Bellak, L. (1975). *The TAT, CAT, and SAT in clinical use* (3rd ed.). New York: Grune & Stratton.

Bellak, L. (1986). *The TAT, CAT, and SAT in clinical use* (4th ed.). New York: Grune & Stratton.

Bellak, L., & Bellak, S. S. (1973). *Manual: Senior Apperception Technique.* Larchmont, NY: CPS.

Bem, D. J., & Allen, A. (1974). On predicting some of the people some of the time: The search for cross-situational consistencies in behavior. *Psychological Review, 81,* 506–520.

Bem, D. J., & Funder, D. C. (1978). Predicting more of the people more of the time: Assessing the personality of situations. *Psychological Review, 85,* 485–501.

Bendell-Estroff, D., Greenfield, D. B., Hogan, A. E., & Claussen, A. H. (1989). Early assessment of sensorimotor and cognitive development in high-risk infants. *Journal of Pediatric Psychology, 4,* 549–557.

Ben-Porath, Y. S., & Butcher, J. N. (1989). The comparability of MMPI and MMPI-2 scales and profiles. *Psychological Assessment: Journal of Consulting and Clinical Psychology, 1,* 1–3.

Ben-Porath, Y. S., & Butcher, J. N. (1991). The historical development of personality assessment. In C. E. Walker (Ed.), *Clinical psychology: Historical and research foundations.* New York: Plenum.

Bentler, P. M. (1987, April). *Causal modeling.* Paper presented at the Health Services Research Methodology Conference, Tucson, AZ.

Bentler, P. M. (1990). Comparative fit indexes in structural models. *Psychological Bulletin, 107*(2), 238–246.

Bentler, P. M. (1991). Modeling of intervention effects. *Nida Research Monograph, 107,* 159–182.

Bentler, P. M. (1994). On the quality of test statistics in covariance structure analysis: Caveat emptor. In C. R. Reynolds (Ed.), *Cognitive assessment: A multidisciplinary perspective. Perspectives on Individual differences* (pp. 237–260). New York: Plenum Press.

Bergan, A., McManis, D. L., & Melchert, P. A. (1971). Effects of social and token reinforcement on WISC block design performance. *Perceptual and Motor Skills, 32,* 871–880.

Bergan, J. R., & Parra, E. B. (1979). Variations in IQ testing and instruction and the letter learning and achievement of Anglo and bilingual Mexican-American children. *Journal of Educational Psychology, 71,* 819–826.

Berger, M. (1970). The third version of the Stanford-Binet (Forms L-M): Some methodological limitations and their practical implications. *Bulletin of the British Psychological Society, 23,* 17–26.

Bergner, M., Babbitt, R. A., Carter, W. B., & Gilson, B. S. (1981). The Sickness Impact Profile: Development and final revision of a health status measure. *Medical Care, 19,* 787–788.

Bernheimer, L. P., & Keogh, B. K. (1988). Stability of cognitive performance of children with developmental delays. *American Journal of Mental Retardation, 92,* 539–542.

Bersoff, D. N. (1979). Regarding psychologists testily: Legal regulation of psychological assessment in the public schools. In B. Sales & M. Novick (Eds.), *Perspectives in law and psychology: Testing and evaluation* (Vol. 3). New York: Plenum.

Bersoff, D. N. (1981). Testing and the law. *American Psychologist, 36,* 1047–1057.

Beutler, L. E. & Berren, M. R. (Eds). (1995). *Integrative assessment of adult personality.* New York: Guilford Press.

Beutler, L. E., Crago, M., & Arizmendi, T. G. (1986). Research on therapist variables in psychotherapy. In A. E. Bergin & S. L. Garfield (Eds.), *Handbook of psychotherapy and behavior change* (3rd ed., pp. 257–310). New York: Wiley.

Bianchini, J. C. (1976, May). *Achievement tests and differentiated norms.* Paper presented at the U.S. Office of Education invitational conference on achievement testing of disadvantaged and minority students for educational program evaluation, Reston, VA.

Binet, A. (1890a). Perceptions d'enfants. *La Revue Philosophique, 30,* 582–611.

Binet, A. (1890b). Recherches sur les mouvements de quelques jeunes enfants. *La Revue Philosophique, 29,* 297–309.

Binet, A., & Henri, V. (1895). La physchologie individuelle. *L'Annee Psychologique, 2,* 411–463.

Binet, A., & Henri, V. (1896). La psychologie individuelle. *L'Annee Psychologique, 3,* 296–332.

Binet, A., & Simon, T. (1905). Methodes nouvelles pour le diagnostic du niveau intellectuel des anormaux. *L'Annee Psychologique, 11,* 191–244.

Biondi, M., & Pancheri, P (1985). Stress, personality, immunity, and cancer: A challenge for psychosomatic medicine. In R. M. Kaplan & M. H. Criqui (Eds.), *Behavioral epidemiology and disease prevention.* New York: Plenum.

Birk, J. M. (1974). Interest inventories: A mixed blessing. *Vocational Guidance Quarterly, 22,* 280–286.

Birney, R. C. (1968). Research on the achievement motive. In E. F. Borgatta & W. W. Lambert (Eds.), *Handbook of personality theory and research.* Chicago: Rand McNally.

Blais, M. A., Norman, D. K., Quintar, B., & Herzog, D. B. (1995). The effect of the administration method: A comparison of the Rapaport and Exner Rorschach systems. *Journal of Clinical Psychology, 51*(1), 119–121.

Blake, J. (1974). Developmental changes in visual information processing under backyard masking. *Journal of Experimental Child Psychology, 17,* 133–146.

Blanchard, E. B., Gerardi, R. J., Kolb, L. C., & Barlow, D. H. (1986). The utility of the Anxiety Disorders Interview Schedule (ADIS) in the diagnosis of the post-traumatic stress disorder (PTSD) in Vietnam veterans. *Behaviour Research and Therapy, 24,* 577–580.

Blatt, S. J. (1975). The validity of projecture techniques and their research and clinical contributions. *Journal of Personality Assessment, 39,* 327–343.

Blatt, S. J. (1990). The Rorschach: A test of perception or an evaluation of representation? *Journal of Personality Assessment, 55,* 394–416.

Block, J. (1961). *The Q-sort method in personality assessment and psychiatric research.* Springfield, Ill.: Thomas.

Block, J. (1965). *The challenge of response sets: Unconfounding meaning, acquiescence, and social desirability in the MMPI.* New York: Appleton-Century-Crafts.

Bloom, A. S., Allard, A. M., Zelko, F. A., Brill, W. J., Topinka, C. W., & Pfohl, W. (1988). Differential validity of the K-ABC for lower functioning preschool children versus those of higher ability. *American Journal of Mental Retardation, 93,* 273–277.

Bloom, B. S. (1980). The new direction in educational research: Alterable variables. *New Directions for Testing and Measurement, 5,* 17–30.

Bolen, L. M., Hewett, J. B., Hall, C. W., & Mitchell, C. C. (1992). Expanded Koppitz Scoring System of the Bender Gestalt Visual-Motor Test for adolescents: A pilot study. *Psychology in the Schools, 29*(2), 113–115.

Bombardier, C., Ware, J., Russell, I. J., & others. (1986). Auranofin therapy in quality of life for patients with rheumatoid arthritis: Results of a multicenter trial. *American Journal of Medicine, 81,* 565–578.

Boone, D. E. (1993). WAIS-R scatter with psychiatric inpatients II: Intersubtest scatter. *Psychological Reports, 73* (3, Pt. 1), 851–860.

Boor, M., & Schill, T. (1968). Subtest performance on the WAIS as a function of anxiety and defensiveness. *Perceptual and Motor Skills, 27,* 33–34.

Borman, W. C., & Hallman, G. L. (1991). Observational accuracy for assessors of work-sample performance: Consistency across task and individual differences correlate. *Journal of Applied Psychology, 76,* 11–18.

Bornstein, M. H. (1993). [Review of the book *The cultural context of infancy: Vol. 2: Multicultural and interdisciplinary approaches to parent-infant relations*]. *Contemporary Psychology. 38*(6), 616–618.

Bortner, M. (1965). Review of the Progressive Matrices Test. In O. K. Buros (Ed.), *The sixth mental measurements yearbook.* Highland Park, NJ: Gryphon Press.

Bosshardt, M. J., Carter, G. W., Gialluca, K. A., Dunnette, M. D., & others. (1992). Predictive validation of an insurance agent support person selection battery [Special Issue: Test validity yearbook: I]. *Journal of Business & Psychology, 7,* 213–224

Bowers, K. S. (1973). Situationalism in psychology: An analysis and critique. *Psychological Review, 80,* 307–336.

Boyle, G. J. (1989). Confirmation of the structural dimensionality of the Stanford-Binet Intelligence Scale [fourth edition]. *Personality and Individual Differences, 10,* 709–715.

Boyle, G. J. (1990). Stanford-Binet IV Intelligence Scale: Is its structure supported by Lisrel congeneric factor analyses? *Personality and Individual Differences, 11,* 1175–1181.

Bracken, B. A. (1985). A critical review of the Kaufman Assessment Battery for Children (K-ABC). *School Psychology Review, 14,* 21–35.

Bradbury, T. N. & Fincham, F. D. (1990). Attributions in marriage: Review and critique. *Psychological Bulletin, 107*(1), 333.

Brand, C. R. (1981). General intelligence and mental speed: Their relationship and development. In M. P. Friedman, J. P. Das, & N. O'Conner (Eds.), *Intelligence and Teaming.* New York: Plenum.

Braun, P. R., & Reynolds, D. N. (1969). A factor analysis of a 100 item fear survey inventory. *Behaviour Research and Therapy, 7,* 399–402.

Brayfield, A. H. (Ed.). (1965). Testing and public policy. *American Psychologist, 20,* 857–1005.

Brazelton, T. B. (1973). *Neonatal behavioral assessment scale.* Philadelphia: Lippincott.

Brazelton, T. B. (1984, November–December). *Neonatal behavioral assessment scale* (2nd ed.). Philadelphia: Lippincott.

Brazelton, T. B. (1993). Why children and parents must play while they eat: An interview with T. Berry Brazelton, MD. [interview by Nancy I. Hahn] *Journal of the American Dietetic Association, 93*(12), 1385–1387.

Bredemeier, M. (1991, November–December). IQ test ban for blacks called unconstitutional. *California Associations of School Psychologists Today,* pp. 22–23.

Brennan, R. L. (1994). Variance components in generalizability theory. C. R. Reynolds, (Eds.), *Cognitive assessment: A multidisciplinary perspective.* (pp. 175–207). New York: Plenum Press.

Brill, S. (1973). The secrecy behind the college boards. *New York Magazine.* (Reprinted by the NYG Corporation.)

Brillinger, D. R. (Ed.). (1994). *The collected works of John W. Tukey.* Belmont, CA: Wadsworth Advanced Books & Software.

Brim, O. G., Jr. (1965). American attitudes toward intelligence tests. *American Psychologist, 20,* 125–130.

Britt, G. C., & Myers, B. J. (1994) The effects of the Brazelton Intervention: A review. *Infant Mental Health Journal, 15*(3) 278–292.

Brittain, M. (1968). A comparative study of the use of the Wechsler Intelligence Scale for Children and the Stanford-Binet Intelligence Scale (Form L-M) with eight-year-old children. *British Journal of Educational Psychology, 38,* 103–104.

Britton, B. K. & Tidwell, P. (1995). Cognitive structure testing: A computer system for diagnosis of expert-novice differences. P. D. Nichols, S. F. Chipman, R. L. Brennan (Eds.), *Cognitively diagnostic assessment* (pp. 251–278). Hillsdale, NJ: Lawrence Erlbaum Associates.

Broaden, H. E. (1946). On the interpretation of the correlation coefficient as a measure of predictive efficiency. *Journal of Educational Psychology, 37,* 65–76.

Broaden, H. E. (1949). When tests pay off. *Personnel Psychology, 2,* 171–183.

Brown, D. C. (1994). Subgroup Norming: Legitimate testing practice or reverse discrimination? *American Psychologist, 49*(11), 927–928.

Brown, F. G. (1979a). The algebra works—but what does it mean? *School Psychology Digest, 8*(2), 213–218.

Brown, F. G. (1979b). The SOMPA: A system of measuring potential abilities? *School Psychology Digest, 8,* 37–46.

Brown, G. W., Bhrolchain, M. N., & Harris T. (1975). Social class and psychiatric disturbance among women in an urban population. *Sociology, 9,* 225–254.

Brown, G. W., & Harris, T. (1978). *Social origins of depression.* London: Tabistock.

Brown, J. S., & Burton, R. B. (1978). Diagnostic models for procedural bugs in basic mathematical skills. *Cognitive Science, 2,* 155–192.

Bryant, F. B. & Yarnold, P. R. (1995). Principal-components analysis and exploratory and confirmatory factor analysis. L. G. Grimm & P. R. Yarnold (Eds.) *Reading and understanding multivariate statistics* (pp. 99–136). Washington, DC: American Psychological Association.

Buck, J. N. (1948). The H-T-P technique as a qualitative and quantitative scoring manual. *Journal of Clinical Psychology, 4,* 317–396.

Burgemeister, B. B., Blum, L. H., & Lorge, I. (1972). *Columbia Mental Maturity Scale* (3rd ed.). New York: Harcourt Brace Jovanovich.

Burke, M. J., & Doran, L. I. (1989). A note on the economic utility of generalized validity coefficients. *Journal of Applied Psychology, 73*, 171–175.

Burns, R. C., & Kaufman, S. H. (1970). *Kinetic Family Drawings (K-F-D): An introduction to understanding through kinetic drawings.* New York: Brunner/Mazel.

Burns, R. C., & Kaufman, S. H. (1972). *Actions, styles, and symbols in Kinetic Family Drawings (K-F-D).* New York: Brunner/Mazel.

Buros, O. K. (Ed.). (1970). *Personality tests and reviews.* Highland Park, NJ: Gryphon Press.

Buros, O. K. (Ed.). (1972). *The seventh mental measurements yearbook* (2 vols.). Highland Park, NJ: Gryphon Press.

Buros, O. K. (1974). *Tests in print II.* Highland Park, NJ: Gryphon Press.

Buros, O. K. (Ed.). (1975a). *Intelligence tests and reviews.* Highland Park, NJ: Gryphon Press.

Buros, O. K. (Ed.). (1975b). *Personality tests and reviews* (Vol. 2). Highland Park, NJ: Gryphon Press.

Buros, O. K. (Ed.). (1975c). *Vocational tests and reviews.* Highland Park, NJ: Gryphon Press.

Buros, O. K. (Ed.). (1978). *The eighth mental measurements yearbook* (2 vols.). Highland Park, NJ: Gryphon Press.

Burton, D. B., Ryan, J. J., Paolo, A. M., & Mittenberg, W. (1994). Structural equation analysis of the Wechsler Adult Intelligence Scale—Revised in a normal elderly sample. *Psychological Assessment, 6*(4), 380–385.

Burton, E., & Burton, N. W. (1993). The effect of item screening on test scores and test characteristics. P. W. Holland & H. Wainer (Eds.) *Differential item functioning* (pp. 321–335). Hillsdale, NJ: Lawrence Erlbaum Associates.

Burtt, H. E. (1926). *Principles of employment psychology.* Boston: Houghton Mifflin.

Bush, J. W. (1984). Relative preferences versus relative frequencies in health-related quality of life evaluations. In N. K. Wenger, M. E. Mattson, C. D. Furberg, & J. Elinson (eds.), *Assessment of quality of life in clinical trials of cardiovascular therapies.* New York: LaJacq.

Butcher, H. L. (1972). Review of cooperative school and college ability tests: Series 2. In O. K. Buros (Ed.), *The seventh mental measurements yearbook* (Vol. 1). Highland Park, NJ: Gryphon Press.

Butcher, J. N. (1989). *MMPI-2 users guide.* Minneapolis, MN: Natural Computer Systems.

Butcher, J. N. (1990). *MMPI-2 in psychological treatment.* New York: Oxford University Press.

Butcher, J. N. (1995). Interpretation of the MMPI-2. E. Beutler & M. R. Berren (Eds.) *Integrative assessment of adult personality* (pp. 206–239). New York: Guilford Press.

Butcher, J. N., Aidwin, C. M., Levenson, M. R., & Ben-Porath, Y. S. (1991). Personality and aging: A study of the MMPI-2 among older men. *Psychology and Aging, 6*, 361–370.

Butcher, J. N., Graham, J. R., Dahlstrom, W. G., Tellegen, A. M., & Kaemmer, B. (1989). *MMPI-2 manual for administrators and scoring.* Minneapolis: University of Minnesota Press.

Butcher, J. N., Graham, J. R., Williams, C. L., & Ben-Porath, Y. S. (1990). *Development and use of the MMPI-2 Content Scales.* Minneapolis: University of Minnesota Press.

Butcher, J. N., Keller, L. S., & Bacon, S. F. (1985). Current developments and future directions in computerized personality assessment. *Journal of Consulting and Clinical Psychology, 53*, 803–815.

Butters, N., Delis, D. C., & Lucas, J. A. (1995). Clinical assessment of memory disorders in amnesia and dementia. *Annual Review of Psychology, 46*, 493–523.

Cacioppo, J. T., Berntson, G. G., & Anderson, B. L. (1991). Physiological approaches to the evaluation of psychotherapeutic process and outcome, 1991: Contributions from social psychophysiology. *Psychological Assessment: A Journal of Consulting and Clinical Psychology, 3*, 321–336.

Caine, E. D. (1986). Neuropsychology of depression: The pseudodementia syndrome. In I. Grant & K. M. Adams (Eds.), *Neuropsychological assessment of neuropsychiatric disorders.* New York: Oxford University Press.

Caldwell, M. B., & Knight, D. (1970). The effects of Negro and white examiners on Negro intelligence test performance. *Journal of Negro Education, 39*, 177–179.

Callender, J. C., & Dougherty, T. W. (1983). *Effects of interviewer training on interview information, interviewer behavior, and interview ratings: A field investigation.* Proceedings of the Southwest Division of The Academy of Management, Houston, TX.

Camara, W. J., & Brown, D. C. (1995). Educational and employment testing: Changing concepts in measurement and policy. *Educational Measurement: Issues and Practice, 1*, 5–11.

Camara, W. J., & Schneider, D. L. (1994). Integrity tests: Facts and unresolved issues. *American Psychologist, 49*(2), 112–119.

Camara, W. J., & Schneider, D. L. (1995). Questions of construct breadth and openness of research in integrity testing. *American Psychologist, 50*, 459–460.

Cameron, R., & Evers, S. E. (1990). Self-report issues in obesity and weight management: State of the art and future directions. *Behavioral Assessment, 12,* 91–106.

Campbell, D. P. (1974). *Manual for the SVIB-SCII Strong-Campbell Interest Inventory* (2nd ed.). Stanford, CA: Stanford University Press.

Campbell, D. P. (1977). *Manual for the Strong-Campbell Interest Inventory.* Stanford, CA: Stanford University Press.

Campbell, D. P. (1995, August). The Campbell Interest and Skills Survey (SCII). Paper presented at the annual meeting of the American Psychological Association, New York.

Campbell, D. P., Hyne, S. A., & Nilsen, D. (1992). Manual for the Campbell Interest and Skill Survey. Minneapolis, MN: National Computer Systems.

Campbell, D. T., & Fiske, D. W. (1959). Convergent and discriminant validation by the multitrait-multimethod matrix. *Psychological Bulletin, 56,* 81–105.

Campion, J. E. (1972). Work sampling for personnel selection. *Journal of Applied Psychology, 56,* 40–44.

Cane, D. B., Olinger, L. J., Gotlib, I. N., & Kuiper, N. A. (1986). Factor structure of the Dysfunctional Attitude Scale in a student population. *Journal of Clinical Psychology, 42,* 307–309.

Canfield, A. A. (1951). The "sten" scale—a modified C-scale. *Educational and Psychological Measurement, 11,* 295–297.

Cannell, C. F., & Henson, R. (1974). Incentives, motives, and response bias. *Annals of Economic and Social Measurement, 3,* 307–317.

Caprara, G. V., Barbaranelli, C., & Comrey, A. L. (1995). Factor analysis of the NEO-PI Inventory and Comprey Personality

Scales in an Italian sample. *Personality and Individual Differences, 18*(2), 193–200.

Carkhuff, R. R. (1969). *Helping and human relations: I: Selection and training. II: Practice and research.* New York: Holt, Rinehart & Winston.

Carkhuff, R. R., & Berenson, B. C. (1967). *Beyond counseling and therapy.* New York: Holt, Rinehart & Winston.

Carlin, J. B., & Rubin, D. B. (1991). Summarizing multiple-choice tests using three information statistics. *Psychological Bulletin, 110,* 338–349.

Carlson, R. E., Thayer, P. W., Mayfield, E. C., & Peterson, D. A. (1971). Improvements in the selection interview. *Personnel Journal, 50,* 268–275.

Carr, M. A., Sweet, J. J., & Rossini, E. (1986). Diagnostic validity of the Luria-Nebraska Neuropsychological Battery—Children's revision. *Journal of Consulting and Clinical Psychology, 54,* 354–358.

Carroll, J. B., & Horn, J. L. (1981). On the scientific basis of ability testing. *American Psychologist, 36,* 1012–1020.

Carvajal, H., Hardy, K., Harmon, K., Sellers, T. A., & Holmes, C. B. (1987). Relationships among scores on the Stanford-Binet IV, Peabody Picture Vocabulary Test—Revised, and Columbia Mental Maturity Scale. *Bulletin of the Psychonomic Society, 25*(4), 275–276.

Carvajal, H., Hardy, K., Smith, K. L., & Weaver, K. A. (1988). Relationships between scores on Stanford-Binet IV and Wechsler preschool and primary scale of intelligence. *Psychology in the Schools, 25,* 129–131.

Carvajal, H., Karr, S. K., Hardy, K. M., & Palmer, B. L. (1988). Relationships between scores on Stanford-Binet IV and scores on McCarthy Scales of Chil-

dren's Abilities. *Bulletin of the Psychonomic Society, 26*(4), 349.

Carvajal, H., & Weyand, K. (1986). Relationships between scores on Stanford-Binet IV and Wechsler Intelligence Scale for Children—Revised. *Psychological Reports, 59,* 963–966.

Cascio, W. F. (1987). *Applied psychology in personnel management* (3rd ed.). Englewood Cliffs, NJ: Prentice-Hall.

Cascio, W. F. (1994). Executive and managerial assessment: Value for the money? [Special Issue: Issues in the assessment of managerial and executive leadership]. *Consulting Psychology Journal: Practice and Research, 46,* 42–48.

Cascio, W. F., & Ramos, R. A. (1986). Development and application of a new method for assessing job performance in behavioral economic terms. *Journal of Applied Psychology, 71,* 20–28.

Cash, T. F. (1985). The impact of grooming style on the evaluation of women in management. In M. Solomon (Ed.), *The psychology of fashion.* New York: Lexington Press.

Castaneda, A., & Ramirez, M. (1974). *Cultural democracy, bicognitive development, and education.* New York: Academic Press.

Castenell, L. A., & Castenell, N. E. (1988). Norm-referenced testing in low-income blacks. *Journal of Counseling and Development, 67,* 205–206.

Cattell, J. M. (1890). Mental tests and measurements. *Mind, 15,* 373–380.

Cattell, J. M. (1930). Psychology in America. *Scientific Monthly, 30,* 114–126.

Cattell, P. (1940). *The measurement of intelligence of infants and young children.* New York: Psychological Corporation.

Cattell, R. B. (1949). *Manual for forms A and B: Sixteen Personality*

Factors Questionnaire. Champaign, IL: Institute for Personality and Ability Testing.

Cattell, R. B. (1957). *Personality and motivation, structure and measurement.* Yonkers, NY: World Book.

Cattell, R. B., & Bolton, L. S. (1969). What pathological dimensions lie beyond the normal dimensions of the 16 PF? A comparison of MMPI and 16 PF factor domains. *Journal of Consulting and Clinical Psychology, 33,* 18–29.

Cattell, R. B., Eber, H. W., & Tatsuoka, M. M. (1970). *Handbook for the Sixteen Personality Factor Questionnaire (16 PF).* Champaign, IL: Institute for Personality and Ability Testing.

Cattell, R. B., & Scheier, I. H. (1961). *The meaning and measurement of neuroticism and anxiety.* New York: Ronald Press.

Cautela, J. R., & Upper, D. (1976). The behavioral inventory battery: The use of self-report measures in behavioral analyses and therapy. In M. Hersen & A. S. Bellack (Eds.), *Behavioral assessment.* New York: Pergamon Press.

Chambers, L. W. (1993). The McMaster Health Index Questionnaire: An Update. In S. R. Walker & R. M. Rossen (Ed.), *Quality of life assessment: Key issues of the 1990s. (pp. 131–149).* Landcaster, England: Kluwer Academic Publishers.

Chambers, L. W. (1996). The McMaster Health Index Questionnaire. In B. F. Spilker (Eds.), *Quality of life and Pharmcoeconomics in clinical trials* (2nd ed., pp. 267–279). New York: Raven.

Champney, H., & Marshall, H. (1939). Optimal refinement of the rating scale. *Journal of Applied Psychology, 23,* 323–331.

Chasnoff, I. J., Burns, K. A., & Burns, W. J. (1987). Cocaine use in pregnancy: Perinatal morbidity and mortality. *Neurotoxicology and Teratology, 9,* 291–293.

Chattin, S. H., & Bracken, B. A. (1989). School psychologists' evaluation of the K-ABC, McCarthy Scales, Stanford-Binet IV, and WISC-R. *Journal of Psychoeducational Assessment, 7,* 112–130.

Chelune, G. J., & Edwards, P. (1981). Early brain lesions: Ontogenetic-environmental considerations. *Journal of Clinical and Consulting Psychology, 49,* 777–790.

Chun, K., & Campbell, J. B. (1974). Dimensionality of the Rotter Interpersonal Trust Scale. *Psychological Reports, 35,* 1059–1070.

Cialdini, R. B. (1985). *Influence: Science and practice.* Glenview, IL: Scott, Foresman.

Cicchetti, D. V. (1994). Guidelines, criteria, and rules of thumb for evaluating normed and standardized assessment instruments in psychology. *Psychological Assessment, 6*(4), 284–290.

Clarizio, H. F. (1979a). In defense of the IQ test. *School Psychology Digest, 8*(1), 79–88.

Clarizio, H. F. (1979b). SOMPA—A symposium continued: Commentaries. *School Psychology Digest, 8*(2), 207–209.

Clark, K. E. (1961). *The vocational interests of nonprofessional men.* Minneapolis: University of Minnesota Press.

Clark, K. E., & Campbell, D. P. (1965). *Manual for the Minnesota Vocational Interest Inventory.* New York: Psychological Corporation.

Cleary, T. A. (1968). Test bias: Prediction of grades of Negro and white students in integrated colleges. *Journal of Educational Measurement, 5,* 115–124.

Cleary, T. A., Humphreys, L. G., Kendrick, S. A., & Wesman, A. (1975). Educational uses of tests with disadvantaged populations. *American Psychologist, 30,* 15–41.

Cliff, N. (1987). *Analyzing multivariate data.* San Diego: Harcourt, Brace, Jovanovich.

Cohen, F., & Lazarus, R. S. (1994). Active coping processes, coping dispositions, and recovery from surgery. A. Steptoe & J. Wardle (Eds.) *Psychosocial processes and health: A reader* (pp. 348–368). Cambridge, England: Cambridge University Press.

Cohen, I. (1970). The effects of material and non-material reinforcement upon performance of the WISC block design subtest by children of different social classes: A follow-up study. *Psychology, 7*(4), 41–47.

Cohen, J. (1957). The factorial structure of the WAIS between early adulthood and old age. *Journal of Consulting Psychology, 21,* 283–290.

Cohen, J. (1960). A coefficient of agreement for nominal scales. *Educational and Psychological Measurement, 20,* 37–46.

Cohen, S., Kanarack, T., & Mermelstein, R. (1983). A global measure of perceived stress. *Journal of Health and Social Behavior, 24,* 385–396.

Cohen, S., & Lichtenstein, E. (1990). Partner behaviors that support quitting smoking. *Journal of Consulting and Clinical Psychology, 58,* 304–309.

Cole, N. S. (1973). Bias in selection. *Journal of Educational Measurement, 10,* 237–255.

Cole, N. S. (1981). Bias in testing. *American Psychologist, 36,* 1067–1077.

Coleman, J. C. (1973). Life stress and maladaptive behavior. *American Journal of Occupational Therapy, 27,* 169–180.

Coleman, W., & Cureton, E. E. (1954). Intelligence and achievement: The "jangle fallacy" again. *Educational and Psychological Measurement, 14,* 347–351.

Coles, C. D., Smith, I. E., & Falek, A. (1987). Prenatal alcohol exposure and infant behavior: Immediate effects and implications for later development. *Advances in Alcohol and Substance Abuse, 6,* 87–104.

Colvin, C. R., Block, J. & Funder, D. C. (1995). Overly positive self-evaluations and personality: Negative implications for mental health. *Journal of Personality and Social Psychology, 68,* 1152–1162.

Conoley, J. C., & Kramer, J. J. (1989). *Tenth mental measurements yearbook.* Lincoln: University of Nebraska Press.

Constantino, G., Malgady, R. G., Casullo, M. M., & Castillo, A. (1991). Cross-cultural standardization of TEMAS in three Hispanic subcultures. *Hispanic Journal of Behavioral Sciences, 13*(1), 48–62.

Constantino, G., Malgady, R. G., Colon-Malgady, G., & Bailey, J. (1992). Clinical utility of the TEMAS with nonminority children. *Journal of Personality Assessment, 59*(3), 433–438.

Construct validation after 30 years. Paper presented at the Department of Educational Psychology, University of Illinois, Champaign.

Cook, M. L., & Peterson, C. (1986). Depressive irrationality. *Cognitive Therapy and Research, 10,* 293–298.

Cooper, C. L. (1995). Life at the chalkface: Identifying and measuring teacher stress [Special Section: Symposium on teacher stress]. *British Journal of Educational Psychology, 65,* 69–71.

Cooper, D. (1990). Factor structure of the Edwards Personal Preference Schedule in a vocational rehabilitation sample. *Journal of Clinical Psychology, 46,* 421–425.

Cooper, W. H. (1981). Ubiquitous halo. *Psychological Bulletin, 90,* 218–244.

Coplan, J., & Gleason, J. R. (1990). Quantifying language development from birth to 3 years using the Early Language Milestone Scale. *Pediatrics, 86,* 963–971.

Copple, C. E., & Succi, G. J. (1974). The comparative ease of processing standard English and black nonstandard English by lower-class black children. *Child Development, 45,* 1048–1053.

Corbett, D., & Wilson, B. (1995). Make a difference with, not for, students: A plea to researchers and reformers. *Educational Researcher, 24*(5), 12–17.

Cordes, A. K. (1994). The reliability of observational data: I. Theories and methods for speech-language pathology. *Journal of Speech & Hearing Research, 37*(2), 264–278.

Costa, P. T., Jr., & McCrae, R. R. (1985). *The NEO Personality Inventory: Manual.* New York: Psychological Assessment Resources.

Costa, P. T., Jr., & McCrae, R. R. (1995). Domains and facets: Hierarchical personality assessment using the revised NEO Personality Inventory. *Journal of Personality Assessment, 64*(1), 21–50.

Costa, P. T., McCrae, R. R., & Kay, G. G. (1995). Persons, places, and personality: Career assessment using the Revised NEO Personality Inventory. *Journal of Career Assessment, 76*(2), 123–139.

Costello, A. J., Edelbrock, C., Dulcan, M. K., Kalas, R., & Klaric, S. H. (1984). *Development and testing of the NIM# diagnostic interview schedule for children in a clinic population.* Final report (contract #RFP-0881–0027). Rockville, MD: National Institute of Mental Health, Center for Epidemiologic Studies.

Costello, J., & Dickie, J. (1970). Leiter and Stanford-Binet IQ's of preschool disadvantaged children. *Developmental Psychology, 2,* 314.

Cota, A. A., Longman, R. S., Evans, C. R., Dion, K. L., & others. (1995). Using and misusing factor analysis to explore group cohesion. *Journal of Clinical Psychology, 51*(2), 308–316.

Cough, H. G. (1995). Career assessment and the California Psychological Inventory. *Journal of Career Assessment, 3*(2), 101–122.

Craig, R. J., & Olson, R. E. (1995). MCMI-II profiles and typologies for the patients seen in marital therapy. *Psychological Reports, 76*(1), 163–170.

Cramer, P., & Blatt, S. J. (1990). Use of the TAT to measure change in defense mechanisms following intensive psychotherapy. *Journal of Personality Assessment, 54,* 236–251.

Crawford, J. R., & Allan, K. M. (1994). The Mahalanobis Distance index of WAIS-R subtest scatter: Psychometric properties in a healthy UK sample. *British Journal of Clinical Psychology, 33*(1), 65–69.

Cripe, L. I., Maxwell, J. K., & Hill, E. (1995). Multivariate discrimination function analysis of neurologic, pain, and psychiatric patients with the MMPI. *Journal of Clinical Psychology, 51*(2), 258–268.

Crisco, J. J., Dobbs, J. M., & Mulhern, R. K. (1988). Cognitive processing of children with Williams syndrome. *Developmental Medicine and Child Neurology, 30,* 650–656.

Crites, J. O. (1973). *Career Maturity Inventory: Theory and research handbook and administration and use manual.* Monterey, CA: CTB/McGraw-Hill.

Crites, J. O. (1974). The Career Maturity Inventory. In D. E. Super (Ed.), *Measuring vocational maturity for counseling and evaluation.* Washington, DC:

National Vocational Guidance Association.

Crockett, D., Clark, C., & Kalonoff, H. (1981). Introduction-overview of neuropsychology. In F. E. Filskov & T. J. Boll (Eds.), *Handbook of clinical neuropsychology*. New York: Wiley.

Cronbach, L. J. (1951). Coefficient alpha and the internal structure of tests. *Psychometlika, 16,* 297–334.

Cronbach, L. J. (1971). Test validation. In R. L. Thorndike (ed.), *Educational measurement* (2nd ed.). Washington, DC: American Council on Education.

Cronbach, L. J. (1975a). Beyond the two disciplines of scientific psychology. *American Psychologist, 30,* 116–127.

Cronbach, L. J. (1975b). Five decades of public controversy over mental testing. *American Psychologist, 30,* 1–14.

Cronbach, L. J. (1978). Black Intelligence Test of Cultural Homogeneity: A review. In O. K. Buros (Ed.), *The eighth mental measurements yearbook* (Vol. 1). Highland Park, NJ: Gryphon Press.

Cronbach, L. J. (1980). Validity on parole: How can we go straight? *New Directions for Testing and Measurement, 5,* 99–108.

Cronbach, L. J. (1989). Construct validation after thirty years. In R. Linn (Ed.), *Intelligence: Measurement, theory, and public policy*. Urbana: University of Illinois Press.

Cronbach, L. J. (1995). Giving method variance its due. P. E. Shrout & S. T. Fiske (Eds.), *Personality research, methods, and theory: A festschrift honoring Donald W. Fiske* (pp. 145–157). Hillsdale, N.J: Lawrence Erlbaum Associates.

Cronbach, L. J., & Furby, L. (1970). How we should measure "change"—or should we? *Psychological Bulletin, 74,* 68–80.

Cronbach, L. J., & Gleser, G. C. (1965). *Psychological tests and personnel decisions*. Urbana: University of Illinois Press.

Cronbach, L. J., Gleser, G. C., Nanda, H., & Rajaratnam, N. (1972). *The dependability of behavioral measures: Theory of generalizability for scores and profiles*. New York: Wiley.

Cronbach, L. J., & Meehl, P. E. (1955). Construct validity in psychological tests. *Psychological Bulletin, 52,* 281–302.

Croog, S. H., Levine, S., Testa, M. A., Brown, D., Bulpitt, C. J., Jenkins, C. D., Klerman, G. L., & Williams, G. H. (1986). The effects of antihypertensive therapy on quality of life. *New England Journal of Medicine, 314,* 1657–1664.

Cundick, B. P. (1985). Review of Incomplete Sentences Task. In J. V. Mitchell (Ed.), *Ninth mental measurements yearbook* (Vol. 1, pp. 681–682). Highland Park, NJ: Gryphon Press.

Dahlstrom, W. G. (1969a). Invasion of privacy: How legitimate is the current concern over this issue? In J. N. Butcher (Ed.), *MMPI: Research developments and clinical applications*. New York: McGraw-Hill.

Dahlstrom, W. G. (1969b). Recurrent issues in the development of the MMPI. In J. N. Butcher (Ed.), *MMPI: Research developments and clinical applications*. New York: McGraw-Hill.

Dahlstrom, W. G., & Welsh, G. S. (1960). *An MMPI handbook: A guide to use in clinical practice and research*. Minneapolis: University of Minnesota Press.

Dahlstrom, W. G., Welsh, G. S., & Dahlstrom, L. E. (1972). *An MMPI handbook: Vol. 1. Clinical interpretation* (Rev. ed.). Minneapolis: University of Minnesota Press.

Dahlstrom, W. G., Welsh, G. S., & Dahlstrom, L. E. (1975). *An*

MMPI handbook: Vol. 2. Research applications (Rev. ed.). Minneapolis: University of Minnesota Press.

Dalessio, A. T., & Silverhart, T. A. (1994). Combining biodata test and interview information: Predicting decisions and performance criteria. *Personnel Psychology, 47*(2), 303–315.

Damarin, F. (1978a). Review of Bayley Scales of Infant Development. In O. K. Buros (Ed.), *The eighth mental measurements yearbook* (Vol. 1). Highland Park, NJ: Gryphon Press.

Damarin, F. (1978b). Review of Cattell Infant Intelligence Scale. In O. K. Buros (Ed.), *The eighth mental measurements yearbook* (Vol. 1). Highland Park, NJ: Gryphon Press.

Dangel, H. L. (1970). *The biasing effect of pretest information on the WISC scores of mentally retarded children*. Doctoral dissertation, Pennsylvania State University. (University Microfilms No. 7116, 588.)

Daniel, W. W. (1990). *Applied nonparametric statistics* (2nd ed.). Boston: PWS-Kent.

Darlington, R. B. (1971). Another look at "cultural fairness." *Journal of Educational Measurement, 8,* 71–82.

Darlington, R. B. (1978). Cultural test bias: Comment on Hunter and Schmidt. *Psychological Bulletin, 85,* 673–674.

Das, J. P. (1973). Cultural deprivation and cognitive competence. In N. R. Ellis (Ed.), *International review of research in mental retardation* (Vol. 6). New York: Academic Press.

Das, J. P. (1987). Simultaneous and successive processes and K-ABC. *Journal of Special Education, 18,* 229–238.

Datta, L. (1975). Foreword. In E. E. Diamond (Ed.), *Issues of sex bias and sex fairness in career interest measurement*. Washington, DC:

National Institutes of Education.

Davis, R. B. (1979). *Error analysis in high school mathematics, conceived as information processing pathology.* Paper presented at the annual meeting of the American Educational Research Association, San Francisco.

Davis, R. B., Jockusch, E., & McKnight, C. (1978). Cognitive process in learning algebra. *Journal of Children's Mathematics Behavior, 2,* 1–320.

Day, D. V., & Sulsky, L. M. (1995). Effects of frame-of-reference training and information configuration on memory organization and rating accuracy. *Journal of Applied Psychology, 80,* 158–167

Dearborn, G. (1897). Blots of ink in experimental psychology. *Psychological Review, 4,* 390–391.

Dearborn, W. F., & Rothney, J. W. M. (1941). *Predicting the child's development.* New York: Sci-Art Publishers.

Deffenbacher, J. L., Swemer, W. A., Whisman, M. A., Hill, R. A., & Sloan, R. D. (1986). Irrational beliefs and anxiety. *Cognitive Therapy and Research, 10,* 281–292.

deGroot, A. M. (1988). Word association norms with reaction times. *Nederlands-Tiydschrift-voor-de-Psychologie-haar-Grensqebieden, 43,* 280–296.

Delhees, K. H., & Cattell, R. B. (1971a). The dimensions of pathology: Proof of their projection beyond the normal 16 PF source traits. *Personality, 2,* 149–173.

Delhees, K. H., & Cattell, R. B. (1971b). *Manual for the Clinical Analysis Questionnaire (CAQ).* Champaign, IL: Institute for Personality and Ability Testing.

Delis, D. C., Freeland, J., Kramer, J. H., & Kaplan, E. (1988). Integrating clinical assessment with cognitive neuroscience: Construct validation of the California Verbal Learning Test. *Journal of Consulting and Clinical Psychology, 56,* 123–130.

Delis, D. C., Kramer, J. H., Kaplan, E., & Ober, B. A. (1987). *The California Verbal Learning Test* (Research ed.). San Diego: Harcourt Brace Jovanovich.

Delis, D. C., Magsman, P. J., Butters, N., Salmon, D. P., Cermak, L. S., & Kramer, J. H. (1991). Profiles of demented and amnesic patients on the California Verbal Learning Test: Implications for the assessment of memory disorders. *Psychological Assessment: A Journal of Consulting and Clinical Psychology, 3,* 19–26.

DeLongis, A., Covne, J. C., Dakof, G., Folkman, S., & Lazarus, R. S. (1982). Relationship of daily hassles, uplifts, and major life events to health status. *Health Psychology, 1,* 119–136.

DeRosa, A., & Patalano, F. (1991). Effects of familiar proctor on fifth and sixth grade students' test anxiety. *Psychological Reports, 68,* 103–113.

DeVellis, R. F. (1991). Scale development: Theory and applications. Newbury Park, CA: Sage.

Diamond, E. E. (1979). Sex equality and measurement practices. *New Directions for Test and Measurement, 3,* 61–78.

DiBello, L. V., Stout, W. F., & Roussos, L. A. (1995). Unified cognitive/psychometric diagnostic assessment likelihood-based classification techniques. In P. D. Nichols, S. F. Chipman, & R. L. Brennan (Eds.), *Cognitively diagnostic assessment* (pp. 361-389). Hillsdale, NJ: Lawrence Erlbaum Associates.

Dicken, C. F. (1959). Simulated patterns on the Edwards Personal Preference Schedule. *Journal of Applied Psychology, 43,* 372–378.

Dikmen, S. & Machamer, J. E. (1995). Neurobehavioral outcomes and their determinants. *Journal of Head Trauma Rehabilitation, 10,* 74–78.

Diller, L., & Gordon, W. A. (1981). Interventions for cognitive deficits in brain-injured adults. *Journal of Consulting and Clinical Psychology, 49,* 822–834.

DiMatteo, M. R. (1979). A sociopsychological analysis of physician-patient rapport: Toward a science of the art of medicine. *Journal of Social Issues, 85*(1), 12–33.

Dipboye, R. L., Arvey, R. D., & Terpstra, D. E. (1977). Sex and physical attractiveness of raters and applicants as determinants of resume evaluations. *Journal of Applied Psychology, 62,* 288–294.

Dishion, T. J., Andrews, D. W., & Crosby, L. (1995). Antisocial boys and their friends in early adolescence: Relationship characteristics, quality, and interactional process. *Child Development, 66,* 139–151.

Dittmann, A. T. (1962). The relationship between body movements and moods in interviews. *Journal of Consulting Psychology, 26,* 480.

Dobko, P., & Kehoe, J. F. (1983). On the fair use of bias: A comment on Drasgow. *Psychological Bulletin, 93,* 604–608.

Doctor, R. (1972). Review of the Porteus Maze Test. In O. K. Buros (Ed.), *The seventh mental measurements yearbook* (Vol. 1). Highland Park, NJ: Gryphon Press.

Dodrill, C. B., & Warner, M. H. (1988). Further studies of the Wonderlic Personnel Test as a brief measure of intelligence. *Journal of Consulting and Clinical Psychology, 59,* 145–147.

Donahue, D., & Sattler, J. M. (1971). Personality variables affecting WAIS scores. *Journal of Consulting and Clinical Psychology, 36,* 441.

Donion, T. F. (Ed.). (1984). *The College Board technical handbook for the Scholastic Aptitude Test*. New York: College Entrance Examination Board.

Doppelt, J. E., & Wallace, W. L. (1955). Standardization of the Wechsler Adult Intelligence Scale for older persons. *Journal of Abnormal and Social Psychology, 51,* 312–330.

Dorans, N. J., & Drasgow, F. (1980). A note on cross-validating prediction equations. *Journal of Applied Psychology, 65,* 728–730.

Dougherty, T. W., Ebert, R. J., & Callender, J. C. (1986). Policy capturing in the employment interview. *Journal of Applied Psychology, 71,* 9–15.

Dougherty, T. W., Turban, D. B., & Callender, J. C. (1994). Confirming first impressions in the employment interview: A field study of interviewer behavior. *Journal of Applied Psychology, 79*(5), 659–665.

Dove, A. (1968). Taking the Chitling Test. *Newsweek, 72,* 51–52.

Downey, J., Elkin, E. J., Ehrhardt, A. A., Meyer-Bahlburg, H. F., Bell, J. J., & Morishima, A. (1991). Cognitive ability and everyday functioning in women with Turner Syndrome. *Journal of Learning Disabilities, 24,* 3239.

Drake, L. E. (1946). A social I. E. scale for the MMPI. *Journal of Applied Psychology, 30,* 51–54.

Drasgow, F. (1982). Biased test items and differential validity. *Psychological Bulletin, 92,* 526–531.

Dreher, G. F., Ash, R. A., & Hancock, P. (1988). The role of the traditional research design in understanding the validity of the employment interview. *Personnel Psychology, 41,* 315–327.

DuBois, P. H. (1966). A test-dominated society: China 115 B.C.–1905 A.D. In A. Anastasi (Ed.), *Testing problems in perspective*. Washington, DC: American Council on Education.

DuBois, P. H. (1970). *A history of psychological testing*. Boston: Allyn and Bacon.

DuBois, P. H. (1972). Increase in educational opportunity through measurement. *Proceedings of the 1971 Invitational Conference on Testing Problems*. Princeton, NJ: Educational Testing Service.

Dunn, J. A. (1972). Review of the Goodenough-Harris Drawing Test. In O. K. Buros (Ed.), *The seventh mental measurements yearbook* (Vol. 1). Highland Park, NJ: Gryphon Press.

Dunn, L. M. (1959). *Peabody Picture Vocabulary Test manual*. Minneapolis, MN: American Guidance Service.

Dunn, L. M. (1965). *Expanded manual for the Peabody Picture Vocabulary Test*. Minneapolis, MN: American Guidance Service.

Dunn, L. M., & Dunn, I. M. (1981). *Peabody Picture Vocabulary Test—Revised*. Circle Pines, MN: American Guidance Service.

Dunnette, M. D. (1967). The assessment of managerial talent. In F. R. Wickert & D. E. McFarland (Eds.), *Measuring executive effectiveness*. New York: Appleton-Century-Crofts.

Dunnette, M. D. (1972). *Validity study results for jobs relevant to the petroleum refining industry*. Washington, DC: American Petroleum Institute.

Dunnette, M. D., & Borman, W. C. (1979). Personnel selection and classification systems. *Annual Review of Psychology, 30,* 477–525.

Dupue, R. A., & Monroe, S. M. (1986). Conceptualization and measurement of human disorder in life stress research: The problem of chronic disturbance. *Psychological Bulletin, 99,* 36–51.

Dush, D. M. (1985). Review of Incomplete Sentences Task. In J. V. Mitchell (Ed.), *The ninth mental measurements yearbook* (Vol. 1, pp. 682–683). Highland Park, NJ: Gryphon Press.

Dvir, T., Eden, D., & Banjo, M. (1995). Self-fulfilling prophecy and gender: Can women be Pygmalion and Galatea? *Journal of Applied Psychology, 80,* 253–270.

Eaton, N. K., Wing, H., & Mitchell, K. J. (1985). Alternative methods of estimating the dollar value of performance. *Personnel Psychology, 38,* 27–40.

Ebel, R. L. (1972). *Essentials of educational measurement*. Englewood Cliffs, NJ: Prentice-Hall.

Ebel, R. L. (1977). Comments on some problems of employment testing. *Personnel Psychology, 30,* 55–63.

Educational Testing Service. (1991). *Sex, race, ethnicity, and performance on the GRE General Test*. Princeton, NJ: Educational Testing Service.

Edwards, A. L. (1954). *Manual for the Edwards Personal Preference Schedule*. New York: Psychological Corporation.

Edwards, A. L. (1957). *Techniques of attitude scale construction*. New York: Appleton-Century-Crofts.

Edwards, A. L. (1959). *Edwards Personal Preference Schedule*. New York: Psychological Corporation.

Edwards, G. A. (1966). Anxiety correlates of the WAIS. *California Journal of Educational Research, 17,* 144–147.

Egeland, B. R. (1969). Examiner expectancy: Effects on the scoring of the WISC. *Psychology in the Schools, 6,* 313–315.

Egeland, B. R. (1978). Review of Columbia Mental Maturity Scale. In O. K. Buros (Ed.), *The eighth mental measurements yearbook* (Vol. 1). Highland Park, NJ: Gryphon Press.

Egeland, B., Butcher, J. N., & Ben-Porath, Y. S. (1992). *MMPI-2 profiles of women at risk for child abuse*. Unpublished manuscript.

Egerton, D. R. (1994). Effects of limited occupational knowledge on SCII profile patterns. *TCA Journal, 22*(2), 18–22.

Eisenberger, R. (1970). Is there a deprivation-satiation function for social approval? *Psychological Bulletin, 74*, 255–275.

Eisenberger, R. (1972). Explanation of rewards that do not reduce tissue need. *Psychological Bulletin, 77*, 319–339.

Eisenberger, R., Kaplan, R. M., & Singer, R. D. (1974). Decremental and nondecremental effects of noncontingent social approval. *Journal of Personality and Social Psychology, 30*, 716–722.

Ekman, P. (1965a). Communication through nonverbal behavior: A source of information about an interpersonal relationship. In S. S. Tomkins & C. E. Izard (Eds.), *Affect, cognition, and personality*. New York: Springer.

Ekman, P. (1965b). Differential communication of affect by head and body cues. *Journal of Personality and Social Psychology, 2*, 725–735.

Ekman, P., & Friesen, W. V. (1968). Nonverbal behavior in psychotherapy research. In J. Shlien, H. Hunt, J. D. Matarazzo, & C. Savage (Eds.), *Research in psychotherapy* (Vol. 3). Washington, DC: American Psychological Association.

Ekman, P., Levenson, R. W., & Friesen, W. V. (1983). Autonomic nervous system activity distinguishes among emotions. *Science, 221*, 1208–1210.

Ekman, P., & O'Sullivan, M. (1991). Who can catch a liar? *American Psychologists, 46*, 913–920.

Ekren, U. W. (1962). *The effect of experimenter knowledge of subjects' scholastic standing on the performance of a task*. Unpublished master's thesis, Marquette University, WI.

Elashoff, J., & Snow, R. E. (Eds.). (1971). *Pygmalion revisited*. Worthington, OH: C. A. Jones.

Elliot, R. (1988). Tests, abilities, race, and conflict. *Intelligence, 12*, 333–350.

Ellis, A. (1946). The validity of personality questionnaires. *Psychological Bulletin, 43*, 385–440.

Ellis, T. E. (1985). The hopelessness scale and social desirability: More data and a contribution from the Irrational Beliefs Test. *Journal of Clinical Psychogy, 41*, 634–639.

Emory, E. K., Tynan, W. D., & Dave, R. (1989). Neurobehavioral anomalies in neonates with seizures. *Journal of Clinical and Experimental Neuropsychology, 11*, 231–240.

Endicott, J., & Spitzer, R. L. (1978). A diagnostic interview: The schedule for affective disorders and schizophrenia. *Archives of General Psychiatry, 35*, 837–844.

Endler, N. S. (1973). The person versus the situation: A pseudo issue? A response to Alker. *Journal of Personality, 41*, 287–303.

Endler, N. S., & Hunt, J. McV. (1968). S–R inventories of hostility and comparisons of the proportions of variance from persons, responses, and situations for hostility and anxiousness. *Journal of Personality and Social Psychology, 9*, 309–315.

Endler, N. S., Kantor, L., & Parker, J. D. (1994). A. State-trait coping, state-trait anxiety and academic performance. *Personality and Individual Differences, 16*(5), 663–670.

Endler, N. S., & Magnusson, D. (1976). *Interactional psychology and personality*. Washington, DC: Hemisphere.

Endler, N. S., & Parker, J. D. A. (1989). Multidimensional assessment of coping: A critical evaluation. *Journal of Personality and Social Psychology, 58*, 844–854.

Endler, N. S., & Parker, J. D. A. (1990). The analysis of a construct that does not exist: Misunderstanding the multidimensional nature of trait anxiety. *Educational and Psychological Measurement, 50*, 265–271.

Endler, N. S., Parker, J. D. A. (1994). Assessment of multidimensional coping: Task, emotion, and avoidance strategies. *Psychological Assessment, 6*(1), 50–60.

Endler, N. S., Parker, J. D. A., Bagby, R. M., & Cox B. J. (1991). Multidimensionality of state and trait anxiety: Factor structure of the Endler multidimensional anxiety scales. *Journal of Personality and Social Psychology, 60*, 919–926.

Erdberg, S. P. (1969). *MMPI differences associated with sex, race, and residence in a Southern sample*. Unpublished doctoral dissertation, University of Alabama, Birmingham.

Esquivel, G. B., & Lopez, E. (1988). Correlations among measures of cognitive ability, creativity, and academic achievement for gifted minority children. *Perceptual and Motor Skills, 67*, 395–398.

Evans, J. H., Carlsen, R. N., & McGrew, K. S. (1993). Classification of exceptional students with the Woodcock-Johnson Psycho-Educational Battery—Revised. In B. A. Bracken & R. S. McCallum (Eds.), Woodcock-Johnson Psycho-Educational Battery-Revised. *(Monograph). Journal of Psychoeducational Assessment*, 6–19.

Everson, H. T., Millsap, R. E., & Rodriguez, C. M. (1991). Isolating gender differences in test anxiety: A confirmatory factor analysis of the test anxiety inventory. *Educational and Psychological Measurement, 51,* 243–251.

Ewart, C. K. (1991). Social action theory for a public health psychology. *American Psychologist, 46,* 931–946.

Exner, J. E. (1974). *The Rorschach: A comprehensive system.* New York: Wiley.

Exner, J. E. (1976). Projective techniques. In I. B. Weiner (Ed.), *Clinical methods in psychology.* New York: Wiley.

Exner, J. E. (1980). But it's only an inkblot. *Journal of Personality Assessment, 44,* 562–577.

Exner, J. E. (1986). Some Rorschach data comparing schizophrenics with borderline and schizotypal personality disorders. *Journal of Personality Assessment, 50,* 455–471.

Exner, J. E. (1993). *The Rorschach: A comprehensive supplement: Vol. 1. Basic foundations* (3rd ed.). New York: Wiley.

Exner, J. E. (1995). Narcissism in the comprehensive system for the Rorschach—Comment. *Clinical Psychology-Science and Practice, 2*(2), 200–206.

Exner, J. E. (1996). A comment on "The Comprehensive System for the Rorschach: A Critical Examination." *Psychological Science, 7,* 11–13.

Exner, J. E., Gillespie, R., Viglione, D., & Coleman, M. (1982). Some intercorrelational data concerning Rorschach structural variables. *Journal of Personality Assessment, 46,* 3237.

Exner, J. E., & Weiner, I. B. (1981). *The Rorschach: A comprehensive system: Vol. 3. Assessment of children and adolescents.* New York: Wiley.

Exploring fantasies of TAT reliability. *Journal of Personality Assessment, 48,* 365–370.

Eyde, L. D., Moreland, K. L., & Robertson, G. J. (with Primoff, E. S., & Most, R. B.). (1988, December). *Test user qualifications: A data-based approach to promoting good test use.* Washington, DC: American Psychological Association.

Eysenck, H. J. (1959). Review of the Rorschach. In O. K. Buros (Ed.), *The fifth mental measurements yearbook.* Highland Park, NJ: Gryphon Press.

Eysenck, H. J. (1967). Intelligence assessment: A theoretical and experimental approach. *British Journal of Educational Psychology, 37,* 81–98.

Eysenck, H. J. (1990). The prediction of death from cancer by means of personality stress questionnaire: Too good to be true. *Perceptual and Motor Skills, 71,* 216–218.

Eysenck, H. J. (1991). Raising IQ through vitamin and mineral supplementation: An introduction. *Personality and Individual Differences, 12,* 329–333.

Fagan, J. F. (1985). A new look at infant intelligence. In D. K. Detterman (Ed.), *Current topics in human intelligence: Research methodology* (Vol. 1., pp. 223–246). Norwood, NJ: Ablex.

Farrell, A. D. (1989). The impact of computers on professional practice: A survey of current practices and attitudes. *Professional Psychology: Research and Practice, 20,* 172–178.

Farrell, A. D. (1991). Computers and behavioral assessment: Current applications, future possibilities, and obstacles to routine use. *Behavioral Assessment, 13,* 159–179.

Farrell, A. D. (1992). Behavioral assessment with adults. In R. T. Ammerman & M. Hersen (Eds.), *Handbook of behavior therapy with children and adults: A developmental and longitudinal perspective.* New York: Pergamon Press.

Feifel, H., Strack, S., & Nagy, V. T. (1987). Degree of lifethreat and differential use of coping modes. *Journal of Psychosomatic Research, 31,* 91–99.

Feldman, M. J., & Corah, N. L. (1960). Social desirability and the forced choice method. *Journal of Consulting Psychology, 24,* 480–482.

Feldman, S. E., & Sullivan, D. S. (1960). Factors mediating the effects of enhanced rapport on children's performances. *Journal of Consulting and Clinical Psychology, 36,* 302.

Felsten, G., & Wasserman, G. S. (1980). Visual masking: Mechanisms and theories. *Psychological Bulletin, 88,* 329–353.

Ferketich, S. (1991). Focus on psychometrics: Aspects of item analysis. *Research in Nursing and Health, 14,* 165–168.

Field, T. M. (1993). [Review of the book *Touch: The foundation of experience*]. *Contemporary Psychology, 38*(7), 735–736.

Filskov, F. E., & Boll, T. J. *(1981). Handbook of clinical neuropsychology.* New York: Wiley.

Finn, S. E. (1986). Structural stability of the MMPI in adult males. *Journal of Consulting and Clinical Psychology, 54,* 703–707.

Flanagan, J. C. (1954). The critical incident technique. *Psychological Bulletin, 51,* 327–358.

Flanagan, J. C. (1971). The PLAN system of individualizing education. *NCME Measurement in Education, 2*(2), 1–8.

Flanagan, R. (1995). The utility of the Kaufman Assessment Battery for Children (K-ABC) and the Wechsler Intelligence Scales for Linguistically Different Children—Clinical considerations. *Psychology in the Schools, 32*(1) 5–11.

Flaugher, R. L. (1978). The many definitions of test bias. *American Psychologist, 33,* 671–679.

Flaugher, R. L., & Schrader, W. B.

(1978). *Eliminating differentially difficult items as an approach to test bias* (RB-78–4). Princeton, NJ: Educational Testing Service.

Fleishman, E. A., & Quaintance, M. K. (1984). *Taxonomies of human performance: The description of human tasks*. Orlando, FL: Academic Press.

Fleiss, J. L. (1971). Measuring nominal scale agreement among many raters. *Psychological Bulletin, 76*, 378–382.

Fletcher, J., Levin, H. S., & Satz, P. (1989). Neuropsychological and intellectual assessment of children. In H. I. Kaplan & B. J. Sadock (Eds.), *Comprehensive textbook of psychiatry* (5th ed., Vol. 1, pp. 513–525). New York: Guilford Publications.

Fletcher, J. M., Taylor, H. G., Levin, H., & Satz, P. (1995). Neuropsychological and intellectual assessment of children. In H. I. Kaplan and B. J. Saddock (Eds.), *Comprehensive textbook of psychiatry* (6th ed., pp. 581–601). Baltimore: Williams & Wilkens.

Flett, G. L., & Blankstein, K. R. (1994). Worry as a component of test anxiety: A multidimensional analysis. G. C. L. Davey, & Frank Tallis (Eds.) *Worrying: Perspectives on theory, assessment and treatment* (pp. 219–239). Chichester, England: Wiley.

Folkman, S., & Lazarus, R. S. (1980). An analysis of coping in a middle aged community sample. *Journal of Health and Social Behavior, 21*, 219–239.

Follick, M. J., Gorkin, L., Smith, T., Capone, R. J., Visco, J., & Stabein, D. (1988). Quality of life post-myocardial infarction: The effects of a transtelephonic coronary intervention system. *Health Psychology, 7*, 169–182.

Foltz, D. (1981, June–July). Courts take psychologists' side in copyright, confidentiality fight. *APA Monitor*, p. 13.

Forrester, B. J., & Klaus, R. A. (1964). The effect of race of the examiner on intelligence test scores of Negro kindergarten children. *Peabody Papers in Human Development, 2*, 1–7.

Forsterling, F. (1988). *Attribution theory in clinical psychology*. New York: Wiley.

Forsyth, R. A. (1991). Do NAEP scales yield valid criterion-referenced interpretations? *Educational Measurement: Issues and Practice, 10*, 16.

Fowler, R. D. (1985). Landmarks in computer-assisted psychological assessment. *Journal of Consulting and Clinical Psychology, 53*, 748–759.

Fowler, R. D., & Coyle, F. A. (1969). Collegiate normative data on MMPI content scales. *Journal of Clinical Psychology, 25*, 62–63.

Fowles, G. P., & Tunick, R. H. (1986). WAIS-R and Shipley estimated IQ correlations. *Journal of Clinical Psychology, 42*, 647–649.

Fox, L. H. (1985). Review of Developing Cognitive Abilities Test. In J. V. Mitchell (Ed.), *The ninth mental measurements yearbook* (Vol. 1). Highland Park, NJ: Gryphon Press.

Francis-Williams, J. (1974). *Children with specific learning disabilities* (2nd ed.). Oxford, England: Pergamon Press.

Frank, G. (1995). On the assessment of self representations and object representations from the Rorschach: A review of the research and commentary. *Psychological Reports, 76*(2), 659–671.

Frank, G. H. (1970). The measurement of personality from the Wechsler tests. In B. A. Mahrer (Ed.), *Progress in experimental personality research*. New York: Academic Press.

Frank, G. H. (1976). Measures of intelligence and conceptual

thinking. In I. B. Weiner (Ed.), *Clinical methods in psychology*. New York: Wiley.

Frank, L. K. (1939). Projective methods for the study of personality. *Journal of Psychology, 8*, 343–389.

Fraser, E. D. (1965). Review of the Stanford-Binet Intelligence Scale, third revision. In O. K. Buros (Ed.), *The sixth mental measurements yearbook*. Highland Park, NJ: Gryphon Press.

Frederiksen, C. (1969). Abilities transfer and information retrieval in verbal learning. *Multivariate Behavioral Research Monographs, 69*, 1–82.

Fredrikson, M. (1991). Physiological responses to stressors: Implications for clinical assessment. *Psychological Assessment: A Journal of Consulting and Clinical Psychology, 3*, 350–355.

Freeman, F. S. (1955). *Theory and practice of psychological testing*. New York: Holt.

French, J. L. (1964). *Manual: Pictorial Test of Intelligence*. Boston: Houghton Mifflin.

Freud, S. (1953). Fragment of an analysis of a case of hysteria. In *The standard edition of the complete psychological works of Sigmund Freud* (Vol. 7). London: Hogarth Press. (Original work published 1905).

Fried, Y., & Tiegs, R. B. (1995). Supervisors' role conflict and role ambiguity differential relations with performance ratings of subordinates and the moderating effect of screening ability. *Journal of Applied Psychology, 80*, 282–296.

Frisch, M. B., & Jessop, N. S. (1989). Improving WAIS-R estimates with the Shirley Hartford and Wonderlic Personnel Tests: Need to control for reading ability. *Psychological Reports, 65*(3), 923–928.

Fuchs, D., & Fuchs, L. S. (1986). Test procedure bias: A meta-analysis of examiner familiarity effects. *Review of Educational Research, 56,* 243–262.

Fuld, P. A., & Fisher, P. (1977). Recovery of intellectual ability after closed head injury. *Developmental Medicine and Child Neurology, 19,* 495–502.

Funder, D. C. (1993). Judgments as data for personality and developmental psychology: Error versus accuracy. In D. C. Funder, R. D. Parke, C. Tomlinson-Keasey, & K. Widaman (Eds.), *Studying lives through time: Personality and development.* APA science volumes (pp. 121–146). Washington, DC: American Psychological Association.

Funder, D. C., Parke, R. D., Tomlinson-Keasey, C., & Widaman, K. (Eds.). (1993). *Studying lives through time: Personality and development.* Washington, DC: American Psychological Association.

Funder, D. C., & West, S. G. (1993). Consensus, self-other agreement, and accuracy in personality judgment: An introduction. [Special Issue: Viewpoints on personality: Consensus, self-other agreement, and accuracy in personality judgment.] *Journal of Personality, 61,* 457–476.

Furnham, A., & Henderson, M. (1982). Content analysis of four personality inventories. *Journal of Clinical Psychology, 38,* 818–825.

Galton, F. (1869). *Hereditary genius: An inquiry into its laws and consequences.* London: Collins.

Galton, F. (1879). Psychometric experiments. *Brain, 2,* 149–162.

Galton, F. (1883). *Inquiries into human faculty and its development.* London: Macmillan.

Gamble, K. R. (1972). The Holtzman Inkblot Technique: A

review. *Psychological Bulletin, 77,* 172–194.

Garcia, J. (1981). The logic and limits of mental aptitude testing. *American Psychologist, 36,* 1172–1180.

Gardner, E. F., Rudman, H. C., Karlsen, B., & Merwin, J. C. (1982). *The Stanford Achievement Test: Seventh edition.* New York: Harcourt Brace Jovanovich.

Gardner, H. (1983). *Frames of mind: The theory of multiple intelligences.* New York: Basic Books.

Gardner, H. (1985). *The mind's new science: A history of the cognitive revolution.* New York: Basic Books.

Gardner, H. (1993). The relationship between early giftedness and later achievement. In *The origins and development of high ability* (pp. 175–186). Ciba Foundation Symposium: Vol. 178. Chichester, England: Wiley.

Gardner, H., Krechevsky, M., Sternberg, R. J., & Okagaki, L. (1994). Intelligence in context: Enhancing students' practical intelligence for school. In K. McGilly (Ed.), *Classroom lessons: Integrating cognitive theory and classroom practice* (pp. 105–127). Cambridge, MA: MIT Press.

Garfield, S. L., & Sineps, J. (1959). An appraisal of Taulbee and Sisson's "configurational analysis of MMPI profiles of psychiatric groups." *Journal of Consulting Psychology, 23,* 333–335.

Gati, I., & Tikotzki, Y. (1989). Strategies for collection and processing of occupational information in making career decisions. *Journal of Counseling Psychology, 36,* 430–439.

Gauvain, M. (1994). [Review of the book *The cultural context of infancy: Vol. 2: Multicultural and interdisciplinary approaches to parent-infant relations*]. *Merrill-Palmer Quarterly Journal of*

Developmental Psychology, 40(4), 568–572.

Geer, J. H. (1965). The development of a scale to measure fear. *Behaviour Research and Therapy, 3,* 45–53.

Geiselman, R. E., Woodward, J. A., & Beatty, J. (1982). Individual differences in verbal memory performance: A test of alternative information-processing models. *Journal of Experimental Psychology: General, 111,* 109–134.

Geisinger, K. F. (1994). Cross-cultural normative assessment: Translation and adaption issues influencing the normative interpretation of assessment instruments. *Psychological Assessment, 6*(4), 304–312.

Georgoff, P. B. (1991). The Rorschach with hospice cancer patients and surviving cancer patients. *Journal of Personality Assessment, 56,* 218–226.

Gerken, K. C., & Eliason, M. J., & Arthur, C. R. (1994). The assessment of at-risk infants and toddlers with the Mental Scale and the Batelle Developmental Inventory: Beyond the data. *Psychology in the Schools, 31*(3), 181–187.

Gesell, A. (1925). Monthly increments of development in infancy. *Journal of Genetic Psychology, 32,* 203–208.

Gesell, A., & Amatruda, C. S. (1941). *Developmental diagnosis: Normal and abnormal child development: Clinical methods and pediatric applications.* New York: Paul B. Hoebler.

Gesell, A., & Amatruda, C. S. (1947). *Developmental diagnosis: Normal and abnormal child development: Clinical methods and pediatric applications* (2nd ed.). New York: Paul B. Hoebler.

Gesell, A., Halverson, H. M., Thompson, H., Ilg, F. L., Castner, B. M., Ames, L. B., & Amatruda, C. S. (1940). *The first five years of life: A guide to the study of the preschool child.* New York: Harper & Row.

Gianetti, R. Z., Klinger, D. E., Johnson, J. H., & Williams, T. A. (1976). The potential for dynamic assessment systems using on-line computer technology. *Behavior Research Methods and Instrumentation, 8,* 101–103.

Gibby, R. G., Miller, D. R., & Walker, E. L. (1953). The examiner's influence on the Rorschach protocol. *Journal of Consulting Psychology, 17,* 425–428.

Gilberstadt, H., & Duker, J. (1965). *A handbook for clinical and actuarial MMPI interpretation.* Philadelphia: Saunders.

Gillingham, W. H. (1970). *An investigation of examiner influence on Wechsler Intelligence Scale for Children scores.* Dissertation, Abstracts International, 31, 2178. (University Microfilms No. 70-20, 458)

Gilmore, D. C., Beehr, T. A., & Love, K. G. (1986). Effects of applicant sex, applicant physical attractiveness, type of job on interview decisions. *Journal of Occupational Psychology, 59,* 103–109.

Glutting, J. J. (1989). Introduction to the structure and application of the Stanford-Binet Intelligence Scale—Fourth Edition. *Journal of School Psychology, 27,* 69–80.

Goddard, H. H. (1908). The Binet and Simon tests of intellectual capacity. *Training School, 5,* 3–9.

Goddard, H. H. (1911). A revision of the Binet scale. *Training School, 8,* 56–62.

Goetcheus, G. (1967). *The effects of instructions and examiners on the Rorschach.* Unpublished master's thesis, Bowling Green State University, OH.

Goldberg, L. R. (1970). Man versus model of man: A rationale, plus some evidence for a method of improving on clinical inferences. *Psychological Bulletin, 73,* 422–432.

Goldberg, L. R. (1972). Parameters of personality inventory construction and utilization: A comparison of prediction strategies and tactics. *Multivariate Behavioral Research Monographs, 72,* 59.

Goldberg, L. R. (1974). Objective personality tests and measures. *Annual Review of Psychology, 25,* 343–366.

Goldberg, L. R., Grenier, J. R., Guion, R. M., Sechrest, L. B., & Wing, H. (1991). Questionnaires used in the prediction of trustworthiness in pre-employment selection decisions: An APA Task Force report. Washington, DC: *American Psychological Association, Science Directorate.*

Golden, C. J. (1981). A standardized version of Luria's neuropsychological tests: Quantitative and qualitative approach in neuropsychological evaluation. In F. E. Filskov & T. J. Boll (Eds.), *Handbook of clinical neuropsychology.* New York: Wiley.

Goldfried, M. R. (1976). Behavioral assessment. In I. B. Weiner (Ed.), *Clinical methods in psychology.* New York: Wiley-Interscience.

Goldman, B. A., & Osbourne, W. (1985). *Unpublished experimental mental measures* (Vol. 4). New York: Human Sciences Press.

Goldman, R. D. (1973). Hidden opportunities in the prediction of college grades for different subgroups. *Journal of Educational Measurement, 10*(3), 205–210.

Goldman, R. D., & Hartig, L. (1976). The WISC may not be a valid predictor of school performance for primary-grade minority children. *American Journal of Mental Deficiency, 80,* 583–587.

Goldman, R. D., & Hewitt, B. (1976). *Culture-free selection of professional school students.*

Unpublished manuscript, University of California, Riverside.

Goldstein, G. (1986). The neuropsychology of schizophrenia. In I. Grant & K. M. Adams (Eds.), *Neuropsychological assessment of neuropsychiatric disorders.* New York: Oxford University Press.

Goldstein, L. H., Canavan, A. G., & Polkey, C. E. (1988). Verbal and abstract designs paired associate learning after unilateral temporal lobectomy. *Cortex, 24,* 41–52.

Gomezbenito, J., & Fornssantacana, M. (1993). Concurrent validity between the Columbia Mental Maturity Scale and the McCarthy Scales of Children's Abilities. *Perceptual and Motor Skills, 76*(3), 1177–1178.

Goodman, J. (1977). The diagnostic fallacy: A critique of Jane Mercer's concept of mental retardation. *Journal of School Psychology, 15,* 197–206.

Goodman, J. (1979). "Ignorance" versus "stupidity"—the basic disagreement. *School Psychology Digest, 8*(2), 218–223.

Gordon, E. W., & Terrell, M. D. (1981). The changed social context of testing. *American Psychologist, 36,* 1167–1171.

Gorsuch, R. L. (1974). *Factor analysis.* Philadelphia: Saunders.

Gotkin, T. D., & Reynolds, C. R. (1981). Factorial similarity of the WISC-R white and black children from the standardization sample. *Journal of Educational Psychology, 73,* 227–231.

Gottfredson, L. S. (1980). Construct validity of Holland's occupational typology in terms of prestige, census, Department of Labor, and other classification systems. *Journal of Applied Psychology, 65,* 697–714.

Gottfredson, L. S. (1994). The science and politics of race-norming. *American Psychologist, 49,* 955–963.

Gottlib, I. H., & Cine, D. B. (1989). Self-report assessment of depression and anxiety. In P. C. Kendill & D. Watson (Eds.), *Anxiety and depression: Distinctive and overlapping features* (pp. 131–169). San Diego: Academic Press.

Gough, H. G. (1957). *California Psychological Inventory manual.* Palo Alto, CA: Consulting Psychologists Press.

Gough, H. G. (1960). The adjective checklist as a personality assessment research technique. *Psychological Reports, 6,* 107–122.

Gough, H. G. (1969). *California Psychological Inventory, revised manual.* Palo Alto, CA: Consulting Psychologists Press.

Gough, H. G. (1987). *California Psychological Inventory, revised manual.* Palo Alto, CA: Consulting Psychologists Press.

Gough, H. G. (1995). Career assessment and the California Psychological Inventory. *Journal of Career Assessments, 3*(2), 101–122.

Gough, H. G., & Heilbrun, A. B., Jr. (1980). *The Adjective Checklist manual (revised).* Palo Alto, CA: Consulting Psychologists Press.

Gould, S. J. (1981). *The mismeasure of man.* New York: Norton.

Graham, F. K., & Kendall, B. S. (1960). Memory-for-Designs test: Revised general manual. *Perceptual Motor Skills, 11,* 147–190.

Graham, F. K., & Kendall, B. S. (1960). Memory-for-Designs test: Revised general manual. *Perceptual Motor Skills, 11,* 147–190.

Graham, J. R. (1990). *MMPI-2 in psychological treatment.* New York: Oxford University Press.

Graham, J. R., Timbrook, R. E., & Ben-Porath, Y. S. (1991). Code-type congruence between MMPI and MMPI-2. Separating fact from artifact. *Journal of Personality Assessment, 57,* 205–215.

Grant, I. (1987). Alcohol and the brain: Neuropsychological correlates. *Journal of Consulting and Clinical Psychology, 55,* 310.

Grant, I., & Adams, K. M. (1986). *Neuropsychological assessment of neuropsychiatric disorders.* New York: Oxford University Press.

Grant, I., & Heaton, R. K. (1990). Human immunodeficiency virustype I (HIV-1) and the brain. *Journal of Consulting and Clinical Psychology, 58,* 22–30.

Grant, I., & Kaplan, R. M. (1988). Statistics and experimental design. In H. I. Kaplan & D. J. Sadock (Eds.), *Comprehensive text book of psychiatry* (5th ed.). Baltimore: Williams & Wilkins.

GRE Guide. (1990). Princeton, NJ: Educational Testing Service.

GRE Guide. (1991). Princeton, NJ: Educational Testing Service.

Greaud, V. A., & Green, B. F. (1986). Equivalence of conventional and computer presentation of speeded tests. *Applied Psychological Measurement, 10,* 23–34.

Green, B. F. (1978). In defense of measurement. *American Psychologist, 33,* 664–670.

Green, B. L., & Kenrick, D. T. (1994). The attractiveness of gender-typed traits at different relationship levels: Androgynous characteristics may be desirable after all. *Personality and Social Psychology Bulletin, 20*(3), 244–253.

Green, D. F., Jr., & Wing, H. (1988). *Analysis of job performance measurement data: Report of a workshop.* Washington, DC: National Academy Press.

Green, D. R., & Draper, J. F. (1972, September). Exploratory studies of bias and achievement. Paper given at the *American Psychological Association,* Honolulu, HI.

Greene, R. L., Weed, N. C., Butchers, J. N., Arredondo, R., & Davis, H. G. (1992). A cross-validation of MMPI-2 Substance Abuse Scales. *Journal of Personality Assessment, 58,* 405–410.

Grieco, A., & Long, C. J. (1984). Investigation of the Karnofsky performance status as a measure of quality of life. *Health Psychology, 3,* 129–142.

Grim, L. G., & Yarnold, P. R. (1995). *Reading and understanding multivariate statistics* (1st ed.). Washington, DC: American Psychological Association.

Groenweg, G., Conway, D. G., & Stan, E. A. (1986). Performance of adults with developmental handicaps on alternate forms of the Peabody Picture Vocabulary Test. *Journal of Speech and Hearing Disorders, 51,* 259–263.

Grossman, L. S., & Craig, R. J. (1995). Comparisons of the MCMI-II and 16 PF validity scales. *Journal of Personality Assessment, 64* (2), 384–389.

Groth-Marnat, G., & Shumaker, J. (1989). Computer-based psychological testing: Issues and guidelines. *American Journal of Orthopsychiatry, 59,* 257–263.

Guertin, W. H., Ladd, C. E., Frank, G. H., Rabin, A. I., & Hiester, D. S. (1966). Research with the Wechsler Intelligence Scales for Adults: 1960–1965. *Psychological Bulletin, 66,* 385–409.

Guertin, W. H., Ladd, C. E., Frank, G. H., Rabin, A. I., & Hiester, D. S. (1971). Research with the Wechsler Intelligence Scales for Adults: 1965–1970. *Psychological Record, 21,* 289–339.

Guertin, W. H., Rabin, A. I., Frank, G. H., & Ladd, C. E. (1962). Research with the Wechsler Intelligence Scales for Adults: 1955–1960. *Psychological Bulletin, 59,* 1–26.

Guilford, J. P. (1940). *An inventory of factors.* Beverly Hills, CA: Sheridan Supply.

Guilford, J. P. (1954). *Psychometric methods* (2nd ed.). New York: McGraw-Hill.

Guilford, J. P. (1959). *Personality.* New York: McGraw-Hill.

Guilford, J. P., & Fruchter, B. (1973). *Fundamental statistics in psychology and education* (5th ed.). New York: McGraw-Hill.

Guilford, J. P., & Martin, H. G. (1943). *The Guilford Martin inventory of factors: GAMIN: Manual of directions and norms.* Beverly Hills, CA: Sheridan Supply.

Guilford, J. P., & Zimmerman, W. S. (1949). *The Guilford Temperament Survey: Manual of instructions and interpretations.* Beverly Hills, CA: Sheridan Supply.

Guilford, J. P., & Zimmerman, W. S. (1956). Fourteen dimensions of temperament. *Psychological Monographs, 70,* (10).

Guion, R. M., & Ironson, G. H. (1983). Latent trait theory for organizational research. *Organizational Behavior and Human Performance, 31,* 54–87.

Gullone, E., & King, N. J. (1992). Psychometric evaluation of a Revised Fear Survey Schedule for children and adolescents. *Journal of Child Psychology and Psychiatry and Allied Disciplines, 33*(6), 987–998.

Gunnison, J. A. (1984). Developing educational intervention from assessments involving the K-ABC. *The Journal of Special Education, 18*(3), 325–343.

Guthrie, R. V. (1976). *Even the rat was white: A historical view of psychology.* New York: Harper & Row.

Guttman, L. (1950). Relation of scalogram analysis to other techniques. In S. A. Stouffer et al. (Eds.), *Measurement and prediction.* Princeton, NJ: Princeton University Press.

Guyatt, G. H., Feeny, D. H., & Patrick, D. L. (1993). Measuring health-related quality of life. *Annals of Internal Medicine, 118,* 622–629.

Guyatt, G., Walter, S., & Norman, G. (1987). Measuring change over time: Assessing the usefulness of evaluative instruments. *Journal of Chronic Diseases, 40,* 171–178.

Gynther, M. D. (1972). White norms and black MMPIS: A prescription for discrimination? *Psychological Bulletin, 78,* 386–402.

Gynther, M. D., & Gynther, R. A. (1976). Personality inventories. In I. B. Weiner (Ed.), *Clinical methods in psychology.* New York: Wiley.

Gynther, M. D., & Shimkunas, A. M. (1965). Age, intelligence, and MMPI F scores. *Journal of Consulting Psychology, 29,* 383–388.

Gyurke, J. S., Stone, B. J., & Beyer, M. (1990). A confirmatory factor analysis of the WPPSI-R. *Journal of Psychoeducational Assessment, 8,* 15–21.

Haber, R. H. (1969). Perception and thought: An information processing analysis. In J. I. Voss *(Ed.), Approaches to thought.* Columbus, OH: Merrill.

Haemmerlie, F. M., & Beamish, P. (1990). The Jenkins Activity Survey and the CPI—Revised: Further evidence of adaptive and maladaptive Type A traits. *Journal of Clinical Psychology, 46,* 573–581.

Hakel, M. D. (1986). Personnel selection and placement. *Annual Review of Psychology, 37,* 351 380.

Haley, S. M., McHorney, C. A., & Ware, J. E. J. (1994). Evaluation of the MOS SF-36 physical functioning scale (PF-10): I. Unidimensionality and reproducibility of the Rasch item scale. *Journal of Clinical Epidemiology, 47,* 671–684.

Hall, J. C. (1957). Correlation of a modified form of Raven's Progressive Matrices (1938) with the Wechster Adult Intelligence Scale. *Journal of Consulting Psychology, 21,* 23–26.

Hall, V. C., Huppertz, J. W., & Levi, A. (1977). Attention and achievement exhibited by middle and lower-class black and white elementary school boys. *Journal of Educational Psychology, 69,* 115–120.

Hambleton, R. K. (1980). Validation of criterion-referenced test score interpretations and standard setting methods. In R. A. Berk (Ed.), *Criterion referenced measurement: The state of the art.* Baltimore: Johns Hopkins University Press.

Hambleton, R. K. (1994). The rise and fall of criterion-referenced measurement? *Educational Measurement: Issues and Practice, 13,* 21–26.

Hammer, A. L., & Marting, M. S. (1985). *Manual for the Coping Resources Inventory.* Palo Alto, CA: Consulting Psychologists Press.

Hampson, E., & Kimura D. (1988). Reciprocal effects of hormonal fluctuations on human motor and perceptual-spatial skills. *Behavioral Neuroscience, 102,* 456–459.

Haney, W. (1981). Validity, vaudeville, and values: A short history of social concerns over standardized testing. *American Psychologist, 36,* 1021–1034.

Hanford, G. H. (1986). The SAT and statewide assessment: The distinction between measurement and evaluation. *Vital Speeches of the Day, 52*(24), 765–768.

Hansen, J.C., Kozberg, J., & Goranson, D. (1994). Accuracy of student recall of Strong Interest Inventory results 1 year after interpretation. *Measurement and Evaluation in Counseling and Development, 26*(4), 235–242.

Hansen, J. C., & Campbell, D. P. (1985). *Manual for the SVIB-SCII*

(4th ed.). Stanford, CA: Stanford University Press.

Hardy, J. B., Welcher, D. W., Mellits, E. D., & Kagan, J. (1976). Pitfalls in the measurement of intelligence: Are standardized intelligence tests valid for measuring the intellectual potential of urban children? *Journal of Psychology, 94,* 43–51.

Hargadon, F. (1981). Test and college admission. *American Psychologist, 36,* 1112–1119.

Harkness, A. R., McNulty, J. L., & Ben-Porath, Y. S. (1995). The personality psychopathology-5 (Psy-5): Construct and MMPI-2 scales. *Psychological Assessment, 7*(1), 104–114.

Harman, H. H. (1967). *Modern factor analysis* (2nd ed.). Chicago: University of Chicago Press.

Harmon, L. W., Cole, N., Wysong, E., & Zytowski, D. G. (1973). AMEG commission report on sex bias in interest measurement. *Measurement and Evaluation in Guidance, 6,* 171–177.

Harris, D. B. (1963). *Children's drawings as measures of intellectual maturity: A revision and extension of the Goodenough Draw-a-Man Test.* New York: Harcourt, Brace, & World.

Harris, F. C., & Lahey, B. B. (1982). Subject reactivity in direct observational assessment: A review and critical analysis. *Clinical Psychology Review, 2,* 523–538.

Harris, M. M. (1989). Reconsidering the employment interview: A review of recent literature and suggestions for future research. *Personnel Psychology, 42,* 691–726.

Harrison, R. (1940a). Studies in the use and validity of the Thematic Apperception Test with mentally disordered patients: II. A quantitative validity study. *Character and Personality, 9,* 122–133.

Harrison, R. (1940b). Studies in the use and validity of the Thematic Apperception Test with mentally disordered patients: III. Validation by blind analysis. *Character and Personality, 9,* 134–138.

Harrison, R. (1965). Thematic apperceptive methods. In B. Wolman (Ed.), *Handbook of clinical psychology.* New York: McGraw-Hill.

Harrison, R., & Rotter, J. B. (1945). A note on the reliability of the Thematic Apperception Test. *Journal of Abnormal and Social Psychology, 40,* 97–99.

Hart, B., & Spearman, C. (1912). General ability, its existence and nature. *British Journal of Psychology, 5,* 51–84.

Hartigan, J., & Wigdor, A. (1989). Fairness in employment testing. *Science, 245,* 14.

Hartlage, L. C., & Steele, C. T. (1977). WISC and WISC-R correlates of academic achievement. *Psychology in the Schools, 14,* 15–18.

Hartman, D. E. (1986a). Artificial intelligence or artificial psychologists? Conceptual issues in clinical microcomputer use. *Professional Psychology: Research and Practice, 17,* 528–534.

Hartman, D. E. (1986b). On the use of clinical psychology software: Practical, legal, and ethical concerns. *Professional Psychology: Research and Practice, 17,* 473–475.

Hartmann, D. P. (1977). Considerations in the choice of interobserver reliability estimates. *Journal of Applied Behavior Analysis, 10,* 103–116.

Harty, H., Adkins, D. M., & Sherwood, R. D. (1984). Predictability of giftedness indentification indices for two recognized approaches to elementary school gifted education. *Journal of Educational Research, 77,* 337–342.

Hase, H. D., & Goldberg, L. R. (1967). Comparative validity of different strategies of constructing personality inventory scales. *Psychological Bulletin, 67,* 231–248.

Hathaway, S. R. (1947). A coding system for MMPI profiles. *Journal of Consulting Psychology, 11,* 334–337.

Hathaway, S. R., & McKinley, J. C. (1943). *Manual for the Minnesota Multiphasic Personality Inventory.* New York: Psychological Corporation.

Hathaway, S. R., & McKinley, J. C. (1967). *Minnesota Multiphasic Personality Inventory, revised manual.* New York: Psychological Corporation.

Hattie, J. (1980). Should creativity tests be administered under testlike conditions? An empirical study of three alternative conditions. *Journal of Educational Psychology, 72,* 87–98.

Hayes, F. B., & Martin, R. P. (1986). Effectiveness of the PPVT-R in the screening of young gifted children. *Journal of Psychoeducational Assessment, 4,* 27–33.

Haynes, S. N. (1990). Behavioral assessment of adults. In A. Goldstein & M. Hersen (Eds.), *Handbook of psychological assessment* (2nd ed., pp. 423–467). New York: Pergamon Press.

Haynes, S. N. (1991). Clinical application of psychophysiological assessment: An introduction. *Psychological Assessment: A Journal of Consulting and Clinical Psychology, 3,* 307–308.

Haynes, S. N. (1991). Behavioral assessment. In M. Hersen, A. Kazdin, & A. Bellack (Eds.), *The clinical psychology handbook* (2nd ed.). New York: Pergamon Press. pp. 430–464.

Haynes, S. N. (1995). Introduction to the special section on chaos theory and psychological assessment. *Psychological Assessment, 7*(1), 3–4.

Haynes, S. N., Blaine, D., & Meyer, K. (1995). Dynamical models for psychological assessment: Phase space functions. *Psychological Assessment, 7*(1), 17–24.

Healy, W., & Fernald, G. M. (1911). Tests for practical mental classification. *Psychological Monographs, 13*(2).

Hearst, E. (1979). One hundred years: Themes and perspectives. In E. Hearst (Ed.), *The first century of experimental psychology*. Hillsdale, NJ: Erlbaum.

Heaton, R. K., & Pendicton, M. G. (1981). Use of neuropsychological tests to predict adult patients' everyday functioning. *Journal of Consulting and Clinical Psychology, 49*, 807–821.

Hebb, D. O. (1981). Reply irrelevant? *American Psychologist, 36*, 423–424.

Heiby, E. M. (1995a). Assessment of behavioral chaos with a focus on transitions in depression. *Psychological Assessment, 7*(1), 10–16.

Heiby, E. M. (1995b). Chaos theory, nonlinear dynamical models, and psychological assessment. *Psychological Assessment, 7*(1), 5–9.

Heider, F. (1944). Social perception and phenomenal causation. *Psychological Review, 51*, 358–374.

Heider, F. (1958). *The psychology of interpersonal relations*. New York: Wiley.

Heilbrun, A. B., Jr. (1972). Edwards Personal Preference Schedule. In O. K. Buros (Ed.), *The seventh mental measurements yearbook* (Vol. 1). Highland Park, NJ: Gryphon Press.

Heimberg, R. C., Keller, K. E., & Peca-Baker, T. (1986). Cognitive assessment of social-evaluative anxiety in the job interview: Job Interview Self-Statement Schedule. *Journal of Counseling Psychology, 33*, 190–195.

Heitzmann, C. A., & Kaplan, R. M. (1988). Assessment of measures for measuring social support. *Health Psychology, 7*, 75–109.

Heller, K. (1971). Laboratory interview research as an analogue to treatment. In A. E. Bergin & S. L. Garfield (Eds.), *Handbook of psychotherapy and behavior change*. New York: Wiley.

Heller, K., Davis, J. D., & Myers, R. A. (1966). The effects of interviewer style in a standardized interview. *Journal of Consulting Psychology, 30*, 501–508.

Henderson, N. B., Fay, W. H., Lindemann, S. J., & Clarkson, Q. D. (1973). Will the IQ test ban decrease the effectiveness of reading prediction? *Journal of Educational Psychology, 65*, 345–355.

Henrichs, T. (1964). Objective configural rules for discriminating MMPI profiles in a psychiatric population. *Journal of Clinical Psychology, 20*, 157–159.

Henry, P., & Bardo, H. R. (1990). Relationship between scores on developing cognitive abilities test and scores on medical college admissions test for nontraditional premedical students. *Psychological Reports, 67*, 55–63.

Henry, P., Bryson, S., & Henry, C. A. (1990). Black student attitudes toward standardized tests. *College Student Journal, 23*, 346–354.

Hensley, W. (1994). Height as a basis for physical attraction. *Adolescence, 29*(114), 469–474.

Herbert, W. (1982). Intelligence tests: Sizing up a newcomer. *Science News, 122*, 280–281.

Hernstein, R. J. (1981). Try again, Dr. Albee. *American Psychologist, 36*, 424–425.

Hernstein, R. J. (1982, August). IQ testing and the media. *Atlantic Monthly*, pp. 68–74.

Herring, J. P. (1922). *Herring revision of the Binet-Simon tests*. Yonkers, NY: World Book.

Herrnstein, R. J. & Murray, C. A. (1994). *The bell curve: Intelligence and class structure in American life*. New York: Free Press.

Hersen, M. (1971). Fear scale norms for an in-patient population. *Journal of Clinical Psychology, 27*, 375–378.

Hersen, M., Kazdin, A. E., & Bellack, A. S. (1991). *The clinical psychology handbook* (2nd ed.). New York: Pergamon Press.

Hersh, J. B. (1971). Effects of referral information on testers. *Journal of Consulting and Clinical Psychology, 37*, 116–122.

Hertz, M. R. (1937). Discussion on "Some recent Rorschach problems." *Rorschach Research Exchange, 2*, 53–65.

Hertz, M. R. (1938). Scoring the Rorschach Inkblot Test. *Journal of Genetic Psychology, 52*, 16–64.

Hertz, M. R. (1986). Rorschach bound: A 50-year memory. *Journal of Personality Assessment, 50*, 396–416.

Hesketh, B., Hesketh, T., Hansen, J. I., & Goranson, D. (1995). Use of fuzzy variables in developing new scales from the Strong Interest Inventory. *Journal of Counseling Psychology, 42*, 85–99.

Higgins, E. T., & Bargh, J. A. (1987). Social cognition and social perception. *Annual Review of Psychology, 38*, 369–425.

Highhouse, S., & Hause, E.L. (1995). Missing information in selection: An application of the Einhorn-Hogarth ambiguity model. *Journal of Applied Psychology, 80*, 86–93.

Hindley, C. B. (1965). Stability and change in abilities up to 5 years: Group trends. *Journal of Child Psychology and Psychiatry, 6*, 85–99.

Hiscock, M. (1978). Imagery assessment through self report: What do imagery questionnaires measure? *Journal of Consulting and Clinical Psychology, 46*, 223–230.

Hoaglin, D. C., Mosteller, F., & Tukey, J. W. (Eds.). (1983). *Understanding robust and exploratory data analysis* [Wiley series in probability and mathematical statistics]. New York: Wiley.

Hoaglin, D. C., Mosteller, F., & Tukey, J. W. (Eds.) (1991). *Fundamentals of exploratory analysis of variance* [Wiley series in probability and mathematical statistics]. New York: Wiley.

Hodges, K. (1985). *Manual for the child assessment schedule (CAS).* Unpublished manuscript, University of Missouri, Columbia.

Hodges, K. (1994). Structured interviews for assessing children. *Journal of Child Psychology and Psychiatry and Allied Disciplines, 34*(1), 49–68.

Hodges, W., & Spielberger, C. (1969). Digit span: An indication of trait or state anxiety? *Journal of Consulting and Clinical Psychology, 33,* 430–434.

Hodos, W., & Campbell, C. B. G. (1969). Scala naturae: Why there is no theory in comparative psychology. *Psychological Review, 76,* 337–350.

Hofer, P. J., & Green, B. I. (1985). The challenge of competence and creativity in computerized psychological testing. *Journal of Consulting and Clinical Psychology, 53,* 826–838.

Hoffman, H., Loper, R. G., & Kammeier, M. L. (1974). Identifying future alcoholics with MMPI alcoholism scales. *Quarterly Journal of Studies on Alcohol, 35,* 490–498.

Hogan, J., & Quigley, A. M. (1986). Physical standards for employment and the courts. *American Psychologist, 41,* 1193–1217.

Holahan, C. J. (1986). Environmental psychology. *Annual Review of Psychology, 37,* 381–407.

Holahan, C. J., & Moos, R. H. (1986). Personality, coping, and family support in stress resistance: A longitudinal analysis. *Journal of Personality and Social Psychology, 51,* 389–395.

Holland, J. L. (1975). *Manual for the Vocational Preference Inventory.* Palo Alto, CA: Consulting Psychologists Press.

Holland, J. L. (1985a). *Making vocational choices* (2nd ed.). Englewood Cliffs, NJ: Prentice-Hall.

Holland, J. L. (1985b). *The Self-Directed Search, professional manual.* Odessa, FL: Psychological Assessment Resources.

Holland, J. L., & Gottfredson, G. D. (1976). Using a typology of persons and environments to explain careers: Some extensions and clarifications. *Counseling Psychologist, 6,* 20–29.

Holland, J. L., & Nichols, R. C. (1964). Prediction of academic and extracurricular achievements in college. *Journal of Educational Psychology, 55,* 55–65.

Holland, P. W., & Wainer, H. (1993). *Differential item functioning.* Hillsdale, NJ: Lawrence Erlbaum Associates.

Hollingworth, H. L. (1922). *Judging human character.* New York: Appleton-Century-Crofts.

Holmes, T. S., & Rahe, R. H. (1967). The Social Readjustment Rating Scale. *Journal of Psychosomatic Research, 11,* 213–218.

Holt, R. R. (1967). Diagnostic testing: Present status and future prospects. *Journal of Nervous and Mental Disease, 141,* 444–464.

Holt, R. R. (1970). Yet another look at clinical and statistical prediction: Or, is clinical psychology worthwhile? *American Psychologist, 25,* 337–349.

Holtzman, W. H., Thorpe, J. S. Swartz, J. D., & Herron, E. W. (1961). *Inkblot perception and personality.* Austin: University of Texas Press.

Holzberg, J. D., & Belmont, L. (1952). The relationship between factors on the Wechsler-Bellevue and Rorschach having a common psychological rationale. *Journal of Consulting Psychology, 16,* 23–30.

Hooper, S. R., Conner, R. E., & Umansky, W. (1986). The Cattell Infant Intelligence Scale: A review of the literature. *Developmental Review, 6,* 146–164.

Hooper, S. R. & March, J. S. (1995). Neuropsychology. J. S. March (Ed.), *Anxiety disorders in children and adolescents* (pp. 35–60), New York: Guilford Press.

Horn, J. L., & Cattell, R. B. (1966). Refinement and test of the theory of fluid and crystallized intelligence. *Journal of Educational Psychology, 57,* 253–276.

Horowitz, M. J., & Wilner, N. (1980). Life events, stress, and coping. In L. Poon (Ed.), *Aging in the eighties.* Washington, DC: American Psychological Association.

Hosey, G. M., Freeman, W. L., Stracqualursi, F., & Gohdes, D. (1990). Designing and evaluating diabetes education material for American Indians. *Diabetes Educator, 16,* 407–414.

Hotelling, H. (1933). Analysis of a complex statistical variable into principal components. *Journal of Educational Psychology, 24,* 417–441, 498–520.

Houldin, A. D., & Forbes, E. J. (1990). Nursing students' personalities as measured by the California Psychological Inventory: Participants vs. nonparticipants in a program of research. *Psychological Reports, 67,* 1119–1122.

Howell, K. W. (1985). Review of the Watkins-Bender Gestalt Scoring System. In J. V. Mitchell (Ed.), *The ninth edition mental measurements yearbook* (Vol. 1). Highland Park, NJ: Gryphon Press.

Hunt, E. (1980). Intelligence as an

information-processing concept. *British Journal of Psychology, 71*, 449–474.

Hunt, T. V. (1978). Review of McCarthy Scales of Children's Abilities. In O. K. Buros (Ed.), *The eighth mental measurements yearbook* (Vol. 1). Highland Park, NJ: Gryphon Press.

Hunter, J. E., & Hunter, R. F. (1984). Validity and utility of alternative predictors of job performance. *Psychological Bulletin, 96*, 72–98.

Hunter, J. E., & Schmidt, F. L (1976). Critical analysis of statistical and ethical implications of various definitions of test bias. *Psychological Bulletin, 83*, 1053–1071.

Hunter, J. E., & Schmidt, F. L. (1978). Bias in defining test bias: Reply to Darlington. *Psychological Bulletin, 85*, 675–676.

Hurt, S. W., Reznikoff, M., & Clarkin, J. F. (1995). The Rorschach. L. E. Beutler & M. R. Berren (Eds.), *Integrative assessment of adult personality* (pp. 187–205). New York: Guilford Press.

Hutchinson, T. A., Boyd, N. F., & Feinstein, A. R. (1979). Scientific problems in clinical scales as demonstrated in the Karnofsky Index of Performance Status. *Journal of Chronic Diseases, 32*, 309–312.

Hyde, L., Wolf, J., McCracken, S., & Yesner, R. (1973). Natural course of inoperable lung cancer. *Chest, 64*, 309–312.

Hynd, T. W., & Obrzut, J. E, (1981). *Neuropsychological assessment and the school-age child: Issues and procedures.* New York: Grune & Stratton.

Iacono, W. G. (1991). Psychophysiological assessment of psychopathology. *Psychological Assessment: A Journal of Consulting and Clinical Psychology, 3*, 309–320.

Imada, A. S., & Hakel, M. D. (1977). Influences of nonverbal communication and rater proximity on impressions and decisions in simulated employment interviews. *Journal of Applied Psychology, 62*, 295–300.

Ingram, R. E. (1980). *The GRES: Are we weighing them too heavily in graduate psychology admissions?* Unpublished manuscript, University of Kansas, Lawrence.

Insurance license exams will be revised. (1984, November 29). *Los Angeles Times*, Part I, p. 5.

Ironson, G. H., & Sebkovial, N. J. (1979). A comparison of several methods for assessing item bias. *Journal of Educational Measurement, 16*, 209–225.

Irwin, M., Daniels, M., Bloom, E. T., Smith, T. L., & Weiner, H. (1987). Life events, depressive symptoms, and immune function. *American Journal of Psychiatry, 144*, 437–441.

Iverson, G. L., Franzen, M. D., & Hammond, J. A. (1995). Examination of inmates' ability to malinger on the MMPI-2. *Psychological Assessment, 7*(1), 118–121.

Ivnik, R. J., Smith, G. E., Malec, J. F., Petersen, R. C., & Tangalos, E. G. (1995). Long-term stability and intercorrelations of cognitive abilities in older persons. *Psychological Assessment, 7*(2), 155–161.

Jaccard, J., & Wan, C. K. (1995). Measurement error in the analysis of interaction effects between continuous predictors using multiple regression: Multiple indicator and structural equation approaches. *Psychological Bulletin, 117*(2), 348–357.

Jackson, D. N. (1967). *Personality Research Form Manual.* Goshen, NY: Research Psychologists Press.

Jackson, D. N. (1970). A sequential system for personality scale development. In C. D. Spielberger (Ed.), *Current topics in clinical and community psychology* (Vol. 2). New York: Academic Press.

Jackson, D. N. (1976a). *Jackson Personality Inventory.* Goshen, NY: Research Psychologists Press.

Jackson, D. N. (1976b). *Manual for the Jackson Personality Inventory.* Goshen, NY: Research Psychologists Press.

Jackson, D. N., & Livesley, W. J. (1995). Possible contributions from personality assessment to the classification of personality disorders. W. J. Livesley (Ed.), *The DSM-IV personality disorders. Diagnosis and treatment of mental disorders* (pp. 459–481). New York: Guilford Press.

Jackson, D. N., & Messick, S. (Eds.). (1967). *Problems in human assessment.* New York: McGraw-Hill.

Jackson, E. W. (1980). Identification of gifted performance in young children. In W, C. Roedell, N. E. Jackson, & H. B. Robinson (Eds.), *Gifted young children.* New York: Teachers College Press.

Jaffe, J. (1968). Computer assessment of dyadic interaction rules from chronographic data. In J. Shlien, H. Hunt, J. D, Matarazzo, & C. Savage (Eds.), *Research in psychotherapy* (Vol. 3). Washington, DC: American Psychological Association.

Janssen, E., Everaerd, W., Vanlunsen, R. H. W., & Oerlemans, S. (1994). Validation of a psychophysiological Waking Erectile Assessment (WEA) for the diagnosis of Male Erectile Disorder. *Urology, 43*(5), 686–695.

Jennings, J. R. (1986). Bodily changes during attention. in M. G. H. Coles, E. Donchin, & S. W. Porges (Eds.), *Psychophysiology: Systems, processes, and applications.* New York: Guilford Press.

Jensen, A. R. (1965). Review of the Rorschach. In O. K. Buros (Ed.), *The sixth mental measurements yearbook*. Highland Park, NJ: Gryphon Press.

Jensen, A. R. (1969). How much can we boost IQ and scholastic achievement? *Harvard Educational Review, 39*, 1–23.

Jensen, A. R. (1972). *Genetics and education*. New York: Harper & Row.

Jensen, A. R. (1979). *g*—Outmoded theory or unconquered frontier? *Creative Science and Technology, 2*, 16–29.

Jensen, A. R. (1980). *Bias in mental testing*. New York: Free Press.

Jensen, A. R. (1982). Reaction time and psychometric "g." In H. J. Eysenck (Ed.), *A model for intelligence*. New York: Springer-Verlag.

Jensen, A. R. (1984). The black-white difference on the K-ABC: Implication for future tests. *Journal of Special Education, 18*, 377–408.

Jensen, A. R. (1985). The nature of black-white differences on various psychometric tests: Spearman's hypothesis. *The Behavioral and Brain Sciences, 8*, 193–263.

Jensen, A. R. (1986). The "g" beyond factor analysis. In J. C. Conoley, J. A. Glover, & R. R. Ronnings (Eds.), *The influence of cognitive psychology on testing and measurement*. Hillsdale, NJ: Erlbaum.

Jensen, A. R. (1991). Spearman G and the problem of educational equality. *Oxford Review of Education, 17*, 169–187.

Jensen, A. R., & Munro, E. (1979). Reaction time, movement time, and intelligence. *Intelligence, 3*, 121–126.

Jensen, A. R. (1988). Editorial: Psychometric "g" as a focus of concerted research effort. *Intelligence*

Johansson, C. B. (1976). *Manual for the Career Assessment Inventory*. Minneapolis, MN: National Computer Systems.

Johansson, C. B., & Johansson, J. C. (1978). *Manual supplement for the Career Assessment Inventory*. Minneapolis, MN: National Computer Systems.

Johansson, G., Johnson, J. V., & Hall, E. M. (1991). Smoking and sedentary behavior as related to work organization. *Social Science and Medicine, 32*(7), 837–846.

Johnson, J. G., & Bernstein, B. F. (1991). Does daily stress independently predict psychopathology? *Journal of Social and Clinical Psychology, 10*, 58–74.

Johnson, J. L. (1994). The Thematic Apperception Test and Alzheimers Disease. *Journal of Personality Assessment, 62*(2), 314–319.

Johnson, N. E., Saccuzzo, D. P., Larson, G. E., Guertin, T. L., Christianson, L., & Longley, S. (1993). *The San Diego Test of Reasoning Ability (S.A.N.T.R.A.)*. [Available from N. E. Johnson, Ph.D., & D. P. Saccuzzo, Ph.D., 6363 Alvarado Court, Suite 103; San Diego, CA 92120–4913].

Jones, E. E., & Nisbett, R. E. (1971). *The actor and observer: Divergent perceptions of the causes of behavior*. Morristown, NJ: General Learning Press.

Jones, R. A. (1968). A *factored measure of Ellis' irrational belief system with personality and maladjustment correlates*. Unpublished doctoral dissertation, Texas Technological College, Lubbock.

Judiesch, M. K., Schmidt, F. L., & Hunter, J. E. (1993). Has the problem of judgment in utility analysis been solved? *Journal of Applied Psychology, 78*, 903–911.

Jung, C. G. (1910). The association method. *American Journal of Psychology, 21*, 219–269.

Kagan, J., Moss, H. A., & Siegel, I. E. (1963). Psychological signifi-cance of styles of conceptualization. *Monographs of the Society for Research in Child Development, 28*(2, Serial No. 86), 73–124.

Kaiser, H. F. (1958). A modified stanine scale. *Journal of Experimental Education, 26*, 261.

Kallingal, A. (1971). The prediction of grades for black and white students at Michigan State University. *Journal of Educational Measurement, 8*, 263–265.

Kamhi, A. G., Minor, J. S., & Mauer, D. (1990). Content analysis and intratest performance profiles on the Columbia and the TONI. *Journal of Speech and Hearing Research, 33*, 375–379.

Kamin, L. J. (1974). *The science and politics of IQ*. Hillsdale, NJ: Eribaum.

Kammeier, M. L., Hoffman, H., & Loper, R. G. (1973). Personality characteristics of alcoholics as college freshmen and at time of treatment. *Quarterly Journal of Studies on Alcohol, 34*, 390–399.

Kamphaus, R. W., & Reynolds, C. R. (1984). Development and structure of the Kaufman Assessment Battery for Children. *The Journal of Special Education, 18*(3), 213–228.

Kanfer, F. H., & Saslow, G. (1969). Behavioral diagnosis. In C. M. Franks (Ed.), *Behavior therapy: Appraisal and status*. New York: McGraw-Hill.

Kanner, A. D., Coyne, J. C., Schaeffer, C., & Lazarus, R. S. (1981). Comparison of two modes of stress measurement: Daily hassles and uplifts versus major life events. *Journal of Behavioral Medicine, 4*, 1–39.

Kaplan, C. (1993). Reliability and validity of test-session behavior observations: Putting the horse before the cart. *Journal of Psychoeducational Assessment, 11*(4), 314–322.

Kaplan, O. J. (1979). Psychological testing in seniles. In O. J. Kaplan (Ed.), *Psychopathology and aging.* New York: Academic Press.

Kaplan, R. M. (1973). Components of trust: Note on use of Rotter's scale. *Psychological Reports, 33,* 13–14.

Kaplan, R. M. (1982). Nader's raid on the Educational Testing Service: Is it in the best interest of the consumer? *American Psychologist, 37,* 15–23.

Kaplan, R. M. (1984). The connection between clinical health promotion and health status: A critical overview. *American Psychologist, 39,* 755–765.

Kaplan, R. M. (1985). The controversy related to the use of psychological tests. In B. B. Wolman (ed.), *Handbook of Intelligence: Theories, measurements, and applications.* New York: Wiley.

Kaplan, R. M. (1987). Basic statistics for the behavioral sciences. Newton, MA: Allyn and Bacon.

Kaplan, R. M. (1988a). New health promotion indicators: The general health policy model. *Health Promotion, 3,* 35–49.

Kaplan, R. M. (1988b). The value dimension in studies of health promotion. In S. Spacapan & S. Oskamp (Eds.), *The Social Psychology of Health.* Beverly Hills, CA: Sage.

Kaplan, R. M. (1990). Behavior as the central outcome in health care. *American Psychologist, 45,* 1211–1220.

Kaplan, R. M. (1992). A quality-of-life approach to health resource allocation. In M. A. Strosberg, J. M. Wiener, R. Baker, & I. A. Fein (Eds.), *Rationing America's medical care: The Oregon plan and beyond.* Washington, DC: The Brookings Institution.

Kaplan, R. M. (1993). *The hippocratic predicament.* San Diego, CA: Academic Press.

Kaplan, R. M. (1994a). Measures of health outcome in social support research. In S. A. Schumaker & S. M. Czajkowski (Eds.), *Social support and cardiovascular disease: Plenum series in behavioral psychophysiology and medicine* (pp. 65–94). New York: Plenum Press.

Kaplan, R. M. (1994b). The Ziggy theorem: toward an outcomes-focused health psychology. *Health Psychology, 13,* 451–460.

Kaplan, R. M. (1995). Utility assessment for estimating quality-adjusted life years. In F. Sloan (Ed.), *Valuing health care: Costs, benefits, and effectiveness of pharmaceuticals and other medical technologies* (pp. 31–61). Boston: Cambridge University Press.

Kaplan, R. M., & Anderson, J. P. (1990). The general health policy model: An integrated approach. In B. Spilker (Ed.), *Quality of life assessments in clinical trials* (pp.131–149). New York: Raven Press.

Kaplan, R. M., Anderson, J. P., & Ganiats, T. G. (1993). The Quality of Well-being Scale: Rationale for a single quality of life index. In S. R. Walker & R. M. Rosser (Eds.), *Quality of life assessment: Key issues in the 1990s* (pp. 65–94). London: Kluwer Academic Publishers.

Kaplan, R. M., Anderson, J. P., Patterson, T. L., McCutchan, J. A., Weinrich, J. D., Heaton, R. K., Atkinson, J. H., Thal, L., Chandler, J., & Grant, I. (1995). Validity of the Quality of Well-Being Scale for persons with human immunodeficiency virus infection. HNRC Group. HIV Neurobehavioral Research Center. *Psychosomatic Medicine, 57,* 138–147.

Kaplan, R. M., Anderson, J. P., Wu, A. W., Mathews, W. C., Kozin, F., & Orenstein, D. (1989). The Quality of Well-being Scale: Applications in AIDS, cystic fibrosis, and arthritis. *Medical Care, 27*(Suppl. 3), S27–S43.

Kaplan, R. M., Atkins, C. J., & Timms, R. M. (1984). Validity of a quality of well-being scale as an outcome measure in chronic obstructive pulmonary disease. *Journal of Chronic Diseases, 37,* 85–95.

Kaplan, R. M., Bush, J. W., & Berry, C. C. (1976). Health status: Types of validity for an index of well-being. *Health Services Research, 11,* 478–507.

Kaplan, R. M., & Ernst, J. (1983). Do category rating scales produce biased preference weights for a health index? *Medical Care, 21,* 193–207.

Kaplan, R. M., & Grant, I. (1995). Statistics and Experimental Design. In B. J. Sadock, and H. Kaplan (Eds.), *Comprehensive Textbook of Psychiatry* (6th ed.). Baltimore: Williams & Wilkens.

Kaplan, R. M., Hartwell, S. H., Wilson, D. K., & Wallace, J. P. (1987). Effects of diet and exercise interventions upon control and quality of life in non-insulin-dependent diabetes mellitus. *Journal of General Internal Medicine, 2,* 220–228.

Kaplan, R. M., McCordick, S., & Twitchell, M. (1979). Is it the cognitive or the behavioral component which makes cognitive behavior modification effective in test anxiety? *Journal of Counseling Psychology, 26,* 371–377.

Kaplan, R.M., & Ries, A. L. (1996). Cognitive-behavioral interventions and the quality of life of patients with chronic obstructive pulmonary disease. In J. Bach (Ed.), *Pulmonary rehabilitation: The obstructive and paralytic conditions* (pp. 133–144). Philadelphia: Hanley and Delfus.

Kaplan, R. M., Ries, A. L., Prewitt, L. M., & Eakin, E. (1994). Self-efficacy expectations predict survival for patients with chronic obstructive pulmonary disease. *Health Psychology, 13*, 366–368.

Kaplan, R. M., & Toshima, M. T. (1992). Does a reduced fat diet cause retardation in child growth? *Preventive Medicine, 21*, 33–52.

Kaplanestrin, M., Jacobson, S. W., & Jacobson, J. L. (1994). Alternative approaches to clustering and scoring the Bayley Infant Behavior Record. *Infant Behavior and Development, 17*(2), 149–157.

Kappelman, M. M. (1993). [Review of the book *Touchpoints: The essential reference: Your Child's Emotional and Behavioral Development*]. *Journal of Developmental and Behavioral Pediatrics, 14*(5), 350–351.

Kareken, D. A., Gur, R. C., & Saykin, A. J. (1995). Reading on the Wide-Range Achievement Test—Revised and parental education as predictors of IQ: Comparisons with the Barona formula. *Archives of Clinical Neuropsychology, 10*(2), 147–157.

Kaszniak, A. W. (1986). The neuropsychology of dementia. In I. Grant & K. M. Adams (Eds.), *Neuropsychological assessment of neuropsychiatric disorders*. New York: Oxford University Press.

Kaszniak, A. W., & Christenson, G. (1994). Differential diagnosis of dementia and depression. In M. Storandt & G. R. VandenBos (Eds.), *Neuropsychological assessment of dementia and depression in older adults: A clinician's guide* (pp. 81-117). Washington, DC: American Psychological Association.

Katz, S. T., Downs, H., Cash, H., & Grotz, R. (1970). Progress and development of an index of EDL. *Gerontologist, 10*, 20–30.

Katz, S. T., Ford, A. D., Moskowitz, R. W., Jackson, B. A., & Jaffe, M.

W. (1963). Studies of illness in the aged: The index of ADL. *Journal of the American Medical Association, 185*, 914–919.

Kaufman, A. S. (1975). Factor structure of the McCarthy Scales of Children's Abilities. *Educational and Psychological Measurement, 35*, 641–656.

Kaufman, A. S. (1978). Review of Columbia Mental Maturity Scale. In O. K. Buros (Ed.), *The eighth mental measurements yearbook* (Vol. 1). Highland Park, NJ: Gryphon Press.

Kaufman, A. S. (1984). K-ABC and controversy. *The Journal of Special Education, 18*(3), 409–444.

Kaufman, A. S., & Kaufman, N. L. (1983a). *K-ABC administration and scoring manual*. Circle Pines, MN: American Guidance Service.

Kaufman, A. S., & Kaufman, N. L. (1983b). *K-ABC interpretive manual*. Circle Pines, MN: American Guidance Service.

Kaufman, A. S., Kaufman, R. W., & Kaufman, N. L. (1985). The Kaufman Assessment Battery for Children (K-ABC). In C. S. Newmark (Ed.), *Major psychological assessment instruments*. Newton, MA: Allyn and Bacon.

Kazdin, A. E. (1977). Artifact, bias, and complexity of assessment: The ABC's of reliability. *Journal of Applied Behavior Analysis, 10*, 141–150.

Kehoe, J. F., & Tenopyr, M. L. (1994). Adjustment in assessment scores and their usage: A taxonomy and evaluation methods [Special Section: Normative assessment]. *Psychological Assessment, 6*(4), 291–303.

Keir, G. (1949). The Progressive Matrices as applied to school children. *British Journal of Psychology*, (Statistical Section 2), 140–150.

Keiser, R. E., & Prather, E. N. (1990). What is the TAT? A review of ten years of research.

Journal of Personality Assessment, 55, 800–803.

Kelley, T. L (1927). *Interpretation of educational measurements*. Yonkers, NY: World Book.

Kelly, E. L (1972). Personality Research Form. In O. K. Buros (Ed.), *The seventh mental measurements yearbook* (Vol. 1). Highland Park, NJ: Gryphon Press.

Kelly, H. H. (1967). Attribution theory in social psychology. In D. Levine (Ed.), *Nebraska Symposium on Motivation*. Lincoln: University of Nebraska Press.

Kendall, P. C., & Korgeski, G. P. (1979). Assessment and cognitive-behavioral interventions. *Cognitive Therapy and Research, 1*, 1–21.

Kendall, P. C., Williams, S., Pechacek, T. F., Graham, L. G., Shisslak, C. S., & Herzoff, N. (1979). Cognitive-behavioral and patient education interventions in cardiac catheterization procedures: The Palo Alto medical psychology project. *Journal of Consulting and Clinical Psychology, 47*, 49–58.

Kennedy, R. S., Baltzley, D. R., Turnage, J. J., & Jones, M. B. (1989). Factor analysis and predictive validity of microcomputer-based tests. *Perceptual and Motor Skills, 69*, 1059–1074.

Kennedy, W. A., Van de Riet, V., & White, J. C., Jr. (1963). A normative sample of intelligence and achievement of Negro elementary school children in the Southeast United States. *Monographs of the Society for Research in Child Development, 28*(6, Serial No. 90).

Kent, G. H., & Rosanoff, A. J. (1910). A study of association in insanity. *American Journal of Insanity, 67*, 37–96, 317–390.

Kent, R. N., Kanowitz, J., O'Leary, K. D., & Cheiken, M. (1977). Observer reliability as a function of circumstances of assessment. *Journal of Applied Behavior Analysis, 10*, 317–324.

Kent, R. N., O'Leary, K. D., Diament, C., & Dietz, A. (1974). Expectation biases in observational evaluation of therapeutic change. *Journal of Consulting and Clinical Psychology, 42*, 774–780.

Kerner, D., Patterson, T. L., Grant, I., & Kaplan, R. M. (1995). Validity of the Quality of Well-being Scale in Alzheimer's disease. Manuscript submitted for publication.

Kerner, J. (1857). Klexographien (Pt. VI). In R. Pissin (Ed.), *Kerners Werke*. Berlin, Germany: Bong.

Keyser, D. J., & Sweetland, R. C. (Eds.). (1985). *Test critiques* (Vol. 1). Kansas City, MO: Test Corporation of America.

Kiersh, E. (1979, January 15). Testing is the name, power is the game. *The Village Voice*.

King, N. J., Josephs, A., Gullone, E., & Madden, C. (1994). Assessing the fears of children with disability using the Revised Fear Survey Schedule for Children: A comparative study. *British Journal of Medical Psychology, 67*, 377–386.

Kirkpatrick, E. A. (1900). Individual tests of school children. *Psychological Review, 7*, 274–280.

Kleijn, W., van der Ploeg, H. M., & Topman, R. M. (1994). Cognition, study habits, test anxiety, and academic performance. *Psychological Reports, 75*, 1219–1226.

Klieger, D. M., & Franklin, M. E. (1993). Validity of the Fear Survey Schedule in phobia research: A laboratory test. *Journal of Psychopathology and Behavioural Assessment, 15*(3), 207–217.

Klieger, D. M., & McCoy, M. L. (1994). Improving the concurrent validity of the Fear Survey Schedule—III. *Journal of Psychopathology and Behavioral Assessment, 16*(3), 201–220.

Kline, P. (1994). *An easy guide to factor analysis*. London: Routledge.

Kline, R. B. (1989). Is the Fourth Edition Stanford-Binet a four-factor test? Confirmatory factor analyses of alternative methods for ages 2 through 23. *Journal of Psychoeducational Assessment, 7*, 4–13.

Klingberg, G. (1994). Reliability and validity of the Swedish version of the dental subscale of the Children's Fear Survey Schedule, CFSS-DS. *Acta Odontologica Scandinavica, 52*(4), 255–256.

Klinger, E. (1978). Modes of normal conscious flow. In K. S. Pope & J. L. Singer (Eds.), *The stream of consciousness: Scientific investigations into the flow of human experience*. New York: Plenum.

Klinger, E., Barta, S., & Mahoney, T. (1976). Motivation, mood, and mental events: Patterns and implications for adaptive processes. In G. Serban (Ed.), *Psychopathology of human adaptation*. New York: Plenum.

Klopfer, B., & Davidson, H. H. (1944). Form level rating: A preliminary proposal for appraising mode and level of thinking as expressed in Rorschach records. *Rorschach Research Exchange, 8*, 164–177.

Klopfer, B., & Kelley, D. (1942). *The Rorschach technique*. Yonkers, NY: World Book.

Knauper, B., & Wittchen, H. U. (1994). Diagnosing major depression in the elderly: Evidence for response bias in standardized diagnostic interviews? *Journal of Psychiatric Research, 28*(2), 147–164.

Knobloch, H., & Pasamanick, B. (1974). *Gesell and Amatruda's developmental diagnosis: The evaluation and management of normal and abnormal neuropsychologic development in infancy and early childhood* (3rd ed.). New York: Harper & Row.

Knotek, P. C., Bayles, K. A., & Kaszniak, A. W. (1990). Response consistency on a semantic memory task in persons with dementia of the Alzheimer type. *Brain and Language, 38*, 465–475.

Knox, H. A. (1914). A scale based on the work at Ellis Island for estimating mental defect. *Journal of the American Medical Association, 62*, 741–747.

Knutson, J. F. (1972). Review of the Rorschach. In O. K. Buros (Ed.), *The seventh mental measurements yearbook* (Vol. 1), Highland Park, NJ: Gryphon Press.

Kohs, S. C. (1923). *Intelligence measurement: A psychological and statistical study based upon the block-design tests*. New York: Macmillan.

Kok, F. (1992). Differential item functioning. L. Verhoeven, J. H. A. L. De Jong (Eds.), *The construct of language proficiency: Applications of psychological models to language assessment* (pp. 115–124). Amsterdam, Netherlands: John Benjamins Publishing Company.

Koksal, F., & Power, K. G. (1990). Four Systems Anxiety Questionnaire (FSAQ): A self-report measure of somatic, cognitive, behavioral, and feeling components. *Journal of Personality Assessment, 54*, 534–545.

Koller, P. S., & Kaplan, R. M. (1978). A two-process theory of learned helplessness. *Journal of Personality and Social Psychology, 36*, 1077–1083.

Komaroff, A. L., Masuda, M., & Holmes, T. H. (1968). The Social Readjustment Rating Scale: A comparative study of Negro, Mexican, and white Americans. *Journal of Psychosomatic Research, 12*, 121.

Koppitz, E. M. (1964). *The Bender*

Gestalt test for young children. New York: Grune & Stratton.

Kraepelin, E. (1912). *Lehrbuch der psychiatrie.* Leipzig: Barth.

Kraiger, K., Hakel, M. D., & Cornelius, E. T., III. (1984). Exploring fantasies of TAT reliability. *Journal of Personality Assessments, 48,* 365–370.

Kramer, J. J., & Conoley, J. C. (Eds.). (1992). *The eleventh mental measurements yearbook.* Lincoln, NE: Buros Institute of Mental Measurements.

Krinsky, S. G. (1990). The feeling of knowing in deaf adolescents. *American Annals of the Deaf, 135,* 389–395.

Kuder, G. F. (1979). *Manual, Kuder Occupational Interest Survey, 1979 revision.* Chicago: Science Research Associates.

Kuder, G. F., & Richardson, M. W. (1937). The theory of the estimation of reliability. *Psychometrika, 2,* 151–160.

Kuhlmann, F. (1912). A revision of the Binet-Simon system for measuring intelligence of children. *Journal of Psycho-Asthenics Monograph Supplement, 1(1),* 1–41.

Kuhlmann, F. (1922). A *handbook of mental tests.* Baltimore: Warwick & York.

Kusyszyn, I. (1968). Comparison of judgmental methods with endorsements in the assessment of personality traits. *Journal of Applied Psychology, 52,* 227–233.

Laily, M., & Nettelbeck, T. (1977). Intelligence, reaction time, and inspection time. *American Journal of Mental Deficiency, 82,* 273–281.

Lakotis, L. (1987). *Quality of life and depression for patients undergoing gastric restriction surgery.* Unpublished master's thesis, San Diego State University, CA.

Lamp, R. E., & Traxler, A. J. (1973). The validity of the Slosson Intelligence Test for use

with disadvantaged Head Start and first grade children. *Journal of Community Psychology, 1,* 27–30.

Lancaster, A. R., & Drasgow, F. (1994). Choosing a norm group for counseling: Legislation, regulation, and nontraditional careers. *Psychological Assessment, 6(4),* 313–320.

Landis, C. (1936). Questionnaires and the study of personality. *Journal of Nervous and Mental Disease, 83,* 125–134.

Landis, C., Zubin, J., & Katz, S. E. (1935). Empirical evaluation of three personality adjustment inventories. *Journal of Educational Psychology, 26,* 321–330.

Landy, F. J. (1986). Stamp collecting versus science: Validation as hypothesis testing. *American Psychologist, 41,* 183–192.

Landy, F. J., Farr, J. L., & Jacobs, R. (1982). Utility concepts in performance measurement. *Organizational Behavior and Human Performance, 30,* 15–40.

Landy, F. J., & Shankster, L. J. (1994). Personnel selection and placement. *Annual Review of Psychology, 45,* 261–296.

Landy, F. J., Vance, R. J., Barnes-Farrell, J. L., & Steele, J. W. (1980). Statistical control of halo error in performance ratings. *Journal of Applied Psychology, 65,* 501–506.

Lang, P. J., & Lazovik, A. D. (1963). Experimental desensitization of a phobia. *Journal of Abnormal and Social Psychology, 66,* 519–525.

Lanyon, B. P., & Lanyon, R. I. (1980). *Incomplete Sentences Task: Manual.* Chicago: Stoelting.

Larkin, J. E., & Pines, H. A. (1994). Affective consequences of self-monitoring style in a job interview setting. *Basic & Applied Social Psychology, 15(3),* 297–310.

Larrabee, L. L., & Kleinsaser, L. D. (1967). *The effect of experimenter*

bias on WISC performance. Unpublished manuscript.

Latham, V. M. (1987). Interviewee training: A review of some empirical literature. *Journal of Career Development, 14,* 96–107.

Lautenschlager, G. J., and Flaherty, V. L. (1990). Computer administration of questions: More desirable or more social desirability? *Journal of Applied Psychology, 75,* 310–314.

Lautenschlager, G. J., Flaherty, V. L., & Park, D. G. (1994). IRT differential item functioning: An examination of ability scale purifications. *Educational and Psychological Measurement, 54,* 21–31.

Lawlis, G. F. (1971). Response styles of a patient population on the Fear Survey Schedule. *Behaviour Research and Therapy, 9,* 95–102.

Lawshe, C. L. (1985). Inferences from personnel tests and their validities. *Journal of Applied Psychology, 70,* 237–238.

Lazarus, R. S. (1995). Psychosocial factors play a role in health, but we have to tackle them with more sophisticated research and thought. *Advances, 11(2),* 14–18.

Lazarus, R. S., Delongis, A., Folkman, S., & Gruen, A. (1985). Stress and adaptational outcomes: The problem of confounded measures. *American Psychologist, 40,* 770–779.

Lazarus, R. S., & Folkman, S. (1984). *Stress, appraisal, and coping.* New York: Springer-Verlag.

Lee, J. A., Moreno, K, E., & Sympson, J. B. (1986). The effects of mode of test administration on test performance. *Educational and Psychological Measurement, 46,* 467–473.

Lefever, D. W. (1959). Review of the Henmon-Nelson Test of Mental Ability, revised edition. In O. K. Buros (Ed.), *The fifth mental measurements yearbook.* Highland Park, NJ: Gryphon Press.

Leichsenring, F. (1990). Discriminating borderline from neurotic patients: A study with the Holtzman Inkblot Technique. *Psychopathology, 23,* 21–26.

Leichsenring, F. (1991). Primary process thinking, primitive defensive operations and object relations in borderline and neurotic patients. *Psychopathology, 24,* 39–44.

Leman, N. (1995, September). The Great Sorting. *Atlantic Monthly,* pp. 84–100.

Lemke, S., & Moos, R. H. (1986). Quality of residential settings of elderly adults. *Journal of Gerontology, 41,* 268–276.

Leong, C., & Joshi, R. (1995). *Developmental and acquired dyslexia: Neuropsychological and neurolinguistic perspectives.* Dordrecht, Netherlands: Kluwer Academic Publishers.

Lerner, B. (1979). Tests and standards today: Attacks, counterattacks, and responses. *New Directions in Testing and Measurement, 1*(3), 15–31.

Lerner, B. (1981). The minimum competence testing movement: Social, scientific, and legal implications. *American Psychologist, 36,* 1057–1066.

Lesser, G. S., Fifer, G., & Clark, D. H. (1965). Mental abilities of children from different social-class and cultural groups. *Monographs of the Society for Research in Child Development, 30*(4, Serial No. 102).

Levenson, H., Olkin, R., Herzoff, N., & DeLancy, M. (1986). MMPI evaluation of erectile dysfunction: Failure of organic vs. psychogenic decision rules. *Journal of Clinical Psychology, 42,* 752–754.

Levin, H. S., Benton, A. L., Fletcher, J. N., & Satz, P. (1989). Neuropsychological and intellectual assessment of adults. In H. I. Kaplan & B. J. Sadock (Eds.), *Comprehensive textbook of Psychiatry* (5th ed., Vol. 1, pp. 496–512). Baltimore: Williams & Wilkins.

Levy, S. (1979). E.T.S. and the "coaching" cover-up, *New Jersey Monthly, 3*(5), 4–7.

Lewandowski, D. G., & Saccuzzo, D. P. (1975). Possible differential WISC patterns for retarded delinquents. *Psychological Reports, 37,* 887–894.

Lewandowski, D. G., & Saccuzzo, D. P. (1976). The decline of psychological testing: Have traditional procedures been fairly evaluated? *Professional Psychology, 7,* 177–184.

Lewinsohn, P. N., & Teri, L. (1982). Selection of depressed and non-depressed subjects on the basis of self-report data. *Journal of Consulting and Clinical Psychology, 50,* 590–591.

Lewis, C. D., & Lorentz, S. (1994). Comparisons of the Leiter International Performance Scale and the Wechsler Intelligence Scales. *Psychological Reports, 74*(2), 521–522.

Lezak, M. D. (1976). *Neuropsychological assessment.* New York: Oxford University Press.

Lezak, M. D. (1983). *Neuropsychological assessment* (2nd ed.). New York: Oxford University Press.

Lezak, M. D. (1995). *Neuropsychological assessment* (3rd ed.). New York: Oxford University Press.

Liebert, R. M., & Morris, L. W. (1967). Cognitive and emotional components of test anxiety: A distinction and some initial data. *Psychological Reports, 20,* 975–978.

Likert, R. (1932). A technique for the measurement of attitudes. *Archives of Psychology,* No. 40.

Lilienfeld, S. O., Alliger, G., & Mitchell, K. (1995). Why integrity testing remains controversial. *American Psychologist, 50*(6), 457–458.

Lincoln, R. K., Crosson, B., Bauer, R. M., & Cooper, P. V. (1994). Relationship between WAIS-R subtests and language measures after blunt head injury. *Clinical Neurospychologist, 8*(2), 140-152.

Lindgren, S., Harper, D. C., Richman, L. C., & Stehbens, J. A. (1986). "Mental imbalance" and the prediction of recurrent delinquent behavior. *Journal of Clinical Psychology, 42,* 821–825.

Lindzey, G. (1952). The Thematic Apperception Test: Interpretive assumptions and related empirical evidence. *Psychological Bulletin, 49,* 1–25.

Linn, R. L. (1980). Test design and analysis for measurement of educational achievement. *New Directions for Testing and Measurement, 5,* 81–92.

Linn, R. L. (1994a). Criterion-referenced measurement: A valuable perspective clouded by surplus meaning. Annual Meeting of the American Educational Research Association: Criterion-referenced measurement: A 30-year retrospective (1993, Atlanta, Georgia). *Educational Measurement: Issues & Practice, 13,* 12–14

Linn, R. L. (1994b). Fair test use: Research and policy. M. G. Rumsey, C. B. Walker, & J. H. Harris (Eds.) *Personnel selection and classification* (pp. 363–375). Hillsdale, NJ: Lawrence Erlbaum Associates.

Linn, R. L. & Burton, E. (1994). Performance-based assessment: Implications of task specificity. *Educational Measurement: Issues & Practice, 13,* 15.

Lipsitz, J. D., Dworkin, R. H., & Erlenmeyer-Kimling, L. (1993). Wechsler comprehension and picture arrangement subtests and social adjustment. *Psychological Assessment, 5*(4), 430–437.

Lipsitz, S. (1969). *Effect of the race of the examiner on results of intel-*

ligence test performance of Negro and white children. Unpublished master's thesis, Long Island University, NY.

Liss, P. H., & Haith, M. M. (1970). The speed of visual processing in children and adults: Effects of backward and forward masking. *Perception and Psychophysics, 8,* 396–398.

Little, K. B., & Shneidman, E. S. (1959). Congruencies among interpretations of psychological test and anamnestic data. *Psychological Monographs, 73*(6, Whole No. 476).

Litz, B. T., Penk, W. E., Walsh, S., Hyer, L., Blake, D. D., Marx, B., Keane, T. M., & Bitman, D. (1991). Similarities and differences between Minnesota Multiphasic Personality Inventory (MMPI) and MMPI-2: Applications to the assessment of posttraumatic steps disorder. *Journal of Personality Assessment, 57,* 238–253.

LoBello, S. G., & Gulgoz, S. (1991). Factor analysis of the Wechsler Preschool and Primary Scale of Intelligence—Revised. *Psychological Assessment: A Journal of Consulting and Clinical Psychology, 3,* 130–132.

Lochman, J. E. (1995). Conduct Problems Prevention Research Group: Screening of child behavior problems for prevention programs at school entry. [Special Section: Prediction and prevention of child and adolescent antisocial behavior]. *Journal of Consulting and Clinical Psychology, 63,* 549–559.

Locke, S. D. & Gilbert, B. O. (1995). Method of psychological assessment, self-disclosure, and experiential differences: A study of computer, questionnaire, and interview assessment formats. *Journal of Social Behavior and Personality, 10,* 255–263.

Lohr, J. M., & Bonge, D. (1982).

The factorial validity of the Irrational Beliefs Test: A psychometric investigation. *Cognitive Therapy and Research, 6,* 225–230.

Long, K. A. Graham, J. R., & Reilley, R. R. (1994). Socioeconomic status and MMPI-2 interpretation. *Measurement and Evaluation in Counseling and Development, 27*(3), 158–177.

Long, P. A., & Anthony, J. J. (1974). The measurement of retardation by a culture-specific test. *Psychology in the Schools, 11,* 310–312.

Loper, R. G., Kammeier, M. L., & Hoffman, H. (1973). MMPI characteristics of college freshman males who later became alcoholics. *Journal of Abnormal Psychology, 82,* 159–162.

Lord, E. (1950). Experimentally induced variations in Rorschach performance. *Psychological Monographs, 64*(10, Whole No. 316).

Lord, F. M. (1950). *Efficiency of prediction when a regression equation from one sample is used in a new sample* (Research Bulletin 50–40). Princeton, NJ: Educational Testing Service.

Lord, F. M. (1978). *A prediction interval for scores on a parallel test form* (Research Bulletin RB-785). Princeton, NJ: Educational Testing Service.

Lotsoff, E. (1953). Intelligence, verbal fluency and the Rorschach test. *Journal of Consulting Psychology, 17,* 21–24.

Lotus, E. F. (1991). The glitter of everyday memory . . . and the gold. *American Psychologist, 46,* 19–26.

Loughmiller, G. C., Ellison, R. L., Tavlor, C. W., & Price, P. B. (1970). Predicting career performances of physicians using the biographical inventory approach. *Proceedings of the American Psychological Association, 5,* 153–154.

Lowman, R. L. (1991). *The clinical*

practice of career assessment. Washington, DC: American Psychological Association.

Loy, D. L. (1959). The validity of the Taulbee-Sisson MMPI scale pairs in female psychiatric groups. *Journal of Clinical Psychology, 15,* 306–307.

Lubin, B. (1965). Adjective checklists for measurement of depression. *Archives of General Psychiatry, 12,* 57–62.

Lubin, B., Larsen, R., & Matarazzo, J. (1984). Patterns of psychological test usage in the United States: 1935–1982. *American Psychologist, 39,* 451–454.

Lubin, B., Larsen, R. M., Matarazzo, J. D., & Seever, M. (1985). Psychological test usage patterns in five professional settings. *American Psychologist, 40,* 857–861.

Lubin, B., & Sands, E. W. (1992). Bibliography of the psychometric properties of the Bender Visual-Motor Gestalt Test: 1970–1991. *Perceptual and Motor Skills, 75*(2), 385–386.

Lubin, B., Wallis, H. R., & Paine, C. (1971). Patterns of psychological test usage in the United States: 1935–1969. *Professional Psychology, 2,* 70–74.

Lumsden, J. (1978). Review of Illinois Test of Psycholinguistic Abilities. In O. K. Buros (Ed.), *The eighth mental measurements yearbook* (Vol. 1). Highland Park, NJ: Gryphon Press.

Lunemann, A. (1974). The correlational validity of I.Q. as a function of ethnicity and desegregation. *Journal of School Psychology, 12,* 263–268.

Lunneborg, C. (1978). Some information-processing correlates of measures of intelligence. *Multivariate Behavioral Research, 13,* 153–161.

Lunz, M. E., & Bergstrom, B. A. (1994). An empirical study of computerized adaptive test administration conditions. *Jour-*

nal of Educational Measurement, 31, 251–263.

Luria, A. R. (1966). *Higher cortical functions in man*. New York: Basic Books.

Luria, A. R. (1973). *The working brain*. New York: Basic Books.

Lyman, B., Hatlelid, D., & Macundy, C. (1981). Stimulus-person cues in first-impression attraction. *Perceptual and Motor Skills, 52*, 59–66.

Lyons, J. A., & Scotti, J. R. (1994). Comparability of two administration formats of the Keane Posttraumatic Stress Disorder Scale. *Psychological Assessment, 6(3)*, 209–211.

Machover, K. (1949). *Personality projection in the drawings of the human figure: A method of personality investigation*. Springfield, IL: Thomas.

MacKinnon, R. A. (1980). Psychiatric interview. In H. I. Kaplan, A. M. Freedman, & B. J. Sadock (Eds.), *Comprehensive textbook for psychiatry* (Vol. 3). Baltimore: Williams & Wilkins.

MacKinnon, R. A., & Michels, R. (1971). *The psychiatric interview in clinical practice*. Philadelphia: Saunders.

Mackintosh, N. J. (1981). A new measure of intelligence. *Nature, 289(5798)*, 529–530.

Magnusson, D., & Endler, N. S. (1977). Interactional psychology: Present status and future prospects. In D. Magnusson & N. S. Endier (Eds.), *Personality at the crossroads: Current issues in interactional psychology*. Hillsdale, NJ: Erlbaum.

Mahoney, M. J. (1974). *Cognition and behavior modification*. Cambridge, MA: Ballinger.

Maisto, S. A., McKay, J. R., & Connors, G. J. (1990). Self-report issues in substance abuse: State of the art and future directions. *Behavioral Assessment, 12*, 117–134.

Majovski, L. V. (1984). The K-ABC: Theory and implications for child neuropsychological assessment and research. *The Journal of Special Education, 18(3)*, 257–268.

Malgady, R., Barcher, P. R., Davis, J., & Towner, G. (1980). Validity of the vocational adaptation rating scale: Prediction of mentally retarded workers' placement in sheltered workshops. *American Journal of Mental Deficiency, 84*, 633–640.

Malgady, R. G., Constantino, G., & Rogler, L. H. (1984). Development of a Thematic Apperception Test (TEMAS) for urban Hispanic children. *Journal of Consulting and Clinical Psychology, 52(6)*, 986–996.

Malinchoc, M., Oxford, K. P., Colligan, R. C., & Morse, R. M. (1994). The Common Alcohol Logistic—Revised Scale (CAL-R): A revised alcoholism scale for the MMPI and MMPI-2. *Journal of Clinical Psychology, 50(3)*, 436–445.

Maloney, M. P., & Ward, M. P. (1976). *Psychological assessment: A conceptual approach*. New York: Oxford University Press.

Mandes, E., & Gessner, T. (1988). Differential effects on verbal performance achievement levels on the WAIS-R as a function of progressive error rate on the Memory for Designs Test (MFD). *Journal of Clinical Psychology, 44*, 795–798.

Mandler, G., & Sarason, S. B. (1952). A study of anxiety and learning. *Journal of Abnormal and Social Psychology, 47*, 166–173.

Mannheim, K. (1936). *Ideology and utopia*. London: Kegan, Paul, Trench, Trubner.

Mapou, R. L., & Spector, J. (1995). *Clinical neuropsychological assessment: A cognitive approach*. New York: Plenum Press.

Marchall et al. v. Georgia. U.S. District Court for the Southern District of Georgia, CV482–233, June 28, 1984, Affd (11th cir no 84–8771), Oct. 29, 1985.

Mark, J. C. (1993). [Review of the book *The Thematic Apperception Test, the Children's Apperception Test, and the Senior Apperception Technique in clinical use, 5th Edition*]. *Contemporary Psychology, 38(9)*, 971–972.

Marlett, N. J., & Watson, D. (1968). Test anxiety and immediate or delayed feedback in a test-avoidance task. *Journal of Personality and Social Psychology, 8*, 200–203.

Marshalek, B., Lohman, D. F., & Snow, R. E. (1983). The complexity continuum in the Radex and hierarchical models of intelligence. *Journal of Intelligence, 7*, 107–127.

Martin, P., Johnson, M., Poon, L. W., Clayton, G. M., & others, (1994). Group or individual testing: Does it make a difference? *Educational Gerontology, 20*, 171–176.

Mask, N., & Brown, C. E. (1984). Comparison of the WISC-R and the Leiter International Performance Scale with average and above-average students. *Journal of Clinical Psychology, 40*, 303–305.

Masters, B. N. (1988). Item discrimination: One more is worse. *Journal of Educational Measurement 25*, 15–29.

Masters, W., & Johnson, V. (1966). *Human sexual response*. Boston: Little, Brown.

Matarazzo, J. D. (1972). *Wechsler's measurement and appraisal of adult intelligence* (5th ed.). Baltimore: Williams & Wilkins.

Matarazzo, J. D. (1986). Computerized clinical psychological test interpretations: Unvalidated plus all mean and no sigma. *American Psychologist, 41*, 14–24.

Matarazzo, J. D. (1990). Psychological assessment versus psychological testing: Validation from Binet to the school, clinic, and court room. *American Psychologist, 45,* 999–1017.

Matarazzo, J. D. (1991). Psychological assessment is reliable and valid: Reply to Ziskin and Faust. *American Psychologist, 46,* 882–884.

Matarazzo, J. D., & Herman, D. O. (1984). Relationship of education and IQ in the standardization sample. *Journal of Consulting and Clinical Psychology 52,* 631–634.

Matarazzo, J. D., & Wiens, A. N. (1972). *The interview: Research on its anatomy and structure.* Chicago: Aldine-Atherton.

Matarazzo, J. D., Wiens, A. N., Matarazzo, R. G., & Saslow, G. (1968). Speech and silence behavior in clinical psychotherapy and its laboratory correlates. In J. Shlien, H. Hunt, J. D. Matarazzo, & C. Savage (Eds.), *Research in psychotherapy* (Vol. 3). Washington, DC: American Psychological Association.

Matias, R., & Turner, S. M. (1986). Concordance and discordance in speech anxiety assessment: The effects of demand characteristics on the tripartite assessment method. *Behavior Research and Therapy, 24,* 537–545.

Maurer, T. J., & Alexander, R. A. (1991). Contrast effects in behavioral measurement: An investigation of alternative process explanations. *Journal of Applied Psychology, 76,* 3–10.

Maurer, T. J., Alexander, R. A., Callahan, C. M., Bailey, J. J., and others. (1991). Methodological and psychometric issues in setting cutoff scores using the Angoff method. *Personnel Psychology, 44*(2), 235–262.

Mayfield, E. C. (1964). The selection interview: A re-evaluation of published research. *Personnel Psychology, 17,* 239–260.

Mayman, M., & Kutner, B. (1947).

Reliability in analyzing TAT stories. *Journal of Abnormal and Social Psychology, 42,* 365–368.

McCall, R. B. (1980). *Fundamental statistics for psychology* (3rd ed.). New York: Harcourt Brace Jovanovich.

McCall, R. B. (1979). The development of intellectual functioning in infancy and the prediction of later IQ. In J. D. Osofsky (Ed.), *Handbook of infant development.* New York: Wiley.

McCall, R. B., Hogarty, P. S., & Hurlburt, N. (1972). Transitions in infant sensorimotor development and the prediction of childhood IQ. *American Psychologist, 27,* 728–748.

McCall, R. B. (1994). *Fundamental statistics for behavioral sciences.* (6th ed.). Fort Worth, TX: Harcourt Brace College Publishers.

McCall, W. A. (1939). *Measurement.* New York: Macmillan.

McCallum, R. S. (1990). Determining the factor structure of the Stanford-Binet: Fourth Edition—The right choice. *Journal of Psychoeducational Assessment, 8,* 436–442.

McCallum, R. S., & Karnes, F. (1987). Comparison of intelligence tests: Responses of gifted pupils to the Stanford-Binet Intelligence Scale (4th ed.), the British Ability Scales, and the Wechsler Intelligence Scale for Children—Revised. *School Psychology International, 8,* 133–139.

McCallum, R. S., Karnes, F. A. & Oehler-Stinnett, J. (1985). Construct validity of the K-ABC for gifted children. *Psychology in the Schools, 22,* 254–259.

McCandless, B. B. (1949). The Rorschach as a predictor of academic success. *Journal of Applied Psychology, 33,* 43–50.

McCarty, J. R., Noble, A. C., & Huntley, R. M. (1989). Effects of item wording on sex bias. *Journal of Educational Measurement, 26,* 285–293.

McClelland, D. C. (1951a). Measuring motivation in phantasy: The achievement motive. In H. Guetzkow (Ed.), *Groups, leadership, and men.* Pittsburgh, PA: Carnegie University Press.

McClelland, D. C. (1951b). *Personality.* New York: William Sloane Associates.

McClelland, D. C. (1958). Methods of measuring human motivation. In J. W. Atkinson (Ed.), *Motives in fantasy, action, and society.* New York: Van Nostrand Reinhold.

McClelland, D. C. (1985). How motives, skills, and values determine what people do. *American Psychologist, 40,* 812–825.

McClelland, D. C. (1994). The knowledge-testing-educational complex strikes back. *American Psychologist, 49*(1), 66–69.

McClelland, D. C., Atkinson, J. W., Clark, R. A., & Lowell, E. L. (1953). *The achievement motive.* New York: Appleton-Century-Crofts.

McCordick, S., Kaplan, R. M., Smith, S., & Finn, M. B. (1981). Variations in cognitive behavior modification for test anxiety. *Psychotherapy: Theory, Research and Practice, 18,* 170–178.

McCormick, E. J., & Iigen, D. (1980). *Industrial psychology* (7th ed.). Englewood Cliffs, NJ: Prentice-Hall.

McCrowell, K. L., & Nagle, R. J. (1994). Comparability of the WPPSI-R and the S-B: IV among preschool children. *Journal of Psychoeducational Assessment, 12*(2), 126–134.

McDaniel, M. A, (1989). Biographical constructs for predicting employee suitability. *Journal of Applied Psychology, 74,* 964–970.

McDaniel, M. A., Whetzel, D. L., Schmidt, F. L., & Maurer, S. D. (1994). The validity of employment interviews: A comprehensive review and meta-analysis.

Journal of Applied Psychology, 79, 599–616.

McEwen, J. (1992). The Nottingham Health Profile. In S. R. Walker & R. M. Rosser (Eds.), *Quality of life assessment: Key issues for the 1990s.* Dordreht, The Netherlands: Kluwer Academic Publishers.

McEwen, J., & McKenna, S. P. (1996). Nottingham health profile. In B. Spilker (Ed.), *Quality of life and pharmacoeconomics in clinical trials* (2nd ed., pp. 281–286). Philadelphia: Lippincott-Raven.

McFall, R. M., & Lillesand, D. B. (1971). Behavior rehearsal with modeling and coaching in assertion training. *Journal of Abnormal Psychology, 77,* 313–323.

McFall, R. M., & McDonell, A. (1986). The continuous search for units of analysis in psychology: Beyond persons, situations, and their interactions. In R. O. Nelson & S. C. Hays (Eds.), *Conceptual foundations of behavioral assessment.* New York: Guilford Press.

McGhee, R. (1993). Fluid and crystallized intelligence: Confirmatory factor analyses of the Differential Abilities Scale, Detroit Tests of Learning Aptitude-3, and Woodcock-Johnson Psycho-Educational Battery—Revised. In B. A. Bracken & R. S. McCallum (Eds.), *Woodcock-Johnson Psycho-Educational Battery—Revised [Monograph]. Journal of Psychoeducational Assessment* (pp. 20–38).

McGivern, R. F., Berka, C., Langlais, M. L., & Chapman, S. (1991). Detection of deficits in temporal pattern discrimination using the seashore rhythm test in young children with reading impairments. *Journal of Learning Disabilities, 24,* 58–62.

McGrath, R. E., & O'Malley, W. B. (1986). The assessment of denial and physical complaints: The validity of the HY Scale and associated MMPI signs. *Journal of Clinical Psychology, 42,* 754–760.

McGrew, K. S. (1986). Investigation of the verbal/nonverbal structure of the Wookcock-Johnson: Implications for subtest interpretation and comparisons with the Wechsler scales. *Journal of Psychoeducational Assessment, 3*(1), 65–71.

McGrew, S. (1993). The relationship between the Woodcock-Johnson Psycho-Educational Battery—Revised *Gf-Gc* cognitive clusters and reading achievement across the lifespan. In B. A. Bracken & R. S. McCallum (Eds.), *Woodcock-Johnson Psycho-Educational Battery—Revised [Monograph]. Journal of Psychoeducational Assessment,* 39–53.

McHenry, J. J. & Schmitt, N. (1994). Multimedia testing. In M. G. Rumsey, C. B. Walker, & J. H. Harris (Eds.), *Personnel selection and classification* (pp. 193–232). Hillsdale, NJ: Lawrence Erlbaum Associates.

McHorney, C. A. & Ware, J. E. J. (1995). Construction and validation of an alternate form general mental health scale for the Medical Outcomes Study Short-Form 36-Item Health Survey. *Medical Care, 33,* 15–28.

McKelvie, S. J. (1989). The Wonderlic Personnel Test: Reliability and validity in an academic setting. *Psychological Reports, 65*(1), 161–162.

McKelvie, S. J. (1994). Validity and reliability findings for an experimental short form of the Wonderlic Personnel Test in an academic setting. *Psychological Reports, 75*(2), 907–910.

McKenna, P., Clare, L., & Baddeley, A. D. (1995). Schizophrenia. In A. D. Baddeley, B. A. Wilson, & F. N. Watts (Eds.), *Handbook of memory disorders* (pp. 271–292). Chichester, England: Wiley.

McMahon, R. C., Davidson, R. S., Gersh, D., & Flynn, P. (1991). A comparison of continuous and episodic drinkers using the MCMI, MMPI, and ALCEVAL-R., *Journal of Clinical Psychology, 47,* 148–159.

McMichael, A. J., Baghurst, P. A., Wigg, N. R., Vimpani, G. V., Robertson, E. F., & Roberts, R. J. (1988). Port Pirie Cohort Study: Environmental exposure to lead and children's abilities at the age of four years. *New England Journal of Medicine, 319,* 468–475.

McNemar, O. W., & Landis, C. (1935). Childhood disease and emotional maturity in the psychopathic woman. *Journal of Abnormal and Social Psychology, 30,* 314–319.

McNemar, Q. (1942). *The revision of the Stanford-Binet scale.* Boston: Houghton Mifflin.

McNemar, Q. (1969). *Psychological statistics* (4th ed.). New York: Wiley.

Meehl, P. E. (1951). *Research results for counselors.* St. Paul, MN: State Department of Education.

Meehl, P. E. (1954). *Clinical versus statistical prediction: A theoretical analysis and a review of the evidence.* Minneapolis: University of Minnesota Press.

Meehl, P. E. (1956). Wanted—a good cookbook. *American Psychologist, 11,* 263–272.

Meehl, P. E. (1957). When shall we use our heads instead of the formula? *Journal of Counseling Psychology, 4,* 268–273.

Meehl, P. E., (1995). Utiles, hedons, and the mind-body problem, or, who's afraid of Vilfredo? In P. E. Shrout & S. T. Fiske (Eds.), *Personality research, methods, and theory: A festschrift honoring Donald W. Fiske* (pp. 45–66). Hillsdale, NJ: Lawrence Erlbaum Associates.

Meehl, P. E., & Dahlstrom, W. G. (1960). Objective configural rules for discriminating psychotic from neurotic MMPI profiles. *Journal of Consulting Psychology, 24,* 375–387.

Meehl, P. E., & Rosen, A. (1955). Antecedent probability and the efficiency of psychometric signs, patterns or cutting scores. *Psychological Bulletin, 52,* 194–216.

Megargee, E. I. (1972). *The California Psychological Inventory Handbook.* San Francisco: Jossey-Bass.

Mehrens, W. A. (1984). A critical analysis of the psychometric properties of the K-ABC. *The Journal of Special Education, 18*(3), 297–310.

Meichenbaum, D. (1972). Cognitive modification of test-anxious college students. *Journal of Consulting and Clinical Psychology, 39,* 370–380.

Meichenbaum, D. (1976). A cognitive-behavior modification approach to assessment. In M. Hersen & A. S. Bellack (Eds.), *Behavioral assessment.* New York: Pergamon Press.

Meichenbaum, D. (1977). *Cognitive-behavior modification.* New York: Plenum.

Meichenbaum, D., & Butler, L. (1980). Toward a conceptual model for the treatment of test anxiety: Implications for research and treatment. In I. G. Sarason (Ed.), *Test anxiety: Theory, research, and applications.* Hillsdale, NJ: Erlbaum.

Meichenbaum, D., & Turk, D. (1976). The cognitive-behavioral management of anxiety, anger, and pain. In P. Davidson (Ed.), *Behavioral management of anxiety, depression and pain.* New York: Brunner/Mazel.

Meikle, S., & Gerritse, R. (1970). MMPI cookbook pattern frequencies in a psychiatric unit. *Journal of Clinical Psychology, 26,* 82–84.

Meinhardt, M., Hibbett, C., Koller, J., & Busch, R. (1993). Comparison of the Woodcock-Johnson Psycho-Educational Battery—Revised and the Wechsler Intelligence Scale for Children—Revised with incarcerated adolescents. In B. A. Bracken & R. S. McCallum (Eds.), *Woodcock-Johnson Psycho-Educational Battery-Revised [Monograph]. Journal of Psychoeducational Assessment,* 64–70.

Melei, J. P., & Hilgard, E. R. (1964). Attitudes toward hypnosis, self predictions, and hypnotic susceptibility. *International Journal of Clinical and Experimental Hypnosis, 12,* 99–108.

Meloy, J. R., & Singer, J. (1991). A psychoanalytic view of the Rorschach Comprehensive System "Special Scores." *Journal of Personality Assessment, 56,* 202–217.

Mercer, J. R. (1971). Sociocultural factors in labeling mental retardates. *Peabody Journal of Education, 48,* 188–203.

Mercer, J. R. (1972, September). *Anticipated achievement: Computerizing the self-fulfilling prophecy.* Paper presented at the meeting of the American Psychological Association, Honolulu, HI.

Mercer, J. R. (1973). *Labeling the mentally retarded: Clinical and social system perspective on mental retardation.* Berkeley: University of California Press.

Mercer, J. R. (1979). In defense of racially and culturally nondiscriminatory assessment. *School Psychology Digest, 8*(1), 89–115.

Mercer, J. R. (1988). Ethnic differences in IQ scores: What do they mean? (A response to Lloyd Dunn) [Special Issue: Achievement testing: Science vs ideology]. *Hispanic Journal of Behavioral Sciences, 10,* 199–218.

Merl, J., & Trombley, W. (1992, September 29). Law school's admissions plan unfair, U.S. finds. *Los Angeles Times,* pp. A1, A26.

Messick, S. (1988). Validity. In R. L. Linn (Ed.), *Educational measurement.* New York: Macmillan.

Messick, S. (1994). Foundations of validity: Meaning and consequences in psychological assessment. Second Conference of the European Association of Psychological Assessment Keynote Address (1993, Groningen, Netherlands). *European Journal of Psychological Assessment, 10*(1), 1–9.

Messick, S., & Jungeblut, A. (1981). Time and method in coaching for the SAT. *Psychological Bulletin, 89,* 191–216.

Meunier, C., & Rule, B. G. (1967). Anxiety, confidence, and conformity. *Journal of Personality, 35,* 498–504.

Michell, J. V., Jr. (1983). *Tests in print III: An index to tests, test reviews, and the literature on specific tests.* Lincoln, NE: Buros Institute of Mental Measurements.

Milgrom, P., Jie, Z., Yang, Z., Tay, K. M. (1994). Cross-cultural validity of a Parent's Version of the Dental Fear Survey Schedule for Children in Chinese. *Behaviour Research and Therapy, 32*(1), 131–135.

Miller, A. B. (1991). Is routine mammography screening appropriate for women 40–49 years of age? *American Journal of Preventive Medicine, 91,* 55–62.

Miller, J. O., & Phillips, J. (1966). *A preliminary evaluation of the Head Start and other metropolitan Nashville kindergartens.* Unpublished manuscript, George Peabody College for Teachers, TN.

Millman, J. (1974). Criterion-referenced measurement. In W. J. Popham (Ed.), *Evaluation and education.* Berkeley, CA: McCutchan.

Millman, J. (1979). Reliability and validity of criterion-referenced test scores. *New Directions in Testing and Measurement, 1*(4), 75–92.

Millon, T. (1969). *Modern psychopathology: A biosocial approach to maladaptive learning and functioning.* Philadelphia: Saunders.

Millon, T. (1983). *Millon Clinical Multiaxial Inventory Manual* (2nd ed.). Minneapolis, MN: National Computer Systems.

Millon, T. (1985). The MCMI provides a good assessment of DSM-III disorders: The MCMI-II will prove even better. *Journal of Personality Assessment, 49,* 379–391.

Millon T. (1987). *Millon Clinical Multiaxial Inventory—II (Manual).* Minneapolis, MN: National Computer Systems.

Minton, H. L., & Schneider, F. W. (1980). *Differential psychology.* Pacific Grove, CA: Brooks/Cole.

Mischel, W. (1968). *Personality and assessment.* New York: Wiley.

Mischel, W. (1984). Convergences and challenges in the search for consistency. *American Psychologist, 39,* 351–364.

Mitchell, J. V. (Ed.). (1985). *The ninth mental measurements yearbook.* Highland Park, NJ: Gryphon Press.

Mitchell, S. K. (1979). Interobserver agreement, reliability, and generalizability of data collected in observational studies. *Psychological Bulletin, 86,* 376–390.

Mitchell, W. G., Chavez, J. M., Lee, H., & Guzman, B. L. (1991). Academic underachievement in children with epilepsy. *Journal of Child Neurology, 6,* 65–72.

Monroe, S. M., & Simons, A. D. (1991). Diathesis-stress theories in the context of life stress research: Implications for the depressive disorders. *Psychological Bulletin, 110,* 406–425.

Moos, R. H. (1973). Conceptualizations of human environment.

American Psychologist, 28, 652–665.

Moos, R. H. (1986a). *Group Environment Scale* (2nd ed.). Palo Alto, CA: Consulting Psychologist Press.

Moos, R. H. (1986b). *Work Environment Scale* (2nd ed.). Palo Alto, CA: Consulting Psychologist Press.

Moos, R. H. (1987a). *Community-oriented Programs Environment Scale Manual* (2nd ed.). Palo Alto, CA: Consulting Psychologist Press.

Moos, R. H. (1987b). *Correctional Institutions Environment Scale Manual* (2nd ed.). Palo Alto, CA: Consulting Psychologist Press.

Moos, R. H. (1987c). *University Residents Environment Scale* (2nd ed.). Palo Alto, CA: Consulting Psychologist Press.

Moos, R. H. (1987d). *Ward Atmosphere Scale Manual* (2nd ed.). Palo Alto, CA: Consulting Psychologist Press.

Moos, R. H., Finney, J. W., & Cronkite, R. C. (1990). *Alcoholism treatment: Context, process, and outcome.* New York: Oxford University Press.

Moos, R. H., & Lemke, S. (1984). Supportive residential settings for older people. *Human behavior & Environment: Advances in Theory and Research, 7,* 159–190.

Moos, R. H., & Lemke, S. (1994). Group residences for older adults: *Physical features, policies, and social climate.* New York: Oxford University Press.

Moos, R. H., & Moos, B. (1986). *Family Environment Scale Manual* (2nd ed.). Palo Alto, CA: Consulting Psychologist Press.

Moos, R. H., & Truckett, E. (1986). *Classroom Environment Scale* (2nd ed.). Palo Alto, CA: Consulting Psychologist Press.

Morales, A. (1994). Validation of a psychophysiological Waking

Erectile Assessment (WEA) for the diagnosis of Male Erectile Disorder: Comment. *Urology, 43*(5), 695–696.

Moreland, K. L. (1985). Validation of computer-based test interpretations: Problems and prospects. *Jounral of Consulting and Clinical Psychology, 53,* 816–825.

Moreland, K. L., Reznikoff, M., & Aronow, E. (1995). Integrating Rorschach interpretation by carefully placing more of your eggs in the content basket. *Journal of Personality Assessment, 64*(2), 239–242.

Morgan, D. (1984). What do the SATs mean? SATs are getting in the way of education. *Current,* pp. 9–13.

Morris, G. L., & Alcorn, M. B. (1995). Raven Progressive Matrices and inspection time: P200 slope correlates. *Personality and Psychological Measurement, 18*(1), 81–87.

Morrison, T., & Morrison M. (1995). A meta-analytic assessment of the predictive validity of the quantitative and verbal components of the Graduate Record Examination with graduate grade point average representing the criterion of graduate success. *Educational and Psychological Measurement, 55*(2), 309–316.

Mortensen, E. L., & Kleven, M. (1993). A WAIS longitudinal study of cognitive development during the life span from ages 50 to 70. *Developmental Psychology, 9*(2), 115–130.

Moses, J. A., Pritchard, D. A., & Faustman, W. O. (1994). Modal profiles for the Luria-Nebraska Neuropsychological Battery. *Archives of Clinical Neuropsychology, 9,* 15–30.

Motowidlo, S. J., Carter, G. W., Dunnette, M. D., Tippins, N., & others, (1992). Studies of the structured behavioral interview. *Journal of Applied Psychology, 77,* 571–587.

Mullins, C. J., Weeks, J. L., & Wilbourn, J. M. (1978). *Ipsative rankings as an indicator of job-worker match* (Tech. Rep. 7870). El Paso, TX: U.S. Air Force Human Relations Laboratory.

Mungas, D. M., Trontel, E. H., & Winegardner, J. (1981). Multi-variable-multimethod analysis of the dimensions of interpersonal behavior. *Journal of Research in Personality, 15,* 107–121.

Munley, P. H., Bains, D. S., Bloem, W. D., & Busby, R. M. (1995). Post-traumatic stress disorder and the MMPI-2. *Journal of Traumatic Stress, 8*(1), 171–178.

Munsinger, H. (1975). The adopted child's I.Q.: A critical review. *Psychological Bulletin, 82,* 623–659.

Murphy, L. L., Conoley, J. C., & Impara, J. C. (1994). *Tests in print IV: an index to tests, test reviews, and the literature on specific tests* Lincoln, NE: Buros Institute of Mental Measurements.

Murray, H. A. (1938). *Explorations in personality.* New York: Oxford University Press.

Murray-Jobsis, J. (1991). An exploratory study of hypnotic capacity of schizophrenic and borderline patients in a clinical setting. *American Journal of Clinical Hypnosis, 33,* 150–160.

Murstein, B. I. (1963). *Theory and research in projective techniques.* New York: Wiley.

Museum of Modern Art. (1955). *The family of man.* New York: Maco Magazine Corporation.

Myers, I. B. (1976). *Introduction to type.* Palo Alto, CA: Consulting Psychologists Press.

Myers, I. B. (1977). *The Myers Briggs Type Indictor: Supplementary Manual.* Palo Alto, CA: Consulting Psychologists Press.

Myers, I. B., & Briggs, K. C. (1962). *The Myers-Briggs Type Indicator.* Palo Alto, CA: Consulting Psychologists Press. (Originally published in 1943.)

Myers, J. K. & Weissman, M. M. (1980). Use of a self-report symptom scale to detect depression in a community sample. *American Journal of Psychiatry, 137,* 1081–1084.

Naglieri, J. A. (1984). Concurrent and predictive validity of the Kaufman Assessment Battery for children with a Navajo sample. *Journal of School Psychology, 22,* 373–380.

Naglieri, J. A. (1985). Review of the Gesell Preschool Test. In J. V. Mitchell (Ed.), *The ninth mental measurements yearbook* (Vol. 1). Highland Park, NJ: Gryphon Press.

Naliboff, B. D., Benton, D., Solomon, G. F., & Morley, J. E. (1991). Immunological changes in young and old adults during brief laboratory stress. *Psychosomatic Medicine, 53,* 121–132.

National Cancer Institute. (1991). *Cancer Statistics Review:* 1973–1988. Bethesda, MD. Unpublished government report.

National Commission on Testing and Public Policy. (1990). *From gatekeeper to gateway: Transforming testing in America.* Chestnut Hill, MA: National Computer Systems, Boston College.

Neisser, U. A. (1967). *Cognitive psychology.* New York: Appleton-Century-Crofts.

Neisser, U. A. (1991). A case of misplaced nostalgia. *American Psychologist, 46,* 34–36.

Nellis, L., & Gridley, B. E. (1994). Review of the Bayley Scales of Infant Development, Second Edition. *Journal of School Psychology, 32*(2), 201–209.

Nelson, E., Conger, B., Douglass, R., Gephart, D., Kirk, J., Page, R., Clark, A., Johnson, K., Stone, K., Wasson, J., & others. (1983). Functional health status levels of primary care patients. *Journal of the American Medical Association, 249,* 3331–3338.

Nelson, L. D. (1994). Introduction to the special section on normative assessment. *Psychological Assessment, 6*(4), 283.

Nettelbeck, T. (1982). Inspection time: An index for intelligence? *Quarterly Journal of Experimental Psychology, 34A,* 299–312.

Nettelbeck, T., & Laily, M. (1976). Inspection time and measured intelligence. *British Journal of Psychology, 67,* 17–22.

Nevo, B., & Jager, R. S. (Eds.). (1993). *Educational and psychological testing: The test taker's outlook.* Gottingen, Germany: Huber Publishers.

Nezworski, M. T., & Wood, J. M. (1995). Narcissism in the comprehensive system for the Rorschach. *Clinical Psychology—Science and Practice, 2,* 179–199.

Nolan, R. F., Watlington, D. K., & Willson, V. L. (1989). Gifted and nongifted race and gender effects on item functioning on the Kaufman Assessment Battery for Children. *Journal of Clinical Psychology, 45,* 645–650.

Norton, E. H. (1978, July). *The Bakke decision and the future of affirmative action.* Statement of the Chair, U.S. Equal Employment Opportunity Commission, at the National Association for the Advancement of Colored People convention.

Novaco, R. W. (1995). Clinical problems of anger and its assessment and regulation through a stress coping skills approach. In W. O'Donohue & L. Krasner (Eds.), *Handbook of psychological skills training: Clinical techniques and applications.* Newton, MA: Allyn & Bacon.

Novick, M. R. (1981). Federal guidelines and professional standards. *American Psychologist, 36,* 1035–1046.

Nunnally, J. C. (1978). *Psychometric theory*. New York: McGraw-Hill.

Nunnally, J. C. (1982). *Psychometric theory* (2nd ed.). New York: McGraw-Hill.

Nunnally, J. C., & Bernstein, I. H. (1994). *Psychometric theory* . (3rd ed.). New York: McGraw-Hill.

Nurius, P. S. (1990). A review of automated assessment. *Computers in human services, 6,* 265–281.

Nykodym, N., & Ruud, W. N. (1985). Intraview: Career development through business communication. *Journal of Employment Counseling, 22,* 161–165.

Nykodym, N., & Simonetti, J. L. (1981). *Communication: The key to business and organizational effectiveness.* Toledo, OH: Management Skills Books.

Oakland, T. (1979). Research on the ABIC and ELP: A revisit to an old topic. *School Psychology Digest 8,* 209–213.

Oakland, T., & Feigenbaum, D. (1979). Multiple sources of test bias on the WISC-R and the Bender-Gestalt test. *Journal of Consulting and Clinical Psychology, 47,* 968–974.

Oakland, T., & Parmelee, R. (1985). Mental measurement of minority-group children. In B. B. Wolman (Ed.), *Handbook of intelligence: Theories, measurements, and applications.* New York: Wiley-Interscience.

O'Brien, M. L. (1989). Psychometric issues relevant to selecting items and assembling parallel forms of language proficiency instruments. *Educational and Psychological Measurement, 49,* 347–353.

O'Donnell, J., Hawkins, J. D., & Abbott, R. D. (1995). Predicting serious delinquency and substance use among agressive boys. [Special Section: Prediction and prevention of child and adolescent antisocial behavior]. *Journal of Consulting and Clinical Psychology, 63,* 529–437.

Oei, T. P. S., Evans, I., & Crook, G. M. (1990). Utility and validity of the STAI with anxiety disorder patients. *British Journal of Clinical Psychology, 29,* 429–432.

Oei, T. P. S., Moylan, A., & Evans, L. (1991). Validity and clinical utility of the Fear Questionnaire for anxiety-disorder patients. *Psychological Assessment: A Journal of Consulting and Clinical Psychology, 3,* 391–397.

O'Leary, K. D., & Kent, R. N. (1973). Behavior modification for social action: Research tactics and problems. In L. A. Hamerlynck, P. O. Davidson, & L. E. Acker (Eds.), *Critical issues in research and practice.* Champaign, IL: Research Press.

O'Leary, K. D., Kent, R. N., & Kanowitz, J. (1975). Shaping data collection congruent with experimental hypotheses. *Journal of Applied Behavior Analysis, 8,* 43–51.

Olmedo, E. L. (1981). Testing linguistic minorities. *American Psychologist, 36,* 1078–1085.

Ones, D. S., Chockalingam, V., & Schmidt, F. L. (1995). Integrity tests: Overlooked facts, resolved issues, and remaining questions. *American Psychologist, 50*(6), 456–457.

Ones, D. S., Mount, M. K., Barrick, M. R., & Hunter, J. E. (1994). Personality and job performance: A critique of the Tett, Jackson, and Rothstein (1991) meta-analysis. *Personnel Psychology, 47,* 147–156.

Opton, E. (1977, April). From California, two views. *APA Monitor,* pp. 5–18.

Opton, E. (1979, December). A psychologist takes a closer look at the recent landmark *Larry P.* opinion. *APA Monitor,* pp. 1–4.

Osipow, S. H. (1983). *Theories of career development* (3rd ed.). Englewood Cliffs, NJ: Prentice-Hall.

Osipow, S. H. (1987). Counselling psychology: Theory, research, and practice in career counselling. *Annual Review of Psychology, 38,* 257–278.

Owen, D. (1985). *None of the above: Behind the myth of scholastic aptitude.* Boston: Houghton Mifflin.

Owings, S., & Siefker, J. M. (1991). Criterion-referenced scoring vs. norming: A critical discussion. *Vocational Evaluation and Work Adjustment Bulletin, 24*(3), 109–111.

Palmer, F. H. (1970). Socioeconomic status and intellectual performance among Negro preschool boys. *Developmental Psychology, 3,* 1–9.

Paolo, A. M., & Ryan, A. M. (1994). WAIS-R digit symbol patterns for persons 75 years and older. *Journal of Psychoeducational Assessment, 12*(1), 67–75.

Parducci, A. (1968). The relativism of absolute judgments. *Scientific American, 219*(6), 84–90.

Parducci, A. (1982). Category ratings: Still more contextual effects! In B. Wegener (Ed.), *Social attitudes in psychophysical measurements.* Hillsdale, NJ: Erlbaum.

Parker, J. D., Endler, N. S.; Bagby, R. M. (1993). If it changes, it might be unstable: Examining the factor structure of the Ways of Coping Questionnaire. *Psychological Assessment, 5*(3), 361–368.

Parker, K. (1983). A meta-analysis of the reliability and validity of the Rorschach. *Journal of Personality Assessment, 42,* 227–231.

Parkinson, C. N. (1957). The short list, or principles of selection. In C. N. Parkinson (Ed.), *Parkinson's law.* Boston: Houghton Mifflin.

Parsons, O. A. (1970). Clinical neuropsychotogy. In C. D.

Spielberger (Ed.), *Current topics in clinical and community psychology* (Vol. 2). New York: Academic Press.

Pasamanick, B. A., & Knobloch, H. (1955). Early language behavior in Negro children and the testing of intelligence. *Journal of Abnormal and Social Psychology, 50,* 401–402.

Patterson, C. H. (1974). *Relationship counseling and psychotherapy.* New York: Harper & Row.

Patterson, T., Slate, J. R., Jones, C. H., & Steger, H. S. (1996). The effects of practice administrations in learning to administer and score the WAI–R: A partial replication. *Educational and Psychological Measurement, 55,* 32–37.

Pattishall, E. (1992). Smoking and body weight. *Health Psychology,* (suppl. 32)3.

Paul, G. L., & Eriksen, C. W. (1964). Effects of test anxiety on "real life" examinations. *Journal of Personality, 32,* 480–494.

Paul, S. M. (1985). The Advanced Raven's Progressive Matrices: Normative data for an American university population and an examination of the relationship with Spearman's "g." *Journal of Experimental Education, 54,* 95–100.

Payne, D. A., Goolsby, C. E., Evans, K. A., & Barton, R. M. (1990). Multivariate analyses of cognitive style variables based on hemisphere specialization theory predictive of success in a college developmental studies program. *Perceptual and Motor Skills, 71,* 545–546.

Pearson, K. (1896). Mathematical contributions to the theory of evolution: Ill. Regression, heredity and panmixia. *Philosophical Transactions, A,* 187, 253–318.

Pedhazer, E. J. (1982). *Multiple regression in behavioral research*

(2nd ed.). New York: Holt, Rinehart & Winston.

Pedhazur, E. J. (1991). *Measurement, design, and analysis: An integrated approach.* Hillsdale, NJ: Lawrence Erlbaum Associates.

Pennington, B. F. & Welsh, M. (1995). Neuropsychology and developmental psychopathology. In D. Cicchetti & D. J. Cohen (Eds.), *Developmental psychopathology* (Vol 1, pp. 254–290). New York: Wiley.

Peoples, V. Y. (1975). Measuring the vocational interest of women. In S. H. Osipow (Ed.), *Emerging women: Career analysis and outlooks.* Columbus, OH: Merrill.

Perry, W., Sprock, J., Schaible, D., & McDougall, A. (1995). Amphetamine on Rorschach measures in normal subjects. *Journal of Personality Assessment, 64*(3), 456–465.

Pettigrew, T. F. (1964). A *profile of the American Negro.* New York: Van Nostrand Reinhold.

Pfeifer, C., & Sediacek, W. (1971). The validity of academic predictors for black and white students at a predominantly white university. *Journal of Educational Measurement, 8,* 253–261.

Pfister, H. (1995). New technology for administering group tests. *Australian Psychologist, 30,* 24–26.

Phelps, L. (1989). Comparison of scores for intellectually gifted students on the WISC-R and the Fourth Edition of the Stanford-Binet. *Psychology in Schools, 26,* 125–129.

Phelps, L. (1994). MMPI-2 and MMPI-A computerized interpretation: An adjunct to quality mental health service. *Measurement and Evaluation in Counseling and Development, 27*(3), 186–189.

Phillips, S. E. (1994). High-stakes testing accommodations: Valid-

ity versus disabled rights. *Applied Measurement in Education, 7*(2), 93–120.

Pierce, J. P., Burns, D., Gilpen, E., Rosenberg, B., Johnson, M., & Bal, D. (1992). *California baseline tobacco survey.* Unpublished report. University of California, San Diego.

Pinizzotto, A. J., & Finkel, N. J. (1990). Criminal personality profiling: An outcome and process study. *Law and Human Behavior, 14,* 215–234.

Piotrowski, C. (1984). The status of projective techniques: Or, "wishing won't make it go away." *Journal of Clinical Psychology, 40,* 1495–1499.

Piotrowski, C., Sherry, D., & Keller, J. W. (1985). Psychodiagnostic test usage: Survey of the Society for Personality Assessment. *Journal of Personality Assessment, 49,* 115–119.

Piotrowski, Z. (1947). Rorschach compendium. *Psychiatric Quarterly, 21, 79*–101.

Piotrowski, Z. (1964). Digital computer interpretation of inkblot test data. *Psychiatric Quarterly, 38,* 1–26.

Pirozzolo, F. J., Campanella, D. J., Christensen, K., & Lawson-Kerr, K. (1981). Effects of cerebral dysfunction on neurolinguistic performance in children. *Journal of Consulting and Clinical Psychology, 49,* 791–806.

Plaisted, J. R., Gustavson, J. L., Wilkening, G. N., & Golden, C. J. (1983). The Luria-Nebraska Neuropsychological Battery Children's revision: Theory and current research findings. *Journal of Clinical Child Psychology, 12,* 13–21.

Polansky, N., Freeman, W., Horowitz, M., Irwin, L., Papanis, N., Rapaport, D., & Whaley, F. (1949). Problems of interpersonal relations in research on groups. *Human Relations, 2,* 281–291.

Polyson, J., Peterson, R., & Marshall, C. (1986). MMPI and Rorschach: Three decades of research. *Professional Psychology: Research and Practice, 17,* 476–478.

Pomerlau, A., Leahey, L., & Malcuit, G. (1994). Evaluation of infant development during the 1st 12 months: Use of the Bayley Scales. *Canadian Journal of Behavioural Science—Revue Canadienne des sciences du Comportement, 26*(1) 85–103.

Pons, L. (1989). Effects of age and sex upon availability of responses on a word-association test. *Perceptual and Motor Skills, 68,* 85–86.

Popham, W. J. (1994). The instructional consequences of criterion-referenced clarity. *Educational Measurement: Issues and Practice, 13*(4), 15-18, 30.

Power, M. J., Katz, R., McGuffin, P., & Duggan, C. F. (1994). The Dysfunctional Attitude Scale (DAS): A comparison of Form-A and Form-B and proposals for a new subscaled version. *Journal of Research in Personality, 28*(3), 263–276.

Prediger, D. J. (1994). Multicultural assessment standards: A compilation for counselors [Special Issue: Multicultural assessment]. *Measurement and Evaluation in Counseling and Development, 27,* 68–73.

Prewett, P. N., & Farhney, M. R. (1994). The concurrent validity of the Matrix Analogies Test—Short Form with the Stanford Binet: Fourth Edition and KTEA-BF (academic achievement). *Psychology in the Schools, 31*(1), 20–25.

Prewett, P. N., & Matavich, M. A. (1994). A comparison of referred students' performance on the WISC-III and the Stanford Binet Intelligence Scale: Fourth Edition. *Journal of Psychoeducational Assessment, 12*(1), 42–48.

Price, K. H., & Garland, H. (1983). Compliance with a leader's suggestions as a function of perceived leader/member competence and potential reciprocity. *Journal of Applied Psychology, 66,* 329–336.

Prince, R. J., & Guastello, S. J. (1990). The Barnum effect in a computerized Rorschach interpresentation system. *The Journal of Psychology, 124,* 217–222.

Prout, H. T., & Sheldon, K. L. (1984). Classifying mental retardation in vocational rehabilitation: A study of diagnostic practices and their adherence to accepted guidelines. *Rehabilitation Counseling Bulletin, 28,* 125–128.

Pugh, R. C. (1968). Evidence for the validity of the behavioral dimensions of Teaching-Characteristics Schedule Scales. *Educational and Psychological Measurement, 28*(4), 1173–1179.

Pugliese, M. D., Lifshitz, F., Grad, G., Fort, P., & Marks-Katz, M. (1983). Fear of obesity: A cause of short stature and delayed puberty. *New England Journal of Medicine, 309,* 513–518.

Quay, L. C. (1971). Language dialect, reinforcement, and the intelligence-test performance of Negro children. *Child Development, 42,* 5–15.

Radcliffe, J. A. (1965). Edwards Personal Preference Schedule. In O. K. Buros (Ed.), *The sixth mental measurements yearbook.* Highland Park, NJ: Gryphon Press.

Raggio, D. J., Massingale, T. W., & Bass, J. D. (1994). Comparison of Vineland Adaptive Behavior Scales-Survey Form age equivalent and standard score with the Bayley Mental Development Index. *Perceptual and Motor Skills, 79*(1), 203–206.

Rahe, R. H. (1972). Subjects' recent life changes and their near-future illness reports. *Annals of Clinical Research, 4,* 250–265.

Raju, N. S., Burke, M. J., Normand, J., & Lezotte, D. V. (1993). What would be if what is wasn't? Rejoinder to Judiesch, Schmidt, and Hunter (1993). *Journal of Applied Psychology, 78,* 912–916.

Raju, N. S., Normand, J., & Burke, M. J. (1990). A new approach for utility analysis. *Journal of Applied Psychology, 75,* 3–12.

Ralston, S. M. (1988). The effect of applicant race upon personnel selection decisions: A review with recommendations. *Employee Responsibilities and Rights Journal, 1,* 215–226.

Rapaport, D., Gill, M. M., & Schafer, R. (1945–1946). *Diagnostic psychological testing* (2 vols.). Chicago: Yearbook Publishers.

Rapaport, D., Gill, M. M., & Schafer, R. (1968). *Diagnostic psychological testing* (Rev. Ed., R. R. Holt, Ed.). New York: International Universities Press.

Rappaport, N. B., & McAnulty, D. P. (1985). The effect of accented speech on the scoring of ambiguous WISC-R responses by prejudiced and nonprejudiced raters. *Journal of Psychoeducational Assessment, 3,* 275–283.

Rathus, S. A. (1973). A thirty-item schedule for assessing assertive behavior. *Behavior Therapy, 4,* 398–406.

Raven, J. (1986). *Manual for Raven's Progressive Matrices and Vocabulary Scales: Research Supplement No. 3.* London: H. K. Lewis.

Raven, J. (1990). *Raven Manual Research Supplement 3: American and International Norms.* London: Oxford Psychologist Press.

Rebok, G., Brandt, J., & Folstein, M. (1990). Longitudinal cognitive decline in patients with Alzheimer's disease. *Journal of*

Geriatric Psychiatry and Neurology, 3, 91–97.

Recase, M. D. (1977). Procedures for computerized testing. *Behavior Research Methods and Instrumentation, 9,* 148–152.

Redfield, J., & Paul, G. L. (1976). Bias in behavioral observation as a function of observer familiarity with subjects and typically of behavior. *Journal of Consulting and Clinical Psychology, 44,* 156.

Ree, M. J., & Carretta, T. R. (1994). Factor analysis of the ASVAB: Confirming a Vernon-like structure. *Educational and Psychological Measurement, 54*(2) 459–463.

Ree, M. J., & Carretta, T. R. (1995). Group differences in aptitude factor structure on the ASVAB. *Educational and Psychological Measurement, 55*(2), 268–277.

Reid, J. B. (1970). Reliability assessment of observation data: A possible methodological problem. *Child Development, 41,* 1143–1150.

Reid, J. B., & DeMaster, B. (1972). The efficacy of the spotcheck procedure in maintaining the reliability of data collected by observers in quasinatural settings: Two pilot studies. *Oregon Research Institute Research Bulletin, 12.*

Reid, N. (1986). Testing the test: Wide Range Achievement Test: 1984 Revised Edition. *Journal Counseling and Development, 64,* 538–540.

Reitan, R. M. (1968). Theoretical and methodological bases of the Halstead-Reitan Neuropsychological Test Battery. In I. Grant & K. N. Adams (Eds.), *Neuropsychological assessment of neuropsychiatric disorders.* New York: Oxford University Press.

Reitan, R. M. (1976a). Neurological and physiological bases of psychopathology. *Annual Review of Psychology, 27,* 189–216.

Reitan, R. M. (1976b). Neuropsychology: The vulgarization that Luria always wanted. *Contemporary Psychology, 21,* 737–738.

Reitan, R. M., & Wolfson, D. (1985). *The Halstead-Reitan Neuropsychological Battery: Theory and clinical interpretation.* Tucson, AZ: Tucson Neuropsychological Press.

Reitan, R. M., & Wolfson, D. (1995). Category Test and Trail Making Test as measures of frontal lobe functions. *Clinical Neuropsychologist, 9*(1), 50–56.

Reschly, D. J. (1981). Psychological testing in educational classification and placement. *American Psychologist, 36,* 1094–1102.

Reschly, D. J., Kicklighter, R., & McKee, P. (1988). Recent placement of litigation part III: Analysis of differences in Larry, P., Marshal and S-1, and implications for future practices. *School Psychology Review, 17,* 39–50.

Reschly, D. J., & Sabers, D. L. (1979). Analysis of test bias in four groups with the regression definition. *Journal of Educational Measurement, 16,* 1–9.

Reschly, D. J., & Ward, S. M. (1991). Use of adaptive behavior measures and overrepresentation of black students in programs for students with mild mental retardation. *American Journal on Mental Retardation, 96,* 257–268.

Research and Education Association (1981). *Handbook of psychiatric rating scales.* New York: Research and Education Association.

Retzlaff, P., Sligner, N., & Gibertini, M. (1986). Predicting WAIS-R scores from the Shipley Institute of Living Scale in a homogeneous sample. *Journal of Clinical Psychology, 42,* 357–359.

Reynolds, C. R. (1980). An examination of bias in a pre-school battery across race and sex.

Journal of Educational Measurement, 17, 137–146.

Reynolds, C. R. (1982). Determining statistically reliable strengths and weaknesses in the performance of single individuals on the Luria-Nebraska Neuropsychological Battery. *Journal of Consulting and Clinical Psychology, 50,* 525–529.

Reynolds, C. R. (1986). Wide Range Achievement Test (WRAT-R), 1984 edition. *Journal of Counseling and Development, 64,* 540–541.

Reynolds, C. R., & Nigl, A. J. (1981). A regression analysis of differential validity: An intellectual assessment for black and white inner-city children. *Journal of Clinical and Child Psychology, 10,* 176–179.

Richman, L, C., & Stehbens, J. A. (1986). "Mental imbalance" and the prediction of recurrent delinquent behavior. *Journal of Clinical Psychology, 42,* 821–825.

Rieke, M. L., & Guastello, S. J. (1995). Unresolved issues in honesty and integrity testing. *American Psychologist, 50,* 458–459.

Rinn, W. E. (1988). Mental decline in normal aging: A review. *Journal of Geriatric Psychiatry and Neurology, 1,* 144–158.

Ritzler, B. A., Sharkey, K. J., & Chudy, J. F. (1980). A comprehensive projective alternative to the TAT. *Journal of Personality Assessment, 44,* 358–362.

Ritzler, B. A., & Alter, B. (1986). Rorschach teaching in APA-approved clinical graduate programs: Ten years later. *Journal of Personality Assessment, 50,* 44–49.

Robinson, J. P., Shaver, P. R., & Wrightsman, L. S. (1991). *Measures of personality and social psychological attitudes.* New York: Academic Press.

Rock, D. A., & Nelson, J. (1992). Applications and extensions of

NAEP concepts and technology. Special Issue: National Assessment of Educational Progress. *Journal of Educational Statistics, 17,* 219–232.

Rocklin, T. R., O'Donnell, A. M., & Holst, P. M. (1995). Effects and underlying mechanisms of self-adapted testing. *Journal of Educational Psychology, 87,* 103–116.

Roe, A., & Klos, D. (1969). Occupational classification. *The Counseling Psychologist, 1,* 84–92.

Roe, A., & Seigelman, M. (1964). *The origin of interests.* Washington, DC: American Personnel and Guidance Association.

Rogers, C. R. (1959a). A tentative scale for the measurement of process in psychotherapy. In E. A. Rubinstein & M. B. Parloff (Eds.), *Research in psychotherapy.* Washington, DC: American Psychological Association.

Rogers, C. R. (1959b). A theory of therapy, personality, and interpersonal relationships, as developed in the client-centered framework. In S. Koch (Ed.), *Psychology: A study of science* (Vol. 3). New York: McGraw-Hill.

Rogers, C. R. (1961). *On becoming a person.* Boston: Houghton Mifflin.

Rogers, C. R. (1980). A *way of being.* Boston: Houghton Mifflin.

Rorschach, H. (1921). *Psycho-diagnostik.* Bern: Bircher.

Roscoe, A. H. (1993). Heart rate as a psychophysiological measure for in-flight workload assessment. *Ergonomics, 36*(9), 1055–1062.

Rosenfeld, P., Doherty, L. M., Vicino, S. M., Kantor, J., & others. (1989). Attitude assessment in organizations: Testing three microcomputer-based survey systems. *The Journal of General Psychology, 116,* 145–154.

Rosenman, R. H., & Chesney, M. A. (1985). Type A behavior pattern: Its relationship to coro-

nary heart disease and its modification by behavioral and pharmacological approaches. In M. R. Zales (Ed.), *Stress in health and disease.* New York: Brunner/Mazel.

Rosenstein, R., & Glickman, A. S. (1994). Type size and performance of the elderly on the Wonderlic Personnel Test. *Journal of Applied Gerontology, 13*(2), 185–192.

Rosenthal, R. (1966). *Experimenter effects in behavioral research.* New York: Appleton-Century-Crofts.

Rosenthal, R., & Fode, K. L. (1963). The effects of experimenter bias on the performance of the albino rat. *Behavioral Science, 8,* 183–189.

Rosenthal, R., Hall, J. A., DiMatteo, M. R., Rogers, P. L., & Archer, D. (1980). *Sensitivity to nonverbal communication: The PONS test.* Baltimore: Johns Hopkins University Press.

Rosenthal, R., & Jacobson, L. (1968). *Pygmalion in the classroom.* New York: Holt, Rinehart & Winston.

Rosenthal, R., & Rosnow, R. L. (1991). *Essentials of behavioral research: Method and data analysis* (2nd ed.). New York: McGraw-Hill.

Rothlisberg, B. A., & Deran, R. S. (1989). Lateral preference and processing style. *International Journal of Neuroscience, 48,* 243–245.

Rotter, J. B. (1966). Generalized expectancies for internal versus external control of reinforcement. *Psychological Monographs, 80*(1, Whole No. 609).

Rotter, J. B. (1967). A new scale for the measurement of interpersonal trust. *Journal of Personality, 35,* 651–665.

Rotter, J. B., & Rafferty, J. E. (1950). *Manual: The Rotter Incomplete Sentences Blank.* San Antonio, TX: Psychological Corporation.

Rourke, B. P., & Gates, R. D. (1981). Neuropsychological research in school psychology. In G. W. Hynd & J. E. Obrzut (Eds.), *Neuropsychological assessment and the school-age child: Issues and procedures.* New York: Grune & Stratton.

Rourke, B. P., Young, G. C., Stang, J. D., & Russel, D. L. (1986). Adult outcomes of central processing deficiencies in children. In I. Grant & K. M. Adams (Eds.), *Neuropsychological assessment of neuropsychiatric disorders.* New York: Oxford University Press.

Rowe, D. C. (1987). Resolving the person-situation debate: Invitation to an interdisciplinary dialogue. *American Psychologist, 42,* 218–227.

Rubin, Z. (1970). Measurement of romantic love. *Journal of Personality and Social Psychology, 16,* 265–273.

Rubin, Z. (1973). *Liking and loving: An invitation to social psychology.* New York: Holt, Rinehart & Winston.

Rubin, Z. (1979, February 21). Los Angeles says it with love on a scale. *Los Angeles Times.*

Rushton, J. P. (1991). Do r-K strategies underlie human race differences? *Canadian Psychology, 32,* 29–42.

Russell, L. B. (1986). *Is prevention better than cure?* Washington, DC: Brookings Institution.

Rutter, M. (1978). Prevalence of types of dyslexia. In A. L. Benton & D. Pearl (Eds.), *Dyslexia: An appraisal of current knowledge.* New York: Oxford University Press.

Ryan, J. J., & Rosenberg, S. J. (1983). Relationship between the WAIS-R and Wide-Range Achievement Test in a sample of mixed patients. *Perceptual and Motor Skills, 56,* 623–626.

Ryan, J. J., Paolo., A. M., & Van Fleet, J. N. (1994). Neurodiagnostic implications of abnormal verbal-performance IQ discrepancies on the WAIS-R: A comparison with the standardization sample. *Archives of Clinical Neuropsychology, 9*(3), 251–258.

Saarnio, P. K. (1994). An asymmetry between the WAIS digit symbol and block design scores in alcoholics. *Perceptual & Motor Skills, 78*(3, Pt. 1), 875–880.

Saccuzzo, D. P. (1975). Canonical correlation as a method of assessing the correlates of good and bad therapy hours. *Psychotherapy: Theory, Research and Practice, 12*, 253–256.

Saccuzzo, D. P. (1976, April). *The practice of psychological testing in America: Issues and trends.* Paper presented at the meeting of the California Psychological Association, Los Angeles.

Saccuzzo, D. P. (1977). The practice of psychotherapy in America: Issues and trends. *Professional Psychology, 8*, 297–306.

Saccuzzo, D. P. (1981). Input capability and speed of processing in mental retardation: A reply to Stanovich and Purcell. *Journal of Abnormal Psychology, 90*, 172–174.

Saccuzzo, D. P. (1986). Information-processing theories of schizophrenia. In R. Ingram (Ed.), *Information processing approaches to clinical psychology.* New York: Academic Press.

Saccuzzo, D. P. (1993). Measuring individual differences in cognition in schizophrenia and other disordered states: Backward masking paradigm. In D. K Determan (Ed.), *Individual differences and cognition: Current topics in human intelligence* (Vol. 3, pp. 219–237). Norwood, NJ: Ablex.

Saccuzzo, D. P. (1994, August). *Coping with complexities of contemporary psychological testing: Negotiating shifting sands.*

Invited presentation for G. Stanley Hall Lecture Series, American Psychological Association 102nd Annual Meeting, Los Angeles.

Saccuzzo, D. P., & Brat, D. L. (1981). Early information processing deficits in schizophrenia: New findings using schizophrenic subgroups and manic controls. *Archives of General Psychiatry, 38*, 175–179.

Saccuzzo, D. P., & Brat, D. L. (1986). Information-processing abnormalities in schizophrenia and psychotic patients: Trait and state dependent components. *Schizophrenia Bulletin, 12*, 447–458.

Saccuzzo, D. P., Brat, D. L., Shine, A., & Lewandowski, D. G. (1981, April). *A differential WISC pattern in the retarded as a function of sex and race.* Paper presented at the meeting of the Western Psychological Association, Los Angeles.

Saccuzzo, D. P., Hirt, M., & Spencer, T. J. (1974). Backward masking as a measure of attention in schizophrenia. *Journal of Abnormal Psychology, 83*, 512–522.

Saccuzzo. D. P., & Johnson, N. E. (in press). The backward masking paradigm in psychopathology: Theories, methodologies and applications from cognitive development studies. In M. Spitzer & B. Maher (Eds.), *Experimental Psychopathology.* Boston: Cambridge University Press.

Saccuzzo, D. P., & Johnson, N. E. (1995). Traditional psychometric test and proportionate representation: An intervention and program evaluation study. *Psychological Assessment, 7*(2), 183–194.

Saccuzzo, D. P., & Kaplan, R. M. (1984). *Clinical psychology.* Boston: Allyn and Bacon.

Saccuzzo, D. P., Johnson, N. E., &

Guertin, T. L. (1994). Information-processing in gifted versus nongifted African-American, Latino, Filipino, and white children: Speeded versus nonspeeded paradigms. *Intelligence, 19*, 219-243.

Saccuzzo, D. P., Johnson, N. E., & Russell, G. (1992). Verbal versus performance IQs for gifted African-American, Caucasian, Filipino, and Hispanic children. *Psychological Assessment, 4*, 239–244.

Saccuzzo, D. P., Kerr, M., Marcus, A., & Brown, R. (1979). Input capability and speed of information processing in mental retardation. *Journal of Abnormal Psychology, 88*, 312–317.

Saccuzzo, D. P., & Larson, G. E. (1987, November). *Analysis of test-retest reliability for a battery of cognitive speed tests.* (Technical Report 88-10). San Diego, CA: Navy Personnel Research and Development Center.

Saccuzzo, D. P., Larson, G. E., & Rimland, B. (1986). Visual, auditory and reaction time approaches to the measurement of speed of information-processing and individual differences in intelligence. *Personality and Individual Differences, 2*, 659–668.

Saccuzzo, D. P., & Lewandowski, D. G. (1976). The WISC as a diagnostic tool. *Journal of Clinical Psychology, 32*, 115–124.

Saccuzzo, D. P., & Marcus, A. (1983). *Speed of visual information-processing improves with practice in mental retardation.* Paper presented at the 91st Annual Convention of the American Psychological Association, Anaheim, CA.

Saccuzzo, D. P., & Michael, B. (1984). Speed of information-processing and structural limitations in retarded and dual diagnosis retarded-schizophrenic persons. *American Jour-*

nal of Mental Deficiency, 89, 187–194.

Saccuzzo, D. P., & Miller, S. (1977). Critical interstimulus interval in delusional schizophrenics and normals. *Journal of Abnormal Psychology, 86,* 261–266.

Saccuzzo, D. P., & Schubert, D. (1981). Backward masking as a measure of slow processing in the schizophrenia spectrum of disorders. *Journal of Abnormal Psychology, 90,* 305–312.

Saccuzzo, D. P., & Schulte, R. (1978). The value of a master's degree for the Ph.D. pursuing student in psychology. *American Psychologist, 33,* 862–864.

Sackett, P. R. & Wilk, S. L. (1994). Within-group norming and other forms of score adjustment in preemployment testing. *American Psychologist, 49,* 929–954.

Saigal, S., Szatmari, P., Rosenbaum, P., Campbell, D., & King, S. (1991). Cognitive abilities and school performance of extremely low birth weight children and matched term control children at age 8 years: A regional study. *Journal of Pediatrics, 118,* 751–760.

Saklofske, D. H., Schwean, V. L., Yackulic, R. A., & Quinn, D. (1994). WISC-III and SV: FE performance of children with attention deficit hyperactivity disorder. *Canadian Journal of School Psychology, 10*(2), 167–171.

Sands, W. A., & Gade, P. (1983). An application of computerized adaptive testing in U.S. Army recruiting. *Journal of Computer Based Instruction, 10,* 87–89.

Sands, W. L. (1972). Psychiatric history and mental status. In A. M. Freedman & I. I. Kaplan (Eds.), *Diagnosing mental illness* (pp. 20–40). New York: Atheneum.

Sarason, B. R., Pierce, G. R., Ban-nerman, A., & Sarason, I. G. (1993). Investigating the antecedents of perceived social support: Parents' views of and behavior toward their children. *Journal of Personality and Social Psychology, 65*(5), 1071–1085.

Sarason, B. R., & Sarason, I. G. (1994). Assessment of social support. In S. A. Shumaker & S. M. Czajkowski, (Eds), *Social support and cardiovascular disease* [Plenum series in behavioral psychophysiology and medicine]. (pp. 41–63). New York: Plenum Press.

Sarason, I. G. (1958). Effects on verbal learning of anxiety, reassurance, and meaningfulness of material. *Journal of Experimental Psychology, 56,* 472–477.

Sarason, I. G. (1959). Intellectual and personality correlates of test anxiety. *Journal of Abnormal and Social Psychology, 59,* 272–275.

Sarason, I. G. (1961). The effects of anxiety and threat on solution of a difficult task. *Journal of Abnormal and Social Psychology, 62,* 165–168.

Sarason, I. G. (1975). Test anxiety, attention, and the general problem of anxiety. In C. D. Spielberger & I. G. Sarason (Eds.), *Stress and anxiety* (Vol. 1). New York: Halsted.

Sarason, I. G. (Ed.). (1980). *Test anxiety: Theory, research, and applications.* Hillsdale, NJ: Erlbaum.

Sarason, I. G., Johnson, J. H., & Siegel, J. M. (1978). Assessing the impact of life change: Development of the Life Experiences Survey. *Journal of Consulting and Clinical Psychology, 46,* 932–946.

Sarason, I. G., Levine, H. M., Bashhnan, R. B., & Sarason, B. R. (1983). Assessing social support: The social support questionnaire. *Journal of Personality and Social Psychology, 44,* 127–139.

Sarason, I. G., & Palola, E. G. (1960). The relationship of test and general anxiety, difficulty of task, and experimental instructions to performance. *Journal of Experimental Psychology, 59,* 185–191.

Sarason, I. G., Pierce, G. R., & Sarason, B. R. (1994). General and specific perceptions of social support. In W. R. Avison & I. H. Gotlib (Eds.), *Stress and mental health: Contemporary issues and prospects for the future* (pp. 151–177). New York: Plenum Press.

Sarason, I. G., & Sarason, B. R. (1980). *Abnormal psychology* (3rd ed.). Englewood Cliffs, NJ: Prentice-Hall.

Sarason, I. G., & Sarason, B. R. (1985a). Life change, social support, coping, and health. In R. M. Kaplan & M. H. Criqui (Eds.), *Behavioral epidemiology and disease prevention.* New York: Plenum.

Sarason, I. G., & Sarason, B. R. (1985b). *Social support: Theory, research, and applications.* Boston: Martinjus Nijhoff International.

Sarason, I. G., & Sarason, B. R. (1990). Test anxiety. In H. Leitenberg (Ed.), *Handbook of social and evaluation anxiety* (pp. 475–495). New York: Plenum Press.

Sarason, I. G., Sarason, B. R., & Pierce, G. R. (1990). *Social support: An interactional view.* New York: Wiley.

Sarason, I. G., Sarason, B. R., & Pierce, G. R. (1994). Social support: Global and relationship-based levels of analysis. *Journal of Social and Personal Relationships, 11,* 295–312.

Sarason, I. G., Smith, R. E., & Diener, E. (1975). Personality research: Components of variance attributable to the person and the situation. *Journal of Personality and Social Psychology, 3,* 199–204.

Sattler, J. M. (1970). Racial "experimenter effects" in experimentation, testing, interviewing, and psychotherapy. *Psychological Bulletin, 73,* 137–160.

Sattler, J. M. (1973a). Examiners' scoring style, accuracy, ability, and personality scores. *Journal of Clinical Psychology, 29,* 38–39.

Sattler, J. M. (1973b). Intelligence testing of ethnic minority-group and culturally disadvantaged children. In L. Mann & D. Sabatino (Eds.), *The first review of special education* (Vol. 2). Philadelphia: JSE Press.

Sattler, J. M. (1973c). Racial experimenter effects. In K. S. Miller & R. M. Dreger (Eds.), *Comparative studies of blacks and whites in the United States.* New York: Seminar Press.

Sattler, J. M. (1977). The effects of therapist-client racial similarity. In A. S. Gurman & A. M. Razin (Eds.), *Effective psychotherapy. A handbook of research* (pp. 252–290). Elmsford, NY: Pergamon Press.

Sattler, J. M. (1978). Review of McCarthy Scales of Children's Abilities. In O. K. Buros (Ed.), *The eighth mental measurements yearbook* (Vol. 1). Highland Park, NJ: Gryphon Press.

Sattler, J. M. (1979a, April). *Intelligence tests on trial:* Larry P. et al. *v.* Wilson Riles et al. Paper presented at the meeting of the Western Psychological Association, San Diego, CA.

Sattler, J. M. (1979b). Standard intelligence tests are valid for measuring the intellectual potential of urban children: Comments on pitfalls in the measurement of intelligence. *Journal of Psychology, 102,* 107–112.

Sattler, J. M. (1980, November). Intelligence tests on trial: An interview with judges Robert F. Peckham and John F. Grady. *APA Monitor,* pp. 7–8.

Sattler, J. M. (1982). *Assessment of children's intelligence and special abilities.* Boston: Allyn and Bacon.

Sattler, J. M. (1988). *Assessment of children* (3rd ed.). San Diego, CA: Sattler.

Sattler, J. M. (1992). *Assessment of children* (3rd ed.). San Diego, CA: J. M. Sattler.

Sattler, J. M. (in press). *Interviewing.* San Diego, CA: Sattler.

Sattler, J. M., & Gwynne, J. (1982). Ethnicity and Bender Visual Motor Test performance. *Journal of School Psychology, 20,* 69–71.

Sattler, J. M., Hillix, W. A., & Neher, L. A. (1970). Halo effect in examiner scoring of intelligence test responses. *Journal of Consulting and Clinical Psychology, 34,* 172–176.

Sattler, J. M., & Theye, F. (1967). Procedural, situational, and interpersonal variables in individual intelligence testing. *Psychological Bulletin, 68,* 347–360.

Sattler, J. M., & Winget, B. M. (1970). Intelligence testing procedures as affected by expectancy and I.Q. *Journal of Clinical Psychology, 26,* 446–448.

Satz, P., & Fletcher, J. M. (1981). Emergent trends in neuropsychology: An overview. *Journal of Consulting and Clinical Psychology, 49,* 851–865.

Saunders, B. T., & Vitro, F. T. (1971). Examiner expectancy and bias as a function of the referral process in cognitive assessment. *Psychology in the Schools, 8,* 168–171.

Sawyer, J. (1966). Measurement and prediction, clinical and statistical. *Psychological Bulletin, 66,* 178–200.

Sax, G. (1989). *Principles of educational and psychological measurement and evaluation* (3rd ed.). Belmont, CA: Wadsworth.

Scarr-Salapatek, S. (1971). Race, social class and I.Q. *Science, 174,* 1285–1295.

Scheuneman, J. D. (1981). New look at bars and aptitude tests. *New Directions in Testing and Measurement, 12,* 5–25.

Scheuneman, J. D. (1987). An experimental, exploratory study of causes of bias in test items. *Journal of Educational Measurement, 24,* 97–118.

Schinka, J. A., Vanderploeg, R. D., & Curtiss, G. (1994). Wechsler Adult Intelligence Scale— Revised subtest scatter as a function of maximum subtest scaled score. *Psychological Assessment, 6*(4), 364–367.

Schmidt, F. L., & Hunter, J. E. (1983). Individual differences in productivity: An empirical test of estimates derived from studies of selection procedure utility. *Journal of Applied Psychology, 68,* 407–414.

Schmidt, F. L., Hunter, J. L., McKenzie, R. C., & Muldrow, T. W. (1979). Impact of valid selection procedures on work-force productivity. *Journal of Applied Psychology, 64,* 609–626.

Schmidt, F. L., Law, K., Hunter, J. E., Rothstein, H. R., & others. (1993). Refinements in validity generalization methods: Implications for the situational specificity hypothesis. *Journal of Applied Psychology, 78,* 3–12.

Schmidt, F. L. & Rothstein, H. R. (1994). Application of validity generalization to biodata scales in employment selection. In G. S. Stokes, M. D. Mumford, & W. A. Owens (Eds.), *Biodata handbook: Theory, research, and use of biographical information in selection and performance prediction* (pp. 237–260). Palo Alto, CA: CPP Books.

Schmitt, N. (1976). Social and situational determinants of interview decisions: Implications for the employment interview. *Personnel Psychology, 29,* 79–101.

Schmitt, N., & Robertson, I. (1990). Personnel selection. *Annual*

Review of Psychology, 41, 289–391.

Schneider, L. M., & Briel, J. B. (1990). *Validity of the GRE: 1988–89 Summary Report.* Princeton, NJ: Educational Testing Service.

Schoggen, P. (1979). Roger G. Barker and behavioral settings: A commentary. *Journal of Personality and Social Psychology, 37,* 2158–2160.

Schroeder, H. E., & Kleinsaser, L. D. (1972). Examiner bias: A determinant of children's verbal behavior on the WISC. *Journal of Consulting and Clinical Psychology, 39,* 451–454.

Schuerger, J. M., Tait, E., & Tavernelli, M. (1982). Temporal stability of personality by questionnaire. *Journal of Personality and Social Psychology, 43,* 176–182.

Schuler, H. (1993). Is there a dilemma between validity and acceptance in the employment interview? In B. Nevo & R. S. Jager (Eds.), *Educational and psychological testing: The test taker's outlook* (pp. 239–250). Gottingen, Germany: Huber.

Schultz, C. B., & Sherman, R. H. (1976). Social class, development, and differences in reinforcer effectiveness. *Review of Educational Research, 46,* 25–59.

Schwab-Stone, M., Fallon, T., Briggs, M., & Crowther, B. (1994). Reliability of diagnostic reporting for children aged 6–11 years: A test-retest study of the Diagnostic Interview Schedule for Children— Revised. *American Journal of Psychiatry, 151*(7), 1048–1054.

Schwartz, R., & Gottman, J. (1976). Toward a task analysis of assertive behavior. *Journal of Consulting and Clinical Psychology, 44,* 910–920.

Science Agenda. (1991). Department of Labor inundated with comments on GATB. *Assessing Assessments, 4,* 6–7.

Scott, L. H. (1981). Measuring intelligence with the Goodenough-Harris Drawing Test. *Psychological Bulletin, 89,* 483–505.

Scott, P., Burton, R. V., & Yarrow, M. (1967). Social reinforcement under natural conditions. *Child Development, 38,* 53–63.

Seguin, E. (1907). *Idiocy: Its treatment by the physiological method.* New York: Bureau of Publications, Teachers College, Columbia University. (Original work published 1866).

Self, P. A., & Horowitz, F. D. (1979). The behavioral assessment of the neonate: An overview. In J. D. Osofsky (Ed.), *Handbook of infant development.* New York: Wiley.

Seligman, M. E. P. (1975). *Helplessness: On depression, development, and death.* San Francisco: Freeman.

Seligmann, J., Coppola, V., Howard, L., & Lee, E. D. (1979, May 28). A really final exam. *Newsweek,* pp. 97–98.

Sexton, M., Fox, N. L., & Hebel, J. R. (1990). Prenatal exposure to tobacco: II. Effects on cognitive functioning at age three. *International Journal of Epidemiology, 19,* 72–77.

Shaffer, D. (1994). Structured interviews for assessing children. *Journal of Child Psychology and Psychiatry and Allied Disciplines, 35*(4), 783–784.

Shaffer, L. (1953). Of whose reality I cannot doubt. *American Psychologist, 8,* 608–623.

Shakow, D., Hilgard, E. R., Kelly, E. L., Sanford, R. N., & Shaffer, L. F. (1947). Recommended graduate training in clinical psychology. *American Psychologist, 2,* 539–558.

Shapiro, S. K., & Simpson, R. G. (1994). Patterns and predictors of performance on the Bender-Gestalt and the Developmental Test of Visual Motor Integration in a sample of behaviorally and emotionally disturbed adolescents. *Journal of Psychoeducational Assessment, 12*(3), 254–263.

Share, J. B., Webb, A., & Koch, R. (1964). The longitudinal development of infants and young children with Down's syndrome. *American Journal of Mental Deficiency, 68,* 689–692.

Sharkey, K. J., & Ritzier, B. A. (1985). Comparing diagnostic validity of the TAT and a new Picture Projective Test. *Journal of Personality Assessment, 49,* 406–412.

Shaywitz, B. A., Fletcher, J. M., & Shaywitz, S. E. (1995). Defining and classifying learning disabilities and attention-deficit/hyperactivity disorder. *Journal of Child Neurology, 10,* S50–S57.

Sheehan, K. M., & Lewis, C. (1992). Computerized mastery testing with nonequivalent testlets. *Applied Psychological Measurement, 16*(1), 65–76.

Shiffman, S., Fischer, L. A., Paty, J. A., Gnys, M., & others. (1995). Drinking and smoking: A field study of their association. *Annals of Behavioral Medicine, 16*(3), 203–209.

Shisslak, C. M., Pazda, S. L., & Crago, M. (1990). Body weight and bulimia as discriminators of psychological characteristics among anorexic, bulimic, and obese women. *Journal of Abnormal Psychology, 99,* 380–384.

Shrout, P. E., Spitzer, R. L., & Fleiss, J. L. (1987). Quantification of agreement in psychiatric diagnosis revisited. *Archives of General Psychiatry, 44*(2):172–177.

Shumaker, S. A., & Berzon, R. (1995). *The international assessment of health-related quality of life: Theory, translation, measurement and analysis.* New York: Oxford University Press.

Sidick, J. T., Barrett, G. V., & Doverspike, D. (1994). Three-alternative multiple choice tests: An attractive option. *Personnel Psychology, 47,* 829–835.

Siegel, S. N., & Castellan, J. (1988). *Nonparametric statistics for the behavioral sciences* (2nd ed.). New York: McGraw-Hill.

Silva, J. M. & Jacobs, R. R. (1993). Performance as a function of increased minority hiring. *Journal of Applied Psychology, 78,* 591–601.

Silver, N. C., & Dunlap, W. P. (1987). Averaging correlation coefficients: Should Fisher's Z transformation be used? *Journal of Applied Psychology, 72,* 146–148.

Silverstein, A. B. (1978). Review of McCarthy Scales of Children's Abilities. In O. K. Buros (Ed.), *The eighth mental measurements yearbook* (Vol. 1). Highland Park, NJ: Gryphon Press.

Silverstein, A. B. (1982). Factor structure of the Wechsler Adult Intelligence Scale—Revised. *Journal of Counseling and Clinical Psychology, 50,* 661–664.

Simon, A. J., & Bass, L. G. (1956). Toward a validation of infant testing. *American Journal of Orthopsychiatry, 26,* 340–350.

Simon, W. E. (1969). Expectancy effects in the scoring of vocabulary items: A study of scorer bias. *Journal of Educational Measurement, 6,* 159–164.

Sines, J. O. (1970). Actuarial versus clinical prediction in psychopathology. *British Journal of Psychiatry, 116,* 129–144.

Singh, L. (1986). Standardization of n-power measuring instrument (T.A.T.). *Journal of Psychological Researches, 28,* 14–20.

Sinha, D. K. (1986). Relationships of graduation requirements and course offerings to Scholastic Aptitude Test performance of seniors in high schools. *The Journal of Educational Research, 80,* 5–9.

Sinnett, E. R., Holen, M. C., & Albott, W. L. (1995). MMPI scores of female victims. *Psychological Reports, 76*(1), 139–144.

Sloan, P., Arsenault, L., Hilsenroth, M., & Harvill, L. (1995). Rorschach measures of post-traumatic stress in Persian Gulf War veterans. *Journal of Personality Assessment, 64*(3), 397–414.

Sloman, J., Bellinger, D. C., & Krentzel, C. P. (1990). Infantile colic and transient developmental log in the first year of life. *Child Psychiatry and Human Development, 21,* 25–36.

Slosson, R. L (1963). *Slosson Intelligence Test (SIT) for children and adults.* New York: Slosson Educational Publications.

Smith, A. E., & Knight-Jones, E. B. (1990). The abilities of very low-birthweight children and their classroom controls. *Developmental Medicine and Child Neurology, 32,* 590–601.

Smith, B., & Sechrest, L. (1991). Treatment of aptitude X treatment interactions. *Journal of Consulting and Clinical Psychology, 59,* 233–244.

Smith, D. (1981). Unfinished business with informed consent procedures. *American Psychologist, 36,* 22–26.

Smith, G. A., & Stanley, G. (1983). Clocking "g": Relating intelligence and measures of timed performance. *Intelligence, 7,* 353–358.

Smith, J. E., Hillard, M. C., Walsh, R. A., Kubacki, S. R., & Morgan, C. D. (1991). Rorschach assessment of purging and nonpurging bulimics. *Journal of Personality Assessment, 56,* 277–288.

Smith, R. E., Ascough, J. C., Ettinger, R. F., & Nelson, D. A. (1971). Humor, anxiety, and task performance. *Journal of Personality and Social Psychology, 19,* 243–246.

Smith, R. M. (1994). A comparison of the power of Rasch total and between-item fit statistics to detect measurement distur-bances. *Educational and Psychological Measurement, 54*(1), 42–55.

Smith, S. H. (1977). *Refining cognitive behavior modification treatments for test anxiety.* Unpublished master's thesis, San Diego State University, CA.

Smith, T. W., & Zurawski, R. M. (1983). Assessment of irrational beliefs: The question of discriminant validity. *Journal of Clinical Psychology, 39,* 976–979.

Snow, R. E. (1969). Review of *Pygmalion in the Classroom* by R. Rosenthal and L. Jacobson. *Contemporary Psychology, 14,* 197–199

Snow, R. E. (1991). Aptitude-treatment interaction as a framework for research on individual differences in psychotherapy. *Journal of Consulting and Clinical Psychology, 59,* 205–216.

Snyderman, M., & Rothman, S. (1987). Survey of expert opinion in intelligence and aptitude testing. *American Psychologist, 42,* 137–144.

Sostek, A. M. (1978). Review of the Brazelton Neonatal Assessment Scale. In O. K. Buros (Ed.), *The eighth mental measurements yearbook* (Vol. 1). Highland Park, NJ: Gryphon Press.

Spearman, C. E. (1904a). General intelligence objectively determined and measured. *American Journal of Psychology, 15,* 201–293.

Spearman, C. E. (1904b). The proof and measurement of association between two things. *American Journal of Psychology, 15,* 72–101.

Spearman, C. E. (1923). *The nature of intelligence and the principles of cognition.* London: Macmillan.

Spearman, C. E. (1927). *The abilities of man.* New York: Macmillan.

Sperry, R. W. (1968). Hemisphere deconnection and unity in conscious awareness. *American Psychologist, 23,* 723–733.

Spielberger, C. D. (1972). Anxiety as an emotional state. In C. D. Spielberger (Ed.), *Anxiety: Current trends in theory and research.* New York: Academic Press.

Spielberger, C. D., Anton, W. B., & Bedell, J. (1976). The nature and treatment of test anxiety. In M. Zuckerman & C. D. Spielberger (Eds.), *Emotions and anxiety: New concepts, methods and applications.* Hillsdale, NJ: Erlbaum.

Spielberger, C. D., Auerbach, S. M., Wadsworth, A. P., Dun, T. M., & Taulbee, E. S. (1975). Emotional reactions to surgery. *Journal of Consulting and Clinical Psychology, 40,* 33–38.

Spielberger, C. D., Gorsuch, R. L., & Lushene, R. E. (1970). *Manual for the State-Trait Anxiety Inventory.* Palo Alto, CA: Consulting Psychologists Press.

Spielberger, C.D., & Reheiser, E. C. (1994). The Job Stress Survey: Measuring gender differences in occupation stress. *Journal of Social Behavior and Personality, 9,* 199–218.

Spielberger, C. D., & Reheiser, E. C. (1995). Measuring occupational stress: The Job Stress Survey. In R. Crandall & P. L. Perrewe (Eds.) *Occupational stress: A handbook* (pp. 51–69). Philadelphia: Taylor & Francis.

Spielberger, C. D., & Sydeman, S. J.(1994). State-Trait Anxiety Inventory and State-Trait Anger Expression Inventory. In M. E. Maruish (Ed.), *The use of psychological testing for treatment planning and outcome assessment* (pp. 292–321). Hillsdale, NJ: Lawrence Erlbaum Associates.

Spiers, P. A. (1982). The Luria-Nebraska Neuropsychological Battery revisited: A theory in practice or just practicing? *Journal of Consulting and Clinical Psychology, 50,* 301–306.

Spiker, D. G., & Ehler, J. G. (1984).

Structured psychiatric interviews for adults. In G. Goldstein & M. Hersen (Eds.), *Handbook of psychological assessment* (pp. 291–304). New York: Pergamon Press.

Spilker, B., & Scheonfelder, J. (Eds.). (1991). *Data collection forms in clinical trials.* New York: Raven Press.

Spilker, B. (1990a). *Quality of life assessment in clinical trials.* New York: Raven Press.

Spilker, B. (1990b) Quality of life bibliography and indexes. *Medical Care, 28,* (Suppl. 12), 1–77.

Spilker, B. (Ed.) (1996). *Quality of like and pharmacoeconomics in clinical trials* (2nd ed.). New York: Raven.

Spitzer, R. L., Williams, J. B. W., Gibbon, M., & First, M. B. (1990a). *Structured clinical interview for DSM-III-R—patient edition* (SCID-P, 9/1/89 version). Washington DC: American Psychiatric Press.

Spitzer, R. L., Williams, J. B. W., Gibbon, M., & First, M. B. (1990b). *Structured clinical interview for DSM-III-R—personality disorders* (SCID-II, 9/1/89 version). Washington, DC: American Psychiatric Press.

Spreen, O., Risser, A. H., & Edgell, D. (1984). *Developmental neuropsychology.* New York: Oxford University Press.

SPSS. (1995). *Statistical Package for the Social Sciences reference guide.* Chicago: Statistical Package for the Social Sciences.

Squire, L. R., & Butters, N. (1984). *The neurosychology of memory.* New York: Guilford Press.

Stallones, R. A., (1983). Ischemic heart disease and lipids in blood and diet. *Annual Review of Nutrition, 3,* 155–185.

Standage, K. (1989). Structured interviews and the diagnosis of personality disorders. *Canadian Journal of Psychiatry, 34,* 906–912.

Stanford-Binet: Fourth Edition Students with learning disabilities. (1992). *Journal of Learning Disabilities, 22,* 260–261.

Stanley, J. C. (1971). Reliability. In R. L. Thorndike (Ed.), *Educational measurement.* Washington, DC: American Council on Education.

Stanley, J. C., & Hopkins, K. D. (1972). *Educational and psychological measurement and evaluation.* Englewood Cliffs, NJ: Prentice-Hall.

Stanley, K. E. (1980). Prognostic factors for survival in patients with inoperable lung cancer. *Journal of the National Cancer Institute, 65,* 25–32.

Steinberg, L., & Thissen, D. (1995). Item response theory in personality research. In P. E. Shrout & S. T. Fiske (Eds.), *Personality research, methods, and theory: A festschrift honoring Donald W. Fiske.* Hillsdale, NJ: Lawrence Erlbaum Associates.

Stephenson, W. (1953). *The study of behavior.* Chicago: University of Chicago Press.

Steptoe, A., & Johnston, D. (1991). Clinical applications of cardiovascular assessment. *Psychological Assessment: A Journal of Consulting and Clinical Psychology, 3,* 337–349.

Stern, W. (1912). *Die psychologische Methoden der Intelligenzprufung.* Leipzig, Germany: Barth.

Sternberg, R. J. (1981). Testing and cognitive psychology. *American Psychologist, 36,* 1181–1189.

Sternberg, R. J. (1984). The Kaufman Assessment Battery for Children: An information processing analysis and critique. *The Journal of Special Education, 18*(3), 269–279.

Sternberg, R. J. (1985). *Beyond IQ: A triarchic theory of human intelligence.* New York: Cambridge University Press.

Sternberg, R. J. (1986). *Intelligence applied: Understanding and increasing your intellectual skills.* San Diego: Harcourt Brace Jovanovich.

Sternberg, R. J. (1988). *The triarchic mind: A theory of human intelligence.* New York: Viking.

Sternberg, R. J. (1991). Death, taxes, and bad intelligence tests. *Intelligence, 15,* 257–269.

Sternberg, R. J., & Gardner, M. K. (1982). A componential interpretation of the general factor in human intelligence. In H. J. Eysenck (Ed.), *A model for intelligence.* New York: Springer-Verlag.

Stevens, S. S. (1966). A metric for the social consensus. *Science, 151,* 530–541.

Stevenson, I. (1971). *The diagnostic interview.* New York: Harper & Row.

Stevenson, J. D. (1986). Alternate form reliability and concurrent validity of the PPVT-R for referred rehabilitation agency adults. *Journal of Clinical Psychology, 42,* 650–653.

Stewart, A. L., & Ware, J. E. (Eds.). (1992). *Measuring functioning and well-being: The medical outcomes study approach.* Durham, NC: Duke University Press.

Stewart, A. L., Ware, J. E., Brook, R. H., & Davies-Avery, A. (1978). *Conceptualization and measurement of health for adults: Vol. 2. Physical health in terms of functioning.* Santa Monica, CA: RAND Corporation.

Stokols, D. (1978). Environmental psychology. *Annual Review of Psychology, 29,* 253–295.

Stokols, D. (1992). Establishing and maintaining healthy environments: Toward a social ecology of health promotion. *American Psychologist, 47*(1), 6–22.

Stone, A. A. (1995). Measurement of affective response. In S. Cohen, R. C. Kessler, & L. U. Gordon (Eds.), *Measuring stress: A guide for health and social scien-*

tists (pp. 148–171). New York: Oxford University Press.

Stone, A. A., Kennedy-Moore, E., & Neale, J. M. (1995). Association between daily coping and end-of-day mood. *Health Psychology, 14*(4), 341–349.

Stone, A. A., & Shiffman, S. (1994). Ecological momentary assessment (EMA) in behavorial medicine. *Annals of Behavioral Medicine, 16*(3), 199–202.

Strassberg, D. S., Ross, S., & Todt, E. H. (1995). MMPI performance among women with bulimia: A cluster-analytic study. *Addictive Behaviors, 20*(1), 137–140.

Strauss, M. E., & Brandt, J. (1990). Are there neuropsychologic manifestations of the gene for Huntington's disease in asymptomatic, at-risk individuals? *Archives of Neurology, 47,* 905–908.

Strauss, M. E., Gynther, M. D., & Wallhermfechtel, J. (1974). Differential misdiagnosis of blacks and whites by the MMPI. *Journal of Personality Assessment, 38,* 55–60.

Strauss, M., Lessen-Firestone, J., Starr, R., Jr., & Ostrea, E., Jr. (1975). Behavior of narcotics-addicted newborns. *Child Development, 46,* 887–893.

Streiner, D. L., & Miller, H. R. (1989). The MCMI-II: How much better than the MCMI? *Journal of Personality Assessment, 53,* 81–84.

Stricker, L. J. (1965). Edwards Personal Preference Schedule. In O. K. Buros (Ed.), *The sixth mental measurements yearbook.* Highland Park, NJ: Gryphon Press.

Strong, E. K., Jr., & Campbell, D. P. (1966). *Manual for Strong Vocational Interest Blank.* Stanford, CA: Stanford University Press.

Subkoviak, M. J. (1980). The reliability of mastery classification decisions. In R. A. Burk (Ed.),

Criterion-referenced measurement: The state of the art. Baltimore: Johns Hopkins University Press.

Sud, A. (1994). Attentional skills training/cognitive modeling: Short term therapeutic cognitive interventions for test anxiety. *Psychological Studies, 39,* 1–7.

Suinn, R. M. (1969a). The relationship between fears and anxiety: A further study. *Behaviour Research and Therapy, 7,* 317–318.

Suinn, R. M. (1969b). The STABS, a measure of test anxiety for behavior therapy: Normative data. *Behaviour Research and Therapy, 7,* 335–339.

Sundberg, N. D. (1961). The practice of psychological testing in clinical services in the United States. *American Psychologist, 16,* 79–83.

Super, D. E. (1953). A theory of vocational development. *American Psychologist, 8,* 185–190.

Super, D. E., & Hall, D. T. (1978). Career development: Exploitation and planning. *Annual Review of Psychology, 29,* 333–372.

Svanum, S., & Dallas, C. L (1981). Alcoholic MMPI types and their relationship to patient charactertistics, polydrug abuse, and abstinence following treatment. *Journal of Personality Assessment, 45,* 278–287.

Swanson, D. B., Norman, G. R., & Linn, R. L. (1995). Performance-based assessment: Lessons from the health professions. *Educational Researcher, 24*(5), 5–11.

Sweet, R. C. (1970). *Variations in the intelligence test performance of lower-class children as a function of feedback or monetary reinforcement.* (University Microfilms No. 70–37, 21) Dissertation Abstracts International, *31*(2A), 648–649.

Sweetland, R. C., & Keyser, D. J. (Eds.). (1983). *Tests: A comprehensive reference for assessment in psychology, education and business.* Kansas City, MO: Test Corporation of America.

Sweetland, R. C., & Keyser, D. J. (1991). *Tests: A comprehensive reference for assessment in psychology, education, and business* (3rd ed.). Austin, TX: Pro-Ed Publishers.

Symonds, P. M. (1924). On the loss of reliability in ratings due to coarseness of the scale. *Journal of Experimental Psychology, 7,* 456–461.

Synodinos, N. E., Papacostas, C. S., & Okimoto, G. M. (1994). Computer-administered versus paper-and-pencil surveys and the effect of sample selection. *Behavior Research Methods, Instruments and Computers, 26,* 395–401.

Szasz, T. S. (1961). *The myth of mental illness.* New York: Harper & Row.

Tabachnick, B. G., & Fidell, L. S. (1989). *Using multivariate statistics* (2nd ed.). New York: Harper & Row.

Tannenbaum, A. J. (1968). Review of the IPAT Culture Fair Intelligence Test. In O. K. Buros (Ed.), *The sixth mental measurements yearbook.* Highland Park, NJ: Gryphon Press.

Taplin, P. S., & Reid, J. B. (1973). Effects of instructional set and experimenter influence on observer reliability. *Child Development, 44,* 547–554.

Tasto, D. L. (1977). Self-report schedules and inventories. In A. R. Ciminero, K. D. Calhoun, & H. E. Adams (Eds.), *Handbook of behavioral assessment,* New York: Wiley-Interscience.

Taulbee, E. S., & Sisson, L. (1957). Configurational analysis of MMPI profiles of psychiatric groups. *Journal of Consulting Psychology, 21,* 413–417.

Taylor, C. W., Price, P. B., Richards, J. M., Jr., & Jacobsen,

T. L. (1965). An investigation of the criterion problem for a group of medical general practitioners. *Journal of Applied Psychology, 49,* 399–406.

Taylor, H. C., & Russell, J. T. (1939). The relationship of validity coefficients to the practical effectiveness of tests in selection: Discussion and tables. *Journal of Applied Psychology, 23,* 565–578.

Taylor, J. A. (1951). The relationship of anxiety to the conditioned eyelid response. *Journal of Experimental Psychology, 41,* 81–92.

Taylor, J. A. (1953). A personality scale of manifest anxiety. *Journal of Abnormal Psychology, 48,* 285–290.

Taylor, R. L., Sternberg, L., & Partenio, I. (1986). Performance of urban and rural children on the SOMPA: Preliminary investigation. *Perceptual and Motor Skills, 63,* 1219–1223.

Temp, G. (1971). Test bias: Validity of the SAT for blacks and whites in thirteen integrated institutions. *Journal of Educational Measurement, 8,* 245–251.

Templer, D. I., Schmitz, S. P., & Corgiat, M. D. (1985). Comparison of the Stanford-Binet with the Wechsler Adult Intelligence Scale—Revised: Preliminary report. *Psychological Reports, 57,* 335–336.

Teng, E. L., Wimer, C., Roberts, E., Damasio, A. R., Eslinger, P. J., Folstein, M. F., Tune, L. E., Whitehouse, P. J., Bardolph, E. L., & Chui, H. C. (1989). Alzheimer's dementia: Performance on parallel forms of the dementia assessment battery. *Journal of Clinical and Experimental Neuropsychology, 11,* 899–912.

Tenopyr, M. L. (1984, November). *So let it be with content validity.* Paper presented at the Content Validity III Conference, Bowl-

ing Green State University, Bowling Green, OH.

Tenopyr, M. L. (1993). Construct validation needs in vocational behavior theories [Special Issue: The Theory of Work Adjustment]. *Journal of Vocational Behavior, 43*(1), 84–89.

Tenopyr, M. L. (1994). Big Five, structural modeling, and item response theory. In G. S. Stokes, M. D. Mumford, & W. A. Owens (Eds.), *Biodata handbook: Theory, research, and use of biographical information in selection and performance prediction* (pp. 519– 533). Palo Alto, CA: CPP Books,.

Teplin, L. A., & Schwartz, J. (1989). Screening for severe mental disorder in jails: The development of the Referral Decision Scale. *Law and Human Behavior, 13,* 118.

Terman, L. M. (1916). *The measurement of intelligence.* Boston: Houghton Mifflin.

Terman, L. M., & Merrill, M. A. (1937). *Measuring intelligence.* Boston: Houghton Mifflin.

Terman, L. M., & Merrill, M. A. (1953). Tests of intelligence: B. 1937 Stanford-Binet scales. In A. Weider (Ed.), *Contributions toward medical psychology* (Vol. 2). New York: Ronald Press.

Terman, L. M., & Merrill, M. A. (1960). *Stanford-Binet intelligence scale.* Boston: Houghton Mifflin.

Terrell, F., Taylor, J., & Terrell, S. L. (1978). Effects of type of social reinforcement on the intelligence test performance of lower-class black children. *Journal of Consulting and Clinical Psychology, 46,* 1538–1539.

Thompson, D. E., & Thompson, T. A. (1982). Court standards for job analysis in test validation. *Personnel Psychology, 35,* 865– 874.

Thorndike, E. L. (1904). *An introduction to the theory of mental and social measurements.* New York: Science Press.

Thorndike, E. L. (1920). A constant error in psychological rating. *Journal of Applied Psychology, 4,* 25–29.

Thorndike, E. L. (1921). Intelligence and its measurement: A symposium. *Journal of Educational Psychology, 12,* 123–147, 195–216.

Thorndike, R. L. (1968). Review of *Pygmalion in the Classroom* by R. Rosenthal and L. Jacobson. *American Educational Research Journal, 5,* 708–711.

Thorndike, R. L. (1971). Concepts of culture-fairness. *Journal of Educational Measurement, 8,* 63–70.

Thorndike, R. L. (1972). Review of the Torrance Tests of Creative Thinking. In O. K. Buros (Ed.), *The seventh mental measurements yearbook* (Vol. 1). Highland Park, NJ: Gryphon Press.

Thorndike, R. L. (1973). *Stanford-Binet Intelligence Scale, Form L-M, 1972 norms tables.* Boston: Houghton Mifflin.

Thorndike, R. L., Hagen, E. P., & Sattler, J. M. (1986). *Technical manual: Stanford Binet Intelligence Scale: Fourth Edition.* Chicago: Riverside.

Thorndike, R. M. (1990a). Origins of intelligence and its measurement. *Journal of Psychoeducational Assessment, 8,* 223–230.

Thorndike, R. M. (1990b). Would the real factors of the Stanford-Binet Fourth Edition please come forward? *Journal of Psychoeducational Assessment, 8,* 412–435.

Thumin, F. J. (1969). MMPI scores as related to age, education and intelligence among male job applicants. *Journal of Applied Psychology, 53,* 404–407.

Thurstone, L. L. (1938). Primary mental abilities. *Psychometric Monographs, 1.*

Tiber, N., & Kennedy, W. A. (1964). The effects of incentives on the intelligence test performance of different social groups. *Journal of Consulting Psychology, 28,* 187.

Timbrook, R. E., & Graham, J. R. (1994). Ethnic differences on the MMPI-2? *Psychological Assessment, 6*(3), 212–217.

Tittle, C. K. (1983). Studies of the effects of career interest inventories: Expanding outcome criteria to include women's experience. *Journal of Vocational Behavior, 22,* 148–158.

Tomkins, S. S. (1947). *The Thematic Apperception Test: The theory and technique of interpretation.* New York: Grune & Stratton.

Topp, R. (1989). Effects of relaxation or exercise on undergraduates' test anxiety. *Perceptual and Motor Skills, 69,* 35–41.

Torgerson, W. S. (1958). *Theory and methods of scaling.* New York: Wiley.

Torrance, E. P. (1970). Broadening concepts of giftedness in the 70's. *Gifted Child Quarterly, 14,* 199–208.

Torrance, E. P. (1977). *Discovery and nurturance of giftedness in the culturally different.* Reston, VA: Council for Exceptional Children.

Traub, R. E., & Lam, Y. R. (1985). Latent structure and item sampling models for testing. *Annual Review of Psychology, 36,* 19–48.

Triandis, H. C., Dunnette, M. D., & Hough, L. M. (1994). *Handbook of industrial and organizational psychology* (Vol. 4, 2nd ed.). Palo Alto, CA: Consulting Psychologists Press.

Tronick, E. Z. (1987). The neonatal behavioral assessment scale as a biomarker of the effects of environmental agents on the newborn. *Environmental Health Perspectives, 74,* 185–189.

Tronick, E., & Brazelton, T. B. (1975). Clinical uses of the Brazelton Neonatal Behavioral Assessment. In B. Friedlander, G. Sterritt, & G. Kirk (Eds.), *Exceptional infant* (Vol. 3). New York: Brunner/Mazel.

Trott, D. M., & Morf, M. E. (1972). A multimethod factor analysis of the Differential Personality Inventory, Personality Research Form, and Minnesota Multiphasic Personality Inventory. *Journal of Counseling Psychology, 19,* 94–103.

Truax, C. B., & Carkhuff, R. R. (1967). *Toward effective counseling and psychotherapy: Training and practice.* Chicago: Aldine-Atherton.

Truax, C. B., & Mitchell, K. M. (1971). Research on certain therapist interpersonal skills in relation to process and outcome. In A. E. Bergin & S. L. Garfield (Eds.), *Handbook of psychotherapy and behavior change.* New York: Wiley.

Tryon, W. W. (1991). *Activity measurement in psychology and medicine.* New York: Plenum.

Tukey, J. W. (1977). *Exploratory data analysis.* Reading, MA: Addison-Wesley.

Turkheimer, E. (1991). Individual and group differences in adoption studies of IQ. *Psychological Bulletin, 110,* 392–405.

Turner, J. A., Herron, L., & Weiner, P. (1986). Utility of the MMPI Pain Assessment Index in predicting outcomes after lumbar surgery. *Journal of Clinical Psychology, 42,* 764–769.

Turner, J. H. (1970). Entrepreneurial environments and the emergence of achievement motivation in adolescent mates. *Sociometry, 33,* 147–165.

Turner, R. J. (1981). Social support as a contingency in psychological well-being. *Journal of Health and Social Behavior, 22,* 357–367.

Turpin, G. (1991). The psychophysiological assessment of anxiety disorders: Three-systems measurement and beyond. *Psychological Assessment: A Jour-*

nal of Consulting and Clinical Psychology, 3, 366–375.

Tutty, L. M. (1995). Theoretical and practical issues in selecting a measure of family functioning. *Research on Social Work Practice, 5,* 80–106

Tyler, L. E. (1969). *The work of the counselor* (3rd ed.). New York: Appleton-Century-Crofts.

Tyler, L. E., & Walsh, W. B. (1979). *Tests and measurements* (3rd ed.). Englewood Cliffs, NJ: Prentice-Hall.

Uhl, N., & Eisenberg, T. (1970). Predicting shrinkage in the multiple correlation coefficient. *Educational and Psychological Measurement, 30,* 487–489.

Ulrich, L., & Trumbo, D. (1965). The selection interview since 1949. *Psychological Bulletin, 63,* 100–116.

Valencia, R. R. (1988). The McCarthy Scales and Hispanic children: A review of psychometric research. *Hispanic Journal of Behavioral Sciences, 10,* 81–104.

Valencia, R. R., & Lopez, R. (1992). Assessment of racial and ethnic minority students: Problems and prospects. In M. Zeidner & R. Most (Eds.), *Psychological testing: An inside view.* Palo Alto, CA: Consulting Psychologists Press.

van Baar, A. (1990). Development of infants of drug dependent mothers. *Journal of Child Psychology and Psychiatry and Allied Disciplines, 31,* 911–920.

Vandenburg, S. G., & Vogler, G. P. (1985). Genetic determinants of intelligence. In B. B. Wolman (Ed.), *Handbook of intelligence.* New York: Wiley.

Vandevijer, F. J. R., & Harsveld, M. (1994). The incomplete equivalence of the paper-and-pencil and computerized versions of the General Aptitude Test Battery. *Journal of Applied Psychology, 79*(6), 852–859.

Varble, D. L. (1971). Current status of the Thematic Apperception Test. In P. McReynolds (Ed.), *Advances in psychological assessment* (Vol. 2). Palo Alto, CA: Science and Behavior Books.

Verschuren, W. M., Jacobs, D. R., Bloemberg, B. P., Kromhout, D., Menotti, A., Aravanis, C., Blackburn, H., Buzina, R., Dontas, A. S., Fidanza, F., & others. (1995). Serum total cholesterol and long-term coronary heart disease mortality in different cultures. Twenty-five-year follow-up of the seven countries study. *Journal of the American Medical Association, 274*(2), 131–136.

Vickers, D., Nettelbeck, T., & Willson, R. J. (1972). Perceptual indices of performance: The measurement of "inspection time" and "noise" in the visual system. *Perception, 1,* 263–295.

Wade, T. C., & Baker, T. B. (1977). Opinions and uses of psychological tests: A survey of clinical psychologists. *American Psychologist, 32,* 874–882.

Wagner, E. E., Alexander, R. A., Roos, G., & Adair, H. (1986). Optimum split-half reliabilities for the Rorschach: Projective techniques are more reliable than we think. *Journal of Personality Assessment, 50,* 107–112.

Wagner, E. E., & Flamos, O. (1988). Optimized split-half reliability for the Bender Visual Motor Gestalt Test: Further evidence for the use of the maximization procedure. *Journal of Personality Assessment, 52,* 454–458.

Wagner, P. A. (1994). Adaptations for administering the Peabody Picture Vocabulary Test— Revised to individuals with severe communications and motor dysfunctions. *Mental Retardation, 32*(2) 107–112.

Wagner, R. (1949). The employment interview: A critical review. *Personnel Psychology, 2,* 17–46.

Wainer, H., & Braun, H. I. (Eds.). (1988). *Test validation.* Hillsdale, NJ: Erlbaum.

Waldman, I. D., Weinberg, R. A., & Scarr, S. (1994). Racial-group differences in IQ in the Minnesota Transracial Adoption Study: A reply to Levin and Lynn. *Intelligence, 19,* 29–44.

Walker, A. M., Rablen, R. A., & Rogers, C. R. (1960). Development of a scale to measure process changes in psychotherapy. *Journal of Clinical Psychology, 16,* 79–85.

Walker, S., & Rosser, R. (1992). *Quality of life assessment: Key issues for the 1990s.* Dordrect, Netherlands: Kluwer Press.

Wallace, W. L. (1972). Review of the SAT. In O. K. Buros (Ed.), *The seventh mental measurements yearbook* (Vol. 1). Highland Park, NJ: Gryphon Press.

Ward, L. C. (1995). Correspondence of the MMPI-2 and MCMI-II male substance abusers. *Journal of Personality Assessment, 64*(2), 390–393.

Ward, T. J., et al. (1989). The effect of computerized tests on the performance and attitudes of college students. *Journal of Educational Computing Research, 5,* 327–333.

Ware, J. E., Jr. (1991). Conceptualizing and measuring generic health outcomes. *Cancer, 67,* 774–779.

Ware, J. E. (1996). The SF-36 health survey. In B. F. Spilker (Ed.), *Quality of life and pharmcoeconomics in clinical trials* (2nd ed., pp. 337–345). New York: Raven.

Ware, J. E. J., Kosinski, M., Bayliss, M. S., McHorney, C. A., Rogers, W. H., & Raczek, A. (1995).

Comparison of methods for the scoring and statistical analysis of SF-36 health profile and summary measures: Summary of results from the Medical Outcomes Study. *Medical Care, 33,* AS264–AS279.

Wasik, B. H., Ramey, C. T., Bryant, D. M., & Sparling, J. J. (1990). A longitudinal study of two early intervention strategies: Project CARE. *Child Development, 61,* 1682–1696.

Wasserman, A. L., Wilimas, J. A., Fairclough, D. L., Mulhern, R. K., & Wang, W. (1991). Subtle neuropsychological deficits in children with sickle cell disease. *American Journal of Pediatric Hematology/Oncology, 13,* 14–20.

Watson, C. W., & Klett, W. G. (1975). The Henmon-Nelson, Cardall-Miles, Slosson, and Quick Tests as predictors of NAIS IQ. *Journal of Clinical Psychology, 31,* 310–313.

Watson, D., & Friend, R. (1969). Measurement of social-evaluative anxiety. *Journal of Consulting and Clinical Psychology, 33,* 448–451.

Watson, R. I. (1951). *The clinical method in psychology.* New York: Harper & Row.

Webb, J. T. (1970, April). *The relation of MMPI two-point codes to age, sex, and education level in a representative nationwide sample of psychiatric outpatients.* Paper presented at the meeting of the Southeastern Psychological Association, Louisville, KY.

Webster, E. C. (1964). *Decision making in the employment interview.* Montreal: Canada: Industrial Relations Center, McGill University.

Webster, J. S., & Dostrow, V., (1982). Efficacy of a decision-tree approach to the Luria-Nebraska Neuropsychological Battery. *Journal of Consulting and Clinical Psychology, 50,* 313–315.

Wechsler, D. (1939). *The measurement of adult intelligence.* Baltimore: Williams & Wilkins.

Wechsler, D. (1943). Non-intellective factors in general intelligence. *Journal of Abnormal and Social Psychology, 38,* 101–103.

Wechsler, D. (1955). *Manual: Wechsler Adult Intelligence Scale.* New York: Psychological Corporation.

Wechsler, D. (1958). *The measurement and appraisal of adult intelligence* (4th ed.). Baltimore: Williams & Wilkins.

Wechsler, D. (1981). *Wechsler Adult Intelligence Scale—Revised.* New York: Psychological Corporation.

Wechsler, D. (1991). *WISC-III manual.* San Antonio, TX: The Psychological Corporation.

Weekley, J. A., Frank, B., O'Connor, E. J., & Peters, L. H. (1985). A comparison of three methods of estimating the standard deviation of performance in dollars. *Journal of Applied Psychology, 70,* 122–126.

Weeks, J. R., Morison, S. J., Millson, W. A., & Fettig, D. M. (1995). A comparison of Native, Metis, and Caucasian offender profiles on the MCMI. *Canadian Journal of Behavioural Science— Revue Canadienne des Sciences du Comportement, 27*(2), 187–198.

Weiner, B. (1991). Metaphors in motivation and attribution. *American Psychologist, 46,* 921–930.

Weiner, B. (1994). Ability versus effort revisited: The moral determinants of achievement evaluation and achievement as a moral system. *Educational Psychologist, 29*(3), 163–172.

Weiner, B., Graham, S., Peter, O., & Zmuidinas, M. (1991). Public confession and forgiveness. *Journal of Personality, 59,* 281–312.

Weiner, B., & Kukla, A. (1970). An attributional analysis of achievement motivation. *Journal of Personality and Social Psychology, 15,* 1–20.

Weiss, D. J. (Ed.). (1983). *New horizons in testing.* New York: Academic Press.

Weiss, D. J. (1985). Adaptive testing by computer. *Journal of Consulting and Clinical Psychology, 53,* 774–789.

Weiss, D J., & Yoes, M. E. (1991). Item response theory. In R. K. Hambleton & J. N. Zaal (Eds.), *Advances in educational and psychological testing: Theory and applications. Evaluation in education and human services series* (pp. 69–95). Boston, MA: Kluwer Academic Publishers.

Weissman, A. N. (1979). The Dysfunctional Attitude Scale: A validation study. *Dissertation Abstracts International, 40,* 1389A–1390B. (University Microfilms No. 79–19, 533)

Weissman, A. N., & Beck, A. T. (1978, November). *Development and validation of the Dysfunctional Attitude Scale: A preliminary investigation.* Paper presented at the meeting of the Association for the Advancement of Behavior Therapy, Chicago.

Weissman, M. M., Sholomskas, D., Pottenger, M., Prusoff, B. A., & Locke, B. Z. (1977). Assessing depressive symptoms in five psychiatric populations: A validation study. *American Journal of Epidemiology, 106,* 203–214.

Welsh, G. S. (1948). An extension of Hathaway's MMPI profile coding system. *Journal of Consulting Psychology, 12,* 343–344.

Welsh, G. S. (1956). Factor dimensions A and R. In G. S. Welsh & W. G. Dahlstrom (Eds.), *Basic readings on the MMPI in psychology and medicine.* Minneapolis: University of Minnesota Press.

Welsh, K., Butters, N., Hughes, J., Mobs, R., & Hayman, A. (1991). Detection of abnormal memory decline in mad cases of Alzheimer's disease using CERAD Neuropsychological Measures. *Archives of Neurology, 48,* 278–281.

Wermiel, S., & Trost, C. (1986, June 20). Justices say hostile job environment due to sex harrassment violates rights. *Wall Street Journal,* p. 2.

Werner, H. (1937). Process and achievement: The basic problem of education and developmental psychology. *Hayward Educational Review, 7,* 353–368.

Wesman, A. G. (1971). Writing the test item. In R. L. Thorndike (Ed.), *Educational measurement* (2nd ed.). Washington, DC: American Council on Education.

Wessel, I. & Mersch, P. (1994). A cognitive-behavioural group treatment for test-anxious adolescents. *Anxiety, Stress and Coping: An International Journal, 7,* 149–160.

Westen, D. (1991). Clinical assessment of object relations using the TAT. *Journal of Personality Assessment, 56,* 56–74.

Wetzler, S. (1990). The Millon Clinical Multiaxial Inventory (MCMI): A review. *Journal of Personality Assessment, 55,* 445–464,

Wheeler, L., & Reitan, R. M. (1962). A presence and alaterality of brain damage predicted from response to a short aphasia screening test. *Perceptual and Motor Skills, 15,* 783–799.

Whipple, G. M. (1910). *Manual of mental and physical tests.* Baltimore: Warwick & York.

Wicker, A. W. (1979). Ecological psychology: Some recent and prospective developments. *American Psychologist, 34,* 755–765.

Wicker, A. W., & Kirmeyer, S. L. (1976). From church to laboratory to national park. In S. Wapner, S. B. Conen, & B.

Kaplan (Eds.), *Experiencing the environment.* New York: Plenum.

Wickham, T. (1978). *WISC patterns in acting-out delinquents, poor readers, and normal controls.* Unpublished doctoral dissertation, United States International University, San Diego.

Wiederholt, J. L. (1978). Review of Illinois Test of Psycholinguistic Abilities. In O. K. Buros (Ed.), *The eighth mental measurements yearbook* (Vol. 1). Highland Park, NJ: Gryphon Press.

Wiens, A. N. (1976). The assessment interview. In I. B. Weiner (Ed.), *Clinical methods in psychology.* New York: Wiley.

Wiens, A. N., Matarazzo, J. D., & Saslow, G. (1965). The interaction recorder: An electronic punched paper tape unit for recording speech behavior during interviews. *Journal of Clinical Psychology, 21,* 142–145.

Wiesner, W. H., & Cronshaw, S. F. (1988). A meta-analytic investigation of the impact of interview format and degree of structure on the validity of the employment interview. *Journal of Occupational Psychology, 61,* 275–290.

Wiggins, J. G. (1994). Would you want your child to be a psychologist? *American Psychologist, 49*(6), 485–492.

Wiggins, J. S. (1973). *Personality and prediction: Principles of personality assessment.* Reading, MA: Addison-Wesley.

Wiggins, N. (1966). Individual viewpoints of social desirability. *Psychological Bulletin, 66,* 68–77.

Wiggins, N., & Kohen, E. S. (1971). Man versus model of man revisited: The forecasting of graduate school success. *Journal of Personality and Social Psychology, 19,* 100–106.

Wild, C. L., McPeek, W. M., Kofler, S. L., Braun, H. I., & Cow-

ell, W. (1989). Concurrent validity of verbal item types for ethnic and gender subgroups. *GRE Publication Report 84–10p.* Princeton, NJ: Educational Testing Service.

Wilder, J. (1950). The law of initial values. *Psychosomatic Medicine, 12,* 392–401.

Wilkinson, S. J., Downes, J., James, O., Davies, M. G., & Davies, A. D. M. (1986). Rating reliability for life events and difficulties in the elderly. *Psychological Medicine, 16,* 101–105.

Wilkinson, S. J., James, O., & Davies, A. D. M. (1985). Life stress and depression in the elderly: Experiences from a community survey. In A. Butler (Ed.), *Aging: Recent advances and creative responses.* London: Croom Helm.

Williams, J. E. (1994). Anxiety measurement: Construct validity and test performance. *Measurement and Evaluation in Counseling and Development, 27,* 302–307.

Williams, R. L. (1974). Scientific racism and I.Q.: The silent mugging of the black community. *Psychology Today, 7,* 32–41.

Williamson, W. D., Wilson, G. S., Lifschitz, M. H., & Thurbers, S. A. (1990). Nonhandicapped very-low-birth-weight infants at one year of age developmental profile. *Pediatrics, 85,* 405–410.

Wine, J. D. (1980). Cognitive-attentional theory of test anxiety. In I. G. Sarason (Ed.), *Test anxiety: Theory, research, and applications.* Hillsdale, NJ: Erlbaum.

Wing, K. R. (1976). *The law and the public's health.* St. Louis, MO: Mosby.

Winter, D. G., & Stewart, A. J. (1977). Power motive reliability, as a function of retest instructions. *Journal of Consulting and Clinical Psychology, 42,* 436–440.

Wishner, J. (1948). Rorschach intellectual indicators in neurotics. *American Journal of Orthopsychiatry, 18*, 265–279.

Wissler, C. (1901). The correlation of mental and physical tests. *Psychological Review, 3*(Monograph Supp. 16).

Witmer, J. M., Bernstein, A. V., & Dunham, R. M. (1971). The effects of verbal approval and disapproval upon the performance of third and fourth grade children of four subtests of the Wechsler Intelligence Scale for Children. *Journal of School Psychology, 9*, 347–356.

Witt, J. C. (1986). Review of the Wide Range Achievement Test—Revised. *Journal of Psychoeducational Assessment, 4*, 88–90.

Witt, J. C., & Gresham, F. M. (1985). Review of the Wechsler Intelligence Scale for Children—Revised. In J. V. Mitchell (Ed.), *The ninth mental measurements yearbook* (Vol. 1). Highland Park, NJ: Gryphon Press.

Wolk, R. L., & Wolk, R. B. (1971). *Manual: Gerontological Apperception Test*. New York: Behavioral Publications.

Wolkind, S. (1974). Review of the Brazelton Neonatal Assessment Scale. *British Journal of Psychiatry, 125*, 216–217.

Wolpe, J. (1969). *The practice of behavior therapy*. New York: Pergamon Press.

Wolpe, J., & Lang, P. J. (1964). A fear survey schedule for use in behavior therapy. *Behaviour Research and Therapy, 2*, 27–30.

Wood, D. J. (1982), Talking to young children. *Developmental Medicine and Child Neurology, 24*, 856–859.

Wood, J. M., Nezworski, T., & Stejskal, W. J. (1996). The comprehensive system for the Rorschach: A critical examination. *Psychological Science, 7*, 3–10.

Wood, P. S., Smith, W. L., Alt-

maier, E. M., Tarico, V. S., & Franken, E. A. (1990). A prospective study of cognitive and non-cognitive selection criteria as predictors of resident performance. *Investigative Radiology, 25*, 855–859.

Woodcock, R. W. (1977). *Woodcock-Johnson Psycho-Educational Battery: Technical report*. Allen, TX: DLM Teaching Resources.

Woodcock. R. W., & Johnson, M. (1989). *Woodcock-Johnson Psycho-Educational Battery—Revised*. Chicago: Riverside.

Woodworth, R. S. (1920). *Personal data sheet*. Chicago: Stoelting.

World Health Organization (1948). *Constitution of the World Health Organization*. Geneva, Switzerland: WHO Basic Documents.

Wright, O. R., Jr. (1969). Summary of research on the selection interview since 1964. *Personnel Psychology, 22*, 391–413.

Wright, T. L., & Tedeschi, R. G. (1975). Factor analysis of the interpersonal trust scale. *Journal of Consulting and Clinical Psychology, 43*, 470–477.

Yates, J. W., Charmer, B., & McKegney, F. P. (1980). Evaluation of patients with advanced cancer using the Karnofsky Performance Status. *Cancer, 45*, 2220–2224.

Yerkes, R. M. (Ed.). (1921). Psychological examining in the United States Army. *Memoirs of the National Academy of Sciences, 15*.

Zales, M. R. (1985). *Stress in health and disease*. New York: Brunner/Mazel.

Zedeck, S., & Blood, M. R. (1974). *Foundations of behavioral science research in organizations*. Pacific Grove, CA: Brooks/Cole.

Zedeck, S., and Cascio, W. F. (1984). Psychological issues in personnel decisions. *Annual*

Review of Psychology, 35, 461–518.

Zedeck, S., Tziner, A., & Middlestadt, S. E. (1983). Interviewer validity and reliability: An individual analysis approach. *Personnel Psychology, 36*, 355–370.

Zeidner, M. (1987). Test of the cultural bias hypothesis: Some Israeli findings. *Journal of Applied Psychology, 72*, 38–48.

Zeidner, M. (1990). Does test anxiety bias scholastic aptitude performance by gender and sociocultural group? *Journal of Personality Assessment, 55*, 145–160.

Zeidner, M., & Hammer, A. (1990). Life events and coping resources as predictors of stress symptoms in adolescents. *Personality and Individual Differences, 11*, 693–703.

Zimet, G. D., Powell, S. S., Farley, G. K., Werkmen, S., & Berkoff, K. A. (1990). Psychometric characteristics of the multidimensional scale of perceived social support. *Journal of Personality Assessment, 55*, 610–617.

Zimmerman, I. L., Woo-Sam, J. M., & Glasser, A. J. (1973). *Clinical interpretation of the Wechsler Adult Intelligence Scale*. New York: Grune & Stratton.

Zimmerman, M., & Coryell, W. (1987). The inventory to diagnose depression (IDD): A self-report scale to diagnose major depressive disorders. *Journal of Consulting and Clinical Psychology, 55*, 55–59.

Ziskin, J. (1995). *Coping with psychiatric and psychological testimony*. Los Angeles: Law and Psychology Press.

Zores, L. S., & Williams, P. B. (1980). A look at the content bias in IQ tests. *Journal of Educational Measurement, 17*, 313–322.

Zubin, J. (1972). Discussion of symposium on newer approaches to personality assessment. *Journal of Personality Assessment, 36,* 427–434.

Zuckerman, M. (1960). The development of an affect adjective check list measure of anxiety. *Journal of Consulting Psychology, 24,* 457–462.

Zuckerman, M. (1971). Physiological measures of sexual arousal in the human. *Psychological Bulletin, 75,* 297–329.

Zuckerman, M. (1990). Some dubious premises in research and theory on racial differences. *American Psychologist, 45,* 1297–1303.

Zytowski, D. G. (1976). Predictive validity of the Kuder Occupational Interest Survey: A 12–19 year follow-up. *Journal of Counseling Psychology, 23,* 221–233.

Zytowski, D. G. (1977). The effects of being interest inventoried. *Journal of Vocational Behavior, 11,* 153–158.

Zytowski, D. G. (1985). *Kuder Occupational Interest Survey Form DD manual supplement.* Chicago: Science Research Associates.

Zytowski, D. G. (1992). Three generations: The continuing evolution of Frederic Kuder's interest inventories. [Special issue: Wellness throughout the life span]. *Journal of Counseling and Development, 71,* 245–248.

Name Index

Janssen, E., 479
Jennings, J. R., 479
Jensen, A. R., 318, 319, 436,
   482, 536, 544, 625
Johansson, C. B., 382
Johansson, G., 389
Johansson, J. C., 382
Johnson, J. G., 501
Johnson, J. H., 500
Johnson, J. L., 455
Johnson, L., 568
Johnson, M., 326
Johnson, N. E., 13, 252, 285,
   298, 359, 360, 361, 449,
   482, 483, 621
Johnson, V., 479
Johnston, D., 479
Jones, E. E., 387, 388
Jones, R. A., 476
Joshi, R., 511
Judiesch, M. K., 185
Jung, C., 427–428, 458
Jungeblut, A., 599

Kagan, J., 538
Kaiser, H., 557
Kallingal, A., 544
Kalonoff, H., 509
Kamhi, A. G., 319
Kamin, L. J., 536, 563, 582,
   587
Kammeier, M. L., 417
Kamphaus, R. W., 316
Kanarack, T., 501
Kanfer, F. H., 464, 467, 474,
   485
Kanner, A. D., 501
Kanowitz, J., 205
Kantor, L., 487
Kaplan, C., 117
Kaplan, O. J., 200
Kaplan, R. M., 24, 59, 90, 105,
   138, 140, 143, 146, 147,
   157, 187, 199, 202, 496,
   499, 503, 504, 521, 524,
   529, 530
Kaplan, S., 356
Kaplanestrin, M., 310
Kappelman, M. M., 306
Karaken, D. A., 331
Karnes, F. A., 318
Karr, S. K., 269
Kaszniak, A. W., 321, 509
Katz, S. E., 406
Katz, S. T., 524, 527
Kaufman, A. S., 316–319, 320
Kaufman, N. L., 316–319
Kaufman, R. W., 316, 318
Kaufman, S. H., 459
Kay, G. G., 431

Kazdin, A. E., 203
Kehoe, J. F., 541
Keiser, R. E., 451, 455
Keller, J. W., 437, 619
Keller, K. E., 240
Keller, L. S., 484
Kelley, D., 439
Kelley, T. L., 19
Kelly, E. C., 428
Kelly, H. H., 387
Kendall, B. S., 329
Kendall, P. C., 484
Kennedy, W. A., 198
Kennedy-Moore, E., 503
Kenrick, D. T., 223
Kent, G. H., 458
Kent, R. N., 204, 205
Keogh, B. K., 307
Kerner, D., 147
Kerner, J., 438
Keyser, D. J., 188, 189, 191
Kicklighter, R., 589
Kimura, D., 203
King, N. J., 470
Kirkpatrick, E. A., 438
Kirmeyer, S. L., 389
Kleinsaser, L. D., 198
Klett, W. G., 345
Kleven, M., 282
Klieger, D. M., 470
Kline, P., 91
Kline, R. B., 268
Klingberg, G., 470
Klopfer, B., 439, 460
Klos, D., 386
Knauper, B., 233
Knight, D., 194
Knight-Jones, E. B., 315
Knobloch, H., 308
Knotek, P. C., 321
Knox, H. A., 305
Knutson, J. F., 436
Kohen, E. S., 610
Kohs, S. C., 283
Kok, F., 540
Koksal, F., 490
Koller, P. S., 199
Komaroff, A. L., 499
Koppitz, E. M., 328
Korgeski, G. P., 484
Kraepelin, E., 16
Kraiger, K., 456
Kramer, J. J., 188
Krentzel, C. P., 311
Krinsky, S. G., 321
Kuder, G. F., 100, 110, 111, 378
Kuhlmann, F., 255

Lahey, B. B., 204
Lally, M., 483

Lambert, N., 582, 583
Lamp, R. E., 546
Lancaster, A. R., 212
Landis, C., 406
Landy, F. J., 133, 137, 148,
   150, 206
Lang, P. J., 471
Lanyon, B. P., 459
Lanyon, R. I., 459
Larkin, J. E., 240
Larrabee, L. L., 198
Larsen, R., 448
Larsen, R. M., 404, 437
Larson, G. E., 482, 483
Latham, V. M., 241
Lautenschlager, G. J., 201
Lauter, D., 592, 595, 596
Lawlis, G. F., 470
Lawshe, C. L., 133, 148
Lazarus, R. S., 501, 502
Leahey, L., 310
Lee, J. A., 483
Leichsenring, F., 451
Lemke, S., 391
Leong, C., 511
Lerner, B., 601
Lesser, G. S., 539
Lester, B. M., 306
Levenson, H., 417
Levenson, R. W., 479
Levi, A., 546
Levin, H. S., 509
Levy, D., 21, 439
Lewandowski, D. G., 24, 25,
   256, 286, 288, 444, 449,
   464
Lewinsohn, P. N., 136
Lewis, C. D., 323
Lezak, M. D., 327, 384, 509,
   517, 518
Lichtenstein, E., 390
Liebert, R. M., 492, 495
Likert, R., 156
Lilienfield, S. O., 206
Lillesand, D. B., 472
Lincoln, R. K., 287
Lindgren, S., 417
Lindzey, G., 455, 461
Linn, R. L., 19, 62, 169, 171
Lipsitz, J. D., 288
Lipsitz, S., 194
Liss, P. H., 483
Little, K. B., 456, 610
Lively, W. J., 381
LoBello, S. G., 299
Lochman, J. E., 179
Locke, S. D., 202
Lohman, D. F., 359
Lohr, J. M., 476
Long, C. J., 526, 527

Subject Index

Credits

This page constitutes an extension of the copyright page. We have made every effort to trace the ownership of all copyrighted material and to secure permission from copyright holders. In the event of any question arising as to the use of any material, we will be pleased to make the necessary corrections in future printings. Thanks are due to the following authors, publishers, and agents for permission to use the material indicated.

62: Figure 2-10 from Publiese et al., 1983, p. 514; reprinted by permission of *The New England Journal of Medicine, 309,* 513–518, 1983.

166: Figure 6-4 from *Introduction to Measurement Theory* by M.J. Allen and W.M. Yen, 1979, Brooks/Cole Publishing Company, Pacific Grove, CA 93950, a division of International Thomson Publishing Inc.

168: Figure 6.8: From "Adaptive Testing by Computer," by D. J. Weiss, *Journal of Consulting and Clinical Psychology,* 1985, *53,* 775. Reprinted by permission of the American Psychological Association and the author.

181: Figure 7-1: Data from National Cancer Institute, Cancer Statistics Review 1973–1988 (Bethesda, MD: July 1991, Table 11-40).

235: Table 9-6 from Spitzer R., Williams J.B.W., Gibbon M., et al: Structured Clinical Interview for DSM-II-R. Washington, D.C., American Psychiatric Press, 1990. Copyright 1990 American Psychiatric Press, Inc. (1990a). Copyright 1990 American Psychiatric Association.

276: Figure 11-2 from the WAIS-R Expanded Record Form © 1981, 1977 by The Psychological Corporation. Reproduced by permission. All rights reserved.

283: Table 11-2. Wechsler Adult Intelligence Scale-Revised. Copyright © 1981, 1955 by The Psychological Corporation. Reproduced by permission. All rights reserved.

294: Figure 11-7. Simulated items similar to those in the Wechsler Intelligence Scales for Adults and Children. Copyright 1949, 1955, 1974, 1981, and 1989 by The Psychological Corporation. Reprinted. by permission. All rights reserved.

295: Figure 11-8. Wechsler Intelligence Scale for Children: Third Edition. Copyright © 1989 by The Psychological Corporation. All rights reserved. Reproduced by permission.

392: Figure 14-1 from the Multiphasic Environmental Assessment Procedure (MEAP) Manual by R. H. Moos and S. Lemke, p. 22. Copyright 1984 by the Social Ecology Laboratory, Stanford University School of Medicine, Palo Alto, California. Reproduced with permission.

525: Table 19-4 from S. Katz et al. (1963). Studies of Illness in the Aged. The Index of ADL: A Standardized Measure of Biological and Psychosocial Function. *Journal of the American Medical Association, 185,* 914–915. Copyright 1963, American Medical Association.

585–587: Focused Example 21-4 from "Different Opinions for Different Judges: Judges Peckham (*Larry P.* v. *Wilson Riles*) and Grady (*Parents in Action for Special Education* v. *Hannon*)" by J. Sattler. In *American Psychological Association Monitor,* 1980, *11* (11), 7–8. Copyright 1980 by the American Psychological Association. Reprinted by permission.

TO THE OWNER OF THIS BOOK:

I hope that you have found *Psychological Testing: Principles, Applications, and Issues,* Fourth Edition, useful. So that this book can be improved in a future edition, would you take the time to complete this sheet and return it? Thank you.

School and address: _____

Department: _____

Instructor's name: _____

1. What I like most about this book is: _____

_____

_____

2. What I like least about this book is: _____

_____

_____

3. My general reaction to this book is: _____

_____

4. The name of the course in which I used this book is: _____

_____

5. Were all of the chapters of the book assigned for you to read? _____

   If not, which ones weren't? _____

6. In the space below, or on a separate sheet of paper, please write specific suggestions for improving this book and anything else you'd care to share about your experience in using the book.

_____

_____

_____

_____

_____

Optional:

Your name:_____ Date:_____

May Brooks/Cole quote you, either in promotion for *Psychological Testing: Principles, Applications, and Issues,* Fourth Edition, or in future publishing ventures?

Yes:_____ No:_____

Sincerely

Robert M. Kaplan
Dennis R. Saccuzzo